Capital, Efficiency
and Growth

List of Contributors

Clopper Almon, University of Maryland
Anthony Barbera, University of Maryland
Barbara Fraumeni, Boston College
George von Furstenberg, Indiana University
Patric Hendershott, Purdue University
Sheng-Cheng Hu, Purdue University
Dale Jorgenson, Harvard University
Burton Malkiel, Princeton University
Ishaq Nadiri, New York University
Harry Watson, George Washington University

Capital, Efficiency and Growth

Edited by
George M. von Furstenberg

Volume III in the Series on Capital Investment and Saving
Sponsored by the American Council of Life Insurance

Ballinger Publishing Company • **Cambridge, Massachusetts**
A Subsidiary of Harper & Row, Publishers, Inc.

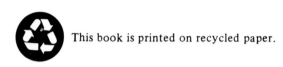 This book is printed on recycled paper.

International Standard Book Number: 0−88410−677−2

Library of Congress Catalog Card Number: 79−26371

Printed in the United States of America

Library of Congress Cataloging in Publication Data

Main entry under title:

Capital, efficiency and growth.

   (Series on capital investment and saving; v. 3)
   "Sponsored by the American Council of Life Insurance."
   Includes index.
   1. Capital—United States—Addresses, essays, lectures. 2. Capital investment—United States—Addresses, essays, lectures. 3. United States—Economic condition—1945− —Addresses, essays, lectures. I. Von Furstenberg, George M., 1941− II. American Council of Life Insurance. III. Series.
HC110.C3C36   332'.041'0973   79−26371
ISBN 0−88410−677−2

Contents

Chapter 3
Accounting for Capital—*Dale W. Jorgenson*

Part II   Malallocations of Capital by Sector and Function

Chapter 4
Government-Induced Biases in the Allocation of the Stock of Fixed Capital in the United States
—*Patric H. Hendershott and Sheng-Cheng Hu*

Chapter 5
Contributions and Determinants of Research and Development Expenditures in the U.S. Manufacturing Industries—*M. Ishaq Nadiri*

List of Tables

List of Figures

Foreword

In 1976, the American Council of Life Insurance through its Subcommittee on Economic Research explored the possibility of a study of capital investment and saving requirements focused on the prospects for continuing economic growth. The subcommittee prepared and discussed drafts for such a project, which in many ways was considered to be a renewal of a similar study in the 1950s, sponsored by the life insurance business, under the direction of Professor Simon Kuznets.

To guide in the planning and development of the project, an Advisory Committee was established which consisted of the following: Professor James S. Duesenberry (Harvard), Dr. Solomon Fabricant (National Bureau of Economic Research), Professor Paul W. McCracken (University of Michigan), Dr. Robert A. Rennie (Nationwide), Dr. Francis H. Schott (The Equitable Life Assurance Society), Professor Ezra Solomon (Stanford), Mr. Albert T. Sommers (The Conference Board), Professor Murray L. Weidenbaum (Washington University), and Dr. Kenneth M. Wright (American Council of Life Insurance). In the summer of 1976, Dr. George M. von Furstenberg, then Professor of Economics at Indiana University, agreed to serve as Project Director to organize the research for this study.

To carry out this project, Dr. von Furstenberg assembled a distinguished group of scholars both in the United States and abroad. In the tradition of Simon Kuznets's study, the present project probes the underlying causes and determinants of saving, investment, and economic growth and examines the ways in which government and other institutions affect capital formation.

Under Dr. von Furstenberg, this work has been carried out with thoroughness and insight. The council is indeed pleased to see the completion and publication of the three volumes that comprise this study.

Kenneth M. Wright
American Council of Life Insurance
Washington, D.C.

Preface

Because of the sharp decline in productivity growth and the deterioration of economic performance during recent years, capital formation has moved to the forefront of national economic concerns. The diagnosis of the current malaise involves many facets, not all of which are limited to the United States.

Volume I, *Social Security versus Private Saving*, examines how the rapid growth of social insurance wealth and of other government debt may have reduced the supply of private saving available for capital formation. This investigation analyzes the experience of several postindustrial democracies and advances the theoretical work with life cycle and macroeconomic models of saving across generations.

Volume II, *The Government and Capital Formation*, places fiscal and monetary policy impacts on saving into a broader context to examine their ultimate effects on potential output and capital intensity. The government's own infrastructure investments are considered also, as are investment resources from abroad. Specific studies of inflation effects on saving and of tax incentives and regulatory disincentives to investment conclude this volume.

Volume III, *Capital, Efficiency and Growth*, joins the issues at the highest level by documenting the importance of capital and technological progress to economic growth through detailed analyses, sector by sector. It also shows how and why the decline in some of the traditional sources of growth makes capital all the more important to what growth there is. The implication is that increased investment in tangible capital and in research and development, as well as an improved allocation of investment resources, are indispensable to restoring some of the buoyancy of living standards and opportunity characteristic of earlier decades.

The purpose of all three volumes is to improve and broaden the analytical base for addressing current policy issues in the area of saving and capital and to bring new evidence and policy alternatives before the public. To meet these objectives in both a coherent and unbiased fashion, outlines of each of the interlocking studies were agreed upon with the editor. Subsequently, however, editorial comments and the comments of outside readers were designed only to improve the technical quality and stylistic appearance of the work submitted. All contributors cooperated by making extensive revisions with alacrity and a quest for perfection. Much of the retyping was supervised by Mrs. Linda Steinwachs of Indiana University, who also provided valuable editorial assistance throughout the three-year work phase of the project.

George M. von Furstenberg
Indiana University
Bloomington

Chapter 1

Introduction

For the U.S. economy, the past decade was a period of relative decline. If this decline could be attributed primarily to shifts in resources toward sectors of slow productivity growth, such as some service industries, it might be part of a pattern frequently attributed to advanced industrial societies. Alternatively, if the slowing in the rate of economic growth were due to lower growth of physical inputs such as labor and capital, the explanation would be even simpler.

The studies in this volume show that these causes are not telling. Shifts in the composition of demand toward the output of low productivity-growth sectors or toward leisure or nonmarket activities do not explain past events or make them any less disappointing. Society has not acquiesced to slower growth of living standards, and shoring up that growth has remained of vital political concern.

Effective remedial actions and coherent strategies will be difficult to devise institutionally and intellectually demanding. They will have to stimulate the efficiency of capital and labor and the rate of technical change and not just simply increase the availability of inputs in the aggregate. Higher saving and investment rates may be necessary conditions for faster growth but they are not sufficient for maintaining that growth. Unless the distribution of investment is made more efficient and technology oriented, curing the "capital shortage" will not, by itself, provide a lasting cure for the "growth shortage."

TECHNICAL DIMENSIONS OF THE
GROWTH PROBLEM

While physical labor inputs, particularly by women, grew much faster than projected a decade ago and young persons entered the labor force in record numbers, lower growth in the average efficiency of labor inputs offset the benefits of faster growth in total hours worked. Like labor quality, the growth in capital quality decreased gradually from 1970 on. In the lead chapter by Barbara Fraumeni and Dale Jorgenson in this volume a change in capital quality is identified as the change in the factor of proportionality between the annual flow of capital services and the start-of-period value of the net capital stock. If this factor of proportionality grows less rapidly, increased growth of physical capital need not produce higher growth in capital inputs. After 1973, however, the growth in the stock of capital also began to shrink. Although the quantitative evidence for the entire peak-to-peak cycle that started in 1973 is not yet in, it is unlikely that all of the decline registered in the early years of that cycle has since been reversed.

The most dramatic part of the detailed sectoral evidence produced by Fraumeni and Jorgenson which is based on the consistent growth and value accounting framework laid out by Jorgenson in Chapter 3 relates, however, to the decline in the rate of technical change. The rate of technical change accounts for that part of the growth of private-sector output that cannot be attributed to the growth of capital and labor inputs. Holding inputs constant requires that both the quality and quantity components of such inputs are held fixed to determine what technical change has occurred over time. On this basis it is found that while technical change was the single most important source of economic growth during the decade 1957–1966, the rate of technical change essentially disappeared as a source of economic growth after 1966. Furthermore, in 1976 the level of technology was still lower than before 1973.

This outcome may be due in part to the repercussions of the energy shock on the efficiency of resources. Reduced rates of investment in research and development in the face of continuing high rates of return to R&D in the manufacturing sector, which are documented by Ishaq Nadiri for a longer period, also undoubtedly played a part. Still, some of the causes of this decline are not yet understood, and this presents a new challenge to both analysis and policy.

The effectiveness of policy measures designed to raise the rate of growth of business capital has been documented repeatedly in the past, and the inventory of stimulative tax devices (accelerated depreciation, the investment tax credit, and so on) is well known.[a] However, there is little precedent for the concerted development and implementation of new technology at the level of individual industrial sectors. Fraumeni and Jorgenson define finding such measures as the central problem facing policymakers in the 1980s if the dismal record of the 1970s is not to be repeated.

MALALLOCATIONS OF THE EXISTING STOCK OF CAPITAL BY SECTOR

Over the period 1948–1976, the capital stock grew at an average annual rate of 3.68 percent per year for households, 2.80 percent for corporate business, and 1.42 for noncorporate business. Because the (derived) income and output elasticities of demand for capital services may differ by sector, there is no reason why these growth rates should be the same. Nevertheless, it is disquieting that household capital (primarily residences) has grown almost twice as rapidly as business capital. According to the estimates by Patric Hendershott and Sheng-Cheng Hu in Chapter 4, the result has been that the average risk-adjusted net returns of capital are now more than twice as high on corporate structures and equipment than on owner-occupied housing. Furthermore, a rise in the expected rate of inflation increases the real value of the subsidies implicit in homeowners' deductions for mortgage interest while the prohibition of replacement-cost accounting for depreciation denies tax relief to business.

The total loss resulting from misallocations of capital between the housing sectors and the corporate and noncorporate business sectors has thus risen from 0.32 percent of the net national product in 1964–1965 to 0.68 percent in 1976–1977. With an NNP of just under $2,000 billion, eliminating the misallocation to achieve a roughly 10 percent rate of return (with some variation for risk) in all sectors would increase the return on existing capital by as much as $142 billion of new capital would have generated if its allocation were no different from that of existing capital.

Before declaring a generalized capital shortage, one should also recognize that there is relatively too much capital in sectors with low efficiency. More investment should be directed toward the high-productivity uses, and not indiscriminately to all uses. This can be done by making the tax system less biased against business capital

[a]For documentation see the studies by Patric Hendershott, Sheng-Cheng Hu, and Jeffery Green in the companion volume, *The Government and Capital Formation.*

and investment in technology on which the growth of living standards ultimately depends.

INVESTMENT BY INDUSTRY AND FUNCTION

Investment has been misdirected not only by sector but also by function. Thus Nadiri documents in Chapter 5 that the average annual rate of growth of R&D expenditures has fallen from 6.5 percent in 1958–1965 to 1.7 percent in 1966–1975 even though the social rate of return on such investment has not declined. Had the earlier growth rate of R&D inputs been sustained, output might have grown 0.5 percent faster in the manufacturing sector, *ceteris paribus.*

There is also likely to be a close positive association between the rate of growth of the stock of capital, the valuation which financial investors put on that capital relative to its replacement cost (a valuation ratio that has come to be known as Tobin's q) and the rate of R&D spending. As calculated by George von Furstenberg, Burton Malkiel, and Harry Watson in Chapter 6, q ratios are highest in chemicals and in the electrical and nonelectrical machinery industries. These industries are also characterized by above-average growth rates of output and capital stock over the period 1956–1976 as a whole. By expanding markets and creating demand for new products, industrial frontrunners can gain temporary monopoly profits based on successful innovation ahead of the international competition.

High R&D, a high q, and high rates of growth of industry output and capital thus mutually condition each other. One is difficult to maintain without the other in the unregulated sectors of the economy (as distinct from the utility sector).

From this point of view it is perhaps alarming that the q ratio of even the most R&D-intensive sectors has declined relentlessly in recent years along with the q ratios of all other two-digit industries examined. Rather than signifying equilibration of the industry q values to a common level, the decline in the q of the postwar growth leaders thus appears to be indicative of a deterioration in their international position that is not compensated by higher growth opportunities for other U.S. industries.

The q theory of investment is related to the neoclassical theory of investment[b] in the sense that a decline in the user cost of capital

---

[b]For a full description see the Appendix to the paper by Jeffery Green in the companion volume, *The Government and Capital Formation.*

should raise q and hence investment under both theories.[c] How changing the user cost of capital would affect the allocation of business fixed investment between eighty-seven industries out to 1990 is one of the issues explored by Clopper Almon and Anthony Barbera in the last chapter. Overall, a gradual decrease in the real rate of interest from 0.035 in 1976 to 0.025 in 1990 that might be induced by a tax policy more favorable to saving would make the total stock of business capital only about 1.5 percent higher than it would be at a constant real interest rate in 1990. However, the rates of increase estimated for individual sectors are extremely diverse. The effects of raising the rate of the investment tax credit from 10 to 15 percent are more than twice as strong on average but just as diverse, with the durable goods industries generally least responsive.

Since some of the most technology-intensive industries produce durable goods it is not clear that their research and development expenditures can be stimulated very much by such devices as the investment tax credit for plant and equipment even though Nadiri has found a complementary relationship between R&D and the capital stock of firms. This again suggests that general measures to stimulate saving and business investment may have to be supplemented by specific measures to raise private investment in R&D. For investment as a whole and for the long-term economic growth of the nation, where the "money" is put may be quite as important as how much is invested in total.

---

[c]However, the theories are not equivalent in applications since Tobin's q can change also when the required rate of return changes in relation to the actual rate of return for reasons not normally entering into the construction of the user cost of capital variable.

Part I

The Contribution of Capital to Economic Growth

Chapter 2

The Role of Capital in U.S. Economic Growth, 1948–1976

Barbara M. Fraumeni and
Dale W. Jorgenson

Rapid growth of the U.S. economy during the postwar period has been sustained by the highest rate of capital formation in U.S. economic history. The postwar performance of the U.S. economy is all the more remarkable in view of the experience of the 1930s, when growth was negligible and the rate of capital formation was severely depressed. Capital formation in the form of tangible assets dropped precipitously after the cyclical peak in economic activity in 1973 and economic growth has slowed measurably. The revival of capital formation is clearly the key to reestablishment of postwar trends in economic growth in the United States.

The purpose of this study is to analyze the interrelationship between capital formation and economic growth in the United States over the period 1948–1976.[a] We begin with a brief overview of the historical record. The growth of the U.S. economy from 1948 to 1976, as measured by the average rate of growth of gross private domestic product, was 3.65 percent per year. By contrast Laurits Christensen and Jorgenson [24, 1970; 25, 1973] have shown that the average annual rate of growth of gross private domestic product from 1929 to 1939 was slightly negative. Simon Kuznets [48, 1961] has estimated that the growth rate of gross national product from 1869 to 1948 averaged 4.23 percent per year.

To assess the role of capital formation in the growth of the U.S. economy from 1948 to 1976, we analyze the contribution of growth

[a]We thank Nelda Hoxie and Betsy Rossen for their expert research assistance on all phases of this study. Helen Lau also contributed by updating the labor date base.

Table 2-1. Characteristics of Capital Input

Legal Forms of Organization:

(1) Corporate
(2) Noncorporate
(3) Household
(4) Institutions

Asset Type:

(1) Producers' durable equipment
(2) Consumers' durables
(3) Tenant-occupied residential structures and nonresidential structures
(4) Owner-occupied residential structures
(5) Inventories
(6) Land

Industry:

(1) Agricultural production
(2) Agricultural services, horticultural services, forestry and fisheries
(3) Metal mining
(4) Coal mining
(5) Crude petroleum and natural gas extractions
(6) Nonmetallic mining and quarrying, except fuel
(7) Construction
(8) Food and kindred products
(9) Tobacco manufactures
(10) Textile mill products
(11) Apparel and other fabricated textile products
(12) Paper and allied products
(13) Printing, publishing, and allied industries
(14) Chemicals and allied products
(15) Petroleum and coal products
(16) Rubber and miscellaneous plastic products
(17) Leather and leather products
(18) Lumber and wood products, except furniture
(19) Furniture and fixtures
(20) Stone, clay, and glass products
(21) Primary metal industries
(22) Fabricated metal industries
(23) Machinery except electrical
(24) Electrical machinery, equipment, and supplies
(25) Transportation equipment, except motor vehicles, and ordnance
(26) Motor vehicles, and motor vehicle equipment
(27) Professional photographic equipment and watches
(28) Miscellaneous manufacturing industries
(29) Railroads and railway express service
(30) Street railway, bus lines, and taxicab service
(31) Trucking service, warehousing and storage
(32) Water transportation
(33) Air transportation
(34) Pipelines, except natural gas
(35) Services incidental to transportation
(36) Telephone, telegraph, and miscellaneous communication services
(37) Radio broadcasting and television
(38) Electric utilities

Table 2–1. continued

Industry: *(continued)*

(39) Gas utilities
(40) Water supply, sanitary services, and other utilities
(41) Wholesale trade
(42) Retail trade
(43) Finance, insurance, and real estate
(44) Services
(45) Private households
(46) Nonprofit institutions

in capital input to the growth of output. We first analyze the contribution of capital input to the growth of output for forty-six industrial sectors of the U.S. economy listed in Table 2–1. We then combine the results for all sectors to analyze the contribution of capital to the growth of the output of the private domestic sector of the U.S. economy. At both sectoral and aggregate levels we compare the contribution of capital with the contributions of other productive inputs and the rate of technical change, defined as the rate of growth of output, holding all inputs fixed.

At the sectoral level the growth of inputs, including capital input, is far more important than the rate of technical change in accounting for the growth of output. The sum of the contributions of capital and labor inputs exceeds the contribution of the rate of technical change for twenty-six of the forty-five industries for which we measure the rate of technical change. At the aggregate level the contribution of capital input exceeds that of the rate of technical change for sixteen of the twenty-eight years included in our study. For the period as a whole the average contribution of capital input exceeds that of the rate of technical change.

In Section I we compile data on investment for the forty-six industrial sectors listed in Table 2–1 for the period 1948–1976. For each sector we have broken down investment by four legal forms of organization—corporate business, noncorporate business, private households, and nonprofit institutions. We have separated investment by six asset types—producers' durable equipment, consumers' durables, tenant-occupied residential and nonresidential structures, owner-occupied residential structures, inventories, and land. In Section II we estimate the stock of capital goods in each sector on the basis of past investments.

In Section III we combine estimates of investment for the individual sectors into estimates for the economy as a whole, broken down by the six legal forms of organization and six types of assets listed in Table 2–1. In Section IV we combine estimates of capital stock for the individual sectors into estimates for the economy as a whole, also broken down by legal form of organization and type of asset. We find that capital stock grows at the rate of 3.68 percent per year for households for the period 1948–1976, 2.80 percent for corporate business, 2.77 percent for nonprofit institutions and 1.42 percent for noncorporate business.

In Section V we combine estimates of capital formation through the acquisition of tangible assets in the private domestic sector with estimates of capital formation through acquisition of net claims on governments and the rest of the world to obtain capital formation for the private national sector of the U.S. economy. For the U.S. economy as a whole capital formation is equal to saving. We estimate net capital formation, defined as capital formation less replacement, where replacement is the loss in efficiency of capital goods with age. We also estimate net saving, defined as saving net of depreciation, where depreciation is defined as the loss in value of capital goods with age.

We present estimates of changes in wealth for the private domestic sector of the U.S. economy. Changes in wealth are the sum of saving net of depreciation and revaluations of assets as changes in capital goods prices take place. While saving has been a stable proportion of the national product, depreciation has risen from slightly over half of saving in 1947 to more than two-thirds in 1975. The proportion of net saving in the national product has fallen steadily over this period. By contrast the revaluation of existing capital goods has risen as a proportion of the change in U.S. national wealth, reflecting increases in the rate of inflation of capital goods prices.

Wealth in the private sector of the U.S. economy includes tangible assets employed in the private domestic sector and net claims on government and the rest of the world. Claims on governments and the rest of the world amounted to almost one-fourth of private national wealth in 1947 and fell steadily until 1974, amounting to less than one-eighth of the national wealth in that year. In 1975 capital formation in the form of net claims on governments and the rest of the world rose to a historic high of $82.8 billion, exceeding net capital formation in the form of private domestic tangible assets of $42.2 billion in that year.

Given estimates of capital stock for each industrial sector and for the private domestic sector of the U.S. economy, our next task is to assess the contribution of the services of capital to the growth of output at both sectoral and aggregate levels. In Section VI we compile data on compensation for the services of capital by individual producing sectors for the period 1948–1976. For each of the forty-six industry sectors we combine data on compensation by the four legal forms of organization and six types of assets as enumerated in Table 2—1.

In Section VII we combine data on property compensation for each industrial sector witn information on the tax structure for property compensation and estimates of revaluation of existing stocks of capital goods to obtain estimates of rates of return to capital for individual producing sectors. We present nominal rates of return for each sector, including earnings on capital assets, and gains from revaluation of these assets, and own rates of return, including only earnings on assets, for each sector. Nominal rates of return have risen with rising rates of inflation over the period 1948—1976. By contrast own rates of return have been stable throughout the period.

In Section VIII we combine rates of return, data on the tax structure, and the prices of capital goods to obtain prices of capital services by type of asset and legal form of organization for each of the forty-six industrial sectors listed in Table 2—1. Finally, we combine prices of capital services with stocks of capital to obtain indexes of the price and quantity of capital input for each sector. We express capital input as the product of a sectoral index of the quality of capital stock and sectoral capital stock at the beginning of the period. The quality of sectoral capital stock transforms sectoral capital stock at the beginning of the period into capital input.

In Section IX we allocate the growth of output in each of the forty-six industrial sectors listed in Table 2—1 among the contributions of intermediate, capital, and labor inputs, and the rate of sectoral technical change, defined as the rate of growth of sectoral output, holding all inputs constant. In Section X we divide the contribution of capital input between the contribution of growth in sectoral capital stock and the growth in the quality of capital stock. Both growth in capital stock and its quality are important contributors to the growth in output at the sectoral level.

In Section XI we combine data on property and labor compensation for all sectors, net of taxes, with data on consumer outlays and saving to obtain national aggregates for income and expenditure. Property income is a stable proportion of national income over the period 1948—1976, varying from 29 to 35 percent of the total. The share of property income generated by private households and nonprofit institutions increases over the period 1948—1976. The share of property income generated by corporate business and by net claims on governments and the rest of the world is stable, while the share of income generated by noncorporate business falls over the period.

We assess the role of capital in the growth of the private domestic sector of the U.S. economy in 1948–1976. For this purpose we combine prices and quantities of capital and labor services for individual producing sectors into prices and quantities of capital and labor services for the economy as a whole. We measure the output of the private domestic sector as the sum of value added over all sectors, where value added in each sector is combined with intermediate output to produce sectoral output. We allocate the growth of aggregate output among the contributions of aggregate capital and labor inputs and the rate of aggregate technical change (Section XII).

The contribution of capital input to the growth of output of the private domestic sector of the U.S. economy is 1.61 percent per year for the period 1948–1976. The contribution of labor input is 0.75 percent per year during this period. The rate of growth of aggregate technical change is 1.14 percent per year. To analyze the contribution of capital input in greater detail we divide the contribution into components associated with growth in capital stock and growth in the quality of capital stock. The contribution of growth in capital stock is 1.08 percent per year during the period 1948–1976 while the contribution of the quality of capital stock was 0.53 percent per year (Section XIII).

I. SECTORAL INVESTMENT

Our first step in measuring sectoral capital input for the U.S. economy is to construct estimates of sectoral capital stocks. We construct estimates of capital stock for assets cross-classified by the four legal forms of organization, six asset types, and forty-six industrial sectors listed in Table 2–1. Estimates of capital stock require data on investment, replacement rates, and initial levels of capital stock. The purpose of this section is to describe the investment data for all classes of assets.

We begin our description of investment data by presenting the sources of data for investment in producers' durable equipment, nonresidential structures, and tenant-occupied residential structures by industrial sector. Our primary data source for investment in these assets is a study by Jack Faucett Associates and the Bureau of Labor Statistics [22, BLS, 1979]. We have revised the allocation of investment among industrial sectors employed in this study and brought the study up to date.

We continue our discussion of investment data by presenting the sources of data for investment in inventories and land by industrial sector. These data are based on estimates of inventory stocks by the

Bureau of Economic Analysis [49, 1972] and estimates of land stocks by Raymond Goldsmith [30, 1962]. We have constructed estimates of investment in inventories and land on the basis of differences between stocks of these assets held by each industrial sector at the beginning and the end of each year.

An important objective of our study is to preserve consistency between our estimates of investment by industrial sectors and national totals for investment in the corresponding assets. For the economy as a whole the amount of land is constant, so that the total of investment in this asset over all sectors is equal to zero. Our final estimates of investment for all other classes of assets are controlled to totals based on the U.S. national income and product accounts.

Households and institutions pose special problems for measuring investment. Consumers' durables and owner-occupied residential structures are employed only in private households. We base our estimates of investment in both classes of assets on national totals from the U.S. national income and product accounts. Nonprofit institutions employ small amounts of nonresidential structures, producers' durable equipment, and land. We separate investment in these classes of assets by nonprofit institutions from investment by business.

In the following section we describe the sources of data on replacement rates and initial levels of capital stock for all classes of assets. We present data on capital stocks for each of the forty-six industrial sectors listed in Table 2–1. Finally, we analyze patterns of growth in capital stock among industries for the period 1948–1976 as a whole and among subperiods of time for each industry.

Equipment and Structures

Producers' durable equipment, nonresidential structures and tenant-occupied residential structures represent the largest investment categories for individual industries of the U.S. economy. Our primary source for depreciable investment originating and remaining in the private sector is the work of Jack Faucett Associates and Kenneth Rogers of the Bureau of Labor Statistics [22, BLS, 1979].[b] The Faucett/BLS investment data [22, BLS, 1979] are available in current and constant dollars for 156 three- or four-digit manufactur-

---

[b]The forthcoming Bureau of Labor Statistics Bulletin [22, 1979] describes the study which is the source for depreciable investment originating in the private sector for all industries except real estate. The controlling procedure employed in this study resulted in negative investment data for real estate for some of the years before 1971. As a result we use data from the earlier Jack Faucett Associates study [43, 1973b] in conjunction with past 1971 growth rates from the later work [22, 1979].

ing industries from the Standard Industrial Classification and thirty-two nonmanufacturing aggregates. The structure series are available for the years 1890–1974. The equipment series are available for the years 1921–1974. Tenant-occupied nonhousekeeping residential structures investment—hotels, motels, and dormitories—is included, while tenant-occupied housekeeping residential structures invest-ment, normally generated by nonprofit institutions and the real estate industry, is excluded.

Current dollar manufacturing investment series are extended through 1975 using the growth rates of the corresponding *Annual Survey of Manufactures* [5, Bureau of the Census, 1975; 6, Bureau of the Census, 1976] investment series. Current dollar nonmanufactur-ing investment series are extended through 1975 using growth rates from the Bureau of Economic Analysis plant and equipment expen-diture survey [57, John Woodward, 1977]. The Bureau of Economic Analysis investment data are available only for the sum of plant and equipment on a company basis for the majority of the large indus-trial aggregates.

We use Faucett/BLS deflators [22, BLS, 1979] from 1890 or 1921 through 1974. The deflator series are extended through 1976 using methodology parallel to that employed in the Faucett/BLS study [22, BLS, 1979]. For 1975 and 1976 implicit deflators for investment expenditures from the U.S. national income and product accounts, Tables 7.13 and 7.14 of the *Survey of Current Business* [20, BEA], are combined, using Faucett/BLS asset weights [22, BLS, 1979]. These weights are constant over time and sum to unity. The weights are developed by averaging the shares of investment expenditures from the 1963 and 1967 *Capital Transactions Matrix* [14, BEA, 1975]. For nonresidential structures the nineteen Faucett/BLS asset weights [22, BLS, 1979] are aggregated to correspond to the eleven U.S. national income and product account investment deflators from Table 7.13 of the *Survey of Current Business* [20, BEA]. No information is entered that is specific to the tenant-occu-pied residential structures investment included in the Faucett/BLS data. For producers' durable equipment the twenty-two Faucett/BLS asset weights [22, BLS, 1979] correspond precisely to twenty-two U.S. national income and product accounts deflators from Table 7.14 of the *Survey of Current Business* [20, BEA]. The product of the asset weights and the U.S. national income and product accounts deflators are summed for each year to create the initial 1974–1976 investment deflators. The final step is to scale the 1974–1976 de-flators such that the 1974 Faucett/BLS implicit deflators and the generated 1974 deflators correspond exactly.

Information for tenant-occupied housekeeping residential structures investment is taken directly from the *Capital Stock Study* of the Bureau of Economic Analysis [16, BEA, 1976a]. The whole of the tenant-occupied housekeeping investment, aside from that originating in nonprofit institutions, is allocated to the real estate industry. Unpublished *Capital Stock Study* data [16, BEA, 1976a] are available from 1890–1977 in both current and constant prices. The implicit *Capital Stock Study* deflators [16, BEA 1976a] are used for all years for this portion of residential structures investment.

The Faucett/BLS industry categories do not match the industry categories listed in Table 2–1 in the case of agriculture, services, and nonprofit institutions. We discuss services and nonprofit institutions below. The Faucett/BLS data [22, BLS, 1979] on investment in agriculture are divided between agricultural production and agricultural services, horticultural services, forestry and fisheries in proportion to the ratio of capital consumption allowances in each industry to the total of capital consumption allowances in both industries. Capital consumption allowances by industry in current dollars are available from the Bureau of Economic Analysis as part of its study *Fourteen Current Dollar Components of Gross Product Originating by Industry* [19, 1979].

The establishment of control totals for structures and producers' durable equipment proceeds in two stages. First, the investment data are controlled using U.S. national income and product accounts totals [17, BEA, 1976b; 20, BEA] and *Capital Stock Study* shares [16, BEA, 1976a]. Second, the distribution of investment among nonmanufacturing industries is adjusted to reflect capital consumption allowances in those industries. At the aggregate level investment in structures and equipment is controlled to totals for structures and producers' durable equipment from the U.S. national income and product accounts [17, BEA, 1976b; 20, BEA]. The *Capital Stock Study* [16, BEA, 1976a] includes information on investment by type of asset, legal form of organization, and by manufacturing versus nonmanufacturing industries. Control totals for investment in these categories are derived by applying *Capital Stock Study* shares [16, BEA, 1976a] to the control totals from the U.S. national income and product accounts.[c]

For producers' durable equipment shares in current and constant prices were calculated from the *Capital Stock Study* [16, BEA, 1976a] for the following sectors of the economy: households, institutions, manufacturing industries, and nonmanufacturing industries.

[c]The issue of assets sold or transferred from the public to the private sector, or vice-versa, will be discussed later.

For structures, shares in current and constant prices were calculated from the *Capital Stock Study* investment data [16, BEA, 1976a] for the following categories: owner-occupied residential structures assigned to households, tenant-occupied housekeeping and non-housekeeping residential structures and nonresidential structures assigned to institutions, nonresidential structures assigned to manufacturing industries, and tenant-occupied housekeeping and non-housekeeping residential structures and nonresidential structures assigned to nonmanufacturing industries.

Tenant-occupied nonhousekeeping residential structures investment is allocated among several industries in the Faucett/BLS data [22, BLS, 1979]. We add tenant-occupied housekeeping residential structures investment to investment in the finance, insurance, and real estate industry.[d] All investment in residential structures is included in our accounts.

Institutional investment from the *Capital Stock Study* [16, BEA, 1976a] includes only nonprofit institutions serving persons, while the Faucett/BLS [22, BLS, 1979] category "Medical and educational services and nonprofit organizations" includes social and fraternal clubs and excludes residential structures. To reconcile these classifications, we deducted institutional investment from the *Capital Stock Study* [16, BEA, 1976a], net of residential structures, from the sum of the Faucett/BLS nonprofit institutions and service industry investment [22, BLS, 1979], to generate service industry investment figures as a residual. Household and institutional investment as described above are generated in the same manner as the investment series included in the Christensen-Jorgenson national income accounting system [23, 1969; 25, 1973].

The second step in imposing control totals is to redistribute plant and equipment investment among the nonmanufacturing industries. For manufacturing, the investment series from the *Annual Survey of Manufactures* [5, Bureau of the Census, 1975; 6, Bureau of the Census, 1976] serve as a source for sectoral data and as a basis for comparison. For nonmanufacturing, no comparable source exists. As a consequence, we redistribute investment for all industries except households and institutions and for all types of plant and equipment except for tenant-occupied housekeeping residential structures. We first estimate capital consumption allowances for each nonmanufacturing industry at historical cost on the basis of our initial estimates of investment for that industry. To redistribute investment among industries we multiply investment for each industry by the

[d]As previously noted, the Faucett/BLS investment data do not include tenant-occupied housekeeping residential structures.

ratio of capital consumption allowances from the study *Fourteen Current Dollar Components of Gross Product Originating by Industry* [19, 1979] to our estimate of capital consumption allowances at historical cost for the period 1948—1976. Finally, we control total investment for all nonmanufacturing industries to the same totals as before.

Difficulties in the measurement of the sale or transfer of assets from the public to the private sector, or vice versa, result from the differences in the accounting conventions used by the primary sources. In the U.S. national income and product accounts [17, BEA, 1976b; 20, BEA] assets transferred or sold are valued at the price actually paid for the asset at the time of the transfer or sale. In the *Capital Stock Study* [16, BEA, 1976a] assets transferred or sold are valued according to the characteristics of the asset. Government assets not well suited to peacetime uses are valued at an estimate of the price private business would be willing to pay for an asset of equal productivity. The value of all other assets transferred or sold is based on the original acquisition price. Government owned, privately operated, assets are transferred to the private sector only at the time of sale following the rules of valuation described above. The *Capital Stock Study* [16, BEA, 1976a] includes transfers both to and from the private sector.

We use the Jack Faucett Associates series [43, 1973b] for government owned, privately operated investment, later sold to the private sector. This investment is transferred to private industry as of the date it was first leased, valued at original acquisition cost. Jack Faucett Associates did not separate nonmanufacturing government owned, privately operated investment, later sold, from investment originating and remaining in the private sector [43, 1973b]. We control private manufacturing investment and nonmanufacturing investment, including a small component of government owned, privately operated, manufacturing investment, to private investment from the U.S. national income and product accounts [17, BEA, 1976b; 20, BEA]. We add government owned, privately operated, later sold manufacturing investment from Jack Faucett Associates [43, 1973b].[e]

To obtain estimates of the quantity of government owned, privately operated, later sold investment, we apply the 1972 based three-digit SIC investment deflators from the more recent Faucett/BLS study [22, BLS, 1979] to the corresponding current dollar gov-

[e]We employ estimates of government-owned, privately operated, later sold, investment from the earlier Jack Faucett Associates study [43, 1973b] as more recent data had not yet been released at the time of this research project. The earlier data extend through 1970, covering the period during which a significant amount of this type of investment occurred. See Table 2-4.

ernment owned, privately operated, later sold manufacturing investment series.

Inventories and Land

Inventory investment for all producing industries except for farm
is constructed in two stages. First we estimate the quantity of corporate and noncorporate inventory stocks for all industries. Second
we control the quantity of corporate and noncorporate inventory
investment to totals derived from the U.S. national income and
product accounts [17, BEA] and from unpublished Bureau of Economic Analysis data. We obtained prices and quantities of corporate
and noncorporate capital stocks for twenty-one manufacturing industries of our study and for nine nonmanufacturing aggregates from
John Hinrichs of the Bureau of Economic Analysis. For the four
industries requiring further disaggregation,[f] we use constant dollar
capital stock distributions available from the report of Jack Faucett
Associates, *Measures of Working Capital* [44, 1973c], and constant
dollar value added distributions available from Table 6.2 of the *Survey of Current Business* [17, BEA, 1976b; 20, BEA]. We use these
distributions to generate industry splits for total inventory stocks.
The ratio of noncorporate capital consumption allowances to the
total of corporate plus noncorporate capital consumption allowances
[see (19, BEA, 1978)] is used to divide inventory stocks between the
noncorporate and corporate components of each sector. The sectoral
noncorporate and corporate data are then scaled so that the aggregate inventory stocks for each sector are allocated between the two
components.

We estimate sectoral inventory investment by taking first differences of sectoral inventory stocks. We employ control totals for the
quantity of corporate and noncorporate nonfarm inventory investment from the Christensen-Jorgenson aggregate national income
accounts [23, 1969; 25, 1973]. Christensen and Jorgenson [23,
1969; 25, 1973] derive noncorporate inventory investment by taking
the first differences of stock figures available from John Hinrichs and
Shirley Loftus [48, Loftus, 1972]. Corporate inventory investment
is obtained by taking the change in nonfarm business inventories
from Table 1.2 of the Survey of Current Business [17, BEA, 1976b;

---

[f]We use the Jack Faucett Associates report [44, 1973c] to disaggregate mining and the public utilities half of communications and public utilities. We use
Table 6.2 [17, BEA, 1976b; 20, BEA] to disaggregate agriculture, transportation, and the communications half of communications and public utilities. The
remaining five aggregates: construction, wholesale trade, retail trade, finance,
insurance and real estate and services correspond to one of our forty-six industries.

20, BEA] less the estimated noncorporate figure. It should be noted that aggregate inventory stock figures available from Hinrichs and Loftus will not match stocks generated from the U.S. national income and product accounts data [17, BEA, 1976b; 30, BEA]. This is mainly due to small differences in the inventory valuation adjustment component of inventory investment. Farm inventory investment is taken directly from Table 1.1 and Table 1.2 of the *Survey of Current Business* [17, BEA, 1976b; 20, BEA] and allocated to the noncorporate sector. The sectoral implicit investment deflators are derived from the unpublished industry level Bureau of Economic Analysis data. The deflators are scaled such that the value of inventory investment equals the figure available from Table 1.1 of the *Survey of Current Business* [17, BEA, 1976b; 20, BEA].[g]

Sectoral land investment is derived from data on land stocks. The construction of estimates of stocks of land begins with estimates of the value of land for the economy as a whole generated by Christensen and Jorgenson [23, 1969; 25, 1973]. Christensen and Jorgenson [23, 1969; 25, 1973] based their estimates on the earlier studies of Goldsmith [30, 1962] and Allen Manvel [50, 1968].

> To establish a benchmark for land we assume that land is 39 percent of the value of all private real estate in 1956. This is based on a study of the value of real estate and land by Manvel. Taking the value of residential and non-residential structures in 1956 to be 61 percent of the value of all private real estate, we obtain a benchmark for the value of land in 1956. . . . [23, 1969, p. 296]

The land stock is then allocated among the four legal forms of organization presented in Table 15 in proportion to date reported for 1956 by Goldsmith [30, 1962]. We assume that the relative distribution of land among legal forms of organization remains constant and that the quantity of land is fixed over time. These stock estimates provide control totals for our estimates of land stock by industry.

We employ balance sheet data from the Internal Revenue Service *Statistics of Income* [38, 39, 41] to distribute the market value of land for the economy as a whole among industrial sectors. Balance sheet data on book value of land by industrial sector are available for

[g]In that the data in Table 1.1 are presented in millions while the data in Table 1.2 are presented in billions, the implicit inventory deflator in the base year, 1972, will not equal 1.000. A similar problem did not present itself in the case of plant and equipment, as implicit price deflators normalized to 1.000 in the base year are available from Table 7.13 and Table 7.14 of the Survey of Current Business [17, BEA, 1976b; 20, BEA]. See Table 2–6.

corporations for all years for the period 1947–1973; however, the data are classified by industries defined on a company rather than establishment basis. We transform balance sheet data to an establishment basis, using the 1958 establishment-company ratios available in the Bureau of the Census *Enterprise Statistics* [4, 1958]. *The Statistics of Income* [38, 39] detail for nonmanufacturing industries is less than the detail used throughout this study; therefore the book value of land is distributed among subindustries using current dollar shares in the value of plant. Finally, the book values for each industry are adjusted so that their sum equals the control total for corporate land. We assume that the ratio of market value to book value is constant for all industries at each point of time.

Noncorporate land data for partnerships and proprietorships are available separately from the *Statistics of Income* [41] for four years for partnerships and two years for proprietorships. We begin by generating a consistent set of industry data for each of the benchmark years (1953, 1959, 1963 and 1965) according to a method first suggested by Hulten:

> (1) The Statistics of Income estimates are inflated from partnership with balance sheets to the level of all partnerships using the ratio of total receipts for the latter to total receipts for the former. (2) The resulting estimates are then adjusted to include sole proprietorships (to bring the estimates up to the noncorporate level). This is accomplished by calculating the ratio of total receipts of proprietorships and partnerships to total receipts of partnerships and using the result to inflate the partnership land estimates. (3) Data for missing industries are then estimated by allocating the total unaccounted-for-land in the same proportion as the corresponding corporate book values. The result is a consistent set of benchmarks for the book values of non-corporate land. [37, 1973b, p. 67]

We then interpolate and extrapolate using the book value growth rates for the corporate land held by the corresponding industry to obtain complete noncorporate land stocks by industry. We assume that the value of land held by the noncorporate sector of an industry is zero when the value of noncorporate capital consumption allowances is zero for that industry.

We employ a single land deflator for all industries. We extend Goldsmith's private land stock series [30, 1962] in current and constant dollars from 1958–1976, employing the average growth rates of land stocks calculated by Goldsmith [31, 1978] for the periods 1954–1964 and 1965–1975. Sectoral investment in land is estimated by first differencing data on stocks.

Households and Institutions

We allocate investment in consumers' durables and owner-occupied residential structures to households. Investment in land associated with owner-occupied residential structures is zero, since we assume that the stock of such land is constant. We treat expenditures on consumers' durables as investment, following Christensen and Jorgenson [23, 1969; 25, 1973]. This treatment differs from that in the U.S. national income and product accounts [17, BEA, 1976b; 20, BEA]. Owner-occupied residential structures investment data are generated by applying shares from the *Capital Stock Study* [16, BEA, 1976a] to residential structures investment totals from the U.S. national income and product accounts [17, BEA, 1976b; 20, BEA]. We do not allocate producers' durable equipment, residential structures or inventory investment to the household industry.

We allocate producers' durable equipment associated with residential and nonresidential structures investment and nonresidential and tenant-occupied housekeeping and nonhousekeeping residential structures investment to nonprofit institutions serving persons. Land investment is zero since we assume that the stock of such land is constant. As with households, we assume that institutions do not hold any inventories.

II. SECTORAL CAPITAL STOCK

Our next objective is to construct estimates of capital stock for each of the forty-six industrial sectors of the U.S. economy listed in Table 2–1. Our estimates are based on the system of vintage accounts for capital presented by Jorgenson [47, 1980] in the next chapter in this volume. In this system each capital good is characterized by the relative efficiency of capital goods of different ages in production. The system encompasses prices as well as quantities of capital goods that appear in our sectoral production accounts.

For capital in the form of equipment and structures we assume that the efficiency of capital goods declines geometrically with the age of the asset. We estimate capital stock A_t at the end of each period as a weighted sum of past investments $A_{t-\tau}$,

$$A_t = \sum_{\tau=0}^{\infty} (1-\delta)^\tau I_{t-\tau},$$

where δ is the rate of decline in efficiency of capital goods with age, t is time, and τ is the age of an asset.

The change in capital stock from period to period is equal to the difference between the acquisition of investment goods and replacement requirements R_t,

$$A_t - A_{t-1} = I_t - R_t ,$$

$$= I_t - \delta A_{t-1} ,$$

where δ is the rate of replacement. The rate of replacement is constant and equal to the rate of decline in efficiency of an asset with age.

To construct estimates of sectoral capital stock in the form of equipment and structures we require data on investment, replacement rates, and initial levels of capital stock for each industrial sector. We assume that capital goods in the form of inventories and land do not decline in efficiency with age, so that the change in capital stock from period to period is equal to the acquisition of investment goods. For these assets we require only data on investment and the initial levels of capital stock for each sector.

In the preceding section we have described investment data for all classes of assets for each of the forty-six industrial sectors listed in Table 2–1. In this section we discuss estimates of rates of replacement for equipment and structures in each sector. Our estimates of replacement rates are based on the double declining balance pattern of relative efficiency of assets of different ages. The replacement rate takes the form:

$$\delta = \frac{2}{L} ,$$

where L is the lifetime of the asset.

We next present data on capital stocks for the forty-six industrial sectors included in our study. We analyze the pattern of growth of capital stock across industries for the time period 1948–1976. Second, we analyze the pattern of growth across subperiods of time for individual industries. For this purpose we divide the period as a whole into seven subperiods corresponding to the years between cyclical peaks of the U.S. economy. In Sections III and IV below we combine estimates of sectoral investment and capital stock to obtain corresponding estimates for the U.S. economy as a whole.

Asset Lifetimes

Information on asset lifetimes by industry is obtained from a study by Jack Faucett Associates [43, 1973b]. Asset lifetimes are available for sixteen types of producers' durable equipment and twelve types of nonresidential structures. Asset weights, similar to those described from the more recent Faucett/BLS study [22, BLS, 1979], are also available by industry.[h] Jack Faucett Associates adjusted the asset lifetimes to insure a close correspondence between their capital stock estimates and the gross asset book values reported in the *Annual Survey of Manufactures*. In general these asset lifetimes are longer than those employed in the *Capital Stock Study* [16, BEA, 1976a]. For those industries for which the Jack Faucett Associates industry classification [43, 1973b] is more detailed than our industry classification, we proceed in several steps. First for each Jack Faucett Associates industry subaggregate, we take the simple summation of the asset lifetimes weighted by the appropriate asset weight. We then determine the relative share of each detailed industry's asset lifetime in the total by calculating shares based on the 1958 constant dollar gross capital stocks from the same Jack Faucett Associates study [43, 1973b]. The aggregate lifetime is then determined by applying these shares to the detailed industry lifetimes. The rate of replacement for tenant-occupied housekeeping residential structures, assigned to households and institutions, are generated from *Capital Stock Study* [16, BEA, 1976a] assets lifetimes. The rates of replacement for other assets of households and institutions are taken from the Christensen-Jorgenson national income accounts [23, 1969].

The capital stock benchmarks for depreciable investment for producing industries are taken to be zero in 1890 for tenant-occupied residential structures and nonresidential structures and zero in 1921 for producers' durable equipment. The benchmarks for assets assigned to households and institutions are taken from the Christensen-Jorgenson accounts [23, 1969, pp. 294–97]. Capital stocks for depreciable assets are allocated between noncorporate and corporate components of each industry in proportion to the capital consumption allowances in each component. Data on capital consumption allowances are obtained from the Bureau of Economic Analysis study *Fourteen Current Dollar Components of Gross Product Originating by Industry* [19, 1978].

The investment deflators are used as asset deflators without modification, except in the case of inventory stocks.[i] For the farm inven-

[h] The asset weights were constructed from the 1958 and 1963 *Capital Transactions Matrices* [21, BLS, 1968; 14, BEA, 1975a].

[i] We distinguish between investment and asset deflators when the valuation of investment differs significantly from the valuation of capital stocks, as in the case of inventories.

tory asset deflator, following Christensen and Jorgenson [23, 1969; 25, 1973], we employ the Bureau of Labor Statistics wholesale price index for farm products, set to unity in 1972. For the nonfarm inventory asset deflator, again following Christensen and Jorgenson, we employ the Bureau of Labor Statistics wholesale price index for industrial commodities, taken equal to unity in 1972. We scale the Bureau of Economic Analysis sectoral asset reflators to produce sectoral asset deflators in such a way that the Bureau of Labor Statistics wholesale price index is the aggregate nonfarm inventory asset deflator.[j] Multiplying the quantity of sectoral gross inventory investment by the ratio of the aggregate inventory investment deflator to the aggregate inventory asset deflator as it enters into the capital stock calculation insures that the value of the addition to aggregate inventory stocks will equal the value of aggregate inventory investment in any period.

Growth in Capital Stock

Table 2–2 presents the rates of growth for the quantity of sectoral capital stock for the following eight periods: the whole period, 1948–1976, and seven subperiods—1948–1953, 1953–1957, 1957–1960, 1960–1966, 1966–1969, 1969–1973, and 1973–1976. Annual data for the price and quantity of sectoral capital stock are given in Appendix A. Table 2–3 classifies the rates of growth of the quantity of sectoral capital stock by average rate of growth categories, for the periods listed above. The three earlier subperiods: 1948–1953, 1953–1957, 1957–1960, and the 1966–1969 time period show a high degree of dispersion of the sectoral rates of growth. The dispersion of the latter time period, 1966–1969, is skewed toward higher rates of growth.

Referring to Table 2–2, the sectors experiencing significantly lower or higher than average rates of growth of capital stock for the whole time period, 1948–1976, can be identified. The industries, predominantly in the transportation sector, that have experienced a decline in capital stock include leather and leather products, railroads and railway express service, street railway, bus lines and taxicab service, and pipelines except natural gas. The three transportation industries exhibit lower than average rates of growth of capital stock for each of the seven subperiods. Leather and leather products shows a high rate of growth of capital stock for one subperiod, 1966–1969. That subperiod is followed by a significant downturn in the next.

[j] We begin with asset reflators from the Bureau of Economic Analysis. We produce investment and asset deflators, employing separate scaling procedures.

Table 2-2.   Sectoral Capital Stock: Rates of Growth (*Average Annual Rates of Growth*)

Industry	1948-1976	1948-1953	1953-1957	1957-1960	1960-1966	1966-1969	1969-1973	1973-1976
Agricultural production	.0127	.0256	-.0024	.0093	.0102	.0226	.0009	.0261
Agricultural services	.0295	-.0089	.0308	.0570	.0409	.0482	.0337	.0168
Metal mining	.0453	.0557	.0729	.1616	.0547	.0017	-.0143	-.0213
Coal mining	.0210	.0473	-.0543	.0143	.0569	-.0065	.0407	.0536
Crude petroleum and natural gas	.0096	.0117	.0161	.0078	.0153	.0063	-.0031	.0078
Nonmetallic mining and quarrying	.0702	.1190	.0981	.0789	.0717	.0520	.0233	.0206
Contract construction	.0655	.1052	.0654	.0708	.0715	.0579	.0550	.0038
Food and kindred products	.0098	.0137	-.0022	.0085	.0100	.0171	.0139	.0075
Tobacco manufacturers	.0152	.0219	.0031	.0083	.0144	-.0202	.0211	.0565
Textile mill products	.0192	.0459	-.0035	-.0302	.0201	.0617	.0267	-.0004

Table 2-2. continued

Industry	1948-1976	1948-1953	1953-1957	1957-1960	1960-1966	1966-1969	1969-1973	1973-1976
Apparel and other fabr. textile prod.	.0259	.0254	.0142	-.0003	.0362	.0752	.0393	-.0189
Paper and allied products	.0422	.0590	.0560	.0364	.0327	.0526	.0292	.0274
Printing and publishing	.0124	.0007	.0059	-.0058	.0224	.0457	.0190	-.0007
Chemicals and allied products	.0341	.0247	.0314	.0233	.0403	.0686	.0239	.0310
Petroleum and coal products	.0196	.0017	.0444	-.0103	.0188	.0756	.0015	.0162
Rubber and misc. plastic products	.0508	.0485	.0331	.0569	.0471	.0775	.0635	.0361
Leather and leather products	.0022	.0133	-.0054	-.0301	-.0034	.0453	-.0364	.0049
Lumber and wood prod., ex. furniture	.0224	.0393	.0288	-.0269	.0105	.0095	.0510	.0334
Furniture and fixtures	.0264	.0190	.0234	.0072	.0192	.0477	.0452	.0303
Stone, clay, and glass products	.0321	.0397	.0597	.0432	.0200	.0234	.0153	.0267

Table 2–2. continued

Industry	1948–1976	1948–1953	1953–1957	1957–1960	1960–1966	1966–1969	1969–1973	1973–1976
Primary metal industries	.0168	.0255	.0254	.0167	.0073	.0384	.0022	.0082
Fabricated metal industries	.0290	.0304	.0360	.0054	.0277	.0517	.0185	.0352
Machinery, ex. electrical	.0433	.0461	.0405	.0166	.0375	.0824	.0309	.0579
Elec. machinery, eqpt. and supplies	.0426	.0723	.0351	.0071	.0450	.0860	.0195	.0214
Trans. eqpt. & ord., ex. motor vehicles	.0216	.0222	.0202	-.0169	.0081	.1666	-.0193	-.0026
Motor vehicles and equipment	.0300	.0396	.0554	-.0283	.0318	.0481	.0244	.0241
Prof. photographic eqpt. and watches	.0599	.0853	.0778	.0343	.0420	.0922	.0416	.0474
Misc. manufacturing industries	.0166	-.0211	.0364	-.0029	.0141	.1164	.0080	-.0105
Railroads and rail express service	-.0044	-.0087	-.0054	-.0162	-.0086	.0037	-.0074	.0200
Street rail., bus lines, and taxicabs	-.0060	.0186	-.0411	-.0273	-.0111	.0129	-.0062	.0124

Table 2-2. continued

Industry	1948-1976	1948-1953	1953-1957	1957-1960	1960-1966	1966-1969	1969-1973	1973-1976
Trucking services and warehousing	.0503	.0589	.0232	.0674	.0330	.0704	.0220	.1075
Water transportation	.0134	-.0203	-.0148	.0368	.0141	.0270	.0149	.0664
Air transportation	.1061	.1076	.1147	.1982	.1041	.2048	.0249	.0078
Pipelines, ex. natural gas	-.0041	-.0073	-.0151	-.0364	-.0075	.0163	.0188	.0038
Transportation services	.0244	-.0333	.0264	.0342	.0237	.0689	-.0086	.1086
Te. and tel. and misc. comm. services	.0602	.0170	.0334	.0391	.0740	.0782	.0959	.0958
Radio broadcasting and television	.0953	.0776	.2121	.1015	.0995	.0985	.0295	.0388
Electric utilities	.0318	.0218	.0168	.0190	.0159	.0449	.0684	.0514
Gas utilities	.0138	.0197	-.0524	.0298	.0010	.0073	.0512	.0584
Water supply and sanitary services	.0543	.1072	-.0071	.0814	.0401	.0533	.0524	.0530

Table 2–2. continued

Industry	1948–1976	1948–1953	1953–1957	1957–1960	1960–1966	1966–1969	1969–1973	1973–1976
Wholesale trade	.0510	.0847	.0419	.0316	.0504	.0725	.0400	.0211
Retail trade	.0355	.0656	.0370	.0072	.0292	.0412	.0376	.0161
Finance, insurance, and real estate	.0117	.0066	.0114	.0075	.0118	.0077	.0233	.0128
Services excl. priv. hh., inst.	.0286	-.0101	.0126	.0410	.0512	.0457	.0390	.0255
Private households	.0368	.0531	.0420	.0282	.0300	.0332	.0353	.0307
Institutions	.0277	.0280	.0313	.0374	.0444	.0585	.0117	-.0099

Table 2–3.   Classification of Rates of Growth of Sectoral Capital Stock by Periods, 1948–1976

Average Rate of Growth of Capital Stock	1948–1976	1948–1953	1953–1957	1957–1960	1960–1966	1966–1969	1969–1973	1973–1976
Less than −2 percent	0	3	3	6	0	1	1	1
−2 to less than 0 percent	4	5	8	6	4	1	6	6
0 to less than 2 percent	12	9	7	13[a]	14	9	12	12
2 to less than 4 percent	16[a]	12[a]	15[a]	10	13[a]	6[a]	16[a]	16[a]
4 to less than 6 percent	9	8	7	4	10	13	8	7
6 to less than 8 percent	3	3	3	3	3	9	2	1
8 percent or more	2	6	3	4	2	7	1	3

[a] Denotes the category which contains the average rate of growth of aggregate capital stock for the period.

Not all transportation industries can be characterized as experiencing lower than average rates of growth of capital stock. Air transportation exhibits the highest rate of growth of capital stock for the period as a whole. The other industries which experience a high rate of growth for the period as a whole include nonmetallic mining and quarrying, except fuel, construction, and both communication sectors—telephone, telegraph, and miscellaneous communication services, and radio broadcasting and television. Of this group, radio broadcasting and television is the only industry which has a higher than average rate of growth for each of the seven subperiods.

Three industries show lower than average growth rates of capital stock only for the most recent periods: nonmetallic mining and quarrying, except fuel, construction, and air transportation. Telephone, telegraph, and miscellaneous communication services exhibits a lower than average rate of growth of capital stock only for the first subperiod 1948–1953. This industry demonstrates a pattern of increasing growth of capital stock over time, until the most recent period, 1973–1976.

For the seven subperiods we consider in detail those industries which exhibit average rates of decline of capital stock of more than 2 percent or average rates of growth of capital stock of 8 percent or more. During the 1948–1953 subperiod, the three industries falling in the lowest category for the average rate of growth of capital stock are miscellaneous manufacturing industries, water transportation, and transportation services. During the same period, the six industries falling in the highest category are nonmetallic mining and quarrying, construction, professional photographic equipment and watches, air transportation, water supply and sanitary services, and wholesale trade. Construction, water supply and sanitary services, and wholesale trade exhibit their highest average rate of growth of capital stock of the whole period.

During the 1953–1957 subperiod, the three industries with average rates of growth of capital stock less then −2 percent are coal mining, street railway, bus lines and taxicabs, and gas utilities. All energy industries, with the exception of petroleum, experienced lower than average rates of growth of capital stock during this period. The three industries with average rates of growth of capital stock of 8 percent or more for this subperiod are among those industries experiencing significantly higher than average rates of growth of capital stock for the period as a whole. These are nonmetallic mining and quarrying, air transportation, and radio broadcasting and television.

Six industries had negative average rates of growth of capital stock of −2 percent or more from 1957–1960: textile mill products, lumber and wood products except furniture, leather and leather products, motor vehicles, street railway, bus lines and taxicab service, and pipelines, except natural gas. The decline of capital stock in the lumber and wood product industry reflects the large decrease in the average rate of growth of owner-occupied residential capital stocks, beginning in 1953—1957 and continuing through the 1966—1969 subperiod. During the subperiod 1957—1960 the four industries with rates of growth of 8 percent or more are metal mining, air transportation, radio broadcasting and television, and water supply and sanitary services.

During the 1960—1966 period, no industries had average rates of growth of capital stock less than −2 percent; the two industries with average rates of growth of 8 percent or more are among those industries experiencing significantly higher than average rates of growth of capital stock for the period as a whole: air transportation and radio broadcasting and television.

Only tobacco manufacturers falls in the lowest category for 1966—1969. The seven industries falling in the highest category are: machinery, except electrical; electrical machinery, equipment, and supplies; transportation equipment and ordnance, except motor vehicles; professional photographic equipment and supplies; miscellaneous manufacturing industries; air transportation; radio broadcasting and television. The last two industries are included in the group with significantly higher than average rates of growth of capital stock for the period as a whole; the other industries are durable goods manufacturing industries. All the durable goods manufacturing industries had higher than average rates of growth of capital stock during this period except for lumber and stone, clay and glass products.

During the 1969—1973 period, only leather and leather products had an average growth rate of capital stock less than −2 percent, and only telephone, telegraph, and miscellaneous communication services had an average growth rate greater than 8 percent. Both industries experienced rates of growth of capital stock which differ significantly from the average for the period as a whole. Only metal mining had a growth rate below −2 percent for the subperiod 1973—1976. Three industries had growth rates of 8 percent or more: trucking services and warehousing, transportation services, and telephone and telegraph and miscellaneous communication services.

III. AGGREGATE INVESTMENT

In this section we combine estimates of sectoral investment to obtain estimates of investment for the U.S. economy as a whole. Investment for the private domestic sector of the U.S. economy is equal to the sum of gross private domestic investment and personal consumption expenditures on consumers' durables from the U.S. national income and product accounts and a small amount of manufacturing investment in assets owned by the government, employed by government contractors, and later transferred or sold to the private sector.

We present data on investment annually for the private domestic sector of the U.S. economy for the period 1947—1975. We also present data on investment annually for three legal forms of organization—corporate and noncorporate business, households, and institutions—and five classes of assets—producers' durable equipment, consumers' durables, tenant-occupied residential and nonresidential structures, owner-occupied residential structures, and inventories. We recall that the stock of land is constant for the economy as a whole, so that investment in land is equal to zero at the aggregate level.

We analyze the pattern of growth of investment across legal forms of organization and classes of assets at the aggregate level for the time period 1947—1975. Investment by households has grown considerably more rapidly than investment by corporate and noncorporate business during this period. Investment in producers' and consumers' durables has grown more rapidly than investment in structures during the period with investment in consumers' durables growing more rapidly than investment in any other class of assets.

We also analyze patterns of growth in investment over seven subperiods—1947—1952, 1952—1956, 1956—1959, 1959—1965, 1965—1968, 1968—1972, and 1972—1975—by legal form of organization and class of asset. The final subperiod, 1972—1975, is characterized by a sharp decline in levels of investment for all legal forms of organization. Levels of investment in structures declined during this subperiod, while growth rates of producers' and consumers' durables fell from those of the preceding subperiod, 1968—1972.

In Section IV we combine estimates of sectoral capital stocks to obtain estimates of capital stock for the U.S. economy as a whole. We present data on capital stocks cross-classified by asset types and legal forms of organization. Finally, we analyze patterns of growth in capital stock for the private domestic sector of the U.S. economy and for each asset type and each legal form of organization. In Section V we combine our data on investment with data on saving to provide accumulation and wealth accounts for the private national sector of the U.S. economy.

Investment

The price and quantity of gross private domestic investment are obtained by aggregating over the forty-six industrial sectors listed in

Table 2–1. The quantity and value of gross private domestic investment are equal to the sum of the quantity and value respectively of gross private domestic investment and personal consumption expenditures on consumers' durables from the U.S. national income and product accounts [17, BEA, 1976b; 20, BEA] plus the quantity and value respectively of government owned, privately operated, later sold, manufacturing investment [43, 1973b]. An implicit deflator is derived as the ratio of the value series to the quantity series. Prices and quantities of investment by class of asset and legal form of organization are derived by the same method.

In Table 2–4 we present the price and quantity of gross private domestic and government owned, privately operated, later sold, manufacturing investment.[k] In Table 2–5 we present the price and quantity of gross private domestic investment by legal form of organization, where corporate and noncorporate investment are aggregated and government owned, privately operated, later sold, investment is included in corporate and noncorporate investment. In Table 2–6 we present the price and quantity of gross private domestic investment by the six asset types listed in Table 2–1, excluding land. Government owned, privately operated, later sold, investment is included in the appropriate asset type category. Land investment is zero as land stocks are assumed to be constant.

Growth in Investment

In Table 2–7 we present the rates of growth of the quantity of gross investment by legal form of organization and asset type for the period 1947–1975 and for the following seven subperiods: 1947–1952, 1952–1956, 1956–1959, 1959–1965, 1965–1968, 1968–1972, and 1972–1975. Considering the rates of growth of investment in Table 2–7, the high variability of the rate of growth over time and the downturn in 1972–1975 are the most significant features. Each decrease or increase in the rate of growth is followed by an increase or decrease in the following subperiod. The downturn in 1972–1975 represents by far the largest change in the rate of growth from the previous period in both absolute and relative terms. Rates of growth are significantly negative for the first subperiod among those included in Table 2–7. Investment for all legal forms of

[k]The value of gross private domestic investment implicit in Table 2-4 in 1959 is not exactly equal to the sum of the value of government-owned, privately operated, later sold, manufacturing investment plus the value of consumers' durables and gross private domestic investment in Table 1.1 of the *Survey of Current Business* [20] because the implicit farm inventory investment deflator derived from Tables 1.1 and 1.2 [20] is zero. This does not affect our analysis as we employ a farm inventory asset deflator that is different from zero.

Table 2–4.   Gross Private Domestic Investment (constant prices of 1972), 1947–1975

Year	Gross Private Domestic		Government Owned, Privately Operated, Later Sold, Manufacturing	
	Price	Quantity	Price	Quantity
1947	.540	100.764	.000	.000
1948	.595	115.396	.000	.000
1949	.593	101.799	.521	.013
1950	.616	137.197	.000	.000
1951	.664	134.039	.000	.000
1952	.665	122.191	.571	.002
1953	.667	128.640	.000	.000
1954	.666	126.906	.593	.018
1955	.685	156.223	.625	.006
1956	.713	152.723	.000	.000
1957	.739	146.988	.668	.096
1958	.737	134.068	.000	.000
1959	.754	159.233	.635	.026
1960	.757	157.860	.000	.000
1961	.753	153.844	.000	.000
1962	.762	173.208	.606	.026
1963	.765	185.227	.000	.000
1964	.773	197.801	.632	.001
1965	.782	223.428	.716	.000
1966	.800	240.274	.836	.004
1967	.820	232.339	.703	.000
1968	.854	249.736	.000	.000
1969	.891	259.889	.000	.000
1970	.927	243.625	.000	.000
1971	.970	264.996	.000	.000
1972	1.000	299.474	.000	.000
1973	1.045	328.990	.000	.000
1974	1.136	296.179	.000	.000
1975	1.268	255.252	.000	.000

Table 2–5.   Gross Private Domestic Investment by Legal Form of Organization (constant prices of 1972), 1947–1975

Year	Corporate and Noncorporate		Household		Institutions	
	Price	Quantity	Price	Quantity	Price	Quantity
1947	.467	49.579	.616	49.351	.454	1.834
1948	.552	57.632	.644	55.374	.500	2.391
1949	.520	42.377	.652	56.547	.503	2.875
1950	.568	61.417	.663	71.835	.510	3.945
1951	.629	66.302	.706	63.924	.563	3.813
1952	.616	56.345	.714	62.274	.575	3.572
1953	.609	57.759	.722	67.125	.584	3.756
1954	.620	52.799	.707	69.729	.579	4.379
1955	.651	69.010	.719	82.787	.592	4.426
1956	.688	70.544	.740	77.409	.639	4.769
1957	.716	66.857	.760	74.933	.668	5.198
1958	.711	56.569	.763	71.905	.661	5.594
1959	.735	69.823	.776	83.440	.668	5.970
1960	.738	70.238	.781	81.172	.666	6.450
1961	.727	69.183	.785	77.830	.663	6.831
1962	.735	80.737	.799	84.801	.666	7.670
1963	.736	84.653	.799	92.700	.673	7.874
1964	.744	90.578	.807	98.485	.684	8.739
1965	.759	107.929	.814	106.144	.694	9.354
1966	.783	121.905	.826	108.689	.720	9.680
1967	.801	114.384	.845	108.951	.749	9.004
1968	.833	117.621	.879	120.657	.784	9.459
1969	.871	127.786	.917	122.775	.834	9.328
1970	.913	116.200	.942	118.525	.895	8.901
1971	.962	120.379	.978	139.030	.948	5.587
1972	1.000	133.775	1.000	159.982	1.000	5.717
1973	1.047	155.719	1.042	168.009	1.069	5.262
1974	1.150	141.534	1.120	150.068	1.250	4.577
1975	1.339	106.164	1.212	144.969	1.410	4.120

Table 2–6. Gross Private Domestic Investment by Asset Type (constant prices of 1972), 1947–1975

Year	Producers' Durable Equipment		Consumers' Durables		Tenant-Occupied Residential and Nonresidential Structures	
	Price	Quantity	Price	Quantity	Price	Quantity
1947	.490	31.871	.668	30.585	.448	19.741
1948	.534	32.978	.691	33.075	.497	21.545
1949	.564	28.436	.691	36.247	.496	21.216
1950	.582	31.227	.708	43.438	.508	23.535
1951	.621	32.601	.747	39.912	.559	23.815
1952	.630	31.845	.748	38.968	.571	23.772
1953	.642	34.139	.755	43.045	.580	25.876
1954	.659	32.193	.732	43.497	.573	27.185
1955	.670	36.302	.740	52.191	.586	29.433
1956	.714	37.536	.760	49.851	.628	31.977
1957	.757	38.359	.792	49.664	.652	32.196
1958	.769	32.967	.794	46.406	.644	31.095
1959	.785	36.718	.819	51.814	.649	32.675
1960	.796	37.765	.821	52.508	.644	34.622
1961	.795	36.806	.827	50.270	.643	36.308
1962	.796	40.658	.839	55.665	.648	39.548
1963	.799	43.317	.848	60.651	.653	41.410
1964	.803	48.345	.857	65.718	.659	43.672
1965	.808	56.720	.856	73.348	.671	49.263
1966	.822	64.325	.857	78.953	.697	50.560
1967	.844	63.152	.874	79.686	.725	48.236
1968	.874	66.947	.907	88.197	.762	51.432
1969	.901	71.194	.931	91.813	.824	55.320
1970	.935	68.109	.955	88.933	.885	52.691
1971	.976	67.345	.990	98.068	.945	51.921
1972	1.000	75.345	1.000	111.241	1.000	54.747
1973	1.016	86.777	1.016	121.766	1.085	57.705
1974	1.091	89.209	1.084	112.547	1.274	48.902
1975	1.259	77.399	1.177	112.692	1.434	42.685

Table 2-6. continued

Year	Owner-Occupied Residential Structures		Inventories	
	Price	Quantity	Price	Quantity
1947	.530	18.766	2.716	-.200
1948	.575	22.298	.834	5.500
1949	.581	20.300	.675	-4.400
1950	.595	28.397	.759	10.600
1951	.638	24.012	.796	13.700
1952	.658	23.306	.776	4.300
1953	.663	24.080	.712	1.500
1954	.666	26.231	.587	-2.200
1955	.682	30.597	.788	7.700
1956	.705	27.558	.749	5.800
1957	.708	25.268	.968	1.500
1958	.707	25.499	.724	-1.900
1959	.706	31.625	.861	6.400
1960	.709	28.664	.866	4.300
1961	.709	27.561	.751	2.900
1962	.711	29.136	.869	8.200
1963	.705	32.049	.794	7.800
1964	.708	32.767	.784	7.300
1965	.720	32.796	.869	11.300
1966	.742	29.736	.860	16.700
1967	.767	29.264	.843	12.000
1968	.804	32.459	.891	8.700
1969	.875	30.961	.899	10.600
1970	.904	29.592	.946	4.300
1971	.948	40.962	.985	6.700
1972	1.000	48.741	1.003	9.400
1973	1.110	46.243	1.026	16.500
1974	1.227	37.521	1.355	8.000
1975	1.332	32.276	1.262	-9.800

Table 2–7. Rates of Growth of Investment by Periods by Legal Form of Organization and Asset Type, 1948–1976

Legal Form of Organization or Asset Type	*1947–1975*	*1947–1952*	*1952–1956*	*1956–1959*	*1959–1965*	*1965–1968*	*1968–1972*	*1972–1975*
Total	0.0332	0.0386	0.0558	0.0139	0.0565	0.0344	0.0474	-0.0532
Corporate and noncorporate	0.0272	0.0256	0.0562	-0.0034	0.0726	0.0287	0.0322	-0.0771
Households	0.0385	0.0465	0.0544	0.0250	0.0401	0.0427	0.0705	-0.0328
Institutions	0.0289	0.1333	0.0722	0.0749	0.0748	0.0037	-0.1259	-0.1092
Producers' durable equipment	0.0317	-0.0002	0.0411	-0.0073	0.0725	0.0553	0.0295	0.0090
Consumers' durables	0.0466	0.0484	0.0616	0.0129	0.0579	0.0615	0.0580	0.0043
Tenant-occupied residential and non-residential structures	0.0275	0.0372	0.0741	0.0072	0.0684	0.0144	0.0156	-0.0830
Owner-occupied residential structures	0.0194	0.0433	0.0419	0.0459	0.0061	-0.0034	0.1016	-0.1374
Inventories	—	—	0.0748	0.0328	0.0948	-0.0872	0.0193	—

organization and all asset types shows very low or negative rates of growth for this subperiod. All categories show a substantial downturn, with the exception of the institutions category which experienced a large, negative rate of growth of gross investment for the previous period as well. The high variability of the rate of growth of gross investment and the downturn in 1972–1975 will be discussed further with reference to capital stock.

Corporate and noncorporate investment represents between 42 and 51 percent of total investment over the period 1947–1975. Prior to the 1968–1972 subperiod, the rate of growth of corporate and noncorporate investment shows higher variability than the rate of growth for total investment. Considering the importance of the business sector in economic growth, the negative rate of growth of −0.0771 in the subperiod 1972–1975 is particularly significant.

Household investment represents between 45 and 57 percent of total investment over the period 1947–1975. Consumers' durables investment dominates household investment, representing between 60 and 78 percent of household investment over the subperiods prior to the 1968–1972 subperiod. Household investment shows lower variability than the rate of growth of total investment. During the first three subperiods this is primarily due to the stability of the rate of growth of investment in owner-occupied residential structures. For the next two subperiods, consumers' durables investment contributes to the relative stability of the rate of growth of household investment.

Institutional investment represents between 2 and 4 percent of total investment over the period 1947–1975. Institutional investment shows little if any cyclical variation. Except for the 1952–1956 subperiod, the rate of growth of institutional investment decreases steadily over the period 1947–1972 from a high positive rate in the 1947–1952 subperiod to a very low negative rate in the 1968–1972 subperiod. In the 1972–1975 subperiod the rate of decrease in institutional investment slows somewhat.

Producers' durable equipment investment represents between 23 and 32 percent of gross investment over the period 1947–1975. The share of producers' durable equipment in total investment does not increase over time. During the first four subperiods the rate of growth of producers' durable equipment investment shows a high degree of variability; however, from the 1968–1972 subperiod to the 1972–1975 subperiod the rate of growth declines by only 0.0205. We conclude that producers' durable equipment investment is not as susceptible to the forces that have caused a dramatic downturn in other categories of investment.

For the 1947–1975 period as a whole, the growth of consumers' durables as a proportion of total investment is the most significant trend. Consumers' durables investment exhibits the largest average rate of growth for the period as a whole and represents an increasing share of total investment. In 1947 consumers' durables investment represents 30 percent of gross investment; by 1975 consumers' durables represents 44 percent of gross investment. With the exception of the 1956–1959 subperiod, consumers' durables investment has sustained a higher than average rate of growth over all seven subperiods we have considered.

Tenant-occupied residential and nonresidential structures investment represents between 16 and 24 percent of total investment over the period 1947–1975. The rate of growth shows a high degree of variability for the first five subperiods. Unlike the rate of growth of producers' durable equipment investment, which is the other major influence on the rate of growth of corporate and noncorporate investment, the rate of growth of tenant-occupied residential and nonresidential structures investment exhibits a substantial decline from the 1968–1972 subperiod to the 1972–1975 subperiod.

Owner-occupied residential structures investment represents between 12 and 21 percent of total investment over the period 1947–1975. The stable rate of growth over the first three subperiods noted earlier is associated with the high rate of family formation during the early postwar years. The next two subperiods exhibit low, but relatively stable, rates of growth. The dramatic increase in the rate of growth of owner-occupied residential structures investment in the 1968–1972 period is followed by an even more dramatic decrease in the rate of growth in the 1972–1975 period.

The rate of growth of inventory investment exhibits greater variability than that of any other category of investment.

IV. AGGREGATE CAPITAL STOCK

Our next objective is to construct estimates of capital stock for the U.S. economy as a whole. Capital stock for the private domestic sector of the U.S. economy is the sum of capital stocks for all forty-six industrial sectors given in Table 2–1. Similarly, capital stock for the four legal forms of organization given in Table 2–1 is the sum of stocks from the corresponding components of all industrial sectors. Finally, capital stock for the six classes of assets given in Table 2–1 is the sum of the corresponding components for all sectors.

We present data on capital stock annually for the private domestic sector of the U.S. economy for the period 1948–1976. We also present data on capital stock annually for corporate business, noncorporate business, private households, and nonprofit institutions. Finally, we present data on capital stock annually for producers' durable equipment, consumers' durables, tenant-occupied residential and nonresidential structures, owner-occupied residential structures, inventories, and land. For the economy as a whole the stock of land is constant.

We analyze the pattern of growth of capital stock across legal forms of organization and classes of assets at the aggregate level for the period 1948–1976. Considering growth by legal form of organization, we find that capital stock held by private households is the most rapidly growing component of aggregate capital stock, while capital stock held by noncorporate business is the most slowly growing component. The growth of capital stock held by corporations and nonprofit institutions is similar to that for the economy as a whole.

Turning to the growth of capital stock by class of assets, we find that consumers' durables is the most rapidly growing component of capital stock, while the owner-occupied residential structures is the next most rapidly growing component. These two classes of assets make up the capital stock of the household sector, so that these trends are reflected in the relative growth of capital stocks by legal form of organization. Since the stock of land is constant for the economy as a whole, its growth rate is zero, the lowest for any class of assets.

We also analyze patterns of growth in capital stock over seven subperiods—1948–1953, 1953–1957, 1957–1960, 1960–1966, 1966–1969, 1969–1973, and 1973–1976. The average rate of growth of capital stock during the final subperiod, 1973–1976, does not yet reflect the sharp downturn in investment portrayed in the preceding section. This subperiod includes a year of exceptionally slow growth, 1975–76, and years of above-average growth. Given the slowdown in investment, the growth of capital stock has continued to decline after 1976.

In Section III we presented data on investment in tangible assets held by the private domestic sector of the U.S. economy. In this section we present data on the corresponding stocks of capital. The assets of the private national economy also include net claims on governments and the rest of the world. In the following section we present data on investment and stocks of capital in the form of net claims on governments and the rest of the world. We combine data on investment and capital stock with data on saving, depreciation, and revaluation to obtain a complete set of accumulation and wealth accounts for the U.S. private national economy.

Capital Stocks

The quantity and value of aggregate capital stocks are constructed from the industry level accounts as the sum of quantities and values of sectoral capital stocks. The price of capital stock is equal to the ratio of the value to the quantity of capital stock. Government owned, privately operated, later sold, manufacturing stocks are included in the appropriate categories.

In Table 2–8 we present the price and quantity of private domestic capital stock for the total and for the four legal forms of organization presented in Table 2–1.

In Table 2–9 we present price and quantity indexes of capital stocks by the six asset types presented in Table 2–1.

Growth in Capital Stock

In Table 2–10 we present the rates of growth of the quantity of beginning-of-period capital stock by legal form of organization and asset type for the period 1948–1976 and for the following seven subperiods: 1948–1953, 1953–1957, 1957–1960, 1960–1966, 1966–1969, 1969–1973, and 1973–1976.

In considering the rates of growth of capital stock it is useful to refer to the basic accounting identities to place these figures in the proper perspective. End-of-period capital stock is equal to beginning-of-period capital stock plus net investment. Gross investment is equal to the sum of replacement and net investment. In Table 2–7 we have presented the rates of growth of the quantity of gross investment by legal form of organization and asset type for seven subperiods. It should not be surprising that net investment reflects the variation in the level of gross investment. Rates of growth of capital stock are lower and show less variation than the corresponding rates for gross investment due to the size of the capital stock base. The level of net investment is the key determinant affecting the rates of growth of capital stock.

We have previously discussed the rates of growth of capital stock. The 1973–1976 subperiod warrants additional comment. The decline in the rate of growth of total capital stock from the 1969–1973 subperiod to the 1973–1976 subperiod does not seem particularly significant. Looking at the annual rate of growth, however, the reverse is true. The rate declines from 0.0387 in 1973–74, to 0.0238 in 1974–75, to 0.0099 in 1975–76. The rate of growth in 1975–76 is the lowest for any annual rate over the entire 1948–1976 period.

Table 2-8.   Private Domestic Capital Stock by Legal Form of Organization *(constant prices of 1972)*, 1948–1976

Year	Private Domestic		Corporate		Noncorporate	
	Price	Quantity	Price	Quantity	Price	Quantity
1948	.483	1616.505	.508	524.023	.497	565.960
1949	.483	1674.299	.511	543.874	.486	574.284
1950	.512	1711.526	.536	538.377	.522	588.693
1951	.556	1778.854	.582	547.612	.566	605.740
1952	.571	1837.129	.594	563.826	.580	619.105
1953	.576	1878.696	.603	577.186	.580	623.373
1954	.580	1922.962	.605	587.876	.585	630.156
1955	.593	1961.864	.618	596.839	.592	632.743
1956	.617	2026.752	.650	614.196	.607	642.384
1957	.638	2082.280	.674	636.271	.623	646.975
1958	.645	2127.250	.680	647.150	.629	657.057
1959	.655	2155.192	.688	657.716	.633	655.329
1960	.664	2206.645	.695	672.896	.639	661.893
1961	.670	2253.193	.694	691.903	.642	664.017
1962	.679	2291.746	.698	706.096	.649	668.125
1963	.687	2347.279	.704	728.371	.653	674.743
1964	.697	2410.478	.710	750.066	.660	683.962
1965	.718	2481.358	.727	785.882	.688	683.313
1966	.745	2572.243	.753	820.004	.723	699.267
1967	.775	2671.667	.781	869.417	.755	711.690
1968	.813	2753.431	.815	904.832	.796	725.201
1969	.862	2843.081	.859	947.744	.845	731.134
1970	.905	2935.221	.906	988.274	.894	745.279
1971	.954	3001.629	.956	1015.305	.945	756.908
1972	1.000	3082.935	1.000	1036.395	1.000	775.669
1973	1.067	3190.930	1.058	1064.010	1.079	798.341
1974	1.185	3316.938	1.204	1107.877	1.195	822.145
1975	1.302	3396.910	1.354	1143.213	1.293	834.777
1976	1.370	3430.874	1.419	1146.612	1.345	842.986

Table 2–8. continued

Year	Household		Institutions	
	Price	Quantity	Price	Quantity
1948	.454	472.240	.353	54.282
1949	.463	500.947	.351	55.195
1950	.491	527.741	.373	56.515
1951	.535	566.695	.415	58.807
1952	.553	593.394	.430	60.804
1953	.562	615.710	.439	62.427
1954	.565	640.804	.445	64.126
1955	.583	665.907	.462	66.335
1956	.611	701.722	.500	68.450
1957	.632	728.269	.529	70.766
1958	.640	749.686	.538	73.357
1959	.657	765.975	.556	76.171
1960	.669	792.678	.570	79.178
1961	.681	814.812	.584	82.462
1962	.696	831.621	.601	85.905
1963	.706	854.209	.619	89.955
1964	.721	882.519	.639	93.931
1965	.738	913.668	.663	98.494
1966	.761	948.975	.696	103.338
1967	.790	982.390	.731	108.169
1968	.829	1011.414	.770	111.983
1969	.882	1048.215	.823	115.988
1970	.916	1082.089	.885	119.579
1971	.960	1106.924	.945	122.492
1972	1.000	1148.984	1.000	121.887
1973	1.068	1207.036	1.070	121.542
1974	1.159	1266.074	1.227	120.842
1975	1.255	1299.353	1.371	119.567
1976	1.339	1323.306	1.429	117.969

Table 2–9. Capital Stock by Asset Type (constant prices of 1972), 1947–1975

Year	Producers' Durable Equipment		Consumers' Durables		Tenant-Occupied Residential and Nonresidential Structures	
	Price	Quantity	Price	Quantity	Price	Quantity
1948	.508	135.847	.691	104.319	.505	294.847
1949	.544	151.688	.691	116.531	.506	301.688
1950	.564	160.489	.708	129.472	.518	307.844
1951	.601	170.684	.747	147.015	.565	316.029
1952	.627	180.528	.748	157.524	.574	324.113
1953	.631	188.075	.755	164.987	.584	331.756
1954	.643	197.124	.732	175.035	.581	341.124
1955	.660	202.950	.740	183.525	.598	351.352
1956	.696	212.001	.760	199.011	.633	363.337
1957	.747	220.952	.792	209.060	.654	377.267
1958	.761	229.354	.794	216.912	.647	390.734
1959	.778	231.229	.819	219.935	.649	402.437
1960	.787	236.699	.821	227.762	.651	415.145
1961	.785	242.397	.827	234.718	.645	429.196
1962	.788	246.344	.839	238.044	.649	444.252
1963	.793	253.613	.848	246.100	.654	461.815
1964	.795	262.455	.857	257.531	.660	480.393
1965	.804	275.108	.856	271.743	.673	500.340
1966	.819	294.444	.857	290.742	.698	524.896
1967	.839	318.669	.874	311.547	.726	549.537
1968	.870	338.387	.907	328.924	.762	570.600
1969	.894	359.211	.931	351.337	.824	593.756
1970	.930	381.185	.955	372.882	.883	619.619
1971	.972	396.757	.990	387.239	.945	641.567
1972	1.000	409.286	1.000	407.859	1.000	661.621
1973	1.015	427.811	1.016	437.528	1.086	683.596
1974	1.090	454.797	1.084	471.788	1.284	707.548
1975	1.270	480.428	1.177	489.978	1.431	721.584
1976	1.363	490.681	1.244	504.675	1.444	728.772

Table 2–9. continued

Year	Owner-Occupied Residential Structures		Inventories		Land	
	Price	*Quantity*	*Price*	*Quantity*	*Price*	*Quantity*
1948	.575	148.802	.718	121.136	.386	811.554
1949	.581	165.297	.754	127.541	.375	811.554
1950	.595	179.150	.791	123.017	.412	811.554
1951	.638	200.560	.863	133.011	.441	811.554
1952	.658	216.750	.846	146.659	.456	811.554
1953	.663	231.603	.817	150.721	.459	811.554
1954	.666	246.650	.828	151.475	.466	811.554
1955	.682	263.262	.820	149.221	.475	811.554
1956	.705	283.591	.843	157.258	.485	811.554
1957	.708	300.089	.879	163.358	.496	811.554
1958	.707	313.654	.882	165.041	.507	811.554
1959	.706	326.921	.877	163.115	.520	811.554
1960	.709	345.796	.905	169.688	.534	811.554
1961	.709	360.974	.857	174.353	.549	811.554
1962	.711	374.457	.874	177.094	.564	811.554
1963	.705	388.989	.844	185.207	.580	811.554
1964	.708	405.868	.856	192.676	.597	811.554
1965	.720	422.806	.879	199.807	.637	811.554
1966	.742	439.113	.888	211.494	.679	811.554
1967	.767	451.723	.881	228.636	.724	811.554
1968	.804	463.370	.914	240.595	.772	811.554
1969	.875	477.758	.917	249.464	.823	811.554
1970	.904	490.087	.956	259.893	.878	811.554
1971	.948	500.566	.981	263.945	.937	811.554
1972	1.000	522.005	1.000	270.610	1.000	811.554
1973	1.110	550.388	1.073	280.052	1.064	811.554
1974	1.227	575.166	1.198	296.083	1.135	811.554
1975	1.332	590.255	1.323	303.110	1.212	811.554
1976	1.430	599.512	1.442	295.679	1.295	811.554

Table 2–10.   Rates of Growth of Capital Stock by Periods, by Legal Form of Organization and Asset Type, 1948–1976

Legal Form of Organization or Asset Type	1948–1976	1948–1953	1953–1957	1957–1960	1960–1966	1966–1969	1969–1973	1973–1976
Total including land	0.0269	0.0301	0.0257	0.0193	0.0256	0.0334	0.0289	0.0242
Corporate	0.0280	0.0193	0.0244	0.0187	0.0331	0.0480	0.0185	0.0249
Noncorporate	0.0142	0.0193	0.0093	0.0076	0.0092	0.0149	0.0220	0.0181
Households	0.0368	0.0531	0.0420	0.0282	0.0300	0.0332	0.0353	0.0307
Institutions	0.0277	0.0280	0.0313	0.0374	0.0444	0.0385	0.0117	-0.0099
Total excluding land	0.0421	0.0564	0.0437	0.0311	0.0388	0.0477	0.0395	0.0320
Producers' durable equipment	0.0459	0.0651	0.0403	0.0229	0.0364	0.0663	0.0437	0.0457
Consumers' durables	0.0563	0.0917	0.0592	0.0286	0.0407	0.0631	0.0548	0.0476
Tenant-occupied residential and non-residential structures	0.0323	0.0236	0.0321	0.0319	0.0391	0.0411	0.0352	0.0213
Owner-occupied residential structures	0.0498	0.0885	0.0648	0.0473	0.0398	0.0281	0.0354	0.0285
Inventories	0.0319	0.0437	0.0201	0.0127	0.0367	0.0550	0.0289	0.0181

With replacement investment, which is relatively stable, growing at a relatively high rate, 0.0384 for 1974–75, the slowdown in growth of aggregate capital stock indicates the likelihood of slower economic growth.

We now turn our attention to the rates of growth by legal form of organization and asset type. Corporate capital stock represents between 30 and 34 percent of total capital stock over the period 1948–1976. The rate of growth of corporate capital stock shows greater variability than the rate of growth for total capital stock. The rate of growth for corporate capital stock during the 1973–1976 subperiod is very close to the economy average, yet on an annual basis the decline in the rate of growth from the 1974–75 subperiod (0.0314) to the 1975–76 subperiod (0.0030) is the most rapid for that of any legal form of organization. Noncorporate capital stock represents between 25 and 35 percent of total capital stock over the period 1948–1976; its share is declining over time. The rate of growth of noncorporate capital stock is lower than the rate of growth of total capital stock for all time periods.

Household capital stock represents between 30 and 39 percent of total capital stock over the period 1948–1976. The rate of growth of household capital stock is higher than the rate of growth of total capital stock for all subperiods except 1966–1969. The decline in the rate of growth of household capital stock during the 1966–1969 subperiod is explained by the lower than average rate of growth of owner-occupied residential structures during this period. Table 2–7 shows that the rate of growth of owner-occupied residential structures investment is low or negative during the 1959–1965 and 1965–1968 subperiods, leading to the lower than average rate of growth of capital stock during the 1966–1969 subperiod. Consumers' durables stock represents an increasing share of household capital stock over time. In 1948 consumers' durables stock represents 22 percent of household stock. By 1976 consumers' durables stock represents 38 percent of household stock. Institutional capital stock represents between 3 and 4 percent of total capital stock over the period 1948–1976. The rate of growth of institutional capital stock increases over the first four subperiods, then declines over the last three subperiods.

The share of producers' durable equipment capital stock in total capital stock increases over time, from 8 percent in 1948 to 14 percent in 1976. The share of consumers' durables capital stock in total capital stock increases over time, from 6 percent in 1948 to 15 percent in 1976. As noted earlier, the growing importance of consumers' durables is the most significant trend of the period.

Tenant-occupied residential and nonresidential structures capital stock represents between 18 and 21 percent of total capital stock over the period 1948–1976. The rate of growth of tenant-occupied residential and nonresidential capital stock is below average for all subperiods except 1957–1960 and 1960–1966. During these two subperiods the rates of growth are very similar to the rate of growth of total capital stock, excluding land. The share of tenant-occupied residential and nonresidential capital stock is declining relative to other asset types and legal forms of organization. Owner-occupied residential capital stock represents between 9 and 17 percent of total capital stock over the period 1948–1976. The rate of growth of owner-occupied residential capital stock is higher than average for the first four subperiods. The rate of growth of owner-occupied residential capital stock does not show the substantial variation seen in the rate of growth of owner-occupied residential structures investment. Finally, capital stock in the form of inventories represents between 7 and 9 percent of total capital stock.

V.   ACCUMULATION AND
WEALTH ACCOUNTS

Capital formation in the private sector of the U.S. economy takes place through the purchase of new capital goods, the accumulation of inventories, and the acquisition of claims on governments and the rest of the world. In Section III we presented estimates of capital formation through the acquisition of tangible assets in the private domestic sector. In this section we combine these estimates with estimates of capital formation through acquisition of claims on governments and the rest of the world to obtain an accumulation account for the U.S. economy as a whole.

Our accumulation account includes capital formation net of replacement, where replacement is defined as the loss of efficiency of capital goods with age. The accumulation account also includes saving net of depreciation, where depreciation is defined as the loss in value of capital goods with age. Our estimates of depreciation are based on the system of vintage accounts for capital presented by Jorgenson [47, 1980] in the next chapter of this volume. This system encompasses prices of capital goods, which provide the basis for our estimates of depreciation, as well as quantities of capital goods, which provide the basis for our estimates of replacement.

We have assumed that for capital in the form of equipment and structures, the efficiency of capital goods declines geometrically with the age of the asset. Under this assumption the rate of depreciation is constant and equal to the rate of replacement. With constant rates of replacement and depreciation the values of replacement and depreciation are equal and depend only on the price of acquisition of new capital goods and the stock of capital:

$$p_{A,t} R_t = \delta p_{A,t} A_{t-1} = p_{D,t} A_{t-1} \ ,$$

where $p_{A,t}$ and $p_{D,t}$ are the prices of acquisition of new capital goods and depreciation. For the U.S. economy as a whole saving is equal to capital formation, so that the value of saving net of depreciation is equal to the value of capital formation net of replacement.

Our accumulation account includes data on capital formation and saving. It also includes changes in wealth through revaluation of capital goods as changes in capital goods prices take place. The value of wealth is the product of the price of acquisition of new capital goods $p_{A,t}$ and the stock of capital A_t. The change in wealth from period to period,

$$p_{A,t} A_t - p_{A,t-1} A_{t-1} = p_{A,t} (A_t - A_{t-1}) + (p_{A,t} - p_{A,t-1}) A_{t-1} \ ,$$

is the sum of capital formation and revaluation.

We present annual data on capital formation, replacement, saving, and depreciation for the private sector for the period 1947–1975. Depreciation as a proportion of saving has risen from slightly over half in 1947 to more than two-thirds in 1975. We also present annual data on changes in wealth and revaluation of capital goods. During four of the five years from 1947 to 1951 and again for the eight years 1968 to 1975, revaluation of existing capital goods exceeds net capital formation as a proportion of the change in U.S. national wealth, reflecting rapid inflation in capital goods prices in those years.

Wealth in the private sector of the U.S. national economy includes tangible assets that generate capital services in the producing sectors of the economy and claims on governments and the rest of the world. In Section IV we presented estimates of capital stock in the form of tangible assets. In this section we combine these estimates with estimates of the stock of net claims to obtain a wealth account for the U.S. economy as a whole. We present annual data on private national wealth for the period 1948–1976. Claims on governments and the rest of the world amounted to almost one-fourth of national wealth in 1947 and fell steadily until 1974, amounting to less than one-eighth of national wealth in that year.[1]

---

[1]For a more detailed discussion of the system of accounts, see Jorgenson [47, 1980].

In the following three sections we combine estimates of sectoral capital stock with data on sectoral property compensation to obtain estimates of sectoral rates of return and sectoral prices of capital input. The price of capital input is a rental rate for the use of capital stock. Sectoral property compensation can be divided between price and quantity components corresponding to the price and quantity of sectoral capital input. Annual data for the sectoral nominal and own rates of return, capital quality and the price, quantity and value of capital input are given in Appendix A. In Section IX we combine estimates of aggregate capital stock with data on aggregate property compensation to obtain aggregate rates of return and price and quantity components corresponding to the price and quantity of aggregate capital input. In Sections X through XII our objective is to analyze the interrelationship between capital formation and economic growth in the United States. We analyze the role of growth in sectoral capital input in the growth of sectoral output in Section X. In Section XI we present an income and expenditure account for the private sector of the U.S. economy, giving income and its distribution between consumer outlays and saving. Finally, in Section XII we analyze the role of growth of aggregate capital input in the growth of output for the U.S. economy as a whole.

Accumulation Account

The components of the value of gross private national saving and gross private national capital formation are presented in Table 2–11, along with the value of depreciation, revaluation, and the change in wealth. The annual change in wealth has been described as the sum of net capital formation and revaluation. Annual estimates of these magnitudes for private domestic tangible assets and for net claims on the government and the rest of the world sectors are presented in Table 2–12.

We have discussed the division of our concept of gross private capital formation between price and quantity components. We construct price indexes for claims on the government and the rest of the world sectors from data on change in the value of claims from period to period and data on the corresponding components of capital formation from the U.S. national income and product accounts. We set the price of claims of each type equal to unity in 1972 and the quantity in 1972 equal to the value of outstanding claims in that year. These price indexes are then used to deflate the corresponding values for net claims on governments and the rest of the world sectors.

To construct an index of the quantity of gross private national capital formation, we take an unweighted sum of the quantity of

Table 2-11. Gross Private National Capital Formation, Saving, and Revaluation (billions of current dollars), 1947–1975

Year	Gross Private National Saving and Capital Formation	Replacement and Depreciation	Net Private National Saving and Capital Formation	Revaluation	Change in Wealth
1947	52.908	28.857	24.051	94.065	118.115
1948	65.628	33.868	31.760	52.099	83.859
1949	66.941	38.202	28.738	-8.439	20.299
1950	75.700	42.372	33.328	49.937	83.264
1951	87.850	49.710	38.140	71.838	109.978
1952	89.883	53.878	36.005	20.712	56.717
1953	94.956	56.546	38.410	9.148	47.558
1954	94.625	59.081	35.544	2.822	38.366
1955	107.583	62.690	44.893	23.857	68.750
1956	110.305	69.629	40.676	45.150	85.826
1957	116.026	76.349	39.677	39.406	79.083
1958	112.288	79.565	32.723	13.284	46.007
1959	122.651	82.452	40.200	22.483	62.683
1960	123.001	85.691	37.310	18.041	55.351
1961	125.367	88.459	36.908	10.064	46.972
1962	142.388	91.013	51.375	20.858	72.233
1963	150.374	94.800	55.574	13.547	69.121
1964	167.992	99.596	68.396	19.242	87.638
1965	185.176	105.242	79.934	46.132	126.066
1966	207.877	113.558	94.319	65.231	159.550
1967	218.012	124.226	93.786	69.791	163.576
1968	227.407	136.027	91.380	101.965	193.345
1969	235.344	150.093	85.251	143.119	228.370
1970	248.456	164.615	83.841	132.205	216.046
1971	282.270	178.662	103.608	145.497	249.105
1972	308.270	191.446	116.824	129.374	246.198
1973	361.947	210.012	151.935	216.478	368.414
1974	360.163	243.863	116.300	402.675	518.975
1975	406.395	281.363	125.032	407.846	532.877

Table 2−12.   Change in Private National Wealth (*billions of current dollars*), 1947−1975

Year	Change in Value of Private Domestic Tangible Assets	Net Capital Formation Private Domestic Tangible Assets	Revaluation Private Domestic Tangible Assets
1947	122.641	25.526	97.116
1948	87.779	34.842	52.937
1949	13.838	22.128	−8.290
1950	87.295	42.197	45.098
1951	110.375	39.284	71.091
1952	47.430	27.380	20.050
1953	36.143	29.302	6.841
1954	28.570	25.485	3.085
1955	67.192	44.311	22.881
1956	82.937	39.280	43.657
1957	71.019	32.237	38.782
1958	30.585	19.197	11.388
1959	58.219	37.639	20.580
1960	49.675	33.862	15.813
1961	37.151	27.449	9.702
1962	59.580	40.894	18.686
1963	62.449	46.836	15.613
1964	74.548	53.329	21.219
1965	117.257	69.559	47.698
1966	145.003	78.585	66.418
1967	141.415	66.249	75.167
1968	177.638	75.494	102.144
1969	217.844	81.585	136.259
1970	185.913	61.130	124.783
1971	224.171	78.394	145.777
1972	247.890	108.070	139.820
1973	347.907	133.701	214.205
1974	486.089	92.727	393.362
1975	440.258	42.195	398.064

gross private domestic investment and the quantity indexes of net claims on government and the rest of the world. The value of gross private national capital formation is calculated as an unweighted sum of the same components. An implicit price index is derived as the ratio of value to quantity. Similarly, the quantity and value of replacement are calculated as unweighted sums of the components of replacement. The price of replacement is derived as the ratio of value to quantity. The price and quantity of gross private national capital formation and replacement are presented in Table 2−13.

The value of gross private national saving is taken from the income and expenditure account. To construct prices and quantities for the saving side of the accumulation account we begin with the price and quantity of gross private national capital formation. The capital for-

Table 2–12. continued

Year	Change in Value of Net Claims on Governments and Rest of World	Net Capital Formation Net Claims on Governments and Rest of World	Revaluation Net Claims on Governments and Rest of World
1947	-4.526	-1.475	-3.051
1948	-3.920	-3.082	-.838
1949	6.461	6.610	-.149
1950	-4.031	-8.869	4.839
1951	-.397	-1.144	.747
1952	9.287	8.625	.662
1953	11.415	9.108	2.307
1954	9.796	10.059	-.263
1955	1.558	.582	.976
1956	2.889	1.396	1.493
1957	8.064	7.440	.624
1958	15.422	13.526	1.896
1959	4.464	2.561	1.903
1960	5.676	3.448	2.228
1961	9.821	9.459	.362
1962	12.653	10.481	2.172
1963	6.672	8.738	-2.066
1964	13.090	15.067	-1.977
1965	8.809	10.375	-1.566
1966	14.547	15.734	-1.187
1967	22.161	27.537	-5.376
1968	15.707	15.886	-.179
1969	10.526	3.666	6.860
1970	30.133	22.711	7.422
1971	24.934	25.214	-.280
1972	-1.692	8.754	-10.446
1973	20.507	18.234	2.273
1974	32.886	23.573	9.313
1975	92.619	82.837	9.782

mation and saving sides of the accumulation account are equal in both current and constant prices. To complete the accumulation and revaluation account in constant prices we must construct accounts for the price and quantity of depreciation and revaluation of assets. Although the value of depreciation is equal to the value of replacement, the price and quantity components of depreciation differ from the price and quantity components of replacement.

We construct the quantity index of depreciation as an index of the quantities of beginning-of-period capital stocks with depreciation shares as weights. The quantity of replacement is an unweighted sum of the quantities of replacement. The price index of depreciation is computed as the ratio of the value of depreciation to the quantity of depreciation. We construct a quantity index of revaluation as an

Table 2–13.   Gross Private National Capital Formation (constant prices of 1972), 1947–1975

Year	Gross Private National Capital Formation		Replacement	
	Price	Quantity	Price	Quantity
1947	.533	99.219	.546	52.818
1948	.585	112.158	.579	58.477
1949	.616	108.749	.593	64.416
1950	.591	128.054	.612	69.230
1951	.661	132.863	.657	75.679
1952	.686	131.030	.671	80.350
1953	.689	137.887	.676	83.591
1954	.690	137.130	.672	87.912
1955	.686	156.812	.684	91.633
1956	.716	154.129	.714	97.454
1957	.751	154.463	.747	102.158
1958	.761	147.567	.750	106.055
1959	.758	161.772	.764	107.907
1960	.763	161.254	.768	111.630
1961	.768	163.144	.769	115.085
1962	.776	183.442	.774	117.539
1963	.776	193.814	.779	121.646
1964	.790	212.695	.786	126.701
1965	.792	233.730	.792	132.876
1966	.812	255.949	.804	141.238
1967	.838	260.175	.826	150.474
1968	.862	263.802	.860	158.190
1969	.893	263.535	.896	167.507
1970	.935	265.824	.931	176.896
1971	.975	289.655	.973	183.579
1972	1.000	308.228	1.000	191.446
1973	1.043	347.137	1.037	202.439
1974	1.128	319.205	1.133	215.158
1975	1.214	334.694	1.258	223.580

index of the various beginning-of-period capital stocks with revaluation shares as weights. The price index of revaluation is computed as the ratio of the value of revaluation to the quantity of revaluation. Price and quantity index numbers of gross private national savings, depreciation, and revaluation are presented in Table 2–14.

Wealth Account

Wealth of private households and institutions is included among the assets of the producing industries. Private domestic wealth as a result includes the tangible assets of the producing industries, including government owned, privately operated, later sold, assets, as well as the tangible assets of households and institutions. Private national wealth includes private domestic wealth and net claims on governments and the rest of the world. The value of the components of private domestic and private national wealth are presented in Table 2–15.

We construct the quantity and value of total wealth by summing the quantities and values of the components of wealth. The implicit prices are then derived as ratios of values to quantities. In Table 2–16 we present the price and quantity of wealth for the aggregates, for net claims on government and the rest of the world, and for the four legal forms of organization.

VI. SECTORAL PROPERTY COMPENSATION

Our next step in measuring sectoral capital input for the U.S. economy is to construct estimates of sectoral rates of return for the forty-six industrial sectors listed in Table 2–1. Estimates of sectoral rates of return require data on sectoral property compensation and on taxation of sectoral assets and property income. These estimates also require data on depreciation for plant and equipment as capital assets age and data on revaluation of all assets within each sector as capital goods prices change. Our first objective in this section is to describe data on sectoral property compensation.

We begin our description of data on property compensation by presenting the sources of data on property compensation for corporate and noncorporate business by industrial sector. Our primary data source is a study by the Bureau of Economic Analysis [19, 1978]. We have supplemented this study with additional data on indirect business taxes allocated to capital assets. Finally, we have allocated noncorporate income between property compensation and the labor compensation of self-employed persons.

To estimate rates of return by sector for corporate and noncorporate business we combine data on sectoral property compensation

Table 2–14.   Gross Private National Saving, Depreciation, and Revaluation (constant prices of 1972), 1947–1975

Year	Gross Private National Saving		Depreciation		Revaluation	
	Price	Quantity	Price	Quantity	Price	Quantity
1947	.533	99.219	.052	551.853	.040	2378.691
1948	.585	112.158	.055	610.981	.021	2476.604
1949	.616	108.749	.057	673.033	-.003	2483.889
1950	.591	128.054	.059	723.328	.021	2497.635
1951	.661	132.863	.063	790.706	.029	2497.796
1952	.686	131.030	.064	839.512	.008	2572.963
1953	.689	137.887	.065	873.373	.003	2657.891
1954	.690	137.130	.064	918.519	.001	2717.701
1955	.686	156.812	.065	957.399	.009	2706.452
1956	.716	154.463	.068	1018.213	.016	2798.775
1957	.751	147.567	.072	1067.365	.014	2887.120
1958	.761	161.772	.072	1108.073	.005	2923.931
1959	.758	161.254	.073	1127.430	.008	2931.307
1960	.763	163.144	.073	1166.324	.006	2954.703
1961	.768	183.442	.074	1202.420	.003	2958.112
1962	.776	193.814	.074	1228.060	.007	2964.152
1963	.776	212.695	.075	1270.978	.005	2972.742
1964	.790	233.730	.075	1323.786	.006	2982.615
1965	.792	255.949	.076	1388.311	.015	3012.020
1966	.812	260.175	.077	1475.674	.021	3070.376
1967	.838	263.802	.079	1572.169	.022	3148.187
1968	.862	263.535	.082	1652.794	.032	3217.435
1969	.893	265.824	.086	1750.141	.043	3308.184
1970	.935	289.655	.089	1848.239	.039	3397.945
1971	.975	308.228	.093	1918.062	.042	3472.270
1972	1.000	347.137	.096	2000.253	.036	3547.862
1973	1.043	319.205	.099	2115.114	.059	3651.181
1974	1.128	334.694	.108	2248.001	.106	3788.501
1975	1.214		.120	2335.999	.105	3892.094

Table 2–15.   Private Domestic and Private National Wealth (*billions of current dollars*), 1947–1975

Year	Private National Wealth	Net Claims on Governments and Rest of World	Private Domestic Wealth	Corporate Tangible Assets
1947	968.650	239.636	729.014	248.308
1948	1052.509	235.716	816.793	277.623
1949	1072.808	242.176	830.631	274.664
1950	1156.072	238.146	917.926	293.836
1951	1266.050	237.749	1028.301	329.526
1952	1322.767	247.036	1075.731	343.173
1953	1370.325	258.451	1111.874	354.276
1954	1408.691	268.247	1140.444	360.851
1955	1477.441	269.805	1207.636	380.640
1956	1563.267	272.694	1290.573	414.319
1957	1642.350	280.758	1361.592	436.650
1958	1688.357	296.180	1392.177	446.770
1959	1751.039	300.644	1450.395	464.326
1960	1806.390	306.320	1500.070	481.728
1961	1853.363	316.141	1537.222	490.493
1962	1925.596	328.794	1596.802	509.128
1963	1994.717	335.466	1659.251	529.034
1964	2082.355	348.556	1733.799	558.903
1965	2208.421	357.365	1851.056	598.252
1966	2367.971	371.912	1996.059	656.893
1967	2531.547	394.073	2137.474	708.210
1968	2724.892	409.780	2315.112	772.772
1969	2953.262	420.306	2532.956	849.316
1970	3169.308	450.439	2718.869	919.720
1971	3418.413	475.373	2943.040	991.115
1972	3664.611	473.681	3190.930	1064.010
1973	4033.025	494.188	3538.837	1170.191
1974	4552.000	527.074	4024.926	1374.736
1975	5084.877	619.693	4465.184	1552.038

Table 2–15. continued

Year	Noncorporate Tangible Assets	Household Tangible Assets	Institutions Tangible Assets
1947	261.463	201.673	17.570
1948	287.085	232.479	19.606
1949	287.093	248.826	20.048
1950	317.634	284.205	22.251
1951	351.859	321.391	25.524
1952	362.099	343.392	27.067
1953	365.878	363.353	28.368
1954	370.309	379.498	29.785
1955	381.246	413.861	31.890
1956	392.922	447.678	35.654
1957	410.059	475.741	39.141
1958	412.270	491.860	41.278
1959	419.015	522.708	44.346
1960	424.010	547.024	47.308
1961	428.823	567.531	50.375
1962	437.938	595.485	54.250
1963	447.193	624.717	58.306
1964	451.042	660.717	63.136
1965	481.760	702.389	68.655
1966	514.769	749.005	75.392
1967	547.531	799.846	81.887
1968	582.452	870.572	89.316
1969	629.847	955.349	98.444
1970	676.674	1014.070	108.404
1971	733.112	1103.618	115.195
1972	798.341	1207.036	121.542
1973	887.342	1352.010	129.293
1974	997.677	1505.781	146.732
1975	1091.196	1660.231	161.719

Table 2–16. Private Domestic and Private National Wealth (constant prices of 1972), 1947–1975

Year	Private National Wealth		Net Claims on Governments and Rest of World		Private Domestic Wealth	
	Price	Quantity	Price	Quantity	Price	Quantity
1947	.519	1867.427	.449	250.923	.451	1616.505
1948	.548	1921.983	.477	247.684	.488	1674.299
1949	.546	1966.161	.510	254.634	.485	1711.526
1950	.571	2024.345	.504	245.491	.516	1778.854
1951	.608	2081.445	.574	244.316	.560	1837.129
1952	.620	2131.850	.607	253.154	.573	1878.696
1953	.627	2185.363	.584	262.401	.578	1922.962
1954	.630	2234.489	.584	272.625	.581	1961.864
1955	.642	2299.966	.594	273.214	.596	2026.752
1956	.663	2356.900	.638	274.620	.620	2082.280
1957	.682	2409.345	.699	282.095	.640	2127.250
1958	.689	2450.787	.614	295.595	.646	2155.192
1959	.699	2504.780	.638	298.134	.657	2206.645
1960	.707	2554.721	.672	301.529	.666	2253.193
1961	.712	2602.574	.665	310.829	.671	2291.746
1962	.722	2668.342	.728	321.063	.680	2347.279
1963	.728	2740.128	.759	329.650	.688	2410.478
1964	.737	2825.901	.816	344.543	.699	2481.358
1965	.754	2927.088	.832	354.845	.720	2572.243
1966	.778	3042.187	.840	370.520	.747	2671.667
1967	.803	3151.787	.849	398.356	.776	2753.431
1968	.836	3257.503	.828	414.422	.814	2843.081
1969	.881	3353.290	.843	418.069	.863	2935.221
1970	.921	3441.896	.973	440.267	.906	3001.629
1971	.964	3547.862	1.008	464.927	.955	3082.935
1972	1.000	3664.611	1.000	473.681	1.000	3190.930
1973	1.059	3808.766	1.325	491.828	1.067	3316.938
1974	1.164	3911.764	1.379	514.854	1.185	3396.910
1975	1.263	4025.170	1.482	594.297	1.301	3430.874

Table 2–16. continued

Year	Corporate Tangible Assets		Noncorporate Tangible Assets	
	Price	Quantity	Price	Quantity
1947	.474	524.023	.462	565.960
1948	.510	543.874	.500	574.284
1949	.510	538.377	.488	588.893
1950	.537	547.612	.524	605.740
1951	.584	563.826	.568	619.105
1952	.595	577.186	.581	623.373
1953	.603	587.876	.581	630.156
1954	.605	596.839	.585	632.783
1955	.620	614.196	.593	642.384
1956	.651	636.271	.607	646.975
1957	.675	647.150	.624	657.057
1958	.679	657.716	.629	655.329
1959	.690	672.896	.633	661.893
1960	.696	691.903	.639	664.017
1961	.695	706.096	.642	668.125
1962	.699	728.371	.649	674.743
1963	.705	750.066	.654	683.962
1964	.711	785.882	.660	683.313
1965	.729	820.664	.689	699.267
1966	.756	869.417	.723	711.690
1967	.783	904.832	.755	725.201
1968	.815	947.744	.797	731.134
1969	.859	988.274	.845	745.279
1970	.906	1015.305	.894	756.908
1971	.956	1036.395	.945	775.669
1972	1.000	1064.010	1.000	798.341
1973	1.056	1107.877	1.079	822.145
1974	1.203	1143.213	1.195	834.777
1975	1.354	1146.612	1.294	842.986

Table 2–16. continued

Year	Households Tangible Assets		Institutions Tangible Assets	
	Price	Quantity	Price	Quantity
1947	.427	472.240	.324	54.282
1948	.464	500.947	.355	55.195
1949	.471	527.741	.355	56.515
1950	.502	566.695	.378	58.807
1951	.542	593.394	.420	60.804
1952	.558	615.710	.434	62.427
1953	.567	640.804	.442	64.126
1954	.570	665.907	.449	66.335
1955	.590	701.722	.466	68.450
1956	.615	728.269	.504	70.766
1957	.635	749.686	.534	73.357
1958	.642	765.975	.542	76.171
1959	.659	792.678	.560	79.178
1960	.671	814.812	.574	82.462
1961	.682	831.621	.586	85.905
1962	.697	854.209	.603	89.955
1963	.708	882.519	.621	93.931
1964	.723	913.668	.641	98.494
1965	.740	948.975	.664	103.338
1966	.762	982.390	.697	108.169
1967	.791	1011.414	.731	111.983
1968	.831	1048.215	.770	115.988
1969	.883	1082.089	.823	119.579
1970	.916	1106.924	.885	122.492
1971	.961	1148.984	.945	121.887
1972	1.000	1207.036	1.000	121.542
1973	1.068	1266.074	1.070	120.842
1974	1.159	1299.353	1.227	119.567
1975	1.255	1323.306	1.371	117.960

with data on the value of sectoral tangible assets, including depreciation and revaluation of assets, described in Sections I through V above. For corporate business we define the return to capital as corporate property compensation before taxes, less indirect corporate business taxes, corporate profits tax liability, and depreciation on corporate assets—plus the revaluation of corporate assets.

We define the nominal rate of return for corporate business by sector as the return to capital divided by the value of corporate assets. We define the own rate of return for corporate business as the return to capital, excluding revaluation of corporate assets, divided by the value of corporate assets. The nominal rate of return reflects gains that result from earnings on assets and gains that accrue through revaluation of assets. The own rate of return reflects only earnings on assets. Revaluations of assets are reflected in our data on the value of assets and wealth. Only earnings are reflected in our data on capital input.

We assume that the nominal rate of return for noncorporate business by sector is the same as the nominal rate of return for corporate business. On the basis of this assumption we allocate noncorporate income between property and labor compensation. The return to capital for noncorporate business is defined as noncorporate property compensation before taxes less indirect noncorporate business taxes and depreciation on noncorporate assets, and plus the revaluation of noncorporate assets. Own rates of return for noncorporate business by sector are defined as noncorporate return to capital, excluding revaluation of noncorporate assets, divided by the value of noncorporate assets.

We continue our discussion of data on property compensation by presenting the sources of data on property compensation for private households and nonprofit institutions. To estimate rates of return for private households and nonprofit institutions we combine data on property compensation with data on the value of tangible assets for these sectors, including depreciation and revaluation, described in Sections I through V. For private households we define the return to capital on owner-occupied dwellings as space rental value less property taxes and depreciation on owner-occupied dwellings, and plus the revaluation of these dwellings. We define the nominal rate of return for private households as the rate of return to owner-occupied dwellings divided by the value of these dwellings.

We assume that the nominal rate of return for consumers' durables held by private households is the same as for owner-occupied dwellings. Similarly, we assume that the nominal rate of return by nonprofit institutions is the same as that for private households. On the basis of these assumptions we impute the value of property compensation for private households and nonprofit institutions. By excluding revaluation of assets in each sector for the return to capital we define own rates of return that reflect only earnings on these assets.

Property Compensation

In our sectoral production accounts property compensation is defined from the point of view of the producer. Sectoral property compensation before taxes for any producing industry is defined as the sum of

net interest
+ capital consumption allowances
+ inventory valuation adjustment
+ business transfer payments
+ corporate profits before tax
+ rental income of persons
+ indirect business taxes allocated to capital assets
+ return to capital of self-employed persons
+ subsidies
+ statistical discrepancy allocated to property compensation.

These components of property compensation are taken directly from the Bureau of Economic Analysis study *Fourteen Current Dollar Components of Gross Product Originating by Industry* [19, 1978] with the exception of indirect business taxes allocated to capital assets, return to capital of self-employed persons and statistical discrepancy allocated to property compensation. The Bureau of Economic Analysis study *Fourteen Current Dollar Components of Gross Product Originating by Industry* [19, 1978] presents information only for public utilities as a whole. We allocate components of property compensation before taxes among electric utilities, gas utilities, and water and sanitary services in proportion to value added in these industries from a study by Jack Faucett Associates [42, 1973a].[m]

Indirect business taxes allocated to capital assets are estimated from unpublished worksheet data by industry provided to us by Walter Surrat of the Bureau of Economic Analysis. These taxes include property taxes, motor vehicle taxes, and other taxes such as corporate franchise, occupational and business, and severance taxes. Income of self-employed persons is available only as the sum of labor and property compensation. We present the methodology for divid-

[m] The 1971 distribution is used for all subsequent years.

ing the total between labor and property compensation in our discussion of the measurement of the rate of return. The statistical discrepancy allocated to property compensation is also determined as a by-product of the rate of return calculations. We distribute the total statistical discrepancy across all producing industries in proportion to each industry's share of income of self-employed persons. The division of the statistical discrepancy between property compensation and labor compensation is determined in measuring the rate of return.[n] The statistical discrepancy must be allocated to factor outlay in order to satisfy the identity that the value of input is equal to the value of output for each sector.

For each industrial sector the sum of corporate plus noncorporate property compensation is equal to total property compensation. Corporate property compensation before taxes for any industry is defined as the sum of

corporate net interest
+ corporate capital consumption allowances
+ corporate inventory valuation adjustment
+ business transfer payments
+ corporate profits before tax
+ indirect business taxes allocated to corporate capital assets.

Noncorporate property compensation before taxes for any industry is defined as the sum of

noncorporate net interest
+ noncorporate capital consumption allowances
+ noncorporate inventory valuation adjustment
+ rental income of persons
+ indirect business taxes allocated to noncorporate capital assets
+ return to capital of self-employed persons
+ subsidies
+ statistical discrepancy allocated to property compensation.

Several components of property compensation are allocated either to corporate or to noncorporate property compensation. We assume

[n]This practice is consistent with the convention adopted by the Bureau of Economic Analysis in determining the value added split among employee compensation, property-type income, and indirect business taxes in the construction of the 1967 input-output matrix [12, 1974a]. Property-type income is defined to include noncorporate profits, which is the sum of the return to capital and labor of self-employed persons and the statistical discrepancy. As a result we distribute the statistical discrepancy in proportion to a subcomponent of profit-type income, noncorporate profits.

all business transfer payments accrue to the corporate sector. We allocate all rental income of persons,[o] return to capital of self-employed persons, subsidies, and statistical discrepancy allocated to property compensation to the noncorporate sector. Net interest and indirect business taxes allocated to capital assets are not available for corporate and noncorporate business separately. We allocate these components of property compensation in proportion to capital consumption allowances for the two legal forms of organization.[p]

We employ totals for corporate financial, corporate nonfinancial, noncorporate financial and noncorporate nonfinancial net interest from Table 1.15 of the *Survey of Current Business* [17, BEA, 1976b; 20, BEA] to control our estimates of net interest. It is important to control financial and nonfinancial net interest separately, as the control totals for the two categories are opposite in sign. We include the following financial industries in the finance, insurance, and real estate industry: banks, credit agencies, holding and investment companies, security and commodity dealers, insurance carriers and insurance agents.

We employ totals from the Christensen-Jorgenson aggregate level national income accounting system [23, 1969; 25, 1973] for corporate and noncorporate indirect business taxes allocated to capital assets to control our estimates. Christensen and Jorgenson [23, 1969; 25, 1973] use unpublished estimates from the Bureau of Economic Analysis for the value of corporate property taxes from 1948 to the present. Other indirect business taxes are allocated in proportion to the value of beginning-of-period capital stock in the corporate and noncorporate sectors.

We take our measure of household and institutional property compensation before taxes directly from the Christensen-Jorgenson aggregate level national income accounting system [23, 1969; 25, 1973].

Household property compensation before taxes is defined to be the sum of

space rental value of owner-occupied farm residential structures
+ space rental value of owner-occupied nonfarm residential
  structures

---

[o] The portion of rental income of persons resulting from the imputed value of owner-occupied housing is allocated to the household industry.

[p] The information on capital consumption allowances comes from the Bureau of Economic Analysis study [19, 1978]. The noncorporate/corporate ratio we describe here is used throughout this study.

  − associated purchases of goods and services, owner-occupied farm residential structures
  − associated purchases of goods and services, owner-occupied non-farm residential structures
  + service flow from consumers' durables.

The income components related to nonfarm residential structures and space rental value of owner-occupied farm residential structures, including a net rent value, are taken from Table 8.3 of the *Survey of Current Business* [17, BEA, 1976b; 20, BEA]. The figure for associated purchases of goods and services for owner-occupied farm residential structures is generated by Christensen and Jorgenson under the assumption that such purchases are proportional to space rental value. The space rental value includes the value of owner-occupied residential structures property taxes, which are considered a part of factor outlay.

We transfer household property compensation components from the real estate industry to the household industry to maintain consistency between capital accounts and production accounts. The service flow from consumers' durables is imputed from the rate of return on real estate held by households and from the value of total personal property taxes. The rate of return derivation will be discussed in a later section. Personal property taxes include the following state and local taxes listed in Table 3.4 of the *Survey of Current Business* [17, BEA, 1976b; 20, BEA]: personal motor vehicle licenses, personal property, and personal other taxes.

Institutional property compensation before taxes is defined to be the sum of

  space rental value of institutional structures
  + equity return on implicit rental of institutional real estate
  + service flow from institutional producers' durable equipment.

The space rental figures are taken from Table 8.3 of the *Survey of Current Business* [17, BEA, 1976b; 20, BEA]. Net rent is not included in the imputation of space rental value by the Bureau of Economic Analysis. We impute space rental value from the rate of return on real estate held by households. The service flow from institutional producers' durable equipment is also imputed from the rate of return on real estate held by households.

In order to maintain consistency between capital accounts and production accounts we reallocate income components not associated with institutions serving persons in the Bureau of Economic

Analysis study *Fourteen Current Dollar Components of Gross Product Originating by Industry* [19, 1978] from nonprofit institutions to the service industry. We also reallocate income representing space rental value from the real estate industry to institutions.[q]

Nominal Rates of Return

Following Christensen and Jorgenson [23, 1969; 25, 1973], the sectoral nominal rate of return on corporate capital assets after corporate profits taxes and indirect business taxes allocated to corporate capital assets can be defined as follows:

r_t = [corporate property compensation before taxes
  − corporate indirect business taxes allocated to property
    compensation
  − corporate depreciation
  + corporate revaluation
  − corporate profits tax liability]
  / [current value of corporate capital stock at beginning
    of period].

The sectoral rates of return are defined from the point of view of the producer. The value of capital service flows is equal to property compensation before taxes.

We have discussed the derivation of components of the nominal rate of return with the exception of the corporate profits tax liability. To construct corporate profits tax liabilities for all producing industries we begin with data from Table 6.20 of the *Survey of Current Business* [17, BEA, 1976b; 20, BEA]. Data on corporate profit tax liabilities for 1976 are available only for the following aggregates: agriculture, forestry and fisheries; mining; construction; manufacturing nondurables; manufacturing durables; transportation; communication; utilities; trade; finance; insurance and real estate; and services. We allocate corporate tax liabilities among the detailed industries in proportion to the 1975 distribution of these liabilities.

To translate the corporate tax liability from Table 6.20 from a company to establishment basis, we first calculate the ratio of corporate profits before taxes on an establishment basis from the Bureau of Economic Analysis study *Fourteen Current Dollar Components of Gross Product Originating by Industry* [19, 1978] to corporate profits before taxes on a company basis from Table 6.18 of the *Survey of Current Business* [17, BEA, 1976b; 20, BEA]. Anomalies in these ratios, such as negative values, are corrected by interpolation or extrapolation between adjacent values. The corpo-

---

[q]Nonprofit institutions not serving persons include such groups as fraternal organizations and clubs.

rate tax liability figures are then multiplied by the ratios of establishment to company basis liability to produce an initial estimate of
the value of corporate profits tax liability on an establishment basis.
As a final step these estimates are controlled so that the sum across
all producing industries equals the value of total corporate profits
tax liability.

As previously noted, we must determine the division between
income of self-employed persons allocated to property compensation
and that allocated to labor compensation. We could assume that self-
employed workers earn the same wages per hour as wage and salary
workers or, alternatively, that corporate and noncorporate nominal
rates of return on capital assets are equal for each sector. We select
the second of these two alternatives, so that we employ the corporate rate of return to obtain noncorporate property compensation
before taxes, including the income of self-employed persons allocated to property compensation. The portion of income of self-
employed persons allocated to labor compensation is determined as a
residual.[r]

Due to the high degree of vertical integration of the petroleum and
primary metal industries we assume that capital assets are correctly
allocated within these industries, but that property income is not
appropriately allocated to the capital assets that generate the income.
We calculate the corporate nominal rate of return and income tax
rate jointly for the crude and refined petroleum industries and for
the metal mining and primary metal industries. The company to
establishment ratio applied to corporate profits tax liability is calculated for the sum of the crude and refined petroleum industries and
for the sum of metal mining and primary metal industries.

The nominal rate of return on residential structures and land held
by households after property taxes is employed as the household and
institutional rate of return for all types of assets. Our derivation follows that of Christensen and Jorgenson [23, 1969; 25, 1973]. The
rate of return on residential structures and land held by households
is defined as follows:

r_t = [space rental value for owner-occupied residential property
      − property taxes, owner-occupied residential property
      − depreciation, owner-occupied residential property
      + revaluation, owner-occupied residential property]
    / [current value of beginning-of-period capital stock, owner-
      occupied residential property].

---

[r]For industries with very small noncorporate sectors, the imputed figures for
income of self-employed persons allocated to labor compensation are occasion-
ally negative, probably due to the limits imposed by the accuracy of the data.

Space rental value is defined as the sum of the components of household property compensation, excluding services from consumers' durables. Property taxes on owner-occupied residential structures and the associated land are obtained from Table 8.3 of the *Survey of Current Business* [17, BEA; 1976b; 20, BEA]. It is assumed that all indirect business taxes and nontaxes reported in Table 8.3 are property taxes. The terms for the value of depreciation, revaluation, and the current value of beginning-of-period capital stock include the values of owner-occupied residential structures and the value of associated land.

VII. SECTORAL RATES OF RETURN

Our next objective is to construct estimates of rates of return for each of the forty-six industrial sectors of the U.S. economy listed in Table 2–1. Our estimates are based on the data for sectoral property compensation described in Section VI and data on the value of sectoral assets, including depreciation and revaluation of assets, described in Sections I through V above. We employ the definition of nominal rates of return presented in Section VI. Nominal rates of return include earnings on assets and gains that accrue through revaluation of assets. Own rates of return include only earnings on assets.

We present data on nominal and own rates of return for the forty-six industrial sectors included in our study. We analyze the pattern of nominal and own rates of return across industries for the time period 1948–1976. Second, we analyze the pattern of growth across subperiods of time for individual industries. For this purpose we divide the period as a whole into seven subperiods, corresponding to the years between cyclical peaks of the U.S. economy.

We are able to identify six industries that experienced average nominal rates of return above 15 percent for the period 1948–1976: nonmetallic mining, lumber and wood, motor vehicles, local transportation, broadcasting, and water supply and other utilities. Industries with rates of return less than 6 percent for the period as a whole include transportation equipment, air transportation and finance, insurance, and real estate. There is no clear-cut association between average rates of growth of capital stock and average rates of return to capital.

In these cases we assume self-employed labor compensation moves in proportion to wage and salary labor compensation. As a result we define a noncorporate rate of return which differs from the corporate rate of return for the affected years.

In comparing rates of return across subperiods of time we find that the distribution of average nominal rates of return has shifted upward between the 1950s and the 1960s and between the 1960s and the 1970s, reflecting increasing rates of increase in the prices of capital goods between these periods. The distribution of average own rates of return, which excludes gains from the revaluation of assets, does not exhibit a similar trend. This distribution appears to be relatively stable over time, reflecting the stability of earnings on assets.

In the following section we employ sectoral nominal rates of return in order to divide sectoral property compensation between price and quantity components. The price components of property compensation is the price of capital input into the sector. The quantity component is the quantity of capital input, which corresponds to the services of capital assets employed in the sector. In Section IX below we combine data on sectoral property compensation and the value of sectoral assets to obtain estimates of aggregate rates of return and the price and quantity of aggregate capital input.

Nominal Rates of Return

Table 2—17 presents the annual averages of sectoral nominal rates of return for the period 1948—1976 and for seven subperiods— 1948—1952, 1953—1956, 1957—1959, 1960—1965, 1966—1968, 1969—1972, and 1973—1976. Table 2—18 classifies industries by average nominal rates of return for these same periods. The aggregate nominal rate of return for the period 1948—1976 is 0.0848; for the seven subperiods the aggregate nominal rates of return are 0.0859 for 1948—1952, 0.0577 for 1953—1956, 0.0563 for 1957—1959, 0.0647 for 1960—1965, 0.1011 for 1966—1968, 0.1038 for 1969— 1972, and 0.1309 for 1973—1976. The distributions of nominal rates of return across industries reflect the aggregate rates. The distributions are concentrated at relatively low levels for the subperiods 1953—1956, 1957—1959, and 1960—1965. Distributions for the remaining subperiods are higher, reflecting higher rates of inflation in asset prices. The majority of industries realize a nominal rate of return that is higher than the aggregate nominal rate of return. The value of capital input series in Appendix B indicates that two industires—finance, insurance, and real estate; and private households— account for the major portion of factor outlay for capital services for the economy as a whole. These industries realize significantly lower than average nominal rates of return for the period as a whole, pulling down the aggregate rate of return.

Sectors experiencing significantly lower or higher than average nominal rates of return for the periods as a whole, 1948—1976, can

Table 2–17. Sectoral Nominal Rates of Return: Annual Averages

Industry	1948–1976	1948–1953	1953–1957	1957–1960	1960–1966	1966–1969	1969–1973	1973–1976
Agricultural production	.0749	.0755	.0229	.0290	.0450	.0969	.1015	.1624
Agricultural services	.0693	.0314	-.0061	.0360	.0630	.1060	.1250	.1433
Metal mining	.0900	.1145	.1056	.0574	.0556	.0961	.0739	.1316
Coal mining	.1424	.1711	.0753	.1142	.0736	.0893	.1359	.3443
Crude petroleum and natural gas	.1240	.1236	.1157	.1014	.0812	.1199	.1176	.2233
Nonmetallic mining and quarrying	.1522	.2971	.1803	.1115	.0866	.1174	.0945	.1561
Contract construction	.1471	.2482	.1329	.1460	.0916	.1410	.1293	.1412
Food and kindred products	.1031	.0965	.0610	.0726	.0874	.1193	.1220	.1690
Tobacco manufacturers	.1350	.0636	.0793	.1071	.1214	.1486	.2244	.2215
Textile mill products	.0903	.1361	.0402	.0509	.0703	.1111	.1010	.1163

Table 2-17. continued

Industry	1948-1976	1948-1953	1953-1957	1957-1960	1960-1966	1966-1969	1969-1973	1973-1976
Apparel and other fabr. textile prod.	.1052	.0956	.0668	.0733	.0993	.1493	.1434	.1170
Paper and allied products	.1283	.1761	.1401	.1006	.0892	.1186	.1039	.1670
Printing and publishing	.1069	.0935	.0726	.0662	.0961	.1388	.1241	.1635
Chemicals and allied products	.1322	.1376	.1215	.1241	.1239	.1322	.1157	.1713
Petroleum and coal products	.1240	.1236	.1157	.1014	.0812	.1199	.1176	.2233
Rubber and misc. plastic products	.1052	.1362	.0912	.0837	.0791	.1085	.1013	.1368
Leather and leather products	.0980	.0853	.0798	.0646	.0981	.1501	.0863	.1296
Lumber and wood prod., ex. furniture	.2045	.2257	.1586	.1053	.1401	.2191	.2533	.3555
Furniture and fixtures	.1137	.1459	.1017	.0702	.1007	.1562	.1126	.1072
Stone, clay, and glass products	.1123	.1240	.1296	.1097	.0953	.0954	.1051	.1278

Table 2-17. continued

Industry	1948-1976	1948-1953	1953-1957	1957-1960	1960-1966	1966-1969	1969-1973	1973-1976
Primary metal industries	.0900	.1145	.1056	.0574	.0556	.0961	.0739	.1516
Fabricated metal industries	.1051	.1455	.0907	.0679	.0701	.1230	.0958	.1450
Machinery, ex. electrical	.1460	.1935	.1318	.1055	.1287	.1657	.1575	.1509
Elec. machinery, eqpt., and supplies	.1212	.1369	.0934	.0890	.0872	.1526	.1507	.1715
Trans. eqpt. & ord., ex. motor vehicles	.0535	.0572	.0543	.0487	.0566	.0912	.0533	.0458
Motor vehicles and equipment	.2846	.2823	.2150	.1283	.3406	.4018	.3162	.2602
Prof. photographic eqpt. and watches	.1420	.1086	.1285	.1164	.1463	.2580	.1560	.1243
Misc. manufacturing industries	.1382	.1648	.1159	.1121	.1161	.1417	.1560	.1793
Railroads and rail express service	.0747	.0844	.0556	.0596	.0355	.0755	.0954	.1510
Street rail, bus lines, and taxicabs	.1712	.0699	.0657	.1245	.1641	.2536	.2779	.2705

Table 2-17. continued

Industry	1948-1976	1948-1953	1953-1957	1957-1960	1960-1966	1966-1969	1969-1973	1973-1976
Trucking services and warehousing	.1435	.1315	.0968	.1350	.1176	.1686	.1894	.1858
Water transportation	.0727	.0103	-.0002	.0511	.0685	.1385	.1148	.1544
Air transportation	.0199	.0832	-.0358	.0178	-.0146	.0557	.0091	.0484
Pipelines, ex. natural gas	.1106	.0533	.0523	.0675	.0679	.1619	.2175	.1917
Transportation services	.0983	.0419	.0696	.0913	.0854	.1241	.1116	.1895
Te. and tel. and misc. comm. services	.1460	.0664	.0941	.1287	.1641	.2014	.1930	.1947
Radio broadcasting and television	.1514	.1802	.2118	.1568	.1304	.1256	.1160	.1371
Electric utilities	.1306	.1043	.1108	.1083	.0979	.1553	.1549	.2060
Gas utilities	.1454	.0823	.0977	.1168	.1176	.1936	.2039	.2404
Water supply and sanitary services	.1824	.1343	.1380	.1739	.1695	.2049	.2282	.2501

Table 2–17. continued

Industry	1948–1976	1948–1953	1953–1957	1957–1960	1960–1966	1966–1969	1969–1973	1973–1976
Wholesale trade	.1269	.1586	.0893	.0960	.0899	.1182	.1203	.2169
Retail trade	.1017	.1360	.0742	.0717	.0777	.1089	.1153	.1258
Finance, insurance, and real estate	.0560	.0704	.0324	.0298	.0559	.0780	.0778	.0733
Services excl. priv. hh., inst.	.0913	.0734	.0599	.0633	.0708	.1123	.1128	.1594
Private households	.0793	.0702	.0544	.0518	.0644	.0915	.1012	.1274
Institutions	.0793	.0702	.0544	.0518	.0644	.0915	.1012	.1274

Table 2-18.   Classification of Annual Averages for Sectoral Nominal Rates of Return by Period, 1948-1976

Average Rate of Growth of Nominal Rates of Return	1948-1976	1948-1952	1953-1956	1957-1959	1960-1965	1966-1968	1969-1972	1973-1976
Less than 3 percent	1	1	4	3	1	0	1	0
3 to less than 6 percent	2	4	8[a]	9[a]	6	1	1	2
6 to less than 9 percent	6[a]	12[a]	10	11	19[a]	3	4	1
9 to less than 12 percent	15	7	13	15	10	18[a]	19[a]	3
12 to less than 15 percent	16	12	8	6	6	10	10	14[a]
15 to less than 18 percent	3	4	0	2	3	7	2	11
18 to less than 21 percent	2	2	1	0	0	3	3	5
21 percent or more	1	4	2	0	1	4	6	10

[a] Denotes the category which contains the annual average for the aggregate nominal rate of return for the period.

be identified. The industries experiencing average nominal rates of return of less than 6 percent are the following: transportation equipment, except motor vehicles, and ordnance; air transportation; and finance, insurance, and real estate. These three industries exhibit lower than average nominal rates of return for each of the seven subperiods. The average nominal rate of return for air transportation is significantly below average for all periods except for 1948–1952. Air transportation experiences the highest rate of capital stock growth for the period as a whole coupled with the lowest average nominal rate of return. Finance, insurance, and real estate shows a lower than average rate of growth of capital stock for each period and a lower than average nominal rate of return for each period. The rate of growth of capital stock for transportation equipment, except motor vehicles and ordnance, is highly variable.

The industries experiencing average nominal rates of return of greater than 15 percent for the period as a whole are the following: nonmetallic mining and quarrying, except fuel; lumber and wood products; motor vehicles and motor vehicle equipment; street railway, bus lines and taxicab service; radio broadcasting and television; and water supply, sanitary services, and other utilities. All these industries experience higher than average nominal rates of return during each of the seven subperiods with the exception of nonmetallic mining and quarrying and street railway, buslines, and taxicab service. For nonmetallic mining, 1969–1972 is the only period which shows a lower than average nominal rate of return. The average nominal rate of return of street railway, bus lines, and taxicab services increases over time, although the progression is not strictly monotone.

Nonmetallic mining and radio broadcasting both combine a significantly higher than average rate of growth of capital stock for the period as a whole with significantly higher than average nominal rates of return. Street railway, bus lines and taxicab services experiences a significantly lower than average rate of growth of capital stock for the period as a whole with significantly higher than average nominal rates of return. Lumber and wood products, excluding furniture, sustains a higher than average rate of growth of capital stock for all periods except those from 1957 through 1969. Motor vehicles and motor vehicle equipment sustains a higher than average rate of growth of capital stock for the period as a whole, experiencing a lower than average rate of growth only during the 1957–1960 period. Water supply, sanitary services, and other utilities sustains clearly higher than average rates of growth of capital stock over all periods, with the exception of the 1953–1957 period.

There is no clear association between higher (lower) than average rates of growth of capital stock and higher (lower) than average nominal rates of return. We have not yet discussed the experience of all industries with significantly lower or higher average rates of growth of capital stock. Leather and leather products combines a significantly lower than average rate of growth of capital stock for the period as a whole with a higher than average nominal rate of return for all periods, except 1969–1972 and 1973–1976. Railroads and railway express service, on the other hand, combines a significantly lower than average rate of growth of capital stock for the period as a whole with a lower than average nominal rate of return for the period as a whole. The decline in the capital stock of pipelines, except natural gas, ceases in 1966–1969. The capital stock of pipelines, except natural gas, increases in the subperiods 1966–1969, 1969–1973, and 1973–1976. The nominal rate of return is significantly above average during these three subperiods. Pipelines, except natural gas, effectively combines lower than average rates of growth of capital stock with higher than average nominal rates of return, the exceptions being 1948–1952 and 1953–1956. Construction combines a significantly higher than average rate of growth of capital stock for the period as a whole with a higher than average rate of return for the period as a whole. Telephone, telegraph, and miscellaneous communication services combines a significantly higher than average rate of growth of capital stock for the period as a whole with a higher than average nominal rate of return for all periods, except 1948–1952.

For the seven subperiods we consider in detail those industries which exhibit average nominal rates of return of either less than 3 percent or 21 percent or more. During the 1948–1952 period only water transportation falls in the lowest category for the average nominal rate of return. This industry also sustained a significantly lower than average rate of growth of capital stock during this period. During the same period, the four industries falling in the highest category are nonmetallic mining and quarrying, construction, lumber and wood products, and motor vehicles and motor vehicle equipment. Construction is the only industry of this group which is not also among those industries experiencing significantly higher than average rates of growth of capital stock for the period as a whole. Nonmetallic mining and quarrying and construction experience significantly higher than average rates of growth of capital stock during this same period.

During the 1953–1956 period, the four industries falling in the lowest category for the average nominal rate of return are both agriculture sectors—agricultural production and agricultural services—and water transportation, and air transportation. Air transportation experiences significantly higher than average rate of growth of capital stock during this period. During this same period the two industries falling in the highest category for the average nominal rate of return are motor vehicles and motor vehicle equipment and radio broadcasting and television. Radio broadcasting and television experiences a significantly higher than average rate of growth of capital stock during this period.

During the 1957—1959 period, the three industries falling in the lowest category for the average nominal rate of return are agricultural production; air transportation; and finance, insurance, and real estate. This is the second consecutive period during which the first two industries have fallen in the lowest category for the average nominal rate of return. Air transportation again experiences a significantly higher than average rate of growth of capital stock during this period. The lower than average nominal rate of return for the finance, insurance, and real estate industry could be in part explained by the dramatic decrease in the rate of growth of tenant-occupied residential and nonresidential structures from the 1952—1956 period to the 1956—1959 period. During this period no industries fall in the highest average nominal rate of return category.

Only air transportation falls in the lowest category for the average nominal rate of return in the period 1960—1965. Air transportation continues to experience a significantly higher rate of growth of capital stock. During the same period, only motor vehicles and motor vehicle equipment falls in the highest category for the average nominal rate of return. During the 1966—1968 period, no industries fall in the lowest category for the average nominal rate of return. The four industries falling in the highest category for the average nominal rate of return are lumber and wood products, except furniture; motor vehicles and motor vehicle equipment; professional photographic equipment and watches; and street railway, bus lines, and taxicab service. With the exception of professional photographic equipment and watches, these industries are those which experience significantly higher than average nominal rates of return for the period as a whole. Professional photographic equipment and watches sustains significantly higher than average rate of growth of capital stock during this period.

Only air transportation falls in the lowest category for the average nominal rate of return from 1969—1972. The six industries falling in the highest category for the average nominal rate of return are tobacco manufactures; lumber and wood products, except furniture;

motor vehicles and motor vehicle equipment; street railway, bus lines, and taxicab service; pipelines, except natural gas; and water supply, sanitary services, and other utilities. During the 1973–1976 period, revaluation plays a major role in determining the level of the nominal rates of return. During this period, no industries fall in the lowest category for the average nominal rate of return. Ten industries fall in the highest category for the average nominal rate of return, with energy and utility industries accounting for one-half of the total. The ten industries are coal mining; crude petroleum and natural gas; tobacco manufactures; petroleum and coal products; lumber and wood products, except furniture; motor vehicles and motor vehicle equipment; street railway, bus lines, and taxicab service; gas utilities; water supply, sanitary services, and other utilities; and wholesale trade.

Own Rates of Return

Sectoral own rates of return are defined by excluding revaluation from the ratio defining nominal rates of return. Table 2–19 presents the annual averages for sectoral own rates of return for the period 1948–1976 and for seven subperiods—1948–1952, 1953–1956, 1957–1959, 1960–1965, 1966–1968, 1969–1972, and 1973–1976. Table 2–20 classifies industries by average own rates of return for these same periods. The aggregate own rate of return for the period 1948–1976 is 0.0478; for the seven subperiods the aggregate own rates of return are 0.0432 for 1948–1952, 0.0414 for 1953–1956, 0.0313 for 1957–1959, 0.0515 for 1960–1965, 0.0605 for 1966–1968, 0.0514 for 1969–1972, and 0.0484 for 1973–1976. Since revaluation is excluded from the numerator in the own rate of return, the aggregate own rate of return shows much less variation over time than the aggregate nominal rate of return. The subperiods 1960–1965, 1960–1968 and 1969–1972 are characterized by high average own rates of return. The most recent subperiod, 1973–1976, has a distribution of own rates of return that is similar to that of the subperiods 1948–1952, 1953–1956, and 1957–1959.

We can identify the sectors experiencing significantly lower or higher than average own rates of return for the period as a whole, 1948–1976. The industries experiencing average own rates of return of less than 3 percent are transportation equipment, except motor vehicles, and ordnance, air transportation, finance, insurance and real estate. These industries exhibit lower than average own rates of return for each of the seven subperiods. The industries experiencing average own rates of return greater than 12 percent are lumber and wood products; motor vehicle and motor vehicle equipment; street

Table 2–19.   Sectoral Own Rates of Return: Annual Averages

Industry	1948–1976	1948–1953	1953–1957	1957–1960	1960–1966	1966–1969	1969–1973	1973–1976
Agricultural production	.0350	.0259	.0103	.0141	.0271	.0419	.0420	.0866
Agricultural services	.0388	.0003	.0109	.0217	.0544	.0674	.0686	.0532
Metal mining	.0462	.0518	.0710	.0472	.0454	.0620	.0205	.0285
Coal mining	.1021	.1304	.0509	.0932	.0711	.0550	.0749	.2336
Crude petroleum and natural gas	.0812	.0793	.0960	.0801	.0732	.0799	.0559	.1075
Nonmetallic mining and quarrying	.1135	.2556	.1536	.0835	.0928	.0797	.0364	.0518
Contract construction	.1078	.1983	.1148	.1215	.0877	.0984	.0724	.0502
Food and kindred products	.0667	.0562	.0516	.0624	.0729	.0889	.0721	.0667
Tobacco manufacturers	.1085	.0523	.0723	.0952	.1142	.1144	.1824	.1377
Textile mill products	.0577	.0964	.0270	.0344	.0639	.0878	.0589	.0241

Table 2–19. continued

Industry	1948-1976	1948-1953	1953-1957	1957-1960	1960-1966	1966-1969	1969-1973	1973-1976
Apparel and other fabr. textile prod.	.0809	.0757	.0632	.0626	.0953	.1236	.0864	.0595
Paper and allied products	.0864	.1257	.1083	.0774	.0784	.0845	.0578	.0642
Printing and publishing	.0654	.0382	.0472	.0498	.0823	.0996	.0712	.0722
Chemicals and allied products	.0950	.0990	.0966	.1039	.1163	.1029	.0731	.0659
Petroleum and coal products	.0812	.0793	.0960	.0801	.0732	.0799	.0559	.1075
Rubber and misc. plastic products	.0660	.0716	.0666	.0732	.0724	.0794	.0624	.0368
Leather and leather products	.0724	.0847	.0659	.0414	.0856	.1313	.0231	.0722
Lumber and wood prod., ex. furniture	.1648	.1710	.1171	.0919	.1308	.1601	.2042	.2746
Furniture and fixtures	.0741	.0932	.0714	.0574	.0919	.1089	.0638	.0227
Stone, clay, and glass products	.0738	.0840	.1017	.0846	.0840	.0574	.0549	.0407

Table 2–19. continued

Industry	1948–1976	1948–1953	1953–1957	1957–1960	1960–1966	1966–1969	1969–1973	1973–1976
Primary metal industries	.0462	.0518	.0710	.0472	.0454	.0620	.0205	.0285
Fabricated metal industries	.0595	.0806	.0482	.0417	.0606	.0886	.0464	.0471
Machinery, ex. electrical	.1068	.1336	.0978	.0831	.1220	.1376	.0979	.0634
Elec. machinery, eqpt., and supplies	.0825	.0860	.0604	.0764	.0804	.1203	.0860	.0761
Trans. eqpt. & ord., ex. motor vehicles	.0127	-.0233	.0156	.0255	.0491	.0602	.0097	-.0421
Motor vehicles and equipment	.2450	.2241	.1848	.1076	.3331	.3721	.2693	.1830
Prof. photographic eqpt. and watches	.1052	.0635	.1059	.0961	.1392	.2029	.1148	.0296
Misc. manufacturing industries	.1030	.1224	.0978	.0937	.1087	.1131	.0967	.0810
Railroads and rail express service	.0346	.0420	.0379	.0266	.0376	.0502	.0352	.0114
Street rail, bus lines, and taxicabs	.1352	.0272	.0320	.0893	.1679	.2362	.2222	.1963

Table 2–19. continued

Industry	1948–1976	1948–1953	1953–1957	1957–1960	1960–1966	1966–1969	1969–1973	1973–1976
Trucking services and warehousing	.1031	.0862	.0717	.1071	.1118	.1371	.1231	.0945
Water transportation	.0455	.0030	.0136	.0230	.0726	.1126	.0453	.0568
Air transportation	-.0152	-.0053	.0079	-.0167	-.0092	.0089	-.0504	-.0415
Pipelines, ex. natural gas	.0697	-.0011	.0150	.0231	.0763	.1367	.1674	.0898
Transportation services	.0632	.0044	.0570	.0775	.0809	.0948	.0525	.0923
Te. and tel. and misc. comm. services	.1126	.0405	.0747	.1079	.1595	.1614	.1365	.1130
Radio broadcasting and television	.1188	.1560	.2004	.1309	.1261	.0868	.0599	.0539
Electric utilities	.0836	.0429	.0597	.0650	.1005	.1233	.1113	.0912
Gas utilities	.0988	.0235	.0524	.0774	.1186	.1615	.1548	.1229
Water supply and sanitary services	.1399	.0907	.1163	.1386	.1637	.1756	.1595	.1440

Table 2–19. continued

Industry	1948–1976	1948–1953	1953–1957	1957–1960	1960–1966	1966–1969	1969–1973	1973–1976
Wholesale trade	.0936	.1226	.0764	.0779	.0855	.0877	.0745	.1220
Retail trade	.0677	.0959	.0579	.0571	.0716	.0749	.0667	.0404
Finance, insurance, and real estate	.0178	.0229	.0188	.0172	.0198	.0239	.0184	.0023
Services excl. priv. hh., inst.	.0533	.0295	.0389	.0501	.0621	.0715	.0553	.0709
Private households	.0442	.0323	.0387	.0321	.0475	.0540	.0541	.0514
Institutions	.0309	.0197	.0246	.0237	.0392	.0414	.0337	.0334

Table 2–20. Classification of Annual Averages for Sectoral Own Rates of Return by Period, 1948–1976

Average Rate of Growth of Own Rates of Return	1948–1976	1948–1952	1953–1956	1957–1959	1960–1965	1966–1968	1969–1972	1973–1976
Less than 0 percent	1	3	0	1	1	0	1	2
0 to less than 3 percent	2	9	9	8	2	2	5	8
3 to less than 6 percent	11[a]	9[a]	12[a]	10[a]	7[a]	6	15[a]	11[a]
6 to less than 9 percent	15	10	11	15	19	16[a]	12	11
9 to less than 12 percent	13	5	11	9	9	8	4	6
12 to less than 15 percent	2	5	0	3	4	7	2	4
15 to less than 18 percent	1	2	1	0	3	4	3	0
18 percent or more	1	3	2	0	1	3	4	4

[a]Denotes the category which contains the annual average for the aggregate own rate of return for the period.

railway, bus lines, and taxicab service; and water supply, sanitary services, and other utilities. These industries exhibit above average own rates of return for each of the seven subperiods. Aside from nonmetallic mining and quarrying, except fuel, and radio broadcasting and television, industries with own rates of return significantly different from the average also have similar differences in nominal rates of return.

For the seven subperiods we consider in detail those industries which exhibit negative average own rates of return or average own rates of return of 18 percent or more. During the 1948–1952 period, the three industries experiencing negative average own rate of return are transportation equipment, except motor vehicles and ordnance; air transportation; and pipelines, except natural gas. The three industries falling in the highest category for the average own rate of return are nonmetallic mining and quarrying, except fuel; construction; and motor vehicles and motor vehicle equipment. The list for the highest category again matches that for the average nominal rate of return except for lumber and wood products.

No industries experienced negative average own rates of return from 1953–1956. The two industries with average own rates of return exceeding 18 percent are motor vehicle and motor vehicle equipment and radio broadcasting and television. This list includes all industries in the corresponding list for nominal rates of return. During the periods 1957–1959 and 1960–1965 only air transportation experienced a negative average own rate of return.

During the period 1960–1965 only motor vehicles and motor vehicle equipment had an average own rate of return of 18 percent or more. These lists are identical to those for the nominal rates of return. During the 1966–1968 period, motor vehicles and motor vehicle equipment; professional photographic equipment and watches; and street railway, bus lines, and taxicab service had average own rates of return exceeding 18 percent.

Only air transportation had a negative average own rate of return for the period 1969–1972. The industries experiencing significantly higher average own rate of return include tobacco manufactures; lumber and wood products, except furniture; motor vehicles and motor vehicle equipment; and street railway, bus lines, and taxicab service. Finally, during the 1973–1976 period, average own rates of return were experienced by transportation equipment, except motor vehicle equipment, and by ordnance and air transportation. Industries with own rates of return exceeding 18 percent are coal mining; lumber and wood products, except furniture; motor vehicles and motor vehicle equipment; and street railway, bus lines, and taxicab service. The corresponding list for nominal rates of return includes energy and utility sectors. Revaluation clearly plays a role in determining average nominal rates of return for the energy and utility sectors during this last subperiod.

VIII.   SECTORAL CAPITAL INPUT

Our final step in measuring sectoral capital input for the U.S. economy is to construct estimates of sectoral prices of capital input for the forty-six industrial sectors listed in Table 2-1. Estimates of sectoral prices of capital input require data on sectoral own rates of return broken down by the four legal forms of organization and six asset types listed in Table 2-1. These data are based on estimates of sectoral rates of return presented in the preceding section and estimates of the value of sectoral assets described in Sections I through V above.

The prices of sectoral capital input incorporate data on sectoral own rates of return and data on the tax structure for each sector. Data on the tax structure include the effective corporate income tax rate, the present value of depreciation deductions on investment, the investment tax credit, and the rate of indirect business taxes allocated to capital assets. Our first objective in this section is to describe the sources of data on the tax structure for the four legal forms of organization, six asset types, and forty-six industrial sectors listed in Table 2-1.

In generating data on sectoral rates of return we have assumed that the value of sectoral capital input for all legal forms of organization and all asset types is equal to the value of sectoral property compensation. In dividing sectoral property compensation between price and quantity components we first construct prices of sectoral capital input for the four legal forms of organization and six asset types listed in Table 2-1. We then combine these prices with quantities of sectoral capital stocks broken down in the same way. Our final estimates of the price and quantity of sectoral capital input are index numbers that combine prices of sectoral capital input and quantities of sectoral capital stocks.

More specifically, we can express sectoral capital input, say K_i, as a translog function of its components, say K_{ki}, following the Jorgenson formulation [47, 1980] described in the next chapter of this volume. The subscript i ranges over the forty-six industries and the subscript k ranges over the four legal forms of organization and the six classes of assets given in Table 2-1. For each of the components of capital input the flow of capital services during the current period, say $K_{ki,\,t}$, is proportional to capital stock at the beginning of the period, say $A_{ki,\,t-1}$:

$$K_{ki,\,t} = Q^i_{Kk} \cdot A_{ki,\,t-1} \; ,$$

where the constants of proportionality, Q_{Kk}, transform capital stock into a flow of capital services.

Considering data on individual capital inputs at any two discrete points in time, we can express the difference between successive logarithms of sectoral capital input as a weighted average of differences between successive logarithms of individual sectoral capital inputs in the two periods:

$$\ln K_{i,\,t} - \ln K_{i,\,t-1} = \Sigma\, \bar{v}^i_{Kk}\, [\ln K_{ki,\,t} - \ln K_{ki,\,t-1}] \; ,$$

where the weights $\bar{v}^i_{Kk}$ are given by

$$\bar{v}^i_{Kk} = \tfrac{1}{2}[v^i_{Kk,\,t} + v^i_{Kk,\,t-1}] \; ,$$

and

$$v^i_{Kk} = \frac{p^i_{Kk}\, K_{ki}}{\Sigma p^i_{Kk}\, K_{ki}} \; ,$$

so that these weights depend on the prices of sectoral capital input p^i_{Kk}. The weights are given by the average share of the value of each capital input $p^i_{Kk}\, K_{ki}$ in the value of all capital inputs in the ith sector $\Sigma p^i_{Kk}\, K_{ki}$. The price of sectoral capital input p^i_K is defined as the ratio of the value of all capital inputs to the translog index of sectoral capital input K_i.

The translog index of sectoral capital input can be expressed in terms of sectoral capital inputs broken down by legal form of organization and class of asset or, alternatively, in terms of the corresponding sectoral capital stocks:

$$\ln K_{i,\,t} - \ln K_{i,\,t-1} = \Sigma\, \bar{v}^i_{Kk}\, [\ln K_{ki,\,t} - \ln K_{ki,\,t-1}] \; ,$$

$$= \Sigma\, \bar{v}^i_{Kk}\, [\ln A_{ki,\,t-1} - \ln A_{ki,\,t-2}] \; .$$

These two expressions are equivalent, since the flow of capital services from an individual capital input $K_{ki,t}$ is proportional to the stock of the corresponding asset at the beginning of the period $A_{ki,\,t-1}$.

We can define sectoral capital stock for the ith sector, say A_i, as an unweighted sum of its components:

$$A_i = \sum_i A_{ik} \ .$$

We can express sectoral capital input for the ith sector K_i as the product of a sectoral index of the quality of capital stock, say $Q^i_{K,\,t}$, and sectoral capital stock at the beginning of the period:

$$K_{i,\,t} = Q^i_{K,\,t} \cdot A_{i,\,t-1} \ .$$

The sectoral index of the quality of capital stock transforms sectoral capital stock at the beginning of the period into sectoral capital input during the period.

Our definition of the sectoral quality of capital stock, $Q^i_{K,\,t}$, is analogous to the definition of the constants of proportionality, Q^i_{Kk}, that transform capital stock into a flow of capital services for individual assets. While the quality of capital stock for a single asset within a sector is constant, the quality of capital stock for the sector as a whole is a function of time and depends on changes in the composition of capital input through time. As capital services with relatively high prices become more important in the total flow of capital services, our index of sectoral quality of capital stock rises. As capital services with relatively low prices become more important, our index falls.

In Section II above we presented data on the growth of sectoral capital stocks for all forty-six industries listed in Table 2–1 for the period 1948–1976 and for seven subperiods within this time period. In this section we present data on the growth of the quality of sectoral capital stocks for all forty-six industries for the period as a whole and for seven subperiods. We analyze the pattern of growth in the quality of capital across industries for the period 1948–1976. Second, we analyze the pattern of growth across periods of time for individual industries.

In order to measure sectoral capital input, sectoral property compensation must be separated into price and quantity components. The price of capital services from an asset held by the corporate sector of any industry is defined by Christensen and Jorgenson [23, 1969; 25, 1973] as

$$p_{K,t} = [\frac{1 - u_t z_t - k_t - y_t}{1 - u_t}][p_{A,t-1}\ r_t + p_{A,t-1}\ \delta - (p_{A,t} - p_{A,t-1})] + p_{A,t}\ \tau_t$$

where u_t is the effective corporate income tax rate, z_t is the present value of depreciation deductions on one dollar of investment, k_t is the investment tax credit rate, $y_t = k_t u_t z_t$ for 1962 and 1963 and zero otherwise, τ_t is the rate of indirect business taxes allocated to capital assets, $p_{A,t}$ is the investment deflator, and r_t is the nominal rate of return. This expression for the price of capital service flows represents the sum of terms that reflect the cost of capital, depreciation, revaluation, and indirect business taxes allocated to capital assets.

The investment tax credit k_t is different from zero only for producers' durable equipment. Depreciation deductions z_t are different from zero only for producers' durables and structures. For the noncorporate sector the terms involving the corporate tax structure— u_t, z_t, k_t, and y_t—are zero.

Taxation of Property Compensation

We have already discussed the derivation of the nominal rate of return r_t and the rate of depreciation δ. The investment tax credit rate, k_t, is calculated as the ratio of the value of the corporate investment tax credit to the value of corporate investment in producers' durable equipment. The investment tax credit was not established until 1962. We obtain information on the corporate investment tax credit from the *Corporate Statistics of Income* [38, IRS; 39, IRS]. Where necessary, we divide the corporate investment tax credit data among industries in proportion to the share of each industry in current dollar producers' durable equipment investment. We then translate the corporate investment tax credit data from a company to an establishment basis by means of the same company to establishment ratio that we applied to corporate profits tax liability. We control the sum of our establishment basis corporate investment tax credit data over producing industries to unpublished totals obtained from Robert Parker and Kenneth Petrick of the Bureau of Economic Analysis. We obtain an estimate of the value of corporate investment in producers' durable equipment by multiplying the value of total producers' durable equipment gross investment by the ratio of corporate capital consumption allowances to total corporate and noncorporate capital allowances. Information on capital consumption allowances is obtained from the Bureau of Economic Analysis study *Fourteen Current Dollar Components of Gross Product Originating by Industry* [19, 1978]. Since we were unable to obtain preliminary estimates of corporate investment tax credit by industry for 1976, we assume that the investment tax credit rate by industry for 1976 is equal to the 1975 rate.

In order to calculate the present value of depreciation deductions on one dollars worth of investment, z_t, we must create a weighted average of the present value of the prevailing depreciation methods used for tax purposes over time. This requires information on which depreciation methods and tax asset lives have been used, which we obtain from the industry level production accounts described by Frank Gollop and Jorgenson [33, 1980]. Depreciation methods for producers' durable equipment are estimated using several sources. Before 1952 the straight-line formula was the only depreciation method allowed by law. Beginning in 1952, double declining and sum-of-years digits depreciation formulas were allowed as well.

A Treasury report by Thomas Vasquez [55, 1975] compares the depreciation methods and asset lives of producers' durable equipment used by corporate taxpayers during 1954, 1954–1959, 1970, and 1971. The percentage of taxpayers employing the various depreciation methods over the period 1954–1959 for eight industry aggregates from Vasquez [55, 1974] is interpolated over the six years by means of annual total manufacturing and nonmanufacturing data presented by Allan Young [58, 1968]. We have assumed that the distribution of depreciation methods is identical for each industry within each of the eight aggregates. A similar procedure is employed to interpolate the distribution of depreciation methods between the 1959 breakdowns and those presented for 1971 for thirty-six industries by the Office of Tax Analysis of the Treasury Department [53, 1973]. The distribution for 1971 is held constant through 1976.

The only source of information on depreciation methods for structures is the study by Young [58, 1968]. Young's estimates of the distribution of depreciation methods for total manufacturing and nonmanufacturing annually 1954–1959 and an average for 1960–1966 are applied to each industry. The 1960–1966 average is extrapolated through 1971. The 1971 figure is used for 1972–1976. It is assumed that taxpayers using accelerated methods employ double declining balance depreciation methods.

Young [58, 1968], Vasquez [55, 1974], and the Office of Tax Analysis [53, 1973] provide information on tax lives for producers' durable equipment. Vasquez's figures [55, 1974] for tax lives for producers' durable equipment for ten industries in 1954 are used as benchmarks from which tax lives are estimated prior to 1954 based upon Young's figures [58, 1968] for average economy-wide changes in producers' durable equipment tax lives. After 1954, interpolation is performed between Vasquez's estimates [55, 1974] of 1954–1959 average tax lives for eight industry aggregates and the Office of Tax Analysis estimates [53, 1973] of 1970 average tax lives for thirty-six industries in proportion to Young's figures [58, 1968]. The 1971–1976 figures for producers' durable equipment are set equal to the 1971 estimates from the Office of Tax Analysis [53, 1973].

The estimates of tax lives for all producing industry structures are based upon information from Young [58, 1968] and Christensen and Jorgenson [23, 1969]. Young [58, 1968] calculates the 1945, 1950, 1952, 1955, 1957, 1960, 1961, and 1962–1966 economy-wide tax lives as a percentage of the 1940 economy-wide tax life. Using the 1953 benchmark for nonresidential structures (35.3 years) from Christensen and Jorgenson [23, 1969], these percentages are converted into tax lives. The missing years prior to 1966 are created via interpolation and the 1967–1976 structure tax lives are set equal to the 1966 value.

Given the final data series on depreciation methods and tax lives for structures and equipment, we calculate the present value of tax depreciation deductions on one dollar's worth of investment. The weights used in the computation are the percentages of taxpayers employing straight-line, 150 percent declining balance, double declining balance, and sum-of-years digits methods. The formulas for calculating the present value of depreciation deductions are taken from Robert Hall and Jorgenson [34, 1967], where the formulas have been adjusted for the "half-year convention." In these formulas it is assumed that the nominal rate of return is ten percent after taxes.[8]

[8] Formulas for the present values of depreciation deductions are:

straight line:

$$\frac{1}{rL} \left(1 - \left(\frac{1}{1+r}\right)^L\right)$$

sum of the years' digits:

$$\frac{2}{rL} \left[1 - \frac{1+r}{r(L+1)} \left(1 - \frac{1}{1+r}\right)^{L+1}\right]$$

We have previously discussed the generation of the corporate profits tax liability on an establishment basis by industry. The corporate profits tax liability is adjusted for the effect of the corporate investment tax credit. The effective corporate income tax rate is calculated on a base of corporate property compensation net of indirect business taxes allocated to capital assets, adjusted for the value of imputed depreciation deductions and the investment tax credit. The parameter y_t adjusts the value of the investment tax credit rate to account for the fact that the value of an asset for depreciation purposes in 1962 and 1963 was calculated net of the value of the investment tax credit.

We assume that the tax rate of indirect business taxes allocated to capital assets, τ_t, is equal across all types of assets for a particular industry and legal form of organization. The rate for any industry is computed as the value of corporate or noncorporate indirect business taxes allocated to capital assets divided by the current value of beginning-of-period corporate or noncorporate capital stock.

The prices of capital service for household owner-occupied residential structures and for consumers' durables are analogous to those for noncorporate business. As noted previously, the rate of return on all household and institutional assets is assumed to be equal to the rate of return on residential structures and the associated land held by households. We assume that the rate of indirect business taxes allocated to capital assets, τ_t, is equal for owner-occupied residential structures and the associated land. We calculate this rate as the ratio of the value of property taxes on owner-occupied residential structures and the associated land to the current value of beginning-of-period capital stocks for the same assets. For consumers' durables, we calculate the rate as the ratio of total personal property taxes to the current value of beginning-of-period capital stock of consumers' durables. The prices of capital services for all institutional assets are analogous to those for households, except that no indirect business taxes are paid on assets.

---

150 percent declining balance:

$$\frac{\frac{1.5}{L}}{r + \frac{1.5}{L}} \left[1 - \left(\left[\frac{1}{1+r}\right]\left[1 - \frac{1.5}{L}\right]\right)^{L^+}\right] + \frac{(1 - \frac{1.5}{T})^{L^+}}{r(L-L^+)} \left[\left(\frac{1}{1+r}\right)^{L^+} - \left(\frac{1}{1+r}\right)^L\right],$$

where r = discount rate, L = lifetime allowable for tax purposes, L^+ = optimal switchover point from 150 percent declining balance to straight-line depreciation. At the rate of discount we have employed, 10 percent after taxes, the sum of the years' digits has the highest present value; see Hall and Jorgenson [34, 1967].

Growth in Capital Quality

In Table 2–21 we present the rates of growth of sectoral capital quality for the period 1948–1976 and for seven subperiods—1948–1953, 1953–1957, 1957–1960, 1960–1966, 1966–1969, 1969–1973, and 1973–1976. In Table 2–2 we presented the rates of growth of sectoral lagged capital stocks for the same time periods.

Table 2–22 classifies the average rates of growth of capital quality presented in Table 2–21 by average rate of growth categories for the period 1948–1976 and for the seven subperiods. The average rate of growth of aggregate capital quality is 0.0132 for the period 1948–1976. For the seven subperiods the average rates of growth are 0.0206 for 1948–1953, 0.0136 for 1953–1957, 0.0080 for 1957–1960, 0.0121 for 1960–1966, 0.0172 for 1966–1969, 0.0107 for 1969–1973, and 0.0071 for 1973–1976. The time pattern for the average rate of growth of aggregate capital quality is similar to that for aggregate capital stock. The rate of growth of aggregate capital quality decreases from the highest value of the seven subperiods in 1948–1953 to a low in 1957–1960. The rate of growth of capital quality then increases to a high in 1966–1969. The rate of growth of capital quality then decreases to the lowest value of the seven subperiods in 1973–1976. The distributions of rates of growth of sectoral quality of capital stock reflect this time pattern. The location of the aggregate average rate of growth of capital quality in the sectoral distribution can be explained by the predominant effect of the private household and finance, insurance and real estate industries.

Referring to Table 2–22, the sectors experiencing average rates of growth of capital quality of less than −1 percent or 1 percent or more for the period 1948–1976 can be identified. Although the average rates of growth of aggregate capital quality and capital stock exhibit similar trends, the lists of industries with exceptionally high or exceptionally low rates of growth are not the same. The three industries experiencing a decline in capital quality of 1 percent or more include textile mill products; rubber and miscellaneous plastic products; and transportation equipment, except motor vehicles and ordnance. The six industries experiencing an average rate of growth of capital quality of at least 1 percent include agricultural services, horticultural services, and forestry and fisheries; leather and leather products; fabricated metal industries; gas utilities; finance, insurance and real estate; and private households. Finance, insurance, and real estate is the only industry which sustains a higher than average rate of growth of capital quality.

Table 2–21.   Sectoral Quality of Capital: Rates of Growth   (Average Annual Rates of Growth)

Industry	1948–1976	1948–1953	1953–1957	1957–1960	1960–1966	1966–1969	1969–1973	1973–1976
Agricultural production	-.0004	.0035	-.0006	-.0045	.0048	.0038	-.0120	-.0018
Agricultural services	.0185	.0943	-.0176	.0074	.0060	.0093	.0045	.0040
Metal mining	.0026	.0135	-.0025	.0223	.0017	.0010	-.0143	-.0019
Coal mining	.0030	.0083	.0160	.0088	.0162	-.0033	-.0054	.0051
Crude petroleum and natural gas	-.0000	-.0021	-.0014	.0000	.0001	.0065	-.0036	.0035
Nonmetallic mining and quarrying	.0051	.0085	-.0023	.0096	.0051	.0023	-.0000	.0148
Contract construction	-.0013	.0025	-.0057	.0009	-.0070	.0017	.0006	.0016
Food and kindred products	.0097	.0102	.0095	.0045	.0063	.0123	.0094	.0187
Tobacco manufacturers	-.0003	.0019	-.0022	.0017	.0004	-.0002	-.0022	-.0022
Textile mill products	-.0194	.0109	.0054	-.0124	.0075	.0014	-.0490	-.1451

Table 2–21. continued

Industry	1948–1976	1948–1953	1953–1957	1957–1960	1960–1966	1966–1969	1969–1973	1973–1976
Apparel and other fabr. textile prod.	.0045	.0060	.0013	.0052	.0052	-.0019	.0080	.0065
Paper and allied products	-.0005	-.0019	.0001	-.0035	.0030	.0042	-.0021	-.0055
Printing and publishing	.0032	.0026	.0010	.0042	.0056	.0065	.0032	.0021
Chemicals and allied products	.0033	.0167	.0032	-.0026	.0024	-.0001	.0030	-.0071
Petroleum and coal products	-.0027	.0039	-.0112	.0006	-.0122	-.0133	.0121	.0040
Rubber and misc. plastic products	-.0110	-.1340	.0110	-.0150	.0069	.0055	-.0011	.1033
Leather and leather products	.0108	.0305	.0043	.0024	.0030	.0014	.0251	.0032
Lumber and wood prod., ex. furniture	.0052	.0103	.0018	.0111	.0015	.0030	.0054	.0047
Furniture and fixtures	.0043	-.0028	.0031	.0078	.0059	.0045	.0055	.0092
Stone, clay, and glass products	.0035	.0088	.0030	-.0019	.0020	.0049	.0042	.0012

Table 2-21. continued

Industry	1948-1976	1948-1953	1953-1957	1957-1960	1960-1966	1966-1969	1969-1973	1973-1976
Primary metal industries	.0033	.0019	.0029	.0009	.0032	.0128	.0010	.0026
Fabricated metal industries	.0107	.0054	.0041	.0112	.0040	.0001	.0046	.0600
Machinery, ex. electrical	.0014	.0062	.0034	.0062	.0059	.0021	.0047	-.0279
Elec. machinery, eqpt., and supplies	.0050	.0046	.0126	-.0006	.0039	.0030	.0051	.0049
Trans. eqpt. & ord., ex. motor vehicles	-.0101	-.0858	.0025	.0195	.0029	-.0026	.0039	.0176
Motor vehicles and equipment	.0033	.0037	.0052	.0033	.0017	-.0044	.0026	.0121
Prof. photographic eqpt. and watches	.0090	.0141	.0040	-.0018	.0033	-.0005	.0026	.0477
Misc. manufacturing industries	.0066	.0094	.0015	.0054	.0109	.0036	.0025	.0094
Railroads and rail express service	.0028	.0014	.0028	-.0004	.0077	.0098	-.0029	-.0006
Street rail, bus lines, and taxicabs	-.0051	-.0077	-.0126	-.0089	-.0043	-.0005	-.0009	.0010

Table 2-21. continued

Industry	1948-1976	1948-1953	1953-1957	1957-1960	1960-1966	1966-1969	1969-1973	1973-1976
Trucking services and warehousing	-.0047	-.0054	-.0034	.0002	-.0068	-.0128	-.0106	.0100
Water transportation	-.0043	-.0068	-.0131	.0024	-.0026	-.0016	.0000	-.0064
Air transportation	-.0070	-.0150	-.0053	.0158	-.0131	.0248	-.0319	-.0056
Pipelines, ex. natural gas	.0037	.0140	.0028	-.0056	.0043	.0044	-.0017	.0023
Transportation services	.0011	-.0275	-.0152	.0235	.0256	.0088	-.0369	.0418
Te. and tel. and misc. comm. services	.0061	.0201	.0041	.0069	.0038	.0023	-.0009	.0023
Radio broadcasting and television	-.0000	-.0057	.0037	-.0002	-.0011	.0026	-.0039	.0093
Electric utilities	.0062	.0183	.0106	.0022	.0007	.0017	.0027	.0040
Gas utilities	.0159	.0480	.0094	.0133	.0044	.0008	.0143	.0136
Water supply and sanitary services	-.0013	-.0314	.0171	-.0045	.0045	.0130	.0017	-.0029

Table 2–21. continued

Industry	1948-1976	1948-1953	1953-1957	1957-1960	1960-1966	1966-1969	1969-1973	1973-1976
Wholesale trade	.0031	-.0044	-.0004	.0011	.0064	.0187	-.0002	.0040
Retail trade	.0054	.0008	.0060	.0051	.0062	.0089	.0039	.0099
Finance, insurance, and real estate	.0289	.0444	.0268	.0091	.0291	.0268	.0467	.0033
Services excl. priv. hh., inst.	.0056	.0024	.0059	.0041	.0076	.0124	.0010	.0079
Private households	.0149	.0327	.0167	.0068	.0096	.0154	.0102	.0074
Institutions	.0030	.0109	.0039	.0039	.0070	.0044	-.0047	-.0110

Table 2–22.   Classification of Rates of Growth of Sectoral Capital Quality by Periods, 1948–1976

Average Rate of Growth of Capital Quality	1948–1976	1948–1953	1953–1957	1957–1960	1960–1966	1966–1969	1969–1973	1973–1976
Less than −1.5 percent	1	4	3	0	0	0	3	2
−1.5 to less than −1.0 percent	2	1	3	2	2	2	3	1
−1 to less than −0.5 percent	2	4	2	3	2	1	2	4
−0.5 to less than 0 percent	8	4	7	9	3	8	10	5
0 to less than 0.5 percent	17	11	19	15	20	20	18	16
0.5 to less than 1.0 percent	10	7	6	10[a]	15	7	5	8[a]
1.0 to less than 1.5 percent	3[a]	7	3[a]	3	1[a]	4	3[a]	4
1.5 percent or more	3	8[a]	2	4	3	4[a]	2	6

[a] Denotes the category which contains the annual average for the aggregate capital quality for the period.

For the seven subperiods we consider in detail those industries which exhibit average rates of decline of capital quality of more than 1.5 percent or average rates of growth of capital quality of 1.5 percent or more. During the 1948–1953 period, one-fourth of the industries experienced very low or high average rates of growth of capital quality. The four industries falling in the lowest category for the average rate of growth of capital quality are rubber and miscellaneous plastic products; transportation equipment, except motor vehicles and ordnance; services incidental to transportation; and water supply, sanitary services, and other utilities. The eight industries falling in the highest category for the average rate of growth of capital quality are agricultural services, horticultural services, and forestry and fisheries; chemicals and allied products; leather and leather products; telephone, telegraph, and miscellaneous communication services; electric utilities; gas utilities; finance, insurance, and real estate; and private households. During this period 1948 and 1949 stand out as being years during which capital quality varies widely from the norm. The rates of growth of capital quality for several industries show the effects of the postwar housing boom. Only three industries—transportation services, finance insurance and real estate, and private households—sustain the low or high rate of growth during the following period.

During the 1953–1957 period, the three industries falling in the lowest category for the average rate of growth of capital quality are agricultural services, horticultural services, and forestry and fisheries; coal mining; and services incidental to transportation. The three industries falling in the highest category for the average rate of growth of capital quality are water supply, sanitary services, and other utilities; finance, insurance, and real estate; and private households.

The four industries with average rates of growth of capital quality of 1.5 percent or more for the period 1957–1960 are metal mining; transportation equipment, except motor vehicles and ordnance; air transportation; and services incidental to transportation. Transportation services, after two periods of low rates of growth of capital quality, sustains high rates of growth of capital quality for two periods. The three industries falling in the highest category for the average rate of growth of capital quality for the period 1960–1966 are coal mining; services incidental to transportation; and finance, insurance, and real estate. Finance, insurance, and real estate sustains a high rate of growth of capital quality during the next two periods as well.

During the 1966–1969 period the four industries falling in the highest category for the average rate of growth of capital quality are air transportation; wholesale trade; finance, insurance, and real estate; and private households. No industries have average rates of decline of capital quality greater than 1.5 percent during these three subperiods. Three industries with average rates of decline of capital quality of 1.5 percent or more for the period 1969–1973 are textile mill products, air transportation, and services incidental to transportation. The two industries with average rates of growth of capital quality of at least 1.5 percent during this period are leather and leather products, and finance, insurance, and real estate. During the 1973–1976, the two industries falling in the lowest category for the average rate of growth of capital quality are textile mill products; and machinery, except electrical. This is the second consecutive period during which textile mill products has a low rate of growth of capital quality. The six industries falling in the highest category for the average rate of growth of capital quality are food and kindred products; rubber and miscellaneous plastic products; fabricated metal industries; transportation equipment, except motor vehicles and ordnance; professional photographic equipment and watches; and services incidental to transportation.

IX. SECTORAL PRODUCTION ACCOUNTS

Our next objective is to analyze the role of capital in the growth of sectoral output in the U.S. economy. Our first step is to combine the data on sectoral capital input described in the preceding section with data on sectoral output and sectoral intermediate and labor inputs. These data taken together comprise a complete sectoral production account for each of the forty-six sectors listed in Table 2–1. The production accounts include data on sectoral output and sectoral intermediate, capital, and labor inputs in current and constant prices.[t]

The fundamental accounting identity for production accounts at the sectoral level is that the value of output is equal to the value of input. We define the value of output and input from the point of view of the producer. We measure revenue as proceeds to the producing sector, including subsidies paid to producers and excluding indirect business taxes on output. Similarly, we measure expenditures as outlay on intermediate, capital, and labor inputs by the sector, including all taxes on these inputs. Our concept of output is inter-

[t]For further information on the production accounts, see Jorgenson [47, 1980], this volume.

mediate between output valued at market prices and output valued at factor cost, as these terms are conventionally employed.

Given our definition of output and input, the accounting identity for the ith producing sector, where the subscript i ranges over the forty-six industries listed in Table 2–1, can be represented in the form

$$p_i Z_i = p_X^i X_i + p_K^i K_i + p_L^i L_i \ ,$$

where p_i, p_X^i, p_K^i, and p_L^i are the prices of output, intermediate input, capital input, and labor input for the ith sector and Z_i, X_i, K_i and L_i are the corresponding quantities. The value of output $p_i Z_i$ is equal to the sum of the values of outlay on intermediate input $p_X^i X_i$, capital input $p_K^i K_i$, and labor input $p_L^i L_i$.

In Section VI above we described the data sources for implementing our definition of sectoral property compensation before taxes from the point of view of the producer. We estimate the value of sectoral labor compensation as the sum of wages, salaries, and supplements from a study by the Bureau of Economic Analysis [19, 1978] and the labor compensation of self-employed persons. Finally, we estimate the values of sectoral intermediate input and output from the point of view of the producer using the methodology and data sources employed by Gollop and Jorgenson [33, 1980].

In the preceding section we described the separation of sectoral property compensation before taxes into price and quantity components, corresponding to the price and quantity of sectoral capital input. In this section we present data on the price and quantity components of sectoral output, sectoral outlay on intermediate input, and sectoral labor compensation. These data are constructed using the methodology and data sources employed by Gollop and Jorgenson [33, 1980].

To complete the construction of sectoral production accounts in constant prices, we introduce a production model for each industrial sector, following Jorgenson [47, 1980]. We take sectoral output to be a translog function of sectoral intermediate, capital, and labor inputs for each of the forty-six industries listed in Table 2–1. We combine the sectoral production functions with necessary conditions for producer equilibrium. These conditions imply that shares of intermediate, capital, and labor inputs in the value of output are equal to the elasticities of sectoral output with respect to these inputs. We define the sectoral rate of technical change as the rate of growth of sectoral output, holding all inputs constant.

Considering data on sectoral output and sectoral inputs at any two discrete points of time, we can express the difference between successive logarithms of sectoral output as the sum of a weighted average of differences between successive logarithms of sectoral inputs and the average sectoral rate of technical change in the two periods:

$$\ln Z_{i,t} - \ln Z_{i,t-1} = \bar{v}_X^i \,[\ln X_{i,t} - \ln X_{i,t-1}] + \bar{v}_k^i \,[\ln K_{i,t} - \ln K_{i,t-1}]$$

$$+ \bar{v}_L^i \,[\ln L_{i,t} - \ln L_{i,t-1}] + \bar{v}_T^i \,,$$

where the weights $\bar{v}_X^i, \bar{v}_K^i, \bar{v}_L^i$ are given by

$$\bar{v}_X^i = \tfrac{1}{2}\,[v_{X,t}^i + v_{X,t-1}^i] \,,$$

$$\bar{v}_K^i = \tfrac{1}{2}\,[v_{K,t}^i + v_{K,t-1}^i] \,,$$

$$\bar{v}_L^i = \tfrac{1}{2}\,[v_{L,t}^i + v_{L,t-1}^i] \,,$$

and

$$v_X^i = \frac{p_X^i \, X_i}{p_i \, Z_i} \,,$$

$$v_K^i = \frac{p_K^i \, K_i}{p_i \, Z_i} \,,$$

$$v_L^i = \frac{p_L^i \, L_i}{p_i \, Z_i} \,,$$

We refer to this expression for the average sectoral rate of technical change v_T^i as the *translog index of the sectoral rate of technical change*.

Given sectoral production accounts in constant prices for all forty-six industrial sectors listed in Table 2–1, we can express the growth of sectoral output for each sector, $\ln Z_{i,t} - \ln Z_{i,t-1}$, as the sum of the contribution of sectoral intermediate input, $\bar{v}_X^i \,[\ln X_{i,t} - \ln X_{i,t-1}]$, the contribution of sectoral capital input, $\bar{v}_K^i \,[\ln K_{i,t} - \ln K_{i,t-1}]$, the contribution of sectoral labor input $\bar{v}_L^i \,[\ln L_{i,t} - \ln L_{i,t-1}]$, and the sectoral rate of technical change, $\bar{v}_T^i$. In this section we present data on the growth of output, the growth of intermediate, capital, and labor inputs, and the rate of technical change for all forty-six sectors. We also present data on the contributions of sectoral intermediate, capital, and labor inputs to the growth of sectoral output for all sectors.

Growth in Output

In Table 2–23 we present the average annual rate of growth for sectoral output, input, and productivity for 1948–1976. The rates of growth for output and inputs are computed from the unweighted successive log differences. Table 2–24 classifies the average rates of growth of output, inputs and technical change by average rate of growth categories. Positive growth rates predominate for output, intermediate input, and capital input during the period 1948–1976. Only five industries sustained negative rates of growth for one or more of these categories during this period. These industries are textile mill products—capital input; leather and leather products—output and intermediate input; railroads and railway express service—intermediate input and capital input; street railway, bus lines, and taxicab service—output, intermediate input; and pipelines, except natural gas—capital input. Only three industries have positive average rates of growth of output of 6 percent or more. These industries are chemicals and allied products; air transportation; and telephone, telegraph, and miscellaneous communications services. Six industries experience rates of growth of intermediate input of at least 6 percent, only two of which sustain rates of growth of 6 percent or more for output or capital input. Professional photographic equipment and watches sustains a high rate of growth for intermediate input and capital input. Air transportation sustains a high rate of growth for output, the highest rate for intermediate input and capital input. The other industries which have average rates of growth of capital input of at least 6 percent are the following: nonmetallic mining and quarrying, except fuel; construction; professional photographic equipment and watches; and radio broadcasting and television.

The average rate of growth of labor input is negative over the whole period 1948–1976 for thirteen industries. The three industries which sustain rates of decline of labor input of more than 2 percent are the following: agricultural production, coal mining, and railroads. Agricultural production has positive rates of growth for all other categories in Table 2–23. Coal mining has positive rates of growth for all other categories except technical change. In contrast, railroads experiences average negative rates of growth for all types of inputs.

Table 2–23.   Sectoral Output, Inputs, and Productivity: Rates of Growth, 1948–1976 (Average Annual Rates of Growth)

Industry	Output	Intermediate Input	Capital Input	Labor Input	Rate of Technical Change
Agricultural production	.0254	.0223	.0123	-.0313	.0210
Agricultural services	.0161	.0335	.0479	.0211	-.0124
Metal mining	.0107	.0033	.0479	-.0002	.0008
Coal mining	.0008	.0216	.0240	-.0254	-.0004
Crude petroleum and natural gas	.0175	.0373	.0096	.0208	-.0075
Nonmetallic mining and quarrying	.0427	.0415	.0753	.0084	.0029
Contract construction	.0261	.0252	.0642	.0144	.0023
Food and kindred products	.0288	.0184	.0195	-.0016	.0137
Tobacco manufacturers	.0152	.0386	.0150	-.0058	-.0081
Textile mill products	.0303	.0295	-.0002	-.0104	.0138

Table 2–23. continued

Industry	Output	Intermediate Input	Capital Input	Labor Input	Rate of Technical Change
Apparel and other fabr. textile prod.	.0327	.0334	.0305	.0039	.0087
Paper and allied products	.0430	.0582	.0417	.0169	-.0031
Printing and publishing	.0343	.0390	.0156	.0151	.0075
Chemicals and allied products	.0638	.0593	.0375	.0233	.0159
Petroleum and coal products	.0418	.0616	.0169	.0043	-.0084
Rubber and misc. plastic products	.0541	.0566	.0398	.0302	.0077
Leather and leather products	-.0017	-.0036	.0086	-.0149	.0052
Lumber and wood prod., ex. furniture	.0252	.0476	.0276	-.0063	.0003
Furniture and fixtures	.0331	.0456	.0307	.0072	.0032
Stone, clay, and glass products	.0405	.0636	.0355	.0095	.0012

Table 2–23. continued

Industry	Output	Intermediate Input	Capital Input	Labor Input	Rate of Technical Change
Primary metal industries	.0214	.0384	.0202	.0003	-.0056
Fabricated metal industries	.0293	.0321	.0397	.0168	.0029
Machinery, ex. electrical	.0361	.0470	.0447	.0173	.0015
Elec. machinery, eqpt., and supplies	.0494	.0435	.0476	.0253	.0126
Trans. eqpt. & ord., ex. motor vehicles	.0505	.0630	.0115	.0245	.0044
Motor vehicles and equipment	.0424	.0370	.0333	.0103	.0124
Prof. photographic eqpt. and watches	.0593	.0663	.0689	.0349	.0080
Misc. manufacturing industries	.0353	.0357	.0232	.0033	.0134
Railroads and rail express service	.0054	-.0039	-.0016	-.0359	.0197
Street rail., bus lines, and taxicabs	-.0302	-.0186	-.0111	-.0168	-.0121

Table 2–23. continued

Industry	Output	Intermediate Input	Capital Input	Labor Input	Rate of Technical Change
Trucking services and warehousing	.0462	.0269	.0456	.0244	.0174
Water transportation	.0221	.0099	.0091	−.0118	.0177
Air transportation	.0894	.0743	.0990	.0504	.0198
Pipelines, ex. natural gas	.0527	.0115	−.0004	−.0101	.0495
Transportation services	.0069	.0401	.0254	.0261	−.0290
Te. and tel. and misc. comm. services	.0646	.0468	.0663	.0188	.0223
Radio broadcasting and television	.0409	.0344	.0953	.0424	−.0077
Electric utilities	.0597	.0581	.0380	.0132	.0192
Gas utilities	.0566	.0615	.0296	.0214	.0090
Water supply and sanitary services	.0350	.0052	.0530	.0103	.0042

Table 2–23. continued

Industry	Output	Intermediate Input	Capital Input	Labor Input	Rate of Technical Change
Wholesale trade	.0448	.0325	.0541	.0251	.0125
Retail trade	.0241	.0100	.0410	.0098	.0103
Finance, insurance, and real estate	.0429	.0596	.0405	.0334	-.0059
Services excl. priv. hh., inst.	.0412	.0453	.0342	.0284	.0068
Private households	.0445	.0000	.0517	-.0198	.0000
Institutions	.0517	.0428	.0308	.0443	.0124

Table 2–24.   Classification of Rates of Growth in Sectoral Output, Inputs, and Productivity, 1948–1976

Average Rates of Growth	Output	Intermediate Input	Capital Input	Labor Input	Rate of Technical Change
Less than −4 percent	0	0	0	0	0
−2 to less than −4 percent	1	0	0	3	1
0 to less than −2 percent	1	3	4	10	10
0 to less than 2 percent	7	6	9	17	31
2 to less than 4 percent	15	16	16	13	2
4 to less than 6 percent	19	14	11	3	1
6 to less than 8 percent	2	6	4	0	0
More than 8 percent	1	0	2	0	0

No industries experience average rates of growth of labor input of 6 percent or more. The three industries having average rates of growth of labor input of 4 percent or more are the following: air transportation, radio broadcasting and television, and nonprofit institutions.

The average rate of growth of technical change is negative over the whole period 1948–1976 for eleven industries. These industries are the following: agricultural services, horticultural services, and forestry and fisheries; coal mining; crude petroleum and natural gas extractions; tobacco manufactures; paper and allied products; petroleum and coal products; primary metal industries; street railway, bus lines, and taxicab service; services incidental to transportation; radio broadcasting and television; and finance, insurance, and real estate. Aside from agricultural services, local transportation and transportation services, all negative rates of growth of technical change are between 0 and −1 percent. Only three industries sustain rates of growth of technical change of at least 2 percent. These industries are the following: agricultural production; pipelines, except natural gas; and telephone, telegraph, and miscellaneous communication services.

Contribution to Output Growth

In Table 2–25 we present the contributions of sectoral inputs and productivity to growth in output. The contributions for inputs represent the successive log differences from Table 2–23 weighted by the average value shares. By definition the sum of the contribution of capital input, labor input, intermediate input, and productivity equals the log difference in the quantity of output.

The contribution of factor inputs to growth in sectoral output can be separated into quality and level components. Since we are concerned primarily with the role of capital in economic growth, we decompose only capital input into its component parts. In Table 2–26 we present the contribution of sectoral quality of capital stock to economic growth for the period 1948–1976 and for seven subperiods—1948–1953, 1953–1957, 1957–1960, 1960–1966, 1969–1973, and 1973–1976. In Table 2–27 we present the contribution of the level of capital stock to economic growth for the same time periods.

The average value shares of sectoral intermediate and capital inputs in the value of output for the whole period 1948–1976 are given in the first two columns of Table 2–25. The average value share of sectoral labor input is equal to one minus the sum of the average value shares of sectoral intermediate and capital inputs. The value share of intermediate input is the largest of the three shares for

Table 2–25.   Contributions to Economic Growth in Sectoral Output: Rates of Growth, 1948–1976 (Average Annual Rates of Growth)

Industry	Average Value Shares		Contributions to Growth in Output			
	Intermediate Input	Capital Input	Intermediate Input	Capital Input	Labor Input	Rate of Technical Change
Agricultural production	.5608	.1318	.0127	.0019	-.0101	.0210
Agricultural services	.4076	.1264	.0133	.0053	.0098	-.0124
Metal mining	.5063	.2056	.0018	.0087	-.0005	.0008
Coal mining	.4156	.1585	.0111	.0051	-.0149	-.0004
Crude petroleum and natural gas	.4995	.3555	.0187	.0035	.0029	-.0075
Nonmetallic mining and quarrying	.3845	.2769	.0156	.0212	.0029	.0029
Contract construction	.5787	.0540	.0153	.0034	.0051	.0023
Food and kindred products	.7730	.0627	.0141	.0012	-.0003	.0137
Tobacco manufacturers	.5241	.2775	.0210	.0036	-.0013	-.0081
Textile mill products	.6486	.0770	.0186	.0009	-.0030	.0138

Table 2–25. continued

Industry	Average Value Shares		Contributions to Growth in Output			
	Intermediate Input	Capital Input	Intermediate Input	Capital Input	Labor Input	Rate of Technical Change
Apparel and other fabr. textile prod.	.6527	.0365	.0216	.0012	.0012	.0087
Paper and allied products	.6201	.1328	.0362	.0058	.0042	-.0031
Printing and publishing	.5053	.1032	.0191	.0017	.0060	.0075
Chemicals and allied products	.6127	.1712	.0365	.0065	.0049	.0159
Petroleum and coal products	.7436	.1331	.0474	.0024	.0003	-.0084
Rubber and misc. plastic products	.5639	.0951	.0321	.0040	.0103	.0077
Leather and leather products	.6068	.0510	-.0023	.0006	-.0052	.0052
Lumber and wood prod., ex. furniture	.4934	.1473	.0231	.0044	-.0026	.0003
Furniture and fixtures	.5648	.0729	.0251	.0022	.0026	.0032
Stone, clay, and glass products	.5149	.1424	.0311	.0053	.0030	.0012

Table 2–25. continued

Industry	Average Value Shares		Contributions to Growth in Output			
	Intermediate Input	Capital Input	Intermediate Input	Capital Input	Labor Input	Rate of Technical Change
Primary metal industries	.6427	.1129	.0245	.0024	.0000	-.0056
Fabricated metal industries	.5066	.0957	.0160	.0038	.0066	.0029
Machinery, ex. electrical	.4823	.1260	.0225	.0058	.0063	.0015
Elec. machinery, eqpt., and supplies	.5334	.1013	.0233	.0049	.0086	.0126
Trans. eqpt. & ord., ex. motor vehicles	.6082	.0497	.0378	.0005	.0078	.0044
Motor vehicles and equipment	.6649	.1295	.0240	.0044	.0016	.0124
Prof. photographic eqpt. and watches	.4017	.1318	.0268	.0088	.0156	.0080
Misc. manufacturing industries	.5458	.0941	.0191	.0019	.0010	.0134
Railroads and rail express service	.5516	.1121	-.0018	-.0002	-.0123	.0197
Street rail., bus lines, and taxicabs	.5644	.1251	-.0118	-.0012	-.0051	-.0121

Table 2–25. continued

Industry	Average Value Shares		Contributions to Growth in Output			
	Intermediate Input	Capital Input	Intermediate Input	Capital Input	Labor Input	Rate of Technical Change
Trucking services and warehousing	.5855	.1146	.0164	.0053	.0071	.0174
Water transportation	.6825	.0645	.0068	.0007	-.0031	.0177
Air transportation	.5826	.1190	.0427	.0119	.0150	.0198
Pipelines, ex. natural gas	.4732	.3463	.0047	.0005	-.0020	.0495
Transportation services	.6413	.1091	.0251	.0036	.0071	-.0290
Te. and tel. and misc. comm. services	.2250	.3531	.0105	.0243	.0076	.0223
Radio broadcasting and television	.4741	.1644	.0170	.0161	.0156	-.0077
Electric utilities	.3823	.3930	.0231	.0144	.0030	.0192
Gas utilities	.6476	.2232	.0382	.0063	.0030	.0090
Water supply and sanitary services	.1757	.5253	.0001	.0276	.0031	.0042

Table 2-25. continued

Industry	Average Value Shares		Contributions to Growth in Output				
	Intermediate Input	Capital Input	Intermediate Input	Capital Input	Labor Input	Rate of Technical Change
Wholesale trade	.2232	.1900	.0075	.0103	.0145	.0125
Retail trade	.3566	.1306	.0033	.0054	.0050	.0103
Finance, insurance, and real estate	.5476	.2712	.0316	.0111	.0061	-.0059
Services excl. priv. hh., inst.	.3251	.0926	.0146	.0031	.0166	.0068
Private households	.0000	.9557	.0000	.0492	-.0007	.0000
Institutions	.1827	.3597	.0078	.0112	.0203	.0124

The Role of Capital in U.S. Economic Growth, 1948–1976   123

Table 2–26. Contribution to Economic Growth, Sectoral Capital Quality: Rates of Growth (Average Annual Rates of Growth)

Industry	1948–1976	1948–1953	1953–1957	1957–1960	1960–1966	1966–1969	1969–1973	1973–1976
Agricultural production	.0000	.0004	−.0001	−.0002	.0007	.0007	−.0015	−.0002
Agricultural services	.0012	.0034	−.0009	.0006	.0012	.0017	.0008	.0007
Metal mining	.0003	.0017	−.0002	.0041	.0001	−.0001	−.0024	−.0004
Coal mining	.0007	.0011	−.0019	.0012	.0029	−.0001	−.0006	.0011
Crude petroleum and natural gas	−.0000	−.0009	−.0005	.0000	.0000	.0022	−.0011	.0012
Nonmetallic mining and quarrying	.0015	.0027	−.0006	.0020	.0015	.0007	−.0001	.0050
Contract construction	−.0001	.0002	−.0003	.0001	−.0003	.0001	.0000	.0001
Food and kindred products	.0006	.0006	.0006	.0003	.0004	.0009	.0005	.0009
Tobacco manufacturers	−.0001	.0003	−.0006	.0005	.0001	−.0001	−.0008	−.0005
Textile mill products	−.0011	.0009	.0004	−.0010	.0006	.0001	−.0027	−.0086

Table 2-26. continued

Industry	1948-1976	1948-1953	1953-1957	1957-1960	1960-1966	1966-1969	1969-1973	1973-1976
Apparel and other fabr. textile prod.	.0002	.0002	.0000	.0002	.0002	-.0001	.0003	.0003
Paper and allied products	-.0000	-.0003	.0000	-.0005	.0004	.0005	-.0002	-.0006
Printing and publishing	.0003	.0003	.0001	.0004	.0005	.0007	.0003	-.0002
Chemicals and allied products	.0007	.0032	.0006	-.0005	.0004	-.0000	.0004	-.0007
Petroleum and coal products	-.0004	.0005	-.0017	.0001	-.0014	-.0016	.0013	.0002
Rubber and misc. plastic products	-.0011	-.0111	.0010	-.0016	.0007	.0006	-.0001	.0071
Leather and leather products	.0005	.0017	.0002	.0000	.0002	.0001	.0008	.0002
Lumber and wood prod., ex. furniture	.0008	.0015	.0002	.0014	.0003	.0006	.0010	.0009
Furniture and fixtures	.0003	-.0002	.0002	.0005	.0005	.0004	.0003	.0005
Stone, clay, and glass products	.0005	.0014	.0005	-.0003	.0003	.0006	.0005	.0001

Table 2–26. continued

Industry	1948–1976	1948–1953	1953–1957	1957–1960	1960–1966	1966–1969	1969–1973	1973–1976
Primary metal industries	.0004	.0002	.0004	.0001	.0004	.0013	.0001	.0003
Fabricated metal industries	.0010	.0006	.0004	.0009	.0004	.0000	.0004	.0051
Machinery, ex. electrical	.0003	.0009	.0004	.0007	.0008	.0003	.0006	-.0023
Elec. machinery, eqpt., and supplies	.0005	.0005	.0012	-.0003	.0004	.0003	.0005	.0004
Trans. eqpt. & ord., ex. motor vehicles	-.0007	-.0048	.0000	.0011	.0001	-.0002	.0002	.0002
Motor vehicles and equipment	.0003	.0005	.0006	.0002	.0003	-.0007	.0003	.0008
Prof. photographic eqpt. and watches	.0008	.0015	.0006	-.0003	.0005	-.0001	.0004	.0034
Misc. manufacturing industries	.0007	.0011	.0001	.0005	.0010	.0003	.0002	.0013
Railroads and rail express service	.0004	.0002	.0004	-.0000	.0009	.0011	-.0002	-.0000
Street rail, bus lines, and taxicabs	-.0005	-.0006	-.0011	-.0011	-.0006	-.0001	-.0001	.0001

Table 2–26. continued

Industry	1948-1976	1948-1953	1953-1957	1957-1960	1960-1966	1966-1969	1969-1973	1973-1976
Trucking services and warehousing	-.0005	-.0005	-.0003	.0000	-.0008	-.0015	-.0013	.0012
Water transportation	-.0002	-.0004	-.0007	.0002	-.0002	-.0001	.0000	-.0004
Air transportation	-.0008	-.0015	-.0007	.0016	-.0019	.0030	-.0033	-.0006
Pipelines, ex. natural gas	.0011	.0038	.0009	-.0018	.0015	.0017	-.0007	.0008
Transportation services	.0005	-.0030	-.0015	.0021	.0038	.0017	-.0030	.0039
Te. and tel. and misc. comm. services	.0019	.0052	.0012	.0026	.0016	.0009	-.0003	.0008
Radio broadcasting and television	.0000	-.0009	.0006	-.0000	-.0002	.0004	-.0005	.0015
Electric utilities	.0023	.0066	.0044	.0009	.0003	.0007	.0010	.0012
Gas utilities	.0037	.0122	.0023	.0031	.0010	.0002	.0028	.0025
Water supply and sanitary services	-.0001	-.0131	.0083	-.0023	.0025	.0078	.0010	-.0015

Table 2–26. continued

Industry	1948–1976	1948–1953	1953–1957	1957–1960	1960–1966	1966–1969	1969–1973	1973–1976
Wholesale trade	.0005	-.0009	-.0000	.0002	.0011	.0033	-.0001	.0010
Retail trade	.0007	.0001	.0007	.0006	.0008	.0012	.0005	.0012
Finance, insurance, and real estate	.0081	.0157	.0081	.0026	.0075	.0066	.0106	.0006
Services excl. priv. hh., inst.	.0005	.0003	.0005	.0004	.0007	.0012	.0001	.0007
Private households	.0142	.0304	.0158	.0065	.0093	.0148	.0099	.0072
Institutions	.0011	.0035	.0013	.0014	-.0000	.0018	-.0020	-.0033

Table 2–27. Contribution to Economic Growth, Sectoral Capital Stock: Rates of Growth (*Average Annual Rates of Growth*)

Industry	1948–1976	1948–1953	1953–1957	1957–1960	1960–1966	1966–1969	1969–1973	1973–1976
Agricultural production	.0018	.0028	-.0001	.0007	.0012	.0037	.0006	.0047
Agricultural services	.0041	-.0017	.0021	.0049	.0064	.0083	.0073	.0030
Metal mining	.0083	.0091	.0119	.0285	.0133	-.0013	-.0022	-.0043
Coal mining	.0044	.0075	-.0071	.0023	.0069	.0003	.0075	.0119
Crude petroleum and natural gas	.0035	.0045	.0065	.0026	.0054	.0023	-.0006	.0018
Nonmetallic mining and quarrying	.0197	.0368	.0269	.0181	.0189	.0152	.0059	.0077
Contract construction	.0035	.0058	.0035	.0038	.0036	.0034	.0030	.0001
Food and kindred products	.0006	.0008	-.0001	.0006	.0007	.0011	.0010	.0004
Tobacco manufacturers	.0037	.0040	.0007	.0025	.0044	-.0063	.0063	.0139
Textile mill products	.0019	.0050	-.0002	-.0020	.0018	.0057	.0021	.0001

Table 2–27. continued

Industry	1948–1976	1948–1953	1953–1957	1957–1960	1960–1966	1966–1969	1969–1973	1973–1976
Apparel and other fabr. textile prod.	.0010	.0007	.0004	.0000	.0015	.0035	.0017	-.0009
Paper and allied products	.0058	.0095	.0084	.0049	.0042	.0068	.0032	.0029
Printing and publishing	.0014	-.0001	.0006	-.0006	.0026	.0052	.0019	-.0002
Chemicals and allied products	.0058	.0049	.0060	.0043	.0073	.0110	.0034	.0035
Petroleum and coal products	.0028	.0008	.0072	-.0015	.0022	.0097	.0005	.0020
Rubber and misc. plastic products	.0051	.0059	.0034	.0061	.0046	.0080	.0057	.0026
Leather and leather products	.0001	.0009	-.0002	-.0012	-.0002	.0029	-.0011	.0000
Lumber and wood prod., ex. furniture	.0036	.0062	.0035	-.0032	.0013	.0009	.0087	.0067
Furniture and fixtures	.0019	.0016	.0018	.0005	.0016	.0041	.0030	.0012
Stone, clay, and glass products	.0048	.0062	.0101	.0072	.0030	.0028	.0018	.0024

Table 2-27. continued

Industry	1948-1976	1948-1953	1953-1957	1957-1960	1960-1966	1966-1969	1969-1973	1973-1976
Primary metal industries	.0021	.0033	.0035	.0024	.0009	.0041	.0002	.0006
Fabricated metal industries	.0028	.0033	.0031	.0005	.0029	.0055	.0016	.0029
Machinery, ex. electrical	.0055	.0068	.0051	.0020	.0052	.0110	.0037	.0048
Elec. machinery, eqpt., and supplies	.0044	.0083	.0034	.0006	.0042	.0095	.0019	.0018
Trans. eqpt. & ord., ex. motor vehicles	.0012	.0006	.0011	-.0008	.0007	.0096	-.0010	-.0000
Motor vehicles and equipment	.0041	.0051	.0067	-.0027	.0055	.0074	.0029	.0014
Prof. photographic eqpt. and watches	.0080	.0092	.0106	.0046	.0067	.0169	.0056	.0030
Misc. manufacturing industries	.0012	-.0025	.0035	-.0005	.0011	.0105	.0008	-.0027
Railroads and rail express service	-.0006	-.0011	-.0007	-.0019	-.0010	.0005	-.0006	.0013
Street rail., bus lines, and taxicabs	-.0007	.0013	-.0036	-.0031	-.0017	.0021	-.0009	.0016

Table 2–27. continued

Industry	1948–1976	1948–1953	1953–1957	1957–1960	1960–1966	1966–1969	1969–1973	1973–1976
Trucking services and warehousing	.0058	.0063	.0023	.0075	.0042	.0086	.0026	.0131
Water transportation	.0009	-.0013	-.0008	.0024	.0011	.0020	.0008	.0041
Air transportation	.0127	.0124	.0142	.0204	.0142	.0259	.0025	.0009
Pipelines, ex. natural gas	-.0006	-.0019	-.0040	-.0112	-.0019	.0061	.0081	.0013
Transportation services	.0031	-.0034	.0027	.0035	.0041	.0094	-.0008	.0109
Te. and tel. and misc. ccmm. services	.0224	.0046	.0103	.0139	.0303	.0317	.0352	.0345
Radio broadcasting and television	.0161	.0096	.0381	.0187	.0183	.0158	.0044	.0062
Electric utilities	.0120	.0081	.0069	.0080	.0069	.0184	.0256	.0154
Gas utilities	.0026	.0049	-.0128	.0069	.0002	.0016	.0101	.0106
Water supply and sanitary services	.0277	.0450	-.0032	.0419	.0224	.0318	.0305	.0288

Table 2–27. continued

Industry	1948-1976	1948-1953	1953-1957	1957-1960	1960-1966	1966-1969	1969-1973	1973-1976
Wholesale trade	.0098	.0183	.0076	.0056	.0084	.0128	.0077	.0051
Retail trade	.0047	.0092	.0046	.0010	.0040	.0055	.0050	.0016
Finance, insurance, and real estate	.0030	.0023	.0034	.0021	.0030	.0019	.0052	.0025
Services excl. priv. hh., inst.	.0026	-.0010	.0012	.0038	.0048	.0042	.0034	.0023
Private households	.0351	.0494	.0398	.0268	.0288	.0320	.0342	.0299
Institutions	.0101	.0091	.0105	.0137	.0169	.0155	.0042	-.0032

thirty-seven of the forty-six industries. The value share of capital input is the largest of the three shares for three of the forty-six industries. These industries include two utility industries—electric utilities and water supply, sanitary services, and other utilities—and private households. The value share of labor input is the largest of the three shares for six of the forty-six industries. These industries include coal mining; telephone, telegraph, and miscellaneous communication services; wholesale trade; retail trade; services; and nonprofit institutions.

The average contribution of growth in sectoral intermediate, capital, and labor inputs to the growth in output are given in the third, fourth, and fifth columns of Table 2-25. The average rate of technical change is given in the sixth column of Table 2-25. The average contribution of growth in sectoral intermediate input is clearly the most significant source of growth in sectoral output. For the industries for which intermediate input is measured, the average contribution of growth in sectoral intermediate input exceeds the average rate of technical change for thirty-two of forty-five industries. The thirteen industries for which the average rate of technical change exceeds the average contribution of growth in sectoral intermediate input include agricultural production; leather and leather products; the following six transportation industries—railroads and railway express service; street railway, bus lines, and taxicab service; trucking service; warehousing and storage; water transportation; pipelines, except natural gas; services incidental to transportation—and telephone, telegraph and miscellaneous communication services; water utilities; wholesale trade; retail trade; and nonprofit institutions.

The average contributions of growth in sectoral capital and labor inputs can be compared to the average rate of technical change. The sum of the average contributions of growth in sectoral capital and labor inputs exceeds the average rate of technical change for twenty-six of the forty-five industries for which we have a measure of the rate of technical change. For ten of the twenty-six industries the average contributions of capital and labor inputs taken alone both exceed the average rate of technical change. For four of the twenty-six industries the average contribution of capital input taken alone exceeds the average rate of technical change. For five of the twenty-six industries the average contribution of labor input taken alone exceeds the average rate of technical change. The rate of technical change is clearly not a predominant source of growth in sectoral output. By far the most important contribution to growth in sectoral output is made by intermediate input. Significant contributions to growth in sectoral output are made by capital and labor input as well.

X. THE ROLE OF CAPITAL IN GROWTH OF SECTORAL OUTPUT

Our final step in analyzing the role of capital in the growth of sectoral output is to divide the contribution of capital input into components that can be identified with the contributions of growth of capital stock and the growth of the quality of capital stock. The contribution of sectoral capital input to the growth of sectoral output is the sum of the contributions of these two components.

In Section VIII above we introduced sectoral indexes of the quality of capital stock, $Q_{K,t}^i$, that transform sectoral capital stocks at the beginning of each period, $A_{i,t-1}$, into sectoral capital inputs during the period $K_{i,t}$:

$$K_{i,t} = Q_{K,t}^i \cdot A_{i,t-1} \quad .$$

Considering data at any two discrete points of time, we can express the difference between successive logarithms of sectoral capital input as the sum of successive logarithms of the sectoral index of the quality of capital stock and successive logarithms of sectoral capital stocks:

$$1n\, K_{i,t} - 1n\, K_{i,t-1} = 1n\, Q_{K,t}^i - 1n\, Q_{K,t-1}^i + 1n\, A_{i,t-1} - 1n\, A_{i,t-2} \quad .$$

In the preceding section we have introduced the contribution of sectoral capital input to the growth of sectoral output $\bar{v}_K^i$ [$1n\, K_{i,t} - 1n\, K_{i,t-1}$]. Using our decomposition of the growth of capital input into the sum of components that can be identified with the growth of the quality of capital stock and the growth of capital stock, we can express the contribution of capital input in the form

$$\bar{v}_K^i\,[1n\, K_{i,t} - 1n\, K_{i,t-1}] = \bar{v}_K^i\,[1n\, Q_{K,t}^i - 1n\, Q_{K,t-1}^i]$$

$$+ \bar{v}_K^i\,[1n\, A_{i,t-1} - 1n\, A_{i,t-2}] \quad .$$

The contribution of sectoral capital input is the sum of the contribution of growth in the quality of sectoral capital stock,

$$\bar{v}_K^i \, [1n \, Q_{K,\,t}^i - 1n \, Q_{K,\,t-1}^i]\,,$$

and the contribution of growth in sectoral capital stock,

$$\bar{v}_K \, [1n \, A_{i,\,t-1} - 1n \, A_{i,\,t-2}]\,.$$

In this section we present data on the contributions of the growth in the quality and quantity of the capital stock to the growth of output for the period 1948–1976 and for the seven subperiods for the forty-six sectors listed in Table 2–1. We analyze the pattern of these contributions to the growth of sectoral output across industries for the period 1948–1976. Second, we analyze the pattern of growth across periods of time for individual industries.

Growth in Capital Quality

Table 2–26 presents the average contribution of growth in capital quality to the growth in output for the period 1948–1976 and for seven subperiods—1948–1953, 1953–1957, 1957–1960, 1960–1966, 1966–1969, 1969–1973, and 1973–1976. The average contribution of growth in sectoral capital quality is 0.0028 for 1948–1976 and 0.0041 for 1948–1953, 0.0027 for 1953–1957, 0.0017 for 1957–1960, 0.0027 for 1960–1966, 0.0038 for 1966–1969, 0.0023 for 1969–1973 and 0.0014 for 1973–1976. The average growth in sectoral capital quality accounts for approximately one-third of the total contribution of growth in sectoral capital input to growth in output. The average rate of growth of technical change for the period as a whole exceeds the average contribution of growth in sectoral capital quality to growth in output for industries for which we measure technical change for all industries except finance, insurance, and real estate. The average contribution of growth in sectoral capital quality exceeds 0.5 percent for the period as a whole, 1948–1976, for only two industries: finance, insurance, and real estate; and private households. The average contribution of growth in sectoral capital quality for private households exceeds 0.5 percent for all subperiods. The average contribution of growth in sectoral capital quality for finance, insurance, and real estate exceeds 0.5 percent for all subperiods except 1957–1960 and 1973–1976. With the exception of these two industries, the contribution of growth in sectoral capital quality to growth in output is not significant, although it is positive.

The 1948−1953 and 1973−1976 subperiods are the only periods during which the contribution of sectoral capital quality to growth in output for more than one industry other than finance, insurance, and real estate or private households exceeds or equals 0.5 percent. During the 1948−1953 subperiod, the five other industries falling in this category include rubber and miscellaneous plastic products; telephone, telegraph, and miscellaneous communication services; and the three utilities—electric utilities; gas utilities; and water supply, sanitary services, and other utilities. During the 1953−1957 subperiod, the only other industry falling in this category is water supply, sanitary services, and other utilities. During the 1957−1960 and 1960−1966 subperiods no other industries fall in this category. During the 1966−1969 subperiod, the only other industry falling in this category is services incidental to transportation. During the 1969−1973 subperiod no other industries fall in this category. During the 1973−1976 subperiod the four other industries falling in this category include nonmetallic mining and quarrying, except fuel; textile mill products; rubber and miscellaneous plastic products; and fabricated metal industries.

Growth in Capital Stock

Table 2−27 presents the average contribution of growth in capital to the growth in output for the period 1948−1976 and for seven subperiods—1948−1953, 1953−1957, 1957−1960, 1960−1966, 1966−1969, 1969−1973, and 1973−1976. The average contribution of growth in sectoral capital stock is 0.0056 for 1948−1976 and 0.0059 for 1948−1953, 0.0052 for 1953−1957, 0.0041 for 1957−1960, 0.0056 for 1960−1966, 0.0074 for 1966−1969, 0.0062 for 1969−1973, and 0.0049 for 1973−1976. Growth in capital stock is generally a significant and positive contributor to growth in output. The growth in sectoral capital stock accounts for the majority of the total contribution of growth in sectoral capital input to growth in output. For industries for which we measure technical change the average contribution of growth in sectoral capital stock to growth in output for the period as a whole exceeds the average rate of technical change for twelve of forty-five industries. During the period 1948−1976 the average contribution of growth in sectoral capital stock to growth in output exceeds 1 percent for eight of forty-six industries. The three industries whose average contribution exceeds 2 percent for the period as a whole include telephone, telegraph, and miscellaneous communication services; water supply, sanitary services, and other utilities; and private households. The average contribution of telephone, telegraph, and miscellaneous communication services is above

2 percent for the last four subperiods—1960–1966, 1966–1969, 1969–1973, and 1973–1976. The average contribution of water supply, sanitary services, and other utilities is above 2 percent for all subperiods except the second—1953–1957. The average contribution of private households is above 2 percent for all subperiods.

During the subperiods there is little variation in the list of 1948–1953 subperiod, the average contribution exceeds 1 percent for five of forty-six industries. The only industry other than water supply and private households whose average contribution exceeds 2 percent is nonmetallic mining and quarrying, except fuel. During the 1953–1957, 1957–1960, and 1960–1966 subperiods, the average contribution exceeds 1 percent for eight of forty-six industries. During the 1953–1957 subperiod the two industries other than private households whose average contribution exceeds 2 percent include nonmetallic mining and quarrying, except fuel, and radio broadcasting and television. During the 1957–1960 subperiod, the two industries other than water supply and private households whose average contribution exceeds 2 percent include metal mining and air transportation. During the 1960–1966 and 1966–1969 subperiods the industries whose average contribution exceeds 2 percent include only the three industries whose average contribution exceeds 2 percent for the period 1948–1976. During the 1966–1969 subperiod, the average contribution exceeds 1 percent for thirteen of forty-six industries. During the 1969–1973 subperiod, the average contribution exceeds 1 percent for five of forty-six industries.

Electric utilities is the only industry other than telephone and telegraph; water supply; and private households whose average contribution exceeds 2 percent. During the 1973–1976 subperiod, the average contribution exceeds 1 percent for nine of forty-six industries. During the 1973–1976 subperiod the industries whose average contribution exceeds 2 percent include only the three industries whose average contribution exceeds 2 percent for the period as a whole.

XI. INCOME AND EXPENDITURE ACCOUNT

Our final objective is to analyze the role of capital in the growth of output of the U.S. economy. Our first step is to construct an income and expenditure account for the U.S. private national economy. The fundamental accounting identity for the income and expenditure account is that consumer receipts are equal to consumer expenditures. Consumer receipts are defined as the sum of income from the supply of capital and labor services, net of taxes, and transfer payments. Consumer expenditures are defined as the sum of consumer outlays for goods and services and saving.

Consumer receipts and consumer expenditures are linked through property compensation and saving. Saving results in the accumulation of tangible assets and financial claims; accumulated assets generate future property income. Saving must be defined in a way that is consistent with property compensation. Saving enters the accumulation account we presented in Section V above, while the value of property compensation is included in the aggregate production account in Section XII below.

In this section we present annual data on gross private national income, divided between property and labor income, and gross private national expenditures, divided between consumer outlays and saving. Property income is a stable proportion of national income over the period 1948–1976, varying from 29 to 35 percent of the total. Saving is a stable proportion of national expenditures, varying from 25 to 30 percent of the total.

To provide information on the generation of property income, we divide property income among income from corporate business, noncorporate business, private households, nonprofit institutions, and net claims on governments and the rest of the world. The share of income generated by private households and nonprofit institutions increases over the period 1948–1976. The share of income generated by corporate business and by net claims on governments and on the rest of the world is stable, while the share of income generated by noncorporate business falls over the period 1948–1976.

To divide property income between price and quantity components we first estimate nominal and own rates of return by legal form of organization, excluding all taxes on property and on income from property. As before, nominal rates of return incorporate gains from revaluation of assets, while own rates of return exclude these gains. We present annual data on rates of return for the period 1948–1976 for the private national economy as a whole and for corporate business, noncorporate business, private households, nonprofit institutions, and net claims on governments and the rest of the world.

Nominal rates of return are relatively high during the period 1948–1951, fall to the lowest levels attained during the period 1948–1976, and then rise gradually to peaks attained in 1973–1975 before falling in 1976. These trends are common to nominal rates of return for all legal forms of organization and reflect the underlying rate of inflation for the economy as a whole at various points of time throughout the period 1948–1976. Own rates of return exhibit no trend over time, rising to historic peaks for the private national economy in 1966, but reaching levels during the 1970s that are comparable to average own rates of return through the period 1948–1976.

Our second step in dividing property income between price and quantity components is to measure the prices of capital services from the point of view of the owner of the asset. The price of capital services is the sum of the own rate of return, multiplied by the price of capital goods at the beginning of the period, plus the price of depreciation. We present annual data on prices of capital services by the six classes of assets and the four legal forms of organization given in Table 2–1, together with net claims on governments and the rest of the world.

Our final step in separating price and quantity components of private national property income is to construct price and quantity indexes of property income. Here the subscript i ranges over the four legal forms of organization given in Table 2–1 and net claims on governments and rest of the world and the subscript k ranges over the six classes of assets given in Table 2–1. We have already described the construction of data on the prices of capital inputs, say q_{Kk}^i. We can express the quantity of property income K as a translog function of the capital stocks, A_{ki}:

$$\ln K_t - \ln K_{t-1} = \Sigma\Sigma \, \bar{v}_{Kk}^i \, [\ln A_{ki, \, t-1} - \ln A_{ki, \, t-2}] \;,$$

where

$$\bar{v}_{Kk}^i = \tfrac{1}{2} \, [v_{Kk, \, t}^i + v_{Kk, \, t-1}^i] \;,$$

and

$$v_{Kk}^i = \frac{p_{Kk}^i \, A_{ki, \, t-1}}{\Sigma\Sigma \, p_{Kk}^i \, A_{ki, \, t-1}} \;.$$

The corresponding price index is the ratio of the value of property income to the translog quantity index. We present annual data on prices and quantities of property income by legal form of organization and for the private national sector of the U.S. economy.

Income and Expenditure

We have defined consumer receipts as the sum of income from the supply of factor services, net of taxes, and transfer payments.

Property and labor compensation are generated as outlays by the forty-six industrial sectors listed in Table 2—1 for capital and labor services. After these outlays have been reduced by direct and indirect taxes, the remainder accrues to households and institutions as property and labor income. Our income account also includes income generated by the supply of factor services to governments and the rest of the world. We include in our measure of income all receipts from the supply of factor services, whether or not they are available for current consumption or have been distributed to consumers.

We include social insurance funds in the private sector of the U.S. economy. Contributions to social insurance funds are included in gross private national income, while benefits paid by these funds are excluded from transfer payments. Investment income from claims on governments by social insurance funds are included in income. Gross private national consumer receipts are equal to the sum of gross private national income plus transfer payments from governments, other than benefits paid by social insurance payments.

Our definition of private national consumer expenditures differs from that of personal consumption expenditures in the U.S. national income and product accounts. We exclude purchases of consumers' durables from consumer expenditures and include the value of the services of these durables, the services of producers' durable equipment employed by nonprofit institutions, and the equity return to real estate held by nonprofit institutions. We preserve the accounting identity that consumer expenditures is equal to consumer receipts by defining gross private national saving as gross private national consumer receipts less private national consumer outlays.

Our income account, as presented by Jorgenson [47, 1980], in the next chapter of this volume, includes property compensation from the taxes on property and property income. These taxes include corporate profits taxes, business property taxes, personal income taxes assigned to property income, personal property taxes, and wealth taxes. The income account also includes property compensation generated by net claims on governments and the rest of the world, net of taxes. Investment income of social insurance funds less transfers to general government is allocated to property income. Finally, the income account includes labor compensation, excluding personal income taxes assigned to labor income. We employ the allocation of personal income taxes between property and labor income developed by Christensen and Jorgenson [23, 1969; 25, 1973].

We present annual data on gross private national income, divided between property and labor income, and gross private national receipts for the period 1948—1976 in Table 2—28. We also present

Table 2–28. Gross Private National Receipts and Expenditures (*billions of current dollars*), 1948–1976

Year	Gross Private National Income	Labor Income	Property Income
1948	231.129	160.831	70.298
1949	232.747	159.025	73.722
1950	254.889	174.480	80.409
1951	287.480	205.200	82.280
1952	305.263	210.533	94.730
1953	317.465	222.948	94.517
1954	331.990	225.473	106.517
1955	354.436	239.512	114.924
1956	371.945	255.875	116.070
1957	388.648	269.594	119.054
1958	405.190	274.414	130.775
1959	428.931	288.249	140.681
1960	451.803	301.868	149.936
1961	466.371	313.271	153.101
1962	499.555	334.843	164.712
1963	523.572	350.794	172.779
1964	567.764	377.347	190.417
1965	616.963	402.593	214.370
1966	675.874	445.138	230.736
1967	710.932	470.166	240.766
1968	759.507	510.378	249.129
1969	825.402	551.194	274.208
1970	865.927	593.371	272.556
1971	943.872	640.842	303.030
1972	1040.060	693.143	346.917
1973	1185.059	798.293	386.766
1974	1242.293	851.300	390.994
1975	1360.372	900.335	460.037
1976	1516.843	991.343	525.500

Table 2–28. continued

Year	Gross Private National Receipts and Expenditures	Consumption Expenditures	Consumer Outlays	Gross Private National Saving
1948	239.085	172.092	173.534	65.551
1949	240.493	172.168	173.546	66.947
1950	262.618	185.564	186.873	75.745
1951	294.081	204.913	206.246	87.835
1952	311.777	220.463	221.866	89.911
1953	323.867	227.368	228.946	94.921
1954	338.632	242.394	244.084	94.548
1955	361.540	252.176	253.909	107.631
1956	379.090	266.819	268.833	110.257
1957	396.171	277.931	280.188	115.983
1958	413.256	298.591	300.982	112.273
1959	437.203	312.328	314.650	122.553
1960	460.232	334.799	337.251	122.981
1961	475.284	347.216	349.932	125.352
1962	508.707	363.278	366.385	142.322
1963	533.208	379.461	382.860	150.348
1964	578.029	406.297	410.127	167.902
1965	628.037	438.565	442.819	185.218
1966	687.798	474.978	479.871	207.927
1967	724.878	500.978	506.871	218.007
1968	775.207	541.172	547.805	227.402
1969	843.655	600.721	608.315	235.340
1970	888.844	631.483	640.331	248.513
1971	971.465	678.895	689.143	282.322
1972	1070.709	750.792	762.443	308.266
1973	1218.119	843.303	856.186	361.933
1974	1281.955	907.853	921.798	360.157
1975	1410.885	988.973	1004.467	406.418
1976	1570.434	1112.112	1129.352	441.082

annual estimates of gross private national consumer expenditures, consumer outlays, and saving. Property income remains in stable proportion to gross private national income over the period 1948–1976, varying between 29 and 35 percent of the total. Gross private national saving remains in stable proportion to gross private national expenditures, varying between 25 and 30 percent of the total. Transfer payments as a proportion of income and nontax payments as a proportion of consumer outlays are small in magnitude throughout the period.

Property Income

Our next objective is the measurement of property compensation from the point of view of the owner of the asset by legal form of organization; to achieve this objective we must allocate taxes on income and wealth. We first implement a detailed allocation of personal income taxes on property compensation to the various types of property compensation. The tax base for personal income taxes on property compensation includes corporate and noncorporate sectors. The tax base also includes the net interest paid domestically by the government and the sum of corporate profits and net interest paid in the rest of world sector. Using this tax base, a total effective rate of tax on property compensation is computed taking into account the deductibility of state and local taxes at the federal level and the investment tax credit. This total effective tax rate is then applied to tax bases which are specific to each legal form of organization. We add corporate profits taxes for the corporate sector, and subtract the investment tax credit for the noncorporate sector. It must be noted that although property income from assets in the household sector is not subject to personal income taxation, household property taxes are deductible from the base on personal income taxes on property compensation. By taking this into account we construct a rate of personal taxation on household property which is effectively negative, that is, an implicit subsidy. Finally we allocate federal and state and local estate and gift taxes to property compensation in proportion to the value of the corresponding asset included in total private national wealth.[u]

Property income by legal form of organization is presented annually in Table 2–29. The household sector accounts for the largest share of property compensation after taxes, followed by the corporate sector. While the share of household property compensation in gross private national property compensation is generally increasing

[u] See Table 3-4 in Jorgenson [47, 1980], this volume, for a comparison of property compensation before and after taxes.

Table 2–29.   Gross Private National Property Income by Legal Form of Organization (billions of current dollars), 1948–1976

Year	Corporate	Noncorporate	Households	Institutions	Net Claims on Government and Rest of World
1948	24.137	14.898	25.333	.922	5.008
1949	24.997	17.219	24.803	1.344	5.359
1950	23.906	18.598	31.140	1.296	5.469
1951	25.462	13.794	35.982	1.037	6.005
1952	26.515	18.405	41.495	1.979	6.336
1953	26.849	18.520	41.016	1.834	6.298
1954	29.308	18.014	50.265	2.397	6.533
1955	35.312	20.246	50.064	2.410	6.893
1956	34.818	18.566	53.773	1.533	7.380
1957	36.687	19.142	53.271	1.810	8.143
1958	37.015	20.716	62.320	3.387	7.357
1959	42.758	24.542	62.237	3.162	7.982
1960	42.179	22.878	72.446	3.993	8.440
1961	43.200	22.822	74.464	4.208	8.407
1962	49.891	23.891	77.039	4.382	9.509
1963	53.172	24.933	80.187	4.254	10.233
1964	59.632	27.485	87.015	4.991	11.294
1965	68.307	31.314	97.001	5.735	12.014
1966	75.111	31.410	105.624	6.094	12.497
1967	76.327	34.527	109.844	6.843	13.226
1968	77.729	33.288	116.366	7.853	13.893
1969	77.346	32.612	139.967	9.586	14.698
1970	78.383	33.100	137.775	6.067	17.231
1971	89.217	37.662	148.656	8.778	18.717
1972	100.230	43.622	172.809	10.720	19.536
1973	105.987	36.806	202.676	14.496	26.800
1974	104.072	47.932	204.323	5.565	29.101
1975	138.060	70.700	209.907	8.507	32.863
1976	153.641	72.269	244.495	19.370	35.724

over time, the share of corporate property compensation is fairly stable over time. The share of noncorporate property compensation in gross private national property compensation is generally decreasing over time. The shares of institutional property compensation and property compensation on net claims on governments and on the rest of the world are small in magnitude, representing less than 5 percent and 10 percent, respectively, over the period 1948–1976.

Rates of Return

The nominal rate of return from the point of view of the owner of the asset is calculated after corporate profits taxes, business and personal property taxes, personal income taxes, and estate and gift taxes. The nominal rate of return from the point of view of the owner of the asset can be derived from the nominal rate of return from the point of view of the producer, by excluding personal income and wealth taxes from the return to capital. Own rates of return from the point of view of the owner of the asset is calculated by excluding revaluation of assets from the return to capital. This definition parallels that for the own rate of return from the point of view of the producer. In Table 2–30 we present nominal and own rates of return from the point of view of the owner of the asset for corporate, noncorporate, households, institutions, total net claims, and the private national economy.

The corporate nominal rate of return is in general the highest of the nominal rates of return after taxes by legal form of organization or for net claims. The net claims nominal rate of return after taxes is in general the lowest. The noncorporate nominal rate of return is lower than the households nominal rate of return for all years after 1951. The households and institutional nominal rates of return after all taxes are very similar as we constrain the nominal rates of return after property taxes to be equal. The household and institutional nominal rates of return from the point of view of the owner of the asset are much closer to the aggregate nominal rate of return than in the case of the nominal rates of return from the point of view of the producer in that the tax burdens of these two sectors are small when compared to the tax burdens of the corporate and noncorporate sectors. The own rate of return after all taxes for the private national economy shows much less variation than the corresponding nominal rate of return. When comparing the sectoral own and nominal rates of return from the point of the producer at the level of individual industries, the reverse seemed to be the case. The private national economy own rates of return are lower than the corresponding nominal rates of return after 1953, indicating that revaluation is positive

Table 2-30. Gross Private National Property Compensation after Taxes, Rates of Return on Capital by Legal Form of Organization, 1948-1976

Year	Private National Economy	Nominal Rates of Return				
		Corporate	Noncorporate	Households	Institutions	Net Claims on Government and Rest of World
1948	.091	.124	.119	.101	.101	.017
1949	.025	.053	.007	.019	.018	.022
1950	.081	.092	.108	.076	.075	.043
1951	.092	.127	.101	.099	.098	.028
1952	.049	.056	.046	.059	.058	.029
1953	.043	.050	.023	.036	.036	.035
1954	.036	.043	.025	.047	.046	.024
1955	.054	.074	.038	.066	.064	.029
1956	.063	.094	.042	.073	.072	.033
1957	.053	.077	.043	.054	.052	.032
1958	.039	.044	.025	.050	.048	.033
1959	.048	.061	.032	.058	.055	.033
1960	.046	.046	.029	.064	.061	.035
1961	.042	.040	.027	.062	.059	.029
1962	.051	.057	.034	.066	.064	.037
1963	.048	.062	.031	.059	.057	.025
1964	.055	.069	.038	.070	.068	.028
1965	.075	.095	.077	.079	.077	.030
1966	.083	.107	.081	.089	.087	.032
1967	.079	.097	.077	.092	.089	.021
1968	.085	.096	.081	.101	.098	.035
1969	.098	.097	.082	.129	.124	.053
1970	.082	.090	.074	.089	.084	.059
1971	.085	.095	.076	.101	.097	.041
1972	.083	.090	.080	.101	.101	.019
1973	.107	.099	.087	.143	.139	.061
1974	.135	.164	.120	.141	.135	.078
1975	.131	.169	.114	.125	.122	.081
1976	.093	.087	.063	.118	.114	.086

Table 2–30. continued

			Own Rates of Return			
Year	Private National Economy	Corporate	Noncorporate	Households	Institutions	Net Claims on Government and Rest of World
1948	.038	.060	.034	.038	.012	.021
1949	.034	.053	.035	.021	.029	.023
1950	.036	.047	.038	.035	.023	.023
1951	.028	.044	.014	.032	.001	.025
1952	.032	.040	.023	.038	.034	.027
1953	.029	.037	.023	.029	.024	.025
1954	.035	.041	.019	.050	.040	.025
1955	.037	.054	.024	.042	.035	.026
1956	.031	.045	.017	.038	.001	.027
1957	.027	.041	.014	.027	.002	.030
1958	.031	.037	.017	.040	.040	.026
1959	.034	.047	.026	.035	.029	.027
1960	.037	.042	.021	.049	.043	.028
1961	.036	.041	.021	.047	.042	.027
1962	.040	.053	.023	.047	.040	.030
1963	.041	.055	.024	.047	.031	.031
1964	.046	.063	.028	.051	.038	.034
1965	.052	.074	.035	.058	.042	.034
1966	.053	.072	.031	.061	.039	.035
1967	.049	.064	.032	.056	.040	.036
1968	.045	.056	.025	.053	.045	.035
1969	.046	.045	.019	.067	.055	.036
1970	.037	.036	.015	.052	.009	.041
1971	.039	.041	.018	.053	.028	.042
1972	.046	.045	.021	.064	.042	.041
1973	.048	.044	.007	.075	.069	.057
1974	.037	.029	.013	.055	.011	.059
1975	.039	.039	.028	.042	.005	.062
1976	.044	.041	.025	.051	.071	.058

for these years. The relationships between the own rates of return presented in Table 2–30 are similar to the relationships between the nominal rates of return. The corporate own rate of return is in general the highest of the own rates of return. The net claims own rate of return is the lowest for the majority of the years being considered. The institutional own rate of return is the lowest for several years and shows a high degree of variability.

Capital Services

Excluding both direct and indirect taxes, the price of capital services from the point of view of the owner of the asset becomes

$$p_{k,t} = p_{A,t-1}\, r_t + p_{A,t}\, \delta - (p_{A,t} - p_{A,t-1})$$

For inventories and land and for net claims on government and rest of world the depreciation rate is equal to zero. In Table 2–31 we present the price of capital service flows from the point of view of the owner of the asset by legal form of organization and asset. For any legal form of organization, the price of capital service flows is generally highest for the equipment category and lowest for land.

We construct price and quantity indexes for property income by expressing the quantity of aggregate property income as a translog index of the quantities of capital stock at the beginning of the period, broken down by class of asset and legal form of organization. The price of property income is defined at the ratio of private national property income to the translog quantity index. Similarly, we can express the quantity of property income by legal form of organization as a translog function of capital stocks by class of asset for each legal form of organization. The corresponding price of property income is defined as the ratio of property income by legal form of organization to the translog quantity index. The price and quantity indexes for property compensation after taxes by corporate, non-corporate, households, institutions, net claims on government and rest of world and private national property compensation are presented in Table 2–32. The price of property compensation after taxes is highest for households, lowest for net claims, and shows the most variability for institutions.

XII.   CAPITAL AND U.S. ECONOMIC GROWTH

Our final objective is to analyze the role of capital in the growth of the U.S. economy over the period 1948–1976. For this purpose we

Table 2–31. Capital Service Flow Prices by Legal Form of Organization and Asset Type, 1948–1976

| Year | Corporate | | | |
	Producers' Durable Equipment	Tenant-Occ. Res. and Nonres. Structures	Inventories	Land
1948	.079	.033	.027	.022
1949	.065	.054	.045	.037
1950	.103	.061	.034	-.002
1951	.109	.043	.013	.027
1952	.102	.050	.059	.012
1953	.096	.050	.029	.022
1954	.089	.062	.028	.018
1955	.118	.061	.036	.033
1956	.105	.045	.035	.045
1957	.103	.059	.037	.036
1958	.114	.070	.033	.018
1959	.126	.069	.034	.028
1960	.122	.068	.037	.020
1961	.130	.060	.038	.016
1962	.142	.065	.046	.026
1963	.144	.069	.051	.030
1964	.150	.073	.051	.035
1965	.171	.085	.066	.020
1966	.174	.082	.069	.029
1967	.163	.076	.069	.024
1968	.160	.072	.061	.025
1969	.171	.055	.054	.027
1970	.165	.059	.046	.023
1971	.171	.072	.055	.029
1972	.190	.081	.054	.025
1973	.212	.070	.031	.042
1974	.231	.054	-.064	.108
1975	.177	.129	.071	.120
1976	.208	.148	.035	.030

Table 2–31. continued

Year	Household			Producers' Durable Equipment	Institutions	
	Consumers' Durables	Owner-Occupied Residential Structures	Land		Tenant-Occ. Res. and Nonres. Structures	Land
1948	.183	.031	.009	.079	.024	.007
1949	.151	.027	.012	.058	.040	.012
1950	.177	.053	-.004	.105	.055	-.006
1951	.180	.041	.008	.104	.019	.006
1952	.193	.043	.008	.114	.052	.008
1953	.171	.045	.011	.099	.042	.011
1954	.205	.054	.005	.103	.066	.004
1955	.188	.054	.007	.124	.057	.005
1956	.186	.054	.007	.103	.027	.005
1957	.167	.063	.001	.099	.042	.003
1958	.196	.064	-.000	.130	.077	-.001
1959	.185	.069	.003	.135	.068	-.005
1960	.214	.070	-.000	.147	.079	-.003
1961	.210	.072	-.001	.158	.077	-.004
1962	.211	.073	.001	.160	.072	-.002
1963	.210	.076	-.003	.153	.066	-.006
1964	.221	.074	.003	.161	.070	-.001
1965	.240	.072	.009	.168	.072	-.005
1966	.247	.071	.016	.170	.067	.011
1967	.236	.073	.019	.168	.072	.014
1968	.237	.072	.028	.173	.077	.021
1969	.279	.067	.053	.206	.081	.042
1970	.250	.084	.021	.170	.048	.012
1971	.259	.084	.034	.184	.074	.024
1972	.294	.087	.041	.212	.095	.029
1973	.330	.076	.084	.263	.121	.070
1974	.292	.087	.087	.213	.015	.071
1975	.278	.101	.074	.139	.069	.060
1976	.321	.115	.070	.256	.202	.055

Table 2–31. continued

Year	Producers' Durable Equipment	Noncorporate Tenant-Occ. Res. and Nonres. Structures	Inventories	Land
1948	.049	.027	.035	.020
1949	.016	.027	.092	.016
1950	.089	.064	.052	.005
1951	.074	.025	.031	.015
1952	.076	.039	.078	.007
1953	.057	.030	.074	.008
1954	.055	.047	.028	.008
1955	.070	.036	.059	.014
1956	.041	.010	.028	.016
1957	.049	.032	.012	.017
1958	.066	.052	.005	.007
1959	.067	.045	.053	.011
1960	.069	.052	.024	.010
1961	.077	.047	.028	.008
1962	.079	.045	.017	.012
1963	.074	.044	.036	.011
1964	.079	.047	.034	.015
1965	.109	.069	.035	.009
1966	.103	.059	.022	.012
1967	.093	.057	.090	.010
1968	.091	.055	.044	.014
1969	.098	.037	.027	.015
1970	.088	.040	.044	.010
1971	.089	.049	.046	.012
1972	.117	.065	.001	.017
1973	.136	.050	.197	.030
1974	.115	.002	.022	.061
1975	.034	.048	.110	.058
1976	.091	.103	.059	.001

Table 2–32.   Gross Private National Property Income by Legal Form of Organization (constant prices of 1972) 1948–1976

Year	Private National Economy		Corporate		Noncorporate	
	Price	Quantity	Price	Quantity	Price	Quantity
1948	.054	1288.481	.059	408.521	.034	443.750
1949	.054	1367.889	.059	426.135	.037	466.122
1950	.056	1435.117	.055	434.056	.039	475.429
1951	.054	1538.252	.057	447.236	.027	501.621
1952	.059	1617.171	.057	467.758	.035	519.467
1953	.056	1678.018	.055	485.061	.035	525.176
1954	.061	1750.928	.059	500.967	.034	537.006
1955	.063	1814.052	.069	512.825	.037	542.414
1956	.061	1909.940	.065	537.279	.034	547.865
1957	.061	1984.205	.066	554.417	.034	562.204
1958	.064	2051.945	.064	576.799	.037	564.214
1959	.067	2092.991	.073	586.037	.043	564.650
1960	.069	2162.105	.070	606.594	.040	566.281
1961	.069	2226.577	.069	626.501	.040	569.953
1962	.072	2277.100	.078	643.680	.042	571.719
1963	.074	2354.299	.080	668.755	.043	577.270
1964	.078	2445.622	.086	690.970	.046	593.549
1965	.084	2556.775	.095	722.621	.052	607.692
1966	.086	2700.493	.098	769.554	.050	629.362
1967	.084	2861.790	.092	829.513	.053	650.729
1968	.083	2999.684	.089	876.027	.050	671.212
1969	.087	3151.965	.084	925.279	.047	691.266
1970	.083	3300.077	.080	978.833	.046	715.159
1971	.089	3413.469	.088	1010.333	.051	743.491
1972	.098	3547.862	.097	1036.395	.056	775.669
1973	.105	3722.282	.099	1072.327	.045	819.375
1974	.100	3922.968	.092	1134.484	.057	839.268
1975	.115	4053.705	.117	1179.933	.082	858.336
1976	.127	4159.708	.129	1192.592	.083	871.188

Table 2–32. continued

Year	Households		Institutions		Net Claims on Government and Rest of World	
	Price	Quantity	Price	Quantity	Price	Quantity
1948	.081	312.865	.029	31.986	.020	250.923
1949	.072	345.830	.041	33.173	.022	247.684
1950	.082	380.586	.037	35.042	.022	254.634
1951	.084	430.661	.027	38.420	.025	245.491
1952	.090	461.086	.049	40.784	.026	244.316
1953	.085	484.139	.043	42.685	.025	253.154
1954	.098	512.942	.054	44.727	.025	262.401
1955	.093	539.895	.051	47.519	.026	272.625
1956	.092	583.185	.031	50.147	.027	273.214
1957	.087	613.833	.034	53.116	.030	274.620
1958	.098	638.602	.060	56.743	.026	282.095
1959	.095	653.724	.052	60.649	.027	295.595
1960	.106	682.263	.061	64.946	.029	298.134
1961	.105	706.350	.060	69.593	.028	301.529
1962	.107	722.115	.059	74.452	.031	310.829
1963	.107	748.058	.053	80.295	.032	321.063
1964	.111	782.213	.058	86.103	.034	329.650
1965	.118	821.587	.062	92.849	.035	344.543
1966	.121	869.941	.061	99.460	.035	354.845
1967	.120	919.161	.065	105.957	.036	370.520
1968	.121	960.339	.071	110.889	.035	398.356
1969	.138	1012.636	.083	115.923	.036	414.422
1970	.130	1062.066	.050	120.431	.041	418.069
1971	.136	1096.250	.071	124.160	.043	440.267
1972	.150	1148.984	.088	121.887	.042	464.927
1973	.166	1222.283	.120	120.354	.057	473.681
1974	.157	1300.721	.047	117.734	.059	491.828
1975	.156	1342.825	.074	115.092	.064	514.854
1976	.178	1375.167	.171	113.098	.060	594.297

construct an aggregate production account in current and constant prices, following Jorgenson [47, 1980]. The fundamental accounting identity for the aggregate production account is that value added is equal to the sum of property and labor compensation for the private domestic sector of the U.S. economy. Our aggregate production account includes data on aggregate value added and aggregate capital and labor input in current and constant prices. Finally, it includes the rate of aggregate technical change.

In Section X above we have presented sectoral production accounts for the forty-six industrial sectors listed in Table 2–1. These accounts include data on sectoral output and sectoral intermediate, capital, and labor input in current and constant prices together with the rate of sectoral technical change. By combining data from our aggregate production account and from our sectoral production accounts, we can express the rate of aggregate technical change as a weighted sum of rates of sectoral technical change and terms corresponding to the effects of the redistribution of value added, capital input, and labor input among sectors.

Our sectoral production accounts are based on sectoral production functions for each of the forty-six industrial sectors listed in Table 2–1. Following Jorgenson [47, 1980] we employ sectoral value added functions in constructing an aggregate production account. Sectoral value added is expressed as a function of sectoral capital and labor inputs and time. We combine the sectoral value added functions with necessary conditions for producer equilibrium in each sector. These conditions imply that the elasticities of the quantity of sectoral value added with respect to the quantities of sectoral capital and labor inputs are equal to the shares of these inputs in sectoral value added.

Sectoral Value Added
Sectoral value added is defined as the sum of the values of sectoral capital input and sectoral labor input:

$$p_V^i V_i = p_K^i K_i + p_L^i L_i \; ,$$

where p_V^i is the price of sectoral value added and V_i is the quantity. Using the definition of value added and the accounting identity between the value of sectoral output and the sum of the values of sectoral intermediate, capital, and labor inputs presented in Section IX above, we can express sectoral value added as the difference between the value of sectoral output and the value of sectoral intermediate input:

$$p_V^i V_i = p_i Z_i - p_X^i X_i .$$

To separate price and quantity components of sectoral value added we represent sectoral output as a function of the quantity of sectoral value added and intermediate input, following Jorgenson [47, 1980]. Sectoral output is not represented as a function of time, so that changes in technology can be attributed to changes in the sectoral value added functions. We combine the sectoral production functions with necessary conditions for producer equilibrium in each sector. These conditions imply that the elasticities of sectoral output with respect to the quantities of sectoral intermediate input and value added are equal to the shares of the value of intermediate input and value added in the value of sectoral output. We assume that the quantity of sectoral output is a translog function of the quantities of sectoral value added and intermediate input.

Considering data on sectoral output and intermediate input at any two discrete points of time, we can express the difference between successive logarithms of sectoral output as a weighted average of the difference between successive logarithms of sectoral intermediate input and value added with weights given by the average shares of sectoral intermediate input and value added in the value of sectoral output:

$$ln\ Z_{i,t} - ln\ Z_{i,t-1} = \bar{v}_X^i [ln\ X_{i,t} - ln\ X_{i,t-1}] + \bar{v}_V^i [ln\ V_{i,t} - ln\ V_{i,t-1}] ,$$

where

$$\bar{v}_X^i = \tfrac{1}{2} [v_{X,t}^i + v_{X,t-1}^i] ,$$

$$\bar{v}_V^i = \tfrac{1}{2} [v_{V,t}^i + v_{V,t-1}^i] ,$$

and

$$v_X^i = \frac{p_X^i X_i}{p_i Z_i} ,$$

$$v_V^i = \frac{p_V^i V_i}{p_i Z_i} .$$

The difference between successive logarithms of sectoral value added can be expressed in terms of differences between successive logarithms of sectoral output and intermediate input and average value shares of sectoral intermediate input and value added:

$$\ln V_t^i - \ln V_{t-1}^i = \frac{1}{\bar{v}_V^i} \; [\ln Z_{i,t} - \ln Z_{i,t-1}] - \frac{\bar{v}_X^i}{\bar{v}_V^i} \; [\ln X_t^i - \ln X_{t-1}^i] \; .$$

Following Jorgenson [47, 1980], we refer to this expression for the quantity of sectoral value added as the *translog index of sectoral value added.* The corresponding index of the price of sectoral value added is equal to the ratio of sectoral value added to the translog quantity index.

Aggregate Production

Our multi-sectoral model of production and technical change includes value added functions for each of the forty-six industrial sectors listed in Table 2–1. The model also includes market equilibrium conditions:

$$K_k = \Sigma K_{ki} \; ,$$

$$L_\varrho = \Sigma L_{\varrho i} \; .$$

Each type of aggregate capital input K_k is the sum of the corresponding sectoral capital inputs, K_{ki}, where the subscript k ranges over the four legal forms of organization and the six types of assets listed in Table 2–1. Similarly, each type of aggregate capital input, L_ϱ, is the sum of the corresponding sectoral labor inputs, $L_{\varrho i}$, where the subscript ϱ ranges over the different types of labor input described by Gollop and Jorgenson [33, 1980].

We can define the prices of aggregate capital inputs, p_{Kk}, in terms of prices paid for each type of capital input in all forty-six sectors listed in Table 2–1:

$$p_{Kk} K_k = p_{Kk} \, \Sigma K_{ki}$$

$$= \Sigma \, p_{Kk}^i \, K_{ki} \; .$$

The value of each type of aggregate capital input is equal to the sum of values over all sectors. The price of each type of aggregate capital input is equal to the ratio of the sum of values over all sectors to the sum of quantities over all sectors. Similarly, we can define the prices of aggregate labor inputs, $p_{L\varrho}$, in terms of prices paid for each type of labor input in all forty-six sectors $p_{L\varrho}^i$:

$$p_{L\varrho}\, L_{\varrho} \; = \; p_{L\varrho} \; \Sigma \; L_{\varrho i} \; ,$$

$$= \; \Sigma \; p_{L\varrho}^i \; L_{\varrho i} \; .$$

These prices of each type of aggregate labor input are equal to the ratio of the sum of values over all sectors to the sum of quantities over all sectors.

Finally, we can define aggregate value added as the sum of value added in all sectors:

$$p_V V \; = \; \Sigma \, p_V^i \, V_i \; ,$$

where p_V is the price and V is the quantity of aggregate value added. The quantity of aggregate value added is the sum of the corresponding sectoral quantities of value added:

$$V \; = \; \Sigma_i V_i \; .$$

Our aggregate model of production and technical change is based on an aggregate production function, representing the quantity of aggregate value added as a function of the quantities of aggregate capital and labor input and time. We combine the aggregate production function with necessary conditions for producer equilibrium at the aggregate level. These conditions imply that the elasticities of aggregate output with respect to the quantities of aggregate capital and labor input are equal to the shares of the value of these inputs in aggregate value added. We assume that the quantity of aggregate output is a translog function of aggregate capital and labor input.

Considering data on aggregate value added and aggregate capital and labor inputs at any two discrete points of time, we can express the difference between successive logarithms of aggregate output as a weighted average of differences between successive logarithms of aggregate capital and labor input with weights given by average value shares in the two periods, plus the average rate of aggregate technical change:

$$\ln V_t - \ln V_{t-1} = \bar{v}_K [\ln K_t - \ln K_{t-1}] + \bar{v}_L [\ln L_t - \ln L_{t-1}] + \bar{v}_t ,$$

where

$$\bar{v}_K = \frac{1}{2} [v_{K,t} + v_{K,t-1}] ,$$

$$\bar{v}_L = \frac{1}{2} [v_{L,t} + v_{L,t-1}] ,$$

$$\bar{v}_t = \frac{1}{2} [v_{t,t} + v_{t,t-1}] ,$$

and

$$v_K = \frac{p_K K}{p_V V} ,$$

$$v_L = \frac{p_L L}{p_V V} .$$

Following Jorgenson [47, 1980], we refer to this expression for the average rate of aggregate technical change as the *translog index of aggregate technical change.*

Similarly, we represent the quantities of aggregate capital and labor input as functions of the quantities of their components. We combine the aggregate input functions with necessary conditions for producer equilibrium at the aggregate level. These conditions imply that the elasticities of aggregate capital and labor input with respect to the quantities of their components are equal to the shares of the value of these components in the value of the corresponding aggregate input. We assume that the quantities of aggregate capital and labor input are translog functions of their components.

Considering data on aggregate capital and labor inputs at any two discrete points of time, we can express the differences between successive logarithms of these inputs as weighted averages of differences between successive logarithms of their components with weights given by average value shares in the two periods:

$$\ln K_t - \ln K_{t-1} = \Sigma \bar{v}_{Kk} [\ln K_{k,t} - \ln K_{k,t-1}] ,$$

$$\ln L_t - \ln L_{t-1} = \Sigma \bar{v}_{L\varrho} [\ln L_{\varrho,t} - \ln L_{\varrho,t-1}] ,$$

where

$$\bar{v}_{Kk} = \tfrac{1}{2} [v_{Kk,t} + v_{Kk,t-1}] \ ,$$

$$\bar{v}_{L\varrho} = \tfrac{1}{2} [v_{L\varrho,t} + v_{L\varrho,t-1}] \ ,$$

and

$$v_{Kk} = \frac{p_{Kk} K_k}{\Sigma p_{Kk} K_k} \ ,$$

$$v_{L\varrho} = \frac{p_{L\varrho} L_\varrho}{\Sigma p_{L\varrho} L_\varrho} \ .$$

Following Jorgenson [47, 1980], we refer to these indexes as *translog indexes of aggregate capital and labor inputs*, respectively.

We take the values of aggregate capital and labor input to be equal to the sum of the values of their components:

$$p_K K = \Sigma p_{Kk} K_k \ ,$$

$$p_L L = \Sigma p_{L\varrho} L_\varrho \ .$$

The prices of aggregate capital and labor inputs are equal to the ratios of the sum of values over all types of aggregate capital and labor inputs to the corresponding translog quantity indexes.

Combining the translog indexes of aggregate capital and labor inputs with the translog index of aggregate technical change, we can express the rate of aggregate technical change in the form

$$\bar{v}_t = \ln V_t - \ln V_{t-1}$$

$$- \bar{v}_K \cdot \Sigma \bar{v}_{Kk} [\ln K_{k,t} - \ln K_{k,t-1}]$$

$$- \bar{v}_L \cdot \Sigma \bar{v}_{L\varrho} [\ln L_{\varrho,t} - \ln L_{\varrho,t-1}] \ .$$

Growth in Output and Inputs

We first construct an aggregate production account for the private domestic sector of the U.S. economy. In Table 2–33 we give data on the prices and quantities of aggregate value added, capital input, and labor input. We present annual data for rates of growth of aggregate value added, capital input, and labor input and for the rate of aggregate technical change in Table 2—34. Value added grows rapidly throughout the period 1948—1973 with declines in 1949, 1954, 1958, and 1970 followed by sharp recoveries in 1950, 1955, 1959, and 1971—72.

The development of aggregate value added during the period 1973—1976 stands apart from earlier postwar experience. First, the magnitude of the decline in 1974 is without precedent during the period 1948—1973. Declines in 1949, 1954, 1958, and 1970 lasted for a single year and were less than 1 percent in magnitude. The decline in 1974 totaled 3.36 percent and continued into 1975 with a further drop of 0.42 percent. Taken together, these two years represent the most severe downturn of the U.S. economy since the 1930s. The recovery of aggregate value added, beginning with growth of 6.45 percent in 1976, is in line with earlier postwar recoveries, suggesting a permanent loss in growth from the downturn that lasted from 1973 to 1975.

Turning to the growth of capital input, we find that declines in value added during the period 1948—1976 were followed by reductions in the rate of growth of capital input one period later. This pattern continued into the period 1973—1976. The growth rate of capital input reached a peak at 5 percent in 1974, followed by growth rates of 3.02 percent in 1975 and 1.35 percent in 1976. The rate of growth of capital input in 1976 was the smallest over any year during the postwar period; however, the decline in the growth rate of capital input that took place from 1974 to 1976 is not out of line with the declines in value added that took place from 1973 to 1975.

The growth rate of capital input was positive throughout the period from 1948 to 1976. By comparison with the growth of capital input, the growth of labor input is considerably more uneven. Substantial declines in labor input coincided with declines in value added in 1949, 1954, 1958, and 1970; however, declines in labor input also took place in 1957, 1961, and 1971. The pattern of coincidence between declines in value added and in labor input was broken during the period 1973—1976. During this period, labor input declined in 1975, lagging behind the drop in value added that took place in 1974. The decline in labor input that took place in 1975 was modest in relation to the decline in value added in 1974 and 1975 and was not large by comparison with earlier postwar drops.

Finally, considering the pattern of technical change over the postwar period, we find that high rates of technical change are associated

Table 2-33.   Aggregate Input (constant prices of 1972), 1948–1976

Year	Value Added		Capital Input		Labor Input	
	Price	Quantity	Price	Quantity	Price	Quantity
1948	.567	433.460	.538	168.725	.331	468.078
1949	.559	431.110	.515	179.214	.331	448.406
1950	.573	473.440	.583	186.333	.351	464.477
1951	.613	506.596	.583	199.194	.400	486.236
1952	.629	519.333	.603	210.094	.402	496.286
1953	.626	544.783	.592	217.375	.419	507.090
1954	.643	543.214	.612	225.701	.432	489.307
1955	.647	583.907	.655	232.550	.446	504.689
1956	.658	603.884	.634	244.755	.471	513.323
1957	.669	617.530	.623	254.391	.498	511.784
1958	.689	615.540	.641	262.839	.519	493.368
1959	.690	658.980	.691	271.194	.528	511.672
1960	.711	671.549	.706	276.155	.536	527.260
1961	.714	688.859	.704	284.434	.564	516.297
1962	.726	725.385	.738	290.781	.583	535.047
1963	.726	760.729	.753	300.720	.604	539.000
1964	.738	801.465	.788	312.669	.625	551.639
1965	.761	847.455	.843	327.338	.648	569.814
1966	.788	897.541	.863	346.095	.687	594.149
1967	.806	918.834	.847	367.150	.714	601.364
1968	.834	960.071	.863	384.033	.765	613.160
1969	.885	989.125	.900	402.805	.816	628.092
1970	.908	988.608	.846	422.055	.866	624.632
1971	.949	1022.059	.906	435.294	.933	616.898
1972	1.000	1082.066	1.000	450.742	1.000	631.324
1973	1.088	1125.855	1.050	471.870	1.109	657.840
1974	1.183	1088.709	1.020	496.083	1.184	660.205
1975	1.277	1084.151	1.126	511.289	1.255	644.242
1976	1.353	1156.370	1.277	518.239	1.348	669.452

Table 2–34.   Growth in Aggregate Input and the Aggregate Rate of Technical Change, 1949–1976

Year	Value Added	Capital Input	Labor Input	Rate of Technical Change
1948–1949	-.0054	.0603	-.0429	-.0014
1949–1950	.0937	.0390	.0352	.0570
1950–1951	.0677	.0667	.0458	.0138
1951–1952	.0248	.0533	.0205	-.0081
1952–1953	.0478	.0341	.0215	.0215
1953–1954	-.0029	.0376	.0357	.0045
1954–1955	.0722	.0299	.0310	.0417
1955–1956	.0336	.0512	.0170	.0031
1956–1957	.0223	.0386	.0030	.0092
1957–1958	-.0032	.0327	-.0366	.0064
1958–1959	.0682	.0164	.0364	.0398
1959–1960	.0189	.0330	.0300	.0123
1960–1961	.0254	.0295	.0210	.0259
1961–1962	.0517	.0221	.0357	.0215
1962–1963	.0476	.0336	.0074	.0295
1963–1964	.0522	.0390	.0232	.0225
1964–1965	.0558	.0458	.0324	.0177
1965–1966	.0574	.0557	.0418	.0097
1966–1967	.0234	.0591	.0121	.0084
1967–1968	.0439	.0450	.0194	.0138
1968–1969	.0298	.0477	.0241	-.0040
1969–1970	-.0005	.0467	-.0055	.0162
1970–1971	.0353	.0309	.0125	.0283
1971–1972	.0571	.0349	.0231	.0291
1972–1973	.0397	.0458	.0411	-.0034
1973–1974	.0336	.0500	.0036	.0557
1974–1975	-.0042	.0302	-.0245	.0018
1975–1976	.0645	.0135	.0384	.0365

with recoveries in the growth of value added in 1950, 1955, 1959, 1971–72, and 1976. In addition, rapid growth in the level of technology took place during the period 1960–1966, which was also characterized by unusually rapid growth of value added, capital input, and labor input. The rate of technical change for 1973 was a negative 0.34 percent in 1973 at the peak of value added, repeating a pattern that emerged at the previous peak in 1969, when the rate of technical change was a negative 0.40 percent. The magnitude of the decline in the level of technology in 1974 was unprecedented in postwar experience, at 5.57 percent. The continuation of declines in the level of technology for three years—1973, 1974, 1975—was also a new development.

Contribution to Economic Growth

We can express the rate of growth of aggregate value added as a weighted average of rates of growth of aggregate capital and labor inputs plus the rate of technical change. Growth rates of capital and labor inputs are weighted by the corresponding shares of each input in aggregate value added. We define the contributions of capital and labor input to the growth of output as the weighted growth rates of these inputs. In Table 2–35 we present the rate of growth of aggregate value added, the average value share of capital input, the contributions of capital and labor input to the growth of output, and the rate of technical change. The average value share of labor input is equal to unity less the average value share of capital input.

The average value share of capital input is very stable over the period 1948–1976, ranging from 0.3763 for 1948 and 1949 to 0.4251 for 1965 and 1966. Accordingly, the cyclical pattern relating growth in value added to the contributions of capital and labor inputs is virtually identical to the pattern relating growth in value added to growth in capital and labor inputs that we have examined previously. Comparing the contributions of capital and labor inputs and the rate of technical change as sources of growth of value added, we find that the contribution of capital input is positive throughout the period from 1948 to 1976 and relatively steady. By contrast, the contribution of labor input and the rate of technical change are negative for eight and nine of the twenty-eight periods, respectively, and are relatively uneven.

The contribution of capital input provides the largest single contribution to the growth of output in thirteen of the twenty-eight periods from 1948 to 1976. The contribution of labor input provides the largest contribution in four of these periods. Finally, the rate of technical change provides the largest contribution in eleven periods.

Table 2–35. Contribution to Growth in Aggregate Output, 1949–1976

Year	Aggregate Value Added	Average Value Share of Capital Input	Capital Input	Labor Input	Rate of Technical Change
1948–1949	-.0054	.3763	.0227	-.0268	-.0014
1949–1950	.0937	.3914	.0152	.0214	.0570
1950–1951	.0677	.3869	.0258	.0281	.0138
1951–1952	.0248	.3811	.0203	.0127	-.0081
1952–1953	.0478	.3828	.0130	.0133	.0215
1953–1954	-.0029	.3864	.0145	-.0219	.0045
1954–1955	.0722	.3995	.0119	.0186	.0417
1955–1956	.0336	.3972	.0203	.0102	.0031
1956–1957	.0223	.3873	.0150	-.0018	.0092
1957–1958	-.0032	.3903	.0128	-.0223	.0064
1958–1959	.0682	.4015	.0066	.0218	.0398
1959–1960	.0189	.4072	.0134	.0178	-.0123
1960–1961	.0254	.4077	.0120	-.0124	.0259
1961–1962	.0517	.4075	.0090	.0211	.0215
1962–1963	.0476	.4089	.0137	.0044	.0295
1963–1964	.0522	.4133	.0161	.0136	.0225
1964–1965	.0558	.4221	.0194	.0187	.0177
1965–1966	.0574	.4251	.0237	.0240	.0097
1966–1967	.0234	.4213	.0249	.0070	-.0084
1967–1968	.0439	.4171	.0188	.0113	.0138
1968–1969	.0298	.4141	.0198	.0141	-.0040
1969–1970	-.0005	.4059	.0189	-.0033	-.0162
1970–1971	.0333	.4021	.0124	-.0074	.0283
1971–1972	.0571	.4116	.0144	.0136	.0291
1972–1973	.0397	.4105	.0188	.0243	-.0034
1973–1974	.0336	.3987	.0200	.0022	-.0557
1974–1975	-.0042	.4045	.0122	-.0146	-.0018
1975–1976	.0645	.4196	.0057	.0223	.0365

Comparing the contribution of capital input with that of labor input, we find that the contribution of capital input is greater in eighteen of the twenty-eight periods. The contribution of capital input is greater than the rate of technical change in seventeen of the twenty-eight periods. Finally, the contribution of labor input is greater than the rate of technical change in only eleven of the twenty-eight periods.

We conclude that the contribution of capital input is the most important source of growth in output, the rate of technical change is the next most important source, and the contribution of labor input is the least important. This conclusion suggests a useful perspective on the severe recession and partial recovery of the U.S. economy over the period 1973–1976. The steep decline in aggregate value added in 1974 was associated with the sharp reversal in growth in the level of technology that began in 1973, reached its nadir in 1974, and extended into 1975. This was followed by a collapse in the growth in capital input that prolonged the downturn and weakened the recovery. By contrast, the contribution of labor input followed a course from 1973 to 1976 that was little different from that of earlier postwar recessions. To examine the pattern of the contributions of capital input and the rate of technical change in more detail, we can decompose these sources of growth into their components.

Decomposition of Capital Input

First, we can decompose the growth of aggregate capital input into components associated with growth in aggregate capital stock and in the quality of capital stock. We can define the quality of capital stock as an index that transforms aggregate capital stock at the beginning of the period into aggregate capital input during the period:

$$K_t = Q_{K,t} \cdot A_{t-1},$$

where K_t is aggregate capital input, $Q_{K,t}$ is the quality of capital stock, and A_{t-1} is aggregate capital stock at the beginning of the period. Using the fact that the rate of growth of aggregate capital input can be expressed as the sum of the rate of growth of aggregate capital stock and the rate of growth of aggregate capital quality, we can express the contribution of aggregate capital input to the growth of output in terms of weighted rates of growth of aggregate capital stock and aggregate capital quality:

$$\bar{v}_K \left[\ln K_t - \ln K_{t-1} \right] = \bar{v}_K \left[\ln Q_{k,t} - \ln Q_{K,t-1} \right) + v_K \left[\ln A_{t-1} - \ln A_{t-2} \right].$$

We define the contributions of capital stock and its quality as the weighted growth rates of these sources of growth in output.

We present the quantity of capital stock for the private domestic sector of the U.S. economy for the period from 1948 to 1976 in Table 2–36. We also present an index of the quality of aggregate capital stock. In order to analyze the growth of capital input, we also provide rates of growth of capital stock and its quality. Finally, we show the contributions of capital stock and its quality to the growth of value added. We find that the growth of capital quality is an important source of growth of capital input, but it is dominated by the growth of capital stock. Both components of capital input have positive rates of growth throughout the period from 1948 to 1976. By comparison with the contribution of labor input and the rate of technical change, the contributions of both capital stock and its quality are relatively smooth.

We have observed that the growth of capital input declined in 1950, 1955, 1959, and 1971, following the declines in value added in 1949, 1954, 1958, and 1970. We find that the slowdown in the growth of capital input is associated with declines in rates of growth of both capital stock and its quality. This pattern persists into the downturn in the growth of capital input that took place in 1975 and 1976. In both years, the growth rates of capital quality and capital stock declined sharply. The growth rate of capital stock reached its postwar minimum in 1976, while the growth rate of the quality of capital stock in 1976 fell to a lower level than in any year in the postwar period except 1959. Since the average share of capital input in value added is very stable, these patterns carry over directly to the contributions of capital stock and its quality to the growth of value added.

Decomposition of Technical Change

We have decomposed the contribution of capital input, the most important source of growth in value added, into components associated with the contributions of capital stock and its quality. Following Jorgenson [47, 1980], we can express the translog index of aggregate technical change in terms of translog indexes of sectoral

Table 2–36.   Aggregate Capital Quality and Aggregate Capital Stock

Capital Input			Growth in Capital Input			Contributions to Growth in Capital Input	
Year	Capital Quality	Capital Stock	Year	Capital Quality	Capital Stock	Capital Quality	Capital Stock
1948	.714	1616.505	1948–1949	.0252	.0351	.0095	.0132
1949	.732	1674.299	1949–1950	.0170	.0220	.0066	.0086
1950	.745	1711.526	1950–1951	.0282	.0386	.0109	.0149
1951	.766	1778.854	1951–1952	.0210	.0322	.0080	.0123
1952	.782	1837.129	1952–1953	.0117	.0224	.0045	.0086
1953	.791	1878.696	1953–1954	.0143	.0233	.0055	.0090
1954	.803	1922.962	1954–1955	.0099	.0200	.0039	.0080
1955	.811	1961.864	1955–1956	.0186	.0325	.0074	.0129
1956	.826	2026.752	1956–1957	.0116	.0270	.0045	.0105
1957	.836	2082.280	1957–1958	.0113	.0214	.0044	.0083
1958	.845	2127.280	1958–1959	.0034	.0130	.0014	.0052
1959	.848	2155.192	1959–1960	.0094	.0236	.0038	.0096
1960	.856	2206.645	1960–1961	.0087	.0209	.0035	.0085
1961	.863	2253.193	1961–1962	.0051	.0170	.0021	.0069
1962	.868	2291.746	1962–1963	.0097	.0239	.0040	.0098
1963	.876	2347.279	1963–1964	.0124	.0266	.0051	.0110
1964	.887	2410.478	1964–1965	.0169	.0290	.0071	.0122
1965	.902	2481.358	1965–1966	.0197	.0360	.0084	.0153
1966	.920	2572.243	1966–1967	.0211	.0379	.0089	.0160
1967	.940	2671.667	1967–1968	.0148	.0301	.0062	.0126
1968	.954	2753.431	1968–1969	.0157	.0320	.0065	.0133
1969	.969	2843.081	1969–1970	.0148	.0319	.0060	.0129
1970	.983	2935.221	1970–1971	.0085	.0224	.0034	.0090
1971	.992	3001.629	1971–1972	.0081	.0267	.0034	.0110
1972	1.000	3082.935	1972–1973	.0114	.0344	.0047	.0141
1973	1.011	3190.930	1973–1974	.0113	.0387	.0045	.0154
1974	1.023	3316.938	1974–1975	.0064	.0238	.0026	.0096
1975	1.029	3396.910	1975–1976	.0036	.0099	.0015	.0042
1976	1.033	3430.874					

technical change in all sectors and changes in the distribution of value added and primary factors of production among sectors:

$$\bar{v}_t = \Sigma \frac{\bar{w}_j}{\bar{v}_V^j} \cdot \bar{v}_t^j + [\ln V_t - \ln V_{t-1}] - \Sigma \bar{w}_j [\ln V_{j,t} - \ln V_{j,t-1}]$$

$$+ \Sigma \bar{w}_j \cdot \frac{\bar{v}_K^j}{\bar{v}_V^j} \Sigma \bar{v}_{Kk}^j [\ln K_{kj,t} - \ln K_{kj,t-1}] - \bar{v}_K \cdot \Sigma \bar{v}_{Kk} [\ln K_{k,t} - \ln K_{k,t-1}]$$

$$+ \Sigma \bar{w}_j \cdot \frac{\bar{v}_L^j}{\bar{v}_V^j} \Sigma \bar{v}_{L\varrho}^j [\ln L_{\varrho j,t} - \ln L_{\varrho j,t-1}] - \bar{v}_L \cdot \Sigma \bar{v}_{L\varrho} [\ln L_{\varrho,t} - \ln L_{\varrho,t-1}]$$

where

$$\bar{v}_V^j = \tfrac{1}{2} [v_{V,t}^j + v_{V,t-1}^j] \, ,$$

$$\bar{w}_j = \tfrac{1}{2} [w_{j,t} + w_{j,t-1}] \, ,$$

and

$$v_V^j = \frac{p_V^j V_j}{p_j Z_j} \, ,$$

$$w_j = \frac{p_V^j V_j}{\Sigma p_V^j V_j} \, .$$

The first term in the expression we have given above for the aggregate rate of technical change is a weighted sum of sectoral rates of technical change with weights given by the ratio of the value of output in each sector to value added in that sector. The sum of these weights exceeds unity, since technical change in each sector contributes to the growth of sectoral output along the lines we indicated in Section X. It also contributes to the growth of sectoral output in other sectors through deliveries to demand for intermediate goods in these sectors. The second, third, and fourth terms in the expression for the aggregate rate of technical change correspond to differences between rates of growth of aggregate value added, capital input, and labor input and weighted averages of value added, capital input, and labor input in all sectors. These terms represent the contribution of redistributions of value added, capital input, and labor input among sectors to the aggregate rate of technical change. If the prices of value added are the same for all sectors or the quantities of value added in all sectors grow at the same rate, the term associated with the reallocation of value added among sectors is equal to zero. Similarly, the terms associated with reallocation of capital and labor inputs are equal to zero if the prices of these inputs are the same for all sectors or if the quantities of these inputs in all sectors grow at the same rate.[v]

We present data for all four components of the aggregate rate of technical change for the period 1948–1976 in Table 2–37. The sum of these four components is equal to the rate of aggregate technical change given in Table 2–34. The weighted sum of rates of sectoral technical change is by far the most important source of the rate of aggregate technical change over the period 1949–1976. The impact of the reallocation of value added among sectors is negative for twenty of the twenty-eight periods and exceeds the impact of the weighted sum of rates of sectoral technical change in only six of the twenty-eight periods. The impact of the reallocation of capital input on the rate of aggregate technical change is very small in every period and is negative for only five of the twenty-eight periods. The impact of the reallocation of labor input is small but not negligible and is negative for ten of the twenty-eight periods.

The period 1973–1976 stands out from the rest of the postwar period in a number of important respects. First, the decline in the aggregate level of technology in 1973 reflects the impact of a weighted sum of sectoral rates of technical change that was smaller than in any previous postwar period, partially offset by the largest positive contribution of the reallocation of value added during the period and smaller positive contributions of the reallocation of capital and labor inputs. The positive contributions of all three reallocation terms continued into 1974 as the weighted sum of sectoral rates of technical change dropped to 6.98 percent, a drop of more than 5 percent from the previous low in 1973. The negative weighted sum of rates of sectoral technical change continued into 1975, augmented by the negative impact of the reallocation of labor input and diminished by positive impacts of the reallocation of value added and capital input, resulting in a negative rate of aggregate technical change. Reallocations were negligible in 1976 relative to the sharp impact of a positive weighted sum of rates of sectoral technical change.

[v]For further information on reallocation, see Jorgenson [47, 1980], this volume.

Table 2–37.   Contribution to Growth in Aggregate Input and the Aggregate Rate of Technical Change, 1949–1976

Year	Sectoral Rates of Technical Change	Reallocation of: Value Added	Reallocation of: Capital Input	Reallocation of: Labor Input
1948–1949	.0144	-.0174	.0041	-.0025
1949–1950	.0606	-.0080	.0020	-.0024
1950–1951	.0035	-.0064	.0022	-.0016
1951–1952	-.0008	-.0086	.0024	-.0012
1952–1953	.0316	-.0102	.0005	-.0004
1953–1954	.0076	-.0009	.0003	-.0025
1954–1955	.0522	-.0117	.0006	.0006
1955–1956	.0024	-.0015	.0011	.0011
1956–1957	.0087	.0019	.0012	-.0025
1957–1958	.0059	.0041	.0003	-.0038
1958–1959	-.0405	-.0020	.0000	.0012
1959–1960	.0028	.0052	.0007	.0037
1960–1961	.0246	-.0004	.0001	.0008
1961–1962	.0241	-.0027	-.0004	.0005
1962–1963	.0301	-.0013	.0000	.0006
1963–1964	.0238	-.0018	.0001	.0007
1964–1965	.0183	-.0026	-.0009	.0011
1965–1966	.0096	-.0020	.0007	.0013
1966–1967	-.0059	-.0017	.0000	.0010
1967–1968	.0170	-.0039	.0001	-.0007
1968–1969	-.0036	-.0020	-.0000	.0014
1969–1970	.0134	.0001	.0001	-.0041
1970–1971	.0244	-.0002	.0013	.0033
1971–1972	.0281	-.0011	.0008	.0006
1972–1973	-.0197	.0132	.0016	.0026
1973–1974	-.0698	.0109	.0006	.0025
1974–1975	-.0016	.0047	.0013	-.0063
1975–1976	.0375	-.0019	.0005	.0004

XIII. CONCLUSION

In Section XII we analyzed the role of capital in the U.S. economy over the period 1948–1976 on the basis of annual data from an aggregate production account in current and constant prices. In this concluding section we summarize these data for the period as a whole and for the following seven subperiods: 1948–1953, 1953–1957, 1957–1960, 1960–1966, 1966–1969, 1969–1973, and 1973–1976. We present average rates of growth for the period 1948–1976 and for the seven subperiods in Table 2–38. The first part of this table provides data on growth in output and inputs from Table 2–34. The second part gives the contributions of capital and labor inputs to the growth of output from Table 2–35. The third part presents a decomposition of the growth of capital input and its contribution into components associated with capital quality and capital stock from Table 2–36. The final part contains a decomposition of the rate of aggregate technical change based on data from Table 2–37.

For the period 1948–1976 aggregate value added grows at 3.50 percent, while capital input grows at 4.01 percent, indicating that the ratio of capital to output has risen during the postwar period. By contrast labor input grows at only 1.28 percent while the rate of aggregate technical change is 1.14 percent. The average rate of growth of value added reached its maximum at 4.83 percent during the period 1960–1966 and grew at only 0.89 percent during the recession and partial recovery of 1973–1976. The growth of capital input was more even, exceeding 5 percent in 1948–1953 and 1966–1969 and falling to 3.12 percent in 1973–1976. The growth of labor input reached its maximum in the period 1960–1966 and fell to 0.58 percent in 1973–1976, which was above the minimum growth rate of 0.23 percent in the period 1953–1957. Finally, the rate of technical change was a maximum from 1960 to 1966, at 2.11 percent. During the following period, 1966–1969, the rate of technical change was almost negligible, at 0.04 percent. The rate of technical change recovered during 1969–1973, rising to 0.95 percent; finally the rate of technical change fell to a negative 0.70 percent during 1973–1976.

To provide additional perspective on the sources of U.S. economic growth, we next analyze the contributions of capital and labor inputs to the growth of value added. Since the average value share of capital input is very stable over the period 1948–1976, the movements of these contributions among subperiods largely parallel those of the rates of growth of capital and labor inputs. For the period

1948–1976, the contribution of capital input of 1.61 percent is the most important source of growth in aggregate value added. The rate of technical change is the next most important source at 1.14 percent, while the contribution of labor input is the third most important at 0.75 percent. For the seven subperiods, the contribution of capital input is the most important source of growth during five subperiods 1948–1953, 1953–1957, 1966–1969, 1969–1973, and 1973–1976. The rate of technical change is the most important source during two subperiods—1957–1960 and 1960–1966.

Our first conclusion is that the contribution of capital input is the most important source of growth in aggregate value added during the period 1948–1976. This conclusion is supported by our analysis of growth for the period as a whole, for the data by subperiods given in Table 2–38, and for the annual data presented in Table 2–35 in Section XII. In Section V we analyzed the decline in capital formation in the form of tangible assets in the private domestic sector that took place from 1972 to 1975. In Section XI we studied the decline in net saving as a proportion of national income over the postwar period. Finally, we described the decline in growth of capital input during the downturn form 1973–1976 in Section XII. An important key to revival of trends in U.S. economic growth established during the period 1948 to 1966 is to stimulate the growth of capital input through capital formation.

In order to analyze the contribution of capital input to growth in aggregate value added in more detail, we can decompose the rate of growth of capital input into components associated with capital stock and the quality of capital stock. For the period 1948–1976 growth in capital stock accounts for two-thirds of growth in capital input, while growth in the quality of capital stock accounts for one-third of growth in capital input. This quantitative relationship between growth in capital stock and growth in capital quality characterizes most of the postwar period. There is a gradual reduction in the role of growth in capital quality in 1970–1973 and again in 1973–1976. These general conclusions hold for the growth rates of capital stock and capital quality and for the contributions of these two components in the contribution of capital input.

The decline in the rate of growth of aggregate value added from 1960–1966 to 1966–1969 resulted from a dramatic fall in the rate of aggregate technical change during these two periods. The growth of capital input actually increased, while the growth of labor input declined only slightly. The revival of growth in the level of technology during 1969–1973 was offset by declines in the growth of capital and labor inputs, leaving the rate of growth of value added unchanged. The rate of technical change became negative during the recession period 1973–1976. Our second conclusion is that a restoration of the rapid growth that characterized the U.S. economy from 1948 to 1966 will also require accelerated growth in the level of technology. This conclusion is supported by the evidence for subperiods given in Table 2–38 and the data on annual rates of technical change presented in Table 2–35 in Section XII.

We find it useful to decompose the rate of aggregate technical change into four components associated with a weighted sum of rates of sectoral technical change and with reallocations of value added, capital input, and labor input. For the period 1948–1976 sectoral rates of technical change account for almost all of the rate of aggregate technical change. The reallocation of value added is a negative 0.16 percent, while reallocations of capital and labor inputs are a positive 0.08 percent and a negative 0.02 percent, respectively. The collapse in the rate of aggregate technical change after 1966 resulted from a drop in the weighted sum of sectoral rates of technical change from 2.17 percent in 1960–1966 to 0.25 percent in 1966–1969. During 1969–1973 sectoral rates of technical change recovered to 0.48 percent; the most important contribution to the revival of the rate of aggregate technical change between those two periods resulted from the change in the reallocation of value added from a negative 0.25 percent in 1966–1969 to a positive 0.30 percent in 1969–1973. During 1973–1976 the weighted sum of sectoral rates of technical change declined to a negative 1.13 percent. The overall conclusion of our analysis of the rate of aggregate technical change is that accelerated growth in the level of technology for the U.S. economy as a whole will require greatly accelerated growth in the levels of technology at the sectoral level. To provide a summary of our findings on the decline in U.S. economic growth during the past decade, we can observe that this decline took place in two steps. First, the rate of technical change essentially disappeared as a source of economic growth after 1966. This can be traced to a very sizable decline in rates of sectoral technical change that began in 1966–1969 and persisted through 1969–1973. Second, during the period 1973–1976 rates of sectoral technical change nosedived, beginning with a severe decline in 1973, followed by a catastrophic fall in 1974, and continuing with a further decline in 1975—all described in Section XII. The recovery beginning in 1976 was insufficient to restore levels of technology that had prevailed before 1973. We can also note that the recession of 1973 was greatly aggravated by a sizable drop in the rate of growth of capital input, associated with the diversion of capital formation from the acquisition of tangible assets in the private

Table 2-38. Summary

	1948-1976	1948-1953	1953-1957	1957-1960	1960-1966	1966-1969	1969-1973	1973-1976
Growth (Table 2-34)								
Growth in value added	0.0350	0.0457	0.0313	0.0279	0.0483	0.0324	0.0324	0.0089
Growth in capital input	0.0401	0.0507	0.0393	0.0274	0.0376	0.0506	0.0396	0.0312
Growth in labor input	0.0128	0.0160	0.0023	0.0099	0.0199	0.0185	0.0116	0.0058
Rate of technical change	0.0114	0.0166	0.0146	0.0113	0.0211	0.0004	0.0095	-0.0070
Contribution (Table 2-35)								
Contribution of capital input	0.0161	0.0194	0.0154	0.0109	0.0156	0.0211	0.0161	0.0126
Contribution of labor input	0.0075	0.0097	0.0013	0.0057	0.0116	0.0108	0.0068	0.0033
Capital (Table 2-36)								
Growth in capital quality	0.0132	0.0206	0.0136	0.0080	0.0121	0.0172	0.0107	0.0071
Growth in capital stock	0.0269	0.0301	0.0257	0.0193	0.0255	0.0334	0.0288	0.0242
Contribution of capital quality	0.0053	0.0079	0.0053	0.0032	0.0050	0.0072	0.0044	0.0028
Contribution of capital stock	0.0108	0.0115	0.0101	0.0077	0.0106	0.0139	0.0118	0.0097

Table 2–38. continued

	1948– 1976	1948– 1953	1953– 1957	1957– 1960	1960– 1966	1966– 1969	1969– 1973	1973– 1976
Reallocation (Table 2–37)								
Sectoral rates of technical change	0.0124	0.0219	0.0177	0.0145	0.0217	0.0025	0.0048	−0.0113
Reallocation of value added	−0.0016	−0.0075	−0.0030	−0.0010	−0.0016	−0.0025	0.0030	0.0046
Reallocation of capital input	0.0008	0.0022	0.0008	−0.0001	0.0002	0.0001	0.0010	0.0008
Reallocation of labor input	−0.0002	−0.000	−0.0008	−0.0021	0.0008	0.0004	0.0006	−0.0011

domestic sector of the U.S. economy to acquisition of claims on governments and the rest of the world described in Section V.

The prospects for future U.S. economic growth depend on the revival of growth in capital input that characterized the period from 1948 to 1973. The economic policies to stimulate capital formation adopted during the first half of the 1960s were highly successful in stimulating growth of capital input. New policy measures to stimulate capital formation can be designed on the basis of a wide range of past experience with incentives to invest. Future growth prospects will also depend on the resuscitation of improvements in the level of technology that characterized the period from 1948 to 1966. The fall in the rate of technical change after 1966 was severely aggravated by the further decline that began in 1973. Measures to stimulate the development and implementation of new technology at the level of individual industrial sectors must be designed and adopted. This task has no precedent in U.S. economic policy and poses the central problem facing policymakers of the 1980s.

Appendix A

CAPITAL STOCK

(constant prices of 1972), 1948–1976

Capital Stock (*constant prices of 1972*), 1948–1976

Year	Capital Stock for Agricultural Production			Capital Stock for Agricultural Services		
	Price	*Quantity*	*Value*	*Price*	*Quantity*	*Value*
1948	.602	99.167	59.697	.648	3.860	2.502
1949	.569	104.223	59.298	.626	4.815	3.014
1950	.596	105.244	62.746	.645	4.588	2.958
1951	.661	107.322	70.992	.703	4.068	2.859
1952	.660	110.298	72.829	.667	3.721	2.483
1953	.641	112.718	72.210	.638	3.692	2.356
1954	.640	112.585	71.999	.632	3.595	2.273
1955	.635	113.958	72.311	.619	3.445	2.134
1956	.645	114.755	74.027	.635	3.920	2.489
1957	.668	111.636	74.563	.665	4.176	2.777
1958	.680	114.063	77.556	.674	4.546	3.064
1959	.672	115.813	77.802	.664	5.090	3.378
1960	.676	114.780	77.636	.673	4.955	3.336
1961	.678	115.858	78.554	.672	5.420	3.644
1962	.688	115.513	79.468	.678	5.476	3.715
1963	.687	117.838	80.910	.681	6.055	4.123
1964	.691	121.671	84.055	.685	5.981	4.097
1965	.718	120.764	86.724	.700	6.009	4.205
1966	.759	122.016	92.598	.737	6.334	4.667
1967	.768	128.352	98.568	.759	6.685	5.073
1968	.805	126.793	102.124	.798	7.248	5.787
1969	.853	130.565	111.436	.845	7.319	6.184
1970	.892	138.345	123.444	.891	7.926	7.063
1971	.930	138.907	129.120	.936	8.656	8.100
1972	1.000	139.905	139.905	1.000	8.816	8.816
1973	1.165	131.023	152.674	1.079	8.376	9.039
1974	1.276	135.252	172.528	1.204	8.624	10.380
1975	1.357	137.277	186.289	1.333	8.776	11.700
1976	1.409	141.675	199.662	1.384	8.807	12.190

Year	Capital Stock for Metal Mining			Capital Stock for Coal Mining		
	Price	Quantity	Value	Price	Quantity	Value
1948	.496	1.292	.641	.490	3.205	1.572
1949	.513	1.495	.767	.505	3.771	1.903
1950	.546	1.528	.834	.543	3.714	2.018
1951	.569	1.616	.920	.568	4.346	2.468
1952	.591	1.773	1.048	.590	4.293	2.533
1953	.610	1.707	1.042	.614	4.060	2.492
1954	.604	1.701	1.027	.608	3.885	2.362
1955	.639	1.941	1.240	.643	3.703	2.382
1956	.639	2.374	1.518	.648	3.438	2.227
1957	.659	2.285	1.506	.670	3.268	2.188
1958	.663	2.552	1.693	.677	3.418	2.313
1959	.680	2.869	1.951	.692	3.387	2.345
1960	.681	3.711	2.528	.692	3.412	2.362
1961	.686	4.549	3.120	.693	3.396	2.354
1962	.691	4.881	3.374	.698	3.575	2.494
1963	.700	5.129	3.590	.705	3.652	2.575
1964	.687	5.280	3.627	.692	3.685	2.551
1965	.703	5.202	3.655	.712	4.369	3.111
1966	.725	5.152	3.735	.731	4.257	3.112
1967	.750	4.981	3.737	.758	4.501	3.412
1968	.782	4.812	3.762	.789	4.415	3.484
1969	.837	5.179	4.336	.842	4.175	3.516
1970	.888	5.293	4.702	.894	4.042	3.613
1971	.937	5.185	4.860	.950	4.647	4.413
1972	1.000	5.048	5.048	1.000	4.761	4.761
1973	1.060	4.891	5.186	1.055	4.913	5.185
1974	1.217	4.842	5.893	1.198	5.211	6.242
1975	1.409	4.779	6.735	1.418	5.464	7.746
1976	1.445	4.589	6.633	1.508	5.771	8.700

Year	Capital Stock for Crude Petroleum and Natural Gas			Capital Stock for Nonmetallic Mining and Quarrying		
	Price	Quantity	Value	Price	Quantity	Value
1948	.509	33.305	16.966	.492	1.012	.498
1949	.525	33.191	17.416	.517	1.047	.542
1950	.536	33.160	17.788	.558	1.219	.681
1951	.562	33.520	18.831	.584	1.364	.796
1952	.587	33.790	19.847	.609	1.589	.968
1953	.606	35.317	21.411	.633	1.835	1.161
1954	.600	35.846	21.509	.629	2.034	1.280
1955	.631	35.899	22.667	.676	2.269	1.534
1956	.633	37.217	23.571	.677	2.559	1.733
1957	.658	37.664	24.782	.698	2.716	1.896
1958	.671	38.057	25.518	.707	3.018	2.133
1959	.689	38.348	26.429	.738	3.236	2.387
1960	.684	38.553	26.361	.728	3.441	2.506
1961	.687	39.322	27.015	.722	3.484	2.515
1962	.696	40.891	28.441	.726	3.806	2.764
1963	.704	40.833	28.727	.717	4.140	2.969
1964	.689	40.455	27.867	.699	4.482	3.132
1965	.706	41.214	29.115	.712	4.945	3.523
1966	.726	42.255	30.673	.735	5.290	3.887
1967	.753	42.397	31.932	.759	6.033	4.580
1968	.787	43.037	33.879	.798	6.302	5.027
1969	.836	43.061	35.992	.847	6.182	5.237
1970	.888	44.574	39.584	.893	6.328	5.649
1971	.945	43.550	41.166	.936	6.498	6.081
1972	1.000	42.141	42.141	1.000	6.834	6.834
1973	1.046	42.539	44.482	1.064	6.785	7.220
1974	1.189	41.827	49.722	1.243	7.421	9.223
1975	1.416	42.490	60.174	1.519	7.388	11.221
1976	1.641	43.550	71.447	1.455	7.223	10.508

Year	Capital Stock for Contract Construction			Capital Stock for Food and Kindred Products		
	Price	Quantity	Value	Price	Quantity	Value
1948	.495	8.006	3.961	.544	26.737	14.543
1949	.511	8.648	4.419	.524	27.734	14.523
1950	.542	9.262	5.021	.547	27.780	15.201
1951	.571	10.801	6.172	.619	28.203	17.444
1952	.604	12.172	7.355	.624	28.741	17.934
1953	.620	13.546	8.403	.619	28.634	17.720
1954	.611	14.155	8.650	.622	28.037	17.450
1955	.637	15.152	9.650	.609	27.912	16.998
1956	.645	16.299	10.505	.653	28.473	18.599
1957	.665	17.597	11.701	.676	28.378	19.194
1958	.677	19.223	13.006	.682	27.996	19.095
1959	.695	19.764	13.734	.676	28.694	19.403
1960	.690	21.762	15.013	.689	29.110	20.059
1961	.690	23.152	15.963	.690	29.224	20.178
1962	.692	25.670	17.752	.698	29.325	20.470
1963	.698	27.081	18.913	.711	29.935	21.279
1964	.691	28.902	19.965	.719	30.299	21.780
1965	.706	30.542	21.555	.749	31.086	23.271
1966	.730	33.428	24.393	.769	30.909	23.771
1967	.756	35.433	26.780	.795	30.810	24.480
1968	.800	38.781	31.008	.823	31.434	25.873
1969	.843	39.772	33.529	.871	32.533	28.348
1970	.890	42.127	37.477	.908	33.386	30.303
1971	.950	44.161	41.938	.958	34.251	32.827
1972	1.000	45.617	45.617	1.000	35.166	35.166
1973	1.056	49.564	52.364	1.094	34.392	37.625
1974	1.197	50.777	60.774	1.248	34.983	43.644
1975	1.377	50.552	69.626	1.408	34.508	48.583
1976	1.409	50.127	70.621	1.462	35.172	51.424

Year	Capital Stock for Tobacco Manufacturers			Capital Stock for Textile Mill Products		
	Price	*Quantity*	*Value*	*Price*	*Quantity*	*Value*
1948	.667	3.021	2.017	.593	8.104	4.802
1949	.678	3.175	2.154	.573	9.114	5.226
1950	.678	3.186	2.161	.594	9.479	5.633
1951	.693	3.240	2.245	.688	9.813	6.754
1952	.698	3.355	2.343	.666	10.480	6.981
1953	.706	3.371	2.380	.651	10.196	6.637
1954	.701	3.441	2.413	.649	10.204	6.623
1955	.702	3.515	2.467	.649	10.030	6.511
1956	.715	3.375	2.412	.700	10.026	7.014
1957	.704	3.413	2.402	.731	10.056	7.347
1958	.722	3.392	2.450	.726	9.669	7.023
1959	.738	3.364	2.484	.743	9.330	6.929
1960	.757	3.499	2.649	.742	9.186	6.819
1961	.778	3.635	2.828	.751	9.278	6.969
1962	.773	3.855	2.980	.760	9.399	7.142
1963	.755	3.889	2.957	.777	9.561	7.429
1964	.743	3.892	2.892	.786	9.569	7.517
1965	.771	3.930	3.030	.787	9.884	7.776
1966	.810	3.816	3.091	.797	10.364	8.264
1967	.830	3.640	3.022	.826	11.401	9.423
1968	.851	3.708	3.157	.846	11.899	10.070
1969	.874	3.591	3.139	.875	12.473	10.919
1970	.908	3.755	3.410	.902	12.972	11.699
1971	.959	3.580	3.434	.955	13.305	12.707
1972	1.000	3.554	3.554	1.000	13.591	13.591
1973	1.032	3.908	4.034	1.123	13.877	15.578
1974	1.158	4.035	4.672	1.156	13.676	15.810
1975	1.305	4.505	5.878	1.347	14.455	19.467
1976	1.376	4.630	6.372	1.403	13.862	19.453

Year	Capital Stock for Apparel and Other Fabricated Textile Products			Capital Stock for Paper and Allied Products		
	Price	Quantity	Value	Price	Quantity	Value
1948	.653	3.437	2.243	.493	7.355	3.628
1949	.619	3.569	2.209	.488	8.061	3.933
1950	.636	3.585	2.280	.502	8.348	4.189
1951	.725	3.933	2.851	.576	8.756	5.044
1952	.680	3.878	2.638	.578	9.446	5.455
1953	.678	3.902	2.644	.581	9.877	5.743
1954	.666	3.903	2.598	.586	9.928	5.819
1955	.666	4.103	2.733	.592	10.729	6.351
1956	.698	4.234	2.955	.650	11.391	7.403
1957	.713	4.130	2.945	.683	12.358	8.436
1958	.702	4.016	2.819	.690	13.185	9.098
1959	.718	4.030	2.894	.698	13.589	9.483
1960	.714	4.127	2.948	.707	13.785	9.748
1961	.714	4.131	2.951	.707	14.120	9.989
1962	.719	4.136	2.975	.715	14.409	10.296
1963	.729	4.501	3.282	.728	14.989	10.907
1964	.736	4.660	3.431	.740	15.410	11.406
1965	.740	4.850	3.591	.751	15.858	11.917
1966	.757	5.128	3.882	.782	16.768	13.105
1967	.776	5.526	4.286	.810	18.030	14.606
1968	.801	5.805	4.650	.835	19.203	16.029
1969	.826	6.425	5.309	.876	19.632	17.198
1970	.856	6.608	5.654	.921	20.513	18.884
1971	.894	6.770	6.050	.961	21.755	20.908
1972	1.000	7.237	7.237	1.000	21.923	21.923
1973	.995	7.520	7.483	1.047	22.063	23.104
1974	1.061	7.830	8.310	1.190	22.604	26.891
1975	1.212	7.363	8.920	1.405	23.657	33.229
1976	1.260	7.105	8.948	1.472	23.953	35.248

	Capital Stock for Printing and Publishing			Capital Stock for Chemicals and Allied Products		
Year	Price	Quantity	Value	Price	Quantity	Value
1948	.475	9.854	4.678	.527	16.557	8.727
1949	.479	9.873	4.726	.514	16.499	8.485
1950	.495	9.763	4.831	.531	16.773	8.914
1951	.555	9.806	5.442	.606	17.320	10.489
1952	.570	9.897	5.643	.609	18.362	11.177
1953	.575	9.820	5.645	.618	18.738	11.587
1954	.578	9.638	5.575	.623	19.213	11.968
1955	.575	9.645	5.544	.618	20.271	12.527
1956	.629	9.754	6.135	.674	20.835	14.053
1957	.655	10.054	6.584	.708	21.244	15.049
1958	.657	9.988	6.562	.715	21.918	15.664
1959	.662	10.011	6.623	.723	22.172	16.031
1960	.670	9.880	6.616	.734	22.780	16.718
1961	.673	10.021	6.748	.735	23.820	17.499
1962	.681	9.882	6.734	.737	25.160	18.541
1963	.693	9.938	6.884	.750	25.360	19.013
1964	.709	10.255	7.269	.763	25.742	19.629
1965	.723	10.639	7.689	.772	26.734	20.652
1966	.752	11.301	8.496	.801	29.017	23.249
1967	.784	12.066	9.458	.827	31.748	26.256
1968	.812	12.670	10.289	.845	33.994	28.713
1969	.864	12.962	11.202	.878	35.646	31.301
1970	.916	13.609	12.465	.923	37.092	34.244
1971	.962	13.694	13.167	.963	38.668	37.244
1972	1.000	13.959	13.959	1.000	39.225	39.225
1973	1.042	13.984	14.574	1.036	39.216	40.612
1974	1.199	14.412	17.274	1.222	39.950	48.838
1975	1.368	14.291	19.545	1.425	42.296	60.253
1976	1.404	13.953	19.587	1.479	43.034	63.633

Year	Capital Stock for Petroleum and Coal Products			Capital Stock for Rubber and Miscellaneous Plastic Products		
	Price	Quantity	Value	Price	Quantity	Value
1948	.481	17.569	8.442	.517	2.927	1.513
1949	.478	18.461	8.824	.519	3.130	1.624
1950	.495	18.598	9.211	.571	3.014	1.721
1951	.556	17.880	9.950	.632	2.926	1.848
1952	.574	17.729	10.180	.639	3.220	2.058
1953	.574	17.718	10.164	.645	3.730	2.407
1954	.576	19.467	11.218	.645	3.898	2.514
1955	.561	21.127	11.844	.677	3.856	2.609
1956	.619	20.633	12.781	.724	4.034	2.919
1957	.650	21.165	13.760	.749	4.257	3.189
1958	.644	21.413	13.780	.751	4.401	3.305
1959	.636	21.155	13.461	.737	4.878	3.595
1960	.642	20.519	13.163	.747	5.050	3.771
1961	.637	20.613	13.140	.744	5.220	3.886
1962	.641	21.307	13.651	.755	5.366	4.051
1963	.652	21.574	14.060	.762	5.726	4.363
1964	.664	21.614	14.360	.770	5.952	4.585
1965	.688	22.423	15.423	.784	6.245	4.896
1966	.719	22.975	16.512	.814	6.699	5.453
1967	.750	25.678	19.264	.839	7.307	6.131
1968	.785	28.795	22.597	.858	7.871	6.749
1969	.840	28.823	24.213	.895	8.452	7.562
1970	.901	27.320	24.602	.939	9.265	8.696
1971	.951	29.343	27.911	.971	9.797	9.514
1972	1.000	30.543	30.543	1.000	10.160	10.160
1973	1.101	28.996	31.933	1.035	10.895	11.278
1974	1.239	28.854	35.762	1.211	11.896	14.410
1975	1.391	29.836	41.489	1.399	12.331	17.248
1976	1.429	30.438	43.484	1.444	12.142	17.531

Year	Capital Stock for Leather and Leather Products			Capital Stock for Lumber and Wood Products, except Furniture		
	Price	Quantity	Value	Price	Quantity	Value
1948	.608	1.733	1.053	.486	5.628	2.737
1949	.590	1.844	1.088	.479	6.215	2.978
1950	.651	1.834	1.194	.511	6.280	3.211
1951	.751	1.794	1.347	.567	6.537	3.707
1952	.606	1.892	1.147	.576	7.040	4.055
1953	.630	1.852	1.167	.582	6.850	3.985
1954	.590	1.864	1.099	.580	6.899	4.001
1955	.588	1.849	1.088	.587	7.075	4.152
1956	.640	1.815	1.161	.631	7.228	4.562
1957	.646	1.813	1.171	.643	7.688	4.941
1958	.654	1.795	1.173	.649	7.067	4.589
1959	.687	1.697	1.166	.662	7.026	4.655
1960	.668	1.656	1.106	.652	7.091	4.622
1961	.694	1.687	1.170	.652	7.134	4.650
1962	.682	1.650	1.125	.650	8.302	5.394
1963	.663	1.653	1.096	.667	7.749	5.169
1964	.684	1.670	1.142	.684	7.305	4.997
1965	.739	1.631	1.205	.700	7.330	5.129
1966	.748	1.623	1.213	.726	7.551	5.480
1967	.739	1.693	1.251	.758	7.990	6.055
1968	.781	1.799	1.406	.830	7.994	6.638
1969	.810	1.859	1.505	.841	7.769	6.530
1970	.829	1.858	1.540	.868	8.661	7.518
1971	.890	1.868	1.662	.951	9.141	8.695
1972	1.000	1.788	1.788	1.000	9.359	9.359
1973	1.036	1.607	1.664	1.088	9.528	10.367
1974	1.057	1.704	1.802	1.126	9.889	11.137
1975	1.196	1.738	2.077	1.294	10.794	13.969
1976	1.247	1.630	2.033	1.356	10.531	14.275

Year	Capital Stock for Furniture and Fixtures			Capital Stock for Stone, Clay, and Glass Products		
	Price	Quantity	Value	Price	Quantity	Value
1948	.492	2.288	1.125	.468	6.776	3.171
1949	.485	2.265	1.098	.476	7.178	3.413
1950	.521	2.272	1.184	.490	7.303	3.575
1951	.584	2.455	1.434	.551	7.580	4.173
1952	.580	2.521	1.462	.561	8.150	4.574
1953	.592	2.516	1.489	.570	8.264	4.712
1954	.589	2.502	1.473	.576	8.548	4.925
1955	.599	2.572	1.541	.577	8.808	5.079
1956	.655	2.696	1.766	.635	9.455	6.002
1957	.673	2.762	1.858	.666	10.493	6.988
1958	.674	2.774	1.869	.677	11.300	7.650
1959	.684	2.724	1.862	.679	11.661	7.922
1960	.681	2.822	1.921	.685	11.943	8.183
1961	.681	2.849	1.941	.683	12.282	8.394
1962	.688	2.815	1.936	.692	12.587	8.708
1963	.697	2.921	2.038	.703	12.564	8.833
1964	.707	2.957	2.091	.717	12.679	9.090
1965	.720	3.034	2.183	.730	12.986	9.478
1966	.747	3.168	2.365	.759	13.466	10.226
1967	.776	3.441	2.670	.788	14.157	11.162
1968	.827	3.575	2.957	.818	14.470	11.840
1969	.850	3.655	3.106	.862	14.446	12.454
1970	.889	3.965	3.526	.915	14.667	13.417
1971	.960	4.115	3.951	.963	14.876	14.321
1972	1.000	4.120	4.120	1.000	14.900	14.900
1973	1.069	4.379	4.682	1.033	15.358	15.866
1974	1.179	4.696	5.536	1.153	16.130	18.598
1975	1.335	5.106	6.816	1.336	16.702	22.311
1976	1.381	4.796	6.622	1.386	16.636	23.060

Year	Capital Stock for Primary Metal Industries			Capital Stock for Fabricated Metal Industries		
	Price	Quantity	Value	Price	Quantity	Value
1948	.471	32.436	15.263	.442	13.058	5.774
1949	.472	33.243	15.704	.457	13.254	6.057
1950	.486	33.718	16.396	.478	12.919	6.175
1951	.565	33.343	18.832	.535	13.637	7.293
1952	.572	35.081	20.067	.548	15.043	8.238
1953	.579	36.842	21.340	.566	15.201	8.607
1954	.579	38.283	22.160	.574	16.182	9.289
1955	.581	37.654	21.896	.585	16.253	9.504
1956	.657	38.370	25.199	.645	17.150	11.060
1957	.676	40.774	27.564	.680	17.552	11.936
1958	.672	42.986	28.879	.688	17.913	12.326
1959	.677	43.570	29.486	.697	17.698	12.328
1960	.675	42.864	28.917	.702	17.838	12.528
1961	.677	43.880	29.715	.704	18.031	12.689
1962	.681	43.186	29.389	.709	18.041	12.788
1963	.693	42.684	29.592	.719	18.329	13.181
1964	.714	42.645	30.466	.730	18.870	13.774
1965	.729	43.490	31.715	.743	19.669	14.615
1966	.757	44.796	33.906	.775	21.061	16.313
1967	.789	46.569	36.765	.798	22.244	17.760
1968	.813	48.923	39.770	.824	23.225	19.141
1969	.874	50.259	43.908	.867	24.593	21.316
1970	.919	50.411	46.333	.920	25.343	23.322
1971	.966	51.439	49.672	.967	25.969	25.117
1972	1.000	50.901	50.901	1.000	26.002	26.002
1973	1.074	50.696	54.424	1.030	26.494	27.299
1974	1.235	49.684	61.361	1.216	28.146	34.225
1975	1.425	50.556	72.022	1.392	29.751	41.404
1976	1.482	51.962	77.002	1.444	29.445	42.512

Year	Capital Stock for Machinery, except Electrical			Capital Stock for Electrical Machinery, Equipment, and Supplies		
	Price	Quantity	Value	Price	Quantity	Value
1948	.490	11.465	5.613	.516	8.796	4.543
1949	.497	11.941	5.939	.521	8.657	4.506
1950	.515	11.689	6.019	.533	8.312	4.432
1951	.580	12.126	7.032	.603	9.113	5.497
1952	.598	13.790	8.247	.614	11.323	6.949
1953	.610	14.434	8.808	.628	12.629	7.933
1954	.611	15.336	9.366	.628	13.264	8.333
1955	.614	15.327	9.415	.643	12.633	8.119
1956	.678	16.008	10.847	.698	13.132	9.168
1957	.713	16.973	12.108	.720	14.530	10.463
1958	.717	17.419	12.487	.714	14.724	10.511
1959	.727	17.175	12.485	.726	14.232	10.325
1960	.735	17.843	13.114	.728	14.843	10.803
1961	.733	17.875	13.107	.725	15.608	11.315
1962	.738	17.679	13.055	.729	16.199	11.807
1963	.750	18.605	13.953	.738	17.272	12.747
1964	.763	18.980	14.482	.748	17.745	13.281
1965	.779	20.275	15.794	.762	17.878	13.621
1966	.813	22.340	18.163	.792	19.439	15.400
1967	.837	24.974	20.907	.816	22.382	18.259
1968	.854	27.070	23.129	.839	24.160	20.280
1969	.899	28.601	25.715	.884	25.161	22.237
1970	.940	31.007	29.146	.929	26.604	24.712
1971	.971	32.108	31.171	.968	27.124	26.245
1972	1.000	31.336	31.336	1.000	26.618	26.618
1973	1.033	32.370	33.429	1.029	27.210	27.997
1974	1.180	36.077	42.554	1.214	29.814	36.191
1975	1.341	39.242	52.635	1.367	30.440	41.619
1976	1.391	38.510	53.551	1.423	29.016	41.283

Year	Capital Stock for Transportation Eqpt. & Ordnance, ex. Motor Vehicles			Capital Stock for Motor Vehicles and Equipment		
	Price	Quantity	Value	Price	Quantity	Value
1948	.479	9.874	4.734	.489	7.538	3.685
1949	.487	9.051	4.410	.500	7.723	3.859
1950	.501	8.532	4.276	.514	7.162	3.683
1951	.573	8.235	4.715	.578	7.675	4.435
1952	.585	9.904	5.796	.594	8.622	5.123
1953	.603	11.034	6.659	.602	9.189	5.531
1954	.608	11.218	6.826	.608	9.504	5.777
1955	.615	11.458	7.051	.610	9.499	5.795
1956	.680	10.978	7.467	.674	10.698	7.208
1957	.717	11.961	8.578	.703	11.470	8.059
1958	.718	11.956	8.587	.711	11.246	7.990
1959	.724	11.638	8.420	.714	10.504	7.499
1960	.717	11.371	8.155	.726	10.538	7.650
1961	.711	10.813	7.692	.723	10.274	7.428
1962	.715	10.470	7.490	.729	9.919	7.226
1963	.723	10.856	7.855	.734	10.197	7.488
1964	.740	11.366	8.415	.746	10.484	7.816
1965	.758	11.459	8.681	.755	11.529	8.705
1966	.786	11.935	9.383	.783	12.752	9.984
1967	.815	14.597	11.897	.808	13.765	11.116
1968	.841	18.082	15.209	.834	13.924	11.616
1969	.885	19.674	17.407	.870	14.732	12.822
1970	.932	20.951	19.518	.922	15.122	13.945
1971	.968	19.542	18.926	.965	14.988	14.470
1972	1.000	18.448	18.448	1.000	14.714	14.714
1973	1.021	18.209	18.589	1.017	16.243	16.526
1974	1.182	18.187	21.493	1.151	18.045	20.227
1975	1.325	17.954	23.781	1.307	18.542	24.227
1976	1.382	18.067	24.976	1.359	17.462	23.726

Year	Capital Stock for Professional Photographic Equipment and Watches			Capital Stock for Miscellaneous Manufacturing Industries		
	Price	Quantity	Value	Price	Quantity	Value
1948	.515	1.558	.803	.534	3.115	1.662
1949	.516	1.623	.838	.535	2.871	1.536
1950	.530	1.695	.899	.560	2.747	1.537
1951	.596	1.899	1.131	.625	2.763	1.728
1952	.619	2.259	1.397	.635	2.891	1.836
1953	.629	2.387	1.501	.643	2.803	1.802
1954	.633	2.515	1.592	.647	2.859	1.850
1955	.626	2.504	1.567	.649	2.901	1.882
1956	.678	2.954	2.003	.684	3.087	2.111
1957	.708	3.259	2.308	.709	3.243	2.300
1958	.717	3.439	2.464	.728	3.738	2.721
1959	.724	3.464	2.507	.731	3.140	2.295
1960	.734	3.613	2.652	.739	3.214	2.375
1961	.734	3.854	2.830	.741	3.293	2.439
1962	.734	3.886	2.852	.748	3.159	2.362
1963	.740	4.098	3.031	.754	3.263	2.459
1964	.749	4.279	3.207	.764	3.317	2.535
1965	.765	4.313	3.300	.780	3.404	2.657
1966	.796	4.647	3.699	.808	3.499	2.826
1967	.833	5.330	4.439	.833	4.026	3.355
1968	.852	5.799	4.941	.857	4.447	3.813
1969	.891	6.128	5.458	.895	4.961	4.441
1970	.933	6.485	6.051	.930	5.058	4.702
1971	.967	6.841	6.618	.968	4.734	4.584
1972	1.000	6.970	6.970	1.000	4.819	4.819
1973	1.038	7.238	7.514	1.049	5.123	5.371
1974	1.221	7.986	9.751	1.234	5.712	7.051
1975	1.378	8.534	11.762	1.389	6.053	8.407
1976	1.422	8.342	11.863	1.435	4.964	7.124

Year	Capital Stock for Railroads and Rail Express Service			Capital Stock for Street Railways, Bus Lines, and Taxicabs		
	Price	Quantity	Value	Price	Quantity	Value
1948	.523	28.211	14.752	.503	3.778	1.902
1949	.536	27.661	14.833	.533	4.195	2.234
1950	.564	27.249	15.382	.575	4.301	2.473
1951	.582	26.850	15.623	.586	4.173	2.446
1952	.621	26.766	16.633	.623	4.173	2.599
1953	.643	27.006	17.352	.667	4.146	2.765
1954	.625	27.920	17.443	.646	4.047	2.616
1955	.669	26.843	17.967	.686	3.852	2.641
1956	.667	26.684	17.797	.699	3.692	2.582
1957	.686	26.432	18.138	.721	3.518	2.536
1958	.709	26.163	18.559	.740	3.391	2.508
1959	.738	25.342	18.700	.773	3.348	2.589
1960	.726	25.180	18.278	.787	3.241	2.551
1961	.720	24.870	17.901	.761	3.184	2.423
1962	.722	24.225	17.495	.741	3.151	2.336
1963	.730	23.777	17.360	.760	3.121	2.373
1964	.704	23.629	16.642	.723	3.067	2.217
1965	.730	23.810	17.371	.765	3.065	2.345
1966	.754	23.911	18.020	.758	3.033	2.299
1967	.767	24.415	18.725	.782	3.069	2.401
1968	.792	24.675	19.548	.804	3.111	2.502
1969	.833	24.176	20.135	.848	3.153	2.673
1970	.886	24.257	21.488	.894	3.128	2.795
1971	.962	24.027	23.121	.958	3.129	2.997
1972	1.000	23.867	23.867	1.000	3.117	3.117
1973	1.019	23.474	23.910	1.035	3.075	3.182
1974	1.149	23.284	26.750	1.177	3.023	3.560
1975	1.327	24.351	32.308	1.421	3.149	4.474
1976	1.560	24.925	38.893	1.326	3.192	4.231

	Capital Stock for Trucking Services and Warehousing			Capital Stock for Water Transportation		
Year	Price	Quantity	Value	Price	Quantity	Value
1948	.456	6.005	2.740	.647	3.507	2.269
1949	.476	6.515	3.101	.668	3.384	2.260
1950	.512	6.725	3.446	.718	3.233	2.322
1951	.523	7.672	4.012	.692	3.078	2.131
1952	.570	8.056	4.596	.726	3.093	2.244
1953	.611	8.061	4.922	.727	3.169	2.302
1954	.597	8.136	4.860	.694	3.194	2.216
1955	.633	7.936	5.022	.715	3.034	2.170
1956	.626	8.653	5.418	.674	2.979	2.008
1957	.649	8.844	5.743	.685	2.986	2.045
1958	.666	9.492	6.320	.704	3.069	2.160
1959	.681	9.522	6.489	.729	3.223	2.349
1960	.691	10.826	7.483	.732	3.335	2.440
1961	.679	10.761	7.305	.715	3.407	2.438
1962	.684	10.573	7.230	.705	3.421	2.413
1963	.701	11.314	7.928	.722	3.470	2.506
1964	.680	11.546	7.851	.686	3.494	2.398
1965	.702	11.852	8.317	.707	3.519	2.489
1966	.721	13.192	9.510	.716	3.630	2.599
1967	.742	14.245	10.567	.738	3.686	2.719
1968	.769	14.510	11.159	.764	3.730	2.850
1969	.817	16.296	13.320	.802	3.936	3.157
1970	.878	17.300	15.192	.853	4.013	3.425
1971	.942	17.872	16.831	.931	4.152	3.864
1972	1.000	18.968	18.968	1.000	4.162	4.162
1973	1.056	17.796	18.790	1.011	4.177	4.224
1974	1.218	22.318	27.186	1.089	4.294	4.675
1975	1.406	23.931	33.654	1.259	4.727	5.954
1976	1.397	24.567	34.309	1.442	5.097	7.349

Year	Capital Stock for Air Transportation			Capital Stock for Pipelines, except Natural Gas		
	Price	*Quantity*	*Value*	*Price*	*Quantity*	*Value*
1948	.565	1.100	.621	.548	2.689	1.474
1949	.600	1.298	.779	.578	2.596	1.500
1950	.603	1.545	.932	.629	2.537	1.596
1951	.615	1.574	.969	.622	2.554	1.588
1952	.843	1.594	1.343	.634	2.520	1.598
1953	.684	1.884	1.289	.674	2.593	1.748
1954	.656	2.312	1.516	.672	2.740	1.840
1955	.696	2.595	1.807	.719	2.632	1.893
1956	.686	2.613	1.793	.722	2.551	1.843
1957	.709	2.980	2.113	.761	2.441	1.858
1958	.736	3.655	2.691	.792	2.349	1.860
1959	.760	4.118	3.128	.822	2.252	1.852
1960	.749	5.401	4.044	.815	2.188	1.783
1961	.741	6.416	4.758	.816	2.086	1.702
1962	.739	7.392	5.465	.805	1.996	1.606
1963	.746	8.040	5.996	.784	2.023	1.587
1964	.713	8.042	5.737	.743	2.144	1.593
1965	.729	9.192	6.704	.765	2.156	1.650
1966	.747	10.087	7.536	.781	2.092	1.634
1967	.764	11.821	9.026	.799	2.061	1.646
1968	.792	14.802	11.729	.825	2.154	1.776
1969	.833	18.646	15.534	.851	2.196	1.870
1970	.881	20.411	17.991	.885	2.190	1.937
1971	.956	22.749	21.757	.949	2.264	2.149
1972	1.000	21.613	21.613	1.000	2.433	2.433
1973	1.032	20.929	21.598	1.031	2.368	2.442
1974	1.167	21.832	25.480	1.142	2.409	2.752
1975	1.354	21.930	29.690	1.382	2.430	3.358
1976	1.406	21.426	30.128	1.461	2.395	3.498

Year	Capital Stock for Transportation Services			Capital Stock for Telephone & Telegraph & Misc. Comm. Services		
	Price	Quantity	Value	Price	Quantity	Value
1948	.540	1.610	.869	.521	11.614	6.056
1949	.547	1.455	.796	.545	11.877	6.475
1950	.584	1.427	.833	.562	11.901	6.684
1951	.595	1.414	.840	.585	11.761	6.882
1952	.623	1.384	.863	.586	11.785	6.902
1953	.634	1.364	.864	.592	12.643	7.489
1954	.625	1.580	.987	.609	13.080	7.961
1955	.653	1.442	.941	.633	13.506	8.545
1956	.647	1.495	.967	.641	14.165	9.085
1957	.654	1.515	.991	.665	14.449	9.602
1958	.672	1.544	1.038	.671	15.463	10.379
1959	.691	1.547	1.069	.684	15.980	10.930
1960	.707	1.679	1.188	.698	16.245	11.338
1961	.697	1.641	1.144	.705	17.068	12.029
1962	.701	1.606	1.126	.692	18.093	12.526
1963	.707	1.653	1.169	.696	19.223	13.388
1964	.695	1.725	1.200	.707	21.150	14.955
1965	.721	1.791	1.291	.712	22.895	16.300
1966	.747	1.936	1.445	.729	25.318	18.460
1967	.771	1.999	1.541	.755	27.722	20.938
1968	.800	2.438	1.951	.803	29.899	24.004
1969	.839	2.380	1.997	.842	32.014	26.967
1970	.877	2.386	2.091	.885	34.358	30.403
1971	.940	2.301	2.163	.940	37.890	35.602
1972	1.000	2.272	2.272	1.000	42.093	42.093
1973	1.081	2.299	2.487	1.055	46.978	49.566
1974	1.335	2.487	3.319	1.134	52.896	59.999
1975	1.206	2.903	3.501	1.262	58.467	73.808
1976	1.374	3.185	4.377	1.363	62.619	85.365

Year	Capital Stock for Radio Broadcasting and Television			Capital Stock for Electric Utilities		
	Price	Quantity	Value	Price	Quantity	Value
1948	.593	.297	.176	.450	22.251	10.023
1949	.604	.343	.207	.479	22.820	10.931
1950	.594	.391	.232	.519	23.108	12.002
1951	.627	.421	.264	.558	23.526	13.128
1952	.623	.473	.295	.553	23.600	13.050
1953	.621	.438	.272	.588	24.817	14.596
1954	.621	.531	.330	.600	25.692	15.403
1955	.627	.706	.443	.631	25.849	16.306
1956	.652	.926	.604	.681	26.179	17.816
1957	.695	1.024	.711	.737	26.540	19.558
1958	.696	1.227	.854	.751	26.924	20.211
1959	.699	1.315	.920	.778	27.620	21.478
1960	.696	1.388	.966	.786	28.095	22.092
1961	.696	1.603	1.115	.767	28.365	21.758
1962	.700	1.597	1.118	.756	28.704	21.708
1963	.701	1.679	1.176	.747	29.081	21.717
1964	.710	2.053	1.458	.756	29.700	22.449
1965	.717	2.233	1.602	.766	30.131	23.071
1966	.732	2.521	1.846	.779	30.903	24.068
1967	.761	2.731	2.078	.807	32.031	25.833
1968	.804	3.209	2.581	.842	33.846	28.511
1969	.848	3.388	2.874	.870	35.364	30.773
1970	.890	3.552	3.161	.915	37.549	34.343
1971	.946	3.527	3.337	.967	40.160	38.832
1972	1.000	3.621	3.621	1.000	43.279	43.279
1973	1.057	3.813	4.029	1.066	46.502	49.582
1974	1.191	4.038	4.807	1.215	50.117	60.915
1975	1.332	4.211	5.610	1.435	52.773	75.720
1976	1.365	4.283	5.847	1.531	54.252	83.075

Year	Capital Stock for Gas Utilities			Capital Stock for Water Supply and Sanitary Services		
	Price	Quantity	Value	Price	Quantity	Value
1948	.447	12.741	5.692	.488	1.604	.783
1949	.464	12.403	5.761	.491	1.876	.920
1950	.510	12.961	6.604	.526	2.166	1.139
1951	.547	13.114	7.179	.536	2.282	1.223
1952	.547	13.032	7.130	.556	2.337	1.300
1953	.575	14.057	8.083	.573	2.741	1.571
1954	.586	13.277	7.784	.578	2.645	1.530
1955	.618	12.059	7.447	.611	2.524	1.542
1956	.662	11.236	7.435	.616	2.421	1.491
1957	.704	11.399	8.029	.633	2.664	1.687
1958	.719	11.901	8.557	.656	2.910	1.909
1959	.748	12.332	9.229	.679	3.143	2.133
1960	.757	12.464	9.439	.681	3.400	2.317
1961	.745	12.682	9.442	.685	3.346	2.292
1962	.733	12.623	9.257	.687	3.596	2.470
1963	.726	12.462	9.046	.694	3.735	2.594
1964	.734	12.477	9.158	.680	3.897	2.648
1965	.749	12.517	9.373	.703	4.080	2.870
1966	.765	12.537	9.589	.721	4.324	3.117
1967	.792	12.642	10.012	.742	4.616	3.424
1968	.823	12.709	10.456	.769	4.880	3.751
1969	.854	12.813	10.944	.809	5.074	4.103
1970	.905	13.600	12.310	.873	5.588	4.876
1971	.961	14.061	13.516	.936	5.980	5.595
1972	1.000	15.485	15.485	1.000	5.922	5.922
1973	1.074	15.725	16.883	1.048	6.257	6.554
1974	1.235	16.850	20.812	1.195	6.299	7.529
1975	1.450	18.095	26.241	1.443	6.953	10.034
1976	1.542	18.737	28.900	1.483	7.335	10.879

	Capital Stock for Wholesale Trade			Capital Stock for Retail Trade		
Year	Price	Quantity	Value	Price	Quantity	Value
1948	.601	24.943	14.992	.567	56.748	32.172
1949	.587	28.695	16.857	.565	63.222	35.696
1950	.602	30.343	18.259	.582	66.654	38.813
1951	.658	34.625	22.789	.632	74.165	46.843
1952	.661	36.888	24.389	.641	76.793	49.243
1953	.659	38.086	25.109	.641	78.757	50.505
1954	.660	37.999	25.076	.644	81.103	52.233
1955	.668	39.286	26.245	.655	83.646	54.821
1956	.695	43.191	29.997	.683	89.031	60.806
1957	.721	45.040	32.476	.706	91.313	64.489
1958	.723	45.567	32.967	.709	91.027	64.552
1959	.730	46.466	33.905	.714	91.507	65.365
1960	.736	49.513	36.427	.718	93.315	66.979
1961	.733	52.127	38.225	.718	95.470	68.545
1962	.737	52.309	38.564	.721	95.604	68.914
1963	.737	55.094	40.628	.722	99.388	71.801
1964	.745	58.176	43.315	.728	103.368	75.282
1965	.761	63.268	48.142	.739	104.929	77.584
1966	.783	67.011	52.468	.763	111.190	84.840
1967	.804	74.679	60.022	.789	117.679	92.868
1968	.837	77.179	64.607	.823	119.600	98.457
1969	.876	83.296	72.986	.866	125.807	108.980
1970	.917	88.381	81.076	.914	131.075	119.797
1971	.962	90.794	87.370	.959	134.808	129.264
1972	1.000	94.093	94.093	1.000	140.884	140.884
1973	1.078	97.760	105.371	1.056	146.204	154.364
1974	1.246	102.422	127.629	1.209	152.862	184.584
1975	1.382	105.285	145.503	1.337	155.863	208.372
1976	1.432	104.133	149.149	1.378	153.453	211.463

Year	Capital Stock for Finance, Insurance, and Real Estate			Capital Stock for Services, excluding Private Households, Institutions		
	Price	Quantity	Value	Price	Quantity	Value
1948	.470	513.296	241.019	.512	49.912	25.557
1949	.461	518.048	239.059	.514	49.099	25.216
1950	.501	520.536	260.569	.530	48.495	25.720
1951	.536	525.653	281.725	.573	48.420	27.766
1952	.553	531.436	293.828	.587	47.738	28.024
1953	.556	530.477	295.112	.591	47.461	28.043
1954	.564	536.013	302.259	.593	47.260	28.045
1955	.575	540.818	310.964	.612	46.806	28.630
1956	.585	545.479	319.119	.641	48.399	31.025
1957	.598	555.263	332.034	.668	49.922	33.363
1958	.603	560.848	338.318	.665	51.469	34.208
1959	.608	562.463	342.165	.669	52.607	35.181
1960	.618	567.871	350.983	.672	56.461	37.926
1961	.621	572.289	355.564	.676	57.782	39.060
1962	.629	578.108	363.369	.680	60.682	41.264
1963	.635	584.665	371.277	.682	63.993	43.661
1964	.643	591.981	380.930	.690	67.435	46.539
1965	.674	599.770	404.479	.705	72.293	50.945
1966	.709	609.504	432.313	.730	76.758	56.013
1967	.747	610.689	456.458	.758	81.267	61.637
1968	.791	619.637	490.381	.798	83.414	66.543
1969	.840	623.686	524.052	.849	88.025	74.747
1970	.892	629.154	560.926	.901	93.325	84.097
1971	.947	635.532	601.739	.955	97.459	93.043
1972	1.000	652.426	652.426	1.000	99.372	99.372
1973	1.063	684.733	727.626	1.066	102.867	109.658
1974	1.178	698.908	823.626	1.221	107.900	131.717
1975	1.260	707.515	891.466	1.350	110.028	148.544
1976	1.314	711.570	935.072	1.396	111.041	154.963

Year	Capital Stock for Private Households			Capital Stock for Institutions		
	Price	Quantity	Value	Price	Quantity	Value
1948	.454	472.240	214.556	.353	54.282	19.148
1949	.463	500.947	231.835	.351	55.195	19.390
1950	.491	527.741	259.046	.373	56.515	21.094
1951	.535	566.695	303.212	.415	58.807	24.411
1952	.553	593.394	328.036	.430	60.804	26.146
1953	.562	615.710	345.791	.439	62.427	27.388
1954	.565	640.804	362.220	.445	64.126	28.527
1955	.583	665.907	388.537	.462	66.335	30.655
1956	.611	701.722	428.410	.500	68.450	34.195
1957	.632	728.269	459.918	.529	70.766	37.434
1958	.640	749.686	480.080	.538	73.357	39.454
1959	.657	765.975	502.972	.556	76.171	42.371
1960	.669	792.678	530.552	.570	79.178	45.161
1961	.681	814.812	555.221	.584	82.462	48.136
1962	.696	831.621	578.394	.601	85.905	51.596
1963	.706	854.209	603.124	.619	89.955	55.671
1964	.721	882.519	636.546	.639	93.931	60.043
1965	.738	913.668	674.385	.663	98.494	65.341
1966	.761	948.975	721.818	.696	103.338	71.953
1967	.790	982.390	775.725	.731	108.169	79.071
1968	.829	1011.414	838.676	.770	111.983	86.213
1969	.882	1048.215	924.502	.823	115.988	95.476
1970	.916	1082.089	990.887	.885	119.579	105.814
1971	.960	1106.924	1062.879	.945	122.492	115.804
1972	1.000	1148.984	1148.984	1.000	121.887	121.887
1973	1.068	1207.036	1289.699	1.070	121.542	129.994
1974	1.159	1266.074	1467.549	1.227	120.842	148.219
1975	1.255	1299.353	1630.603	1.371	119.567	163.925
1976	1.339	1323.306	1771.266	1.429	117.969	168.631

Appendix B

RATES OF RETURN AND CAPITAL INPUT FOR INDUSTRIAL PRODUCTION,

1948-1976

Rates of Return and Capital Input for Agricultural Production, 1948–1976

Year	Rate of Return		Capital Quality	Capital Input		
	Nominal	Own		Price	Quantity	Value
1948	.117	.039	.973	.040	96.479	3.847
1949	.004	.025	.980	.060	102.135	6.125
1950	.118	.031	.974	.060	102.554	6.183
1951	.095	.025	.987	.018	105.956	1.890
1952	.043	.010	.977	.058	107.780	6.205
1953	.012	.004	.990	.055	111.571	6.119
1954	.026	.016	.993	.042	111.848	4.730
1955	.027	.012	.989	.049	112.681	5.576
1956	.027	.009	.988	.035	113.427	3.948
1957	.034	.013	.987	.029	110.217	3.221
1958	.029	.018	.968	.036	110.389	3.921
1959	.024	.011	.965	.056	111.728	6.282
1960	.034	.022	.974	.051	111.786	5.687
1961	.032	.021	.969	.052	112.295	5.854
1962	.044	.032	.974	.054	112.471	6.028
1963	.031	.020	.970	.055	114.254	6.329
1964	.038	.024	.976	.056	118.779	6.634
1965	.092	.043	.987	.072	119.169	8.521
1966	.107	.055	1.002	.074	122.300	9.034
1967	.089	.034	.992	.093	127.343	11.803
1968	.095	.036	1.018	.075	129.103	9.688
1969	.106	.046	1.014	.077	132.357	10.172
1970	.084	.024	.994	.073	137.577	9.976
1971	.081	.027	1.002	.078	139.235	10.811
1972	.136	.072	1.000	.100	139.905	14.007
1973	.184	.126	.966	.073	126.603	9.195
1974	.163	.061	.961	.144	129.997	18.748
1975	.197	.097	.955	.242	131.108	31.700
1976	.106	.062	.961	.170	136.139	23.116

Rates of Return and Capital Input for Agricultural Services, 1948–1976

Year	Rate of Return		Capital Quality	Capital Input		
	Nominal	Own		Price	Quantity	Value
1948	.080	-.001	.623	.023	2.404	.056
1949	-.097	-.007	1.787	.001	8.604	.009
1950	.048	-.000	.898	.015	4.118	.062
1951	.143	.006	1.075	.031	4.372	.136
1952	-.017	.005	1.078	.015	4.012	.059
1953	.044	.004	.998	.015	3.685	.054
1954	.002	.007	.993	.027	3.572	.097
1955	-.007	.015	.944	.028	3.252	.090
1956	.029	.016	.936	.036	3.670	.130
1957	.056	.019	.930	.045	3.885	.173
1958	.050	.025	.913	.052	4.152	.218
1959	.002	.021	.899	.035	4.575	.161
1960	.034	.028	.951	.050	4.712	.234
1961	.042	.045	.939	.061	5.087	.309
1962	.080	.066	.955	.083	5.232	.434
1963	.054	.058	.952	.075	5.762	.432
1964	.069	.062	.969	.081	5.796	.467
1965	.098	.067	.961	.084	5.777	.486
1966	.135	.088	.986	.105	6.244	.656
1967	.070	.049	.991	.073	6.627	.483
1968	.113	.065	1.001	.093	7.253	.677
1969	.119	.062	1.014	.098	7.419	.727
1970	.120	.066	.994	.106	7.878	.834
1971	.120	.074	.986	.116	8.533	.986
1972	.141	.073	1.000	.127	8.816	1.123
1973	.125	.046	1.032	.109	8.645	.940
1974	.190	.059	1.037	.152	8.947	1.359
1975	.157	.038	1.040	.138	9.132	1.258
1976	.101	.070	1.045	.164	9.201	1.510

Rates of Return and Capital Input for Metal Mining, 1948–1976

Year	Rate of Return		Capital Quality	Capital Input		
	Nominal	Own		Price	Quantity	Value
1948	.159	.050	.887	.179	1.147	.205
1949	.048	.044	.903	.114	1.351	.154
1950	.092	.060	.931	.137	1.423	.196
1951	.222	.068	.932	.309	1.506	.466
1952	.051	.037	.928	.113	1.646	.186
1953	.076	.064	.949	.150	1.621	.243
1954	.050	.050	.940	.158	1.599	.253
1955	.096	.087	.930	.143	1.804	.259
1956	.201	.083	.943	.304	2.239	.681
1957	.100	.071	.940	.174	2.148	.373
1958	.026	.034	.947	.111	2.416	.269
1959	.046	.037	.960	.118	2.755	.325
1960	.036	.039	1.005	.125	3.728	.464
1961	.023	.022	1.029	.105	4.680	.493
1962	.040	.038	1.020	.107	4.979	.530
1963	.061	.044	1.022	.128	5.245	.673
1964	.082	.058	1.020	.172	5.386	.925
1965	.092	.073	1.008	.144	5.243	.755
1966	.118	.082	1.015	.156	5.229	.809
1967	.096	.058	1.007	.136	5.015	.684
1968	.075	.046	1.007	.113	4.847	.548
1969	.103	.030	1.018	.124	5.271	.656
1970	.073	.021	1.023	.104	5.416	.563
1971	.060	.010	1.015	.099	5.265	.523
1972	.059	.021	1.000	.103	5.048	.518
1973	.099	.027	.961	.192	4.701	.902
1974	.207	.056	.982	.297	4.753	1.410
1975	.179	.025	.951	.195	4.547	.887
1976	.041	.006	.956	.230	4.386	1.007

Rates of Return and Capital Input for Coal Mining, 1948–1976

Year	Rate of Return		Capital	Capital Input		
	Nominal	Own	Quality	Price	Quantity	Value
1948	.343	.312	.930	.265	2.979	.788
1949	.107	.090	.949	.114	3.579	.408
1950	.198	.128	.962	.149	3.575	.534
1951	.123	.077	.962	.114	4.181	.478
1952	.085	.046	.949	.093	4.074	.378
1953	.053	.016	.969	.077	3.933	.303
1954	.008	.015	.947	.072	3.679	.263
1955	.114	.052	.926	.105	3.431	.362
1956	.126	.120	.916	.167	3.148	.526
1957	.164	.133	.909	.182	2.970	.541
1958	.099	.090	.897	.145	3.067	.444
1959	.080	.056	.920	.113	3.115	.351
1960	.046	.049	.933	.107	3.183	.339
1961	.069	.070	.942	.125	3.200	.399
1962	.061	.055	.958	.109	3.427	.372
1963	.075	.067	.976	.122	3.563	.434
1964	.096	.116	.985	.160	3.631	.583
1965	.095	.070	1.023	.122	4.469	.544
1966	.114	.088	1.028	.141	4.377	.617
1967	.092	.056	1.045	.116	4.701	.544
1968	.063	.022	1.037	.095	4.580	.433
1969	.070	.002	1.018	.078	4.251	.332
1970	.216	.155	.987	.255	3.992	1.017
1971	.132	.070	1.011	.169	4.698	.793
1972	.126	.073	1.000	.170	4.761	.811
1973	.150	.094	.996	.202	4.895	.990
1974	.490	.351	1.017	.617	5.298	3.270
1975	.477	.291	1.015	.616	5.545	3.417
1976	.260	.198	1.011	.547	5.837	3.190

Rates of Return and Capital Input for Crude Petroleum and Natural Gas, 1948–1976

Year	Rate of Return Nominal	Rate of Return Own	Capital Quality	Capital Input Price	Capital Input Quantity	Capital Input Value
1948	.169	.096	1.001	.109	33.332	3.647
1949	.080	.069	.995	.077	33.016	2.550
1950	.103	.076	.996	.102	33.020	3.375
1951	.157	.082	.996	.130	33.382	4.352
1952	.110	.073	.991	.101	33.497	3.394
1953	.104	.083	.990	.108	34.973	3.770
1954	.088	.092	.986	.123	35.350	4.350
1955	.130	.104	.982	.112	35.268	3.959
1956	.141	.104	.988	.159	36.783	5.833
1957	.130	.090	.985	.123	37.085	4.565
1958	.084	.076	.980	.109	37.278	4.050
1959	.091	.075	.981	.110	37.611	4.135
1960	.072	.076	.985	.127	37.964	4.818
1961	.076	.073	.985	.119	38.716	4.604
1962	.081	.068	.981	.114	40.103	4.557
1963	.081	.068	.983	.122	40.120	4.900
1964	.067	.074	.983	.133	39.769	5.308
1965	.110	.079	.986	.135	40.626	5.421
1966	.107	.073	.985	.137	41.627	5.693
1967	.129	.088	.996	.149	42.236	6.293
1968	.124	.079	.993	.142	42.727	6.089
1969	.128	.064	1.004	.135	43.254	5.861
1970	.124	.058	1.011	.141	45.084	6.366
1971	.109	.047	1.001	.130	43.612	5.648
1972	.110	.055	1.000	.152	42.141	6.423
1973	.137	.069	.990	.211	42.117	8.868
1974	.268	.133	1.001	.302	41.863	12.637
1975	.256	.098	1.001	.257	42.513	10.919
1976	.233	.130	1.001	.322	43.575	14.010

Rates of Return and Capital Input for Nonmetallic Mining and Quarrying, 1948–1976

Year	Rate of Return		Capital	Capital Input		
	Nominal	Own	Quality	Price	Quantity	Value
1948	.325	.297	.897	.292	.908	.265
1949	.314	.286	.916	.287	.959	.275
1950	.318	.251	.930	.285	1.134	.323
1951	.285	.243	.931	.289	1.270	.366
1952	.243	.201	.927	.247	1.473	.363
1953	.176	.141	.936	.207	1.718	.355
1954	.155	.160	.930	.222	1.892	.421
1955	.250	.174	.926	.237	2.102	.498
1956	.141	.140	.932	.214	2.385	.512
1957	.146	.117	.927	.185	2.519	.466
1958	.072	.061	.906	.151	2.735	.414
1959	.116	.073	.951	.145	3.079	.448
1960	.075	.090	.955	.157	3.285	.515
1961	.070	.079	.945	.147	3.294	.484
1962	.094	.088	.945	.155	3.598	.559
1963	.088	.102	.955	.171	3.956	.676
1964	.095	.121	.969	.177	4.344	.770
1965	.096	.078	.978	.140	4.837	.677
1966	.124	.093	.984	.152	5.205	.791
1967	.122	.090	1.005	.154	6.065	.936
1968	.106	.056	1.004	.135	6.330	.853
1969	.115	.053	.991	.141	6.125	.861
1970	.078	.024	.988	.118	6.255	.737
1971	.082	.034	.995	.134	6.467	.867
1972	.102	.034	1.000	.141	6.834	.963
1973	.146	.082	.991	.205	6.723	1.381
1974	.240	.065	1.036	.212	7.687	1.627
1975	.258	.037	1.032	.208	7.627	1.585
1976	-.020	.023	1.036	.199	7.480	1.487

Rates of Return and Capital Input for Contract Construction, 1948–1976

Year	Rate of Return		Capital Quality	Capital Input		
	Nominal	Own		Price	Quantity	Value
1948	.323	.264	1.033	.204	8.274	1.686
1949	.271	.248	1.045	.193	9.040	1.746
1950	.241	.179	1.049	.175	9.718	1.703
1951	.214	.158	1.047	.170	11.311	1.919
1952	.192	.143	1.046	.161	12.735	2.046
1953	.128	.102	1.025	.139	14.174	1.975
1954	.107	.118	1.017	.152	14.503	2.211
1955	.144	.103	1.033	.138	15.417	2.129
1956	.152	.136	1.023	.169	16.836	2.838
1957	.177	.149	1.028	.178	18.001	3.208
1958	.127	.112	1.030	.151	19.756	2.986
1959	.133	.103	1.026	.147	20.351	3.001
1960	.065	.077	1.009	.126	22.321	2.805
1961	.078	.076	.976	.124	23.356	2.902
1962	.096	.086	.976	.129	25.044	3.241
1963	.092	.083	.983	.128	26.434	3.373
1964	.085	.096	.985	.135	28.399	3.843
1965	.133	.109	.983	.147	30.098	4.410
1966	.139	.105	.993	.146	32.874	4.795
1967	.139	.103	.978	.148	35.175	5.221
1968	.145	.087	.988	.141	37.933	5.337
1969	.139	.086	.991	.146	39.309	5.733
1970	.129	.075	.991	.143	41.766	5.985
1971	.132	.064	1.000	.145	43.768	6.364
1972	.117	.064	.991	.151	45.617	6.878
1973	.108	.051	1.004	.143	49.114	7.022
1974	.177	.042	.998	.144	50.981	7.362
1975	.210	.061	.996	.186	50.445	9.394
1976	.069	.046		.186	49.910	9.295

Rates of Return and Capital Input for Food and Kindred Products, 1948–1976

Year	Rate of Return		Capital	Capital Input		
	Nominal	Own	Quality	Price	Quantity	Value
1948	.153	.086	.833	.110	22.284	2.454
1949	.030	.069	.840	.102	23.284	2.377
1950	.094	.050	.859	.096	23.863	2.291
1951	.148	.028	.852	.087	24.593	2.142
1952	.059	.048	.874	.104	25.108	2.621
1953	.036	.047	.877	.106	25.109	2.668
1954	.049	.045	.883	.105	24.756	2.590
1955	.052	.074	.890	.128	24.848	3.186
1956	.107	.041	.903	.106	25.708	2.728
1957	.076	.045	.911	.113	25.844	2.910
1958	.073	.064	.921	.132	25.771	3.396
1959	.068	.079	.919	.146	26.383	3.849
1960	.071	.055	.923	.127	26.872	3.410
1961	.067	.066	.927	.138	27.078	3.731
1962	.079	.073	.937	.140	27.476	3.859
1963	.098	.082	.944	.153	28.246	4.323
1964	.099	.090	.949	.159	28.743	4.583
1965	.111	.071	.951	.147	29.557	4.346
1966	.130	.100	.959	.181	29.640	5.352
1967	.117	.089	.984	.170	30.302	5.149
1968	.111	.078	.997	.170	31.344	5.323
1969	.127	.068	.995	.167	32.372	5.402
1970	.131	.089	.994	.194	33.198	6.427
1971	.132	.077	.998	.186	34.188	6.354
1972	.098	.055	1.000	.164	35.166	5.782
1973	.122	.028	1.033	.147	35.531	5.221
1974	.176	.034	1.058	.170	37.003	6.304
1975	.263	.126	1.095	.312	37.798	11.777
1976	.115	.079	1.093	.293	38.436	11.257

Rates of Return and Capital Input for Tobacco Manufacturers, 1948–1976

Year	Rate of Return		Capital Quality	Capital Input		
	Nominal	Own		Price	Quantity	Value
1948	.062	.053	1.002	.073	3.029	.220
1949	.092	.076	1.004	.089	3.189	.284
1950	.044	.041	1.005	.076	3.201	.245
1951	.062	.041	1.008	.088	3.266	.289
1952	.058	.051	1.011	.092	3.391	.311
1953	.089	.077	1.012	.121	3.410	.412
1954	.071	.076	1.012	.112	3.482	.391
1955	.066	.065	1.011	.111	3.554	.395
1956	.091	.070	1.009	.123	3.406	.420
1957	.069	.043	1.003	.139	3.423	.476
1958	.117	.091	1.003	.157	3.404	.534
1959	.136	.112	1.007	.184	3.387	.624
1960	.130	.105	1.008	.179	3.528	.633
1961	.127	.099	1.008	.184	3.665	.673
1962	.109	.117	1.009	.191	3.890	.744
1963	.115	.138	1.009	.216	3.923	.849
1964	.113	.129	1.007	.199	3.918	.780
1965	.134	.098	1.009	.171	3.965	.679
1966	.154	.102	1.011	.183	3.856	.707
1967	.152	.127	1.011	.219	3.681	.805
1968	.140	.114	1.011	.227	3.747	.849
1969	.131	.155	1.010	.275	3.627	.998
1970	.232	.190	1.002	.320	3.761	1.205
1971	.259	.203	.999	.357	3.577	1.276
1972	.225	.183	1.000	.346	3.554	1.228
1973	.194	.161	1.001	.311	3.913	1.215
1974	.240	.119	.998	.271	4.028	1.092
1975	.268	.141	.994	.342	4.480	1.534
1976	.184	.129	.995	.381	4.605	1.753

Rates of Return and Capital Input for Textile Mill Products, 1948–1976

Year	Rate of Return		Capital Quality	Price	Capital Input	
	Nominal	Own			Quantity	Value
1948	.279	.200	.910	.226	7.375	1.670
1949	.079	.097	.897	.124	8.171	1.014
1950	.074	.026	.919	.106	8.713	.920
1951	.258	.106	.930	.157	9.128	1.430
1952	-.010	.053	.979	.095	10.256	.975
1953	.016	.026	.961	.079	9.799	.770
1954	.006	.007	.955	.057	9.743	.556
1955	.035	.038	.958	.089	9.612	.852
1956	.103	.037	.971	.090	9.736	.873
1957	.062	.025	.982	.078	9.875	.767
1958	.024	.029	.988	.080	9.558	.763
1959	.067	.050	.997	.105	9.298	.974
1960	.044	.047	.946	.118	8.690	1.024
1961	.047	.040	.971	.107	9.006	.966
1962	.060	.053	.969	.122	9.106	1.112
1963	.073	.057	.974	.127	9.315	1.184
1964	.093	.084	.981	.158	9.385	1.480
1965	.105	.103	.980	.182	9.683	1.761
1966	.122	.112	.989	.185	10.253	1.900
1967	.113	.077	.989	.150	11.275	1.691
1968	.099	.075	.989	.165	11.766	1.944
1969	.106	.074	.994	.160	12.393	1.985
1970	.100	.070	.993	.155	12.877	1.996
1971	.111	.052	.996	.142	13.246	1.881
1972	.087	.040	1.000	.137	13.591	1.865
1973	.119	-.003	.817	.130	11.335	1.475
1974	.102	.061	.511	.351	6.993	2.458
1975	.176	.012	.521	.235	7.536	1.773
1976	.068	.027	.529	.300	7.327	2.195

Rates of Return and Capital Input for Apparel and Other Fabricated Textile Products, 1948–1976

Year	Rate of Return		Capital	Capital Input		
	Nominal	Own	Quality	Price	Quantity	Value
1948	.176	.109	.901	.131	3.096	.406
1949	.049	.104	.903	.119	3.224	.382
1950	.038	.002	.902	.064	3.233	.208
1951	.199	.083	.921	.105	3.624	.381
1952	.016	.080	.919	.110	3.565	.390
1953	.055	.062	.928	.095	3.622	.344
1954	.037	.055	.931	.089	3.635	.325
1955	.067	.066	.925	.103	3.797	.393
1956	.109	.070	.934	.103	3.954	.409
1957	.072	.053	.933	.094	3.854	.362
1958	.059	.073	.942	.114	3.783	.431
1959	.089	.062	.942	.110	3.797	.417
1960	.073	.080	.948	.123	3.910	.482
1961	.082	.084	.953	.133	3.937	.524
1962	.112	.105	.951	.154	3.932	.607
1963	.098	.086	.958	.136	4.312	.587
1964	.112	.103	.966	.154	4.503	.693
1965	.120	.114	.972	.166	4.712	.782
1966	.165	.145	.978	.196	5.014	.984
1967	.147	.122	.975	.187	5.387	1.005
1968	.136	.104	.977	.185	5.675	1.049
1969	.121	.089	.972	.163	6.246	1.020
1970	.119	.083	.988	.158	6.525	1.029
1971	.121	.078	.993	.160	6.724	1.078
1972	.213	.095	1.000	.179	7.237	1.295
1973	.045	.050	1.004	.154	7.546	1.161
1974	.106	.040	1.007	.132	7.882	1.041
1975	.217	.083	1.007	.209	7.413	1.548
1976	.100	.065	1.023	.221	7.270	1.608

Rates of Return and Capital Input for Paper and Allied Products, 1948–1976

Year	Rate of Return		Capital		Capital Input	
	Nominal	Own	Quality	Price	Quantity	Value
1948	.242	.159	1.001	.143	7.363	1.049
1949	.108	.116	.995	.113	8.022	.903
1950	.162	.129	.990	.152	8.266	1.253
1951	.280	.129	.992	.204	8.689	1.769
1952	.092	.095	.998	.151	9.424	1.425
1953	.102	.091	.991	.145	9.792	1.418
1954	.108	.100	.995	.147	9.876	1.450
1955	.128	.115	.989	.162	10.607	1.720
1956	.223	.128	.989	.183	11.260	2.064
1957	.131	.086	.992	.146	12.256	1.785
1958	.082	.070	.990	.129	13.059	1.690
1959	.089	.076	.992	.143	13.475	1.921
1960	.080	.071	.981	.137	13.529	1.853
1961	.072	.072	.988	.136	13.945	1.898
1962	.084	.078	.989	.138	14.246	1.967
1963	.094	.076	.988	.134	14.809	1.984
1964	.102	.085	.988	.142	15.226	2.167
1965	.104	.090	.992	.151	15.736	2.368
1966	.134	.097	.999	.163	16.754	2.726
1967	.116	.081	1.003	.144	18.091	2.602
1968	.106	.076	1.007	.148	19.337	2.853
1969	.124	.075	1.012	.152	19.861	3.014
1970	.105	.055	1.013	.132	20.783	2.746
1971	.090	.045	.997	.123	21.694	2.671
1972	.097	.057	1.000	.148	21.923	3.240
1973	.121	.074	1.003	.187	22.136	4.143
1974	.200	.063	1.006	.204	22.736	4.649
1975	.231	.053	.991	.192	23.451	4.493
1976	.116	.067	.987	.240	23.641	5.679

Rates of Return and Capital Input for Printing and Publishing, 1948–1976

Year	Rate of Return		Capital Quality	Price	Capital Input	
	Nominal	Own			Quantity	Value
1948	.133	.047	.914	.083	9.003	.747
1949	.061	.052	.917	.086	9.058	.779
1950	.078	.042	.920	.090	8.978	.805
1951	.139	.022	.924	.089	9.060	.810
1952	.056	.027	.918	.097	9.082	.881
1953	.044	.034	.926	.103	9.089	.936
1954	.044	.039	.925	.105	8.912	.932
1955	.057	.062	.932	.128	8.993	1.147
1956	.146	.055	.933	.128	9.101	1.169
1957	.093	.053	.929	.134	9.344	1.248
1958	.040	.037	.929	.119	9.280	1.104
1959	.066	.059	.936	.144	9.366	1.348
1960	.080	.072	.941	.154	9.298	1.430
1961	.059	.054	.949	.139	9.506	1.324
1962	.075	.067	.964	.151	9.523	1.437
1963	.092	.073	.968	.160	9.618	1.540
1964	.138	.117	.973	.207	9.974	2.063
1965	.153	.111	.975	.208	10.368	2.154
1966	.162	.120	.973	.222	10.997	2.437
1967	.131	.091	.984	.196	11.878	2.325
1968	.124	.088	.986	.208	12.497	2.602
1969	.152	.090	.992	.221	12.861	2.837
1970	.116	.057	.994	.183	13.528	2.476
1971	.119	.069	.997	.210	13.654	2.862
1972	.109	.069	1.000	.222	13.959	3.095
1973	.135	.093	1.005	.259	14.055	3.634
1974	.196	.043	.989	.221	14.260	3.145
1975	.220	.077	.996	.291	14.237	4.145
1976	.103	.075	.999	.333	13.935	4.643

Rates of Return and Capital Input for Chemicals and Allied Products, 1948–1976

Year	Rate of Return		Capital Quality	Capital Input		
	Nominal	Own		Price	Quantity	Value
1948	.183	.110	.891	.137	14.753	2.025
1949	.075	.114	.921	.145	15.204	2.201
1950	.136	.103	.924	.179	15.503	2.774
1951	.227	.091	.924	.206	16.008	3.302
1952	.066	.078	.948	.169	17.400	2.948
1953	.084	.072	.969	.165	18.151	2.990
1954	.100	.092	.974	.169	18.722	3.164
1955	.108	.111	.963	.211	19.515	4.123
1956	.193	.111	.975	.195	20.307	3.965
1957	.148	.104	.981	.195	20.839	4.057
1958	.098	.092	.984	.182	21.566	3.926
1959	.126	.115	.989	.223	21.923	4.899
1960	.111	.100	.973	.206	22.175	4.576
1961	.095	.100	.965	.207	22.996	4.764
1962	.116	.111	.962	.211	24.202	5.095
1963	.130	.120	.972	.225	24.640	5.536
1964	.138	.125	.979	.231	25.193	5.826
1965	.153	.142	.983	.250	26.289	6.564
1966	.162	.127	.988	.236	28.664	6.757
1967	.120	.090	.991	.195	31.448	6.141
1968	.114	.092	.990	.216	33.661	7.279
1969	.120	.080	.988	.203	35.206	7.158
1970	.113	.063	.995	.184	36.910	6.780
1971	.113	.071	.995	.196	38.461	7.547
1972	.116	.078	1.000	.215	39.225	8.420
1973	.116	.080	.999	.235	39.191	9.223
1974	.231	.050	1.017	.218	40.637	8.862
1975	.220	.057	.981	.250	41.503	10.357
1976	.118	.076	.978	.314	42.106	13.224

Rates of Return and Capital Input for Petroleum and Coal Products, 1948–1976

Year	Rate of Return		Capital		Capital Input	
	Nominal	Own	Quality	Price	Quantity	Value
1948	.169	.096	1.131	.056	19.870	1.117
1949	.080	.069	1.117	.073	20.613	1.511
1950	.103	.076	1.126	.059	20.940	1.233
1951	.157	.082	1.115	.049	19.945	.978
1952	.110	.073	1.140	.083	20.204	1.685
1953	.104	.083	1.153	.095	20.435	1.949
1954	.088	.092	1.133	.075	22.061	1.646
1955	.130	.104	1.121	.115	23.679	2.733
1956	.141	.104	1.112	.055	22.941	1.267
1957	.130	.090	1.103	.087	23.338	2.030
1958	.084	.076	1.112	.087	23.821	2.065
1959	.091	.075	1.119	.095	23.663	2.247
1960	.072	.076	1.105	.073	22.670	1.666
1961	.076	.073	1.093	.082	22.535	1.847
1962	.081	.068	1.074	.077	22.883	1.763
1963	.081	.068	1.069	.071	23.067	1.639
1964	.067	.074	1.062	.062	22.964	1.425
1965	.110	.079	1.038	.077	23.285	1.798
1966	.107	.073	1.027	.078	23.588	1.848
1967	.129	.088	.985	.097	25.301	2.456
1968	.124	.079	.964	.099	27.761	2.761
1969	.128	.064	.986	.091	28.431	2.587
1970	.124	.058	1.012	.095	27.636	2.634
1971	.109	.047	1.003	.110	29.424	3.242
1972	.110	.055	1.000	.111	30.543	3.375
1973	.137	.069	1.035	.097	30.019	2.909
1974	.268	.133	1.069	.223	30.846	6.894
1975	.256	.098	1.052	.282	31.395	8.844
1976	.233	.130	1.048	.383	31.893	12.229

Rates of Return and Capital Input for Rubber and Miscellaneous Plastic Products, 1948–1976

Year	Rate of Return		Capital Quality	Capital Input		
	Nominal	Own		Price	Quantity	Value
1948	.148	.076	1.857	.048	5.434	.263
1949	.054	.057	1.875	.040	5.867	.233
1950	.092	.024	1.536	.054	4.630	.249
1951	.304	.125	.834	.262	2.438	.638
1952	.083	.124	.870	.218	2.803	.611
1953	.052	.082	.950	.158	3.542	.561
1954	.034	.033	.949	.103	3.698	.382
1955	.113	.055	.974	.139	3.757	.522
1956	.166	.096	.975	.170	3.935	.671
1957	.097	.071	.992	.148	4.224	.627
1958	.068	.070	.998	.149	4.391	.656
1959	.086	.079	.956	.164	4.663	.763
1960	.073	.067	.949	.144	4.791	.691
1961	.069	.073	.954	.156	4.982	.776
1962	.093	.083	.962	.160	5.163	.824
1963	.076	.072	.969	.148	5.550	.820
1964	.081	.070	.972	.146	5.783	.845
1965	.083	.069	.980	.146	6.121	.896
1966	.115	.079	.989	.164	6.626	1.089
1967	.106	.077	.995	.165	7.267	1.203
1968	.104	.082	.996	.186	7.838	1.457
1969	.124	.082	1.005	.186	8.498	1.579
1970	.089	.040	1.003	.125	9.293	1.165
1971	.096	.061	1.004	.167	9.840	1.638
1972	.096	.066	1.000	.180	10.160	1.830
1973	.102	.067	1.001	.184	10.906	2.004
1974	.189	.018	.995	.130	11.834	1.538
1975	.192	.032	1.353	.120	16.686	1.999
1976	.064	.031	1.365	.132	16.569	2.188

Rates of Return and Capital Input for Leather and Leather Products, 1948–1976

Year	Rate of Return		Capital Quality	Capital Input		
	Nominal	Own		Price	Quantity	Value
1948	.155	.149	.769	.190	1.333	.253
1949	.024	.068	.791	.110	1.459	.160
1950	.073	−.024	.817	.056	1.498	.084
1951	.313	.159	.838	.199	1.503	.299
1952	.139	−.071	.887	.127	1.678	.213
1953	.107	.070	.896	.111	1.660	.185
1954	.020	.086	.896	.126	1.671	.210
1955	.031	.033	.898	.094	1.661	.156
1956	.161	.074	.909	.122	1.651	.202
1957	.078	.070	.912	.123	1.653	.203
1958	.037	.024	.915	.086	1.642	.141
1959	.079	.030	.934	.099	1.586	.158
1960	.072	.100	.918	.151	1.521	.230
1961	.059	.021	.929	.089	1.566	.139
1962	.076	.092	.926	.147	1.527	.224
1963	.108	.136	.926	.183	1.530	.280
1964	.118	.087	.931	.145	1.554	.225
1965	.156	.077	.929	.148	1.515	.224
1966	.144	.133	.935	.206	1.518	.313
1967	.157	.168	.938	.237	1.588	.377
1968	.150	.092	.934	.189	1.681	.317
1969	.105	.069	.939	.158	1.746	.276
1970	.101	.076	.948	.167	1.761	.295
1971	.074	.003	.952	.147	1.778	.262
1972	.065	−.056	1.000	.046	1.788	.082
1973	.110	.075	1.030	.171	1.655	.282
1974	.094	.072	1.034	.165	1.762	.291
1975	.196	.062	1.035	.198	1.798	.355
1976	.119	.079	1.040	.253	1.696	.429

Rates of Return and Capital Input for Lumber and Wood Products Except Furniture, 1948–1976

Year	Rate of Return		Capital	Price	Capital Input	
	Nominal	Own	Quality		Quantity	Value
1948	.355	.258	.888	.200	4.997	1.001
1949	.119	.137	.902	.128	5.603	.720
1950	.245	.170	.903	.180	5.668	1.021
1951	.290	.182	.913	.182	5.966	1.086
1952	.119	.108	.926	.135	6.522	.881
1953	.108	.100	.935	.127	6.402	.811
1954	.095	.098	.930	.129	6.417	.829
1955	.159	.144	.929	.167	6.573	1.096
1956	.192	.126	.937	.149	6.770	1.010
1957	.084	.068	.941	.109	7.238	.790
1958	.098	.093	.956	.135	6.759	.915
1959	.135	.115	.973	.155	6.840	1.060
1960	.099	.113	.973	.145	6.901	1.001
1961	.088	.089	.985	.127	7.030	.894
1962	.110	.099	.921	.132	7.647	1.010
1963	.135	.115	.948	.150	7.343	1.100
1964	.175	.157	.970	.188	7.083	1.331
1965	.233	.211	.976	.234	7.155	1.678
1966	.185	.150	.982	.191	7.416	1.418
1967	.180	.136	.979	.187	7.825	1.467
1968	.292	.195	.979	.266	7.827	2.081
1969	.282	.271	.991	.349	7.698	2.685
1970	.185	.151	.996	.227	8.623	1.958
1971	.259	.158	.984	.257	8.999	2.311
1972	.287	.236	1.000	.368	9.359	3.443
1973	.445	.356	1.013	.541	9.649	5.218
1974	.362	.324	1.016	.508	10.044	5.098
1975	.339	.187	1.021	.355	11.025	3.909
1976	.276	.231	1.027	.463	10.816	5.007

Rates of Return and Capital Input for Furniture and Fixtures, 1948-1976

Year	Rate of Return		Capital		Capital Input	
	Nominal	Own	Quality	Price	Quantity	Value
1948	.180	.077	.913	.095	2.089	.199
1949	.096	.110	.910	.111	2.062	.229
1950	.147	.070	.905	.121	2.055	.249
1951	.209	.101	.889	.143	2.183	.311
1952	.097	.108	.897	.138	2.262	.312
1953	.070	.049	.901	.103	2.266	.233
1954	.067	.070	.907	.116	2.268	.264
1955	.098	.081	.915	.137	2.352	.321
1956	.172	.085	.911	.143	2.456	.351
1957	.100	.076	.912	.138	2.519	.348
1958	.039	.036	.936	.097	2.596	.252
1959	.072	.060	.944	.126	2.570	.324
1960	.058	.059	.934	.120	2.635	.316
1961	.061	.059	.934	.124	2.661	.331
1962	.095	.087	.939	.150	2.645	.397
1963	.107	.092	.940	.157	2.745	.430
1964	.120	.107	.954	.171	2.822	.482
1965	.163	.147	.963	.217	2.921	.634
1966	.162	.125	.967	.207	3.063	.635
1967	.152	.113	.966	.192	3.323	.638
1968	.154	.088	.975	.188	3.486	.655
1969	.135	.108	.980	.218	3.583	.784
1970	.103	.057	.980	.148	3.886	.577
1971	.116	.036	.987	.134	4.063	.546
1972	.096	.055	1.000	.173	4.120	.714
1973	.093	.024	1.001	.133	4.385	.582
1974	.117	.015	1.014	.115	4.764	.550
1975	.161	.030	.996	.145	5.085	.738
1976	.057	.023	1.029	.163	4.936	.805

Rates of Return and Capital Input for Stone, Clay, and Glass Products, 1948–1976

Year	Rate of Return		Capital Quality	Capital Input		
	Nominal	Own		Price	Quantity	Value
1948	.049	.076	.911	.097	6.174	.596
1949	.124	.089	.916	.104	6.576	.684
1950	.155	.115	.926	.148	6.759	.998
1951	.217	.082	.733	.146	7.074	1.035
1952	.077	.059	.941	.119	7.668	.913
1953	.076	.074	.952	.139	7.868	1.091
1954	.107	.091	.953	.146	8.150	1.187
1955	.128	.135	.956	.193	8.418	1.625
1956	.208	.106	.959	.169	9.063	1.536
1957	.135	.078	.964	.146	10.113	1.481
1958	.099	.083	.960	.148	10.848	1.604
1959	.096	.092	.960	.167	11.196	1.869
1960	.092	.076	.958	.147	11.444	1.678
1961	.053	.070	.955	.141	11.729	1.655
1962	.096	.076	.956	.141	12.039	1.695
1963	.093	.089	.964	.156	12.107	1.894
1964	.121	.099	.968	.165	12.277	2.023
1965	.117	.094	.970	.160	12.596	2.021
1966	.111	.073	.970	.140	13.058	1.834
1967	.081	.049	.979	.117	13.853	1.622
1968	.094	.051	.979	.129	14.167	1.827
1969	.111	.063	.984	.150	14.214	2.136
1970	.103	.039	.993	.123	14.563	1.797
1971	.101	.049	.996	.147	14.810	2.174
1972	.106	.069	1.000	.176	14.900	2.628
1973	.106	.069	1.000	.176	15.364	2.702
1974	.132	.028	1.006	.124	16.220	2.013
1975	.191	.029	1.004	.147	16.766	2.472
1976	.082	.037	1.004	.176	16.703	2.940

Rates of Return and Capital Input for Primary Metal Industries, 1948–1976

Year	Rate of Return		Capital Quality	Capital Input		
	Nominal	*Own*		*Price*	*Quantity*	*Value*
1948	.159	.050	.905	.074	29.345	2.160
1949	.048	.044	.906	.070	30.126	2.106
1950	.092	.060	.893	.103	30.102	3.105
1951	.222	.068	.895	.129	29.833	3.839
1952	.051	.037	.903	.093	31.662	2.931
1953	.076	.064	.913	.120	33.642	4.041
1954	.050	.050	.907	.095	34.731	3.303
1955	.096	.087	.913	.143	34.380	4.906
1956	.201	.083	.912	.132	34.996	4.627
1957	.100	.071	.924	.131	37.662	4.927
1958	.026	.034	.928	.091	39.896	3.629
1959	.046	.037	.926	.098	40.331	3.945
1960	.036	.039	.926	.096	39.700	3.811
1961	.023	.022	.924	.079	40.542	3.218
1962	.040	.038	.933	.087	40.280	3.509
1963	.061	.044	.934	.096	39.875	3.836
1964	.082	.058	.937	.108	39.938	4.327
1965	.092	.073	.941	.131	40.913	5.340
1966	.118	.082	.944	.145	42.303	6.129
1967	.096	.058	.958	.119	44.599	5.310
1968	.075	.046	.965	.108	47.225	5.079
1969	.103	.030	.981	.094	49.321	4.651
1970	.073	.021	.997	.086	50.278	4.340
1971	.060	.010	.999	.073	51.384	3.746
1972	.059	.021	1.000	.097	50.901	4.946
1973	.099	.027	.985	.110	49.957	5.507
1974	.207	.056	1.021	.170	50.725	8.609
1975	.179	.025	1.018	.129	51.471	6.648
1976	.041	.006	.993	.116	51.607	5.977

Rates of Return and Capital Input for Fabricated Metal Industries, 1948–1976

Year	Rate of Return		Capital	Capital Input		
	Nominal	Own	Quality	Price	Quantity	Value
1948	.191	.089	.889	.096	11.607	1.112
1949	.112	.078	.887	.084	11.755	.984
1950	.143	.095	.902	.120	11.656	1.401
1951	.200	.083	.902	.136	12.304	1.668
1952	.081	.057	.901	.102	13.555	1.382
1953	.082	.047	.913	.098	13.882	1.365
1954	.066	.051	.914	.093	14.788	1.368
1955	.073	.053	.932	.098	15.152	1.482
1956	.142	.042	.927	.095	15.893	1.508
1957	.100	.046	.928	.103	16.294	1.684
1958	.049	.037	.942	.090	16.868	1.517
1959	.055	.042	.952	.097	16.851	1.631
1960	.045	.037	.960	.087	17.126	1.490
1961	.046	.044	.961	.098	17.336	1.693
1962	.070	.063	.965	.114	17.416	1.990
1963	.077	.064	.969	.118	17.752	2.103
1964	.078	.066	.972	.122	18.340	2.237
1965	.105	.090	.980	.152	19.270	2.934
1966	.135	.094	.984	.164	20.714	3.402
1967	.122	.092	.983	.167	21.876	3.655
1968	.112	.080	.986	.169	22.906	3.861
1969	.114	.063	.984	.149	24.196	3.600
1970	.094	.033	.992	.114	25.150	2.856
1971	.083	.033	.995	.115	25.837	2.976
1972	.091	.057	1.000	.147	26.002	3.828
1973	.095	.065	1.002	.172	26.549	4.556
1974	.186	.006	1.086	.115	30.555	3.527
1975	.198	.056	1.195	.164	35.538	5.844
1976	.101	.061	1.200	.207	35.323	7.306

Rates of Return and Capital Input for Machinery Except Electrical, 1948–1976

Year	Rate of Return		Capital	Price	Capital Input	
	Nominal	Own	Quality		Quantity	Value
1948	.221	.123	.885	.154	10.142	1.563
1949	.163	.145	.889	.159	10.610	1.688
1950	.173	.131	.894	.185	10.455	1.932
1951	.255	.135	.899	.255	10.900	2.782
1952	.154	.135	.908	.238	12.526	2.981
1953	.113	.093	.912	.193	13.167	2.540
1954	.109	.102	.912	.174	13.982	2.430
1955	.102	.090	.922	.169	14.138	2.388
1956	.204	.106	.922	.204	14.763	3.016
1957	.136	.088	.925	.187	15.698	2.930
1958	.069	.064	.931	.147	16.222	2.386
1959	.112	.098	.943	.193	16.198	3.124
1960	.091	.086	.942	.172	16.814	2.892
1961	.088	.090	.943	.179	16.853	3.012
1962	.130	.125	.950	.215	16.791	3.613
1963	.119	.113	.959	.205	17.837	3.664
1964	.163	.149	.962	.252	18.266	4.597
1965	.181	.168	.971	.272	19.695	5.367
1966	.195	.156	.976	.277	21.806	6.050
1967	.170	.146	.983	.253	24.544	6.205
1968	.131	.110	.983	.235	26.619	6.266
1969	.149	.096	.982	.218	28.092	6.117
1970	.140	.097	.985	.207	30.533	6.313
1971	.121	.089	.990	.197	31.777	6.275
1972	.140	.110	1.000	.234	31.336	7.336
1973	.138	.105	1.001	.244	32.396	7.905
1974	.166	.023	.934	.160	33.700	5.382
1975	.205	.069	.909	.243	35.674	8.672
1976	.095	.056	.921	.277	35.451	9.822

Rates of Return and Capital Input for Electrical Machinery, Equipment, and Supplies, 1948–1976

Year	Rate of Return		Capital Quality	Capital Input		
	Nominal	Own		Price	Quantity	Value
1948	.150	.069	.884	.103	7.772	.797
1949	.111	.099	.905	.117	7.833	.918
1950	.136	.109	.917	.179	7.619	1.364
1951	.198	.072	.916	.175	8.344	1.460
1952	.089	.081	.911	.173	10.316	1.783
1953	.082	.060	.904	.149	11.418	1.699
1954	.067	.066	.910	.128	12.071	1.550
1955	.075	.054	.942	.119	11.906	1.415
1956	.149	.062	.946	.129	12.426	1.607
1957	.100	.074	.951	.148	13.819	2.045
1958	.061	.068	.954	.137	14.040	1.922
1959	.106	.088	.961	.173	13.678	2.367
1960	.068	.066	.949	.147	14.090	2.066
1961	.057	.060	.952	.140	14.858	2.075
1962	.081	.077	.953	.151	15.441	2.337
1963	.087	.076	.952	.152	16.439	2.499
1964	.088	.073	.956	.152	16.962	2.582
1965	.143	.129	.969	.220	17.324	3.813
1966	.180	.142	.972	.241	18.892	4.558
1967	.148	.119	.970	.213	21.715	4.631
1968	.129	.100	.975	.202	23.546	4.764
1969	.136	.083	.981	.192	24.675	4.727
1970	.111	.060	.988	.151	26.295	3.971
1971	.124	.082	.994	.187	26.958	5.038
1972	.153	.119	1.000	.246	26.618	6.547
1973	.138	.109	1.001	.242	27.237	6.605
1974	.237	.056	.984	.166	29.328	4.858
1975	.206	.076	1.008	.207	30.687	6.361
1976	.106	.063	1.016	.229	29.473	6.742

Rates of Return and Capital Input for Transportation Equipment and Ordnance, Except Motor Vehicles, 1948–1976

Year	Rate of Return		Capital Quality	Capital Input		
	Nominal	Own		Price	Quantity	Value
1948	.043	−.057	1.377	.016	13.592	.223
1949	−.010	−.028	1.363	.025	12.334	.304
1950	.011	−.019	1.281	.038	10.929	.412
1951	.116	−.025	1.165	.051	9.592	.486
1952	.027	.013	1.000	.084	9.900	.831
1953	.032	.004	.896	.098	9.891	.965
1954	.055	.048	.871	.123	9.774	1.198
1955	.033	.021	.855	.099	9.791	.966
1956	.098	−.011	.902	.086	9.902	.848
1957	.083	.032	.906	.119	10.832	1.287
1958	.041	.035	.944	.109	11.284	1.231
1959	.022	.010	.949	.073	11.049	.811
1960	.016	.019	.960	.074	10.912	.806
1961	.026	.032	.970	.099	10.488	1.035
1962	.073	.069	.982	.134	10.282	1.373
1963	.074	.065	.980	.134	10.642	1.421
1964	.075	.056	.978	.133	11.111	1.477
1965	.075	.055	.984	.138	11.272	1.554
1966	.092	.055	.977	.139	11.657	1.619
1967	.091	.063	.979	.138	14.295	1.968
1968	.091	.062	.967	.141	17.482	2.462
1969	.047	−.002	.969	.063	19.069	1.209
1970	.053	.002	.972	.063	20.369	1.288
1971	.057	.016	1.002	.079	19.573	1.553
1972	.056	.023	1.000	.102	18.448	1.876
1973	.011	−.010	.985	.066	17.927	1.183
1974	.096	−.062	.974	.033	17.719	.579
1975	.086	−.036	.983	.054	17.642	.948
1976	−.017	−.061	1.038	.024	18.755	.453

Rates of Return and Capital Input for Motor Vehicles and Equipment, 1948–1976

Year	Rate of Return		Capital	Capital Input		
	Nominal	Own	Quality	Price	Quantity	Value
1948	.263	.167	.955	.196	7.202	1.412
1949	.320	.296	.961	.299	7.418	2.220
1950	.400	.364	.960	.466	6.878	3.204
1951	.267	.153	.971	.319	7.450	2.379
1952	.162	.141	.974	.294	8.398	2.466
1953	.152	.141	.973	.313	8.942	2.796
1954	.182	.175	.977	.251	9.289	2.327
1955	.322	.309	.981	.481	9.316	4.481
1956	.204	.114	.981	.243	10.498	2.554
1957	.172	.127	.994	.266	11.396	3.026
1958	.033	.022	1.010	.117	11.356	1.326
1959	.181	.173	1.008	.321	10.592	3.404
1960	.214	.204	1.003	.358	10.573	3.781
1961	.181	.182	1.000	.324	10.273	3.333
1962	.326	.319	1.001	.505	9.931	5.016
1963	.397	.391	1.005	.593	10.246	6.071
1964	.422	.408	1.007	.576	10.557	6.077
1965	.504	.494	1.012	.671	11.670	7.826
1966	.463	.427	1.013	.557	12.923	7.200
1967	.352	.316	1.005	.435	13.840	6.019
1968	.408	.373	1.003	.569	13.968	7.943
1969	.362	.317	1.000	.498	14.732	7.343
1970	.230	.171	1.000	.270	15.120	4.077
1971	.328	.281	1.000	.505	15.016	7.580
1972	.345	.309	1.000	.576	14.714	8.472
1973	.274	.257	1.010	.508	16.413	8.331
1974	.185	.051	1.001	.183	18.070	3.331
1975	.255	.115	1.043	.278	19.331	5.378
1976	.351	.310	1.048	.566	18.295	10.357

Rates of Return and Capital Input for Professional Photographic Equipment and Watches, 1948–1976

Year	Rate of Return		Capital Quality	Capital Input		
	Nominal	Own		Price	Quantity	Value
1948	.100	.022	.896	.084	1.397	.118
1949	.074	.070	.910	.110	1.477	.163
1950	.091	.064	.907	.135	1.536	.208
1951	.176	.073	.927	.191	1.760	.335
1952	.102	.088	.963	.181	2.176	.393
1953	.090	.076	.962	.181	2.297	.415
1954	.113	.107	.964	.197	2.423	.477
1955	.122	.124	.972	.212	2.433	.515
1956	.189	.116	.975	.203	2.879	.585
1957	.112	.072	.978	.163	3.186	.518
1958	.097	.088	.979	.177	3.367	.596
1959	.141	.128	.983	.233	3.405	.794
1960	.119	.113	.972	.224	3.512	.786
1961	.108	.110	.973	.203	3.751	.762
1962	.152	.148	.977	.258	3.795	.979
1963	.162	.154	.977	.246	4.004	.986
1964	.134	.122	.978	.223	4.187	.934
1965	.203	.188	.987	.303	4.257	1.290
1966	.271	.234	.991	.373	4.607	1.717
1967	.235	.192	.993	.329	5.294	1.741
1968	.208	.182	.992	.343	5.754	1.973
1969	.231	.183	.990	.365	6.066	2.217
1970	.140	.093	.992	.246	6.433	1.582
1971	.122	.087	.997	.232	6.819	1.580
1972	.130	.097	1.000	.251	6.970	1.752
1973	.118	.080	1.000	.241	7.239	1.748
1974	.152	.025	1.113	.088	8.890	.786
1975	.161	.031	1.128	.170	9.626	1.640
1976	.067	.033	1.154	.209	9.628	2.012

Rates of Return and Capital Input for Miscellaneous Manufacturing Industries, 1948–1976

Year	Rate of Return		Capital Quality	Capital Input		
	Nominal	Own		Price	Quantity	Value
1948	.204	.143	.862	.149	2.685	.400
1949	.132	.135	.877	.141	2.518	.354
1950	.182	.132	.876	.172	2.406	.413
1951	.193	.093	.892	.155	2.465	.382
1952	.114	.109	.899	.153	2.599	.398
1953	.094	.085	.904	.133	2.533	.338
1954	.091	.086	.905	.133	2.588	.345
1955	.126	.122	.905	.169	2.626	.444
1956	.152	.099	.908	.156	2.803	.437
1957	.116	.083	.909	.140	2.947	.414
1958	.091	.084	.905	.133	3.382	.449
1959	.129	.115	.924	.178	2.917	.518
1960	.108	.103	.937	.161	2.969	.477
1961	.134	.136	.949	.195	3.086	.601
1962	.127	.120	.956	.188	2.997	.564
1963	.108	.103	.963	.173	3.119	.540
1964	.108	.096	.978	.163	3.192	.520
1965	.112	.094	.986	.163	3.330	.543
1966	.151	.120	.980	.192	3.451	.661
1967	.147	.118	.990	.187	3.947	.738
1968	.128	.101	.997	.181	4.404	.798
1969	.120	.079	.989	.161	4.946	.795
1970	.117	.075	1.002	.143	5.002	.714
1971	.141	.099	1.000	.194	4.743	.919
1972	.166	.133	1.007	.246	4.819	1.184
1973	.147	.098	.980	.220	5.158	1.134
1974	.216	.038	.980	.151	5.598	.844
1975	.224	.099	.983	.260	5.951	1.544
1976	.131	.088	1.036	.317	5.142	1.630

Rates of Return and Capital Input for Railroads and Rail Express Service, 1948–1976

Year	Rate of Return		Capital	Capital Input		
	Nominal	Own	Quality	Price	Quantity	Value
1948	.079	.041	.915	.078	25.818	2.008
1949	.055	.030	.925	.068	25.580	1.728
1950	.097	.045	.925	.090	25.193	2.270
1951	.075	.044	.922	.094	24.753	2.324
1952	.116	.050	.924	.103	24.719	2.546
1953	.072	.042	.922	.100	24.895	2.488
1954	.000	.026	.915	.076	24.552	1.948
1955	.114	.045	.927	.098	24.879	2.445
1956	.036	.039	.929	.097	24.796	2.394
1957	.063	.035	.932	.092	24.642	2.270
1958	.055	.024	.936	.083	24.489	2.026
1959	.061	.021	.939	.085	23.785	2.011
1960	.003	.017	.931	.078	23.448	1.823
1961	.010	.021	.945	.081	23.507	1.896
1962	.037	.035	.947	.086	22.940	1.965
1963	.053	.042	.946	.095	22.501	2.134
1964	.013	.049	.948	.096	22.410	2.157
1965	.095	.061	.963	.104	22.934	2.395
1966	.100	.071	.975	.115	23.324	2.687
1967	.057	.043	.998	.088	24.364	2.137
1968	.070	.037	1.001	.085	24.694	2.092
1969	.093	.042	1.004	.091	24.283	2.218
1970	.103	.039	1.006	.090	24.406	2.208
1971	.113	.027	1.007	.088	24.206	2.120
1972	.073	.033	1.000	.102	23.867	2.431
1973	.041	.023	.993	.092	23.303	2.133
1974	.140	.012	.991	.092	23.081	2.126
1975	.159	.003	.994	.087	24.200	2.098
1976	.184	.007	.991	.110	24.697	2.714

230 The Contribution of Capital to Economic Growth

Rates of Return and Capital Input for Street Railways, Bus Lines, and Taxicabs, 1948–1976

Year	Rate of Return		Capital	Capital Input		
	Nominal	Own	Quality	Price	Quantity	Value
1948	.035	.048	1.156	.085	4.368	.369
1949	.085	.024	1.143	.067	4.796	.322
1950	.091	.009	1.129	.070	4.855	.342
1951	.050	.028	1.122	.082	4.681	.384
1952	.089	.027	1.115	.090	4.653	.419
1953	.088	.017	1.113	.088	4.614	.408
1954	.012	.016	1.095	.083	4.430	.369
1955	.105	.043	1.073	.104	4.134	.429
1956	.073	.053	1.066	.115	3.937	.455
1957	.100	.069	1.058	.130	3.722	.483
1958	.114	.088	1.052	.146	3.569	.522
1959	.159	.110	1.043	.179	3.490	.625
1960	.139	.119	1.030	.190	3.340	.636
1961	.104	.136	1.018	.207	3.241	.672
1962	.131	.156	1.013	.217	3.191	.693
1963	.186	.159	1.010	.216	3.152	.680
1964	.150	.198	1.006	.248	3.084	.764
1965	.298	.240	1.004	.280	3.076	.861
1966	.277	.236	1.004	.284	3.045	.866
1967	.256	.245	1.005	.291	3.086	.897
1968	.266	.228	1.006	.285	3.130	.893
1969	.282	.212	1.002	.277	3.160	.876
1970	.307	.228	1.001	.303	3.131	.947
1971	.256	.236	1.000	.330	3.130	1.033
1972	.227	.212	1.000	.331	3.117	1.032
1973		.192	.999	.318	3.072	.978
1974	.372	.229	1.000	.378	3.024	1.143
1975	.388	.182	1.003	.360	3.158	1.136
1976	.117	.182	1.002	.407	3.198	1.300

Rates of Return and Capital Input for Trucking Services and Warehousing, 1948–1976

Year	Rate of Return		Capital Quality	Capital Input		
	Nominal	Own		Price	Quantity	Value
1948	.130	.117	1.149	.132	6.901	.911
1949	.115	.077	1.158	.102	7.543	.767
1950	.177	.105	1.154	.135	7.759	1.048
1951	.102	.079	1.125	.118	8.634	1.019
1952	.133	.053	1.123	.119	9.048	1.072
1953	.122	.055	1.119	.131	9.017	1.184
1954	.045	.064	1.101	.139	8.955	1.248
1955	.148	.090	1.094	.159	8.684	1.384
1956	.072	.078	1.108	.152	9.584	1.457
1957	.134	.098	1.103	.165	9.759	1.609
1958	.114	.090	1.102	.161	10.460	1.684
1959	.157	.133	1.096	.209	10.436	2.184
1960	.078	.063	1.104	.162	11.952	1.940
1961	.069	.085	1.093	.179	11.762	2.101
1962	.136	.130	1.081	.208	11.431	2.376
1963	.122	.097	1.081	.188	12.232	2.294
1964	.102	.129	1.067	.209	12.320	2.573
1965	.198	.166	1.060	.238	12.565	2.991
1966	.181	.153	1.060	.232	13.983	3.243
1967	.151	.121	1.052	.215	14.980	3.225
1968	.174	.137	1.032	.235	14.977	3.517
1969	.195	.134	1.020	.236	16.622	3.918
1970	.182	.111	1.009	.228	17.459	3.987
1971	.192	.121	1.003	.258	17.920	4.631
1972	.187	.126	1.000	.284	18.968	5.390
1973	.205	.149	.978	.325	17.400	5.655
1974	.263	.103	.999	.289	22.289	6.444
1975	.215	.062	1.006	.264	24.084	6.363
1976	.061	.065	1.008	.293	24.751	7.249

Rates of Return and Capital Input for Water Transportation, 1948–1976

Year	Rate of Return		Capital Quality	Capital Input		
	Nominal	Own		Price	Quantity	Value
1948	-.105	-.007	1.103	.057	3.868	.220
1949	.040	-.004	1.100	.064	3.722	.240
1950	.073	.005	1.098	.068	3.550	.242
1951	-.009	.025	1.092	.104	3.362	.349
1952	.053	-.001	1.074	.077	3.321	.257
1953	.010	.001	1.066	.074	3.378	.250
1954	-.049	-.010	1.032	.061	3.296	.200
1955	.054	.021	1.027	.091	3.117	.284
1956	.015	.041	1.016	.109	3.026	.331
1957	.017	.001	1.011	.084	3.020	.252
1958	.062	.032	1.013	.090	3.109	.281
1959	.074	.036	1.011	.107	3.257	.349
1960	.043	.038	1.019	.109	3.397	.372
1961	.021	.043	1.011	.111	3.444	.384
1962	.047	.061	1.005	.121	3.440	.416
1963	.103	.078	1.006	.139	3.492	.484
1964	.054	.103	1.004	.159	3.507	.556
1965	.143	.113	1.003	.162	3.530	.570
1966	.121	.108	1.003	.166	3.640	.605
1967	.140	.110	1.002	.166	3.693	.615
1968	.155	.120	1.001	.185	3.734	.690
1969	.116	.061	.998	.136	3.928	.534
1970	.125	.052	1.000	.134	4.013	.537
1971	.108	.035	1.000	.122	4.150	.506
1972	.059	.033	1.000	.131	4.162	.546
1973	.166	.048	.998	.155	4.169	.646
1974	.208	.087	.992	.228	4.260	.972
1975	.185	.055	.990	.193	4.680	.903
1976		.038	.979	.204	4.991	1.018

Rates of Return and Capital Input for Air Transportation, 1948–1976

Year	Rate of Return		Capital	Capital Input		
	Nominal	Own	Quality	Price	Quantity	Value
1948	-.033	-.010	1.153	.068	1.268	.086
1949	.071	.001	1.071	.084	1.390	.117
1950	.014	.010	1.082	.106	1.672	.177
1951	.040	.018	1.068	.128	1.681	.216
1952	.325	.045	1.067	.118	1.702	.201
1953	-.180	-.008	1.070	.124	2.016	.251
1954	.017	.020	1.063	.125	2.458	.307
1955	.066	.003	1.064	.117	2.760	.323
1956	-.012	-.000	1.043	.110	2.726	.301
1957	.020	-.013	1.048	.088	3.122	.276
1958	.018	-.017	1.073	.089	3.921	.347
1959	.015	.020	1.066	.094	4.389	.413
1960	.051	-.033	1.099	.079	5.933	.469
1961	.042	.034	1.087	.076	6.975	.532
1962	-.018	-.016	1.079	.091	7.976	.724
1963	.005	-.015	1.074	.098	8.636	.847
1964	-.025	-.014	1.044	.122	8.394	1.025
1965	.054	.028	1.016	.142	9.337	1.326
1966	.051	.027	1.016	.144	10.244	1.474
1967	.040	.020	1.032	.130	12.194	1.579
1968	.016	-.020	1.055	.092	15.610	1.432
1969	.008	-.044	1.094	.073	20.399	1.488
1970	.003	.060	1.067	.062	21.778	1.352
1971	.027	.057	1.027	.073	23.354	1.711
1972	.005	.041	1.000	.092	21.613	1.983
1973	.003	-.029	.963	.106	20.154	2.136
1974	.094	-.035	.938	.114	20.478	2.344
1975	.094	-.066	.942	.090	20.651	1.869
1976	.003	-.037	.947	.131	20.288	2.649

Rates of Return and Capital Input for Pipelines, Except Natural Gas, 1948–1976

Year	Rate of Return		Capital Quality	Capital Input		
	Nominal	Own		Price	Quantity	Value
1948	.084	−.022	.888	.044	2.387	.104
1949	.042	−.013	.932	.050	2.420	.121
1950	.104	.011	.943	.084	2.391	.200
1951	.005	.010	.935	.090	2.388	.214
1952	.031	.009	.932	.092	2.350	.217
1953	.070	.005	.952	.090	2.468	.221
1954	.019	.012	.952	.088	2.609	.229
1955	.090	.021	.972	.091	2.558	.233
1956	.030	.022	.965	.101	2.462	.248
1957	.071	.016	.963	.103	2.350	.242
1958	.063	.023	.967	.117	2.272	.265
1959	.068	.030	.969	.139	2.183	.303
1960	.034	.035	.947	.147	2.072	.305
1961	.041	.042	.958	.157	1.999	.314
1962	.036	.050	.963	.159	1.922	.306
1963	.081	.099	.957	.210	1.936	.406
1964	.063	.111	.951	.208	2.039	.425
1965	.152	.121	.959	.210	2.068	.434
1966	.150	.132	.972	.221	2.032	.449
1967	.167	.146	.983	.233	2.025	.471
1968	.168	.133	.978	.221	2.106	.466
1969	.184	.150	.984	.247	2.162	.534
1970	.219	.180	.984	.288	2.154	.620
1971	.237	.163	.986	.282	2.233	.630
1972	.231	.177	1.000	.312	2.433	.760
1973	.173	.142	.978	.302	2.315	.698
1974	.182	.073	.983	.251	2.369	.595
1975	.277	.067	.985	.303	2.393	.726
1976	.135	.077	.985	.371	2.358	.875

Rates of Return and Capital Input for Transportation Services, 1948–1976

Year	Rate of Return Nominal	Rate of Return Own	Capital Quality	Capital Input Price	Capital Input Quantity	Capital Input Value
1948	-.013	-.026	1.090	.054	1.755	.095
1949	.003	-.010	1.080	.063	1.572	.100
1950	.079	-.001	1.013	.075	1.446	.109
1951	.066	.034	.923	.103	1.305	.135
1952	.074	.026	.952	.102	1.318	.134
1953	.058	.041	.950	.112	1.295	.145
1954	.048	.044	.882	.111	1.394	.155
1955	.108	.070	.889	.139	1.282	.155
1956	.064	.073	.891	.144	1.332	.179
1957	.107	.099	.894	.162	1.354	.192
1958	.081	.068	.946	.125	1.461	.219
1959	.085	.066	.965	.143	1.494	.182
1960	.086	.056	.959	.138	1.610	.213
1961	.040	.064	.987	.150	1.620	.222
1962	.073	.069	.998	.147	1.603	.243
1963	.088	.081	1.002	.151	1.657	.236
1964	.080	.099	1.006	.160	1.736	.251
1965	.145	.115	1.047	.172	1.876	.278
1966	.119	.094	1.118	.161	2.164	.322
1967	.175	.146	1.147	.192	2.293	.348
1968	.078	.044	1.198	.122	2.919	.441
1969	.096	.044	1.148	.128	2.733	.355
1970	.101	.055	1.110	.140	2.648	.350
1971	.112	.038	1.069	.137	2.459	.371
1972	.137	.072	1.000	.175	2.272	.337
1973	.137	.055	.990	.180	2.277	.397
1974	.373	.132	1.057	.257	2.628	.409
1975	.019	.097	1.102	.246	3.198	.675
1976	.230	.085	1.123	.249	3.576	.786

Rates of Return and Capital Input for Telephone and Telegraph and Miscellaneous Communication Services, 1948–1976

Year	Rate of Return		Capital Quality	Capital Input		
	Nominal	Own		Price	Quantity	Value
1948	.048	.018	.849	.084	9.857	.833
1949	.064	.029	.878	.096	10.433	.997
1950	.076	.048	.887	.121	10.551	1.274
1951	.089	.050	.894	.138	10.514	1.452
1952	.055	.057	.900	.150	10.604	1.593
1953	.063	.063	.938	.154	11.864	1.830
1954	.096	.072	.954	.162	12.478	2.023
1955	.122	.084	.955	.183	12.902	2.362
1956	.096	.081	.953	.186	13.499	2.510
1957	.131	.093	.954	.205	13.783	2.826
1958	.114	.105	.953	.222	14.733	3.268
1959	.141	.125	.961	.253	15.362	3.883
1960	.143	.128	.974	.262	15.820	4.146
1961	.146	.139	.980	.273	16.723	4.573
1962	.135	.154	.982	.283	17.764	5.027
1963	.186	.182	.986	.303	18.952	5.742
1964	.190	.176	.990	.293	20.937	6.145
1965	.184	.178	.992	.290	22.719	6.595
1966	.197	.174	.997	.289	25.230	7.282
1967	.198	.163	1.000	.281	27.713	7.781
1968	.209	.146	1.002	.283	29.952	8.465
1969	.189	.140	1.003	.284	32.124	9.110
1970	.187	.136	1.001	.274	34.385	9.413
1971	.196	.135	1.000	.267	37.877	10.109
1972	.200	.136	1.000	.267	42.093	11.226
1973	.185	.130	1.000	.272	46.969	12.769
1974	.190	.114	1.002	.259	53.021	13.728
1975	.224	.109	1.006	.264	58.822	15.507
1976	.179	.098	1.007	.281	63.045	17.692

Rates of Return and Capital Input for Radio Broadcasting and Television, 1948–1976

Year	Rate of Return		Capital Quality	Price	Capital Input	
	Nominal	Own			Quantity	Value
1948	.209	.157	1.028	.200	.306	.061
1949	.130	.107	1.029	.164	.353	.058
1950	.140	.151	1.033	.205	.403	.083
1951	.253	.192	1.015	.279	.427	.119
1952	.169	.172	1.009	.266	.478	.127
1953	.187	.188	.999	.308	.438	.135
1954	.181	.180	1.007	.291	.534	.156
1955	.265	.258	1.006	.340	.711	.242
1956	.214	.175	1.016	.263	.941	.247
1957	.219	.151	1.014	.256	1.038	.266
1958	.116	.111	1.008	.219	1.237	.271
1959	.136	.131	1.011	.240	1.330	.320
1960	.152	.158	1.014	.267	1.407	.375
1961	.087	.089	1.017	.198	1.630	.323
1962	.161	.153	1.010	.271	1.612	.436
1963	.140	.139	1.006	.275	1.688	.464
1964	.114	.101	1.011	.205	2.075	.426
1965	.128	.118	1.011	.218	2.258	.493
1966	.135	.114	1.007	.214	2.539	.544
1967	.125	.086	1.010	.176	2.758	.486
1968	.117	.060	1.013	.170	3.251	.554
1969	.108	.053	1.015	.173	3.440	.595
1970	.100	.050	1.010	.161	3.587	.576
1971	.113	.050	1.004	.168	3.539	.596
1972	.143	.086	1.000	.232	3.621	.840
1973	.126	.069	.999	.223	3.810	.850
1974	.143	.016	1.011	.195	4.083	.798
1975	.172	.050	1.025	.227	4.316	.980
1976	.107	.081	1.028	.344	4.402	1.515

Rates of Return and Capital Input for Electric Utilities, 1948–1976

Year	Rate of Return		Capital Quality	Capital Input		
	Nominal	Own		Price	Quantity	Value
1948	.147	.040	.854	.080	19.008	1.514
1949	.101	.044	.884	.086	20.184	1.726
1950	.122	.041	.907	.092	20.954	1.934
1951	.115	.041	.917	.103	21.585	2.230
1952	.038	.048	.919	.115	21.694	2.491
1953	.109	.049	.936	.117	23.230	2.713
1954	.076	.059	.954	.127	24.504	3.105
1955	.117	.066	.966	.138	24.973	3.440
1956	.142	.064	.978	.144	25.595	3.695
1957	.144	.061	.976	.150	25.915	3.875
1958	.077	.060	.978	.153	26.345	4.037
1959	.103	.068	.982	.166	27.120	4.514
1960	.091	.079	.983	.182	27.616	5.022
1961	.057	.082	.986	.189	27.959	5.281
1962	.084	.098	.986	.198	28.302	5.617
1963	.093	.106	.988	.204	28.722	5.871
1964	.127	.114	.987	.213	29.314	6.252
1965	.136	.123	.986	.221	29.722	6.580
1966	.144	.127	.987	.228	30.508	6.948
1967	.159	.125	.989	.228	31.684	7.232
1968	.162	.118	.991	.230	33.538	7.726
1969	.149	.117	.992	.234	35.095	8.202
1970	.158	.107	.994	.228	37.317	8.490
1971	.169	.112	.997	.238	40.024	9.540
1972	.143	.110	1.000	.242	43.279	10.484
1973	.171	.105	1.003	.242	46.657	11.311
1974	.215	.074	1.012	.221	50.724	11.216
1975	.280	.097	1.017	.278	53.663	14.917
1976	.158	.088	1.015	.301	55.085	16.599

Rates of Return and Capital Input for Gas Utilities, 1948–1976

Year	Rate of Return		Capital Quality	Capital Input		
	Nominal	Own		Price	Quantity	Value
1948	.119	.019	.667	.069	8.502	.586
1949	.071	.034	.688	.088	8.529	.750
1950	.108	.018	.767	.080	9.942	.794
1951	.091	.020	.829	.092	10.872	.997
1952	.023	.026	.851	.101	11.086	1.124
1953	.077	.027	.848	.104	11.923	1.241
1954	.058	.043	.879	.123	11.666	1.434
1955	.113	.063	.886	.149	10.678	1.589
1956	.143	.076	.885	.176	9.946	1.755
1957	.145	.080	.881	.188	10.038	1.891
1958	.089	.074	.903	.188	10.747	2.024
1959	.116	.079	.924	.200	11.389	2.274
1960	.108	.094	.916	.222	11.422	2.530
1961	.067	.092	.947	.224	12.008	2.684
1962	.101	.114	.936	.238	11.818	2.817
1963	.120	.130	.935	.253	11.650	2.944
1964	.147	.137	.936	.260	11.679	3.038
1965	.163	.144	.940	.267	11.770	3.139
1966	.176	.154	.941	.281	11.798	3.315
1967	.196	.161	.942	.292	11.905	3.482
1968	.209	.170	.944	.313	11.994	3.753
1969	.213	.173	.943	.322	12.087	3.895
1970	.205	.147	.954	.299	12.976	3.885
1971	.219	.158	.966	.321	13.581	4.366
1972	.179	.140	1.000	.310	15.485	4.798
1973	.222	.148	.999	.329	15.711	5.176
1974	.256	.103	1.030	.296	17.349	5.133
1975	.304	.127	1.040	.363	18.816	6.827
1976	.179	.113	1.041	.390	19.502	7.596

Rates of Return and Capital Input for Water Supply and Sanitary Services, 1948–1976

Year	Rate of Return — Nominal	Rate of Return — Own	Capital Quality	Capital Input — Price	Capital Input — Quantity	Capital Input — Value
1948	.134	.088	1.031	.104	1.653	.173
1949	.122	.105	.990	.115	1.856	.213
1950	.167	.077	.950	.100	2.058	.207
1951	.114	.087	.911	.120	2.078	.250
1952	.135	.096	.893	.135	2.087	.281
1953	.122	.088	.881	.128	2.414	.308
1954	.113	.110	.899	.150	2.379	.356
1955	.184	.132	.917	.177	2.315	.410
1956	.133	.135	.942	.189	2.282	.431
1957	.171	.142	.943	.192	2.513	.483
1958	.172	.134	.943	.188	2.744	.515
1959	.179	.140	.939	.202	2.951	.595
1960	.159	.148	.931	.215	3.165	.680
1961	.153	.155	.946	.229	3.166	.724
1962	.169	.161	.935	.228	3.363	.768
1963	.171	.163	.943	.233	3.521	.821
1964	.148	.172	.947	.241	3.692	.890
1965	.216	.182	.950	.244	3.877	.946
1966	.204	.180	.956	.248	4.136	1.024
1967	.201	.173	.965	.242	4.454	1.079
1968	.209	.173	.979	.248	4.780	1.188
1969	.227	.174	.994	.255	5.046	1.287
1970	.232	.152	.997	.244	5.571	1.358
1971	.223	.150	1.002	.255	5.994	1.526
1972	.231	.162	1.000	.283	5.922	1.676
1973	.205	.157	1.001	.289	6.264	1.809
1974	.278	.137	.997	.285	6.282	1.793
1975	.359	.150	.993	.346	6.901	2.385
1976	.159	.132	.993	.365	7.281	2.654

Rates of Return and Capital Input for Wholesale Trade, 1948–1976

Year	Rate of Return		Capital Quality	Price	Capital Input	
	Nominal	Own			Quantity	Value
1948	.245	.179	.929	.188	23.160	4.364
1949	.110	.131	.921	.143	26.435	3.775
1950	.141	.107	.919	.159	27.899	4.438
1951	.196	.102	.918	.161	31.792	5.132
1952	.101	.094	.913	.138	33.695	4.659
1953	.062	.063	.909	.113	34.602	3.912
1954	.072	.070	.902	.116	34.262	3.984
1955	.113	.100	.901	.147	35.392	5.194
1956	.110	.072	.907	.131	39.160	5.115
1957	.104	.066	.907	.127	40.853	5.181
1958	.078	.072	.910	.128	41.469	5.297
1959	.106	.095	.914	.152	42.472	6.476
1960	.083	.079	.910	.132	45.054	5.961
1961	.072	.074	.910	.129	47.446	6.104
1962	.088	.086	.913	.139	47.740	6.644
1963	.079	.081	.925	.132	50.986	6.725
1964	.101	.094	.933	.144	54.272	7.830
1965	.117	.100	.921	.154	58.247	8.972
1966	.126	.099	.946	.155	63.371	9.802
1967	.104	.080	.980	.136	73.208	9.946
1968	.125	.084	.982	.152	75.780	11.492
1969	.120	.072	1.000	.146	83.328	12.149
1970	.110	.063	1.010	.139	89.263	12.379
1971	.110	.061	1.009	.144	91.621	13.173
1972	.141	.101	1.000	.192	94.093	18.104
1973	.188	.110	1.000	.226	97.737	22.062
1974	.278	.122	1.006	.268	103.050	27.570
1975	.224	.115	1.007	.267	106.060	28.336
1976	.177	.141	1.012	.330	105.377	34.798

Rates of Return and Capital Input for Retail Trade, 1948–1976

Year	Rate of Return		Capital	Capital Input		
	Nominal	Own	Quality	Price	Quantity	Value
1948	.215	.141	.892	.138	50.643	6.978
1949	.100	.107	.898	.114	56.791	6.468
1950	.136	.095	.900	.121	59.964	7.234
1951	.150	.069	.902	.099	66.885	6.623
1952	.081	.068	.904	.101	69.414	7.006
1953	.062	.056	.896	.093	70.550	6.592
1954	.063	.059	.909	.095	73.699	6.973
1955	.087	.069	.912	.103	76.250	7.844
1956	.084	.048	.921	.090	81.997	7.381
1957	.083	.049	.917	.093	83.775	7.804
1958	.053	.051	.924	.096	84.154	8.088
1959	.079	.071	.925	.113	84.614	9.576
1960	.066	.061	.932	.103	86.943	8.944
1961	.062	.061	.935	.103	89.300	9.158
1962	.075	.070	.947	.110	90.516	9.995
1963	.072	.070	.949	.111	94.320	10.457
1964	.090	.083	.951	.122	98.304	11.971
1965	.101	.085	.961	.125	100.824	12.642
1966	.103	.074	.967	.118	107.535	12.638
1967	.107	.077	.979	.124	115.187	14.233
1968	.116	.074	.990	.129	118.363	15.301
1969	.120	.070	.993	.129	124.973	16.157
1970	.114	.060	.999	.125	130.972	16.326
1971	.122	.073	.996	.145	134.270	19.509
1972	.106	.064	1.000	.142	140.884	20.003
1973	.103	.048	1.009	.132	147.510	19.449
1974	.156	.009	1.021	.097	155.944	15.171
1975	.159	.052	1.026	.159	159.918	25.502
1976	.085	.053	1.039	.175	159.469	27.985

Rates of Return and Capital Input for Finance, Insurance, and Real Estate, 1948–1976

Year	Rate of Return		Capital Quality	Capital Input		
	Nominal	Own		Price	Quantity	Value
1948	.105	.027	.475	.047	243.632	11.367
1949	.001	.024	.506	.046	261.914	12.168
1950	.104	.026	.530	.049	276.034	13.443
1951	.095	.021	.563	.049	295.718	14.408
1952	.047	.017	.595	.048	316.192	15.121
1953	.027	.020	.593	.052	314.354	16.265
1954	.027	.018	.612	.052	328.117	17.174
1955	.036	.019	.631	.053	341.165	18.142
1956	.039	.018	.641	.054	349.661	18.760
1957	.037	.015	.660	.055	366.246	20.098
1958	.022	.017	.674	.056	378.274	21.322
1959	.030	.019	.674	.060	379.294	22.925
1960	.027	.018	.678	.062	384.946	23.738
1961	.027	.019	.690	.062	395.035	24.412
1962	.031	.020	.701	.065	405.429	26.254
1963	.029	.020	.715	.065	418.184	27.389
1964	.031	.019	.738	.066	436.726	28.658
1965	.070	.024	.779	.067	467.248	31.437
1966	.077	.026	.807	.070	492.082	34.584
1967	.077	.024	.826	.072	504.415	36.145
1968	.080	.022	.853	.074	528.687	39.291
1969	.081	.020	.875	.075	545.761	41.172
1970	.078	.017	.926	.076	582.361	44.005
1971	.079	.019	.958	.081	608.880	49.316
1972	.073	.018	1.000	.081	652.426	52.969
1973	.067	.006	1.055	.070	722.136	50.615
1974	.105	.002	1.048	.072	732.158	52.944
1975	.082	-.000	1.059	.074	749.042	55.300
1976	.040	.002	1.065	.083	757.907	62.847

Rates of Return and Capital Input for Services, Excluding Private Households, Institutions, 1948–1976

Year	Rate of Return		Capital	Capital Input		
	Nominal	Own	Quality	Price	Quantity	Value
1948	.115	.030	.876	.061	43.740	2.655
1949	.025	.032	.885	.063	43.474	2.755
1950	.064	.028	.893	.074	43.312	3.202
1951	.112	.031	.890	.071	43.103	3.059
1952	.051	.027	.892	.074	42.589	3.164
1953	.040	.031	.887	.077	42.086	3.244
1954	.033	.029	.894	.078	42.237	3.300
1955	.077	.050	.889	.093	41.595	3.850
1956	.090	.046	.903	.094	43.708	4.111
1957	.088	.048	.908	.102	45.318	4.633
1958	.038	.042	.913	.100	46.968	4.703
1959	.065	.060	.923	.111	48.569	5.400
1960	.062	.057	.919	.108	51.895	5.612
1961	.053	.049	.935	.103	54.019	5.568
1962	.066	.057	.931	.108	56.494	6.095
1963	.067	.063	.933	.114	59.709	6.799
1964	.082	.071	.934	.119	63.015	7.481
1965	.096	.075	.947	.125	68.439	8.550
1966	.108	.075	.962	.126	73.849	9.325
1967	.108	.070	.977	.126	79.425	10.010
1968	.121	.070	.982	.132	81.890	10.804
1969	.120	.058	.999	.129	87.907	11.377
1970	.110	.050	1.008	.128	94.089	12.080
1971	.112	.051	.998	.136	97.311	13.269
1972	.109	.062	1.000	.153	99.372	15.220
1973	.143	.077	1.003	.175	103.138	18.081
1974	.204	.058	1.024	.169	110.513	18.648
1975	.175	.069	1.026	.201	112.875	22.725
1976	.116	.079	1.027	.237	113.987	27.005

Rates of Return and Capital Input for Private Households, 1948–1976

Year	Rate of Return		Capital Quality	Capital Input		
	Nominal	Own		Price	Quantity	Value
1948	.101	.038	.681	.085	321.385	27.298
1949	.018	.021	.708	.076	354.620	27.091
1950	.075	.034	.738	.086	389.367	33.521
1951	.098	.031	.776	.088	439.498	38.674
1952	.058	.038	.792	.094	470.174	44.391
1953	.036	.029	.802	.090	493.576	44.217
1954	.046	.049	.816	.103	522.589	53.595
1955	.064	.041	.826	.098	549.881	53.827
1956	.072	.037	.845	.098	593.235	57.972
1957	.052	.025	.857	.093	624.015	57.847
1958	.048	.039	.866	.104	648.879	67.304
1959	.055	.033	.867	.102	664.420	67.641
1960	.061	.046	.875	.113	693.256	78.205
1961	.059	.044	.881	.113	717.524	80.766
1962	.064	.045	.882	.114	733.646	83.968
1963	.057	.044	.889	.116	759.557	87.834
1964	.068	.049	.899	.120	793.424	95.502
1965	.077	.057	.911	.128	832.209	106.312
1966	.089	.059	.927	.132	879.406	115.701
1967	.098	.053	.944	.130	926.981	120.563
1968	.124	.049	.956	.132	966.760	127.579
1969	.084	.062	.970	.149	1017.248	151.553
1970	.097	.046	.984	.141	1064.756	150.501
1971	.101	.048	.992	.149	1097.661	163.609
1972	.139	.059	1.000	.164	1148.984	188.275
1973	.135	.070	1.011	.180	1220.289	219.705
1974	.122	.050	1.024	.170	1296.078	220.872
1975	.114	.039	1.029	.173	1336.872	230.682
1976		.047	1.034	.194	1367.927	265.136

Rates of Return and Capital Input for Institutions, 1948–1976

Year	Rate of Return		Capital Quality	Price	Capital Input	
	Nominal	Own			Quantity	Value
1948	.101	.012	.879	.020	47.723	.942
1949	.018	.029	.890	.028	49.142	1.362
1950	.075	.023	.899	.026	50.821	1.312
1951	.098	.001	.917	.020	53.914	1.055
1952	.058	.034	.925	.036	56.238	2.001
1953	.036	.024	.928	.032	57.956	1.858
1954	.046	.040	.931	.041	59.676	2.421
1955	.064	.035	.932	.039	61.857	2.437
1956	.072	−.001	.938	.024	64.225	1.568
1957	.052	.002	.943	.028	66.728	1.851
1958	.048	.040	.947	.049	69.484	3.428
1959	.055	.029	.949	.044	72.323	3.206
1960	.061	.043	.954	.054	75.550	4.050
1961	.059	.042	.959	.054	79.052	4.274
1962	.064	.040	.963	.054	82.748	4.454
1963	.057	.031	.970	.050	87.241	4.336
1964	.068	.038	.977	.055	91.780	5.088
1965	.077	.042	.988	.060	97.352	5.846
1966	.087	.039	.995	.060	102.809	6.216
1967	.089	.040	1.001	.064	108.289	6.971
1968	.098	.045	1.004	.071	112.454	7.987
1969	.124	.055	1.008	.083	116.935	9.739
1970	.084	.009	1.012	.051	121.016	6.228
1971	.097	.028	1.015	.072	124.315	8.978
1972	.101	.042	1.000	.090	121.887	10.950
1973	.139	.069	.989	.122	120.231	14.715
1974	.135	−.011	.973	.049	117.568	5.767
1975	.122	.005	.960	.076	114.786	8.715
1976	.114	.071	.957	.174	112.921	19.600

REFERENCES

1. ANDO, ALBERT, and BROWN, E. CARY. "The Impacts of Fiscal Policy," in *Stabilization Policies*. Edited by E. CARY BROWN et al. Englewood Cliffs, N.J.: Prentice Hall, 1963.

2. BOARD OF GOVERNORS OF THE FEDERAL RESERVE SYSTEM. *Federal Reserve Bulletin*, various monthly issues, Washington, D.C.

3. ____. *Flow of Funds Accounts, 1946-1975.* Washington, D.C.: FRS, 1976.

4. BUREAU OF THE CENSUS. *Enterprise Statistics: 1958, Part 3 Link of Census Establishment and IRS Corporation Data.* Series ES3, No. 3. Washington, D.C.: U.S. Department of Commerce, 1963.

5. ____. *Annual Survey of Manufactures, 1975.* Washington, D.C.: U.S.G.P.O., 1975.

6. ____. *Annual Survey of Manufactures, 1976.* Washington, D.C.: U.S. G.P.O., 1976.

7. BUREAU OF ECONOMIC ANALYSIS. "Transactions Table of 1958 Input-Output Study and Revised Direct and Total Requirement Data," *Survey of Current Business*, Sept. 1965, *45*(9), pp. 33-49, 56.

8. ____. *Input-Output Transactions: 1961*, Staff Paper in Economics and Statistics, No. 16. Washington, D.C.: U.S. Department of Commerce, 1968.

9. ____. "Input-Output Structure of the U.S. Economy: 1963," *Survey of Current Business*, Nov. 1969, *49*(11), pp. 16-47.

10. ____. *The Input-Output Structure of the United States Economy: 1947.* Washington, D.C.: U.S. Department of Commerce, March 1970.

11. ____. *Input-Output Transactions: 1966.* Staff Paper in Economics and Statistics, No. 19. Washington, D.C.: U.S. Department of Commerce, Feb. 1972.

12. ____. "The Input-Output Structure of the U.S. Economy: 1967," *Survey of Current Business*, Feb. 1974a, *54*(2), pp. 24-56.

13. ____. *The Input-Output Structure of the U.S. Economy: 1967, A Supplement to the Survey of Current Business.* Volume 1-2. Washington, D.C.: U.S. Department of Commerce, 1974b.

14. ____. *Interindustry Transactions in New Structures and Equipment, 1963 and 1967, Supplement to the Survey of Current Business.* Washington, D.C.: U.S. Department of Commerce, Sept. 1975a.

15. ____. *Summary Input-Output Tables of the U.S. Economy: 1968, 1969, 1970.* Bureau of Economic Analysis Staff Paper No. 27. Washington, D.C.: U.S. Department of Commerce, Sept. 1975b.

16. ____. *Fixed Nonresidential Business and Residential Capital in the United States, 1925-1975.* PB-253 725. Washington, D.C.: U.S. Department of Commerce, National Technical Information Service, 1976a.

17. ____. *The National Income and Product Accounts of the United States, 1929-1974: Statistical Tables, A Supplement to the Survey of Current Business.* Washington, D.C.: U.S. Department of Commerce, U.S.G.P.O., 1976b.

18. ____. *Input-Output Table of the U.S. Economy: 1971.* Bureau of Economic Analysis Staff Paper No. 28. Washington, D.C.: U.S. Department of Commerce, March 1977.

19. ____ . *Fourteen Current Dollar Components of Gross Product Originating by Industry.* Workfile 1205-01-03. Washington, D.C.: U.S. Department of Commerce, 1978.

20. ____ . *Survey of Current Business,* various monthly issues.

21. BUREAU OF LABOR STATISTICS. *Capital Flows Matrix, 1958.* Washington, D.C.: Oct. 1968.

22. ____ . *Development of Capital Stocks Series by Industry.* Bureau of Labor Statistics Bulletin. Washington, D.C.: U.S.G.P.O., 1979, forthcoming.

23. CHRISTENSEN, LAURITS R., and JORGENSON, DALE W. "The Measurement of U.S. Real Capital Input, 1929-1967," *Review of Income and Wealth,* Dec. 1969, Series 15 (4), pp. 293-320.

24. ____ . "U.S. Real Product and Real Factor Input, 1929-1967," *Review of Income and Wealth,* March 1970, Series 16 (1), pp. 19-50.

25. ____ . "Measuring the Performance of the Private Sector of the U.S. Economy, 1929-1969," in *Measuring Economic and Social Performance.* Edited by MILTON MOSS. New York: National Bureau of Economic Research, 1973.

26. DIEWERT, W. ERWIN. "Exact and Superlative Index Numbers," *Journal of Econometrics,* May 1976, *4*(2), pp. 115-46.

27. EXECUTIVE OFFICE OF THE PRESIDENT. *Standard Industrial Classification Manual.* Washington, D.C.: Bureau of the Budget, U.S.G.P.O., 1967.

28. ____ . *Standard Industrial Classification Manual.* Washington, D.C.: Bureau of the Budget, U.S.G.P.O., 1972.

29. FRANE, LENORE, and KLEIN, LAWRENCE R. "The Estimation of Disposable Income by Distributive Shares," *Review of Economics and Statistics,* Nov. 1953, *35*(4), pp. 333-37.

30. GOLDSMITH, RAYMOND W. *The National Wealth of the United States in the Postwar Period.* New York: National Bureau of Economic Research, 1962.

31. ____ . *The Balance Sheet of the United States, 1953-1973.* Preliminary draft dated March 1978.

32. GOLDSMITH, RAYMOND W.; LIPSEY, ROBERT E.; and MENDELSON, MORRIS. *Studies in the National Balance Sheet of the United States.* Princeton, N.J.: Princeton Univ. Press, 1963.

33. GOLLOP, FRANK M., and JORGENSON, DALE W. "U.S. Productivity Growth by Industry, 1947-1973," in *New Developments in Productivity Measurement.* Edited by JOHN W. KENDRICK and BEATRICE VACCARA. Chicago: Univ. of Chicago Press, 1980.

34. HALL, ROBERT E., and JORGENSON, DALE W. "Tax Policy and Investment Behavior," *American Economic Review,* June 1967, *57*(3), pp. 391-414.

35. ____ . "Application of the Theory of Optimum Capital Accumulation," in *Tax Incentives and Capital Spending.* Edited by GARY FROMM. Washington, D.C.: The Brookings Institution, 1971, pp. 9-60.

36. HULTEN, CHARLES. "Divisia Index Numbers," *Econometrica,* Nov. 1973a, *41* (6), pp. 1017-26.

37. ____. *The Measurement of Total Factor Productivity in U.S. Manufacturing, 1948-1966*, unpublished Ph.D. dissertation. University of California, Berkeley, 1973b.

38. INTERNAL REVENUE SERVICE. *Preliminary Statistics of Income, Corporation Income Tax Returns*, various annual issues.

39. ____. *Source Book, Statistics of Income, Active Corporation Income Tax Returns*, various annual issues.

40. ____. *Statistics of Income, Individual Returns*, various annual issues.

41. ____. *Statistics of Income, Partnerships and Proprietorships*, various annual issues.

42. JACK FAUCETT ASSOCIATES. *Data Development for the I-O Energy Model, Final Report*. Washington, D.C.: Submitted to the Energy Policy Project, May 1973a.

43. ____. *Development of Capital Stock Series by Industry Sector.* Washington, D.C.: Office of Emergency Preparedness, March 1973b.

44. ____. *Measures of Working Capital.* Washington, D.C.: U.S. Department of the Treasury, 1973c.

45. ____. *Output and Employment for Input-Output Sectors.* Washington, D.C.: U.S. Bureau of Labor Statistics, March 1975.

46. JORGENSON, DALE W. "The Economic Theory of Replacement and Depreciation," in *Econometrics and Economic Theory*. Edited by WILLY SELLEKAERTS. New York: Macmillan, 1973.

47. ____. "Accounting for Capital," in this volume.

48. KUZNETS, SIMON. *Capital in the American Economy*. Princeton, N.J.: Princeton Univ. Press, 1961.

49. LOFTUS, SHIRLEY F. "Stocks of Business Inventories in the United States, 1928-1971," *Survey of Current Business*, Dec. 1972, 52(12), pp. 29-32.

50. MANVEL, ALLEN. "Trends in the Value of Real Estate and Land, 1956-1966," *Three Land Research Studies*, The National Commission on Urban Problems, Washington, D.C.: U.S.G.P.O., 1968.

51. MUSGRAVE, JOHN. "Fixed Nonresidential Business and Residential Capital in the United States, 1925-1975," *Survey of Current Business*, April 1976, 56(4), pp. 46-52.

52. OFFICE OF ECONOMIC GROWTH. *Time Series Data for Input-Output Industries: Output, Price and Employment*. Washington, D.C.: Bureau of Labor Statistics, U.S. Department of Labor, Oct. 1977.

53. OFFICE OF TAX ANALYSIS. Unpublished Tables: "Investment and Asset Life by Industry and Type of Equipment; Use of Depreciation Methods by Industry and Equipment Type; and Investment by Industry." Washington, D.C.: U.S. Department of the Treasury, 1973 (typewritten).

54. UNITED STATES DEPARTMENT OF THE TREASURY. *Treasury Bulletin*, various issues.

55. VASQUEZ, THOMAS. "ADR Paper." Washington, D.C.: U.S. Department of the Treasury, Office of Tax Analysis, May 1974 (typewritten).

56. WALDERHAUG, ALBERT J. "The Composition of Value Added in the 1963 Input-Output Study," *Survey of Current Business*, April 1973, 53(4), pp. 34-44.

57. WOODWARD, JOHN T. "Plant and Equipment Expenditures: 1977 Programs Revised," *Survey of Current Business*, Sept. 1977, *57*(9), pp. 17–22.

58. YOUNG, ALLAN. "Alternative Estimates of Corporate Depreciation and Profits: Part I," *Survey of Current Business*, April 1968, *48*(4), pp. 17–28.

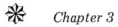 *Chapter 3*

Accounting for Capital

Dale W. Jorgenson

The purpose of this chapter is to present the framework that was used for accounting for the role of capital in the economic growth of the United States over the period 1948–1976 in the preceding chapter. Economic growth is defined as an increase in the national product, consisting of all goods and services delivered to ultimate consumers. The national product includes the consumption of households and institutions, the investment of businesses, the consumption and investment of governments, and net exports to the rest of the world.

Investment is made up of all newly produced capital goods and additions to inventories. The future is linked to the present through the prices of new capital goods. The value of a new capital good reflects the value of its future services as capital input, extending forward in time. At any point in time the services of capital goods are combined with labor services to generate the national product. The past is linked to the present through the stocks of all capital goods currently in existence. Stocks of capital goods are the result of past investments, extending backward in time.

Property and labor compensation comprise the outlay of the production sector on primary factors of production. After this outlay has been reduced by direct and indirect taxes, the remainder accrues to households and institutions as income. National income also includes compensation net of taxes for capital and labor services supplied to governments and to the rest of the world. Total receipts by households and institutions include government transfer payments to persons as well as income generated by the supply of capital and labor services. These receipts are allocated between outlays on consumption and saving. Depreciation, defined as the loss in value of capital goods currently in existence with age, accounts for a substantial portion of national saving.

For the U.S. economy as a whole, saving is identically equal to capital formation. Capital formation takes place through the purchase of new capital goods, the accumulation of inventories, and the acquisition of claims on governments and on the rest of the world. Changes in national wealth can be allocated between net capital formation, defined as capital formation less depreciation, and the revaluation of capital goods as changes in capital goods prices take place. Net capital formation can be divided between the accumulation of tangible assets that generate capital services in the producing sectors of the economy and the accumulation of claims on governments and the rest of the world.

Growth in national product takes place through growth in capital and labor inputs and through changes in technology. Growth in capital input results from additions to the stocks of capital goods through the production of new capital goods. A complete account of the role of capital in U.S. economic growth must include investment in new capital goods, the holding of stocks of capital goods resulting from past investments, and the utilization of services of all capital goods currently in existence. Such an account must also encompass the system of prices for capital goods that determines the allocation of capital in the U.S. economy.

The prices of new capital goods are compared with the prices of consumption goods and services in determining the allocation of the national product between investment and consumption. The prices of the services of capital goods currently in existence are compared with the prices of labor services in selecting the relative proportions of capital and labor services in production. Income from property resulting from past investments and changes in the prices of capital goods determine the return to capital that enters into the choice between consumption and saving. The return to tangible assets employed in production is compared with the return to claims on governments and the rest of the world in allocating the national wealth among different forms of assets.

In the remaining sections of this chapter we present a detailed accounting framework for the role of capital in U.S. economic growth. This framework consists of a system of accounts that encompasses national aggregates for production, income, saving, and wealth. It includes accounts for production by individual sectors of the U.S.

economy. The system of accounts incorporates prices and quantities of investment, capital stock, and capital services at both aggregate and sectoral levels. Accounts for outlay on capital services and for property income include rates of return to capital.

In the first section of the chapter we present a system of accounts for the measurement of output and capital in current prices. This requires production accounts for all industrial sectors and for the economy as a whole, including output and outlay on productive inputs. We first present an aggregate production account that contains data on the value of aggregate output and the value of outlay on primary factor inputs. We also describe sectoral production accounts that include data on the value of sectoral output and the value of sectoral outlay on intermediate input and on primary factor inputs. Second, we consider an aggregate income and expenditure account, incorporating data on income from the supply of factor services, net of taxes, and transfer payments. These receipts are allocated between consumer outlays and saving. The aggregate accumulation account includes data on saving, capital formation, and revaluation of existing assets. Finally, the aggregate wealth account contains data on values of wealth at each point of time.

In the second section of the chapter we outline an approach to the measurement of sectoral output and capital in constant prices. Our approach is based on a system of vintage accounts for prices and quantities of capital goods originated by Christensen and Jorgenson [17, 1973]. The characterization of capital goods that underlies our system of vintage accounts is based on the relative efficiency of capital goods of different ages. Given data on investment in each type of capital and on property compensation in each producing sector, we develop measures of the price and quantity of capital input. These data are combined with measures of output, intermediate input, and labor input to obtain sectoral production accounts in constant prices.

In the third section of the chapter we outline a methodology for incorporating data on property compensation, accumulation and revaluation, and wealth into a complete system of aggregate accounts in constant prices. Finally, we present a methodology for implementation of an aggregate production account. Our methodology encompasses the development of data on the price and quantity of aggregate capital input; these data are combined with measures of aggregate output and labor input to obtain an aggregate production account in constant prices. We analyze the relationship between sectoral production accounts and the aggregate production account by aggregating over sectors to obtain aggregate measures of output, capital input, and labor input.

Our complete accounting system for analyzing the role of capital in U.S. economic growth has been implemented for 1948–1976 by Fraumeni and Jorgenson [33, 1980]. The first step is the compilation of data on investment by individual producing sectors. At each point of time the stock of capital goods in each sector is estimated on the basis of past investments. Data on investment and capital stock at the sectoral level are combined into national aggregates for investment, capital formation and revaluation, capital stock, and wealth. Data on property compensation by individual sectors are combined with information on the tax structure and estimates of revaluation of existing stocks of capital goods to obtain estimates of rates of return to capital for individual sectors and for the economy as a whole. Data on property compensation at the sectoral level are combined with data on consumer outlays and saving to obtain national income and expenditure.

The primary focus of the study of the role of capital in U.S. economic growth presented in the preceding chapter is on the growth of capital input at both sectoral and aggregate levels. The growth of capital input results from capital formation through the acquisition of tangible assets, including new capital goods and inventories. Changes in the value of tangible assets take place through capital formation and the revaluation of capital goods. Capital formation results from saving out of income, while revaluation together with earnings determine rates of return on existing assets. Income is generated through the supply of capital and labor services.

A complete accounting system for the U.S. economy is required to encompass all aspects of the role of capital in the U.S. economy—as input in the production account, a source of income in the income and expenditure account, a use of income in the saving and capital formation account, and a store of wealth in the wealth account. Such an accounting system imposes internal consistency on quantitative measures of capital input, capital formation, and wealth. It also incorporates the interrelationships among the different roles played by capital in the process of economic growth.

I. A SYSTEM OF ACCOUNTS

The first step in accounting for the role of capital in economic growth is to measure output and capital in current prices. This requires a system of four accounts. First, the aggregate production account includes data on the output of all industrial sectors and the outlay of all sectors on factor services. The sectoral production accounts include data on the outlay of individual sectors on intermediate input and on factor services. Second, the aggregate income and expenditure account contains transfer payments and income from factor services; these receipts are allocated between consumer outlays and saving. Third, the aggregate accumulation account includes saving, capital formation, revaluation of existing assets, and the change in wealth from period to period. Finally, successive values of wealth are contained in the aggregate wealth account.

Production Accounts

The aggregate production account contains data on the value of aggregate output and the value of aggregate input; as an accounting identity the value of output is equal to the value of input. The value of output is equal to the sum of value added in all sectors of the economy. The value of input is equal to the sum of factor outlay in all sectors. Value added is equal to the value of all deliveries to final demand, including production of investment goods and production of consumption goods. The two sides of the aggregate production account are linked through investment goods output and compensation for the services of capital. Investment goods output enters the change in wealth from period to period through capital formation. Accumulated wealth generates factor incomes in the form of compensation for the services of capital.

In the U.S. national income and product accounts, total output is divided among services, nondurable goods, durable goods, and structures.[a] The output of services includes the services of owner-occupied dwellings; the output of structures includes the production of new residential housing. Capital formation in the form of residential housing is a component of the change in wealth from period to period; property compensation includes the imputed value of compensation for the use of owner-occupied dwellings. The output of durables includes consumer durables and producer durables used by nonprofit institutions. However, property compensation, as defined in the U.S. national accounts, does not include the imputed value of the services of these durables.

In the U.S. national accounts, the value of the services of owner-occupied residential real estate, including structures and land, is imputed from market rental prices of tenant-occupied residential real estate. The value of these services is allocated among net rent, interest, taxes, and capital consumption allowances. A similar imputation is made for the services of real estate used by nonprofit institutions,

---

[a]All references to the U.S. national income and product accounts are to *The National Income and Product Accounts of the United States, 1929-1974, Statistical Tables, A Supplement to The Survey of Current Business* [11, 1976b].

but the imputed value excludes net rent. To preserve consistency between the accounts for investment goods production and for property compensation we introduce imputations for the value of the services of consumer durables and durables used by nonprofit institutions and the net rent of real estate used by institutions.[b] The value of the services of these assets is included in the output of services, together with the services of owner-occupied dwellings. Property compensation also includes the value of these services. This imputation preserves the accounting identity between the value of output and the value of input.

The sectoral production accounts contain data on the value of sectoral output and the value of sectoral input. The value of output includes the value of intermediate input as well as the value of factor outlay. Value added in each sector is equal to the difference between the value of output and the value of intermediate input; as an accounting identity value added is equal to the value of factor outlay. We implement sectoral production accounts for all sectors of the U.S. private domestic economy, including production activities of U.S. business and household sectors and nonprofit institutions. In principle, similar accounts could be constructed for government and rest of the world sectors of the U.S. economy.

We define the revenue of each sector as proceeds to the sector from the sale of output and the outlay of each sector as gross outlays by the sector on purchases of input. We distinguish between taxes charged against revenue, such as excise or sales taxes on output, and taxes that are part of the outlay on purchases of input. These taxes include property taxes that are part of outlay on capital input and excise or sales taxes that are part of outlay on intermediate input. We exclude taxes on output from the value of gross output since these taxes are not included in the proceeds to the sector. We include taxes on input since these taxes are included in the outlay of the sector. Our concept of output is intermediate between gross output at market prices and gross output at factor cost, as these concepts are usually employed. Output at market prices includes all indirect taxes on the value of output; output at factor cost excludes all indirect taxes.

For the economy as a whole we define revenue as the sum of value added in all sectors of the economy, where value added is the difference between the value of output and the value of intermediate input. Output excludes excise or sales taxes on output, but the value of intermediate input includes excise and sales taxes paid on inter-

---

[b] These imputations are based on those of Christensen and Jorgenson [15, 1969].

mediate input. Value added includes taxes paid on capital and labor input. To be more specific, we exclude all excise and sales taxes, business nontax payments, and customs duties from the value of output and include other indirect business taxes plus subsidies less current surplus of federal and state and local government enterprises. The resulting aggregate production account is given for 1972 in Table 3–1.

As an accounting identity, the value of gross private domestic factor outlay is equal to the value of gross private domestic product. Factor outlay is the sum of income originating in private enterprises and private households and institutions, plus the imputed value of consumer durables, producer durables utilized by institutions, and the net rent on institutional real estate, plus indirect taxes included in factor outlay. Factor outlay includes capital consumption allowances, business transfer payments, and the statistical discrepancy. Capital consumption allowances are part of the rental value of capital services. We include business transfer payments and the statistical discrepancy in factor outlay on capital. The value of gross private domestic factor outlay for the year 1972 is presented in Table 3–1.

The sectoral production accounts are similar in concept to the aggregate production account presented in Table 3–1. For each sector the value of output excludes excise and sales taxes on output, but includes taxes paid on intermediate, capital, and labor inputs. As an accounting identity the value of sectoral output is equal to the value of sectoral outlay on intermediate input and the value of sectoral factor outlay, the outlay on sectoral capital and labor inputs. Sectoral value added is equal to the value of sectoral factor outlay. We achieve consistency between the sectoral and aggregate production accounts by defining value added at the aggregate level as the sum of value added in all sectors. Similarly, outlays on capital and labor inputs at the aggregate level are defined as sums of sectoral outlays on capital and labor inputs over all sectors. These outlays are included in the definition of income for the aggregate income and expenditure account.

Income and Expenditure Account

The income and expenditure account includes data on transfer payments and the value of income from factor services, the value of consumer outlays, and saving. As an accounting identity, the value of consumer receipts is equal to the value of consumer outlays plus saving. The two sides of the income and expenditure account are linked through property compensation and saving. Saving results in the accumulation of tangible assets and financial claims; the accumulated

Table 3—1.   Production Account: Gross Private Domestic Product and Factor Outlay, 1972 *(billions of current dollars)*

		Product	
1.		Private gross national product (Table 1.7, ℓ.1 minus ℓ.12)[a]	1,033.7
2.	−	Compensation of employees in government enterprises (Table 6.5, ℓ.78 and ℓ.81)	15.1
3.	−	Rest of the world gross national product (Table 1.7, ℓ.15)	7.0
4.	+	Services of consumer durables (Christensen–Jorgenson)[b]	121.7
5.	+	Services of durables held by institutions (Christensen–Jorgenson)	2.7
6.	+	Net rent on institutional real estate (Christensen–Jorgenson)	4.5
7.	−	Federal indirect business tax and nontax accruals (Table 3.2, ℓ.12)	20.0
8.	+	Capital stock tax (Table 3.2, footnote 2)	—
9.	−	State and local indirect business tax and nontax accruals (Table 3.4, ℓ.24)	91.0
10.	+	Business motor vehicle licenses (Table 3.4, ℓ.24)	1.5
11.	+	Business property taxes (Table 3.4, ℓ.23)	43.0
12.	+	Business other taxes (Table 3.4, ℓ.25)	4.4
13.	+	Subsidies less current surplus of federal government enterprises (Table 3.2, ℓ.39)	7.8
14.	+	Subsidies less current surplus of state and local government enterprises (Table 3.4, ℓ.48)	−4.2
15.	=	Gross private domestic product	1,082.1

		Factor Outlay	
1.		Compensation of employees (GPO)[c]	562.6
2.	+	Income of self-employed persons allocated to labor compensation (Fraumeni–Jorgenson)[d]	68.7
3.	+	Property compensation before taxes (Fraumeni–Jorgenson)	450.7
4.	=	Gross private domestic factor outlay	1,082.1

[a]All table references are to the U.S. national income and product accounts, [11, 1976b], henceforth NIPA.

[b]These data are taken directly from the Christensen–Jorgenson aggregate national income accounts, [15, 1969; 16, 1970; 17, 1973], henceforth Christensen–Jorgenson.

[c]This series is taken from the Bureau of Economic Analysis study *Fourteen Current Dollar Components of Gross Product Originating by Industry*, [12, 1978], henceforth GPO.

[d]These data are taken from the study of Fraumeni and Jorgenson [33, 1980], henceforth Fraumeni–Jorgenson.

wealth generates future property income. Saving must be defined in a way that is consistent with accounts for property income. Income must include all payments for factor services that result in consumption expenditures or in the accumulation of assets that result in future income.

We implement the income and expenditure account for the U.S. private national economy. For this purpose we consolidate the accounts of private business with those of private households and institutions. Financial claims on the business sector by households and institutions are liabilities of the business sector; in the consolidated accounts these assets and liabilities cancel out. The assets of the private national economy include the tangible assets of the business sector. We treat social insurance funds as part of the private national economy. The claims of these funds on the rest of the governmental sector are treated as assets of the private sector.

In the U.S. national accounts the income and expenditure account of the government sector does not include income from tangible assets owned by government. If capital accounts were available for the government sector, we could construct income and expenditure accounts for that sector which would be analogous to our accounts for the private sector. The income and expenditure account of the rest of the world sector of the U.S. national accounts is comparable to our account for the private sector.

We define income of the private national economy as proceeds from the sale of factor services. We define expenditure of the sector as consumer outlays plus saving. Our concept of income is closer to that underlying the concept of gross private saving in the U.S. national accounts than to the more commonly employed concept of personal disposable income. Accordingly, we refer to our income concept as gross private national income. Outlay on factor services by the production sector includes indirect taxes such as property taxes and motor vehicle licenses. This outlay also includes direct taxes such as corporate and personal income taxes. Our concept of gross private national income excludes both indirect and direct taxes.

To be specific, gross private national income includes labor and property income originating in the private domestic economy and the rest of the world sectors, labor income originating in the government sector, net interest paid by government, and the statistical discrepancy. Income is net of indirect taxes on factor outlay and all direct taxes on incomes. Gross private national income excludes interest paid by consumers and personal transfer payments to foreigners. Income also includes the investment income of social insurance

Table 3–2.   Gross Private National Receipts and Expenditures, 1972
(billions of current dollars)

	Receipts	
1.	Property compensation before taxes (Fraumeni–Jorgenson)	450.7
2. +	Compensation of employees (GPO)	562.6
3. +	Income of self-employed persons allocated to labor compensation (Fraumeni–Jorgenson)	68.7
4. +	Compensation of employees in general government (GPO)	137.4
5. +	Compensation of employees in government enterprises (GPO)	15.1
6. +	Compensation of employees, corporate profits and net interest, rest of world (Table 6.1, ℓ.178, ℓ.180)	7.0
7. +	Net reinvested earnings, rest of world (BOP)[a]	4.0
8. +	Investment income of social insurance funds less transfers to general government (Table 3.10, ℓ.7 and ℓ.18 minus ℓ.10 and ℓ.21)	5.8
9. +	Government owned privately operated, later sold manufacturing investment (JFA)[b]	0.0
10. +	Net interest paid by government (Table 3.1, ℓ.13 minus Table 4.1, Table 4.1, ℓ.13)	9.7
11. −	Corporate profits tax liability (Table 6.20, ℓ.1)	41.5
12. −	Indirect business taxes allocated to capital assets (Fraumeni–Jorgenson)[c]	48.9
13. −	Personal tax and nontax payments (Table 2.1, ℓ.23)	141.2
14. +	Personal nontax payments (Table 3.2, ℓ.8 and Table 3.4, ℓ.8)	10.6
15. =	Gross private national income	1,040.1
16. +	Government transfer payments to persons other than benefits from social insurance funds (Table 3.12, ℓ.2 and ℓ.28 minus ℓ.3 and ℓ.29)	30.6
17. =	Gross private national consumer receipts	1,070.7
	Expenditures	
1.	Personal consumption expenditures (Table 1.1, ℓ.2)	733.0
2. −	Personal consumption expenditures, durable goods (Table 1.1, ℓ.3)	111.2
3. +	Services of consumer durables (Christensen–Jorgenson)	121.7
4. +	Services of institutional durables (Christensen–Jorgenson)	2.7
5. +	Net rent on institutional real estate (Christensen–Jorgenson)	4.5
6. =	Private national consumption expenditure	750.8
7. +	Personal transfer payments to foreigners (Table 2.1, ℓ.28)	1.0
8. +	Personal nontax payments (Table 3.2, ℓ.8 and Table 3.4, ℓ.8)	10.6
9. =	Private national consumer outlays	762.4
10. +	Gross private national saving	308.3
11. =	Private national expenditures	1,070.7

Notes to Table 3–2

[a]This series is taken from the U.S. Balance of Payments Accounts and accompanying article published yearly in the *Survey of Current Business* [13], henceforth BOP.
[b]This series is taken from the study described in Jack Faucett Associates, Inc. *Development of Capital Stock Series by Industry Sector* [44, 1973], henceforth JFA.
[c]Line 12 is equal to Table 1, sum of lines 10, 11, and 12.

funds, less transfers to general government by these funds. Contributions to social insurance are included and transfers from social insurance funds are excluded from income. The value of gross private national income for the year 1972 is presented in Table 3–2.

Consumption is equal to personal consumption expenditures on services and nondurable goods plus our imputation for the services of consumer and institutional durables and the net rent of institutional real estate. Purchases of consumer durables, included in personal consumption expenditures in the U.S. national accounts, are treated as part of saving in our income and expenditure account. The value of consumption includes taxes and excludes subsidies on output; these taxes are excluded from the value of consumption goods output in the production account. Our concept of saving differs from gross private saving as defined in the U.S. national accounts in the treatment of social insurance and the statistical discrepancy. The expenditure account for consuming sector for the year 1972 is presented in Table 3–2.

Our definition of income is similar to the definition underlying the U.S. national accounts concept of gross private saving. Our definition differs from the national accounts concept in the treatment of social insurance and transfer payments and the inclusion of the services of consumer and institutional durables, the net rent on institutional real estate, and the statistical discrepancy. Transfer payments are treated as a nonincome receipt of the consumer sector. The services of durables, net rent, and the statistical discrepancy are treated as part of outlays on capital services. The services of durables are included in output and capital input in order to preserve consistency between the definition of investment goods in the production account and the definition of property compensation in the factor outlay account. Net rent is included in output and factor outlay to preserve consistency between the treatment of owner-occupied residential real estate and institutional real estate. The statistical discrepancy is assigned to factor outlay so that the accounting identity between the value of output and the value of factor outlay is preserved.

Our treatment of social insurance can be compared with the treatment that underlies the U.S. national accounting concepts of personal disposable income and gross private saving. In these concepts the social insurance funds are treated as part of the government sector rather than the private sector. Contributions to social insurance are treated as a tax and benefits paid by these funds are treated as a transfer payment. The financial claims of social insurance funds on other governmental bodies cancel out in a consolidated government wealth account. Our concept of income focuses on the separation of contributions to social insurance from other taxes and on the effects of a future stream of benefits on saving decisions by individuals. The national accounts treatment focuses on the involuntary nature of contributions to social insurance.

We next divide gross private national income between labor and property income. Compensation of employees, including wages, salaries and supplements from the Bureau of Economic Analysis study *Fourteen Current Dollar Components of Gross Product Originating by Industry* [12, 1978] is allocated to labor income. We impute income of self-employed persons allocated to labor compensation as a byproduct of the calculation of property compensation before taxes.[c] Total property compensation before taxes for all industries is included in property income. In addition we assign net reinvested earnings, rest of world, the investment income of social insurance funds less transfers to general government, and net interest paid by government to property income. Net reinvested earnings are the retained earnings of U.S. corporations abroad less the retained earnings of foreign corporations in the U.S. We deduct from property income the corporate profits tax liability, indirect business taxes allocated to property, personal property taxes, and all estate and gift taxes.

We employ figures for personal income taxes from the Christensen and Jorgenson national income accounting system [15, 1969; 17, 1973]. Personal income taxes, which are deducted from income, are allocated between labor and property income in accord with a method developed by Lenore Frane and Lawrence Klein. They describe their method as follows: "The fraction of taxes in each income bracket allocated to wage income is estimated by the ratio of wage and salary income to 'adjusted gross income' in each bracket. Total taxes allocated to wages are the sum of the taxes so allocated in all brackets" [32, 1953, p. 336]. This method has been applied by Albert Ando and Cary Brown [1, 1963] to U.S. data for 1929 to

---

[c]For more detailed discussion, see Fraumeni and Jorgenson [33, 1980]. Alternative methods for imputation are discussed by Christensen [14, 1971] and Irving Kravis [50, 1959].

1958. Their figures have been updated to 1976 in a way that closely approximates this procedure.

Personal income taxes on income from labor services, as estimated by Ando and Brown, are a remarkably stable proportion of total personal income tax receipts. The 1929–1958 figures show an average proportion of 0.755, with a negligible amount of variation. *Statistics of Income* [43, IRS] indicates that the ratio of labor to property income was very stable in the 1951–1958 period and that pattern has continued to the present. A proportion of 0.755 of personal income taxes is allocated to labor income for all years from 1959 to 1976. Prior to 1959, we use the actual proportions estimated by Ando and Brown to allocate personal income taxes to labor income. The remainder of personal income taxes are attributed to property income. The components of labor and property income for 1972 are presented in Table 3–3.

Property Compensation

In production accounts we measure property compensation from the point of view of the producing sectors, so that compensation includes all taxes. In the income and expenditure account we measure property compensation from the point of view of the asset owner so that we exclude all direct and indirect taxes. The tax base for personal income taxes on property compensation includes property compensation in the corporate and noncorporate sectors. It also includes the net interest paid by the government and the sum of corporate profits and net interest paid by the rest of the world. We estimate the effective rate of personal income tax on property compensation as the ratio of personal income taxes on property compensation plus the investment tax credit to the tax base less state and local taxes on property compensation. We allocate personal income taxes on property compensation by legal form of organization by assuming that the effective tax rate is the same for all sectors.

Property compensation on assets held in the household sector is not subject to the personal income tax. However, property taxes and interest paid on these assets are deductible from the base for personal income taxes, creating a subsidy on property compensation from household assets. We allocate federal and state and local gift taxes on property compensation in proportion to the value of the assets included in private national wealth. A detailed breakdown of gross private national property compensation by legal form of organization is presented for 1972 in Table 3–4.

Table 3–3.   Gross Private National Labor and Property Income, 1972
(billions of current dollars)

	Labor Income	
1.	Compensation of employees (GPO)	562.6
2. +	Income of self-employed persons allocated to labor compensation (Fraumeni–Jorgenson)	68.7
3. +	Compensation of employees in general government (GPO)	137.4
4. +	Compensation of employees in government enterprises (GPO)	15.1
5. +	Compensation of employees, rest of world (GPO)	0.0
6. −	Personal income taxes attributed to labor income (Christensen–Jorgenson)[a]	90.7
7. =	Private national labor income	693.1
	Property Income	
1.	Property compensation before taxes (Fraumeni–Jorgenson)	450.7
2. +	Corporate profits, rest of world (GPO)	4.8
3. +	Net interest, rest of world (GPO)	2.2
4. +	Net reinvested earnings, rest of world (BOP)	4.0
5. +	Investment income of social insurance funds less transfers to general government (Table 3.10, ℓ.7 and ℓ.18 minus ℓ.10 and ℓ.21)	5.8
6. +	Net interest paid by government (Table 3.1, ℓ.13 minus Table 4.1, ℓ.13)	9.7
7. −	Corporate profits tax liability (Table 6.20, ℓ.1)	41.5
8. −	Indirect business taxes allocated to capital assets (Fraumeni–Jorgenson)	48.9
9. −	Personal income taxes attributed to property income (Christensen–Jorgenson)[a]	29.4
10. −	Federal estate and gift taxes (Table 3.2, ℓ.7)[a]	5.4
11. −	State and local estate and gift taxes (Table 3.4, ℓ.4)[a]	1.4
12. −	State and local personal motor vehicle licenses, property taxes, and other taxes (Table 3.4, ℓ.5, ℓ.6, and ℓ.7)[a]	3.7
13. =	Gross private national property income	346.9

[a]The sum of line 6 under labor income plus lines 9, 10, 11, and 12 under property income is equal to Table 2, line 13 minus line 14.

Table 3-4. Gross Private National Property Compensation after Taxes by Legal Form of Organization, 1972 *(billions of current dollars)*

Corporate Property Compensation

1.	Corporate property compensation before taxes (Fraumeni-Jorgenson)	184.9
2. −	Corporate profits tax liability (Table 6.20, ℓ.1)	41.5
3. −	Indirect business taxes allocated to corporate capital assets (Fraumeni-Jorgenson)	21.2
4. −	Personal income taxes attributed to corporate property income (Christensen-Jorgenson)	20.0
5. −	Wealth taxes attributed to corporate assets (Fraumeni-Jorgenson)	2.0
6. =	Corporate property compensation after taxes	100.2

Noncorporate Property Compensation

1.	Noncorporate property compensation before taxes (Fraumeni-Jorgenson)	66.6
2. −	Indirect business taxes allocated to noncorporate capital assets (Fraumeni-Jorgenson)	10.6
3. −	Personal income taxes attributed to noncorporate property income (Christensen-Jorgenson)	10.9
4. −	Wealth taxes attributed to noncorporate assets (Fraumeni-Jorgenson)	1.5
5. =	Noncorporate property compensation after taxes	43.6

Household Property Compensation

1.	Household property compensation before taxes (Fraumeni-Jorgenson)	188.3
2. −	Property taxes, owner-occupied dwellings (Table 8.3, ℓ.65 and ℓ.77)	17.1
3. −	Personal property taxes, consumer durables (Table 3.4, ℓ.5, ℓ.6 and ℓ.7)	3.7
4. −	Personal income taxes attributed to household and property income (Christensen-Jorgenson)[a]	−7.5
5. −	Wealth taxes attributed to household assets (Fraumeni-Jorgenson)	2.2
6. =	Household property compensation after taxes	172.8

Institutional Property Compensation

1.	Institutional property compensation after taxes (Fraumeni-Jorgenson)	10.9
2. −	Wealth taxes attributed to institutional assets (Fraumeni-Jorgenson)	0.2
3. =	Institutional property compensation after taxes (Fraumeni-Jorgenson)	10.7

(Table 3-4. continued overleaf)

Table 3—4. continued

Compensation from Net Claims on Government and Rest of World	
1. Net interest paid by government domestically (Table 3.1, ℓ.13 minus Table 4.1, ℓ.13)	9.7
2. + Investment income of social insurance funds less transfers to general government (Table 3.10, ℓ.7 and ℓ.18 minus ℓ.10 and ℓ.21)	5.8
3. + Corporate profits, rest of world (Table 6.1, ℓ.179)	4.8
4. + Net interest, rest of world (Table 6.1, ℓ.180)	2.2
5. + Net reinvested earnings, rest of world	4.0
6. − Personal income taxes attributed to compensation from net claims (Fraumeni–Jorgenson)	6.0
7. − Wealth taxes attributed to net claims (Fraumeni–Jorgenson)	0.9
8. = Compensation from net claims	19.6

[a]The negative tax reflects deductibility of interest and property taxes for owner occupied dwellings.

Accumulation Account

The accumulation account includes data on saving, capital formation, revaluation of existing assets, and the change in wealth from period to period. Gross private national saving is reduced by depreciation to obtain saving as it enters the accumulation account. As an accounting identity, the value of saving is equal to the value of capital formation. The change in wealth from period to period is equal to saving plus the revaluation of existing assets. Although revaluations are part of the change in wealth, they are excluded from income and from saving. In measuring the return from investment in different types of assets, both returns in the form of income and returns from revaluations must be considered.

We implement the accumulation account for the U.S. private national economy. Sources of saving include gross private saving, as defined in the U.S. national accounts, government-owned, privately operated investment, later sold or transferred to the private sector, the surplus of federal and state and local social insurance funds, personal consumption expenditures on durable goods, net reinvested earnings, rest of world, and the statistical discrepancy. Capital formation includes gross private domestic investment, personal consumption expenditures on durable goods, deficits of the federal, state, and local governments excluding social insurance funds, and net foreign investment. Private national saving and capital formation are given for 1972 in Table 3—5.

To estimate the change in wealth from period to period we require estimates of saving net of depreciation and estimates of the revalua-

Table 3–5. Gross Private National Capital Formation, Saving, and Revaluation, 1972 *(billions of current dollars)*

Saving	
1. Personal saving (Table 5.1, ℓ.3)	49.4
2. + Undistributed corporate profits (Table 5.1, ℓ.5)	30.0
3. + Government owned privately operated, later sold manufacturing investment (JFA)	0.0
4. + Net reinvested earnings, rest of world (BOP)	4.0
5. + Corporate inventory valuation adjustment (Table 5.1, ℓ.6)	−6.6
6. + Corporate capital consumption allowances (GPO)	67.9
7. + Noncorporate capital consumption allowances with capital consumption adjustment (Table 5.1, ℓ.9)	40.0
8. + Private wage accruals less disbursements (Table 5.1, ℓ.10)	−0.3
9. + Personal consumption expenditures, durable goods (Table 1.1, ℓ.3)	111.2
10. + Surplus, social insurance funds (Table 3.10, ℓ.11 and ℓ.22)	10.7
11. + Government wage accruals less disbursements (Table 3.1, ℓ.17)	0.3
12. + Statistical discrepancy (Table 1.9, ℓ.8)	1.7
13. = Gross private national saving	308.3
14. − Depreciation (Fraumeni–Jorgenson)	191.4
15. = Net private national saving	116.8
16. + Revaluation (Fraumeni–Jorgenson)	129.4
17. = Change in private national wealth	246.2
Capital Formation	
1. Gross private domestic investment (Table 1.1, ℓ.6)	188.3
2. + Personal consumption expenditures, durable goods (Table 1.1, ℓ.3)	111.2
3. + Government owned privately operated, later sold manufacturing investment (JFA)	0.0
4. + Deficit of federal government (Table 3.2, ℓ.43)	17.3
5. + Deficit of state & local governments (Table 3.4, ℓ.52)	−13.7
6. − Deficit, federal social insurance funds (Table 3.10, ℓ.11)	−2.6
7. − Deficit, state & local social insurance funds (Table 3.10, ℓ.22)	−8.1
8. + Wage accruals less disbursements, federal government (Table 3.2, ℓ.42)	0.5
9. + Wage accruals less disbursements, state & local government (Table 3.4, ℓ.51)	−0.2
10. + Net foreign investment (Christensen–Jorgenson)	−5.8
11. = Gross private national capital formation	308.3
12. − Replacement (Fraumeni–Jorgenson)	191.4
13. = Net private national capital formation	116.8

tion of existing assets due to price changes. Revaluations are not included in the U.S. national accounts, so that an essential link between income and expenditure accounts and wealth accounts is missing. We have estimated the revaluations for private domestic tangible assets as part of our perpetual inventory of capital goods. Our estimates of revaluation for financial claims are based on accounts for stocks of these claims in current prices. We estimate revaluation as the difference between the period to period changes in these stocks and the deficits of the government and rest of the world sectors. The annual change in wealth can be represented as net capital formation plus capital gains or revaluation.

Wealth Account

All of the accounts we have considered up to this point contain data on flows. The production account includes flows of output and input; the income and expenditure account includes the corresponding flows; the flow of saving and changes in wealth from period to period are included in the accumulation account. The wealth account contains data on the stock of wealth in successive periods. The wealth account can be presented in balance sheet form with the value of assets equal to the value of liabilities as an accounting identity. We present only the asset side of the wealth account.

We implement the wealth account for the U.S. private national economy. The wealth accounts of private business are consolidated with those of private households and institutions. Our wealth account includes data on assets in the consolidated account. These assets include the tangible assets of private households and institutions and the tangible assets of private business. In addition, they include net claims on the foreign and government sectors by the private sector. Social insurance funds are treated as part of the private sector rather than as part of government.

Our estimate of the stock of private domestic tangible assets is based on a perpetual inventory of capital goods. Our estimate of net claims on government and the rest of the world is based on the flow of funds accounts of the Board of Governors of the Federal Reserve System [8, 1976], the *Treasury Bulletin* [65, U.S. Department of the Treasury], and the *Survey of Current Business* [11, 1976b; 13, BEA].[d] We distinguish between monetary and nonmonetary claims on the federal government by the private sector. Monetary claims include vault cash of commercial banks, member bank reserves, and currency outside banks [7, Board of Governors of the Federal Re-

---

[d]Historical data on flow of funds are provided by Raymond Goldsmith [34, 1962; 35, 1978; 36, 1963].

serve System; 8, 1976]. Nonmonetary claims on the federal government include U.S. government total liabilities, less U.S. government financial assets, net liabilities of federally sponsored credit agencies, financial assets of included social insurance funds [65, U.S. Department of the Treasury], less U.S. government liabilities to rest of world [13, BEA], U.S. government credits and claims abroad [13, BEA], less monetary liabilities. Private sector claims on state and local governments include state and local government total liabilities, less state and local governmental financial assets [7, Board of Governors of the Federal Reserve System; 8, FFA, 1976] and assets of state and local social insurance funds. Net private claims on the rest of the world include private U.S. assets and investments abroad, less private U.S. liabilities to foreigners [13, BEA]. Table 3–6 presents the private domestic and private national wealth for 1972.

Conclusion

The production and the income and expenditure accounts are related through markets for commodities and factor services. Factor outlay by the producing sector is the most important component of income from the supply of factor services by the consuming sector. Income also includes the value of factor services supplied to the government and rest of the world sectors. The expenditure account is linked to the production account through the market for consumption goods and services. The production of consumption goods also includes goods consumed by the government and the rest of the world sectors. Expenditure on consumption goods includes goods supplied by the rest of the world sector. The expenditure account is also linked to the production account indirectly through saving.

The accumulation account allocates saving among its sources and uses. The uses of saving include capital formation through investment in reproducible tangible assets. Expenditure on investment in these assets is linked to the production account through the market for investment goods output. The production of investment goods is partly consumed by government and rest of the world sectors; part of the supply of these goods originates in the rest of the world sector. The accumulation account is linked to the wealth account through the accounting identity between period to period changes in wealth and the sum of saving and revaluations of existing assets.

The structure of this accounting system can be compared with that of the U.S. national income and product accounts [11, 1976b; 13, BEA].[e] In the production account our measure of gross private

[e]Alternative accounting systems for capital are discussed by Edward Denison [22, 1974], John Kendrick [47, 1961; 48, 1973], and Simon Kuznets [51, 1961].

Table 3−6. Private Domestic and Private National Wealth, 1972
(billions of current dollars)

1.	Private domestic wealth (Fraumeni–Jorgenson)		3,190.9
2.	+ Net claims on the federal, state, and local governments		430.1
	a. Federal, monetary		92.2
	(i) + Vault cash of commercial banks[a]	8.7	
	(ii) + Member bank reserves[a]	25.6	
	(iii) + Currency outside banks[a]	57.9	
	b. Federal, nonmonetary		244.2
	(i) U.S. government total liabilities[a]	392.4	
	(ii) − U.S. government financial assets[a]	94.5	
	(iii) + Net liabilities, federally sponsored credit agencies[a]	−1.2	
	(iv) + Assets of included social insurance funds[b]	56.4	
	(v) − U.S. government liabilities to rest of world[c]	55.7	
	(vi) + U.S. government credits and claims abroad[c]	38.8	
	(vii) − Monetary liabilities[a]	92.2	
	c. State and local		93.8
	(i) State and local government total liabilities[a]	189.0	
	(ii) − State and local government financial assets[a]	95.2	
	(iii) + Assets of cash sickness compensation fund (our imputation)	−0.0	
3.	+ Net claims on the rest of world		43.6
	a. Private U.S. assets and investments abroad[c]	149.7	
	b. − Private U.S. liabilities to foreigners[c]	106.1	
4.	= Private national wealth		3,664.6

[a]Board of Governors of the Federal Reserve System, *Flow of Funds Accounts, 1946–1975*, December 1976, [8, 1976].

[b]U.S. Department of the Treasury, *Treasury Bulletin*, February issues [65].

[c]From *Survey of Current Business*, October issues, "The International Investment Position of the United States" [13].

domestic product differs from the corresponding measure from the U.S. national accounts [11, 1976b; 13, BEA] by the value of services of consumer durables, services of producers' durable equipment utilized by institutions, net rent on institutional structures, and subsidies minus sales and excise taxes. We have presented a reconciliation between the two concepts of national product for 1972 in Table 3-1.

In Table 3-7 we present a reconciliation for gross national product between the income components in the Bureau of Economic Analysis study *Fourteen Current Dollar Components of Gross Product Originating by Industry* [12, 1978] and specific table entries from the U.S. national income and product accounts [11, 1976b; 13, BEA]. The Bureau of Economic Analysis study [12, 1978] is the primary source for our measures of property compensation by industry. The two sources differ in the allocation of inventory valuation and capital consumption adjustments, in the treatment of rental income of persons, and in the definition of surplus of government enterprises and subsidies prior to 1959.

Our definition of income is similar to the widely used concept of personal disposable income, but there are several important differences. First, personal disposable income includes government transfer payments to persons and excludes contributions to social insurance funds. Since we include social insurance funds in the private national economy, we include contributions to social insurance in income but exclude benefits from social insurance funds; we treat other transfer payments as nonincome receipts. In addition, we include investment income of social insurance funds net of transfers to general government in gross private national income. These differences between gross private income and personal disposable income can be summarized as the surplus of social insurance funds plus government transfers to persons other than social insurance benefits. The surplus of social insurance funds is included in private saving and in gross private national income. Similarly, wage accruals less disbursements are included in gross private national income. Table 3-8 presents a reconciliation of personal disposable income presented in the U.S. national income and product accounts [11, 1976b; 13, BEA] and our concept of gross private national income.

Since our concept of gross private national income is very similar to that underlying the concept of gross private saving employed in the U.S. national income and product accounts, our concept of gross private national saving is similar to that of gross private saving in the U.S. National Income and Product Accounts [11, 1976b; 13, BEA]. A reconciliation of the two concepts is presented in Table 3-9.

Table 3–7. Reconciliation of Gross National Product: Fourteen Current Dollar Components of Gross Product Originating by Industry and the National Income and Product Accounts, 1972 *(billions of current dollars)*

1.	Wages and salaries		
	a. Wages and salaries (GPO)	633.8	
	b. Wages and salaries (Table 6.6, ℓ.1)		633.8
2. +	Supplements		
	a. Supplements (GPO)		
	b. Supplements	81.4	
	(i) Compensation of employees (Table 6.5, ℓ.1)		715.1
	(ii) – Wages and salaries (Table 6.6, ℓ.1)		−633.8
3. +	Net interest		
	a. Net interest (GPO)	47.0	
	b. Net interest (Table 1.13, ℓ.29)		47.0
4. +	Corporate capital consumption allowances		
	a. Noncorporate capital consumption allowances (GPO)	32.6	
	b. Noncorporate capital consumption allowances		
	(i) Noncorporate capital consumption allowances with capital consumption adjustment (Table 5.1, ℓ.9)		40.0
	(ii) + Farm, capital consumption adjustment (Table 1.13, ℓ.12)		−2.0
	(iii) + Nonfarm, capital consumption adjustment (Table 1.13, ℓ.16)		2.6
	(iv) + Rental income, capital consumption adjustment (Table 1.13, ℓ.19)		−7.9
6. +	Indirect business taxes		
	a. Indirect business taxes (GPO)	111.0	
	b. Indirect business tax and nontax accruals (Table 3.1, ℓ.4)		111.0
7. +	Business transfer payments		
	a. Business transfer payments (GPO)	4.7	
	b. Business transfer payments (Table 1.9, ℓ.22)		4.7
8. +	Corporate profits		
	a. Corporate profits (GPO)	96.2	
	b. Corporate, profits before tax (Table 1.13, ℓ.22)		96.2
9. +	Noncorporate profits		
	a. Noncorporate profits (GPO)	76.4	
	b. Noncorporate profits		
	(i) Proprietors' income with inventory valuation and capital consumption adjustments (Table 1.13, ℓ.9)		76.1
	(ii) – Farm, capital consumption adjustment (Table 1.13, ℓ.12)		−2.0
	(iii) – Nonfarm, inventory valuation adjustment (Table 1.13, ℓ.15)		−0.7
	(iv) – Nonfarm, capital consumption adjustment (Table 1.13, ℓ.16)		2.5

Table 3−7. continued

10. + Corporate inventory valuation adjustment		
a. Corporate inventory valuation adjustment (GPO)	−6.6	
b. Corporate, inventory valuation adjustment		
(Table 1.13, ℓ.27)		−6.6
11. + Noncorporate inventory valuation adjustment		
a. Noncorporate inventory valuation adjustment (GPO)	−0.7	
b. Nonfarm, inventory valuation adjustment		
(Table 1.13, ℓ.15)		−0.7
12. + Rental income of persons		
a. Rental income of persons (GPO)	29.4	
b. Rental income of persons (Table 1.13, ℓ.18)		29.4
13. + Surplus of government enterprises[a]		
a. Surplus of government enterprises (GPO)	3.2	
b. Current surplus of government enterprises		
(Table 3.1, ℓ.16)		3.2
14. − Subsidies		
a. Subsidies (GPO)	6.8	
b. Subsidies (Table 3.1, ℓ.15)		6.8
15. + Statistical discrepancy (Table 5.1, ℓ.18)[b]	1.7	
		1.7
16. = Gross national product	1,171.1	
(Table 1.1, ℓ.1)		1,171.1

[a]Prior to 1959, the two sources can be reconciled only at the level of surplus of government enterprises minus subsidies.

[b]The statistical discrepancy is not available in GPO [12, 1978].

Table 3−8.   Reconciliation of Personal Disposable Income and Gross Private National Income, 1972 *(billions of current dollars)*

1. Personal disposable income (Table 2.1, ℓ.30)	801.3
2. + Government owned privately operated, later sold manufacturing investment (JFA)	0.0
3. + Surplus of social insurance funds (Table 3.10, ℓ.11 and ℓ.22)	10.7
4. − Government transfer payments to persons other than social insurance funds (Table 3.12, ℓ.2 and ℓ.28 minus ℓ.3 and ℓ.29)	30.6
5. + Undistributed corporate profits with inventory valuation and capital consumption adjustments (Table 5.1, ℓ.4)	25.9
6. + Net reinvested earnings, rest of world (BOP)	4.0
7. + Capital consumption allowances with capital consumption adjustment (Table 1.9, ℓ.2)	105.4
8. + Statistical discrepancy (Table 1.9, ℓ.8)	1.7
9. + Expenditure (items 3, 4, 5 from Table 19 above)	128.9
10. + Government and private wage accruals less disbursements (Table 3.1, ℓ.17 and Table 5.1, ℓ.10)	0.0
11. − Interest paid by consumers to business (Table 2.1, ℓ.27)	17.9
12. + Personal nontax payments (Table 3.2, ℓ.8 and Table 3.4, ℓ.8)	10.6
13. = Gross private national income	1,040.7

Table 3−9.   Reconciliation of Gross Private Saving and Gross Private National Saving, 1972 *(billions of current dollars)*

1. Gross private saving (Table 5.1, ℓ.2)	180.4
2. + Government-owned privately operated, later sold manufacturing investment (JFA)	0.0
3. + Personal consumption expenditures, durable goods (Table 1.1, ℓ.3)	111.2
4. + Surplus, social insurance funds (Table 3.10, ℓ.11 and ℓ.22)	10.7
5. + Government wage accruals less disbursements (Table 3.1, ℓ.17)	0.3
6. + Statistical discrepancy (Table 1.9, ℓ.8)	1.7
7. + Net reinvested earnings, rest of world (Balance of Payments)	4.0
8. = Gross private national saving	308.3

II. SECTORAL PRODUCTION ACCOUNTS

We have described a system of four accounts for measuring output and capital in current prices. The complete system includes production, income and expenditure, accumulation, and wealth accounts. Our next objective is to develop a system of accounts in constant prices, linking output in constant prices to assets in constant prices. Our first step is to construct a measure of capital input for the production accounts. To provide the necessary data on capital we employ a set of vintage accounts encompassing data on prices as well as quantities of capital goods. Quantities of individual assets are estimated from data on past levels of investment. Investment goods prices and data on property compensation are employed to develop the corresponding prices of individual assets by vintage.

Relative Efficiency

We begin the construction of a complete system of income and wealth accounts in constant prices with a description of the price and quantity data required for a single capital good. As in the perpetual inventory method our characterization of a capital good is based on the relative efficiency of capital goods of different ages.[f] In the perpetual inventory method the relative efficiency of a capital good depends on the age of the good and not on the time it is acquired. Replacement requirements are determined by losses in efficiency of existing capital goods as well as actual physical disappearance or retirement of capital goods. When a capital good is retired its relative efficiency drops to zero. The relative efficiency of capital goods of different ages can be described by a sequence of nonnegative numbers:

$$d_0, d_1 \ldots .$$

We normalize the relative efficiency of a new capital good at unity and assume that relative efficiency is nonincreasing, so that

$$d_0 = 1, \quad d_\tau - d_{\tau-1} \leqq 0, \qquad\qquad (\tau = 0, 1 \ldots) .$$

We also assume that every capital good is eventually retired or scrapped so that relative efficiency eventually drops to zero:

$$\lim_{\tau \to \infty} d_\tau = 0 .$$

---

[f]A more detailed discussion of the economic theory of replacement and depreciation is given by Jorgenson [45, 1973].

Subject to these restrictions a wide variety of patterns of decline in efficiency may be employed in the perpetual inventory method.

For illustration we consider "one-hoss shay," straight-line, and declining balance patterns of decline in efficiency. In the "one-hoss shay" pattern efficiency is constant over the lifetime of the capital good. Where T is the lifetime, relative efficiency is

$$d_\tau = 1, \qquad\qquad (\tau = 0, 1 \ldots T{-}1) .$$

In the straight-line pattern efficiency declines linearly over the lifetime of the capital good:

$$d_\tau = 1 - \frac{1}{T} \tau , \qquad\qquad (\tau = 0, 1 \ldots T{-}1).$$

In the declining balance pattern efficiency declines geometrically:

$$d_\tau = (1 - \delta)^\tau , \qquad\qquad (\tau = 0, 1 \ldots) .$$

These patterns of decline in efficiency and many others may be treated as special cases within the framework of our extension of the perpetual inventory method.

Capital goods decline in efficiency at each point of time, giving rise to needs for replacement to maintain productive capacity. The proportion of an investment to be replaced during the τth period after its acquisition is equal to the decline in efficiency during that period. We refer to the decline in relative efficiency as the mortality distribution of a capital good, say m_τ, where

$$m_\tau = -(d_\tau - d_{\tau-1}) , \qquad\qquad (\tau = 1, 2 \ldots) .$$

By our assumption that relative efficiency is nonincreasing, the mortality distribution may be represented by a sequence of nonnegative numbers:

$$m_1, m_2 \ldots ,$$

where

$$\sum_{\tau=1}^{\infty} m_\tau = \sum_{\tau=1}^{\infty} (d_{\tau-1} - d_\tau) = d_0 = 1 .$$

For the patterns of decline in efficiency considered above, we can derive the corresponding mortality distributions. If efficiency is constant over the lifetime of the capital good, the mortality distribution is zero except for period T:

$$m_T = 1 .$$

For linear decline in efficiency the mortality distribution is constant throughout the lifetime of the capital good:

$$m_\tau = \frac{1}{T} , \qquad (\tau = 1, 2 \ldots T) .$$

For geometric decline in efficiency the mortality distribution declines geometrically:

$$m_\tau = \delta (1 - \delta)^{\tau - 1} , \qquad (\tau = 0, 1 \ldots) .$$

Replacement requirements can be expressed in terms of the mortality distribution for capital goods. Requirements can also be expressed in terms of the proportion of an initial investment replaced τ periods after the initial acquisition. This proportion includes replacement of the initial investment and subsequent replacements of each succeeding replacement. We refer to the sequence of these proportions as the replacement distribution of a capital good; each coefficient, say δ_τ, is the rate of replacement of an investment replaced τ periods after initial acquisition. The sequence of replacement rates $\{\delta_\tau\}$ can be computed recursively for the sequence of mortality rates $\{m_\tau\}$. The proportion of an initial investment replaced at time ν and again at time $\tau > \nu$ is $m_\nu \delta_{\tau - \nu}$. The proportion of the stock replaced in the τth period is the sum of proportions replaced first in periods $1, 2, \ldots$, and later at period τ; hence,

$$\delta_\tau = m_1 \delta_{\tau-1} + m_2 \delta_{\tau-2} + \ldots + m_\tau \delta_0 , \qquad (\tau = 1, 2 \ldots) .$$

This equation is referred to as the renewal equation.[g]
For constant relative efficiency over the lifetime of a capital good, the replacement distribution is periodic with period equal to the lifetime of the capital good:

$$\delta_\tau = 1 , \qquad (\tau = T, 2T \ldots) .$$

[g] See William Feller [29, 1957].

For linear decline in efficiency, the replacement distribution may be represented in the form

$$\delta_1 = \frac{1}{T} \, ,$$

$$\delta_2 = \frac{1}{T} \, [1 + \frac{1}{T}] \, ,$$

$$\cdots \cdot$$

For geometric decline in efficiency, the replacement distribution is constant:

$$\delta_\tau = \delta \, , \qquad\qquad\qquad (\tau = 1, 2 \ldots) \, .$$

Vintage Accounting System

The relative efficiency of capital goods of different ages and the derived mortality and replacement distributions are useful in estimating the data required for income and wealth accounts in constant prices. We begin our description of the required capital data with quantities estimated by the perpetual inventory method. First, capital stock at the end of each period, say K_t, is the sum of past investments, say $A_{t-\tau}$, each weighted by its relative efficiency:

$$K_t = \sum_{\tau=0}^{\infty} d_\tau A_{t-\tau} \, .$$

For a complete system of accounts both capital stock and investments in every preceding period are required. For this purpose a system of vintage accounts containing data on investments of every age in every period is essential.

Taking the first difference of the expression for capital stock in terms of past investments, we obtain

$$K_t - K_{t-1} = A_t + \sum_{\tau=1}^{\infty} (d_\tau - d_{\tau-1}) A_{t-\tau} \, ,$$

$$= A_t - \sum_{\tau=1}^{\infty} m_\tau A_{t-\tau} \, ,$$

$$= A_t - R_t \, ,$$

where

$$R_t = \sum_{\tau=1}^{\infty} m_\tau A_{t-\tau}$$

is the level of replacement requirements in period t. The change in capital stock from period to period is equal to the acquisition of investment goods less replacement requirements.

Replacement requirements may also be expressed in terms of present and past changes in capital stock, using the replacement distribution

$$R_t = \sum_{\tau=1}^{\infty} \delta_\tau [K_{t-\tau} - K_{t-\tau-1}] \ .$$

The average replacement rate for capital stock at the beginning of the period

$$\hat{\delta}_t = \frac{R_t}{K_{t-1}} = \sum_{\tau=1}^{\infty} \delta_\tau \frac{[K_{t-\tau} - K_{t-\tau-1}]}{K_{t-1}}$$

is a weighted average of replacement rates with weights given by the relative proportions of changes in capital stock of each vintage in beginning of period capital stock.

We turn next to a description of the price data required for construction of income and wealth accounts in constant prices. For this purpose a system of vintage accounts containing data on prices of capital goods of every age in every period is needed. This system of vintage accounts is dual to the perpetual inventory method in the sense that there is a one-to-one correspondence between the vintage quantities that appear in the perpetual inventory method and the prices that appear in our vintage price accounts.[h] To bring out this correspondence and to simplify the notation we use a system of present or discounted prices. Taking the present as time zero, the discounted price of a commodity, say q_t, is the future price, say p_t, multiplied by a discount factor:

$$q_t = \prod_{s=1}^{t} \frac{1}{1+r_s} p_t \ .$$

[h] The system of vintage price accounts described below was originated by Christensen and Jorgenson [17, 1973].

The notational convenience of present or discounted prices results from dispensing with explicit discount factors in expressing prices for different time periods.

In the correspondence between the perpetual inventory method and its dual or price counterpart the price of acquisition of a capital good is analogous to capital stock.[i] The price of acquisition, say $q_{A,t}$, is the sum of future rental prices of capital services, say $q_{K,t}$, weighted by the relative efficiency of the capital good in each future period:

$$q_{A,t} = \sum_{\tau=0}^{\infty} d_\tau q_{K,t+\tau+1} .$$

This expression may be compared with the corresponding expression giving capital stock as a weighted sum of past investments. The acquisition price of capital goods enters the production account through the price of investment goods output. This price also appears as the price component of capital formation in the accumulation account. Vintage accounts, containing data on the acquisition prices of capital goods of every age at every point of time, are required for a complete system of accounts.

Taking the first difference of the expression for the acquisition price of capital goods in terms of future rentals, we obtain

$$q_{A,t} - q_{A,t-1} = -q_{K,t} - \sum_{\tau=1}^{\infty} (d_\tau - d_{\tau-1}) q_{K,t+\tau} ,$$

$$= -q_{K,t} + \sum_{\tau=1}^{\infty} m_\tau q_{K,t+\tau} ,$$

$$= -q_{K,t} + q_{D,t} ,$$

where

$$q_{D,t} = \sum_{\tau=1}^{\infty} m_\tau q_{K,t+\tau}$$

[i]The dual to the durable goods model was developed by Kenneth Arrow [3, 1964] and Robert Hall [38, 1968] on the basis of earlier work by Harold Hotelling [41, 1925].

is depreciation on a capital good in period t. The period-to-period change in the price of acquisition of a capital good is equal to depreciation less the rental price of capital. Postponing the purchase of a capital good makes it necessary to forego one period's rental and makes it possible to avoid one period's depreciation. In the correspondence between the perpetual inventory method and its price counterpart, investment corresponds to the rental price of capital and replacement corresponds to depreciation.

We can rewrite the expression for the first difference of the acquisition price of capital goods in terms of undiscounted prices and the period-to-period discount rate:

$$p_{K,t} = p_{A,t-1}\, r_t + p_{D,t} - (p_{A,t} - p_{A,t-1}) \; ,$$

where $p_{A,t}$ is the undiscounted price of acquisition of capital goods, $p_{K,t}$ the price of capital services, $p_{D,t}$ depreciation, and r_t the rate of return, all in period t. The price of capital services $p_{K,t}$ is the sum of return per unit of capital $p_{A,t-1}\, r_t$, depreciation $p_{D,t}$, and the negative of revaluation, $(p_{A,t} - p_{A,t-1})$. The service price enters the production and the income and expenditure accounts through the price component of capital input and property compensation. Depreciation enters the accumulation account as the price component of depreciation on existing capital assets. Revaluation enters the accumulation account as the price component of revaluation of existing assets.

Depreciation may also be expressed in terms of present and future changes in the price of acquisition of investment goods, using the replacement distribution

$$q_{D,t} = -\sum_{\tau=1}^{\infty} \delta_\tau\, [q_{A,t+\tau} - q_{A,t+\tau-1}] \; .$$

The average depreciation rate on the acquisition price of a capital good,

$$\bar{\delta}_t = \frac{q_{D,t}}{q_{A,t}} = -\sum_{\tau=1}^{\infty} \delta_\tau\, \frac{[q_{A,t+\tau} - q_{A,t+\tau-1}]}{q_{A,t}} \; ,$$

is a weighted average of replacement rates with weights given by the relative proportions of changes in futures prices in the acquisition price of investment goods in the current period. This expression may be compared with that for the average replacement rate $\hat{\delta}_t$ given above. For a complete system of accounts vintage data on the depreciation of capital goods of every age at every point of time are required.

In the perpetual inventory method data on the quantity of investment goods of every vintage are used to estimate capital formation, replacement requirements, and capital stock. In the price counterpart of the perpetual inventory method data on the acquisition prices of investment goods of every vintage required. The price of acquisition of an investment good of age v at time t, say $q_{A,t,v}$, is the weighted sum of future rental prices of capital prices. The weights are relative efficiencies of the capital good in each future period, beginning with age v:

$$q_{A,t,v} = \sum_{\tau=0}^{\infty} d_{\tau+v} \, q_{K,t+\tau+1} \; .$$

A new investment good has age zero, so that

$$q_{A,t,0} = q_{A,t} \; .$$

Given the acquisition prices, we require estimates of depreciation and the rental price for goods of each vintage.

To calculate depreciation on capital goods of each vintage we take the first difference of the acquisition prices across vintages at a given point in time:

$$q_{A,t,v} - q_{A,t,v+1} = - \sum_{\tau=1}^{\infty} (d_{\tau+v} - d_{\tau+v-1}) \, q_{K,t+v+\tau} \; ,$$

$$= \sum_{\tau=1}^{\infty} m_{\tau+v} \, q_{K,t+v+\tau} \; ,$$

$$= q_{D,t,v} \; ,$$

where $q_{D,t,v}$ is depreciation on a capital good of age v at time t. Again, a new investment good has age zero, so that

$$q_{D,t,0} = q_{D,t} \; .$$

To obtain depreciation in terms of future prices or undiscounted prices, we observe that acquisition prices across vintages at a given point in time and the corresponding depreciation are associated with the same discount factor, so that

$$p_{A,t,v} - p_{A,t,v+1} = p_{D,t,v} .$$

To calculate the capital service price for goods of each vintage we first observe that the rental of a capital good of age v at time t, say $p_{K,t,v}$, is proportional to the rental of a new capital good,

$$p_{K,t,v} = d_v p_{K,t} .$$

with the constant of proportionality given by the efficiency of a capital good of age v relative to that of a new capital good. New and used capital goods are perfect substitutes in production. To calculate the service price for new capital goods we use the formula derived above:

$$p_{K,t} = p_{A,t-1} r_t + p_{D,t} - (p_{A,t} - p_{A,t-1}) .$$

To apply this formula we require a series of undiscounted acquisition prices for capital goods $p_{A,t}$, rates of return r_t, depreciation on new capital goods $p_{D,t}$, and revaluation of existing capital goods $p_{A,t} - p_{A,t-1}$.

To calculate the rate of return in each period we set the formula for the rental price $p_{K,t}$ times the quantity of capital K_{t-1} equal to property compensation. All of the variables entering this equation— current and past acquisition prices for capital goods, depreciation, revaluation, capital stock, and property compensation—except for the rate of return, are known. Replacing these variables by the corresponding data we solve this equation for the rate of return. To obtain the capital service price itself we substitute the rate of return into the original formula along with the other data. This completes the calculation of the service price.

We conclude that acquisition prices for capital goods of each vintage at each point of time provide sufficient information to enable us to calculate depreciation and rental value for capital goods of each vintage. These data together with current investment, capital stock, replacement, and investments of all vintages at each point of time constitute the basic data on quantities and prices required for a complete vintage accounting system. The problem that remains is to describe the role of each of these data in production, income and expenditure, accumulation, and wealth accounts. From this point we consider an accounting system for any number of investment goods. Price and quantity data that we have described above for a single investment good are required for each investment good in the system. The data for all investment goods are used to derive price and quantity indexes that play the role of the price and quantity data for a single investment good outlined above.

Measurement of Capital Input

We have described a methodology for measuring the price and quantity of capital input for a single capital good. To construct production accounts in constant prices we first combine data on capital inputs from different capital goods into a single index of input. We refer to a typical capital good as the kth capital good, where the index ranges from one to the total number of capital goods, say p. We assume that the proportional changes in the individual capital inputs that comprise aggregate capital input result in proportional changes in the aggregate, so that capital input is characterized by constant returns to scale. Where K is the quantity of aggregate capital input and $\{K_k\}$ are the quantities of the individual capital inputs, the aggregate can be represented as a homogeneous function of its components:

$$K = K(K_1, K_2 \ldots K_p) .$$

Data on the quantities of capital input at every point of time are compiled from the vintage accounts for the individual capital goods.

We can define the shares of the individual capital inputs, say $\{v_{Kk}\}$, in the value of the capital aggregate by

$$v_{Kk} = \frac{p_{Kk} K_k}{p_K K} , \qquad (k = 1, 2 \ldots p) ,$$

where p_K is the price of aggregate capital input and $\{p_{Kk}\}$ are the prices of the individual capital inputs. Necessary conditions for producer equilibrium are given by equalities between the shares of the individual capital inputs in the value of the capital aggregate and the elasticities of the aggregate with respect to the individual capital inputs:

$$v_{Kk} = \frac{\partial \ln K}{\partial \ln K_k} \; (K_1, \; K_2 \; \ldots \; K_p) \; , \qquad\qquad (k = 1, 2 \; \ldots \; p) \; .$$

Under constant returns to scale the elasticities and the value shares of all capital inputs sum to unity, so that the value of the capital aggregate is equal to the sum of the values of the individual capital inputs:

$$p_K K = \Sigma p_{Kk} K_k \; .$$

Our data on capital input in current prices satisfy this equality as an accounting identity. The price of aggregate capital input is a function of the prices of the individual capital inputs:

$$p_K = p_K \, (p_{K1}, \; p_{K2}, \; \ldots \; p_{Kp}) \; .$$

This function is homogeneous, so that proportional changes in the prices of the individual capital inputs result in proportional changes in the price of aggregate capital input.[j]

To implement our methodology for aggregation of capital input we consider a specific form for the capital aggregate as a function of individual capital inputs:

$$K = \exp \; [\, \alpha_1 \; \ln K_1 + \alpha_2 \; \ln K_2 + \; \ldots \; + \alpha_p \; \ln K_p$$

$$+ \tfrac{1}{2} \beta_{11} \; (\ln K_1)^2 + \beta_{12} \; \ln K_1 \; \ln K_2 + \; \ldots$$

$$+ \tfrac{1}{2} \beta_{pp} \; (\ln K_p)^2 \,] \; .$$

For this form the quantity of aggregate capital input is a transcendental or, more specifically, exponential function of the logarithms of individual capital inputs. We refer to this form as *transcendental logarithmic capital input* or, more simply, translog capital input.[k]

---

[j]A more detailed discussion of aggregation for capital input is given by Frank Gollop and Jorgenson [37, 1980]. Further discussion and references to the literature are provided by Erwin Diewert [27, 1980].

[k]The transcendental logarithmic production function was introduced by Christensen, Jorgenson, and Lawrence Lau [18, 1971; 19, 1973].

Necessary conditions for producer equilibrium imply that the value shares of individual capital inputs $\{K_k\}$ are equal to the elasticities of aggregate capital input with respect to its components:

$$v_{Kk} = \alpha_k + \beta_{1k} \ln K_1 + \ldots + \beta_{kp} \ln K_p .$$

Aggregate capital input is characterized by constant returns to scale if and only if the parameters of the aggregate satisfy the conditions:

$$\alpha_1 + \alpha_2 + \ldots + \alpha_p = 1 ,$$

$$\beta_{11} + \beta_{12} + \ldots + \beta_{1p} = 0 ,$$

$$\cdot \quad \cdot \quad \cdot \quad \cdot \quad \cdot \quad \cdot \quad \cdot \quad \cdot$$

$$\beta_{1p} + \beta_{2p} + \ldots + \beta_{pp} = 0 .$$

Considering data on individual capital inputs at any two discrete points of time, we can express the difference between successive logarithms of capital input as a weighted average of differences between successive logarithms of individual capital inputs with weights given by the average value shares:

$$\ln K_t - \ln K_{t-1} = \Sigma \bar{v}_{Kk} [\ln K_{k,t} - \ln K_{k,t-1}] ,$$

where

$$\bar{v}_{Kk} = \tfrac{1}{2} [v_{Kk,t} + v_{Kk,t-1}] , \qquad (k = 1, 2 \ldots p) .$$

We refer to this expression for aggregate capital input as the *translog index of capital input.*[1]

The product of price and quantity indexes of capital input must be equal to the sum of the values of individual capital inputs. We can define the price index corresponding to the translog quantity index of capital input as the ratio of the value of capital input to the translog quantity index. The resulting price index of capital input does not have the form of a translog price index, but it can be determined from data on prices and quantities at any two discrete points of time.

[1]Translog quantity indexes were introduced by Irving Fisher [31, 1922] and have been discussed by Tuun Kloek [49, 1966], Henri Theil [63, 1965], and Leo Tornquist [64, 1936]. These indexes were first derived from the translog production function by Diewert [25, 1976].

Intermediate and Labor Inputs

We have defined an aggregate for capital input in terms of individual capital inputs. As the sectoral level we can define aggregates for intermediate and labor inputs that depend on the quantities of individual intermediate and labor inputs. We refer to a typical intermediate input as the jth input and a typical labor input as the ℓth input, where j ranges from 1 to n and ℓ ranges from 1 to q. As before, we assume that proportional changes in all inputs that comprise each aggregate input result in proportional changes in the aggregate, so that aggregate intermediate and labor inputs are characterized by constant returns to scale:

$$X = X(X_1, X_2 \ \ldots \ X_n),$$

$$L = L(L_1, L_2 \ \ldots \ L_q),$$

where X and L are the quantities of the intermediate and labor aggregates and $\{ X_j, L_\varrho \}$ are the quantities of the individual intermediate and labor inputs.

We can define the shares of the individual intermediate and labor inputs, say $\{ v_{xj}, v_{L\varrho} \}$, in the value of the intermediate and labor aggregates by

$$v_{Xj} \ = \ \frac{p_{Xj} X_j}{p_X \ X}, \qquad\qquad (j = 1, 2 \ \ldots \ n),$$

$$v_{L\varrho} \ = \ \frac{p_{L\varrho} L_\varrho}{p_X \ X}, \qquad\qquad (\ell = 1, 2 \ \ldots \ q),$$

where p_X and p_L are the prices of the intermediate and labor aggregates and p_{Xj} and $p_{L\varrho}$ are the prices of the individual intermediate and labor inputs. As before, necessary conditions for producer equilibrium are given by equalities between the shares of individual intermediate and labor inputs in the value of the corresponding aggregates and the elasticities of the aggregate with respect to the individual inputs:

$$v_{Xj} \ = \ \frac{\partial \ln X}{\partial \ln X_j} \ (X_1, \ X_2 \ \ldots \ X_n), \qquad\qquad (j = 1, 2 \ \ldots \ n),$$

$$v_{L\varrho} \ = \ \frac{\ell \ln L}{\partial \ln L_\varrho} \ (L_1, \ L_2 \ \ldots \ L_q), \qquad\qquad (\ell = 1, 2 \ \ldots \ q).$$

Under constant returns to scale the elasticities and value shares of all intermediate inputs and of all labor inputs sum to unity, so that the values of the intermediate and labor aggregates are equal to the sums of the values of the individual intermediate and labor inputs:

$$p_X X = \Sigma \, p_{Xj} X_j \;,$$

$$p_L L = \Sigma \, p_{L\varrho} L_\varrho \;.$$

Our data on intermediate and labor input satisfy these equalities as accounting identities. The prices of aggregate intermediate and labor inputs are functions of the prices of individual intermediate and labor inputs:

$$p_X = p_X \, (p_{X1}, \; p_{X2} \cdots p_{Xn}) \,,$$

$$p_L = p_L \, (p_{L1}, p_{L2} \cdots p_{Lq}) \;.$$

As before, these functions are homogeneous, so that proportional changes in the prices of the individual intermediate and labor inputs result in proportional changes in the prices of aggregate intermediate and labor inputs.

We can consider specific forms for aggregate intermediate and labor inputs as functions of individual intermediate and labor inputs. If these aggregates are translog functions of their components, we can express the difference between successive logarithms of aggregate intermediate and labor inputs in the form

$$\ln X_t - \ln X_{t-1} = \Sigma \, \bar{v}_{Xj} \, [\ln X_{j,t} - \ln X_{j,t-1}] \,,$$

$$\ln L_t - \ln L_{t-1} = \Sigma \, \bar{v}_{L\varrho} \, [\ln L_{\varrho,t} - \ln L_{\varrho,t-1}] \,,$$

where

$$\bar{v}_{Xj} = \tfrac{1}{2} \, [v_{Xj,t} + v_{Xj,\, t-1}] \,, \qquad\qquad (j = 1, \, 2 \, \ldots \, n) \,,$$

$$\bar{v}_{L\varrho} = \tfrac{1}{2} \, [v_{L\varrho,t} + v_{L\varrho,\, t-1}] \,, \qquad\qquad (\varrho = 1, \, 2 \, \ldots \, q) \,.$$

We refer to these expressions for aggregate intermediate and labor input as *translog indexes of intermediate and labor input*. As before, we can define the price indexes corresponding to the translog quantity indexes of intermediate and labor inputs as ratios of the value of each input to the corresponding translog quantity index.

Sectoral Production Model

We have defined intermediate, capital, and labor inputs in constant prices. To complete the methodology for sectoral production accounts in constant prices we introduce a production function for each industrial sector, giving sectoral output as a function of intermediate, capital, and labor inputs and time. We assume that proportional changes in all inputs result in proportional changes in output, so that production is characterized by constant returns to scale. Where Z is the quantity of output, X, K, and L are quantities of intermediate, capital, and labor inputs, and t is time, the quantity of output can be represented as a homogeneous function F of the quantities of inputs:

$$Z = F(X, K, L, t).$$

We can define the shares of intermediate, capital, and labor inputs, say v_X, v_K, and v_L, in the value of output by

$$v_X = \frac{p_X X}{p Z}, \qquad v_K = \frac{p_K K}{p Z}, \qquad v_L = \frac{p_L L}{p Z},$$

where p, p_X, p_K, and p_L denote the prices of output and intermediate, capital, and labor inputs. Output is valued in producers' prices, while inputs are valued in purchasers' prices.

Necessary conditions for producer equilibrium are given by equalities between the shares of each input in the value of output and the elasticity of output with respect to that input:

$$v_X = \frac{\partial \ln Z}{\partial \ln X} \ (X, K, L, t),$$

$$v_K = \frac{\partial \ln Z}{\partial \ln K} \ (X, K, L, t),$$

$$v_L = \frac{\partial \ln Z}{\partial \ln L} \ (X, K, L, t).$$

Under constant returns to scale the elasticities and the value shares for all three inputs sum to unity. Finally, we can define the rate of technical change, say v_t, as rates of growth of output with respect to time, holding intermediate, capital and labor input constant:

$$v_t = \frac{\partial \ln Z}{\partial t} \quad (X, K, L, t) \ .$$

A more restrictive form of our methodology for sectoral production accounts in constant prices is based on the concept of value added.[m] Output is represented as a function of intermediate input and value added:

$$Z = F(X, V) \ ,$$

where V is the quantity of value added. The quantity of value added is represented in turn as a function of capital input, labor input, and time:

$$V = G(K, L, t) \ ,$$

where G is the value added function. Combining the production function and the value added function,

$$Z = F(X, G(K, L, t)) \ ,$$

we observe that time and capital and labor inputs are separable from intermediate input.

We can define the share of value added, say v_V, in the value of output by

$$v_V = \frac{p_V V}{p Z} \ ,$$

where p_V denotes the price of value added. Necessary conditions for producer equilibrium include equality between the share of value added and the elasticity of output with respect to value added:

$$v_V = \frac{\partial \ln Z}{\partial \ln V} \quad (X, Y) \ .$$

[m]A model of production and technical change based on value added has been discussed by Arrow [4, 1974], Michael Bruno [9, 1978], Diewert [26, 1978], Kazno Sato [58, 1976], and Christopher Sims [59, 1969]. Sato provides references to the literature.

Under constant returns to scale the elasticities and the value shares for intermediate input and value added sum to unity.

The necessary conditions for producer equilibrium under constant returns to scale imply that the value of output is the sum of the values of intermediate, capital, and labor input:

$$p Z = p_X X + p_K K + p_L L .$$

Our data on sectoral output, intermediate input, capital input, and labor input in current prices satisfy this equality as an accounting identity. The price of output is a function of the prices of intermediate, capital, and labor inputs and time:

$$p = P(p_X, p_K, p_L, t) .$$

We refer to the function P as the *price function*. This function is homogeneous, so that proportional changes in all input prices result in a proportional change in the price of output.

If a value added aggregate exists, the necessary conditions for producer equilibrium under constant returns to scale imply that the value of output is equal to the sum of the values of intermediate input and value added:

$$p Z = p_X X + p_V V .$$

The price of output is a function of the prices of intermediate input and value added:

$$p = P(p_X, p_V) .$$

As before, we refer to this function as the *price function*. This function is homogeneous in the prices of intermediate input and value added. Similarly, value added is equal to the sum of the values of capital and labor inputs:

$$p_V V = p_K K + p_L L .$$

The price of value added is a function of the prices of capital and labor inputs and time:

$$p_V = p_V (p_K, p_L, t) .$$

We refer to this function as the *price of value added function*. This function is homogeneous in the prices of capital and labor inputs.

Sectoral Production Functions

To implement our methodology for sectoral production accounts in constant prices we consider a specific form for the sectoral production function:

$$Z = \exp\,[\,\alpha_0 + \alpha_X \ln X + \alpha_K \ln K + \alpha_L \ln\ L + \alpha_t \cdot t$$

$$+\ \tfrac{1}{2}\beta_{XX}(\ln X)^2 + \beta_{XK}\ln X \ln K + \beta_{XL} \ln X \ln L$$

$$+\ \ \beta_{Xt}\ln X \cdot t + \tfrac{1}{2}\beta_{KK}(\ln K)^2 + \beta_{KL}\ln K \ln L$$

$$+\ \ \beta_{Kt}\ln K \cdot t + \tfrac{1}{2}\beta_{LL}(\ln L)^2 + \beta_{Lt}\ln L \cdot t + \tfrac{1}{2}\beta_{tt}\cdot t^2\,]\,.$$

For this form of the production function output is a translog function of intermediate, capital, and labor inputs. We refer to this form as the *translog production function*.

Necessary conditions for producer equilibrium imply that the value shares of intermediate, capital, and labor are equal to the elasticities of output with respect to these inputs:

$$v_X\ =\ \alpha_X + \beta_{XX}\ln X + \beta_{XK}\ln K + \beta_{XL}\ln L + \beta_{Xt}\cdot t\ ,$$

$$v_K\ =\ \alpha_K + \beta_{XK}\ln X + \beta_{KK}\ln K + \beta_{KL}\ln L + \beta_{Xt}\cdot t\ ,$$

$$v_L\ =\ \alpha_L + \beta_{XL}\ln X + \beta_{KL}\ln K + \beta_{LL}\ln L + \beta_{Lt}\cdot t\ .$$

Similarly, the rate of technical change is equal to the rate of growth of output, holding all inputs constant:

$$v_t\ =\ \alpha_t + \beta_{Xt}\ln X + \beta_{Kt}\ln K + \beta_{Lt}\ln L + \beta_{tt}\cdot t\ .$$

The production function is characterized by constant returns to scale if and only if the parameters of the function satisfy the conditions:

$$\alpha_X + \alpha_K + \alpha_L\ =\ 1\ ,$$

$$\beta_{XX} + \beta_{XK} + \beta_{XL} = 0 \ ,$$

$$\beta_{XK} + \beta_{KK} + \beta_{KL} = 0 \ ,$$

$$\beta_{XL} + \beta_{KL} + \beta_{LL} = 0 \ ,$$

$$\beta_{Xt} + \beta_{Kt} + \beta_{Lt} = 0 \ .$$

Considering data on output and on intermediate, capital, and labor inputs at two discrete points of time, we can express the difference between successive logarithms of output as a weighted average of the differences between successive logarithms of intermediate, capital, and labor inputs with weights given by average value shares, plus the average rate of technical change:

$$\ln Z_t - \ln Z_{t-1} = \bar{v}_X \left[\ln X_t - \ln X_{t-1} \right] + \bar{v}_K \left[\ln K_t - \ln K_{t-1} \right]$$

$$+ \bar{v}_L \left[\ln L_t - \ln L_{t-1} \right] + \bar{v}_t \ ,$$

where

$$\bar{v}_X = \tfrac{1}{2} \left[v_{X,t} + v_{X,t-1} \right] ,$$

$$\bar{v}_K = \tfrac{1}{2} \left[v_{K,t} + v_{K,t-1} \right] ,$$

$$\bar{v}_L = \tfrac{1}{2} \left[v_{L,t} + v_{L,t-1} \right] ,$$

$$\bar{v}_t = \tfrac{1}{2} \left[v_{t,t} + v_{t,t-1} \right] .$$

We refer to this expression for the average rate of technical change as the *translog index of the rate of technical change*.[n]

To implement the more restrictive form of our methodology based on the concept of value added we consider a specific form for the production function:

$$Z = \exp \left[\alpha_0 + \alpha_X \ln X + \alpha_V \ln V + \tfrac{1}{2} \beta_{XX} (\ln X)^2 \right.$$

$$\left. + \beta_{XV} \ln X \ln V + \tfrac{1}{2} \beta_{VV} (\ln V)^2 \right] .$$

[n]The translog index of technical change was introduced by Christensen and Jorgenson [16, 1970]. This index was first derived from the translog production function by Diewert [27, 1980] and by Jorgenson and Lau [46, 1980].

For this form of the production function output is a translog function of intermediate input. We refer to this form as the *translog production function in terms of value added.*

Necessary conditions for producer equilibrium imply that the value shares of intermediate input and value added are equal to the elasticities of output with respect to intermediate input and value added:

$$v_X = \alpha_X + \beta_{XX} \ln X + \beta_{XV} \ln V,$$

$$v_V = \alpha_V + \beta_{XV} \ln X + \beta_{VV} \ln V.$$

The production function is characterized by constant returns to scale if and only if the parameters of the function satisfy the conditions:

$$\alpha_X + \alpha_V = 1,$$

$$\beta_{XX} + \beta_{XV} = 0,$$

$$\beta_{XV} + \beta_{VV} = 0.$$

Considering data on output and intermediate input at any two discrete points of time, we can express the difference between successive logarithms of output as a weighted average of differences between successive logarithms of intermediate input and value added with weights given by average value shares:

$$\ln Z_t - \ln Z_{t-1}$$

$$= \bar{v}_X [\ln X_t - \ln X_{t-1}] + \bar{v}_V [\ln V_t - \ln V_{t-1}],$$

where

$$\bar{v}_X = \tfrac{1}{2} [v_{X,t} + v_{X,t-1}],$$

$$\bar{v}_V = \tfrac{1}{2} [v_{V,t} + v_{V,t-1}].$$

The difference between successive logarithms of value added can be expressed in terms of differences between successive logarithms of output and intermediate input and average value shares of intermediate input and value added:

$$\ln V_t - \ln V_{t-1}$$

$$= \frac{1}{\bar{v}_V} [\ln Z_t - \ln Z_{t-1}] - \frac{\bar{v}_X}{\bar{v}_V} [\ln X_t - \ln X_{t-1}].$$

We refer to this expression for value added as the *translog index of sectoral value added.*[o] We can define the price index corresponding to the translog quantity index of value added as the ratio of value added to the translog quantity index.

III. AGGREGATE ACCOUNTING SYSTEM

We have presented a methodology for constructing sectoral production accounts in constant prices. This methodology is based on a sectoral model of production and technical change. The next step in the development of a system of accounts in constant prices is to construct measures of property compensation and saving in current and constant prices for the aggregate income and expenditure account. We also wish to construct measures of capital formation and replacement and measures of depreciation and revaluation for the aggregate accumulation account. Finally, we wish to construct measures of capital stock for the aggregate wealth account. As before, we employ a set of vintage accounts encompassing data on prices and quantities of capital goods.

Income, Accumulation, and Wealth Accounts

The quantities of investment goods A_t enter the production account in the period the investment is made through the quantity of investment goods output. An analogous quantity appears as part of capital formation in the accumulation account. The prices associated with investment in the production and accumulation accounts are prices of acquisition of new investment goods $p_{A,t}$. The value of investment goods output is price times quantity, say $p_{A,t} A_t$. The value of capital formation is also equal to price times quantity; the price includes taxes on investment goods output. For several investment goods values of investment goods output and capital formation

---

[o]An alternative approach to the construction of a translog index of sectoral value added has been proposed by Diewert [27, 1980].

are sums of prices times quantities for the individual investment goods. The price and quantity components of these accounts are derived by application of index number formulas to the underlying price and quantity data for the individual investment goods.

Capital stock enters the production account through the quantities of capital service input K_{t-1}; the quantity of capital service input also appears in the income and expenditure account as the quantity component of property compensation. The prices associated with capital services in the production and the income and expenditure accounts are rental prices $p_{K,t}$. The value of capital input and property compensation is price times quantity, say $p_{K,t} K_{t-1}$. The service prices entering the production account are gross of taxes while the prices entering the property compensation account are net of taxes. For several capital goods the values of capital services input and property compensation are sums of prices times quantities for each capital good. The price and quantity components of these accounts are derived by application of index number formulas to the rental price and service quantity data for the individual capital goods.

Capital stock enters the accumulation account as the quantity component of depreciation. In the accumulation account capital stock must be distinguished by vintage so that vintage accounts containing data on investment of every age A_{t-v-1} may be regarded as part of the accumulation account in constant prices. The prices associated with capital stock in the accumulation account are the levels of depreciation $p_{D,t,v}$. The value of depreciation for capital goods of age v is price times quantity, say $p_{D,t,v} A_{t-v-1}$; to obtain the total value of depreciation we sum over vintages, obtaining $\sum_{v=0}^{\infty} p_{D,t,v} A_{t-v-1}$. Even for a single capital good the separation of prices and quantities of depreciation requires application of an index number formula to the underlying vintage data. For several capital goods and the appropriate price and quantity index numbers can be constructed by applying index number formulas to prices and quantities for each capital good derived from vintage data.

Capital stock also enters the accumulation account as the quantity component of revaluation. The prices associated with capital stock in measuring revaluation are the price changes $p_{A,t,v} - p_{A,t-1,v}$. Revaluation for capital goods of age v is price times quantity, say $(p_{A,t,v} - p_{A,t-1,v}) A_{t-v-1}$; to obtain total revaluation we sum over vintages obtaining $\sum_{v=0}^{\infty} (p_{A,t,v} - p_{A,t-1,v}) A_{t-v-1}$. Separation of price and quantity components of revaluation for a single capital good or for several goods requires the application of index number formulas to prices and quantities for each vintage of each capital good, just as in the depreciation account. The prices used for depreciation and revaluation in the accumulation account must be consistent with those used for capital service prices in the production and the income and expenditure accounts.

Replacement appears in the accumulation account as part of capital formation. Gross capital formation is equal to investment. Net capital formation is equal to gross capital formation less replacement. Net capital formation is equal to the period-to-period change in capital stock. Replacement represents the change in the quantity of existing capital goods due to a decline in relative efficiency. Depreciation represents the change in the price of existing capital goods due to present and all future declines in efficiency. We have already described the separation of price and quantity components of gross capital formation. The methods for separation of these components of net capital formation and replacement are strictly analogous; quantities of gross capital formation or investment are replaced by quantities of net capital formation and replacement in index number formulas that also depend on prices of acquisition of investment goods.

Finally, capital stock appears in the wealth account as the quantity component of capital assets. In the wealth account capital stock must be distinguished by vintage so that vintage accounts containing investment of every age in every time period may be regarded as part of both accumulation and wealth accounts. The prices associated with capital stock in the wealth account are the acquisition prices $p_{A,t,v}$. The value of wealth for capital goods of age v is price times quantity, say $p_{A,t,v} A_{t-v}$; to obtain the total value of wealth we sum over vintages, obtaining $\sum_{v=0}^{\infty} p_{A,t,v} A_{t-v}$. For a single capital good or for several capital goods, price and quantity index numbers of wealth can be constructed by applying index number formulas to prices and quantities of capital assets of each vintage at each point of time.

Simplified Accounting System

For capital goods with a full set of data for every time period, including investment of every vintage and the price of acquisition for every vintage, accounts can be compiled for capital input, property compensation, depreciation, capital formation, replacement, and wealth in current and constant prices. Price data corresponding to each of the accounts in constant prices can also be compiled. For capital goods with a less complete set of data a simplified system of accounts can be constructed on the basis of the assumption that decline in efficiency is geometric. Under this assumption the rate of replacement and the rate of depreciation are constant and equal to the rate of decline in efficiency:

$$\hat{\delta}_t = \bar{\delta}_t = \delta .$$

Constant rates of replacement and depreciation lead to substantial simplifications in our system of income and wealth accounts in constant prices. Vintage accounts can be dispensed with since replacement is proportional to capital stock and depreciation is proportional to the current acquisition price of investment goods.

As a first step in construction of a simplified accounting system for income and wealth in constant prices we estimate capital stock at the end of each period as a weighted sum of past investments:

$$K_t = \sum_{\tau=0}^{\infty} (1-\delta)^{\tau} A_{t-\tau} .$$

With a constant rate of replacement, replacement becomes

$$R_t = \delta K_{t-1} .$$

The price of acquisition of new investment goods is a weighted sum of future rentals:

$$q_{A,t} = \sum_{\tau=0}^{\infty} (1-\delta)^{\tau} q_{K, t+\tau+1} .$$

With a constant rate of depreciation, depreciation becomes

$$p_{D,t} = \delta p_{A,t} .$$

The acquisition price of investment goods of age v at time t is

$$p_{A,t,v} = (1-\delta)^{v} p_{A,t} .$$

The service price for new capital goods becomes

$$p_{K,t} = p_{A,t-1} \, r_t + \delta p_{A,t} - (p_{A,t} - p_{A,t-1}) \, .$$

In the complete accounting system for income and wealth in constant prices outlined above, vintage accounts for capital are required for calculating replacement, depreciation, capital formation, revaluation, and wealth. With constant replacement rates δ_τ the values of replacement and depreciation are equal and depend only on the price of acquisition of new capital goods and the stock of capital:

$$p_{A,t} R_t = \delta p_{A,t} K_{t-1} = p_{D,t} K_{t-1} \, .$$

Similarly, the value of wealth is the product of the price of acquisition and the stock of capital, $p_{A,t} K_t$. The change in wealth from period to period,

$$p_{A,t} K_t - p_{A,t-1} K_{t-1} = p_{A,t}(K_t - K_{t-1}) + (p_{A,t} - p_{A,t-1})K_{t-1} \, ,$$

is the sum of capital formation and revaluation. No vintage accounts for capital goods are required under the assumption of constant replacement rates. For several capital goods index number formulas must be employed to separate replacement, depreciation, capital formation, revaluation, and wealth into price and quantity components.

Geometric decline in efficiency is among the patterns most commonly employed in estimating capital stock by the perpetual inventory method.[p] For geometric decline in efficiency depreciation is proportional to the acquisition price of new capital goods and replacement is proportional to capital stock. These properties result from the constancy of the sequence of replacement rates δ_τ. Neither property holds for any other representation of the relative efficiency of capital goods of different ages. A fundamental result of renewal theory is that the sequence of replacement rates δ_τ tends to be constant value for almost any pattern of decline in efficiency.[q] Geometric decline in efficiency, resulting in a constant rate of replacement δ, may provide a useful approximation to replacement

[p]See, for example, the BEA Capital Stock Study [10, 1976a].

[q]See Jorgenson [45, 1973] for a detailed discussion of the application of renewal theory to replacement and depreciation.

requirements and depreciation for a wide variety of patterns of decline in efficiency. Where this approximation is unsatisfactory, a complete accounting system for income and wealth in constant prices requires vintage accounts for capital goods quantities and prices.

Aggregate Production Model

We have outlined a methodology for constructing aggregate income, accumulation, and wealth accounts in constant prices. Our final objective is to develop an aggregate production account in constant prices. For this purpose we introduce a multi-sectoral model of production and technical change based on value added. At this point it is necessary to distinguish between output and input for the economy as a whole and output and input for a single producing sector. We refer to a typical producing sector as the ith sector, where the index i ranges from 1 to the total number of sectors, say n.

Our multi-sectoral model includes value added functions for each of the n sectors. We can represent these functions, say G^i, in the form

$$V_i = G^i(K_i, L_i, t), \qquad\qquad (i = 1, 2 \ldots n),$$

where V_i, K_i, and L_i are the quantities of value added, capital input, and labor input. We represent the individual capital inputs for the economy as a whole by K_k and the corresponding inputs for the individual sectors by K_{ki}. Similarly, we represent the individual labor inputs for the economy as a whole by L_ϱ and the corresponding inputs for the individual sectors by $L_{\varrho i}$. Our multi-sectoral model includes market equilibrium conditions that assure equality between the supply of each factor or production and the demands for that factor by all sectors:

$$K_k = \Sigma K_{ki}, \qquad\qquad (k = 1, 2 \ldots p),$$

$$L_\varrho = \Sigma L_{\varrho i}, \qquad\qquad (\varrho = 1, 2 \ldots q).$$

To derive an aggregate model of production and technical change we first choose a set of quantities of value added for all sectors. We then maximize aggregate output, defined as a proportion of all quantities of value added, subject to the value added functions for all sectors, the market equilibrium conditions, and given supplies of primary factors of production.[r] We can express the maximum value of aggregate output, say λ, as a function of all quantities of value added, all supplies of primary factors of production, and time:

$$\lambda = H(V_1, V_2 \ldots V_n; K_1, K_2 \ldots K_p; L_1, L_2 \ldots L_q; t).$$

The constraints of our maximization problem—sectoral value added functions and market equilibrium conditions—are linear homogeneous functions in the supplies of primary factors of production, sectoral quantities of value added, and demands for factors of production. The function H is homogeneous of degree minus one in the quantities of value added V_i, homogeneous of degree one in the factor supplies K_k and L_ϱ, and homogeneous of degree zero in quantities of value added and factor supplies together. We conclude that our model of aggregate output is characterized by constant returns to scale. Any combination of quantities of value added and supplies of primary factors of production that is proportional to a feasible combination is also feasible. Any combination that is proportional to an efficient combination is also efficient.

A restrictive form of our methodology for aggregate productivity measurement is based on the existence of an aggregate production function. If the production possibility frontier for the economy as a whole can be expressed in terms of aggregate value added, say V, aggregate capital input, say K, and aggregate labor input, say L, we can write the production possibility frontier in the form

$$1 = H(V(V_1, V_2 \ldots V_n), K(K_1, K_2 \ldots K_p), L(L_1, L_2 \ldots L_q), t),$$

where the aggregates V, K, and L are characterized by constant returns to scale. Proportional changes in all components of each aggregate result in a proportional change in the aggregate itself.

Aggregate value added can be expressed as a function, say F, of aggregate capital and labor input and time:

$$V = F(K, L, t).$$

---

[r]The derivation of a production possibility frontier from a multi-sectoral model of production was introduced by Gerard Debreu [20, 1951, p. 285] and has been discussed by Abram Bergson [5, 1961; 6, 1975], Diewert [27, 1980], Franklin Fisher and Karl Shell [30, 1972], and Richard Moorsteen [55, 1961].

This expression defines the *aggregate production function*;[s] the aggregate production function is characterized by constant returns to scale in the aggregate inputs. The quantities of aggregate capital and labor input are functions of the quantities of their components:

$$K = K(K_1, K_2 \ldots K_p),$$

$$L = L(L_1, L_2 \ldots L_q).$$

These functions are also characterized by constant returns to scale.

The existence of an aggregate production function implies that the value added functions of all sectors are identical up to a scalar multiple.[t] Under this condition we can write the sectoral value added functions in the form

$$V_i = G^i(K_i, L_i, t),$$

$$= a_i F(K_i, L_i, t), \qquad (i = 1, 2 \ldots n),$$

where F is the aggregate production function and the constants of proportionality $\{a_i\}$ are fixed. We can choose dimensions for measuring value added in each sector so that these constants are equal to unity for all sectors; for this choice of dimensions all sectoral value added functions are identical to the aggregate production function. In addition sectoral capital and labor inputs $\{K_i\}$ and $\{L_i\}$ are identical functions of their components.

Given the existence of an aggregate production function, we can define the shares of capital and labor input, say v_K and v_L, in value added by

$$v_K = \frac{p_K K}{p_V V},$$

$$v_L = \frac{p_L L}{p_V V},$$

---

[s]An aggregate production function was employed by Robert Solow [60, 1957].

[t]This condition for the existence of an aggregate production function is due to Michael Denny [23, 1972] and Hall [39, 1973]. For further discussion, see Denny and Cheryl Pinto [24, 1978], and Lau [52, 1978].

where p_V, p_K, and p_L denote the prices of aggregate value added, capital input, and labor input. Necessary conditions for producer equilibrium for the economy as a whole are given by equalities between the value shares of each aggregate input and the elasticity of aggregate output with respect to that input:

$$v_K = \frac{\partial \ln V}{\partial \ln K} \quad (K, L, t),$$

$$v_L = \frac{\partial \ln V}{\partial \ln L} \quad (K, L, t).$$

Since the value added functions of all sectors are identical to the aggregate production function, the elasticities and the value shares are identical for all sectors. Under constant returns to scale for the economy as a whole, the elasticities and the value shares for both inputs sum to unity. We can define the rate of technical change for the economy as a whole, say v_T, as the growth of aggregate output with respect to time, holding capital and labor input constant:

$$v_t = \frac{\partial \ln V}{\partial t} \quad (K, L, t).$$

We can define the shares of components of capital and labor input, say v_{Kk} and $v_{L\varrho}$, in the value of the corresponding aggregate by

$$v_{Kk} = \frac{p_{Kk} K_k}{\Sigma p_{Kk} K_k}, \qquad (k = 1, 2 \ldots p),$$

$$v_{L\varrho} = \frac{p_{L\varrho} L_\varrho}{\Sigma p_{L\varrho} L_\varrho}, \qquad (\varrho = 1, 2 \ldots q).$$

Necessary conditions for producer equilibrium for the economy as a whole are given by equalities between the value shares of each component and the elasticities of the aggregate with respect to that component:

$$v_{Kk} = \frac{\partial \ln K}{\partial \ln K_k} \quad (K_1, K_2 \ldots K_p), \qquad (k = 1, 2 \ldots p),$$

$$v_{L\varrho} = \frac{\partial \ln L}{\partial \ln L_\varrho} \quad (L_1, L_2 \ldots L_q), \qquad (\varrho = 1, 2 \ldots q).$$

As before, the elasticities and value shares are identical for all sectors. Under constant returns to scale the elasticities and the value shares sum to unity for each aggregate.

Under constant returns to scale the necessary conditions for producer equilibrium at the aggregate level imply that value added is equal to the sum of the values of capital and labor inputs:

$$p_V V = p_K K + p_L L.$$

Our data on aggregate value added, capital input, and labor input satisfy this equality as an accounting identity. The price of aggregate value added can be expressed as a function, say P, of prices of aggregate capital and labor inputs and time:

$$p_V = P(p_K, p_L, t).$$

We refer to the function P as the *aggregate* price function. This function is homogeneous so that proportional changes in both input prices result in a proportional change in the price of output. Similarly, the prices of aggregate capital and labor input are functions of the prices of their components:

$$p_K = p_K (p_{K1}, p_{K2} \cdots p_{Kp}),$$

$$p_L = p_L (p_{L1}, p_{L2} \cdots p_{Lq}).$$

These functions are also homogeneous.

The existence of an aggregate price function implies that the price of value added functions for all sectors are identical up to a scalar multiple. Under this condition we can represent the sectoral price of value added functions, say $\{ P_V^i \}$, in the form

$$p_V^i = P_V^i (p_K^i, p_L^i, t),$$

$$= b_i P(p_K, p_L, t), \qquad\qquad (i = 1, 2 \ldots n).$$

where P is the aggregate price function, p_K and p_L are the prices of aggregate capital and labor input, and the constants of proportionality b_i are fixed. As before, we can choose dimensions for measuring value added in each sector so that these constants are equal to unity in all sectors; for this choice of dimensions all sectoral price of value added functions are identical to the aggregate price function. In addition, all prices of capital and labor input are identical functions of the prices of their components.

If the prices paid for primary inputs are the same for all sectors, the sectoral prices of value added $\{p_V^i\}$ are identical to the aggregate price of value added p_V. Constant returns to scale for the economy as a whole imply that aggregate value added is equal to the sum of value added in all sectors:

$$p_V V = \Sigma p_V^i V_i .$$

Our data on aggregate value added satisfy this equality as an accounting identity. If all sectoral prices of value added are identical to the aggregate price of value added, this identity implies that the quantity of value added for the economy as a whole can be expressed as the sum of the quantities of value added in all sectors:[u]

$$V = \Sigma V_i .$$

Similarly, constant returns imply that the values of aggregate capital and labor inputs are equal to the sums of the values of their components:

$$p_K K = \Sigma p_{Kk} K_k ,$$

$$p_L L = \Sigma p_{L\ell} L\ell .$$

Again, our data on aggregate capital and labor input satisfy these equalities as accounting identities.

[u]The existence of a value added aggregate equal to the sum of the quantities of value added in all sectors is an implication of John Hicks [40, 1946] aggregation. For further discussion see Bruno [9, 1978] and Diewert [26, 1978].

Aggregate Production Function

To implement our methodology for aggregate production accounts in constant prices we consider a specific form for the aggregate production function:

$$V = \exp [\alpha_0 + \alpha_K \ln K + \alpha_L \ln L + \alpha_t \cdot t + \frac{1}{2} \beta_{KK} (\ln K)^2$$

$$+ \beta_{KL} \ln K \ln L + \beta_{Kt} \ln K \cdot t + \frac{1}{2} \beta_{LL} (\ln L)^2$$

$$+ \beta_{Lt} \ln L \cdot t + \frac{1}{2} \beta_{tt} \cdot t^2] .$$

We refer to this form as the translog production function. The sectoral value added functions are identical to the aggregate production function.

Necessary conditions for producer equilibrium for the economy as a whole are given by equalities between the value shares of each aggregate input and the elasticity of aggregate output with respect to that input:

$$v_K = \alpha_K + \alpha_{KK} \ln K + \alpha_{KL} \ln L + \alpha_{Kt} \cdot t ,$$

$$v_L = \alpha_L + \alpha_{KL} \ln K + \alpha_{LL} \ln L + \alpha_{Lt} \cdot t .$$

Similarly, the rate of aggregate technical change is equal to the rate of growth of output, holding both inputs constant:

$$v_t = \alpha_t + \beta_{Kt} \ln K + \beta_{Lt} \ln L + \beta_{tt} \cdot t .$$

The sectoral value shares and rates of technical change are identical to the corresponding aggregate value shares and rate of technical change.

The aggregate production function is characterized by constant returns to scale if and only if the parameters satisfy the conditions:

$$\alpha_K + \alpha_L = 1 ,$$

$$\beta_{KK} + \beta_{KL} = 0 ,$$

$$\beta_{KL} + \beta_{LL} = 0 \, ,$$

$$\beta_{Kt} + \beta_{Lt} = 0 \, ,$$

If we consider data for the economy as a whole at any two discrete points of time, say t and $t-1$, the difference between successive logarithms of aggregate output can be expressed as a weighted average of the differences between successive logarithms of aggregate capital and labor input, with weights given by average value shares, plus the average rate of aggregate technical change:

$$\ln V_t - \ln V_{t-1} = \bar{v}_K \left[\ln K_t - \ln K_{t-1} \right]$$

$$+ \bar{v}_L \left[\ln L_t - \ln L_{t-1} \right] + \bar{v}_t \, ,$$

where

$$\bar{v}_K = \frac{1}{2} \left[v_{K,t} + v_{K,t-1} \right] \, ,$$

$$\bar{v}_L = \frac{1}{2} \left[v_{L,t} + v_{L,t-1} \right] \, ,$$

$$\bar{v}_t = \frac{1}{2} \left[v_{t,t} + v_{t,t-1} \right] \, .$$

We refer to the expression for the average rate of aggregate technical change $\bar{v}_t$ as the *translog index of the aggregate rate of technical change*.

Similarly, we can consider specific forms for aggregate capital and labor input as functions of their components. For example, the quantity of aggregate capital input can be expressed as a translog function of its components:

$$K = \exp \left[\alpha_1 \ln K_1 + \alpha_2 \ln K_2 + \ldots + \alpha_p \ln K_p \right.$$

$$+ \frac{1}{2} \beta_{11} \left(\ln K_1 \right)^2 + \beta_{12} \ln K_1 \ln K_2 + \ldots$$

$$\left. + \frac{1}{2} \beta_{pp} \left(\ln K_p \right)^2 \right] \, .$$

As before, the corresponding sectoral functions are identical to the aggregate function. Necessary conditions for producer equilibrium

for the economy as a whole imply that the shares of each component of capital input in the value of aggregate capital input are equal
to the elasticities of aggregate value added with respect to its components:

$$w_{Kk} = \alpha_k + \beta_{1k} \ln K_1 + \beta_{2k} \ln K_2 + \ldots + \beta_{pk} \ln K_p ,$$

$$(k = 1, 2 \ldots p).$$

The quantity of capital input for the economy as a whole is characterized by constant returns to scale if and only if the parameters
satisfy the conditions:

$$\alpha_1 + \alpha_2 + \ldots + \alpha_p = 1 ,$$

$$\beta_{11} + \beta_{12} + \ldots + \beta_{1p} = 0 ,$$

$$\beta_{12} + \beta_{22} + \ldots + \beta_{2p} = 0 ,$$

$$\cdot \quad \cdot \quad \cdot \quad \cdot \quad \cdot \quad \cdot \quad \cdot \quad \cdot$$

$$\beta_{1p} + \beta_{2p} + \ldots + \beta_{pp} = 0 .$$

Considering data on capital input at any two discrete points of
time, we can express the difference between successive logarithms of
aggregate capital input as a weighted average of differences between
successive logarithms of its components with weights given by average value shares:

$$\ln K_t - \ln K_{t-1} = \Sigma \bar{v}_{Kk} [\ln K_{k,t} - \ln K_{k,t-1}] ,$$

where

$$\bar{v}_{Kk} = \frac{1}{2} [v_{Kk,t} + v_{Kk,t-1}] , \qquad (k = 1, 2 \ldots p) .$$

Similarly, if aggregate labor input is a translog function of its components, we can express the difference between successive logarithms
of aggregate labor input in the form

$$\ln L_t - \ln L_{t-1} = \Sigma \bar{v}_{L\varrho} [\ln L_{\varrho,t} - \ln L_{\varrho,t-1}] ,$$

where

$$\bar{v}_{L\varrho} = \frac{1}{2} \left[v_{L\varrho,\,t} + v_{L\varrho,\,t-1} \right].$$

We refer to the expressions for aggregate capital input K and labor input L as *translog indexes of aggregate capital input and labor input*.

Using the translog indexes, we can write the translog index of the aggregate rate of technical change in the form

$$\bar{v}_t = \ln V_t - \ln V_{t-1}$$

$$- \bar{v}_K \cdot \Sigma \bar{v}_{Kk} \left[\ln K_{k,\,t} - \ln K_{k,\,t-1} \right]$$

$$- \bar{v}_L \cdot \Sigma \bar{v}_{L\varrho} \left[\ln L_{\varrho,\,t} - \ln L_{\varrho,\,t-1} \right].$$

Again, the sectoral rates of technical change are identical to the aggregate rate of technical change.

The product of price and quantity indexes of aggregate value added, capital input, and labor input must be equal to the sum of the values of value added in all sectors and the sums of values of capital and labor inputs for the economy as a whole. For example, we can define the price index corresponding to the translog quantity index of aggregate capital input as the ratio of the value of capital input in all n sectors to the translog quantity index. The price index corresponding to the translog quantity index of aggregate labor input can be defined in the same way.

Aggregation Over Sectors

Our final objective is to compare the methodology we have developed for constructing a production account in constant prices at the aggregate level with our methodology for constructing production accounts in constant prices at the sectoral level. Our sectoral production accounts are based on models of production and technical change with a sectoral production function giving output as a function of intermediate input, capital input, labor input, and time. The production function for each sector is combined with necessary conditions for producer equilibrium for that sector. A more restrictive model is based on value added functions for each sector, giving the quantity of value added as a function of capital input, labor input, and time.

Our aggregate production account is based on a multi-sectoral model of production and technical change that includes value added functions for all sectors. The multi-sectoral model includes market equilibrium conditions for each factor of production. Our aggregate model is based on a production possibility frontier for the economy as a whole and conditions for producer equilibrium at the aggregate level. A much more restrictive model is based on an aggregate production function. The existence of an aggregate production function implies that all sectoral value added functions are identical and that capital and labor inputs within each sector are identical functions of their components.

Conditions for producer equilibrium at the sectoral level are defined in terms of prices for the output of each sector and prices paid for intermediate goods and for the primary factors of production by each sector. Conditions for producer equilibrium at the aggregate level are defined in terms of prices for value added and for primary factors of production for the economy as a whole. Conditions for producer equilibrium at the sectoral and aggregative levels are equivalent only under the following extremely restrictive conditions. First, value added functions exist for all sectors that are identical to the aggregate production function. Second, capital and labor inputs within each sector are identical functions of their components. Third, the prices paid for primary factor inputs are the same for all sectors.

If conditions for producer equilibrium at sectoral and aggregate levels are equivalent, we can express the rate of technical change for the economy as a whole in terms of sectoral rates of technical change.[v] If prices of value added differ among sectors, due to differences among sectoral value added functions or to differences among sectors in prices paid for primary factors of production, we can express the aggregate rate of technical change in terms of sectoral rates of technical change and changes in the distribution of value added and the primary factors of production among sectors.[w]

---

[v] The relationship between aggregate and sectoral indexes of technical change was first discussed by Wassily Leontief [53, 1953] and Debreu [21, 1954] under the assumption that prices paid for primary factors of production are the same for all sectors.

[w] The relationship between aggregate and sectoral indexes of technical change under the assumption that prices of primary factors of production differ among sectors was first discussed by Kendrick [47, 1961] and Benton Massell [54, 1961].

We can define the price of value added for the economy as a whole p_V in terms of prices of value added in all sectors $\{p_V^i\}$:

$$p_V V = \Sigma p_V^i \, V_i \, .$$

Value added for the economy as a whole is equal to the sum of value added over all sectors. Our data on value added satisfy this equality as an accounting identity. Similarly, we can define the prices of capital inputs for the economy as a whole p_{Kk} in terms of prices paid for each type of capital input in all sectors p_{Kk}^i:

$$p_{Kk} K_k = \Sigma p_{Kk}^i K_{ki}, \qquad (k = 1, 2 \ldots p),$$

and the prices of labor inputs for the economy as a whole $p_{L\varrho}$ in terms of prices paid in all sectors $p_{L\varrho}^i$:

$$p_{L\varrho} L_\varrho = \Sigma p_{L\varrho}^i L_{\varrho i}, \qquad (\varrho = 1, 2 \ldots q).$$

The value of each of the capital inputs for the economy as a whole is equal to the sum of values over all sectors and the value of each of the labor inputs is equal to the sum of values over all sectors. Our data on capital and labor input satisfy these equalities as accounting identities.

We can express the translog index of aggregate technical change in terms of translog indexes of sectoral technical change for all sectors and changes in the distribution of value added and primary factors of production among sectors.[x]

[x]This expression generalizes a formula originally proposed by Evsey Domar [28, 1961], correcting the procedure introduced by Leontief [28, 1953]. Domar's approach, like Leontief's, is based on the assumption that prices paid for primary factors of production are the same for all sectors. Domar's approach has been discussed by Diewert [27, 1980] and Charles Hulten [42, 1978], and has been employed by Mieko Nishimizu [56, 1975] and by Nishimizu and Hulten [57, 1978]. Leontief's approach has been discussed by the Statistical Office of the United Nations [62, 1968], "Gross Output and All Inputs, The Gross System of Productivity Measurement," pp. 69–70, and has been employed by Spencer Star [61, 1974] and Tsunehiko Watanabe [66, 1971]. A closely related approach, based on a sectoral model of production and technical change, was introduced by Bergson [5, 1961], Domar [28, 1961], Kendrick [47, 1961], Massell [54, 1961], and Moorsteen [55, 1961] and has been discussed by Bergson [6, 1975], Fisher and Shell [30, 1972], and Statistical Office of the United

First, we write the sectoral indexes for the quantity of value added in the form

$$\ell n\ V_{j,t} - \ell n\ V_{j,t-1} = \frac{1}{\bar{v}_V^j}\ [\ell n\ Z_{i,t} - \ell n\ Z_{i,t-1}] - \frac{\bar{v}_X^j}{\bar{v}_V^j}\ [\ell n\ X_{j,t} - \ell n\ X_{j,t-1}],$$

$$= \frac{\bar{v}_K^j}{\bar{v}_V^j}\ [\ell n\ K_{j,t} - \ell n\ K_{j,t-1}] + \frac{\bar{v}_L^j}{\bar{v}_V^j}\ [\ell n\ L_{j,t} - \ell n\ L_{j,t-1}]$$

$$+ \frac{\bar{v}_t^j}{\bar{v}_V^j}$$

$$= \frac{\bar{v}_K^j}{\bar{v}_V^j}\ \Sigma \bar{v}_{Kk}^j\ [\ell n\ K_{Kj,t} - \ell n\ K_{kj,t-1}]$$

$$+ \frac{\bar{v}_L^j}{\bar{v}_V^j}\ \Sigma \bar{v}_{L\varrho}^j\ [\ell n\ L_{\varrho j,t} - \ell n\ L_{\varrho j,t-1}] + \frac{\bar{v}_t^j}{\bar{v}_V^j},$$

$$(j = 1, 2, \ldots, n),$$

where

$$\bar{v}_V^j = \frac{1}{2}\ [v_{V,t}^j + v_{V,t-1}^j], \qquad\qquad (j = 1, 2, \ldots, n),$$

and

$$v_V^j = \frac{p_V^j\ V_j}{p_j\ Z_j}, \qquad\qquad (j = 1, 2, \ldots, n).$$

Nations [62, 1968], "Value Added and Primary Inputs: The Net System of Productivity Measurement," p. 69. This approach has been employed by Alan Armstrong [2, 1974], Kendrick [47, 1961; 48, 1973], and Massell [54, 1961].

Multiplying the sectoral indexes of technical change by the ratio of value added in the corresponding sector to value added in all sectors, summing over all sectors and subtracting the results from the index for the economy as a whole, we obtain

$$\bar{v}_t = \Sigma \frac{\bar{w}_j}{\bar{v}_V^j} \cdot \bar{v}_t^j + [\ln V_t - \ln V_{t-1}] - \Sigma \bar{w}_j [\ln V_{j,t} - \ln V_{j,t-1}]$$

$$+ \Sigma \bar{w}_j \cdot \frac{\bar{v}_K^j}{\bar{v}_V^j} \Sigma \bar{v}_{Kk}^j [\ln K_{kj,t} - \ln K_{kj,t-1}] - \bar{v}_K \cdot \Sigma \bar{v}_{Kk} [\ln K_{k,t}$$

$$- \ln K_{k,t-1}]$$

$$+ \Sigma \bar{w}_j \cdot \frac{\bar{v}_L^j}{\bar{v}_V^j} \Sigma \bar{v}_{L\ell}^j [\ln L_{lj,t} - \ln L_{lj,t-1}] - \bar{v}_L \cdot \Sigma \bar{v}_{L\ell} [\ln L_{\ell,t}$$

$$- \ln L_{\ell,t-1}],$$

where

$$\bar{w}_j = \frac{1}{2}(w_{j,t} + w_{j,t-1}), \qquad (j = 1, 2 \ldots n),$$

and

$$w_j = \frac{p_V^j V_j}{\Sigma p_V^j V_j}, \qquad (j = 1, 2 \ldots n).$$

The first term in this expression is a weighted sum of sectoral rates of technical change with weights given by ratios of the value of output in each sector to the value added in all sectors. The sum of these weights exceeds unity, since each sector contributes to the rate of technical change for the economy as a whole both through sectoral technical change and through its deliveries to demand for intermediate goods by other sectors. The remaining terms reflect the contributions of changes in the distribution of value added and primary factors of production among sectors to the rate of technical change for the economy as a whole.

The second term in the expression given above for the translog index of technical change for the economy as a whole is a weighted sum of rates of growth of the quantity of value added in all sectors. The weights reflect the differences between value added at the prices received by each sector $p_V^j V_j$ and value added at an average price received by the economy as a whole $p_V V_j$. Since the sums of these values over all sectors are equal, the weights sum to zero. If rates of growth of the quantity of value added are the same in all sectors, the weighted sum is equal to zero. This sum reflects the contribution of changes in the distribution of value added among sectors to the rate of technical change for the economy as a whole.

Similarly, the third term in the expression given above is a weighted sum of rates of growth of all types of capital input into all sectors. The weights reflect differences between the values of each type of capital input at prices paid by each sector $p_{Kk}^j K_{kj}$ and the values of this type of capital input at an average of prices paid by the economy as a whole $p_{Kk} K_{kj}$. Since the sums of these values over all sectors are equal, the weights sum to zero for each type of capital input. If rates of growth of a given type of capital input are the same for all sectors, the corresponding term in the weighted sum is zero. The weighted sum reflects the contribution of changes in the distribution of all types of capital input among the sectors to the rate of technical change for the economy as a whole.

Finally, the fourth term in the expression for the translog index of technical change is a weighted sum of the rates of growth of all types of labor input into all sectors. The weights reflect differences between the values of each type of labor input at prices paid by each sector $p_{L\varrho}^j L_{\varrho j}$ and values of this type of labor input at an average of prices paid by the economy as a whole $p_{L\varrho} L_{\varrho j}$. As before, the sums of these values over all sectors are equal, so that the weights sum to zero. The weighted sum reflects the contribution of changes in the distribution of each type of labor to the rate of technical change for the economy as a whole.

IV. CONCLUSION

We have presented a detailed accounting framework for the role of capital in U.S. economic growth. This framework is based on a system of vintage accounts for prices and quantities of capital goods originated by Christensen and Jorgenson [17, 1973]. The complete accounting system consists of production accounts for individual industrial sectors and aggregate accounts for production, income and expenditure, accumulation, and wealth. The measurement of capital at both sectoral and aggregate levels is based on vintage accounts for prices and quantities of capital goods broken down by type of asset and by sector.

The sectoral production accounts incorporate data on output and intermediate, capital, and labor input for each industrial sector. The value of output is equal to the value of outlay on all three inputs for each sector. In Section II of this chapter we outlined a methodology for measuring sectoral capital input in current and constant prices. The prices and quantities of sectoral capital input are based on data on investment in each type of asset and on property compensation in each sector. From these data we can measure the prices and quantities of capital input for each type of asset by vintage.

We aggregate over the sectoral production accounts by introducing the concept of value added in each sector, defined as the value of output less the value of outlay on intermediate input. The quantity of value added in each sector depends on the quantities of sectoral output and intermediate input. Value added for the economy as a whole is defined as the sum of value added for all sectors. Outlay on capital and labor input for the economy as a whole is also the sum over all sectors. In Section III of this chapter we presented a methodology for measuring aggregate value added, capital input, and labor input in current and constant prices. The quantities of value added, each type of capital input, and each type of labor input are sums of the corresponding sectoral quantities over all sectors.

Our aggregate production accounts includes outlay in capital and labor inputs. We incorporate these data into an aggregate income and expenditure account that includes income from the supply of factor services, net of taxes, and transfer payments. These receipts are allocated between consumer outlays and saving. For the economy as a whole saving is equal to capital formation through the acquisition of new capital goods, the accumulation of inventories, and the acquisition of claims on governments and the rest of the world. Saving and capital formation are incorporated into an aggregate accumulation account. This account also includes revaluation of existing assets through price changes.

Capital formation and revaluation of existing assets comprise changes in the value of wealth. Our accounting system for the role of capital is completed by a wealth account that incorporates data on wealth in current and constant prices. Prices and quantities of capital goods for each type of asset by vintage are used to estimate capital input as a source of income in the income and expenditure account, capital formation as a use of income in the accumulation account, and capital as a store of wealth in the wealth account. This vintage accounting system provides the data necessary to encompass all aspects of the role of capital in the U.S. economy. Our complete accounting system has been implemented for 1948–1976 by Fraumeni and Jorgenson [33, 1980].

REFERENCES

1. ANDO, ALBERT, and BROWN, E. CARY. "The Impacts of Fiscal Policy," in *Stabilization Policies*. Edited by E. CARY BROWN et al. Englewood Cliffs, N.J.: Prentice Hall, 1963.

2. ARMSTRONG, ALAN. *Structural Change in the British Economy 1948–1968*. Cambridge, England: Chapman and Hall, 1974.

3. ARROW, KENNETH J. "Optimal Capital Policy, The Cost of Capital, and Myopic Decision Rules," *Annals of the Institute of Statistical Mathematics*, 1964, *16*, pp. 21–30.

4. ____ . "The Measurement of Real Value Added," in *Nations and Households in Economic Growth*. Edited by PAUL A. DAVID and MELVIN W. REDER. New York: Academic Press, 1974.

5. BERGSON, ABRAM. *The Real National Income of Soviet Russia Since 1928*. Cambridge: Harvard Univ. Press, 1961.

6. ____ . "Index Numbers and the Computation of Factor Productivity," *Review of Income and Wealth*, Sept. 1975, *21* (3), pp. 259–78.

7. BOARD OF GOVERNORS OF THE FEDERAL RESERVE SYSTEM. *Federal Reserve Bulletin*, various monthly issues.

8. ____ . *Flow of Funds Accounts, 1946–1975*. Washington, D.C.: Federal Reserve System, 1976.

9. BRUNO, MICHAEL. "Quality, Intermediate Inputs and Value-Added," in *Production Economics: A Dual Approach to Theory and Applications*, 2. Edited by MELVYN FUSS and DANIEL MCFADDEN. Amsterdam: North-Holland, 1978.

10. BUREAU OF ECONOMIC ANALYSIS. *Fixed Nonresidential Business and Residential Capital in the United States, 1925-1975*, PB-253 725. Washington, D.C.: U.S. Department of Commerce, National Technical Information Service, 1976a.

11. ____ . *The National Income and Product Accounts of the United States, 1929-1974: Statistical Tables, A Supplement to the Survey of Current Business*. Washington, D.C.: U.S. Department of Commerce, U.S.G.P.O., 1976b.

12. ____ . *Fourteen Current Dollar Components of Gross Product Originating by Industry*, Workfile 1205-01-03. Washington, D.C.: U.S. Department of Commerce, 1978.

13. ____ . *Survey of Current Business*, various monthly issues.

14. CHRISTENSEN, LAURITS R. "Entrepreneurial Income: How Does It Measure Up?" *American Economic Review*, Sept. 1971, *61* (4), pp. 575–85.

15. CHRISTENSEN, LAURITS R., and JORGENSON, DALE W. "The Measurement of U.S. Real Capital Input, 1929-1967," *Review of Income and Wealth*, Dec. 1969, *15* (4), pp. 293–320.

16. _____ . "U.S. Real Product and Real Factor Input, 1929-1967," *Review of Income and Wealth*, March 1970, *16*(1), pp. 19-50.

17. _____ . "Measuring the Performance of the Private Sector of the U.S. Economy, 1929-1969," in *Measuring Economic and Social Performance.* Edited by MILTON MOSS. New York: National Bureau of Economic Research, 1973.

18. CHRISTENSEN, LAURITS R.; JORGENSON, DALE W.; and LAU, LAWRENCE J. "Conjugate Duality and the Transcendental Logarithmic Production Function," *Econometrica*, July 1971, *39*(4), pp. 225- 26.

19. _____ . "Transcendental Logarithmic Production Frontiers, *Review of Economics and Statistics*, Feb. 1973, *55*(1), pp. 28-45.

20. DEBREU, GERARD. "The Coefficient of Resource Allocation," *Econometrica*, July 1951, *19*(3), 273-92.

21. _____ . "Numerical Representations of Technological Change," *Metroeconomica*, Aug. 1954, *6*(11), pp. 45-54.

22. DENISON, EDWARD F. *Accounting for United States Economic Growth 1929-1969.* Washington, D.C.: The Brookings Institution, 1974.

23. DENNY, MICHAEL. Trade and the Production Sector: An Exploration of Models of Multi-Product Technologies. Unpublished Ph.D. dissertation. University of California, Berkeley, 1972.

24. DENNY, MICHAEL, and PINTO, CHERYL. "An Aggregate Model with Multi-Product Technologies," in *Production Economics: A Dual Approach to Theory and Applications, 2.* Edited by MELVYN FUSS and DANIEL MCFADDEN. Amsterdam: North-Holland, 1978.

25. DIEWERT, W. ERWIN. "Exact and Superlative Index Numbers," *Journal of Econometrics*, May 1976, *4*(2), pp. 115-46.

26. _____ . "Hicks Aggregation Theorem and the Existence of a Real Value Added Function," in *Production Economics: A Dual Approach to Theory and Applications, 2.* Edited by MELVYN FUSS and DANIEL MCFADDEN. Amsterdam: North-Holland, 1978.

27. _____ . "Aggregation Problems in the Measurement of Capital," in *The Measurement of Capital.* Edited by DAN USHER. Chicago: Univ. of Chicago Press, 1980.

28. DOMAR, EVSEY D. "On the Measurement of Technological Change," *Economic Journal*, Dec. 1961, *71*(284), pp. 709-29.

29. FELLER, WILLIAM. *An Introduction to Probability Theory and Its Application*, Vol. 1. New York: Wiley, 2nd ed., 1957.

30. FISHER, FRANKLIN M., and SHELL, KARL. *The Economic Theory of Price Indices.* New York: Academic Press, 1972.

31. FISHER, IRVING. *The Making of Index Numbers.* Boston: Houghton Mifflin, 1922.

32. FRANE, L., and KLEIN, L.R. "The Estimation of Disposable Income by Distributive Shares," *Review of Economics and Statistics*, Nov. 1953, *35*(4), pp. 333-37.

33. FRAUMENI, BARBARA M., and JORGENSON, DALE W. "The Role of Capital in U.S. Economic Growth, 1948-1976," in this volume.

34. GOLDSMITH, RAYMOND W. *The National Wealth of the United States in the Postwar Period.* New York: National Bureau of Economic Research, 1962.

35. _____ . *The Balance Sheet of the United States, 1953-1975.* Preliminary draft dated March 1978.

36. GOLDSMITH, RAYMOND W.; LIPSEY, ROBERT E.; and MENDELSON, MORRIS. *Studies in the National Balance Sheet of the United States.* Princeton: Princeton Univ. Press, 1963.

37. GOLLOP, FRANK M., and JORGENSON, DALE W. "U.S. Productivity Growth by Industry, 1947-1973," in *New Developments in Productivity Measurement.* Edited by JOHN W. KENDRICK and BEATRICE VACCARA. Chicago: University of Chicago Press, 1980.

38. HALL, ROBERT E. "Technical Change and Capital from the Point of View of the Dual," *Review of Economic Studies*, Jan. 1968, *35*(101), pp. 35-46.

39. _____ . "The Specification of Technology with Several Kinds of Output," *Journal of Political Economy*, July/Aug. 1973, *81* (4), pp. 878-92.

40. HICKS, JOHN R. *Value and Capital.* Oxford: Oxford Univ. Press, 2nd ed., 1946.

41. HOTELLING, HAROLD S. "A General Mathematical Theory of Depreciation," *Journal of the American Statistical Association*, Sept. 1925, *20*(3), pp. 340-53.

42. HULTEN, CHARLES R. "Growth Accounting with Intermediate Inputs," *Review of Economic Studies*, Oct. 1978, *45*(141), pp. 511-18.

43. INTERNAL REVENUE SERVICE. *Statistics of Income: Individual Income Tax Returns*, various annual issues.

44. JACK FAUCETT ASSOCIATES. *Development of Capital Stock Series by Industry Sector.* Washington, D.C.: Office of Emergency Preparedness, March 1973.

45. JORGENSON, DALE W. "The Economic Theory of Replacement and Depreciation," in *Econometrics and Economic Theory.* Edited by WILLY SELLEKAERTS. New York: Macmillan, 1973.

46. JORGENSON, DALE W., and LAU, LAWRENCE J. *Transcendental Logarithmic Production Functions.* Amsterdam: North-Holland, 1980.

47. KENDRICK, JOHN W. *Productivity Trends in the United States.* Princeton: Princeton Univ. Press, 1961.

48. _____ . *Postwar Productivity Trends in the United States, 1948-1969.* New York: National Bureau of Economic Research, 1973.

49. KLOEK, TUUN. *Indexcijfers: enige methodologisch aspecten.* The Hague: Pasmans, 1966.

50. KRAVIS, IRVING B. "Relative Income Shares in Fact and Theory," *American Economic Review*, Dec. 1959, *49*(5), pp. 917-49.

51. KUZNETS, SIMON. *Capital in the American Economy.* Princeton: Princeton Univ. Press, 1961.

52. LAU, LAWRENCE J. "Applications of Profit Functions," in *Production Economics: A Dual Approach to Theory and Applications, 1.* Edited by MELVYN FUSS and DANIEL MCFADDEN. Amsterdam: North-Holland, 1978.

53. LEONTIEF, WASSILY. "Structural Change," in *Studies in the Structure of the American Economy.* Edited by WASSILY LEONTIEF. New York: Oxford Univ. Press, 1953.

54. MASSELL, BENTON F. "A Disaggregated View of Technical Change," *Journal of Political Economy*, Dec. 1961, *69*(6), pp. 547-57.

55. MOORSTEEN, RICHARD H. "On Measuring Productive Potential and Relative Efficiency," *Quarterly Journal of Economics*, Aug. 1961, *75*(3), pp. 451-67.

56. NISHIMIZU, MIEKO. *Total Factor Productivity Analysis: A Disaggregated Study of the Post-war Japanese Economy with Explicit Consideration of Intermediate Inputs*. Unpublished Ph.D. dissertation. Johns Hopkins University, Baltimore, 1974.

57. NISHIMIZU, MIEKO, and HULTEN, CHARLES R. "The Sources of Japanese Economic Growth: 1955-71," *Review of Economics and Statistics*, Aug. 1978, *60*(3), pp. 351-61.

58. SATO, KAZUO. "The Meaning and Measurement of the Real Value Added Index," *Review of Economics and Statistics*, Nov. 1976, *58*(4), pp. 434-42.

59. SIMS, CHRISTOPHER. "Theoretical Basis for a Double-Deflated Index of Real Value Added," *Review of Economics and Statistics*, Nov. 1969, *51*(4) pp. 470-71.

60. SOLOW, ROBERT M. "Technical Change and the Aggregate Production Function," *Review of Economics and Statistics*. Nov. 1957, *39*(4), pp. 312-20.

61. STAR, SPENCER. "Accounting for the Growth of Output," *American Economic Review*, March 1974, *64*(1), pp. 123-35.

62. STATISTICAL OFFICE OF THE UNITED NATIONS. *A System of National Accounts*. New York: United Nations, 1968.

63. THEIL, HENRI. "The Information Approach to Demand Analysis," *Econometrica*, Jan. 1965, *33*(1), pp. 67-87.

64. TORNQUIST, LEO. "The Bank of Finland's Consumption Price Index," *Bank of Finland Monthly Bulletin*, 1936, *10*, pp. 1-8.

65. UNITED STATES DEPARTMENT OF THE TREASURY. *Treasury Bulletin*, various monthly issues.

66. WATANABE, TSUNEHIKO. "A Note on Measuring Sectoral Input Productivity," *Review of Income and Wealth*, Dec. 1971, *17*(4), pp. 335-40.

Part II

Malallocations of Capital by Sector and Function

Government-Induced Biases in the Allocation of the Stock of Fixed Capital in the United States

*Patric H. Hendershott and
Sheng-Cheng Hu*

During the past eighteen years, legislative changes that directly affect user costs of capital and thus the level and the distribution of the stock of capital in the United States have become more frequent. Pertinent legislation is that directly dealing with or influencing tax rates on individual and corporate income and on capital gains, tax credits, and the tax base. The base is a function of tax depreciation which depends on allowable service lives and depreciation methods, inflation accounting for inventories, financial structure, and the proposed dividend deduction for corporations. Beyond this, relative interest rates, and thus user costs of capital, are influenced by interest rate ceilings, the exemption of state and local government interest payments from federal taxes, and government-sponsored lending and guaranteeing. It would seem important for a nation now especially concerned with capital formation that the impact of government action on user costs of capital be clearly understood.

This chapter is the first stage of a research agenda designed to deduce the impact of government actions, past and proposed, on the level and distribution of the American capital stock. We begin by developing a general expression for calculating net user costs of capital. Specific expressions are derived for six categories of investment: owner-occupied housing, rental housing acquired by noncorporate

Critiques by George von Furstenberg of early versions of this chapter have been most helpful. We also wish to thank Larry Rosenberg of the National Science Foundation, Lewis Johnson of the Federal Reserve Board, and Michael Boskin of Stanford University for arranging seminars that generated a number of useful comments.

business, equipment and structures acquired by corporations, and equipment and structures acquired by noncorporate business, and user costs are computed for these six categories for the 1964–65 and 1976–77 periods.[a] Our framework is then contrasted with that of Martin Feldstein and Lawrence Summers [6, 1978], and our estimates are compared with computations employed in the estimation of the Federal Reserve-MIT-Penn (FMP) quarterly model. Next, estimates are provided of the productivity losses being imposed on the American economy owing to the fact that the American capital stock is not allocated optimally, that is, that the net user costs of capital are not equal for all investments. (Unless the context makes clear otherwise, the attribute "net" by itself refers not to taxes but to depreciation throughout this chapter, with the net user cost of capital tending to equality with the marginal physical product of capital net of depreciation as shown below.) Finally, methods of reducing the differences in net user costs and thus the productivity losses are considered.

I. THE NET COST OF CAPITAL: A GENERAL EXPRESSION

As is well known, the decision to invest depends on whether the present value of the expected revenue from investment, net of direct operating expenses and indirect taxes, exceeds the supply price of capital, and in equilibrium the two will be equal. We assume that inflation is expected to cause both these net revenues and the supply price of capital to rise at the same rate p and that the productivity of the investment and thus real net revenues are expected to decline at the output decay rate of d per year.[b] In the absence of direct taxes we can then write

$$P_k = \sum_{t=1}^{N} \frac{(1+p-d)^{t-1} REV}{(1+r)^t} + (1-\beta) \frac{(1+p-d)^N}{(1+r)^N} P_k, \qquad (1)$$

[a] Because of lack of data for the fourth quarter of 1977, our analysis for the period 1976-77 starts with the fourth quarter of 1975 and ends with the third quarter of 1977. The 1964-65 period includes the impact of Kennedy-Johnson tax cuts and excludes the subsequent years of rapid inflation.

[b] Two expected inflation rates are relevant, those for revenues and asset prices. For cost of capital expressions that allow for different inflation rates, see [12, Hendershott and Hu, 1980].

where

P_k =   current supply price of capital,

REV =   current expected net revenue (operating income),

r =   financing rate (generally the average of an interest rate on debt issues, i, and an equity or own financing rate, e),

p =   annual rate of inflation,

d =   annual rate of economic depreciation,

N =   the years the capital good is held, and

β =   the cost, as a percent of the market price, of selling the capital good in the secondary market.

Because

$$(1 - \frac{(1+p-d)^N}{(1+r)^N}) = (1 - \frac{1+p-d}{1+r}) (\sum_{t=1}^{N} \frac{(1+p-d)^{t-1}}{(1+r)^{t-1}}),$$

$$\sum_{t=1}^{N} \frac{(1+p-d)^{t-1}}{(1+r)^t} = \frac{1-(1+p-d)^N (1+r)^{-N}}{r+d-p}. \tag{2}$$

With the use of equation (2), equation (1) can be rewritten as

$$\gamma P_K = \delta \frac{REV}{r+d-p}, \tag{1a}$$

where $\gamma = 1-(1-\beta)(1+p-d)^N (1+r)^{-N}$ and $\delta = 1-(1+p-d)^N (1+r)^{-N}$. The γ and δ factors, respectively, convert the price of the asset into the net (of the present value of the expected liquidation value) price and the present value of an infinite revenue stream into the present value of an N-period revenue stream. The gross cost of capital is obtained by solving (1a) for REV/P_K:

$$c_G = \frac{\gamma}{\delta} (r+d-p) = \frac{REV}{P_K}. \tag{3}$$

When β is zero (no selling costs) or $N = \infty$ and $r > p - d$, $c_G = r + d - p$. The right side of equation (3) equals the gross marginal product of capital in equilibrium.

Expression (1) ignores the existence of income taxes and investment tax credits. Moreover, when income taxes are introduced, care must be taken to account for the deductibility of interest and depreciation charges allowed under the tax law. The following assumptions are made for the most general case:

1. Income is taxed at the rate τ_y, property is taxed at rate τ_p, and the effective rate of the investment tax credit is μ.

2. A portion α of the net investment $(1-\mu)P_k$ is debt financed (that is, α is the loan-to-value ratio); the debt and equity portions remain constant throughout the life of the asset; and debt financing charges are deductible from the income tax base.

3. Depreciation and property taxes are deductible from the income tax base. The depreciation rate allowed for tax purposes in period t is dx_t.

4. No recapture provisions or capital gain taxes are in effect.[c] With these assumptions the analogue to equation (1) is

$$(4)$$

$$(1-\mu)P_k = \sum_{t=1}^{N} (1+r_a)^{-t} [(1+p-d)^{t-1} (1-\tau_y)REV + d(1+p-d)^{t-1} \tau_y P_k$$

$$- (1-\tau_y)\tau_p (1+p-d)P_k + \tau_y [dx_t - d(1+p-d)^{t-1}] P_k]$$

$$+ (1-\beta) \frac{(1+p-d)^N}{(1+r_a)^N} P_k ,$$

where r_a is now the after-tax average financing rate used to discount after-tax cash flows

$$r_a = (1-\tau_y)\alpha i + (1-\alpha)e_a , \qquad (5)$$

and e_a is the after-tax return on equity. The second term in the brackets in (4) captures the tax saving from the depreciation deduction based on true economic depreciation, the third term the cost (net of the income tax deduction) of property taxes, and the fourth the difference between the value of the depreciation deduction allowed under the tax law and that consistent with true economic

---

[c]Even if there are capital gains taxes, equation (4) would remain unchanged if $(1-\beta)(1+p-d)^N > 1$.

depreciation. Using equation (2), with r_a replacing r, we can derive[d]

$$c_G = \left[\frac{\gamma_a - \mu}{\delta_a}(r_a - p + d) - \tau_y d + (1 - \tau_y)\tau_p - \tau_y\left(\frac{r_a - p + d}{\delta_a}\sum_{t=1}^{N}\frac{dx_t}{(1 + r_a)^t} - d\right)\right]\frac{1}{1 - \tau_y}$$

$$= \frac{REV}{P_k}, \tag{6}$$

where γ_a and δ_a are defined analogously to r and δ but with r_a replacing r. When $\beta = 1$ (the cost of selling the capital good is prohibitive), $\gamma_a = 1$; when $\beta = 0$ (the cost of selling the good is zero), $\gamma_a = \delta_a$; when $N = \infty$ and $r_a > p - d$, $\gamma_a = \delta_a = 1$. The second through fourth terms in the brackets in (6) measure the impacts of true depreciation, property taxes, and the difference between tax and economic depreciation.

The net cost of capital is obtained by subtracting d from both sides of equation (6):

$$c_N = \left[\frac{\gamma_a - \mu}{\delta_a}(r_a - p + d) - d\right]\frac{1}{1 - \tau_y} + \tau_p - (d^* - d)\frac{\tau_y}{1 - \tau_y} = \frac{REV}{P_k} - d,$$

$$\tag{6a}$$

where d^* is the average annual geometric rate of depreciation allowed under tax law. If tax, depreciation, and financial policy were neutral and if all investments were equally risky, then c_N would be equal for all investments in equilibrium.

II. ASSUMPTIONS UNDERLYING SPECIFIC COST-OF-CAPITAL CALCULATIONS

Analogues to equation (6a) are used to compute the net cost of capital for six categories of investment: owner-occupied housing, rental housing held by noncorporate business, equipment held by corporations, equipment held by noncorporate business, structures held by corporations, and structures held by noncorporate business. In com-

---

[d]The continuous-time, infinite-life version of this equation was derived by Dale Jorgenson [13, 1965]. See also Laurits Christensen and Dale Jorgenson [2, 1977].

puting the net costs of capital for investment in a particular asset by a particular economic unit, all the factors affecting equation (6a) must be considered. For convenience we have divided them into three groups: tax rates and the deductibility of expenses, actual and tax depreciation, and financing rates. Each of these is discussed for both the 1964—65 and 1976—77 periods.

Tax Rates and the Deductibility of Interest and Taxes

Homeowners are not required to pay tax on the imputed rental from their own houses. Thus the appropriate discount rate for the cash flows is a before-tax rate. However, homeowners are allowed to deduct mortgage interest from other income when computing their personal tax liability and thus the tax saving from this deduction should appear in equation (4). Further, they may deduct property taxes in computing their tax liability but may not deduct depreciation. As a result, the analogue to equation (6a) for owner-occupied housing is

$$c_N = \frac{\gamma_a}{\delta_a}(r-p) + \frac{\gamma_a - \delta_a}{\delta_a}d + (1-\tau_y)\tau_p. \tag{6b}$$

For business investments, depreciation is tax deductible, as are interest and property tax expenses, but net revenue is also subject to taxation.

The personal income tax rate reflects both the marginal federal and state and local income tax rates. The marginal federal income tax rate varies across investors. For our calculations we assume the most relevant marginal rate to be the weighted average of the marginal effective tax rate paid by the top half of the income distribution (30.3 percent for 1964—65 and 33.5 percent for 1976—77).[e] Owing to the lack of data, we approximate the marginal state and local income tax rate by the average rate computed from the national income and product accounts: 4.3 percent for 1964—65 and 6.9 percent for 1976—77. Taking into consideration the deductibility of state and local taxes from the federal income tax base, the total marginal income tax rate for all noncorporate investments was 33.0 percent for 1964—65 and 38.1 percent for 1976—77.

---

[e]The 1964 and 1965 marginal rates are obtained from [23, U.S. Internal Revenue Service, Tables 22 and 23, 1964 and 1965]; the 1976-77 rates are based on the 1974 rates derived from [23, U.S. Internal Revenue Service, Table 3.18, 1974]. The weights are the share of total adjusted gross income in the respective marginal tax bracket.

The ratio of property tax payments on owner-occupied housing to the value of existing structures, including land, has remained roughly constant between the middle 1960s and 1970s at 0.018.[f] Given a household marginal tax rate of roughly 1/3, the property tax term in equation (6b) is thus 0.012. Knowledge regarding the property tax rates applied to business structures and equipment is limited, but our general impression is that these rates are lower than those for owner-occupied housing. We will take these rates, and thus the property tax term, to have been 0.012 in both periods. Therefore, property taxes are assumed to raise costs of capital for all investments by the same 1.2 percent and have no impact on the allocation of capital (owner-occupied housing is taxed more heavily, but not taxing imputed rents offsets the impact of the higher rate of taxation on the cost of capital).

The marginal federal tax rate on corporate profits was 50 percent in 1964 and 48 percent in 1965 and 1976−77. Again the marginal state and local corporate income tax rate is approximated by the average rate. It was estimated to be 2.7 percent for 1964−65 and 5.7 percent for 1976−77. Thus the total marginal corporate rate was 50.3 percent for 1964−65 and 51.0 percent for 1976−77.

An investment tax credit at a statutory rate of 7 percent (3 percent for utilities) was first established in 1962 to encourage investment in equipment with the full rate being available on equipment with a useful life of eight years or more. The 1962 law required deduction of the credit from the cost of an asset before computing depreciation for tax purposes. But this requirement was eliminated by the 1964 Long Amendment. This tax credit was repealed in 1969 but restored in 1971. It stood at 10 percent (including utilities) during 1976−77. Because of the maximum limitations restrictions of "Section 38" (prohibiting reductions of otherwise taxable income by more than 50 percent, except currently by utilities, through use of the credit) and carryover restrictions and the only partial application of the credit to short-lived equipment, the effective tax credit rate is assumed to be 5.5 percent for 1964−65 and 8.5 percent for 1976−77.[g]

Tax and Economic Depreciation

Only the cost of capital for owner-occupied housing, for which depreciation is not deductible from taxable income, is unaffected by

---

[f]This is based upon a Census Bureau study as reported in the *San Francisco Chronicle*, Jan. 12, 1979, p. 30.

[g]This assumption follows the FMP model [1, 1977]. The effective tax credit rates assumed by Christensen and Jorgenson [2, 1977] were 4.6 percent for 1964−65 and 8.4 percent for 1975.

the method by which tax depreciation is computed. From the derivation in Section I, the average annual geometric rate of tax depreciation over an N-period horizon is

$$d^* = \frac{r_a - p + d}{\delta_a} \sum_{t=1}^{N} \frac{dx_t}{(1 + r_a)^t}, \tag{7}$$

and the reduction in (addition to, if negative) the cost of capital owing to the difference between tax and economic depreciation is

$$TXD = (d^* - d) \frac{\tau_y}{1 - \tau_y}. \tag{8}$$

If tax depreciation were equal to economic depreciation at replacement cost, then $dx_t = d(1+p-d)^{t-1}$ and $d^* = d$ and thus $TXD = 0$. However, under present law tax depreciation is based on historical cost, that is, $dx_t = d(1-d)^{t-1}$. Substituting this expression into (7),

$$d^* = \frac{r_a - p + d}{r_a + d} \eta d, \tag{7a}$$

where

$$\eta = \frac{1 - (1-d)^N (1+r_a)^{-N}}{\delta_a}$$

and

$$TXD = [\eta - 1 - \frac{\eta p}{r_a + d}] \frac{d\tau_y}{1 - \tau_y}. \tag{8a}$$

Another source of distortion between economic and tax depreciation exists. The service life for tax purposes is generally less than the economic service life, and assets may generally be depreciated on an accelerated rate schedule that exceeds the actual depreciation rate schedule. Three frequently used methods for computing tax depreciation are straight line, declining balance, and sum of the years' digits. The accelerated-declining and sum-of-years'-digits methods accelerate depreciation relative to the straight-line method by allowing more depreciation in the early years and less in the later years of an asset's service life. The advantage of these two accelerated methods over the straight-line method is greater the higher the tax rate and the real interest rate and the longer the service life for tax purposes. However, the higher the inflation rate (and the nominal interest rate), the smaller is the tax gain, that is, the higher the inflation rate, the more disadvantageous is historical cost depreciation. All three depreciation methods are discussed and compared in [19, John Shoven and Jeremy Bulow, 1975].

Several changes in the IRS rules have resulted in greater tax gains from depreciation during recent decades. First, the average service life for tax purposes was gradually shortened from 100 percent of the service life in the Treasury Department's 1942 edition of Bulletin F to an average of approximately 64 percent for manufacturing equipment and 75 percent for structures by 1952. Further liberalization occurred in 1954, when business firms were first permitted to switch from the straight-line method to the other depreciation methods. By 1960, approximately 75 percent of new investments used these two methods and by 1975, these methods were used on 90 percent of new investments (see Allan Young [24, 1968] and Shoven and Bulow [20, 1976]). Second, the class-life, asset-depreciation range system was adopted in 1971. This system allows the firm to group assets into vintage accounts and provides a range (plus or minus 20 percent of the guideline life) from which the life may be selected. The effect of such a policy was to reduce the service life for equipment from an average of thirteen years in the 1960s to eleven years [25, Young, 1975]. The service lives for structures and rental housing were relatively unaffected. We assume that the former was thirty-seven years and the latter was thirty-two years during both 1964–65 and 1976–77.[h] One change in depreciation policy that reduced tax gains on depreciation was the decision in 1969 to allow only 150 percent declining balance depreciation on nonresidential structures rather than the previous 200 percent declining balance depreciation.

The choice of true economic depreciation rates is an extremely difficult matter. Table 4–1 contains estimates of geometric decay depreciation rates employed by various researchers. As can be seen there are significant differences, on a percentage basis, most notably for structures. We assume that economic lives are eighty years for owner-occupied housing, sixty-five years for rental housing, fifty

---

[h]A Treasury study completed in 1974 reports these lives as the average lives claimed by taxpayers [22, U.S. Department of the Treasury, 1978, p. 84]. If service lines were taken to be 85 percent of the most recent guideline [3, Commercial Clearing Housing, 1977] then they would be thirty-eight and thirty-four years, respectively, for structures and apartments.

Table 4-1. Geometric-Decay Depreciation Rates (d)

	Christensen and Jorgenson[a]	Feldstein and Summers[b]	FMP	Hulten and Wykoff[c]	Hendershott and Hu[d]
Owner-occupied housing	0.039	—	0.027	—	0.017[d]
Rental housing	0.039	—	0.027	—	0.022[d]
Equipment	0.138	0.13	0.160	—	0.13[e]
Structures	0.056	0.03	0.060	0.030	0.03[d]

[a] DDB depreciation rates (approximately geometric-decay weights).

[b] Assumes geometric decay over lives of ten and thirty years, respectively, and then scrapping at zero value.

[c] Estimates are presented for fifteen classifications of structures. The rates for the major categories were 0.0409 (factories), 0.0297 (office buildings), 0.0273 (retail trade buildings) and 0.0295 (warehouses).

[d] Assumes straight-line depreciation over lives of eighty, sixty-five and fifty years, respectively, converted to equivalent geometric rates over these lives by employing a 4 percent real discount rate.

[e] Assumes geometric decay over a sixteen-year life and then scrapping at zero value.

years for structures, and sixteen years for equipment and that the assets are held for these lives. The lives for the housing components and equipment follow Young [25, 1975]. That for structures is longer than the 42.5 years (85 percent of Bulletin F) suggested by Young. It is further assumed that economic depreciation for equipment occurs at a geometric decay rate over its life, while that for other investment goods follows a straight-line pattern.[i] Exponential decay rates that provide a real present value for depreciation which is equivalent to that provided by straight-line depreciation over the assumed lives of the assets are reported in the far right column of Table 4—1 for investment goods other than equipment. At the end of the assumed lives, the liquidation value is assumed to be zero ($\beta = 1$ and thus $\gamma_a = 1$). As can be seen, these rates for housing are lower than those employed by Christensen and Jorgenson [2, 1977, p. 7] and the FMP [1, 1977]. For structures and equipment, the rates are less than those utilized in these studies, but are equal to those employed by Feldstein and Summers [6, 1978, p. 61] and Charles Hulten and Frank Wykoff [13, 1977, Table 2.1, p. 11].

The estimated expected reductions in (addition to) net costs of capital owing to differences between tax and economic depreciation for 1964—65 and 1976—77 are listed in the first two columns of Table 4—2. As can be seen, the accelerated depreciation method and the shorter tax lives relative to true economic lives reduced the costs of capital by 0.5 to nearly a full percentage point in the 1960s. By the middle 1970s, however, the excess of expected tax depreciation over economic depreciation raised the costs of capital for noncorporate nonresidential investments by over half a percentage point and for corporate investments by three-quarters to one percentage point. This switch is, of course, due to the increase in expected inflation and the use of historical-cost depreciation. The expected inflation rate is calculated as a geometric average of the inflation rates during the current and 19 previous quarters. The rate of change in the NIA implicit price deflator for gross domestic nonfarm business and household products is employed as the basic inflation rate. The resultant expected inflation rates for 1964—65 and 1976—77 are 0.012 and 0.065, respectively.

The remaining columns of Table 4—2 contain the change (decline) in the costs of capital due to changing tax depreciation between the

[i]There is considerable controversy on this point. Christensen and Jorgenson [2, 1977 and earlier work] assume that depreciation follows the double-declining balance pattern (approximately a geometric decay), while others, Paul Taubman and Robert Rasche [21, 1969], for example, contend that even a straight line pattern overstates depreciation in the early years of structures.

Table 4–2. The Effect of Differences between Tax and Economic Depreciation on the Net User Cost of Capital *(in percentage points)*[a]

					Source of Change		
	1964–65	*1976–77*	*Change*	*Financing Rate*	*Inflation Rate*	*Income Tax Rate*	*Service Life and Depreciation Method*
Noncorporate rental housing	0.66	−0.16	−0.82	0.61	−1.34	−0.09	—
Noncorporate equipment	0.45	−0.65	−1.10	0.49	−1.87	−0.17	0.45
Noncorporate structures	0.45	−0.53	−0.98	0.29	−0.90	−0.13	−0.24
Corporate equipment	0.95	−0.89	−1.84	0.53	−3.19	−0.02	0.84
Corporate structures	0.97	−0.77	−1.74	0.19	−1.44	−0.02	−0.47

[a]DDB method assumed except for corporate and noncorporate structures where a switch from DDB to 150 percent DB occurred in 1969.

middle 1960s and 1970s and measures of the importance of the various factors contributing to the change. In this table, the impact of the increase in inflation is measured by the difference between the effect of discrepancies between tax and economic depreciation at the middle 1970s rate of inflation and that evaluated at the middle 1960s rate, with all other variables taking their middle 1970s values. The impacts of changes in tax rates and depreciation law are likewise measured, while the impacts of changes in the financing rates are calculated as the residual. These data confirm that the loss is largely attributable to the increase in inflation and the use of historical-cost depreciation. For structures this loss is reinforced by the switch from double-declining balance to 150 percent declining balance; for equipment, the adoption of the class-life, asset-depreciation range system partially offset the loss.

Financing Rates

The assumed values of debt rates (i), tax rates (τ_y), after-tax debt rates, after-tax equity rates (e_a), loan-to-value ratios (α), and after-tax total financing rates (r_a) for different types of investment are listed in Table 4–3. The debt financing rates employed are the yields on conventional home mortgages (Federal Home Loan Bank Board) for owner-occupied housing, on multifamily and commercial mortgages (Life Insurance Association of America, later the American Life Insurance Association, now the American Council of Life Insurance) for noncorporate rental housing and equipment and structures, and on A-rated utility and industrial bonds (Salomon Brothers and Hutzler) for corporate equipment and structures.

The weights for debt for owner-occupied and rental housing, respectively, could be assumed to be the average loan-to-value ratios for new conventional single and multifamily homes. These weights are about 0.75 (from the FHLBB and LIAA *et seq.* data). However, the ratio of debt to the value of the housing unit tends to decline over time, especially during inflationary periods. For example, the ratio of the stock of 1–4 family mortgage debt to nonfarm owner-occupied residential structures varied between 0.50 and 0.58 between 1963 and 1977.[j] The three-quarter weight would likely overstate the relevant expected debt/market-value ratio over the life of the unit. We have employed two-thirds as the α weight for both single-family and rental housing. No data comparable to the

---

[j]Data on mortgage debt are from the flow of funds accounts; housing stock data are from John Musgrave [16, 1976, p. 51] and later issues of the *Survey of Current Business.*

Table 4–3. Average Financing Rates

		1964–65	1976–77	Change
Owner-occupied housing	τ_y	0.330	0.381	
	i (home mortgage)	5.85	9.01	
	$(1 - \tau_y)i$	3.92	5.58	
	e_a	7.16	11.20	
	α	2/3	2/3	
	r_a	5.00	7.45	2.45
Noncorporate rental housing	τ_y	0.330	0.381	
	i (nonhome mortgage)	5.92	9.71	
	$(1 - \tau_y)i$	3.97	6.01	
	e_a	7.16	12.93	
	α	2/3	2/3	
	r_a	5.03	8.32	3.29
Noncorporate investments	τ_y	0.330	0.381	
	i (nonhome mortgage)	5.92	9.71	
	$(1 - \tau_y)i$	3.97	6.01	
	e_a	7.16	12.93	
	α	1/3	1/3	
	r_a	6.10	10.62	4.52
Corporate investments	τ_y	0.503	0.510	
	i (corporate bond)	4.57	8.69	
	$(1 - \tau_y)i$	2.27	4.26	
	e_a	8.74	15.66	
	α	1/3	1/3	
	r_a	6.58	11.86	5.28

published loan-to-value ratios are available for nonresidential investments. The ratio of the market value of debt of nonfinancial corporations to the replacement cost of their nonfinancial assets (including net non-interest bearing financial claims) has remained quite close to one-quarter during the last fifteen years [7, von Furstenberg, 1977, Table 1, column (5) ÷ column (3)]. Because the ratio of debt to the value of net assets likely declines with the age of firm as well as household assets, one-quarter weight is likely an understatement of the relevant debt-equity ratio. We employ one-third as the α weight (Feldstein and Summers [6, 1978] utilize the same weight) for both corporate and noncorporate nonresidential investments.

The higher debt yields and loan-to-value ratios for housing probably reflect in large measure the lesser marketability of mortgages versus bonds and the greater marketability of housing relatively to plant and equipment. That is, better secondary markets exist for bonds than for mortgages and for housing than for nonresidential capital.

Deducing equity yields is a more difficult task. In the absence of differences between tax and economic depreciation and of tax credits, property taxes, the expected real after-tax rate of return on corporate equity issued to finance an investment project would be

$$e_a - p = \frac{(1 - \tau_y)\,[REV - DEPR - iD] + pD}{E}, \tag{9}$$

where $DEPR$ is depreciation and equals dP_k, D is the debt issued to finance the project and equals αP_k, E is the equity issued and equals $(1-\alpha)P_k$, and the pD term reflects the expected real gains accruing to shareholders owing to the expected erosion in the real value of this debt. Writing REV as $(c_N + d)P_k$, substituting for $DEPR$, D and E, and solving for c_N, we obtain equation (6a) with $\mu = 0$, $\gamma_a / \delta_a = 1$ and $d^* = d$.

The problem is the practical one of estimating $e_a - p$ from available historical data. Under the assumptions that (1) equity investors expect future investments to generate earnings similar to past investments, (2) the inflation rate has been stable, and (3) equilibrium exists continually, the expected real after-tax return on equity to be employed in calculating the equilibrium costs of capital could be approximated by the earnings-price ratio, adjusted for the expected erosion in the market value of debt. That is,

$$e_a - p = \frac{EAT + pMD}{ME}, \tag{9a}$$

where EAT is true after-tax profits, MD is the market value of debt, and ME is the market value of equities. True after-tax profits are obtained by adding to reported after-tax profits (1) the inventory valuation adjustment, which eliminates inventory capital gains, and

(2) the capital consumption adjustment, which eliminates any fictitious profits owing to underdepreciation by converting tax depreciation allowances to replacement-cost depreciation. Dividing the ratio into two parts, approximating MD/ME by $\alpha/(1-\alpha)$, and solving for e_a, we have

$$e_a = (EAT/ME) + \frac{p}{1-\alpha} \ . \qquad (9b)$$

Changes in the expected inflation rate, such as from about a single percentage point in the middle 1960s to the 1976 value of 6.5 percentage points, could cause problems with this approximation. Observed 1976 true after-tax profits might deviate from expected after-tax profits on new investments for two reasons. First, the higher interest rates associated with the greater expected inflation would not yet be fully built into existing debt payments. To illustrate, the 1976 ratio of net interest paid by nonfinancial corporations to the market value of debt was 0.067, two full percentage points below the 0.087 yield on new bond issues.[k] At a debt level of $481 billion, this results in an understatement of "equilibrium" after-tax interest payments of $4.8 billion. To include the gains due to the erosion of the real value of debt in the $e_a - p$ expression while subtracting from earnings debt payments that do not fully reflect current high interest rates associated with the current p would obviously be inappropriate. Second, the long-run expected depreciation charges based on replacement-cost depreciation might not equal the Commerce Department's current capital consumption adjustment. The long-run understatement of depreciation on fixed assets due to historic-cost depreciation is the stock of fixed assets times the ratio of the product of the inflation and depreciation rates to the sum of the inflation, depreciation, and real growth (g) rates.[l] With a p of 0.065, d of 0.085 (an average of the 0.139 for equipment and 0.03 for structures), g of 0.025, and fixed assets of $991 billion, the long-

[k] Net interest paid was $32.4 billion [*Survey of Current Business*, July 1977, p. 25]; the market value of debt is from [7, von Furstenberg, 1977, Table 1, column 5, average of end of 1975 and end of 1976 values].

[l] The understatement of depreciation allowances in any period due to inflation and the use of historic-cost depreciation (INFCC), can be approximated by

$$INFCC = (P-P_{-1})dGINV_{-1} + (P-P_{-2})d(1-d)GINV_{-2} + (P-P_{-3})d(1-d)^2 GINV_{-3}$$

$+ \ldots$, where P is the price of capital goods and $GINV$ is real gross investment. Multiplying the lagged one value of $INFCC$ by $1-d$ and subtracting from $INFCC$

yields $INFCC - (1-d)INFCC_{-1} = (P-P_{-1})dGINV_{-1} + (P-P_{-1})d \sum\limits_{i=1}^{\infty} (1-d)^i$

$GINV_{-i-1} = d\ FIX_{-1} \ \dfrac{\Delta P}{P_{-1}}$, where FIX is the replacement cost value of the

run understatement was $31.4 billion.[m] In contrast, the inflation component of the Commerce Department's depreciation adjustment was $35.3 billion, or $3.9 billion greater.[n] Given the small net magnitude of these factors, no adjustment has been made to true earnings.

A second possible problem with the approximation (9b) is the assumption that equilibrium continually exists such that $REV = P_k(c_N + d)$. It is generally accepted that expected returns on corporate investment were extraordinarily high in the middle 1960s and low in the 1970s ([7, von Furstenberg, 1977] and [15, Burton Malkiel, 1978]). Thus existing earnings-market value ratios in the middle 1960s probably understated the expected rate of return, and the reverse was true in the middle 1970s. An attempt to correct for this bias consists of multiplying the observed earning-price ratios during these periods by the average value of Tobin's "q" as computed by von Furstenberg [7, 1977, Table 1, column 9]. The average values of q are 1.066 for 1964–65 and 0.68 for 1976. We denote the product of q and EAT/ME by $(EAT/ME)'$.

The expected after-tax earnings-market value ratio (EAT/ME) is defined as a geometric average of the observed ratio during the current and previous nineteen quarters. True earnings were defined to include the IVA and CCA adjustments, and the market value of stocks is obtained by dividing dividends on common stock by Standard and Poor's dividend/market-value ratio for common stock. The average value for 1964–65 is 0.0651. For 1976–77 the average is 0.0873. Multiplying by q, the adjusted values are 0.0694 for 1964–65 and 0.0594 for 1976–77. Adding the inflation terms gives e_a's of 0.0874 and 0.1566 for the two periods.[o]

---

fixed capital stock. In the long run, when p equals the actual inflation rate, $INFCC = (1+p+g)INFCC_{-1}$ (g being the real growth rate of capital) and $FIX = (1+p+g)FIX_{-1}$, $INFCC = dpFIX/(d+g+p)$.

[m] The market value of fixed assets is the 1976 year-end value of the current dollar net stock of fixed nonresidential business capital of nonfinancial corporations [*Survey of Current Business*, August 1977, p. 57].

[n] This is obtained by subtracting the adjustment under current-cost depreciation from that with historic-cost depreciation, assuming straight-line depreciation with either Bulletin F or 0.75F lives (*Survey of Current Business*, August 1977, p. 58]. The explanation for the overshooting of the long-run adjustment is the severe actual inflation in capital goods prices that occurred in the 1974–75 period. During 1974, prices of structures rose by 22 percent; during the mid-1974–mid-1975 period prices of equipment increased by over 15 percent.

[o] As a check on these estimates we have compared them with those obtained independently by Burton Malkiel [15, 1978] who applied a variant of the Gordon dividend growth rate model where the growth rate was estimated from the Value Line Investment Survey. Malkiel obtains after-tax nominal rates of 0.083 in 1964–65 and of 0.144 in 1976–77.

To calculate e_a's for noncorporate investments, we assume that the risk-adjusted after-tax expected returns to individuals on equity in different forms are equal. Taking into account the differential treatment of dividends and capital gains, the after-tax return to shareholders on corporate equity, e^s, is

$$e^s = [\theta(1-\tau_h) + (1-\theta)(1-\tau_g)] \, (EAT/ME)' + (1-\tau_g) \, \frac{p}{1-\alpha} , \qquad (10)$$

where θ is the proportion of after-tax earnings that are paid out as dividends, τ_h is the household income tax rate, and τ_g is the "equivalent concurrent" tax rate on capital gains. The underlying data suggest that θ was roughly 0.5 in 1964–65, and 0.7 in 1976–77. We follow Feldstein and Summers [6, 1978, p. 73] by setting τ_g equal to 0.1, and τ_h was discussed earlier. The calculated values for e^s in 1964–65 and 1976–77, respectively, are 0.0707 and 0.1293. The nearly 6 percentage point increase in e^s and the much smaller rise in after-tax yields on bonds implies a significant jump in the risk premium required to induce investors to hold equities. The after-tax risk premium is calculated as $\rho = e^s - (1 - \tau_h)i$, where i is the corporate bond rate. Using the values of the variables specified above, ρ was 0.041 in 1964–65 and 0.075 in 1976–77, a rise of 3.4 percentage points. A rationale for the increase in ρ is the increased uncertainty regarding regulatory costs, energy prices, and economic activity generally in the 1970s [15, Malkiel, 1978].[p]

The next task is to determine relative risk premiums on equity investments in different forms. In general, it is not even clear which investments are the riskiest, much less how much riskier they are. We have simply assumed, with one exception, that all equity investments are equally risky. The exception is owner-occupied housing in the 1970s. To the extent that the increased risk premium on equities vis-à-vis bonds between the middle 1960s and 1970s is attributable to uncertainties regarding environmental and safety regulations of business activity, the increase in the premium is not applicable to owner-occupied housing.[q] We shall treat the calculated values of e^s as the after-tax equity yields for all noncorporate investments in

[p]Another possible explanation is that the willingness of investors to take on a given level of risk declined over this period. An argument against an increase in *p* is the greater uncertainty regarding general inflation which should make equity investments less risky than debt investments [8, Myron Gordon and Paul Halpern, 1976].

[q]Insofar as legislators are expected to continue to protect homeowners from abrupt changes in energy prices, this source of the increase in the risk premium is also not applicable to owner-occupied housing.

1964−65 and for noncorporate investments other than owner-occupied housing in 1976−77. For the latter we will subtract one-half of the 0.034 increase in ρ between the periods from the calculated value of e^s in 1976−77. The resultant yields are listed in Table 4−3.

Comparison of the increases in the after-tax debt, equity, and total financing rates in Table 4−3 with each other and with the 5.29 percentage point increase in the calculated expected inflation rate is interesting. The after-tax business borrowing rates rose by about 2 percentage points, and the after-tax home mortgage rate increased by only 1.69 percentage points. The smaller rise in the latter is due to governmental credit market intervention [11, Patric Hendershott, 1977, Chapter 16]. While the after-tax debt rates have increased by far less than the increase in the expected inflation rate, the after-tax equity rates, except that on owner-occupied housing, have risen by more owning to the 3.44 percentage point increase in the after-tax risk premium associated with equity investments. The increase is about 7 percentage points for corporate investments and 6 percentage points for other business investments, the difference being attributable to the taxation of corporate income at both the firm and personal levels. The total financing rates are averages of the debt and equity rates and thus are higher for the nonhousing investments because these are most heavily equity financed and equity financing is more expensive than debt financing, especially in the middle 1970s. The increase in the after-tax financing rate is least for owner-occupied housing, owing to the relatively smaller increases in the home mortgage and owner-occupied equity rates, and greatest for corporate investments, due to the large increase in that equity yield. One particularly interesting result of our calculations is the similarity of the real after-tax corporate financing rates in 1964−65 and 1976−77, in spite of the fact that the real after-tax debt rate fell sharply from 1.1 percentage points to −2.2 percentage points.

III. THE ESTIMATED RESULTS

Our best estimates of net costs of capital and their changes between the two periods are presented in Table 4−4. A number of relationships stand out. First are the differences in the changes in costs of capital between the periods. There was a 1.5 to 2.5 percentage point decline in c_N for housing investments, a slight rise in the c_N's for nonresidential investments of unincorporated businesses, and 1 to 2 percentage point increases in c_N for corporate investments. The decline in c_N for residential investments follows largely from the high

Table 4-4.   Average Net Costs of Capital

	1964-65	*1976-77*	*Change*
Owner-occupied housing	5.08	2.59	-2.49
Noncorporate rental housing	6.47	4.94	-1.53
Noncorporate structures	8.32	8.84	0.52
Noncorporate equipment	7.98	8.01	0.03
Corporate structures	11.37	13.29	1.92
Corporate equipment	10.84	11.93	1.09

loan-to-value ratios for these investments and the decline in real debt rates; the rise in c_N for corporate investments is due to the extraordinary increase in the equity yield and the high corporate tax rate. Second are the consistent differentials between corporate and noncorporate costs of nonresidential capital, with the cost of capital for a given type of investment being 3 percentage points lower for unincorporated businesses than corporations in the 1960s and 4 to 4.5 percentage points lower in the 1970s. Third is the percentage point excess of the cost of capital for structures (excluding housing) over that for equipment.

Differences in costs of capital can reflect differences in the riskiness and marketability of investments, as well as biases in government tax, depreciation, and financial policies. The riskiness and marketability of the investments are reflected in the interest rates and loan-to-value ratios employed in calculating the financing rates. In an attempt to isolate the impact of governmental policies on the costs of capital, the costs have been recomputed with the same loan-to-value ratio ($\alpha = 0.5$) for all investments and a common debt rate (the corporate bond rate). The one exception is the use of the bond rate less one-half percentage point as the debt rate for owner-occupied housing in 1976-77. This is an attempt to incorporate the impact of the expanded mortgage-support policies of the federal government and its sponsored credit agencies since the middle 1960s. The equity yields are then recomputed for $\alpha = 0.5$ from equations (9b), after multiplying EAT/ME by q, and (10), following the procedures described in the previous section. These adjusted yields are 0.1890 (corporate investments) and 0.1584 (other). The average risk-adjusted costs of capital, so calculated, are listed in Table 4-5.

In the middle of the 1970s a number of substantial differentials remain. First is the roughly 3 percentage point differential in favor of investment in owner-occupied housing versus rental housing and other investments by unincorporated businesses. This reflects a bias

Table 4—5. Average Risk-Adjusted Net Costs of Capital
(in percentage points)

	1964—65	*1976—77*	*Change*
Owner-occupied housing	5.29	5.26	−0.03
Noncorporate rental housing	6.93	7.95	1.02
Noncorporate structures	7.39	8.83	1.46
Noncorporate equipment	7.10	8.01	0.91
Corporate structures	9.97	12.79	2.82
Corporate equipment	9.54	11.51	1.97

in favor of home ownership owing to (1) the failure to tax imputed rental income on owner-occupied housing, and (2) federal support of the home mortgage market. Second is the 3.5 to 4 percentage point differential in favor of noncorporate versus corporate investment. It reflects the greater taxation of corporate income (the "double taxation" of dividends), and the impact of this increased in the 1970s owing to the increase in the corporate payout ratio (θ). Third is a percentage point differential in favor of equipment introduced by application of the investment tax credit to equipment but not structures.

The exact magnitudes of the impacts of the changes in the various variables on the changes in the risk-adjusted net costs of capital between the middle 1960s and the 1970s are presented in Table 4—6. The data in this table are computed in a manner similar to those in Table 4—2. That is, effects of changes in all variables except the real financing rate are calculated with all other variables set at their middle 1970s values, and the unaccounted-for change in the cost of capital is attributed to changes in the real financing rate. The data in Table 4—6 are best interpreted in terms of equations (6a) and (6b). While an increase in p lowers the cost of capital directly, it raises the cost through the *TXD* component (the use of historic cost). Thus even though real after-tax borrowing rates generally fell, the combination of the increases in r_a and p raised costs of capital. The increase is smallest for owner-occupied housing because (1) there is no negative impact of increases in p through a *TXD* term and (2) the increase in the debt rate was relatively small for this form of investment. The effect is larger for equipment than structures because the use of historical-cost raises the cost of capital more for shorter-life investments. The impact is larger for corporate costs than for those of unincorporated businesses owing to the higher tax rate applied to income of the former. The increase in the tax credit lowered the

Table 4-6. Factors Affecting the Change in Net Risk-Adjusted Costs of Capital *(in percentage points)*

	$r_a - p$	μ	τ_y	Service Life and Depreciation Method	Total Effect
Owner-occupied housing	0.38	—	-0.41	—	-0.03
Noncorporate rental housing	1.10	—	-0.08	—	1.02
Noncorporate structures	1.28	—	-0.06	0.24	1.46
Noncorporate equipment	2.15	-0.89	0.10	-0.45	0.91
Corporate structures	2.18	—	0.18	0.46	2.82
Corporate equipment	3.81	-1.18	0.16	-0.82	1.97

costs of capital for equipment by about a percentage point. The increase in the personal income tax rate lowered the cost of capital for owner-occupied housing by nearly a half percentage point (largely via the mortgage interest deduction), but had a negligible impact on costs of capital of unincorporated businesses. The corporate tax rate rose by only a miniscule amount. Finally, the shortening of the average tax life for equipment from thirteen to eleven years lowered corporate costs of capital by more than three-quarters of a percentage point, while the switch from double-declining balance depreciation to 150 percent declining balance for structures raised those costs of capital by nearly half a percentage point.

Feldstein and Summers

Feldstein and Summers [6, 1978, pp. 64–77] recently carried out an analysis that is similar in many respects to ours. They begin with the case in which marginal investments are financed by debt only. Their maximum potential interest rate is defined as the rate that the firm can afford to pay on the loan used to finance the project. Using our symbols, their equation (6) can be written as

$$L_t - L_{t-1} = iL_{t-1} - (1+p-d)^{t-1} REV + \tau_y [(1+p-d)^{t-1} REV - iL_{t-1} -$$

$$dx_t P_k] ,$$

where the initial loan value L_0 equals $(1-\mu) P_k$ and the final loan value is zero. After rearranging terms, it can be seen that net after-tax revenues are just enough to cover the interest payments and repay the loan. For $t = 1$,

$$L_1 = [1 + (1 - \tau_y)i] L_0 - (1 - \tau_y)(1+p-d)^0 REV - \tau_y dx_1 P_k , \qquad (12)$$

and substituting recursively through period N,

$$L_N = [1 + (1 - \tau_y)i]^N L_0 - (1 - \tau_y) [1 + (1 - \tau_y)i]^N REV \, \Sigma \, \frac{(1+p-d)^{t-1}}{[1+(1-\tau_y)i]^t}$$

$$- \tau_y [1 + (1 - \tau_y)i]^N \Sigma \, \frac{dx_t P_k}{[1+(1-\tau_y)i]^t} . \qquad (12a)$$

Setting L_0 equal to $(1-\mu)P_k$ and L_N to 0 (the loan is completely repaid), utilizing relation (2) (but with $(1-\tau_y)i$ replacing r), and letting $\alpha = 1.0$, we can obtain

$$\frac{REV}{P_k} = \frac{1}{\delta'_a}(1-\mu)(i + \frac{d-p}{1-\tau_y}) - \frac{\tau_y}{1-\tau_y}d^*, \tag{13}$$

This expression is the same as our equation (6) with $\alpha = 1.0, \beta = 1.0$ ($\gamma_a = 1$), and $\tau_p = 0.0$. In the case of mixed debt-equity financing, Feldstein and Summers replace i with $\alpha i + (1-\alpha)e_a/(1-\tau_y)$. The resultant expression for REV/P_k is then the same as ours with $\beta = 1.0$ and $\tau_p = 0.0$.

Rather than computing e_a from earnings data and calculating $REV/P_k - d$, Feldstein and Summers begin with a value of $REV/P_k - d$ equal to 0.12 that they calculated in earlier work [5, 1977]. Taking this value for c_N, they then determine i and e_a simultaneously by using equation (13), after substituting $\alpha i + (1-\alpha)e_a/(1-\tau_y)$ for i, and a combination of equations (9b), (10), and the portfolio balance relation $e^s = (1-\tau_h)i + \rho$, assuming different values (0.04, 0.05, and 0.06) of the risk premium ρ.

While Feldstein and Summers employed a value of $REV/P_k - d = 0.12$ in their more recent piece [6, 1978], they calculated annual values in their earlier work [5, 1977]. These "cyclically adjusted" or full employment values, which were 0.136 for 1964–65 and 0.103 for 1976, were calculated as average ex post rates of return. Our rates of return are estimates of expected marginal returns. Giving the cost of capital for equipment a weight of two-thirds and that for structures a weight of one-third to approximate the Feldstein and Summer "sandwich" project, our estimates of $REV/P_k - d$ for corporate capital are 0.110 for 1964–65 and 0.124 for 1976–77.

Comparison with the Measures of c_N Used in the FMP Model

The net costs of capital reported in Table 4–7 are quite different from those employed in the Federal Reserve-MIT-Penn model [1, 1977]. The FMP costs are listed in Table 4–7, as are our estimates less theirs (in parentheses). The differences are over 3 percentage points in four of eight cases, including one of 6.5 percentage points. Given the large differences, we will concentrate on major sources of discrepancy rather than detailing each and every difference.

Table 4−7. Net Costs of Capital in FMP Model and the Difference *(in parentheses)* between Our Costs and Theirs *(in percentage points)*[a]

	1964−65	*1976−77*
Owner-occupied housing (1−4 family)	2.72 (2.36)	2.12 (0.47)
Rental housing (5 or more families)	2.79 (3.68)	4.91 (0.03)
Corporate structures	14.76 (−3.39)	19.80 (−6.51)
Corporate equipment	6.49 (4.35)	11.93 (0.00)

[a]Net user costs are calculated as the difference between gross user costs and depreciation rates. In terms of the FMP symbols and depreciation rates, the net costs are RCH1-2.7 for owner-occupied housing, RCH5-2.7 for rental housing, 100(RTPD/PDD)-16 for equipment and 100(RTPS/PPS)-6 for structures. RCH1, RCH5, RTPD, and RTPS are defined, respectively, in equations II.7, II.8, III.3 and IV.3 in [1, 1977].

For owner-occupied housing the differences are due to two factors. First, the constant term relating to d is 3 percentage points lower in the FMP model than in ours.[r] Second, the FMP model employs the rent component of the consumer price index in determining expected inflation, rather than the NIA private deflator. As a result, the FMP model expected inflation rate is less than ours by over two percentage points in the middle 1970s, largely offsetting the 3 percentage point difference in the constant. These same two factors affect the differences in the costs of capital for rental housing in a roughly similar manner, although the FMP constant term relating to d is now 4 percentage points lower than ours.[s] Moreover, our greater increase in expected inflation has a larger impact because p is multiplied by $1/(1-\tau_y)$ in equation (6) and we employ a higher estimate of τ_y than does the FMP (0.38 versus 0.25). This accounts for the sharp drop in the differences between our estimate and theirs between the middle 1960s and the middle 1970s.

For corporate investment the differences between the FMP method of computing the c_N's and our method are so great as to necessi-

[r]The constant in their equation (II.7) is −0.26 percent rather than 2.7 percent (the value of d).

[s]The constant in their equation (II.8) is −1.24 percent rather than a fraction of 2.7 percent (the fraction would allow for tax gains on accelerated depreciation). It should be noted that their equation refers to all rental housing, corporate as well as noncorporate. Christensen and Jorgenson [2, 1977, Table 3, p. 13] suggest that less than a fifth of rental housing is corporate owned.

tate a presentation of their method, using their equation numbers for identification:

FMP Equipment:

$$c_N = \left\{ [(1 - 0.2\tau_y)\,(r-p) + d]\,(1-\mu) - d \right\} \frac{1}{1-\tau_y} - TXD', \quad \text{(III.3)}$$

$$r - p = 2.0 \left(\frac{\text{dividend}}{\text{price}} \right) + \text{risk premium} - 2.0, \quad \text{(III.5)}$$

FMP Structures:

$$c_N = [(1 - 0.2\tau_y)\,(r-p)]\, \frac{1}{1-\tau_y} - TXD', \quad \text{(IV.3)}$$

$$r - p = 2.0 \left(\frac{\text{dividend}}{\text{price}} \right) + 5.0. \quad \text{(IV.5)}$$

The major difference between the FMP treatment and ours is the definition of the total real financing rate as an equity rate (the dividend price ratio) and the "constants" in their expressions for $r-p$. That is, the differences in costs of capital in parentheses in Table 4–7 result from the $(1-0.2\tau_y)\,(r-p)$ measures for the FMP greatly exceeding our estimates of $r_a - p$ for structures in both periods, but more so in the middle 1970s, and being less than our estimates in the 1960s, before their risk premium jumped.

IV. THE COSTS OF MISALLOCATION OF CAPITAL

The substantial differences in net risk-adjusted costs of capital, ranging from less than 4 percentage points for owner-occupied housing to nearly 11.5 percentage points for corporate structures, and thus in net marginal products, suggests that substantial productivity gains could be achieved by allocating the capital stock more efficiently, that is, toward investments with higher net marginal products. On the other hand, it may be that these differences, which are due to deliberate government policies, are necessary in order to correct for differences in private and social returns, for example, the alleged positive externalities of homeownership. In any event, it is probably of interest to compute the productivity losses so that they might be weighted intelligently, against the alleged benefits.

The general procedure used to evaluate the productivity loss due to government policies is illustrated in terms of Figure 4–1 for the case where there are two capital goods. The two downward sloping curves represent the marginal products and therefore the gross rates of return on the first and the second capital goods, denoted by c_G^1 and c_G^2, respectively. However, when the ordinates start out at d_1 and d_2, respectively, the vertical axes also represent c_N^1 and c_N^2, both measured from a common origin of 0. In the absence of government policy distortions, the two risk-adjusted net rates of return must be equal to the same net cost of capital. Letting the initial equilibrium cost of capital be c_N^*, the equilibrium point for each market is E, and the corresponding equilibrium levels of capital are K_1^* and K_2^*, respectively. Suppose now that a government policy changes the net costs of capital to c_N^1 and c_N^2, respectively, so that the new equilibrium points are at F and the new equilibrium levels of capital are K_1 and K_2. Because the gross rate of return is but the gross cost of capital, c_G, which in equilibrium is equal to the gross marginal physical product of capital (or the value of the marginal product divided by P_k), the increase in the value of output produced by the additional investment in the first capital good is approximately equal to the sum of the areas A_1 and A_2 and the decrease in the value of output produced by the second is approximately equal to $B_1 + B_2$. Thus the total productivity loss, L, equals

$$L = (B_1 + B_2) - (A_1 + A_2).$$

Assuming no change in the level of aggregate investment so that the total value of capital stock remains constant, then

$$B_1 = (A_1 + A_2 + A_3).$$

Substituting, we obtain

$$L = A_3 + B_2. \tag{14}$$

Now suppose the elasticity of demand for gross capital stock is unitary with respect to the gross cost of capital, c_G^i, in all capital goods i considered in this chapter. This would follow if the technology is adequately described by a Cobb-Douglas production function in each sector. The problem of finding the efficient distribution of

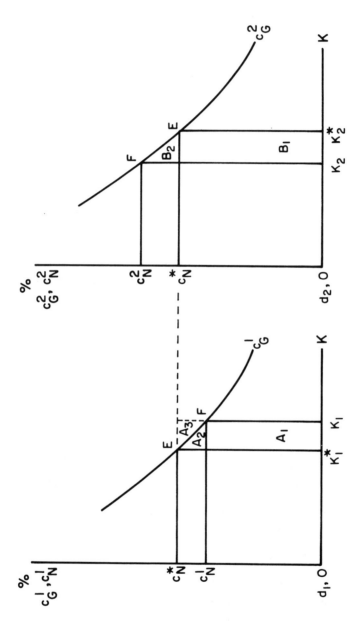

Figure 4–1. The Demand for Capital and the Productivity Loss Due to Government Policies

the existing capital stock then involves finding a distribution such that all c_N^i are equalized. Calling this equilibrium level c_N^*, with unitary elasticities the following equation holds in each capital good i:

$$\frac{c_N^* + d_i}{c_N^i + d_i} = \frac{K_i}{K_i^*} . \tag{15}$$

Hence, considering the total capital stock, $\overline{K}$, as given, the efficient values, K_i^* and c_N^*, can be found from the following system of equations, where the first equation is repeated for each i:

$$K_i^* = \frac{K_i (c_N^i + d)}{c_N^* + d} , \tag{16a-f}$$

$$\sum_i K_i^* = \overline{K} . \tag{17}$$

Further, the welfare loss can be approximated by the following triangle rule:[t]

$$L = \sum \tfrac{1}{2} (\Delta c_G^i \ \Delta K_i)$$

$$= \sum \tfrac{1}{2} (c_N^* - c_N^i) (K_i - K_i^*) .$$

In our computations, c_N^i and d_i are obtained from the preceding section with the costs of capital taken to be their risk-adjusted rates. The K_i are as estimated by John Musgrave [16, 1976] for nonfinancial corporate, noncorporate and residential capital. The average values of these stocks for 1964–65 and 1976–77 are presented in Table 4–8.

We first divide the economy into three sectors: owner-occupied housing, unincorporated business, and corporate business. For each of the two business sectors an undistorted equilibrium cost of capi-

---

[t]A more precise measure of the area $A_3 + B_2$ is the sum of the differences between the integral of K_i from c_G^i to c_G^* and $(c_G^* - c_G^i) K_1^*$ for all i, or

$$L = \sum | (K_i c_G^i) \ \log \ (c_G^i / c_G^*) - (c_G^i \ c_G^*) K_i | .$$

This formula is employed to make the calculations.

Table 4–8. **Actual Stocks of Capital** *(billions of 1972 dollars)*

	1964–65[a]	1976–77[b]
Owner-occupied housing	496.3	699.4
Rental housing	172.0	222.2
Noncorporate equipment	58.6	81.8
Noncorporate structures	128.7	186.1
Corporate equipment	198.7	347.2
Corporate structures	230.6	334.8
	1284.9	1871.5

[a] Average of the stocks at the end of 1964 and at the end of 1965 [16, Musgrave, 1976, pp. 49 and 52].

[b] Average of the stocks at the end of 1975 and at the end of 1976 [*Survey of Current Business*, August 1977, p. 57].

tal (c_N^*), the shift in capital necessary to achieve an efficient distribution of capital ($K^* - K$), and the productivity losses associated with the observed inefficient distribution of capital are calculated. These results are shown in rows (1) and (2) in Table 4–9 for both 1964–65 and 1976–77. The numbers in the $K^* - K$ column refer to the shift from the first listed form of capital (for example, rental housing) into the second listed (for example, other capital). The next step is then to compute similar data for the total business sector and for owner-occupied housing and the aggregate business sector. These results are reported in rows (3) and (4). Finally, rows (1) through (4) are added to give the economy-wide productivity loss in row (5).

The data in rows (1) and (2) suggest that there were only minor misallocations within the noncorporate and corporate sectors. For example, the total productivity losses within these sectors in 1976–77 were only $0.11 (0.04 + 0.07) billion (in 1972 dollars), all of which were due to a total underinvestment in nonresidential structures of $21.1 billion (9.5 + 11.6). However, the substantial excess of the equilibrium cost of capital for corporations over that of unincorporated businesses—2.75 percentage points in 1964–65 and 4 percentage points in 1976–77—was the cause of large overinvestment in noncorporate capital and thus great productivity losses for the total business sector [see row (3)]. This overinvestment nearly doubled, from $46.1 billion in 1964–65 to $81.2 billion in 1976–77, and the productivity loss nearly tripled, from $0.62 billion to $1.74 billion. Even greater was the overinvestment in owner-occupied housing [row (4)], which rose from $112.4 billion in 1964–65 to $230.0 billion in 1976–77. On a percentage basis this overinvestment amounted to 23 percent of the owner-occupied housing stock

Table 4–9. Productivity Losses *(in billions of 1972 dollars),* **Equilibrium Net Costs of Capital** *(in percentage points)* **and Shifts in Capital Stocks** *(in billions of 1972 dollars)*[a]

	1964–65			1976–77		
	c_N^*	K^*-K	Losses	c_N^*	K^*-K	Losses
1. Rental housing versus other capital of unincorporated businesses	7.15	4.8	0.01	8.35	9.5	0.04
2. Corporate equipment versus structures	9.90	3.2	0.01	12.35	11.6	0.07
3. Unincorporated business versus corporate businesses	8.50	46.1	0.62	10.45	81.2	1.74
4. Owner-occupied housing versus total business	7.00	112.4	1.76	8.10	230.0	6.00
5. Total economy	7.00		2.40	8.10		7.85

[a]The number in the K^*-K column indicates the shift out of the first listed form of capital into the second listed.

in 1964—65 and 33 percent in 1976—77.[u] The resulting productivity loss was $6.00 billion in 1976—77, compared with $1.76 billion in 1964—65. Adding together the losses across the entire economy [row (5)], the total loss was $7.85 billion in 1976—77 and $2.40 billion in 1964—65.[v] The comparability of the equilibrium net costs of capital for investments within the unincorporated business sector and across the entire economy, 7.15 versus 7.00 in 1964—65 and 8.35 versus 8.10 in 1976—77, suggests that the overall productivity loss is almost totally due to overinvestment in owner-occupied housing and underinvestment in corporate capital.

In early 1978 dollars the total productivity loss for the second period is $11.5 billion. While $11.5 billion might seem small in a $2 trillion economy, $142 billion of additional net capital earning our average economy-wide net return of 8.10 percent in 1976—77 [row (5)] would be required to generate the $11.5 billion dollar loss. That is, efficient allocation of the existing capital stock would make as great a contribution to economic well-being as increasing the existing inefficiently allocated capital stock by $142 billion (in 1972 dollars), or 5 percent.

V. METHODS OF EQUALIZING NET COSTS OF CAPITAL

If one wished to equalize net costs of capital and thus recapture the productivity loss, then the most obvious step would be remove the present sources of differences. For example, imputed rental income on owner-occupied housing could be taxed (and depreciation could then be made deductible), the double taxation of corporate income could be eliminated, the investment tax credit for equipment could be removed, and all tax depreciation could be computed on a re-placement-cost, true economic life basis. However, political realities might prohibit some of these steps, particularly the taxation of imputed rental income on owner-occupied housing. The question, then, is how can the difference in net costs of capital be narrowed without taxing imputed rental income?

The general procedure is clear: if a housing subsidy cannot be removed, then offsetting subsidies to other investments must be given. Two such subsidies already exist—accelerated depreciation methods and the investment tax credit. The problem is that accelerated de-

---

[u]This result supports the views of Arnold Harberger [10, 1966] and David and Attiat Ott [18, 1975], among others.

[v]If the elasticity of substitution were assumed to be 0.5 instead of unity, then the total productivity loss due to misallocation of capital would be about halved.

preciation is currently more than offset by the use of historical-cost depreciation and the tax credit is available only for equipment. The impacts on costs of capital of switching to replacement-cost depreciation and extending the tax credit to structures are discussed below, but first the impact of eliminating the double taxation of corporate income is considered.

Single Taxation of Corporate Income

It has been proposed that dividends be taxed at only the personal income level and that all corporate earnings be treated as though they were paid out as dividends. The effective result is elimination of both the corporate income tax on equity returns and the retention of earnings. Thus the after-tax risk adjusted returns on equity in all business ventures would be the same. As a first approximation, we hold interest rates and after-tax returns on equity in nonincorporated businesses at their 1976—77 values. Thus the after-tax risk-adjusted return on corporate equity is assumed to decline from 0.1890 to 0.1584. Also, the τ_y in equations (5) and (6a) is now the personal tax rate, 0.38, not 0.51.^{W} These changes would reduce the risk-adjusted net costs of capital by 3.5 percentage points for corporate equipment and 4 percentage points for corporate structures.

Treatment of Depreciation

As indicated by the data in Table 4—2, the impact of differences between tax and economic depreciation changed markedly between the middle 1960s and middle 1970s. Current accelerated depreciation schedules are such that at the inflation and interest rates of the middle 1960s the corporate costs of capital would be nearly a percentage point below that which would exist under true economic depreciation for both equipment and structures. However, the enormous impact that the increase in inflation between the middle 1960s and 1970s has had on the difference between replacement and historical-cost depreciation has far outweighed the impact of accelerated depreciation schedules so that corporate costs of capital are currently one-half to nearly two percentage points higher than they would be with true economic depreciation.

The obvious solution is to switch to replacement-cost depreciation.^{X} The impact on the cost of capital of such a switch is equal to

---

^{W}This analysis assumes state and local taxes for corporations to be the same as for unincorporated businesses.

^{X}The Carter administration has proposed a decrease in the allowable acceleration methods without referring to the problem created by the use of historic-cost depreciation in an inflationary environment [22, U.S. Department of Treasury, 1978, pp. 81-99].

the negative of *TXD* given in equation (8a). At 1976−77 values, the costs of capital for corporate equipment would decline by 3.14 percentage points and that for corporate structures would fall by 1.36 percentage points. Declines in noncorporate costs of capital would be less—roughly 2 and 1 percentage points, respectively—owing to the lower tax rate.

Investment Tax Credits

An extension of the investment tax credit to structures other than owner-occupied housing is a means of reducing the bias in favor of shortlived investments, as well as that in favor of owner-occupied housing.[y] However, applying the same effective rate of the credit to equipment and structures would reduce the cost of capital for equipment by much more than that for structures. In each case a 10 percent credit is an effective 10 percent reduction in the purchase price of the asset, but this onetime gain is spread over a much longer period of years for structures than for equipment. Thus the per annum cost of capital is lowered less for structures.

The importance of the economic life of the asset to the benefit of the tax credit is best shown by contrasting equation (6a) with and without μ. This procedure reveals the impact of introducing a tax credit on the cost of capital to be

$$ -\frac{\mu}{\delta_a} \, (r_a - p + d)/(1 - \tau_y) \, . $$

Because δ_a is smaller the higher is d, this expression indicates that a tax credit cuts the cost of capital more the shorter is the life of the asset. With the risk-adjusted $r_a - p$ at its 1976−77 value of 0.0510 and $\tau_y = 0.51$, the present 8.5 percent credit lowers the cost of capital for corporate equipment ($\delta_a = 0.94$ and $d = 0.13$) by 3.3 percentage points, but would lower that for structures ($\delta_a = 0.96$ and $d = 0.03$) by only 1.5 percentage points. Thus about a 20 percent credit on structures would be needed to lower its cost of capital by as much as the 8.5 percent credit lowers that of equipment on average.

Impact of Proposed Changes on Costs of Capital

Table 4−10 contains estimates of how the costs of capital would be changed if the double taxation of corporate income were elimi-

[y]The Carter administration has proposed both an extension of the tax credit to factory structures and permitting credits to offset up to 90 percent of the taxpayer's tax liability rather than the current maximum of 50 percent [22, U.S. Department of Treasury, 1978, pp. 254-62].

Table 4-10. The Impact of Proposed Changes on Net Costs of Capital
(in percentage points)

	1976-77 Actual	*1976-77 with Proposed Changes*
Owner-occupied housing	5.26	5.26
Rental housing	7.95	5.19
Noncorporate structures	8.83	5.60
Noncorporate equipment	8.01	5.76
Corporate structures	12.79	5.60
Corporate equipment	11.51	5.76

nated, replacement-cost depreciation were allowed, and 20 and 10 percent tax credits were applied, respectively, to structures and equipment. All net costs of capital are computed on a risk-adjusted basis. As can be seen, the differences between corporate and noncorporate costs of capital disappears, the smaller difference in costs of capital for structures and equipment nearly disappears, and the bias in favor of owner-occupied housing is almost eliminated.[z] Recalculation of the productivity loss associated with the differences in the cost of capital in the right-hand column ot Table 4-10 gives a $0.5 billion loss, less than about one-twentieth of the present $11.5 billion loss.

Reducing the costs of capital through the above proposals would stimulate investment and security issues to finance it. This would result in higher debt and equity yields (i's and e's) for all investments [6, Feldstein and Summers, 1978]. The important point, though, is that the yields would tend to rise about equally and thus the final costs of capital would be much closer than they are under present tax and depreciation policies.

VI. SUMMARY

Jorgenson's basic cost of capital formula has been utilized to measure net costs of capital for six different categories of investment goods during the 1964-65 and 1976-77 periods. The six categories are owner-occupied housing, investment by unincorporated businesses in rental housing, equipment and structures, and investment by corporations in equipment and structures. Care is taken to account for differences in tax treatment, tax credits, and tax depreciation,

---

[z]A small bias in favor of rental housing relative to nonresidential structures remains because of the more rapid depreciation method (double declining balance) allowed the former.

to measure economic depreciation and financing rates accurately, and to include expected inflation appropriately. Measurement of equity yields is the most difficult task. We obtain a yield on corporate equity, after considering numerous adjustments to corporate earnings, and then invoke the assumption that after-tax, risk-adjusted yields on equity in different forms will be equal.

Our results indicate that the net (after depreciation) cost of capital is least for owner-occupied housing, owing to the exemption of implicit rents from taxation, and highest for corporate investments, owing to the double taxation of corporate income. Further, the net cost of capital for equipment is less than that for structures because the former is eligible for the investment tax credit. The costs of capital for housing declined between the middle 1960s and 1970s because debt yields rose by less than the increase in the inflation rate and housing is heavily debt financed. The cost of capital for corporate investments rose because these investments are heavily equity financed and equity rates, especially the rate for corporations that is subject to double taxation, rose sharply.

Both the productivity losses owing to the misallocation of capital in response to the differences in costs of capital and the efficient allocation of capital when these differences are eliminated are derived under the assumption of Cobb-Douglas technology. Our results confirm the view that there has been underinvestment in plant and equipment relative to housing and in corporate capital relative to noncorporate capital. The loss resulting from such misallocations increased from 0.32 percent of net national product in 1964–65 to 0.68 percent in 1976–77. Eliminating the misallocation would increase the return on existing capital by as much as $142 billion (in 1978 dollars) of new capital would generate in total.

While politicians are obviously reluctant to tax implicit rents on housing, this subsidy need not be removed to reduce substantially the bias in favor of housing. Rather, the housing subsidy could be offset by extending subsidies to other investments such as (1) continuing the use of accelerated depreciation methods and switching to replacement-cost depreciation and (2) extending a tax credit to structures. This, coupled with removal of the double taxation of corporate income, would roughly equalize net costs of capital.

REFERENCES

1. BOARD OF GOVERNORS OF THE FEDERAL RESERVE SYSTEM. *Quarterly Economic Model*, May 1977 (preliminary).
2. CHRISTENSEN, LAURITS R., and JORGENSON, DALE W. "The Measurement of U.S. Real Capital Input, 1972-75." Unpublished manuscript, Harvard University, 1977.
3. COMMERCIAL CLEARING HOUSE. *1977 U.S. Master Tax Guide.* Chicago: Commerce Clearing House, 1976.
4. FELDSTEIN, MARTIN S.; GREEN, JERRY; and SHESHINSKI, EYTAN. "Inflation and Taxes in a Growing Economy with Debt and Equity Financing," *Journal of Political Economy*, April 1978, *86*(2), pp. S50-S70.
5. FELDSTEIN, MARTIN S., and SUMMERS, LAWRENCE. "Is the Profit Rate Falling?" *Brookings Papers on Economic Activity*, 1977 (1), pp. 221-27.
6. ____. "Inflation, Tax Rules, and the Long-Term Interest Rate," *Brookings Papers on Economic Activity*, 1978 (1), pp. 61-99.
7. VON FURSTENBERG, GEORGE M. "Corporate Investments: Does Market Valuation Matter in the Aggrevate?" *Brookings Papers on Economic Activity*, 1977 (2), pp. 347-97.
8. GORDON, MYRON J. and HALPERN, PAUL J. "Bond Share Yield Spreads under Uncertain Inflation," *American Economic Review*, Sept. 1976, *66*(4), pp. 559-65.
9. HALL, ROBERT E., and JORGENSON, DALE W. "Tax Policy and Investment Behavior," *American Economic Review*, June 1967, *56*(3), pp. 391-414.
10. HARBERGER, ARNOLD C. "Efficiency Effects of Taxes on Income from Capital," in *Effects of Corporate Income Tax.* Edited by M. KRZYZANIAK. Detroit: Wayne State Univ. Press, 1966.
11. HENDERSHOTT, PATRIC H. *Understanding Capital Markets: Volume I: A Flow of Funds Financial Model.* Lexington, Mass.: D.C. Heath, 1977.
12. HENDERSHOTT, PATRIC H., and HU, SHENG-CHENG. "The Relative Impacts of Various Proposals to Stimulate Business Investment," in *The Government and Capital Formation.* Edited by G.M. VON FURSTENBERG. Cambridge: Ballinger Publishing Company, 1980.
13. HULTEN, CHARLES R., and WYKOFF, FRANK. "Economic Depreciation and the Taxation of Structures in U.S. Manufacturing Industries: An Empirical Analysis," Discussion Paper No. 77-02, Department of Economics, University of British Columbia, Feb. 1977.
14. JORGENSON, DALE W. "Anticipation and Investment," in *Brookings Quarterly Econometric Model of the United States.* Edited by J. DUESENBERRY, G. FROMM, L.R. KLEIN, and E. KUH. Chicago: Rand McNally, 1965, pp. 35-92.
15. MALKIEL, BURTON G. "The Capital Formation Problem in the United States," Research Memo No. 25, Financial Research Center, Princeton University, Aug. 1978.

16. MUSGRAVE, JOHN C. "Fixed Nonresidential Business and Residential Capital in the United States," *Survey of Current Business*, April 1976, *56*(4), pp. 46-52.

17. NORDHAUS, WILLIAM. "The Falling Share of Profits," *Brookings Papers on Economic Activity*, 1974 (1), pp. 169-268.

18. OTT, DAVID J. and ATTIAT F. "The Effect of Nonneutral Taxation on the Use of Capital by Sector," *Journal of Political Economy*, July/Aug. 1973, *81*(4), pp. 972-81.

19. SHOVEN, JOHN B., and BULOW, JEREMY J. "Inflation Accounting and Nonfinancial Corporate Profits: Physical Assets," *Brookings Papers on Economic Activity*, 1975 (3), pp. 557-98.

20. _____ . "Inflation Accounting and Non-Financial Corporate Profits: Financial Assets and Liabilities," *Brookings Papers on Economic Activity*, 1976 (1), pp. 15-66.

21. TAUBMAN, PAUL, and RASCHE, ROBERT. "Economic and Tax Depreciation of Office Buildings," *National Tax Journal*, Sept. 1969, *22*(3), pp. 334-46.

22. U.S. DEPARTMENT OF THE TREASURY. *The President's 1978 Tax Program.* Washington, D.C., Jan. 1978.

23. U.S. INTERNAL REVENUE SERVICE. *Statistics of Income: Individual Returns.* Washington, D.C., 1964, 1965, and 1974.

24. YOUNG, ALLAN H. "Alternative Estimates of Corporate Depreciation and Profit, Part I," *Survey of Current Business*, April 1968, *48*(4), pp. 17-28.

25. _____ . "New Estimates of Capital Consumption Allowances in the Benchwork Revision of GNP," *Survey of Current Business*, Oct. 1975, *55*(10), pp. 14-16.

※ *Chapter 5*

Contributions and Determinants of Research and Development Expenditures in the U.S. Manufacturing Industries

M. Ishaq Nadiri

A large body of research has been devoted to discovering the sources of productivity growth in the United States.

Aside from the contributions attributed to a growth in quantity and an improvement in quality of the factors of production, such as capital and labor, it is often argued that a major contributor to growth of output is technological change.[a] The rate of technical progress is determined by diverse factors, and the underlying process that characterizes technical change is complex. However, research and development (R&D) is considered to be a major determinant of technical progress. The bulk of studies surveyed by Edwin Mansfield [24, 1972] came to the conclusion that industrial research and development expenditures contributed significantly to growth of output and productivity resulting in positive and substantial private and social returns.

Since 1971 it has became increasingly apparent that productivity growth in the U.S. private sector has slowed down appreciably. Part of this slowdown is attributed to the substantial decline in the rate of growth of R&D expenditures. Consider the following statistics: from 1953 to 1961 R&D expenditures in real terms increased at an average of about 14 percent for government and 7.1 percent for non-government sponsors; from 1961 to 1967 these growth rates were decidedly lower—5.6 percent for government-funded and 7.4 percent for private R&D. But from 1967 to 1975 the growth rate of

[a]See for further discussion Edward F. Denison [3, 1974], Dale Jorgenson and Zvi Griliches [15, 1967], John Kendrick [17, 1973], Charles Kennedy and A.P. Thirlwall [19, 1972], and M. Ishaq Nadiri [27, 1970].

government and private R&D expenditures dropped to 3 percent and 1.8 percent, respectively.

Given these figures, and the received conventional wisdom of high rates of return to R&D efforts, two questions arise: (1) Have the contributions of R&D to growth of output and productivity remained as high in recent years as suggested in the literature? (2) What factors account for the sharp decline in R&D expenditure since 1967?

To answer these questions it is necessary to review briefly what has been reported in the literature and to provide evidence to validate or contradict, wherever possible, some of the conclusions about the role and determinants of R&D. Specifically, we shall attempt to focus on three issues: first, to provide a summary of the findings of studies on the contribution of R&D expenditures; second, to provide some new estimates for the contribution of R&D to growth of output in total manufacturing, total durables, and total nondurables industries; third, to assess the factors that determine the rate of growth of research and development.

In the first section, we shall briefly examine the findings of the studies reported in the literature since 1970 on the contribution of R&D to growth of output and productivity. A brief survey of the studies that attempts to explain the behavior of R&D expenditures will be presented in Section II. In the third section, we shall examine the results obtained from the econometric production function approach using a sample of pooled cross section-time series data for the period 1955–1975 for the three industry sectors mentioned. The fourth section will pertain to the specification of a demand function for the stock of R&D in order to find out whether growth of output, changes in relative prices, and past stocks of other inputs affect the level and growth of the R&D input. Particular attention will be given to an examination of the effect of publicly funded R&D on private R&D expenditures. The conclusions and some suggestions for policy and future research are stated in Section V.

I. CONTRIBUTION OF R&D TO GROWTH OF PRODUCTIVITY: RECENT EVIDENCE

An ubiquitous finding of all empirical studies summarized several years ago by Mansfield [24, 1972] was that R&D expenditures contribute substantially to the growth of output in a variety of industries. Subsequent studies have confirmed these findings but have gone beyond earlier studies in a number of ways. Their coverage is much broader, for example, one study includes a sample of about 1,000 U.S. industrial firms. More attention has been paid to interindustry technology flows, and distinctions have been drawn between the returns from privately financed and federally financed R&D. The overall findings are that the rate of productivity of a firm or industry increases with an increase in its rate of expenditures on R&D and that the marginal rate of return from investment in R&D is very high. Confirmation of these conclusions becomes more striking when we note that some of the studies analyze individual R&D projects, others firm and industry data.[b] We shall briefly describe some of the specific issues concerning the contributions of R&D to growth of output.

Direct Contributions

Several studies indicate positive but varying contributions of an increase in R&D expenditures to the rate of growth of output in different industries. Using seventeen two-digit industries, William Leonard [20, 1971] analyzed the relationship between growth of productivity and R&D intensity (defined by the ratio of company R&D to net sales or the number of company-financed R&D scientists and engineers per 1,000 employees). He found that productivity growth can be explained by research intensity, total man-hours, and skill level of the employees (measured by median number of school years completed). His correlation analysis indicated that causality runs from R&D spending to industrial growth and not the reverse.[c] Nestor Terleckyj [38, 1974], using a sample of thirty-three industries, correlated growth in total factor productivity for the period 1948–1966 with non-R&D variables, such as percent of sales to the private sector, degree of union membership, annual rate of cyclical change in output, the ratio of investment in plant and equipment to value added, and two types of R&D expenditure: privately financed and government financed. The results showed a strong direct effect of privately financed R&D on growth of factor productivity and no discernible effect by government-financed R&D. The explanation may be that government-financed R&D, unlike privately financed R&D, can be viewed as a distinct output of the performing industry rather than as an investment in its stock of knowledge. The contribution of firm-financed R&D to growth of productivity was calculated

[b] For a sample of these studies, see Nestor Terleckyj [37, 1959; 38, 1974], Zvi Griliches [9, 1964], Edwin Mansfield [23, 1965], Jora Minasian [26, 1969], Murray Brown and Alfred Conrad [2, 1967].

[c] This correlation is positive, strong, and on the average begins in the second year after R&D investment, continuing to rise steadily for at least nine years after the initial input years, reflecting the rising proportion of sales of new products developed through R&D. See William Leonard [20, 1971].

to be about 0.36 percent. Zvi Griliches [10, 1973], using Census data for 883 large R&D-performing companies, reported that the contribution of R&D to growth of productivity differed considerably among industries, as did the estimated output elasticities and derived rates of return for R&D. The main source of productivity differences was the differences in ratio of output to R&D capital stock among the industries. His results indicated that growth of productivity, besides depending on growth of R&D, was affected significantly by growth of plant and equipment of different industries.

Effects of R&D Embodied in Purchased Goods

Measured productivity in a given industry can increase through the purchase of R&D-intensive capital or intermediate goods from other industries. For example, R&D-intensive capital goods such as computers may result in a productivity increase in banking and insurance industries which do not undertake any significant R&D of their own. Research-intensive intermediate goods, such as fertilizers and agriculture and prefabricated structures in the construction industry, contribute greatly to the productivity measured in the industries using them. These indirect spillover effects of industry R&D have not received the attention they deserve, nor is the underlying dynamic process of the transmission of technical change via the industrial input-output structure well understood.

There are a few studies, however, that have begun exploration of these issues. Terleckyj [38, 1974] has estimated the contribution of R&D embodied in purchased goods for thirty-three manufacturing and nonmanufacturing industries for the period 1948–1966. The results indicate a strong effect by R&D-intensive purchased inputs on productivity growth; rates of return of 45 percent in manufacturing, 62 percent for total industries, and 187 percent for nonmanufacturing are attributed to the indirect effect of R&D through purchased inputs. Terleckyj sets the estimated indirect effect of private R&D at 80 percent, more than twice the direct rate of return of 30 percent. These results are in contrast to the estimates obtained by Griliches, which are 20 percent each for direct and indirect R&D, and to rate of return obtained by Mansfield et al. [25, 1977], who estimated a 25 percent rate of return for direct and indirect R&D. Finally, Michael Evans [5, 1976], in his study of contribution of NASA R&D expenditures to growth of aggregate productivity in the United States, suggests a significant effect of R&D expenditures on growth of aggregate output and productivity through the interindustry transmission of technical change.

From these studies, despite their differences and the ambiguity of some of their results, there seems to be some evidence for the indirect or spillover effects of R&D on growth of output and productivity. Also, there is evidence that linkages among industries determine the speed and magnitude of the indirect effects. The tentative implication is that in evaluating the contribution of R&D of an industry both the direct and indirect effects should be considered. However, because of the conceptual and empirical weakness of some of the past work, further studies of the spillover effects are needed to support more expanded government involvement in R&D efforts.

The Contribution of Government-Financed R&D

Government-financed R&D is concentrated in a few defense-oriented industries such as Air Transportation (missiles and space) (SIC 451), Electrical Machinery (SIC 36), Transportation Equipment (SIC 37), Ordnance and Instruments. There is some evidence, mostly negative, on the contribution of R&D financed by the federal government. Terleckyj reports that government-financed research (except in agriculture) had no direct effect on the productivity of the industries conducting it. There is some evidence that the indirect effect of government-financed R&D embodied in purchased inputs on the growth of output in the purchasing industries is very small. This was particularly true in the case of manufacturing industries, while in nonmanufacturing industries the evidence of indirect effects of government-financed R&D on growth of industrial output was not clearly established.

In another study, Griliches [11, 1979] found a statistically significant but negative direct effect on productivity growth of the share of R&D expenditure financed by government. Total factor productivity in manufacturing was correlated with (1) the ratio of R&D to value added (a measure of research intensity) and (2) a dummy variable for a ratio of R&D expenditure to net sales of more than 15 percent to single out the research intensity of the Ordnance (SIC 19) and Aircraft and Guided Missiles Parts (SIC 372) industries, where government-financed R&D is very high. The results suggest that concentrated, government-supported R&D leads to a decline in the growth of productivity. Similarly, in a different study using firm data, Griliches reports a strong depressing effect by publicly supported R&D on the estimated rate of return. The two industries which are the major recipients of federal research funds, Electrical Equipment and Aircraft and Missiles, had the lowest rates of return on R&D investment: 2 percent and 5 percent. In Chemical and

Chemical Products and Fabricated Metals, the rates were about 90 percent and 25 percent, respectively.[d] However, unlike Terleckyj, Griliches calculates a positive but small indirect contribution to private productivity by government financed R&D.

Several features of publicly supported research in the United States should be noted. First, the large gains from public research in some industries, such as agriculture, are well documented. Second, the government R&D expenditures are unevenly distributed; half of all publicly financed R&D has been in defense and space. These are R&D-intensive industries, and the added R&D support may be subject to diminishing return. Third, in these industries, government purchases are very large and, therefore, output is measured not totally by inputs.

In a study evaluating the economic impact of NASA R&D spending, Michael Evans [5, 1976] found a very significant effect by publicly funded space R&D expenditures. Using a combination of macroeconometric and input-output models, Evans carried out two simulation exercises: one holding total government purchases constant but increasing NASA spending by $1 billion for one year and the other increasing the level of NASA R&D spending by $1 billion over a longer period of time. The results of the first simulation showed that simply changing the composition of government spending toward greater NASA spending redistributes demand from lower productivity to higher productivity industries. This shift results in a net increase of 20,000 jobs, higher productivity, and a lower rate of inflation. Under the assumption of sustained higher NASA R&D spending of $1 billion per year will lead in 1984 to the following pattern of changes: 2.1 percent change in output, 0.8 percent change in employment, −2.2 percent change in consumer price index, 2.1 percent change in index of labor productivity, and −0.5 percent change in the unemployment rate. The key factors that make this possible are the increase in productivity due to a shift to high technology industries, such as the space industry, and a shift of demand away from industries with high rates of excess capacity. The rate of return to NASA spending, according to the Evans study, turns out to be about 38 percent.

The rate of return on government R&D is surprisingly high and in sharp conflict with results obtained using the micro-data sets noted

---

[d] Zvi Griliches [11, 1979] has found a somewhat higher elasticity (10 percent) for research-intensive industries (Chemical and Allied Products, Primary Metals Industries, Electrical Equipment, Motor Vehicle and Equipment, and Aircraft & Guided Missiles) and a lower elasticity (4 percent) for other industries.

earlier. There are serious methodological and estimation problems that cast doubt on the accuracy and reasonableness of the results of this study. The estimates are extremely sensitive to small changes in estimation procedure and data classification. The results are also contaminated because of a strong trend in the data used. Further, they lead us to a largely untenable, but enviable public policy prescription. That is, by simply shifting the composition of the government budget, we can solve, to a large degree, the problems of growth, productivity, unemployment, and inflation simultaneously. Nonetheless, the Evans study is one of the few macroeconomic studies that directly assesses the impact of R&D expenditures on aggregate output models of the economy. The analytical framework of this study may be useful in further work. However, it is not possible at present to compare results obtained using macro and micro data. The data, models, and estimation techniques used in each study are quite different. The inconclusive nature of the evidence on the productivity of publicly funded R&D points to the urgent need for further study.

Private and Social Rates of Return

As noted earlier, the direct rate of return to R&D is very high when compared to other types of investment and the direct returns suggest that external benefits of R&D are even more impressive. For example, one study puts the direct rate of return to about 30 percent and indirect return to about 80 percent while another study suggest a median private rate of return of 25 percent and a median social rate of return of 56 percent. The crucial questions are what determines such divergence between the private and social rates of return and why the degree of this divergence differs among different industries. Current research does not provide adequate answers to these questions. However, a recent study by Mansfield et al. [25, 1977] provides some evidence on these issues.

Their study indicates that the social and private rates of return vary greatly for different innovations. In about 30 percent of the cases, the private rate of return was so low that no firm, with the advantage of hindsight, would have invested in innovations, even though the social rate of return from these innovations was fairly high. The gap between social and private rates of return is often explained in terms of the market structure of the innovator's industry, that is, whether the innovation is minor or major and whether the innovation is a new product or a process. To be sure, other factors can also be responsible for this gap, but the statistical results of Mansfield's study [25, 1977] indicate that the differences between the social and private rates of return tend to be greater for more important innovations and for innovations that can be imitated relatively cheaply by competitors. When the cost of initiating research is held constant it makes little difference whether the innovation is patented or not. These results are suggestive, but further research must be done before we can fully explain the substantial differences between social and private benefits of R&D.

Composition of R&D Expenditures and Growth of Productivity

The distribution of R&D expenditures is shifting away from basic research toward developmental research. These compositional shifts, accompanied by the relative decline of total R&D noted earlier, may affect the long-run growth of productivity in the U.S. economy. There is very little empirical evidence on the determinants of different types of R&D expenditures and on how they affect the growth of industrial output. How one stage of R&D leads to the other and with what time lag also remain largely unresolved.

There have been some studies, however, on the determinants of firm R&D for the purposes of designing new products. Several considerations may enter into a firm's decision to develop new products rather than improve existing products or methods of production. Such factors include the nature of the firm's existing product line, the riskiness of demand for these products in comparison with that anticipated for the new product, the potential entry of new competitors and rivalry with existing competitors, the size of the existing R&D program, and other industry characteristics. A study by Jon Rasmussen [35, 1973] suggests that the anticipated demand for new products over a period of six years (as a measure of risk) positively affects R&D decisions for new product development. The more assured the growth of demand for existing products and the greater the profitability of the firm, the less motivation the firm has to attempt new product development. Conversely, more new products tend to be developed if the anticipated demand for them is sufficiently strong and the variability of demand for the existing product is high.

Unfortunately, very little research has been performed on issues related to compositional change in R&D expenditure (that is, among basic, applied, and development research) and its relationship to productivity growth. The implications of a shift in the composition of R&D expenditures away from basic research for the long-run growth of productivity (while total R&D expenditure relative to GNP is declining) require close attention and careful assessment.

Some of the questions which need to be answered are (1) Just how much has the composition of R&D changed, and in which industries? (2) Are the changes from basic to applied research, or to development? How meaningful is the distinction between basic and applied research, anyway? (3) Is the basic research a "pool" from which applied research draws, and does a decline in the growth of basic research lead to a decline in productivity of applied research? There is also an urgent need to explore the underlying processes and the factors that determine the relationship between basic and applied research and new product development.

II. FACTORS INFLUENCING R&D EXPENDITURES: PAST FINDINGS

In addition to the studies that estimate the contribution of R&D growth of output, a considerable amount of recent research has been devoted to finding which factors determine the magnitudes and patterns of R&D expenditures in different industries. The question here is whether and for how long growth of output, changes in relative prices and profits, degree of concentration, extent of regulation, and so on affect the level and rate of growth of R&D expenditures in different industries. Related issues are the pattern of causality that may exist between these variables and R&D decisions and the possible interactions of the existing structure of inputs with the accumulation of technical know-how or innovations.

The Input Demand Functions for R&D

The underlying hypothesis of studies on the demand for R&D expenditures is that R&D, like labor and capital, is considered to be an input in the production process and therefore subject to the influence of economic and technological considerations. The demand functions are derived by an optimization procedure and often estimated with such data as output, relative prices, profits, capital, and unemployment.

Most studies report a strong and positive relationship between R&D and output (sales), suggesting that growth of demand, especially if it is sustained over a period of time, stimulates innovative effort. Empirical evidence for the proposition that either liquidity or profitability is conducive to innovative effort is weak. There are studies, mainly using firm data, that assign an important role to cash flow variables in determining R&D expenditures, while other studies find no significant relationship.[e] However, where evidence of a

---

[e]For further discussion, see Henry Grabowski and Dennis Mueller [7, 1977], J.W. Elliot [4, 1971], and J.D. Howe and D.G. McFetridge [14, 1976].

positive relationship exists, cash flow variables seem to have their strongest effect on R&D during growth periods. This implies that anti-recessionary policies, such as lowering corporate income taxes or increasing depreciation allowances, would buttress R&D programs against cutbacks.

Surprisingly, very few studies, except those of M. Ishaq Nadiri and George Bitros [29, 1979] and Rasmussen [35, 1973], have examined the effect of relative input prices, such as cost of capital and wage rates, on R&D decisions. Both of these studies report evidence that relative prices affect R&D decisions both in the short and long runs. In the first study, the time response of R&D to changes in relative prices is found to be similar to that of investment in plant and equipment, that is, price changes begin to affect R&D decisions after the second year. Rasmussen reports that R&D is sensitive to movements in the prices of labor and capital, and that a capital-saving bias is associated with industrial R&D effort. The evidence implies that public policy, by changing the relative prices through fiscal and monetary policies, could stimulate R&D effort.

Firm Size, Concentration, and Inventive Activity

It is often stated that large size and monopoly power are complementary insofar as R&D is concerned, with the former influencing the breadth of the market for an innovation and the latter influencing its duration. It is also claimed that large diversified firms might undertake more research than small, single-product firms and that large, monopolistic firms would attract the best innovative talent. It is further argued that a certain critical size of an R&D program is required in order to realize positive returns, and that the minimum effort can best be undertaken by large firms.

The theoretical and empirical evidence of several studies on the relationship between the size of the firm and R&D effort as summarized by Morton Kamien and Nancy Schwartz [16, 1975] indicates that the relationship is at best inconclusive, mainly due to the vagueness of the definitions of firm size, monopoly power, and so on used in these studies. Also, more recent studies do not support a positive relationship between a firm's size and its R&D effort. Using concentration ratios as proxies for the extent of innovative rivalry in an industry is generally unsatisfactory. The relationship between R&D activity and industry concentration may also be non-linear. It may be that an intermediate market structure—between monopoly and perfect competition—is most conducive to R&D activity. To argue, therefore, the case of mergers simply on grounds of economies of scale in research could be incorrect unless it is to reach a threshold level below which R&D effort would be uneconomical to undertake.

Existing Factors of Production and R&D Decisions

The existing stocks of capital and labor probably affect both the level and the speed of adjustment of R&D expenditures in a firm. A highly capital-intensive firm may not be able to introduce new techniques which would make a large part of its existing capital obsolete. Also, the training and level of skills of the labor force can influence the R&D intensity of a firm. There are few studies exploring the relationships between the traditional factors of production and R&D expenditures. Nadiri and Bitros [29, 1979], using a general disequilibrium framework, have analyzed the interactions among employment, capital stock, and stock of R&D. Using a sample of 114 firms, they found that R&D, capital, and labor not only respond to changes in output and relative prices but that there are strong interactions among them. The decision with respect to one input, such as R&D, is not independent of the firm's other input decisions and there is an interaction to and from other inputs as R&D, labor, and capital move toward long-run equilibrium values. They also found a strong effect of R&D expenditures on labor productivity both in the short and long runs. The implications of these findings are that a consistent policy should be designed taking account of feedbacks among the inputs, and that a slowdown of the growth of productivity can be partially reversed if more R&D efforts are encouraged.

The Effects of Regulation

Where there is a possibility of natural monopoly due to the presence of economies of scale or an uncertainty of information on the part of consumers and a lack of incentive for firms to provide more adequate information, the forces of the free market will not ensure the proper amount or quality of goods and services at reasonable prices. These forces often lead to what is known as "market failures," and the regulatory bodies are assigned the task of regulating the amount and quality of goods and services to correct such failures. Whatever the merits of regulation on other grounds, there is evidence that the pursuit of regulatory objectives has contributed to an inhibition or distortion of technological innovation in several industries.

In the pharmaceutical industry, according to several studies, the introduction of the Kefauver amendment in 1962 to FDA regulations has led to a sharp decline in the number of new chemical entities (NCEs) approved by the FDA in the period 1963–1975. Martin Bailey's [1, 1972] results show that the level of R&D expenditures necessary to generate a given flow of NCEs has more than doubled as a result of the 1962 amendment. Sam Pelzman's study [34, 1974] of the industry before and after the 1962 amendment shows that the new regulations significantly reduced the flow of NCEs and indicates that the amendment may account for most of the difference between the pre- and post-1962 NCE flow.

Henry Grabowksi, John Vernon, and Thomas Lacy's [8, 1976] comparative study of the introduction of new pharmaceutical products in the United States and the United Kingdom shows that, because of the stringent U.S. regulations, R&D productivity declined about sixfold between 1960–1961 and 1966–1970, while the decrease in the United Kingdom was about threefold. They also show that increased regulation roughly has doubled R&D costs per NCE in the United States. Further, the rising costs and lowered productivity of innovation in this industry have led to a shift in expenditures away from domestic R&D to foreign R&D by U.S. firms. Regulatory differences may also be at least partly responsible for the faster growth of R&D in pharmaceutical products in foreign countries and the acceleration of the U.S. drug firms' investments in manufacturing capacity abroad. Moreover, studies by Bailey [1, 1972] and David Schwartzman [36, 1976] show that there has been a sharp decline in private rates of return to R&D activity in the post-1962 period. Schwartzman's results also show a high variability in sales of NCEs since 1962, which is an indication that a significant "risk" premium is associated for new drug development throughout the post-amendment period.

Similarly, the study by Aaron Gellman [6, 1971] on innovation in railroads concludes that regulation in railroad and truck transport has slowed down and distorted the pace and pattern of technological change. Roger Noll [33, 1971] provides similar conclusions in the case of communications networks. Paul MacAvoy and James Sloss [21, 1967] show that an average of $9.4 million per year (1958–1962) in potential cost-savings were lost through ICC-induced delays of adoptions of unit coal trains by the four major eastern railroads.

The available studies generally point to the negative effects of regulation on the rate and timing of innovations. However, further studies are needed to explore in depth the trade-off between costs and benefits of regulation and to suggest ways of incorporating considerations that promote technological progress as part of the decisionmaking processes of the regulatory agencies.

Summary

Our discussion in the previous two sections points to the following tentative conclusions:

1. There is evidence to confirm the findings of previous studies that R&D contributes positively to growth of output and productivity. The gross rate of return on R&D during the 1960s was very high—twice that of physical capital. Though little is known about the net return, the gross rate of return remained fairly high, as we shall see, in the 1970s. The indirect or spillover effect of R&D from one industry to another is an important source of R&D contributions to growth of productivity.

2. There is evidence that R&D inputs respond to changes in demand, relative prices, and existing input mix. There are interactive adjustments among R&D, employment, and capital.

3. Judging from the results of the available studies, the effect of regulations on the timing and pace of R&D activities appears to be one of inhibiting the rate of technological change.

4. Government-supported R&D contributes marginally to the measured growth of output and productivity. This may be due to the fact that government-financed R&D is concentrated in a few defense-oriented industries. Difficulties lie in measuring "output" in these cases. Another problem is the difficulty of measuring "output" of innovative activities. However, too little is known in this area to be very certain.

5. A strong relationship between R&D intensity and firm size is not supported by the available evidence. Evidence on the relation between market structure and R&D performance is also inconclusive.

III. NEW ESTIMATES OF R&D CONTRIBUTIONS

Most of the studies mentioned in the previous two sections employed data from the 1960s, though the investigations were carried out in the early 1970s. Their conclusions may be dated and may not be applicable to recent years. A closer look is needed at the 1970s data. Production functions will be used to evaluate the conclusions of the literature we have surveyed and to test some new hypotheses. To accomplish this, we have assembled data from different sources on eleven two-digit manufacturing industries for the period 1958–1975. The data are classified into three samples of pooled cross-section time series data for "total manufacturing," "total durables," and "total nondurables."

Three main issues will be examined. The first issue is to explain the contribution of R&D input to growth of output and productivity over the entire period 1958–1975 and the subperiods 1958–1965 and 1966–1976. The subperiods were chosen to see whether the contribution of R&D input to growth of output is different during the first period, when the rate of R&D expenditures was generally increasing, and the second period, when it was decreasing. Second, the factors that may explain the behavior of the R&D input during these periods must be identified. The third task is to explore the effect of government-financed R&D on the private sector decision to undertake R&D expenditures. The question here is whether public financing of R&D positively or negatively affects private R&D expenditures.

The issue of assessing the contribution of R&D input to growth of output is addressed in this section by specifying and estimating a production function. The other two issues are taken up in Section IV, where an input demand model for R&D is specified and estimated. Before presenting and interpreting results of our estimations, we shall describe briefly the nature of out data and the specification of the variables that are used in the econometric production and input functions.

Data and Specification of Explanatory Variables

Annual data on several variables were collected from a variety of sources, indicated below, for the period 1958–1975 for the following eleven industries:

SIC CODE	Industry
Durables	
32	Stone, Clay, and Glass
33	Primary Metals
35	Nonelectrical Machinery
36	Electrical Machinery
37	Transportation Equipment
Nondurables	
20	Food and Beverage
22	Textiles
26	Paper and Products
28	Chemicals and Products
29	Petroleum and Coal Products
30	Rubber and Plastics

The choice of industries was dictated by the availability of consistent time series data on R&D expenditures: "Total Durables" consists of the first five industries, "Total Nondurables" contains the remaining six industries, and "Total Manufacturing" includes all eleven industries. These pooled time-series cross-section samples were designed to provide richer data to estimate the functions under consideration. The individual industry data are highly collinear and the resulting estimates would often be unstable and difficult to interpret. The production and R&D demand functions are estimated using an analysis of covariance technique developed by G.S. Maddala [22, 1971].

The list of variables and their construction are

1. Q is a measure of output constructed from the industry value added data published in *Census of Manufacturers* [39, 1977] and deflated by output price deflators given in *Survey of Current Business* [40, 1977].

2. (W/C) is the relative price variable, where W is a measure of the price of labor and C is the user-cost of capital. W is measured by the average hourly earnings of production workers obtained from different issues of the *Employment Situation*, published by the Bureau of Labor Statistics (BLS). The user cost of capital is constructed following Jorgenson's formulation as

$$C = \frac{p_k (\bar{r} + \delta) (1 - \bar{k} - vz + vzk')}{(1 - v)} ,$$

where p_k is the price of investment goods; $\bar{r}$ is the real rate of interest calculated as $\bar{r} = r - (\dot{p}/p)^e$, where r is the nominal rate of interest on Moody's Aaa-rated industrial bonds and $(\dot{p}/p)^e$ is the measure of expected inflation calculated as a weighted average of past changes in the consumer price index; δ is the rate of depreciation; $\bar{k}$ is the effective rate of investment credit; k' is the tax credit allowance under the Long amendment, which required firms to subtract their total tax credit from their depreciation base. It is equal to $\bar{k}$ during the time when the Long amendment was in effect and 0 at all other times; v is the corporate income tax; and z is the present value of the depreciation per dollar of investment of deductions.[f]

3. L is a measure of total employment excluding employment figures for scientists and engineers in each industry. Total employment figures are constructed by adding total production and non-produc-

[f]For details of constructing the user-cost of capital and source of data, see M. Ishaq Nadiri [28, 1972].

tion workers published in *Earnings & Employment* [41, 1977] minus the number of employed scientists and engineers reported in NSF publications.

4. K_t is the measure of the net capital stock generated for each industry using the perpetual inventory formula

$$K_t = I_t + (1-\delta_1) K_{t-1} .$$

Here annual real investment, I_t , is taken from various issues of the *Survey of Current Business* [40, 1977]; δ_1 is the depreciation rate, and K_{t-1} is the benchmark capital stock. The depreciation rates and benchmark capital stock figures are taken from Bert Hickman [12, 1965, Appendix B].

5. R_t is the measure of the net capital stock of R&D. It is generated by a similar perpetual inventory formula, that is,

$$R_t = D_t + (1 - \delta_2) R_{t-1} .$$

Here D is R&D expenditure deflated by the price index for investment in plant and equipment. The R&D figures for each industry are obtained from National Science Foundation (NSF) publications [31, 1974; 32, 1976]. The choice of the R&D deflator is certainly arbitrary, but unavailability of the appropriate deflator for R&D permits little choice in this matter. It is extremely difficult to measure depreciation rates for stocks of knowledge. We arbitrarily picked a rate of 0.10 and assumed that it prevailed in each of the industries since there is no reliable information about depreciation of the stock of knowledge available to improve on this guess.

Benchmark figures for stocks of R&D are not available either for the aggregate economy or for individual industries. Some authors take the first available observation on real R&D expenditure as the benchmark. This approach has certain shortcomings especially if the rate of growth of R&D is rather slow. We have estimated the benchmark figures for R_{t-1} for each industry using the relation

$$R_{t-1} = \frac{D_0}{\delta_2 + g} ,$$

where D_0 is the first-year R&D expenditures in real terms and g is measured by the average growth rate of capital stock for the years succeeding the benchmark year.

6. R_{p_t} is the measure of stock of private R&D and is generated in a similar way as R_t , using the appropriate R&D expenditures series and the same values of δ_2 . The private R&D expenditure figures are published by NSF [31, 1974].

7. R_{g_t} is the measure of stock of government-financed R&D and is generated in a similar manner as R_{p_t}, using, however, the government-financed R&D figures published by NSF.

8. U_t is a measure of the capacity utilization rate by industry taken from Wharton [42, 1977].

Specification and Estimation Problems

To measure the contribution of R&D to growth of output, we used a simple three-input Cobb-Douglas production function of the form:

$$Q_t = A K_t^{\alpha_1} \, L_t^{\alpha_2} \, R_t^{\alpha_3} \, e^{\rho t} \tag{1}$$

where ρ is the rate of exogenous technical change and t is time; other variables in equation (1) have been defined earlier. The Cobb-Douglas production function is a first order approximation to higher-order logarithmic functions and is simple to interpret.

In estimating equation (1), using the cross-section time series data, we encountered estimation problems due to the high multi-collinearity among the variables. The pairwise correlations among K, L, R, and t often were about 0.90. A consequence of the high degrees of multi-collinearity among these variables is to make some of the variables look statistically insignificant when in fact they should be significant on theoretical grounds. This is what in fact turned out to be the case. The coefficients of employment, L, in each case were very large—above one, and the signs of the coefficients of K and R were sometimes negative and their magnitudes turned out to be statistically insignificant. The coefficient of the time trend also turned out to be statistically insignificant, and the fit of the equation was generally poor.

To meet this estimation problem, we have used the Ridge regression technique to estimate equation (1). Since this method is not very well known, it may be useful to explain some of its main features.[g]

Consider the standard multiple regression model with N observation and K explanatory variables:

$$Y - X\beta + e,$$

[g]For further description of this method, see A.E. Hoerl and R.W. Kennard [13, 1970].

where β is a $(K \times 1)$ vector, X is $(N \times K)$ and of full rank. The expected values are $E(e) = 0$ and $E(ee') = \sigma^2 I$, where σ^2 is the population variance and I the corresponding identity matrix. The least squares estimate of β is given by $\bar{\beta} = (X'X)^{-1} X'Y$. Define the square of the distance from $\bar{\beta}$ to β by $D^2 = (\bar{\beta}-\beta)'(\bar{\beta}-\beta)$. The mean expected value of the square of the distance, called the mean square error, is

$$E(D^2) = \sigma^2 \text{ Trace } (X'X)^{-1} = \sigma^2 \sum_{i=1}^{K} (1/\omega_i)$$

where the ω_i's are the eigenvalues of $X'X$.

If $X'X$ is an ill-conditioned matrix with nonorthogonal data vectors and some small eigenvalues, the distance from $\bar{\beta}$ to β will be large. The least squares estimator is unbiased $(E(\beta) = \bar{\beta})$ and minimizes the residual sum of squares. However, utilizing both unbiasedness and minimum variance criteria, the results are not satisfactory in the presence of multicollinearity.

The ridge regression estimator reduces the distance from β to the estimator of $\bar{\beta}$, at the cost of an increase in the residual sum of squares. However, the greater the nonorthogonality of the matrix of regressors, the further one can move from the least squares estimator without an appreciable increase in the residual sum of squares. Minimizing the sum of squared errors subject to a constraint on the distance, yields the ridge regression estimator, given by

$$\bar{\beta}* = [X'X + \lambda I]^{-1} X'Y$$

where λ is a constant greater than zero.

The diagonal of $X'X$ is augmented by a constant λ. Varying λ results in the estimation of the ridge trace.

The expected value of the distance is given by

$$E[D^2(\lambda)] = E\{(\bar{\beta}* -\beta)'(\bar{\beta}*-\beta)\}$$

$$\sigma^2 [\text{Trace } (X'X + \lambda I)^{-1} - \lambda \text{ Trace } (X'X + \lambda I)^{-2}] + \lambda^2 \beta' (X'X + \lambda I)^{-2} \beta.$$

The first term is the sum of the variances of parameter estimates. The second term is the sum of the squares of the bias. Total variance decreases as λ increases, while the square of the bias increases with λ.

There exists a λ for which the mean square error is less than for the least squares estimator. The choice of the appropriate λ is arbitrary, so that a trace over a range of λ becomes of interest. Major considerations include the following: (1) the sum of squared errors should not be large relative to least-squares regression; (2) the systems should stabilize with some coefficients going to zero and all others become insensitive to small changes in λ; (3) coefficients with incorrect signs or unreasonable magnitudes should have been changed.

The Parameter Estimates and Their Stability
The production function (1) is estimated using the analysis of variance technique. Three sets of cross-section and time series data were employed. The estimated coefficients of the function are shown for three aggregate manufacturing industries in Table 5—1. Experimenting with the ridge regression technique, it was clear that, at very small values of λ, the system of variables exhibited an orthogonal structure. The coefficient of the time trend, t, was often statistically insignificant, and, therefore, equation (1) was estimated without it.

Table 5—1. Generalized Least Squares Estimates of the Cobb–Douglas Production Function, Estimation Period: 1958—1975

Estimated Equation

$$1nQ_t = \alpha_0 + \alpha_1 \, 1nL_t + \alpha_2 \, 1nK_t + \alpha_3 \, 1nR_t$$

Independent Variables	*Total Manufacturing* $1nQ_t$	*Total Durables* $1nQ_t$	*Total Nondurables* $1nQ_t$
Constant	0.37 (2.22)	0.50 (2.83)	−0.07 (1.14)
$1nL_t$	0.65 (35.15)	0.82 (17.76)	0.70 (45.94)
$1nK_t$	0.36 (21.80)	0.22 (8.73)	0.32 (17.31)
$1nR_t$	0.11 (11.17)	0.08 (6.51)	0.19 (11.01)
R^2	0.94	0.98	0.99
SSR^a	219.7	95.8	121.0
λ^b	0.006	0.002	0.005

[a] Sum of squares due to regression.
[b] λ is a constant in the augmented $(X'X)^{-1}$ matrix, i.e., $[(X'X) + \lambda I]^{-1}$.

As can be seen, the fit of the functions is quite good. The coefficients have the correct signs and all are statistically significant. The output elasticity of labor indicated in the second row of Table 5—1 ranges from 0.65 to 0.80, which is close to the share of labor, while the output elasticity of capital ranges from 0.22 to 0.36. However, the output elasticity of stock of R&D is much smaller compared to that of capital and labor in each of the three industries, as would be expected. The magnitude of this elasticity is fairly high in Total Nondurables, perhaps reflecting the significance of R&D in chemical and petroleum industries. To test the sensitivity of the estimates, the production function was fitted using the stock of private R&D in place of the total stock of R&D. The result did not change much except that the coefficients of the R&D variable in each of the sectors were somewhat larger when the stock of private R&D was used. Similarly, when we replaced our capital stock series by the series recently developed by John Kendrick [18, 1973], the parameter estimates and the overall fit of the regressions changed very little.

The production estimates suggest that economies of scale prevail in each of the three industries. The sum of the coefficients of equation (1), $\mu = \alpha + \beta + \gamma$, provides an estimate of the magnitude of economies of scale. It is about 1.12 for Total Manufacturing, 1.11 for Total Durables, and 1.12 for Nondurables. The alternative hypothesis of constant returns to scale was rejected, using an F-test. Basically, the estimates in Table 5—1 suggest that there are constant returns to scale with respect to the traditional inputs, that is, capital and labor. That is, the production function can be written as

$$Q_t = A K_t^{\alpha_1} L_t^{(1-\alpha_1)} R_t^{\alpha_3} e^{\rho t} . \qquad (2)$$

A statistical fit of this equation supported the hypothesis of constant returns to scale with respect to K and L.

From these results, it is quite clear that R&D contributes significantly to the growth of output over the period 1958 to 1975. The output elasticity of stock of R&D is estimated to be 0.11 in Total Manufacturing, about 0.075 in Total Durables, and approximately 0.19 in Total Nondurables. The estimates of the gross rates of return on stock of R&D (calculated as $\psi = \alpha_3 (\overline{Q/R})$, where α_3 is the coefficient of R in each of the production functions and ($\overline{Q/R}$) is the average ratio of output to R&D stock) for the period are 0.20 for Total Manufacturing, 0.12 for Total Durables, and 0.86 for Total

Nondurables. The substantial difference in the rates of return to R&D in the durables and nondurables sectors is partly due to the differences in the output elasticities of R&D but more importantly is due to the large differences in Q/R ratios in the two industries; the growth of stock of R&D compared to growth of output in nondurables has been very small in spite of the fact that some nondurables industries such as chemicals have experienced high rates of growth of R&D in the postwar period.

Another issue that arises here is whether these estimates are stable over time. It is likely that the structure of the production process might have changed at some point during the period of estimation and the decline in R&D expenditure since 1966 may be a response to such a change. To test the stability of the production function over time, we fitted the function to several subperiods: 1958–1962, 1963–1967, 1968–1972, and 1973–1975, as well as to samples of data covering the periods 1958–1965 and 1966–1975. Selection of the exact time when structural changes might have occurred is always difficult and arbitrary. Nonetheless, checking the stability of the coefficients and fit of a function over several subsamples is an appropriate test.

To save space, we have presented in Table 5–2 the parameter estimates of the production function for each of the industries for the periods 1958–1965 and 1966–1975. The estimates in Table 5–2 clearly indicate that the values of the parameters of the production function hardly change over the two periods. The estimates obtained by fitting the model to data for the four subperiods mentioned also exhibit stability and the magnitudes of the coefficients are similar to those indicated in Table 5–2. We conclude that the parameters of the production function are highly stable. Thus, the substantial reduction in R&D expenditures since 1966 has had no effect on the stability of the coefficients. Neither has the gross rate of return on stock of R&D changed substantially since 1966. The values of ψ calculated for the two periods for each of the industries are indicated in Table 5–3. The reason for the stability of ψ in each of the sectors in the two periods is that the output elasticities shown in Table 5–2 have not changed and that $(\overline{Q/R})_i$ has also remained fairly stable. The latter is explained by the slowdown in the growth of the stock of R&D having been accompanied by a similar slowdown in growth of output in the period 1966–1975.

However, the reduction in R&D expenditures since 1966 has greatly reduced the growth of the potential output in these industries. The average annual growth rates of the stock of R&D and real

Table 5-2.   Generalized Least Squares Estimates of the Cobb–Douglas Production Function, Estimation Period: 1958–1965 and 1966–1975

Estimated Equation

$$\ln Q_t = \alpha_0 + \alpha_1 \ln L + \alpha_2 \ln K_t + \alpha_3 \ln R_t$$

Independent Variables	Total Manufacturing $\ln Q_t$		Total Durables $\ln Q_t$		Total Nondurables $\ln Q_t$	
	1958–1965	1966–1975	1958–1965	1966–1975	1958–1965	1966–1975
Constant	0.10 (0.77)	0.55 (2.30)	0.72 (3.48)	0.72 (2.82)	−0.14 (−1.14)	−0.05 (−1.69)
$\ln L_t$	0.65 (38.98)	0.63 (29.63)	0.77 (23.75)	0.75 (13.52)	0.69 (39.45)	0.71 (57.88)
$\ln K_t$	0.38 (26.64)	0.35 (16.86)	0.22 (15.14)	0.23 (7.42)	0.33 (17.95)	0.33 (20.95)
$\ln R_t$	0.11 (13.26)	0.11 (9.47)	0.08 (10.38)	0.09 (6.96)	0.18 (11.13)	0.18 (11.36)
R^2	0.98	0.94	0.99	0.98	0.99	0.99
SSR^a	114.18	137.19	51.01	60.09	57.95	73.96
λ^b	0.001	0.001	0.001	0.001	0.001	0.001

[a]Sum of squares due to regression.
[b]λ is a constant in the augmented $(X'X)^{-1}$ matrix, i.e., $[(X'X) + \lambda I]^{-1}$.

Table 5−3. Gross Rates of Return on R&D in the Manufacturing Industries for the Periods 1958−1965 and 1966−1975 [a]

Industries	1958−1965	1966−1975
Total manufacturing	0.22	0.20
Total durables	0.10	0.12
Total nondurables	0.86	0.85

[a]The value of ψ is calculated by $\alpha_{3i}\ (\overline{Q/R})_i$ where α_{3i} are regression coefficients of stock of R&D for industry i in Table 5-2 and $(\overline{Q/R})_i$ are the associated average value of the ratio of output to the stock of R&D.

R&D expenditures over the periods 1958−1965 and 1966−1975 for the three industries were:

	Growth of Stock of R&D		Growth Rate of R&D Expenditures	
	1958–65	1966–75	1958–65	1966–75
Total Manufacturing	0.07	0.03	0.065	0.017
Total Durables	0.08	0.03	0.070	0.027
Total Nondurables	0.07	0.04	0.065	0.007

These figures indicate that a substantial decline in rates of growth of both R&D expenditures and stock of R&D input has occurred during these two periods. An important factor contributing to these declines has been a substantial cutback in public funding of R&D in most of the durable and nondurable industries.

Tentative estimates of how much extra output would have been generated in each of the industries (assuming everything else remains the same), if the rate of R&D expenditures had not declined since 1966, could be obtained by the following mental experiment. Suppose the stock of R&D for the three industries had increased during 1966−1975 at the same average rate as for the period 1958−1965. Let us assume also that the growth of other inputs would not be affected by the faster growth of R&D input and that the parameters of the production function (1) remained stable between the two periods and their estimated values were equal to those shown for the 1958−1965 period. Our calculations suggest that the yearly output would have grown by 0.005 for Total Manufacturing, 0.004 for Total Durables, and 0.006 for Total Nondurables.

These estimates should be interpreted carefully and only as an exercise; the underlying assumptions for these calculations are extremely weak, especially the notion that the parameter estimates for other inputs would remain the same if the stock of R&D had grown substantially; the complementarity among the inputs, K, L and R, precludes such a possibility. However, as an exercise these figures suggest substantial loss of potential output due to decline in R&D spending. The potential loss is much greater when we note that all manufacturing industries are not included in our samples and that the indirect or spillover effects on other industries are excluded as well.

IV. A MODEL OF R&D INPUT DEMAND

In the previous section we assumed that the quantities of all the inputs—labor, capital, and stock of R&D—were given and explored the contribution of stock of R&D to growth of output. However, there is also the question of what determines the R&D expenditures. Elsewhere, we have developed a complete model of interrelated input demand functions where the determinants of all three inputs are specified and estimated.[h] Here, we shall concentrate only on the demand function for R&D deduced from the complete model.

A Derived Demand Model

Using the general disequilibrium input demand model developed by Nadiri and Rosen [30, 1973], we can formulate the R&D input function as

$$1nR_t = \beta_0 + \beta_1 \; 1nQ_t + \beta_2 \; 1n \; \left(\frac{W}{C}\right)_t + \beta_3 \; 1nL_{t-1} + \beta_4 \; 1nK_{t-1}$$

$$+ \beta_5 \; 1nR_{t-1} + \beta_6 \; 1nU_{t-1} , \tag{3}$$

where R_t is the stock of R&D, Q the level of output, (W/C) the ratio of wage to user cost of capital, L_{t-1} the lagged value of employment, K_{t-1} the lagged value of capital stock, R_{t-1} the lagged values of the dependent variable, and U_{t-1} the lagged value of the utilization rate. This equation is one of a system of four equations which includes the production function (1) and two input equations for capital and labor similar in structure to (3).

The interpretation of equation (3) is that the desired and hence the actual stock of R&D is affected by the level of output and by movements in relative prices. Unfortunately, it is not possible to con-

---

[h] See for further details and specifications, M. Ishaq Nadiri and Sherwin Rosen [30, 1973].

struct a price variable for R&D input, and we have made the arbitrary but convenient assumption that the R&D input price can be approximated by the user-cost of physical capital. The other variables that influence the behavior of R&D in (3) are the lagged values of all factors of production. The lagged values, L_{t-1} and K_{t-1}, depict dynamic forces which affect the adjustment path of R&D to its equilibrium or desired level. That is, whenever there is a disequilibrium in quantities of labor or capital (that is, the actual values are different from their optimum levels) the firm's decision with respect to R&D is affected. Whether R&D expenditures increase or decrease when there is disequilibrium in the firm's input levels of capital and labor depends on the complementary or substitutional relationships that may exist between R&D and capital or R&D and labor. Thus, the sign of the coefficients of $1nL_{t-1}$ and $1nK_{t-1}$ in equation (3) can be positive or negative depending on the relation of R&D with K and L in the production of output. Finally, R&D decisions may be influenced by business cycle developments, that is, when business is expanding, firms increase their R&D expenditures while in periods of recession they may decrease or postpone such expenditures. The capacity utilization variable, U_{t-1}, in equation (3) is to account for these developments.

The rationale for the existence of the dynamic forces in equation (3) requires some explanation. The underlying hypothesis is that the firm must incur some costs over time to change its inputs. When the firm attempts to adjust one of its inputs, the adjustment of its other inputs is affected because the adjustments of the inputs are interdependent if the firm is to remain on its production function. For example, if the firm increases its capital stock, it would create the need to increase its stock of knowledge and to increase or decrease the size of its employment. Thus, there is a feedback system among the inputs, and as the firm attempts to meet its demand, this feedback process traces the dynamic adjustment path of each input.

Equation (3) was estimated by both the generalized least squares and the two-stage least squares procedure to take account of the simultaneous relations that exist between R and output Q. The coefficients of equation (3) were not sensitive to the choice of estimation technique, and therefore only the estimates generated by the two-stage least squares technique are shown in Table 5-4. As can be seen from that table, equation (3) provides a very good explanation of the behavior of total R&D in all three aggregate industries. The fit of the equations is quite good and the coefficients of the explanatory variables have the expected signs and are statistically significant. The estimates indicate that changes in output and relative prices affect

Table 5-4. The Determinants of Total R&D Expenditures, Estimation
Period: 1958-1975

	Estimated Equation		
$\ln R_t = \beta_0 + \beta_1 \ln Q_t + \beta_2 \ln(W/C)_t + \beta_3 \ln L_{t-1} + \beta_4 \ln K_{t-1} + \beta_5 \ln R_{t-1} + \beta_6 \ln U_{t-1}$			

Independent Variables	Total Manufacturing	Total Durables	Total Nondurables
Constant	0.34 (1.87)	0.45 (2.05)	-2.07 (5.57)
$\ln Q_t$	0.05 (3.28)	0.08 (4.62)	0.04 (1.96)
$\ln(W/C)_t$	0.16 (3.76)	-0.12 (2.41)	0.56 (8.95)
$\ln L_{t-1}$	-0.09 (3.62)	-0.05 (1.85)	-0.13 (3.59)
$\ln K_{t-1}$	0.06 (5.00)	0.03 (1.72)	0.14 (8.17)
$\ln R_{t-1}$	0.84 (68.85)	0.89 (68.29)	0.88 (34.99)
$\ln U_{t-1}$	0.04 (1.79)	0.04 (2.12)	0.18 (4.34)
R_2	0.97	0.98	0.94
SSR^a	189.80	79.86	100.81
λ^b	0.00	0.00	0.00

[a] Sum of squares due to regression.
[b] The equations in the table were estimated without resort to the ridge regression technique.

R&D in the short run except in the category of Nondurables, where the effect of changes of output in the short run is statistically insignificant. Surprisingly, relative price changes exert very significant effects, particularly in Nondurables. This may be due in part to collinearity between relative price and output as real wages in natural as opposed to efficiency units have tended to rise relative to the user cost of capital along with output.

The signs of the coefficients associated with labor and capital suggest that a disequilibrium in employment leads to a reduction in R&D investment, while a similar phenomenon in physical capital leads to an increase in R&D expenditure. That is, there is a substitutional relationship between employment and R&D and a complementary relation between R&D and capital stock of the firm. These feedback or cross-adjustment effects are fairly strong and statistically significant. Also, it seems that the average adjustment lags between actual and desired levels of R&D are fairly low—over five years in each of these aggregate industries.

Finally, the degree of capacity utilization influences the stock of R&D positively and significantly, the main effect of capacity utilization on R&D input being felt in the Nondurables sector. The results support the notion that, in the expansionary phase of the business cycle, expenditures on R&D are often increased, while in the contractionary phase such expenditures are generally reduced.

The results shown in Table 5—4 suggest several possibilities for public policy to promote R&D activities. For example, if the fiscal and monetary policies promote sustained growth of the economy and avoid business cycle fluctuations, or if through tax policies the relative prices are changed, R&D expenditures will increase. Also, public policy should recognize the interdependence that exists at least in the short run between different inputs. For instance, a vigorous R&D program may lead to an increase or decrease in investment in plant and equipment or in the level of employment; these indirect effects need to be considered when formulating public policy. Further, the results indicate that fairly long and complicated adjustment lags are involved as R&D adjusts over a period of time. The intertemporal adjustment of R&D is intertwined with that of other inputs, and not recognizing this could lead to erroneous decisions.

The Effect of Government-Financed R&D

As we noted earlier, some believe that public and private R&D are complementary with each other; that is, when opportunities for new innovations arise, public funding enables firms to exploit these opportunities better than if they were to finance the whole undertaking from their own funds. Others argue that firms cut back their own financing of R&D when public funding becomes available. Which of these hypotheses is correct is important for public policy.

We now examine the relationship between publicly funded R&D and privately financed R&D in the three aggregate industries. The same basic model of determinants of R&D as described by equation (3) is utilized to investigate the issue. The modifications that are introduced are: the dependent variable is now the stock of privately financed R&D, R_p, and the stock of government-financed R&D, R_g, is added to the independent variables on the right-hand side of equation (3). The underlying hypothesis is that firms in principle accumu-

Table 5-5. The Determinants of Privately Financed R&D Expenditures,
Estimation Period: 1960-1975

Estimated Equation

$$1nR_t = \gamma_0 + \gamma_1 1nQ_t + \gamma_2 1n(W/C)_t + \gamma_3 1nL_{t-1} + \gamma_4 1nK_{t-1} + \gamma_5 1nR_{g_t} +$$

$$\gamma_6 1nR_{p_{t-1}} + \gamma_7 1nU_{t-1}$$

Independent Variables	Total Manufacturing	Total Durables	Total Nondurables
Constant	-1.01 (4.36)	-0.70 (3.00)	-1.02 (2.81)
$1nQ_t$	0.05 (3.78)	0.11 (6.42)	0.03 (1.48)
$1n(W/C)_t$	0.27 (5.63)	0.01 (0.23)	0.39 (5.72)
$1nL_{t-1}$	-0.07 (2.81)	-0.01 (1.39)	-0.03 (1.82)
$1nK_{t-1}$	0.08 (6.41)	0.04 (3.11)	0.07 (3.68)
$1nR_{g_t}$	0.01 (2.25)	-0.04 (4.34)	0.02 (3.44)
$1nR_{p_{t-1}}$	0.92 (61.54)	0.87 (45.39)	0.85 (27.59)
$1nU_{t-1}$	0.07 (3.35)	0.02 (0.75)	0.12 (2.71)
R^2	0.97	0.99	0.96
SSR^a	153.7	67.9	70.0
λ^b	0.00	0.00	0.00

[a]Sum of squares due to regression.
[b]The equations in the table were estimated without resort to the ridge regression technique.

late two types of stock of knowledge, one financed from their own funds and the other through government financing. We have assumed that government-financed R&D is exogenously given.

The results are shown in Table 5-5. Due to unavailability of suitable data, the sample period for these equations is shorter (1969-1975) than before, and Total Nondurables comprises only five industries instead of six. Further, we have made some crude assumptions to generate the series for the stock of government and privately financed R&D.[i] The results in Table 5-5 are, in general, similar to

[i]See pp. 376-377 for construction of these variables and sources of data.

those presented in Table 5—4. Privately financed R&D is influenced by changes in demand and relative prices. The effects of changes in capital and labor are also strong and statistically significant, and the business cycle effect, captured by the capacity utilization variable, also exerts strong effects except in the durable industries.

The effect of government financed R&D on private R&D differs by sector according to the results in Table 5—5. Based on the data in our sample, it seems that growth of publicly financed stock of R&D has a positive and statistically significant effect on both Total Manufacturing and Total Durables, while its effect is statistically significant and negative in Nondurables. These estimates suggest that whether recent slowdown of government R&D expenditures affects the growth of private R&D in the aggregate economy depends mainly on the industry composition. When publicly financed R&D was lagged one year, its coefficient turned out to be statistically insignificant. This suggests that the effect of government financing of R&D on private R&D decisions is felt within the year. It should be pointed out, however, that the aggregate nature of the data probably conceals the true timing relationship between government-financed and private R&D decisions.

V. SUMMARY AND CONCLUSIONS

From the estimates of the production and input functions we discussed in Sections III and IV, certain conclusions emerge:

1. Contributions of R&D input to growth of output and productivity are substantial in all three major industry sectors, although the size of the contributions differs by sectors.

2. The magnitude of the output elasticities of R&D input has remained fairly stable over the period 1958—1975, though the slower rate of growth of R&D expenditures since 1966 has contributed to the slower growth of potential output since then. The gross rates of return on stock of R&D have not changed in the 1966—1975 period because of slower growth of both output and R&D input.

3. Changes in output and relative input prices do influence R&D activities, which are also influenced by cyclical fluctuations of the economy and by changes in the stock of physical capital and in the employment level.

4. The effect of government financing of R&D on private decisions regarding R&D expenditures differs among different industries. Our results are basically inconclusive on whether government-supported R&D affects positively or negatively the growth of output.

Among the many issues that require further consideration are the processes and effects of public and private cooperation in funding new R&D, the role and method of public funding in areas where R&D is needed (for example, pollution control, housing, urban transportation, energy), and the relationship between the changes in the composition of R&D expenditures (basic, applied, and developmental) and growth of productivity. Extensive research on the influence of government regulations on the rate and timing of innovations and much further examination of the structural relationships between R&D expenditures, production of knowledge, patents, growth of out· ut and productivity are also needed.

The list could be extended. However, the most important barriers to further research into these areas of inquiry are the inadequate state of data and the poor conceptual framework of our models. Better macro and micro data are needed. The measurement errors of the available data are substantial. Careful study of these data, reduction in measurement errors, and new bodies of data are necessary. Considerable progress is also needed at the conceptual level to understand how knowledge differs from and interacts with other production inputs and how it influences the productive process over time.

REFERENCES

1. BAILEY, MARTIN. "Research and Development Cost and Returns: The U.S. Pharmaceutical Industry," *Journal of Political Economy*, Jan./Feb. 1972, *80*(1), pp. 70–85.

2. BROWN, MURRAY, and CONRAD, ALFRED. "The Influence of Research and Education in CES Production Relations," in *The Theory and Empirical Analysis of Production.* Edited by MURRAY BROWN. New York: National Bureau of Economic Research; distributed by Columbia Univ. Press, 1967.

3. DENISON, EDWARD F. *Accounting for United States Growth, 1929–1969.* Washington, D.C.: Brookings Institution, 1974.

4. ELLIOT, JAN W. "Funds Flow vs. Expectational Theories of Research and Development Expenditures in the Firm," *Southern Economic Journal*, April 1971, *37*(4), pp. 409–22.

5. EVANS, MICHAEL. "The Economic Impact of NASA R&D Spending." Bala Cynwyd, Pa.: Chase Econometric Associates, Inc., April 1976, mimeo.

6. GELLMAN, AARON. "Surface Freight Transportation," in *Technological Change in Regulated Industries.* Edited by WILLIAM M. CAPRON. Washington, D.C.: Brookings Institution, 1971.

7. GRABOWSKI, HENRY, and MUELLER, DENNIS. "Rates of Return on Corporate Investment." Durham, N.C.: Duke University, 1977, mimeo.

8. GRABOWSKI, HENRY; VERNON, JOHN; and LACY, THOMAS. "The Effects of Regulatory Policy on the Incentives to Innovate: An International Comparative Analysis," in *Impact of Public Policy on Drug Innovation and Pric-*

ing. Edited by SAM A. MITCHELL and ED A. LINK. Washington, D.C.: American University, 1976.

9. GRILICHES, ZVI. "Research Expenditures, Education and Aggregate Agricultural Production Function," *American Economic Review,* Dec. 1964, *54* (6), pp. 961-74.

10. ____. "Research Expenditures and Growth Accounting," *Science and Technology in Economic Growth.* Edited by BRUCE R. WILLIAMS. New York: John Wiley and Sons, Halsted Press, 1973.

11. ____. "Returns to Research and Development Expenditures in the Private Sector," in *New Developments in Productivity Measurement.* Edited by JOHN KENDRICK and BEATRICE VACCARA. National Bureau of Economic Research. Cambridge, Mass.: Ballinger Publishing Company, 1979.

12. HICKMAN, BERT. *Investment Demand and U.S. Economic Growth.* Washington, D.C.: Brookings Institution, 1965.

13. HOERL, A.E., and KENNARD, R.W. "Ridge Regressions: Applications to Nonorthogonal Problems," *Technometrics,* Feb. 1970, *12* (1), pp. 59-70.

14. HOWE, J.D., and MCFETRIDGE, D.G. "The Determinants of R&D Expenditures," *Canadian Journal of Economics,* Feb. 1976, *9* (1), pp. 57-71.

15. JORGENSON, DALE, and GRILICHES, ZVI. "The Explanation of Productivity Change," *Review of Economic Studies,* July 1967, *34* (99), pp. 249-82.

16. KAMIEN, MORTON, and SCHWARTZ, NANCY. "Market Structure and Innovations: A Survey," *Journal of Economic Literature,* March 1975, *13* (1), pp. 1-37.

17. KENDRICK, JOHN W. *Postwar Productivity Trends in the U.S., 1948-69.* New York: National Bureau of Economic Research; distributed by Columbia Univ. Press, 1973.

18. ____. *The National Wealth of the United States: By Major Sector and Industry.* New York: The National Industrial Conference Board, Inc., 1976.

19. KENNEDY, C., and THIRLWALL, A.P. "Survey in Applied Economics: Technical Progress," *Economic Journal,* March 1972, *82* (325), pp. 11-63.

20. LEONARD, WILLIAM N. "Research and Development in Industrial Growth," *Journal of Political Economy,* March/April 1971, *79* (2), pp. 232-56.

21. MACAVOY, PAUL, and SLOSS, JAMES. *Regulation of Transport Innovation: The ICC and Unit Coal Trains to the East Coast.* New York: Random House, 1967.

22. MADDALA, G.S. "The Use of Variance Components Methods in Pooling: Cross Section and Time Series Data," *Econometrica,* March 1971, *39* (2), pp. 341-77.

23. MANSFIELD, EDWIN. "Rates of Return from Industrial Research and Development," *American Economic Review,* May 1965, *55* (2), pp. 310-22.

24. ____. "Contribution of Research and Development to Economic Growth of the United States," *Papers and Proceedings of a Colloquium: Research and Development and Economic Growth Productivity.* National Science Foundation. Washington, D.C.: U.S.G.P.O., 1972.

25. MANSFIELD, EDWIN; RAPOPORT, JOHN; ROMEO, ANTHONY; WAGNER, SAMUEL; and BEARDSLEY, G. "Social and Private Rates of Re-

turns from Industrial Innovations," *Quarterly Journal of Economics*, May 1977, *91*(2), pp. 221-40.

26. MINASIAN, JORA. "Research and Development Production Functions, and Rates of Return," *American Economic Review*, May 1969, *59*(2), pp. 80-85.

27. NADIRI, M. ISHAQ. "Some Approaches to the Theory and Measurement of Total Factor Productivity: A Survey," *Journal of Economic Literature*, Dec. 1970, *8*(4), pp. 1137-77.

28. _____ . "An Alternative Model of Business Investment Spending," *Brookings Papers on Economic Activity*, 1972 (3), pp. 547-83.

29. NADIRI, M. ISHAQ, and BITROS, GEORGE. "Research and Development Expenditure and Labor Productivity," in *New Developments in Productivity Measurement*. Edited by JOHN KENDRICK and BEATRICE VACCARA. National Bureau of Economic Research. Cambridge, Mass.: Ballinger Publishing Company, 1979.

30. NADIRI, M. ISHAQ, and ROSEN, SHERWIN. *A Disequilibrium Model for Factors of Production*. New York: National Bureau of Economic Research; distributed by Columbia Univ. Press, 1973.

31. NATIONAL SCIENCE FOUNDATION. *R&D In Industry*. Washington, D.C.: U.S.G.P.O., 1974.

32. _____ . *Science Resources Studies Highlight*. Washington, D.C.: U.S. G.P.O., 1976.

33. NOLL, ROGER. *Reforming Regulation: An Evaluation of the Ash Council Proposals*. Washington, D.C.: Brookings Institution, 1971.

34. PELTZMAN, SAM. *Regulation of Pharmaceutical Innovation: The 1962 Amendments*. Washington, D.C.: American Enterprise Institute for Public Research, 1974.

35. RASMUSSEN, JON A. "Applications of a Model of Endogeneous Technical Change to U.S. Industry Data," *Review of Economic Studies*, April 1973, *40*(122), pp. 225-38.

36. SCHWARTZMAN, DAVID. *Innovation in the Pharmaceutical Industry*. Baltimore: Johns Hopkins Univ. Press, 1976, pp. 136-61.

37. TERLECKYJ, NESTOR. "Sources of Productivity Change." New York: Columbia University, 1959, mimeo.

38. _____ . *The Effects of R&D on Productivity Growth of Industries: An Exploratory Study*. Washington, D.C.: National Planning Association, 1974.

39. U.S. DEPARTMENT OF COMMERCE. *Census of Manufacturers*. Washington, D.C.: U.S.G.P.O., 1977.

40. _____ , BUREAU OF ECONOMIC ANALYSIS. *Survey of Current Business*, August 1972, *52*(8), August 1977, *57*(8).

41. U.S. DEPARTMENT OF LABOR. *Earnings & Employment for the U.S. 1909-1965*, and *Monthly Labor Bulletin*, April 1976, *99*(4), April 1977, *100*(4). Washington, D.C.: U.S.G.P.O.

42. WHARTON SCHOOL OF BUSINESS AND COMMERCE. *Capacity Utilization Indexes*. Philadelphia: Univ. of Pennsylvania Press, 1977.

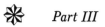 *Part III*

Investment by Industries

Chapter 6

The Distribution of
Investment between Industries:
A Microeconomic Application
of the "q" Ratio

George M. von Furstenberg,
Burton G. Malkiel and
Harry S. Watson

In the last few years a new variable, whose conceptual development and theoretical underpinning are credited to James Tobin, has begun to appear in investment equations. This variable, q, is defined as the market value of the equity securities and bonds of a firm divided by the replacement cost of its assets. In spite of its microeconomic origins, the rationale for q has generally been applied to the investment behavior of the aggregate of nonfinancial corporations [6, Ciccolo, 1975; 45, U.S. President, 1977, pp. 27–30; 18, von Furstenberg, 1977; 46, U.S. President, 1978, pp. 68–70]. It has also been used for integrating financial variables and expectational processes into macroeconomic theory [5, Brainard and Tobin, 1968; 40, Tobin, 1969; 41, Tobin, 1977; 7, Ciccolo, 1978; 28, Malkiel et al., 1979].[a] As a result, with few exceptions, only a single aggregate time series of q has been derived to help explain total investment behavior, and many microeconomic applications of the q-theory, for instance for corporate finance, have hitherto remained unexplored.

Using the Compustat tapes for the years 1956 through 1976 to derive balance sheet data which are revalued to market or to replacement cost as described in the appendix, this study chooses a lower

The authors are indebted to John C. Hinrichs, Frank Ripley, and Gary Fromm for data and other help.

[a]This literature has not yet been joined with ongoing microeconomic explorations of the efficiency of the stock market in the allocation of investment resources. For recent contributions to that literature and references, see Irwin Friend [17, 1972], Joram Mayshar [29, 1978], and Eugene Fama [14, 1978].

level of aggregation. By deriving time series for the q values applicable to the aggregation of Compustat firms by two-digit or three-digit SIC, representative q values are obtained for major manufacturing industries and for the utility sector, which can be related to the aggregate q ratio previously derived for the nonfinancial corporate sector as a whole.

While even more disaggregated analyses such as those conducted by Tobin and William Brainard [4, 1977] and John Ciccolo and Gary Fromm [8, 1979] are useful to explore the microeconomic applications of the q theory, the industry level of analysis can reveal systematic differences between distinct classes of assets. Franco Modigliani and Merton Miller [31, 1958, p. 267] have argued that their concept of fundamental risk classes of assets "while not identical to that of the industry, is at least closely related to it. Certainly the basic characteristics of the probability distributions of the returns on assets will depend to a significant extent on the product sold and the technology used." More recently, Miles Livingston [26, 1977, p. 873] has concluded that "the finding of clearcut residual industry patterns of comovements of stocks implies that security analysis of industry groups makes sense."

It turns out that the industry q's vary closely with the aggregate q. However, there is no observable tendency for the industry q's to converge to the same quasi-permanent equilibrium value. Rather, fast-growing and R&D-intensive industries have tended to maintain above-average q's and rates of return while industries with below-average q's have grown more slowly but still have not appeared to improve their q's. Even though the tendency for q values to be equilibrated between industries is very weak, the level of q that is characteristic for each has important implications not only for the growth rate of its stock of capital but also for how investors appear to react to and interpret changes in corporate financing.

Furthermore, while changes in the own q's have a statistically significant influence on gross investment rates in all industries, changes in own q divided by the coincident value of the aggregate q for the nonfinancial sector as a whole have no significant effect. Changes in these relative q's should signal shifts in the distribution of investment incentives between industries, because they should indicate changes in the fundamental position of industries vis-à-vis the average. Yet, partly because the variation in relative q's in any industry was small over the sample period, such shifts could not be confirmed statistically so that only changes in own q and not in relative q appeared to change industry investment rates.

I. CONSTRUCTION AND RATIONALE OF q

Unlike the older "valuation ratio" [see 13, Eriksson, 1978; 34, Reinhart, 1978], which usually employs readily ascertainable book values in the denominator, the measurement of q is quite difficult because the replacement cost of inventories, land, and of the net stock of plant and equipment owned by a firm is hard to estimate.[b] In the absence of direct price quotations or a ready market for capital assets in stock or in use, market values are approximated by simple procedures such as applying straight-line depreciation to the original cost of fixed capital and then converting the undepreciated balance from historical cost to replacement cost by use of price indexes applicable to broad classes of plant and equipment. Technological obsolescence is rarely dealt with explicitly in such estimates, and the replacement cost of capitalized research and development expenditures, which produce such assets as technical know-how and patents, is never included.[c]

Although the true value of q is thus not observable directly, this loss of precision is readily compensated for by the conceptual advantage of using the replacement cost rather than the book value of net assets in modeling investment decisions. Because of inflation, book values do not represent the market value of existing assets; rather they tend to understate that value systematically and to a sub-

[b] For firms whose securities are privately placed or not traded in a continuous market, the valuation of the liabilities also presents difficulties, but these difficulties are common both to traditional valuation ratios and to q.

[c] Neither the market value of patents nor the replacement cost of patents can readily be determined in most instances. Patents that constitute part of a development chain may be worth more to the firm which owns them than they could possibly be to anyone else, so that the reservation price may exceed the hypothetical price at which the patent can be sold. If all rents received by a firm from its employees, management enterprise, superior organization, market position, or inventiveness were capitalized and treated as part of the replacement cost of the assets of a firm, the measurement of the q ratio would be tautological. The replacement cost of capital would then come to depend on market structure and on the efficiency and profitability with which capital is used. Some balance sheet assets and many hidden assets are therefore excluded from the denominator of q advisedly. However, it is worth keeping in mind that to the extent a firm owes its high q to these excluded factors, it may increase "investment" in its employees, researchers, management, or market position, rather than acquiring more plant and equipment, inventories or net financial assets, all of which appear in the denominator of q. For example, Edward Greenberg et al. [21, 1978, p. 250] have suggested that "value-maximizing behavior may dictate that a firm attempt to change its product's price or income elasticities through advertising or quality changes. A firm may undertake an advertising policy designed to increase the extent to which consumers view its products as a necessity. If successful, such a policy would, *ceteris paribus*, reduce the product's income elasticity and bring about a decrease in the firm's risk."

Table 6−1. Illustration of Stock Dilution through Expansion When $q < 1$

Replacement Cost of Assets	Debt Value	Equity Value	Number of Shares Outstanding	Equity Value Per Share	—Including Dividend[a]
(0) No expansion					
200	50	50	50	1	1.04
(1) Debt-financed expansion					
202	52	49	50	0.98	1.02
(2) Equity-financed expansion					
202	50	51	52.04	0.98	1.02
(3) Internally financed expansion					
202	50	51	50	1.02	1.02

[a]The dividend is 0.04 per share in all cases except (3) where it is zero. It is added to equity value per share so that the holding period rate of return is equal to the entries in the last column minus 1.

stantial degree, particularly for long-lived fixed assets and for firms using the LIFO method of inventory accounting.[d] Thus, the market value of these assets must be inferred from the price of comparable new assets since it would be surprising indeed if the prices of new and existing assets differed systematically.

If the assumption that the prices of comparable units of new and existing assets tend to equality is built right into the construction of q, the same tendency might be expected to obtain between the price a firm is willing to pay for replacing its productive assets and the price financial investors put on claims to the earning power thereof. If financial investors are not willing to accord the firm a dollar increase in its market value for every dollar of new investment it plans to undertake, or, in other words, if the marginal value of q is not at least unity, a firm would create capital losses for present security owners by proceeding to invest.

In the absence of taxes this conclusion holds regardless of how the firm finances the expansion. As shown in the numerical examples of Table 6−1, an increase in short-term borrowing or debt (1), new stock issues (2), and increased earnings retention through suspending dividend payments for one year (3) all dilute equity value per share equally relative to the alternative of no expansion (0), if the marginal

[d]When second-hand assets are acquired through mergers or other means, they are sometimes written up to purchase cost. Thus, book values themselves may be a curious mixture of original cost and market value accounting.

q is less than 1. In that table both the marginal and the average value of q are assumed to be 0.5, and a 1 percent increase in the replacement cost of assets is assumed to be produced by $2.00 of real net investment. In each case the per share value of the equity plus the annual dividend (assumed to be 4 cents per share except when the investment is financed by retention) falls from $1.04 to $1.02 as a result of the marginal expansion from a fixed initial position. If management believes that financial investors are always right and know best what is good for them in both the short and the long run and if it further espouses maximization of risk-adjusted returns per share as its primary responsibility, clearly the investment should not be made.

Having illustrated this proposition, it can now be stated rigorously and generalized using the following notation and assumptions:

A = Replacement cost of net assets,

V = Market value of firm = $S + D$,

S = Market value of equity = $p_s N$,

p_s = Equity value per share (= price per share assuming only a single class of stock),

N = Number of (homogeneous) shares outstanding,

D = Market value of debt, assumed to be short term, so that the effect of changes in borrowing rates on D can be ignored,

q = V/A.

It follows from the definition of (average) q that $qA = V = S + D$. Hence the marginal q, dV/dA, is equal to the change in the market value of the firm produced by a unit increase in the replacement cost of assets, or

$$(dq/dA)A + q = (dp_s/dA)N + p_s(dN/dA) + dD/dA . \qquad (1)$$

Now with debt financing $dD/dA = 1$ and $dN/dA = 0$, so that

$$(dq/dA)A + q - 1 = (dp_s/dA)N . \qquad (2)$$

Dividing both sides of equation (2) by S and expanding on the LHS yields,

$$[((dq/dA)A + q - 1)/A] (A/V) (V/S) = (dp_s/dA)N/(p_s N), \text{ or}$$

$$(dp_s/dA)/(p_s/A) = [(dq/dA)A + q - 1]/[q(S/V)] . \qquad (3)$$

Conversely, with equity financing $p_s(dN/dA) = 1$ and $dD/dA = 0$. Substituting into equation (1) and proceeding as before again yields equation (3).

That equation shows that unless the marginal q, $q + (dq/dA)A$, is at least equal to unity, expansion ($dA > 0$) will reduce equity value per share at any one time when the only effect on q is assumed to stem from real net investment raising A. The relative price change, dp_s/p_s, per percentage change in the replacement cost of assets, dA/A, will be greater the higher the percentage of debt in the market value of the firm (D/V) or the smaller the percentage of equity (S/V). If the marginal q is equal to the average q, so that $dq/dA = 0$, the level of q itself determines whether or not expansion would be beneficial to shareholders. For a given rate of expansion a greater degree of leverage will then produce faster rates of stock dilution if $q < 1$ and higher rates of capital gains if $q > 1$. Thus if, unlike in Table 6−1, the initial leverage ratios differ, expansion will hurt the stockholders of the most highly levered firms or industries most, given a q below unity, as long as the market value of debt remains close to its face value.

Tax asymmetries can scramble these simple results and encourage reinvestment of earnings even when the marginal q is less than 1 [1, Auerbach, 1978]. For instance, if dividends were taxed at a marginal individual income rate of 60 percent while the present value of capital gains tax liabilities, deferred until realization, is 15 percent, the after-tax return per share would be only 1.6 percent with no expansion (0), but 1.7 percent in case (3) of Table 6−1. Earnings retention could thus be preferred to their pay-out as dividends, even though the marginal q is only one-half and the capital gain from reinvestment is only one-half as large as the amount retained.

Disregarding these important ramifications, the essence of Tobin's q theory is therefore that a marginal q of less than 1 deters investment while a marginal q greater than 1 stimulates additions to capacity. This tendency, however, is deduced from optimizing behavior based on the assumption of good stewardship of corporate managers and not on the automatic functioning of markets. Unlike the equilibration of the prices of new and existing assets, the equilibration of the replacement cost of assets and the market value of firms is therefore predicated on complex behavioral assumptions and a round-about adjustment process of capacities to required rates of return over cost established by the valuations of financial investors.

II. PROBLEMS OF APPLICATION

In practice, marginal as opposed to average q's are unobservable. The marginal q cannot even be inferred from changes in the average q over time since changes in the latter may stem not only from differences between the marginal q on new investments and a fixed average q on past investments but also from reassessments of the outlook and risks for a firm's past investments. Should new investment projects signal a major change in management aptitude, strategy or direction to financial investors, any change in q would still be due to the changed prospects for the entire business rather than to the new investment per se. Worse yet, even if the marginal q could be determined *ex post*, management would not generally be able to estimate its magnitude at the time new investments are planned and capital goods orders are placed. Frequently the reception accorded to its plans will transpire only after the investment decision has been taken and its consequences have been evaluated by financial investors. Obviously, therefore, Tobin's q theory would be of little use in explaining actual investment behavior if its empirical application depended on isolating a marginal q which is generally unobservable *ex post* and unknowable *ex ante*.

To surmount these difficulties, Tobin and Brainard [40, 1969; 42, 1977] have used average q values in the expectation that the marginal q's of firms or industries differ cross-sectionally or over time by about as much as the average q's. In other words, a drop in the average q signifies not only that the external cost of capital, particularly equity capital, to the firm has increased but also that the attractiveness of new investments, whether financed internally or externally, has declined.

It is easy to think of exceptions to this correlation. For instance, a drop in the average q may result when tax provisions are liberalized with respect to new investment. However, such a drop would be due to the additional investment induced by the rise in the marginal q relative to its required level. As another example, research intensive firms operating in dynamic markets cannot hope to recover or even to endure if investment is stopped. The laws of survival sometimes induce firms to look harder for new opportunities when the fortunes of their existing operations or products decline. A firm may thus discover highly profitable new investment opportunities just at the time when financial investors take a more jaundiced view of its traditional lines of business or location, causing the average q to fall. That firm, though handicapped by the higher cost of capital, may rationally decide to spend itself out of a low average q rather than attempt to raise its q by abstaining from new investments and shrinking. Industries that face stiff competition from domestic and foreign capacities can hardly count on abstinence to restore profit margins and to lift their q, particularly if there are cost-saving inventions to be embodied in new capacity.

The point of the Tobin-Brainard approach is that such situations are exceptions rather than the rule. It is also quite possible that firms with very low marginal as well as average q's relative to most other firms will continue to invest retained earnings more or less indefinitely. At least two studies [25, Little, 1966; 2, Baumol et al., 1970] have suggested that over certain historical periods there is reason to believe that retained earnings have been used by firms to finance more new investment than would have been efficient. Firms with a low marginal q may sometimes continue to expand their debt perhaps by trading on the "public spiritedness" or "civic responsibility" of hometown bankers or by seeking refuge under the protective umbrella of government regulations, credit guarantees, or contingent subsidies in the form of quotas, tariffs, or price supports. Even stock issues need not stop completely when they are clearly dilutive. Stockholders, one suspects, need not be the most important constituency of management in regulated and government-supported industries. In the utilities industry, for instance, much investment is, in effect, mandated to meet the requirements of the service area whatever the value of marginal q.

For these as well as tax reasons and because the true value of q cannot be determined precisely, it should never be assumed that investment will stop when the average or even the marginal q is less than one. What is important for the empirical application of the Tobin-Brainard theory is only that the estimates of q be sufficiently reliable to make the ranking of industries or firms by the estimated average value of q correspond closely, if not perfectly, with the ranking that would prevail if the true average value of q were known. The ranking by the estimated average values, in turn, must correlate highly with the unknown ranking by the marginal q's if the theory is to be useful operationally.

III. DIFFERENCES IN INDUSTRY q's

Even if the estimated average q's do effectively signal the relevant marginal q's, it may still take many years for firms to correct past investment mistakes that have saddled them with a chronically low q. Because of the heterogeneity and fixity of capital in use, firms cannot instantly convert their existing capital stock to different uses, change location, start new product lines, or divest themselves of unprofitable operations. Such operations may therefore continue as long as short-run marginal costs remain covered even if the market value of the capital stock involved is far below its estimated replacement cost.

Conversely, certain other firms, particularly those that are technological leaders in their fields and are protected from potential competitors by patents, by a considerable headstart, or by high entry costs, may have high q's which show little tendency to decline over time. Such firms may continue to have extraordinarily attractive investment opportunities and the degree of market power that comes from technological leadership [39, Thomadakis, 1977]. Thus the forces tending to drive q values back to equilibrium may be quite weak in many individual instances. Firms in fast-growing technology-intensive new industries may have higher q's than firms in technology-extensive old industries for long periods of time. A positive association between q and the growth rates of the capital stock would exist, but the tendency for q to be equalized between firms and industries would be weak.

The data in Table 6–2 indicate that differences in the q's of industry i (q_i) have, in fact, been pronounced and persistent over the period 1956–1976 covered in this study. While the highest annual q_i is generally at least twice as high as the lowest q_i of each range, the q_i's of textile mill products (22), petroleum and coal products (29), primary metals (33), basic steel and mill products (331), and the utilities (49) fall well short of unity during the entire period. The annual average values of their respective q_i's range from 0.47 to 0.64. By contrast, the q_i's of some other industries were rarely below unity in any year, with averages ranging from 1.43 to 1.65 calculated for chemicals and products (28), nonelectrical machinery (35), and electrical machinery (36).

Throughout Table 6–2 the coincidence of movements in the annual q_i's appears to be high. The q_i's of all but one of the sixteen industries listed in that table (foods) reach a low during the period 1974–1976. All of them show a peak (defined as a q_i value higher than that of the two surrounding years or more) in 1964 or 1965 and most have a second, though generally lower, peak in 1972. Since the aggregate q ratio of the nonfinancial corporate sector as a whole fol-

Table 6–2.   Characteristics of q_i by Industry

Industry (SIC)	Weights[a] w_i	Peak in 1964	Peak in 1965	Peak in 1972	Range of q_i Low (year)	Range of q_i High (year)	Average of q_i
Foods (20)	0.0686		x	x	0.682 (1957)	1.283 (1972)	1.035
Textile mill products (22)	0.0181		x	x	0.361 (1975)	0.850 (1968)	0.589
Paper and products (26)	0.0302	x		x	0.498 (1975)	1.032 (1956)	0.785
Chemicals and products (28)	0.1179	x		x	0.902 (1976)	1.785 (1961)	1.446
Petroleum and coal products (29)	0.3329	x			0.427 (1975)	0.833 (1956)	0.642
Rubber and plastics products (30)	0.0235		x	x	0.387 (1975)	1.186 (1959)	0.818
Clay, stone, and glass products (32)	0.0267	x		x	0.424 (1975)	1.141 (1959)	0.883
Primary metals (33)	0.0962	x		x	0.332 (1975)	0.833 (1956)	0.557
Basic steel & mill products (331)	—	x		x	0.272 (1974)	0.758 (1959)	0.468
Primary nonferrous metals (333)	—	x			0.483 (1975)	1.190 (1956)	0.786
Nonelectrical machinery (35)	0.0930		x	x	0.899 (1975)	2.237 (1968)	1.650
Electrical machinery (36)	0.0595		x	x	0.743 (1975)	1.870 (1965)	1.434
Transportation equipment (37)	0.1334		x	x	0.377 (1975)	1.182 (1965)	0.817
Motor vehicles and parts (371)	—	x			0.373 (1975)	1.254 (1964)	0.836
Aircraft and parts (372)	—		x	x	0.345 (1974)	1.258 (1965)	0.741
Utilities (49)	—		x	x	0.340 (1975)	0.695 (1961)	0.530
Entire nonfinancial corporate sector	—		x	x	0.612 (1975)	1.095 (1965)	0.846

Source: Appendix to this chapter and [18].

[a]These weights indicate the relative importance of each of the two-digit manufacturing industries shown in this table. The weights are shares of the replacement cost of assets (the denominator of q) estimated for 1972 and they add to 1.

lows a similar path, the coherence between movements in the industry q_i's and in the aggregate q is likely to be high.[e]

The high covariance between the q_i's and the aggregate q does not necessarily imply that q_i/q is stationary. Rather, the ratio of q_i to q may have been subject to persistent time trends as the relative attractiveness of particular industries for both real and financial investment may have changed gradually in recent decades. To the extent such trends exist, they are of course only descriptive of the sample period and not suitable for extrapolation since the pattern of industrial evolutions may change. Leaving the derivation of quasi-permanent equilibrium values of the q_i/q ratios to the next subsection, the equation used to reveal relations between the data for 1956 $(t=1)$ through 1976 $(t=21)$ is estimated in natural logarithms (log). Its specification including the error term u_i (not shown in subsequent estimating equations) and the intercept a_{0i} for each industry is

$$\log q_i = a_{0i} + a_{1i} \log q + a_{2i} t + u_i. \tag{4}$$

The results in Table 6-3 show that the a_{1i} coefficients are scattered around unity as expected. The q_i values in paper and products (26), petroleum and coal products (29), the primary metals sectors (33, 331, 333), and the utilities (49) are least responsive to movements in the aggregate q. Surprisingly, most of the annual exponential growth rates a_{2i}, are negative so that negative time trends predominate. Thus there appears to be a fairly widespread tendency for the q_i's of individual industries included in this study to start somewhat higher and to fall somewhat faster than the aggregate q over the sample period. Even the q_i for nonelectrical machinery (35) which includes major portions of the computer industry—also represented in parts of (36) and, to a small extent, in the excluded instruments industry (38)—does not show a positive trend relative to the average. The downward drift in so many q_i's is later shown to be reconcilable

---

[e]Calendar-year averages of the aggregate q were obtained from the quarterly values reported in [18, von Furstenberg, 1977]. With some cyclical interruptions, the q values for the twenty-one years from 1956 through 1976 form a first rising and then declining pattern, cresting in the mid-1960s. They are 0.765, 0.711, 0.727, 0.852, 0.833, 0.923, 0.874, 0.975, 1.042, 1.095, 0.977, 0.976, 0.994, 0.884, 0.710, 0.783, 0.849, 0.816, 0.684, 0.612, 0.680. The zero-order correlation coefficients between these q values and the coincident q_i values of each of the industries identified by its SIC number in parentheses were 0.79(20), 0.83(22), 0.53(26), 0.71(28), 0.56(29), 0.60(30), 0.69(32), 0.32(33), 0.25 (331), 0.40(333), 0.83(35), 0.84(36), 0.84(37), 0.87(371), 0.76(372), and 0.87(49).

Table 6–3.   Regression Results for the Logarithm of Industry q_i's

Industry (SIC)	Intercept a_{0i} (t-value)	Log q a_{1i} (t-value)	t a_{2i} (t-value)	$\bar{R}^2$	D.W.
Foods (20)	0.089 (2.04)	1.178 (8.32)	0.014 (3.80)	0.777	0.75
Textile mill products (22)	−0.436 (−7.64)	1.665 (9.00)	0.017 (3.56)	0.801	0.64
Paper and products (26)	0.054 (1.88)	0.467 (4.98)	−0.023 (−9.52)	0.883	1.78
Chemicals and products (28)	0.663 (17.24)	0.743 (5.95)	−0.018 (−5.63)	0.818	0.86
Petroleum and coal products (29)	−0.173 (−4.32)	0.499 (3.83)	−0.020 (−5.86)	0.762	0.82
Rubber and plastics products (30)	0.279 (5.60)	0.940 (5.80)	−0.035 (−8.54)	0.877	0.53
Clay, stone, and glass products (32)	0.334 (7.45)	1.028 (7.06)	−0.031 (−8.36)	0.890	0.58
Primary metals (33)	−0.131 (−4.23)	0.323 (3.21)	−0.044 (−16.96)	0.946	1.23
Basic steel & mill products (331)	−0.287 (−6.45)	0.216 (1.49)	−0.048 (−13.08)	0.908	0.91
Primary nonferrous metals (333)	0.170 (4.19)	0.446 (3.39)	−0.036 (−10.78)	0.887	1.31
Nonelectrical machinery (35)	0.731 (12.03)	1.322 (6.71)	−0.002 (−0.39)	0.707	0.55
Electrical machinery (36)	0.730 (16.64)	1.213 (8.51)	−0.018 (−5.00)	0.865	0.79
Transportation equipment (37)	0.289 (7.51)	1.410 (11.28)	−0.028 (−8.89)	0.933	1.08
Motor vehicles and parts (371)	0.294 (6.02)	1.573 (9.91)	−0.024 (−5.91)	0.898	1.03
Aircraft and parts (372)	0.215 (2.57)	1.567 (5.78)	−0.030 (−4.37)	0.777	0.85
Utilities (49)	−0.326 (−15.76)	0.541 (5.33)	−0.033 (−9.15)	0.971	1.29

with movements in q since the continuing redistribution of weights from slow-growing, low q_i industries to their opposites shores up the aggregate q.

While such drifts lessen the usefulness of the q_i/q ratios for indicating changes in comparative advantage in subsequent investment equations, they do not necessarily imply that the equilibrium values of q_i/q, inferred in the next subsection, are much below the average for the sample period. Rather the estimated equilibrium value of the relative q_i will be found to be far below its average only in industries such as primary metals (33), particularly basic steel (331), and the utilities (49) in which a strong negative time trend is expected from industry characteristics and confirmed statistically.

The Question of Convergence

To test the degree to which industry q values have tended to converge, annual percentage changes in the q of each industry i, $d \log q_i$, are regressed on percentage changes in the annual q for the nonfinancial corporate sector as a whole, $d \log q$, and on the ratio of q_i to q lagged one year. The resulting specification is

$$d \log q_i = a_{3i} + a_{4i} (d \log q) + a_{5i} (q_i/q)_{-1} . \qquad (5)$$

If there is a tendency for the industry q_i's to converge to q over the sample period 1956–1976, a low level of q_i relative to q should raise the expected percentage change in q_i and vice versa, so that the regression coefficient a_{5i} should be negative. The coefficient a_{4i} is analogous to an (industry) "beta" coefficient used in portfolio analysis; it shows the degree to which the industry q_i changes with the overall (market) q in percentage terms. Its magnitude should be comparable to that of a_{1i} in equation (4). However, the intercept a_{3i} should exceed a_{2i} by the product of a_{5i} and the industry mean of $(q_i/q)_{-1}$ if a_{5i} is negative as expected.

The regression results for equation (5) presented in Table 6–4 are again derived from annual data for the period 1956–1976 (1961–1976 in the utility sector). All two-digit SIC industries in manufacturing for which estimates of real gross investment and capital stocks are available from Data Resources, Inc. (DRI) as well as some three-digit industries in manufacturing plus the utility sector are shown.[f]

---

[f]The manufacturing industries represented here are identical to those analyzed by Robert Resek [35, 1966] for the period 1953–1962.

Table 6—4.   Regression Results for the Percentage Change in Industry q's, $d \log q_i$

Industry (SIC)	Intercept a_{3i} (t-value)	$d \log q$ a_{4i} (t-value)
Foods (20)	0.283 (2.01)	1.007 (5.99)
Textile mill products (22)	0.120 (0.99)	1.219 (6.02)
Paper and products (26)	0.215 (2.27)	0.893 (5.94)
Chemicals and products (28)	0.119 (0.90)	1.084 (6.82)
Petroleum and coal products (29)	0.181 (2.07)	0.849 (6.01)
Rubber and plastics products (30)	−0.039 (−0.43)	0.946 (5.01)
Clay, stone & glass products (32)	−0.018 (−0.18)	0.926 (5.27)
Primary metals (33)	0.048 (0.84)	0.641 (4.15)
Basic steel & mill products (331)	0.016 (0.26)	0.651 (3.38)
Primary nonferrous metals (333)	0.142 (1.60)	0.605 (2.88)
Nonelectrical machinery (35)	0.199 (1.10)	1.212 (5.54)
Electrical machinery (36)	0.142 (0.98)	1.362 (7.22)
Transportation equipment (37)	0.119 (1.08)	1.360 (6.99)
Motor vehicles and parts (371)	0.168 (1.22)	1.465 (6.15)
Aircraft and parts (372)	0.207 (1.54)	1.293 (3.76)
Utilities (49)	0.076 (0.68)	0.725 (5.88)
All 2-digit manufacturing industries[b]	0.001 (1.07)	0.921 (18.62)

[a]Not applicable or meaningless. Figures in second-last column calculated from unrounded numbers.

[b]The weights used in the pooled regression are the industry shares of the replacement cost of assets (the denominator of q) in 1972. They are shown in the first column of Table 6–2.

With twenty observations remaining after the construction of the lagged explanatory variable, the t-values with seventeen degrees of freedom would have to exceed 1.74 for regression coefficients to be significantly different from zero at the 5 percent level in a one-tailed test. On this basis Table 6—4 shows that the beta-like coefficient a_{4i} is highly significant in all industries. It ranges from a high of 1.47 for motor vehicles and parts (371) to a low of 0.61 for primary non-ferrous metals. Pooling the observations, weighted by the 1972 replacement cost of assets, over all two-digit manufacturing industries considered yields a coefficient on $d \log q$ that is almost significantly less than 1. This suggests that the selection of industries may not

Table 6—4. continued

$(q_i/q)_{-1}$			$(q_i/q)^*$	q_i/q
a_{5i} (t-value)	$\bar{R}^2$	D.W.	$-(a_{3i}/a_{5i})$	Average
−0.224 (−1.96)	0.681	1.83	1.266	1.224
−0.168 (−0.97)	0.677	1.45	0.714	0.690
−0.253 (−2.54)	0.649	1.82	0.851	0.936
−0.082 (−1.07)	0.702	1.66	1.455	1.713
−0.267 (−2.39)	0.665	2.05	0.677	0.766
0.006 (0.07)	0.573	1.25	NA[a]	0.964
−0.013 (−0.14)	0.594	1.49	NA[a]	1.040
−0.127 (−1.55)	0.448	1.65	0.381	0.664
−0.085 (−0.78)	0.334	1.40	0.193	0.558
−0.191 (−2.08)	0.310	1.84	0.747	0.936
−0.104 (−1.13)	0.636	1.31	1.910	1.939
−0.093 (−1.11)	0.725	1.42	1.528	1.684
−0.152 (−1.36)	0.713	1.34	0.782	0.954
−0.194 (−1.42)	0.654	1.29	0.865	0.973
−0.281 (−1.89)	0.460	1.53	0.737	0.860
−0.167 (−0.93)	0.719	1.83	0.453	0.607
−0.030 (−3.89)	0.622	NA[a]	NA[a]	1.105

be entirely representative of the nonfinancial corporate sector as a whole.

To the extent percentage changes in q_i and q are similar, there is little room for individual q_i's to converge to q if there are differences between q_i and q to start with. Rather, the initial percentage spreads will tend to be preserved. Thus Table 6—4 shows that the tendency toward convergence is statistically insignificant in most industries and minute in the pooled equation for all manufacturing industries combined. While a_{5i} is almost always negative as expected, only foods (20), paper and products (26), petroleum and coal products (29), primary nonferrous metals (333) and aircraft and parts (372) have q_i's with a significant tendency to converge to q. In these same industries, and only in these, the intercept, a_{3i}, tends to be positive significant. The upward time drifts revealed after adding a_{5i} times the mean of $(q_i/q)_{-1}$ is reined in by a negative a_{5i} if the average of $(q_i/q)_{-1}$ exceeds unity, as in industry (20). In the other four industries a downward time drift is braked by a_{5i} being negative.[g]

The normal level of the ratio of q_i to q can be inferred for all industries by setting $d \log q$ equal to zero in equation (5) and then asking what q_i/q would have to be for $d \log q_i$ to be zero also. The stationary value of that ratio, which may be interpreted as a quasi-permanent equilibrium inferred from the results for the sample period as distinct from a true long-term equilibrium, is therefore

$$(q_i/q)^* = -a_{3i}/a_{5i} . \tag{6}$$

A comparison of the last two columns of Table 6–4 shows that both $(q_i/q)^*$ and the simple twenty-one-year average of the (q_i/q) values for each industry i can differ greatly from unity. Furthermore, the two measures agree quite closely for most i except in a few cases where $(q_i/q)^*$ is implausibly low. Hence, to the extent the estimates of $(q_i/q)^*$ are to be believed, they do not show that the quasi-permanent equilibrium values of q_i/q lie any closer together than the raw averages.

While useful in supporting this conclusion, the $(q_i/q)^*$ values should be treated with some skepticism. One such value was negative (industry 32) and one other dynamically unstable (industry 30) and all the values had to be calculated from coefficients which, with few exceptions, were not significant statistically. Thus it is probably preferable to use the period averages of q_i/q in each industry to represent the quasi-permanent equilibrium of that ratio. The next section, then, attempts to relate enduring industry differences in $(q_i/q)_{av.}$ to differences in industry fundamentals.

IV. FACTORS IN THE GROWTH OF INDUSTRY CAPITAL

If the average annual levels of the relative industry q_i's, $(q_i/q)_{av.}$, show little tendency to converge, there may well be other economic

[g]The mean value of $(q_i/q)_{-1}$ is 1.226 in industry (20), 0.939 in (26), 0.770 in (29), 0.944 in (333), and 0.871 in (372) yielding a time trend of 0.008 in the q_i of industry (20), -0.023 in (26), -0.025 in (29), -0.038 in (333), and -0.038 in (372). These trends are annual exponential rates of growth or decline, and are similar in magnitude to those found in Table 6-3 (a_{2i}) with a simpler specification.

factors, such as growth rates of demand and capital invested, which differ by industry for extended periods. Furthermore, research intensiveness in relation to investment (R/I) and a high rate of return (ρ) presumably make for a high $(q_i/q)_{av.}$. These two variables will be discussed in turn before the matrix showing the zero-order correlation coefficients between all the variables listed in Table 6−5 is presented later in this section. Thereafter, a potentially causal relationship will be estimated between the trend rate of growth of the real gross stock of capital in industry i, g_i, the trend rate of growth of real output, z_i, as well as $(q_i/q)_{av.}$, ρ_i, and $(R/I)_i$. The associative relationship between $(q_i/q)_{av.}$ and the dividend/price ratio, $(DIV/MVE)_i$, as well as the percentage of debt in total market value, $(LD/MVT)_i$, and what it implies for financial analysis in the light of the q theory will be discussed also.

Research Intensiveness

The direction of causation among growth, spending on research, and the level of q_i is difficult to determine. Noting from column 4 of Table 6−5 that research efforts are highest in chemicals (28), aircraft (372), and the machine-building industries (35, 36) suggests, however, that research, expressed as a percentage of gross investment, is highest in fast-changing industries in which patented products and processes coupled with the successful introduction of new products are crucial to the continuing success of a firm and present unusually profitable investment opportunities. Research efforts thus seem designed to capture technological growth opportunities in these industries and to establish and defend market power and international dominance that stem from technological leadership. A high degree of research intensiveness and growth, high industry rates of return on the replacement cost of assets, and a high $(q_i/q)_{av.}$ thus mutually condition and reinforce each other, though as shown by the aircraft industry, the association of research intensiveness with high rates of return may not hold in all instances.

The variable for the research spending by industry was constructed by taking annual averages of the ratio of R&D expenses to total capital expenditures. These ratios can be calculated from the Compustat tapes for most or all of the years since 1972 in each industry. R&D includes development expenses which account for over 90 percent of total R&D in transportation equipment (37) and motor vehicles and parts (371). Development expenses may forge the link from basic and applied R&D to current sales and profits but they are not necessarily the manna of future growth and profits that will nourish q.

Table 6—5. Statistics Estimated by Industry, Annual Averages for
1956—1976 *(percent)*

| Industry | ρ | Exponential Annual Growth Rates | |
		Output $(z)^a$	Capital $(g)^a$
Column:	(1)	(2)	(3)
Foods (20)	5.57	3.24	3.01
Textile mill products (22)	3.90	4.24	1.66
Paper and products (26)	4.55	4.58	4.72
Chemicals and products (28)	5.91	7.24	4.68
Petroleum & coal products (29)	4.56	3.50	2.40
Rubber & plastics products (30)	4.73	8.55	6.59
Clay, stone, & glass products (32)	4.80	3.20	4.23
Primary metals (33)	3.48	2.50	1.75
Basic steel & mill products (331)	3.38	1.69	0.71
Primary nonferrous metals (333)	4.15	3.94	5.08
Nonelectrical machinery (35)	6.27	5.29	6.10
Electrical machinery (36)	6.12	6.68	6.08
Transportation equipment (37)	3.52	3.19	2.85
Motor vehicles and parts (371)	3.98	3.96	2.96
Aircraft and parts (372)	1.37	1.17	4.55
Utilities (49)	3.69	6.26	5.47

[a]The growth rates z for output and g for capital are the regression estimates of a_1 in the log-linear form of $X(t) = a_0 e^{a_1 t}$, where $X(t)$ at time t is either an average annual Federal Reserve [3] index of industrial production (Q) or the DRI estimate of the real gross stock of capital (K) by industries. The lowest t-value on a_1 for Q is 2.23 in industry 372 and the lowest for K is 10.57 in industry 331. Since instantaneous growth rates are reported, the growth rate of the output-capital ratio can be inferred by subtracting each entry in column 3 from the corresponding entry in column 2. To obtain cyclically comparable endpoints, data for 1954 and 1955 were included in all regressions.

We therefore used the National Science Foundation's [32, 1974 et seq.] estimates of the distribution of R&D expenditures by industry among the basic, applied, and development categories to obtain annual percentages of basic and applied R&D in the total.[h] These estimates were available for some or all of the years 1971—1975,

[h]The NSF information was spotty for industries 331, 333, 37, and 371, and the communications industry (48) was included in industry (36). No breakdown was available for the utilities (49) whose minute reported R&D expenses were all assumed to be for basic or applied research rather than for development.

Table 6-5. continued

Research Expense/ Capital Expenditures[b] (R/I)	Common Dividends/ Market Value of Common Equity[c] (DIV/MVE)	(Market Value of) Long-Term Debt/ Total Liabilities[c] (LD/MVT)
(4)	(5)	(6)
3.61	3.21	12.07
11.03	4.26	25.48
3.63	3.57	20.41
34.93	2.82	8.77
3.18	3.96	13.32
8.79	3.31	24.75
6.09	3.39	15.91
11.32	4.28	25.97
6.97	4.85	25.03
13.78	3.60	28.57
15.36	1.85	8.96
27.27	2.53	10.19
10.10	4.73	10.97
3.26	4.96	8.42
33.50	3.07	22.04
0.88	4.80	39.71

[b]Capital expenditures represent the amount spent for the construction and/or acquisition of property, plant, and/or equipment as stated on the Compustat tapes. Research and development expense is the amount charged to operations, with development expenses excluded through the application of percentages derived from [32] as described below.

[c]Compustat and authors' estimates of market values described in the Appendix.

which span one recent business cycle. Averaging the annual percentages of basic and applied research in the total for the years for which such information is available in each industry then yielded factors that were used to net out the development component. The remainder, $(R/I)_i$, is the figure shown in percent of gross investment (annual capital expenditures) in Table 6-5.

Rates of Return

Though combination of a high $(R/I)_i$ with low growth and with low $(q_i/q)_{av.}$ is anomalous, the aircraft industry (372) shows that research intensiveness may fail to boost the relative q if rates of return are low and the dependence on government research contracts high. However, in the absence of significant interindustry differences in required risk premiums,[i] the relation between average rates of return and $(q_i/q)_{av.}$ should be particularly close. Persistent differences in both should correlate positively between industries as financial investors in an efficient market bid up the market value of corporations in industries with high rates of return on the replacement cost of their assets to equalize expected financial returns between assets at current market prices. A high $(q_i/q)_{av.}$, in turn, should be associated with a high trend rate of growth of capital, g_i, since high rates of return may not generally be maintained through restrictive or monopolistic practices checking the expansion of industry capacity.[j] Rather, leadership in the development of new products and markets and generation of new and cost-cutting technological capabilities provides the dynamic foundation for a high relative q_i.

Unfortunately the derivation of the correct real rates of return from Compustat data is fraught with difficulties. The replacement cost of all assets on which the firm must earn a return is available as a by-product of the industry q calculations described in the appendix. Hence construction of the denominator of the rate of return variable presents no new problems. However, adding interest expense and subtracting interest income,[k] an item that is reported on the Compustat tapes since 1969, to earnings before extraordinary items and discontinued operations yields a measure that still does not agree with the economic concept of the after-tax return on total capital invested. The reason, of course, is inflation.

For firms using the first-in, first-out (FIFO) method of inventory accounting, the cost of inventories which is charged against operating revenues is understated to the extent inflation has raised the replacement cost of inventories above their original acquisition cost. Furthermore, even accelerated book depreciation has tended to fall short of straight-line replacement-cost depreciation to an increasing extent since 1974. In the national income accounts, an inventory valuation adjustment (IVA) and a capital consumption adjustment (CCA) are

[i]Kenneth Clarkson [9, 1977, p. 63] finds that risk may have been overstated in previous inquiries into interindustry differentials in rates of return.

[j]Clarkson [9, 1977, p. 22] also observes that "the traditional reasons given for differences in rates of return among industries where prices and entry are not regulated (entry barriers, concentration) do not produce major rate-of-return differentials." However, there seems little question that "a powerful firm, i.e., a large firm and/or a firm in a concentrated industry, seems to be confronted by lower costs to attract capital than a non-powerful firm" [37, Sullivan, 1978].

[k]The netting of interest income against interest expenses matches the netting of short-term liabilities against financial assets in the construction of industry q_i's described in the appendix.

therefore made to reported profits. However, there is simply no information about depreciation rules and service lives that would allow CCA to be calculated for the industry aggregates of Compustat firms. By failing to make this adjustment, the average annual rates of return for the period 1969–1976, shown in Table 6–5, may overstate the true economic rate of return in all or most industries. Fortunately, the overstatement is likely to be slight since the CCA for the non-financial corporate sector as a whole was negative only in the last three years included in the average.

The IVA is more critical for making rates of return comparable between industries. Inventory prices have tended to rise unevenly in different industries. Moreover, inventory accounting methods also differ by industry. To obtain annual estimates of the industry IVAs we first calculated the implicit deflators for inventories. For this, replacement cost data for industry inventories, supplied by the Bureau of Economic Analysis, were related to quarterly constant-cost estimates appearing in the May 1976, August 1976, August 1977, and November 1977 issues of the *Survey of Current Business.*[1] During 1974, the resulting fourth-quarter to fourth-quarter percentage changes in the constructed deflators ranged from a high of 53 percent in petroleum and coal products (29) to a low of 5 percent in textile mill products (22). Furthermore, in recent years, the percentage of industry inventories that was subject to FIFO accounting (the FIFO percentage), which was inferred from codes appearing on the Compustat tapes since 1971, ranged from a high of 96 percent in primary steel (331) to a low of 7 percent in aircraft and parts (372), as best could be determined from Compustat information.[m]

---

[1]Because of missing detail, the deflators for textile mill products (22) and clay, stone, and glass products (32) had to be extracted from the "other non-durables" and "other durables" categories, respectively. The assumptions made for all other industries are the same as those described under item (1) in the appendix.

[m] Since 1971, the inventory accounting methods used by corporations have been identified by codes appearing on the Compustat tapes. Summing all LIFO inventories reported by the corporations in any industry and dividing by total Compustat inventories in that industry then yields the annual LIFO percentage for each. This percentage was generally steady from 1971 through 1973. Because of higher inflation, it then jumped from 1973 to 1974 to a new steady level maintained through 1976. The two percentages, the first of which was assumed to apply to 1969-1973 and the second to 1974-1976 inventories, are reported below with the industry numbers (in parentheses) to which they refer. Only industries (32), (37), (371), and (372) did not follow this two-tier pattern so that the LIFO percentages for these industries had to be reported differently. For the other industries they are 10, 17 (20); 9, 35 (22); 25, 54 (26); 7, 45 (28); 30, 58 (29); 0, 66 (30); 62, 82 (33); 86, 96 (331); 30, 70 (333); 19, 38 (35); 31, 45 (36); 0, 10 (49). For industry (32) the LIFO percentages is 0 for 1969-1972, 14 for 1973, and 67 thereafter. For industries (37), (371), and (372) they are all 0

Assuming a one-year turnover period for inventories, a crude IVA was therefore calculated by multiplying the book value of inventories in each industry by the complement of its LIFO percentage to estimate FIFO inventories which are in turn multiplied by the rate of inventory price inflation in any year. The resulting annual earnings with the IVA, divided by the replacement cost of total assets, were then averaged in each industry over the period 1969–1976 to obtain rough estimates of the rates of return, ρ_i. Given that industry rates of return are still frequently measured in a more hidebound fashion based on book value accounting, we present our estimates of the annual rates of return in Table 6–6. In spite of their crudeness, the impression that real after-tax rates of return on total industry assets generally average less than 6 percent in the United States is overwhelming. It is also broadly compatible with previous estimates [18, von Furstenberg, 1977, p. 397] for the nonfinancial corporate sector as a whole over the period 1952–1976.[n] Nevertheless, the inability to include earlier years in the average used to obtain ρ_i as well as $(R/I)_i$ is regrettable since all the other variables shown in Table 6–5 refer to annual averages for the entire sample period, 1956–1976, within each industry.

Pairwise Correlations and the Growth of Capital

The interindustry correlation between ρ_i and $(q_i/q)_{av.}$ of over 0.7 shown in Table 6–7 suggests a fairly tight correlation between the two, and $(q_i/q)_{av.}$ is, in turn, highly correlated with g_i. This holds for the full set of industries, as well as for the two-digit manufacturing industries, shown in the second panel of the table, alone. In addition, the trend growth rate of output, z_i, correlates closely with g_i between industries and its correlation with both ρ_i and $(q_i/q)_{av.}$ is about one-half. The correlation between $(R/I)_i$ and $(q_i/q)_{av.}$ is also about one-half, but the other pairwise correlations with $(R/I)_i$ are weaker.

In general all of these factors condition and influence each other and the direction of causation is mutual. Nevertheless, one may treat

---

for 1969-1973; 7, 8, and 0 for 1974; 7, 8, and 3 for 1975; and 48, 61, and 7 for 1976, respectively. The complement of these percentages is assumed to be the FIFO percentage used in the calculation of the IVA.

[n]The average rate of return on the replacement cost of depreciable fixed capital, inventories and land was estimated to be 5.3 percent in that source implying a rate of return of 4.7 percent on the replacement cost of total assets, including net non-interest bearing financial assets, which account for about 12 percent of total assets.

Table 6-6. Estimated Rates of Return *(including IVA)* **on the Replacement Cost of Industry Assets, 1969-1976** *(percent)*

Industry (SIC)	1969	1970	1971	1972	1973	1974	1975	1976
Foods (20)	5.30	6.65	5.50	4.70	2.77	2.69	9.06	7.88
Textile mill products (22)	4.56	3.28	4.68	4.24	2.92	5.26	2.35	3.91
Paper and products (26)	4.75	3.82	3.51	4.20	4.39	5.29	5.01	5.45
Chemicals and products (28)	6.20	6.07	5.82	7.07	6.18	2.64	6.37	6.90
Petroleum and coal products (29)	4.62	4.37	4.62	4.15	3.49	5.79	4.42	5.02
Rubber and plastics products (30)	5.84	4.57	5.69	5.57	5.82	2.05	4.31	3.99
Clay, stone, and glass products (32)	5.63	4.70	3.76	4.51	5.42	4.44	4.77	5.16
Primary metals (33)	3.51	3.26	2.55	3.03	3.29	5.65	3.53	3.00
Basic steel & mill products (331)	3.13	2.37	2.30	2.73	3.62	6.14	3.73	3.02
Primary nonferrous products (333)	5.16	5.69	3.35	3.95	3.15	5.17	3.41	3.34
Nonelectrical machinery (35)	6.53	6.26	5.89	6.62	6.28	4.00	7.24	7.35
Electrical machinery (36)	5.62	6.04	6.30	7.84	5.53	4.68	6.08	6.86
Transportation equipment (37)	4.75	2.62	4.61	5.94	3.57	-0.96	2.00	5.60
Motor vehicles & parts (371)	5.16	2.28	5.36	6.61	5.74	-1.72	2.07	6.31
Aircraft and parts (372)	2.75	2.13	1.26	3.93	-1.73	-2.26	1.58	3.28
Utilities (49)	3.50	3.60	3.56	3.68	3.74	3.85	3.73	3.85

Table 6-7. Pairwise Correlations across Industries

	$(q_i/q)_{av.}$	z_i	ρ_i	$(R/I)_i$	$(DIV/MVE)_i$	$(LD/MVT)_i$
	A. Excluding industries (33) and (37)					
g_i	0.533	0.661	0.336	0.324	-0.621	0.017
$(q_i/q)_{av.}$		0.436	0.765	0.535	-0.843	-0.710
z_i			0.595	0.125	-0.290	-0.021
ρ_i				0.013	-0.543	-0.569
$(R/I)_i$					-0.594	-0.285
$(DIV/MVE)_i$						0.500
	B. Excluding industries (331), (333), (371), (372), and (49)					
g_i	0.687	0.790	0.694	0.369	-0.782	-0.300
$(q_i/q)_{av.}$		0.501	0.908	0.681	-0.894	-0.752
z_i			0.531	0.576	-0.555	-0.078
ρ_i				0.516	-0.953	-0.663
$(R/I)_i$					-0.468	-0.420
$(DIV/MVE)_i$						0.511

the trend growth rate of capital, g_i, as the dependent variable, on the theory that a high level of $(q_i/q)_{av.}$, ρ_i, and perhaps $(R/I)_i$, and rapidly growing demand for an industry's products revealed by a large z_i stimulate the growth of the real capital stock by industry. Because there are only eleven observations, equal to the number of two-digit manufacturing industries examined in this chapter, and because multicollinearity is high, alternative pairs of explanatory variables will be run to see which appear to be the most robust. Furthermore, the intercept was suppressed since it proved statistically insignificant in half the runs and minute in all. The estimating equations, weighted by the 1972 replacement cost of the real stock of capital as explained in Table 6−9, will then be selected from

$$g_i = a_6 \, (q_i/q)_{av.} + a_7 \, z_i + a_8 \, \rho_i + a_9 \, (R/I)_i \, . \qquad (7)$$

The results in the top half of Table 6−8 show that interindustry differences in $(R/I)_i$ help explain interindustry differences in g_i only if $(R/I)_i$ is run in conjunction with ρ_i. The latter variable itself pales if run with z_i (run 3). However, relating the trend growth of capital to the trend growth of output alone (run 4) explains very little economically except that interindustry differences in g_i are less than interindustry differences in z_i since the coefficient on z_i is significantly less than 1.

The results in the bottom half of Table 6−8 are more revealing. They show that interindustry differences in g_i are highly correlated with the corresponding differences in $(q_i/q)_{av.}$ and that adding any of the other three variables does not improve the fit. A one point difference in $(q_i/q)_{av.}$, which has not been unusual between high q and low q industries, is associated with a 3 percentage point difference in their g_i's. Although one must be cautious in view of the high degree of collinearity and the small number of observations, we doubt that this result is a quirk or highly sample-specific. Since the input variables themselves generally represent twenty-one-year averages of particular rates, durable relations ought to be revealed by the regressions. The close association between $(q_i/q)_{av.}$ and g_i may very well be causal and it shows that q-type variables may have useful cross-sectional applications, as Michael Lovell [27, 1977, p. 400] has suggested.

Financial Considerations

Since $(q_i/q)_{av.}$ was found to be the single most important determinant of the trend growth rate of capital by industry, the implica-

420 Investment by Industries

Table 6–8. Weighted Regression Results for the Trend Rate of Growth of Real Industry Capital, g_i^a

Run	$(q_i/q)_{av.}$ a_6 (t-value)	z_i a_7 (t-value)	ρ_i a_8 (t-value)	$(R/I)_i$ a_9 (t-value)	$\bar{R}^2$
(1)			0.538 (7.45)	0.051 (1.95)	0.761
(2)		0.775 (8.53)		-0.012 (-0.42)	0.812
(3)		0.609 (2.76)	0.120 (0.62)		0.816
(4)		0.743 (15.14)			0.827
(5)	0.021 (2.64)	0.240 (1.23)			0.892
(6)	0.027 (3.98)		0.070 (0.48)		0.877
(7)	0.033 (11.22)			-0.022 (-0.98)	0.886
(8)	0.030 (18.80)				0.886

[a]The weights used for each of the two-digit industries in manufacturing are shown in Table 6-9. The coefficient of determination, $\bar{R}^2$, is adjusted for degrees of freedom throughout this chapter.

tions of the q theory for financial ratios are worth exploring. From Table 6–7, a strong inverse pairwise correlation is evident between $(q_i/q)_{av.}$ and both the dividend-price ratio, $(DIV/MVE)_i$, and the percentage of long-term debt in the market value of total liabilities, $(LD/MVT)_i$. The lower the relative q_i and hence the marginal q_i compared to other industries, the greater is the dividend-price ratio and the higher is the share of the market value of long-term debt in total value. What can possibly explain this association?

In earlier sections it was shown that if the marginal q_i is less than unity, expansion, no matter how financed, will create capital losses for existing shareholders starting from a given financial position. Furthermore, if the initial leverage ratios differ, stockholders may be hurt more by a given expansion the greater the degree of leverage.

This readily explains why those who hold stock in low $(q_i/q)_{av.}$ industries require a high dividend return on the market value of their common equity. For them, earnings retention does not carry the promise of at least equivalent capital gains on a fixed number of shares but rather the prospect of inadequate returns to stockholders. They would therefore want the firm to use internally generated funds to pay dividends. If the firm does not increase its pay-out ratio and reduce the rate of investment,[o] this dismal prospect will drive down stock prices, thereby raising dividend-price ratios by shrinkage in the denominator. Consequently firms with relatively low q's will tend to have high dividend-price ratios. More generally, increases in pay-out ratios that are accompanied by reduced investment will be welcomed by financial investors if the marginal q is below unity and frowned upon in the opposite case, unless tax considerations [1, Auerbach, 1978] modify this conclusion.[p]

---

[o]In fact, the ratios of dividends paid plus own stock repurchased to total earnings before extraordinary items and discontinued operations, calculated from Compustat information for each of the years 1971 through 1976 and then averaged for each industry, did not vary systematically with $(q_i/q)_{av}$. For instance, the ratio was 43 percent in basic steel (331), which has the lowest relative q, and 42 percent in electrical machinery (36), which has one of the highest. For utilities (49), the estimated ratio of 35 percent is beset with data problems and not comparable on account of the inclusion of allowances for funds used during construction in reported income. Such allowances are capitalized in the rate base, as actual or imputed interest expenses are treated as part of the cost of construction, but they do not add to cash flow in the year made.

[p]The crucial nature of the assumption that expectations are independent from financial policy in proofs of the irrelevance of corporate financial policy has been pointed out by Joseph Stiglitz [36, 1977, p. 861]. If it should turn out that expectations regarding the planned rate of expansion of the real stock of capital are a function of the financial policy of the firm, then its valuation will be affected. Empirically, Phoebus Dhrymes and Mordecai Kurz [10, 1967, p. 463] have found "a significant degree of interdependence between the investment and dividend decisionmaking processes."

These novel implications of the q theory show that the irrelevance of pay-out ratios to share prices, which has been asserted by others, can only be deduced from models in which either the marginal q is assumed to be unity at all times or the rate of investment is independent of the pay-out ratio in spite of considerable empirical evidence to the contrary.[q] Apart from these special cases, anything a firm does to reduce the rate of investment will be beneficial to shareholders if the marginal q is less than 1 and unfavorable otherwise. Increased dividend payments and buy-back of own shares or debt in the open market may be such actions.[r]

The high leverage ratios of many of the industries with low $(q_i / q)_{av.}$ are less readily explained. Certainly stockholders do not favor debt-financed expansion in such industries since it accelerates stock dilution from continuing expansion as leverage rises over time. A firm that has a q of 0.5 and a market value of $50 initially without debt can only issue a maximum of $100 in debt to buy an additional $100 of assets before equity is wiped out if q remains at one-half and

---

[q]Modigliani and Miller [31, 1958, p. 266] have provided a clear statement of this proposition: "As long as management is presumed to be acting in the best interests of shareholders, retained earnings can be regarded as equivalent to fully subscribed, pre-emptive issue of common stock. Hence, for present purposes, the division of the stream between cash dividends and retained earnings in any period is a mere detail." Since they define investment as worth undertaking if the project, as financed, raises the market value of a firm's shares (p. 264), they are assuming that the marginal $q \geq 1$ for firms utilizing retained earnings. This assumption, though appealing in theory, is probably not descriptive of actual firm behavior which is frequently nonoptimal from the standpoint of financial theory. Firms appear to have relatively fixed target pay-out ratios which are rarely changed on account of q. Furthermore, the independence of the average cost of capital to any firm of its capital structure and form of financing postulated by Modigliani and Miller (p. 269) does not easily square with the decision process of corporate managers. In particular, because of transaction costs, the perceived cost of internal funds has frequently been found to be below that of external funds [2, Baumol et al., 1970; 20 Grabowski and Mueller, 1975], though some of the inferences previously drawn from these findings have recently been challenged [30, McFetridge, 1978].

[r]Tobin and Brainard [42, 1977, p. 257] interpret their results for a sample of firms with estimated q's generally far in excess of unity as showing that "the stock market likes leverage (contradicting Modigliani-Miller), and for given leverage prefers pay-out of common stock earnings to their retention." They do not comment on the implications of the q theory for financial structure or link any of their findings to the level of the marginal q. The theoretical implications brought out in the present paper are that while the market should like leverage for firms with $q > 1$, it should be averse to increased pay-out by such firms provided increased pay-out signifies reduced investment. By contrast, Allan Taub's [38, 1975, p. 415] finding that there is a positive impact on the firm's desired debt-equity ratio when the difference between the return to the firm and the long-term rate of interest (and hence q) increases, is entirely in line with our expectations though it is perhaps beclouded by the unclear treatment of financial (leverage) risk.

the debt stays at par.[s] The mere prospect of such a development could quickly reduce the market value of common equity in the total, thereby raising $(LD/MVT)_i$. If the consequences of debt-financed expansion by industries with low q's are potentially so dire for stockholders, why does it still occur?

Systematic explanations are difficult to find. It should be noted, however, that some firms are in effect "forced" to make substantial real investments even when their marginal q's are less than unity because they cannot back out of prior commitments or regulatory impositions. An example would be electric utilities. The public service aspect of their business requires them to invest in sufficient generating capacity to meet the needs of their service area even if such investment does not appear to be in the interests of their shareholders.

Although the considerations entering into rate-setting by regulators have been modeled in several different ways [12, Elton and Gruber, 1971], most utilities are faced with a difficult financing dilemma. Over time these firms have attracted a clientele of shareholders who require maintenance of high dividends since capital gains prospects are dim. This has tended to rule out much use of retained earnings for new investments. Moreover, new issues of equity have appeared far too expensive to utility managements since required rates of return on equity appear to have risen to the 13–15 percent range, whereas allowed rates of return on book value have tended to be considerably lower. In fact, Table 6–6 shows that the (adjusted) real after-tax rates of return on total assets at replacement cost never exceeded 4 percent in any year from 1969 through 1976. In such circumstances many utility managements have been reluctant to sell common stock, especially since such sales would have to be made at prices below book value in recent years, thus diluting not only market value per share but even book value per share.

Utility managements have therefore been left with the alternative of financing investment largely by new debt issues. While they are aware of the proposition that the marginal cost of debt includes the increase in the required return on equity [31, Modigliani and Miller, 1958], they have believed that the marginal cost of debt is lower than the marginal cost of equity because of the tax advantage of debt financing. Furthermore, in the political environment in which utility

---

[s]If expansion continues beyond that point, Penn Central style, bankruptcy becomes a logical possibility. Ironically, the effect of bankruptcy may be to raise q as the assets of the bankrupt firm are eliminated from the industry total or absorbed after substantial write-downs by other firms. The restrictive nature of the assumption of no bankruptcy in proofs of the irrelevance of financial policy has been emphasized by Stiglitz [36, 1974, p. 862].

managements operate, it may not be a particularly desirable public-relations strategy to depict lower earnings per share as being fully compensated by reduced leverage and risk per share. Rather, the decline in earnings per share may be attributed to financial misman-agement by the uninitiated. Thus, electric utilities with marginal q's less than one have tended to continue programs of real investment. The programs have been financed largely with debt, since debt financing has appeared to be the least undesirable financing alterna-tive.

For the utility sector as a whole the average debt ratio of close to 40 percent evaluated at market is by far the highest of all the indus-tries shown in Table 6—5. But other industries must also behave like the utilities in their use of debt. Perhaps it is the assumed tax advan-tage of debt, the perceived difficulty of firms with low q's and poor market reception to arrange the sale of new equity issues with under-writers, or, alternatively, the tendency for entities with inadequate returns and low q's to protect earnings per share regardless of risks that are sufficiently common to make the correlation between $(q_i / q)_{av.}$ and $(LD/MVT)_i$ about -0.7 between all the industries in Table 6—7. While hardest on stockholders, such a financing policy may be easiest for management, particularly in regulated environments.

V. THE RELATIVE q HYPOTHESIS FOR INVESTMENT

Previous sections have shown that interindustry differences in the relative q's, q_i/q, are quasi-permanent and that the sample-period averages of these ratios for each industry correlate positively with average annual industry growth rates, research intensiveness and rates of return on the replacement cost of assets. While percentage changes in q_i and q are often similar in any year so that variations in q_i/q over time are small within most industries, it is interesting to con-sider whether any structural information can be extracted from what variations there are. This investigation then leads to an analysis of whether changes in own q, relative q, or aggregate q matter most for industry investment rates.

Previous work [18, von Furstenberg, 1977] showed that, over the post-Korean period, movements in the aggregate q basically formed a single long wave which crested in the mid-1960s. Deviations from this basic time shape were attributable primarily to cyclical factors, specifically the capacity utilization rate in manufacturing. Hence movements in many of the industry q_i's follow this same pattern. One may now wonder whether corporate managers should react strongly to cyclical movements in q_i when directly observable and more reliable cyclical variables, such as industry capacity utilization rates, CU_i, are available. Conceivably, changes in the own value of q_i over time may convey little new information to the investment equation for industry i when movements in q_i are dominated by cyclical developments and common trends so that q_i/q does not change. Changes in the relative standing of various industries with financial investors may perhaps be more important for long-term investment planning, and such changes are indicated by variations in q_i/q. At the very least it seems reasonable to hypothesize that an increase in q_i is less favorable to investment in industry i if there are parallel increases in other industries. Only when q_i/q rises also would industry i's relative as well as its absolute position have improved.

To test whether relative q_i's matter, the term $a_{12i} \Delta(q_i/q)_{-1}$, with the coefficient a_{12i} expected to be positive, may be added to specification (8) for the change in the gross investment rate, $\Delta(I/K)_i$, below. The basic form of this equation has been reconciled with a rational expectations framework in previous work by the present authors [28, 1979]. That work showed that, contrary to Ciccolo [6, 1975], deviations of output from trend or changes in capacity utilization rates logically belong in investment equations with q and that, contrary to both Ciccolo and von Furstenberg [18, 1977], the estimating equation for gross investment rates should be run in differenced form.

In the present version, CU_i is the Wharton index of capacity utilization in industry i divided by 100, so that the linked-peak trends of the Federal Reserve index of industrial production, which Wharton uses to indicate 100 percent capacity utilization, form a fixed referent of 1.[t] For each industry q_i is divided by its sample-period average, $\bar{q}_i$, to convert changes in q_i to own rates. The basic specification is then

$$100 \Delta(I/K)_i = a_{10i} \Delta(CU_i)_{-1} + a_{11i} \Delta(q_i/\bar{q}_i)_{-1} . \tag{8}$$

[t]Wharton Econometric Forecasting Associates does not provide estimates of capacity utilization rates for industries (331), (333), and (37). We therefore estimated these rates by identifying peaks in the Federal Reserve (FRB) indexes of industrial production [3, 1977] and by following the general procedure described by Lawrence Klein and Ross Preston [24, 1967]. The Wharton index is the ratio of the actual FRB production index to the interpolated linked-peak values of that index, assuming constant exponential growth rates between peaks. Though Wharton uses more sophisticated methods of extrapolation [23, Klein and Long, 1973], these growth rates were continued past the most recent peak if necessary. Peaks were established for the following quarters in (331): 1955-III, 1965-I, 1966-III, 1969-IV, and 1973-IV; in (333): 1955-IV, 1956-IV, 1960-II, 1964-I, 1967-I, 1969-IV, and 1974-IV; in (37): 1955-III, 1957-I, 1966-IV, 1968-IV, 1973-I, and 1977-III.

Before the data can validly be pooled in the weighted run for all two-digit manufacturing industries shown on the last line of Table 6-9, both $\Delta(CU_i)_{-1}$ and $\Delta(q_i/\bar{q}_i)_{-1}$, which denote differences between periods -1 and -2, first have to be multiplied by the ratio of the net to the gross stock of capital in industry i.[u] This ratio, α_i, is derived from Compustat data and is taken to be constant for each industry.[v] Since multiplication by α_i does not affect the goodness of fit in any of the industry regressions, it is omitted in those runs. However, the data cannot efficiently be pooled without adjustment because the size of the regression coefficients would otherwise be expected to differ to the extent α_i differs between industries even if the behavioral response of net investment rates to changes in CU_i or $q_i/\bar{q}_i$ were precisely the same in all. Since the intercept was not statistically significant in any of the two-digit manufacturing industries and since no intercept belongs in the specification barring unexplained time trends in gross investment rates, no industry dummy variables are needed in the pooled regression to capture differences in intercepts.[w] As reported in Table 6-9, the weights used in that regression are the shares of the two-digit manufacturing industries considered in the sum of their 1972 real gross stocks of capital.

The manufacturing industries with the greatest weight are petroleum and coal products (29), primary metals (33), and chemicals and products (28). The results in Table 6-9 show that these are precisely the industries in which changes in capacity utilization rates tend to have large and, except in (29), statistically significant effects on gross investment rates. The large weight of this small minority of manufacturing industries then contributes to the lagged ΔCU_i being highly

---

[u]The assumption that replacement is proportional to net capital enters into the derivation given by the authors [28, 1979]. For criticisms of that assumption see [15, Feldstein, 1974].

[v]The ratios of plant-net to plant-gross calculated for each industry from the Compustat tapes as described in the appendix were averaged over the years 1956 through 1976 to obtain the estimates of α_i shown in Table 6-9. Because of differences in depreciation rules and historical-cost accounting, the resulting values need not agree precisely with the ratio of the corresponding magnitudes of the real net and gross stocks of fixed nonresidential capital, which the Bureau of Economic Analysis has estimated to rise slightly from 0.54 to 0.56 over the period 1956-1976 for the nonfinancial corporate sector as a whole.

[w]Since the intercept was significant for the utilities as shown in the run reported below, industry (49) was excluded from the pooled regression.

$$100\Delta(I/K)_{49} = 0.251 + 17.550\ \Delta(CU_{49})_{-1} + 1.332\ \Delta(q_{49}/\bar{q}_{49})_{-1}\ ;$$
$$\phantom{100\Delta(I/K)_{49} = }(2.23)\quad\ (3.65)\qquad\qquad (0.98)$$

$$\bar{R}^2 = 0.532,\quad D.W. = 1.55.$$

Table 6–9.   Regression Results for Changes in Gross Investment Rates by Industry, $100\Delta(I/K)_i$

Industry (SIC)	$\Delta(CU_i)-1$ a_{10i} (t-value)	$\Delta(q_i/\bar{q}_i)-1$ a_{11i} (t-value)	$\bar{R}^2$	D.W.	w'_i [a]	α_i [a]
Foods (20)	−6.751 (−0.68)	3.026 (3.45)	0.378	2.21	0.0868	0.5674
Textile mill products (22)	2.481 (0.57)	4.123 (2.80)	0.399	1.74	0.0303	0.5164
Paper and products (26)	6.597 (1.31)	5.646 (2.57)	0.429	1.03	0.0616	0.5704
Chemicals and products (28)	8.989 (1.85)	3.551 (2.11)	0.377	0.90	0.1199	0.5134
Petroleum and coal products (29)	6.178 (0.88)	−0.201 (−0.14)	—	1.03	0.2898	0.5417
Rubber and plastics products (30)	−1.239 (−0.24)	7.979 (2.86)	0.291	1.82	0.0290	0.4921
Clay, stone, and glass products (32)	0.979 (0.23)	6.363 (2.98)	0.297	1.54	0.0470	0.5606
Primary metals (33)	5.797 (2.82)	4.444 (2.76)	0.523	0.96	0.1427	0.4916
Basic steel and mill products (331)	4.424 (1.97)	3.197 (1.88)	0.259	1.47	—	0.4619
Primary nonferrous metals (333)	11.453 (1.95)	9.895 (3.15)	0.425	0.81	—	0.5655
Nonelectrical machinery (35)	6.435 (1.36)	3.880 (1.63)	0.145	1.49	0.0742	0.5237
Electrical machinery (36)	4.429 (1.35)	7.476 (4.24)	0.519	2.06	0.0530	0.5009
Transportation equipment (37)	2.827 (1.09)	10.661 (6.42)	0.709	1.59	0.0657	0.4822
Motor vehicles and parts (371)	0.121 (0.04)	12.454 (5.52)	0.651	1.99	—	0.4705
Aircraft and parts (372)	−5.944 (−0.92)	13.039 (6.19)	0.669	1.94	—	0.4370
Utilities (49)	16.347 (2.96)	−0.247 (−0.18)	0.377	1.46	—	0.7727
All 2-digit manufacturing industries [a]	11.741 (4.95)	4.272 (4.58)	0.222	—	—	—

[a] All two-digit industries shown above except 49 are included in the pooled and weighted regression. The weights (w'_i) for each industry are its share of the real gross stock of capital in 1972 where the weights shown in the next to last column of this table add to 1. All independent variables are also multiplied by α_i; the estimated 1956–1976 average ratio of the net to the gross stock of capital, in the pooled regression.

significant in the pooled and weighted regression. Considering that a_{10i} is also large and statistically significant in utilities (49), this may explain why capacity utilization has been found to be a significant determinant of gross investment rates in previous work for the nonfinancial corporate sector as a whole [18, von Furstenberg, 1977] and more important and reliable than q.

While such an ordering of the relative importance of CU and q may be correct for the weighted aggregate, the disaggregated evidence presented in Table 6−9 shows that for most individual industries the ordering is quite the reverse. With few exceptions, most notably petroleum and coal products (29) and utilities (49), a_{11i} is significant and a_{10i} is not. Furthermore, both of the exceptions involve industries that are heavily affected by government regulations and controls. In the utility sector, book values rather than the replacement cost of assets are used to establish "fair" rates of return and much investment is mandated by regulatory bodies regardless of how low the value of its q. This may explain why a positive significant intercept, representing an otherwise unexplained upward drift in gross investment rates, was found only in that industry. In petroleum, foreign governments may require refineries to be built in their countries and capacity can be added in the United States only after many environmental and regulatory hurdles are overcome. The imposed delays and distortions leave little room for actual investment outlays to stay in phase with economic incentives. To explain investment in that industry one should thus use specific information on major project approvals and completion schedules rather than estimate fixed behavioral relationships based on the unconstrained application of economic rationality.

For the other industries, the implications that may be extracted from the results of Table 6−9 for forecasters are as follows: (1) Pay particular attention to expected demand and capacity utilization rates in the utilities (49), but ignore q_i. (2) In chemicals (28) and primary metals (33) and its two major subsectors (331, 333), as well as possibly in paper and products (26) and nonelectrical (35) and electrical (36) machinery, include both CU_i and q_i among the explanatory variables.[x] (3) For all other industries shown, ignore CU_i and

---

[x]The importance of demand-type variables in investment equations for the utilities (49) and primary metals (33) has been noted by others. See, for instance, [11, Eisner, 1971, p. 58]. Raford Boddy and Michael Gort [4, 1974] estimate that the share of capital is 63 percent in utilities and 30 percent in primary metals, making the former extremely capital intensive. Furthermore, the longevity of capital is very high in both industries. The estimated annual depreciation rates of around 4.5 percent for utilities and 6.8 percent for primary metals are the lowest rates reported for any of the twenty-four industries examined by Boddy and Gort.

concentrate on q_i. If the task of estimating q_i on a reasonably current basis proves impossible, use q in lieu of q_i in each of them since q_i and q are highly correlated.

Regardless of whether such a tripartite division is particularly useful to forecasters who want to make use of q, the lesson that the effects of $\Delta(CU_i)_{-1}$ and $\Delta(q_i/\bar{q}_i)_{-1}$ on gross investment rates differ greatly between industries but are most frequently significant for the latter stands out clearly from the results reported in Table 6−9.

Turning to the test of the relative q hypothesis and adding a_{12i} $\Delta(q_i/q)_{-1}$ to the explanatory variables in equation (8) yielded surprising results. Instead of being positive, a_{12i} was negative in all industries except (37), (371), and (49), though statistically insignificant in all but one instance. The relative q hypothesis is thus refuted and there is weak evidence that a given rise in $q_i/\bar{q}_i$ in a particular industry stimulates investment in industry i more if q_i/q rises less because the own q_i's of other industries rise also. Rather than being competitive as we have supposed, the q_i's thus appear to be weakly complementary or "synergistic" in that a rise in the q_i of one industry also stimulates investment in other industries, or at least does not divert investment from them.

If a widespread rise in the q_i's is due to a fall in rates of return required by financial investors or associated with a general improvement in the business and profit outlook and an increase in the supply of saving available for private capital formation, while the isolated rise in a particular q_i is not, such a finding is not entirely unreasonable. It suggests, however, that while q-type variables affect investment in different industries very differently, it may not be so much changes in each industry's individual q_i but the information conveyed by changes in the aggregate q about the economy as a whole which causes changes in industry investment rates.

To test for this possibility, the last term in equation (8), a_{11i} $\Delta(q_i/\bar{q}_i)_{-1}$, was replaced by $a_{11i}^*\Delta(q/\bar{q})_{-1}$. While a_{11i}^* was generally found to be between 20 and 60 percent greater than a_{11i} for $a_{11i} > 0$, it was less significant in all industries except (30), (32), and (35). As a result a_{11i}^* was significantly different from zero in eleven out of the sixteen industries examined, while a_{11i} was significant in thirteen industries. Some useful industry-specific information is clearly lost by substituting $\Delta(q/\bar{q})_{-1}$ for $\Delta(q_i/\bar{q}_i)_{-1}$, but, statistically, the explanatory power added by that information is small. This confirms that, in a pinch, the former variable may be used as a proxy for each of the latter in investment equations as long as it is understood that the theory justifying the presence of q-type variables in such equations remains basically microeconomic. Ideally, the measurement of q should be as disaggregated as the dependent variable whose behavior is being studied since it is changes in the own q's that matter most.

VI. CONCLUSION

Estimates of the aggregate q, originated in the United States, have begun to appear in other countries [33, Oulton, 1978] and will eventually circle the globe. It is important, therefore, to explore the uses of this concept which may one day be factored explicitly into such concrete decisions as whether the U.S. parent of a textile company should locate subsidiaries in South Carolina, or perhaps in South Korea or Brazil, depending on where it gets more "q" for investing its money.

The present paper analyzed some of the financial and real economic correlates of q, including investment behavior, from the perspective of the firm although the observation units are industries. While changes in the q_i values are not equally potent in all industries, they do appear to be the single most important determinant of changes in gross investment rates. Changes in capacity utilizations are a poor second in most industries so that cyclical disturbances in the demand for output rarely trigger statistically significant reductions in the capital stock desired for future years. Nevertheless, the high correlation between almost all of the industry q_i's and the aggregate q for the nonfinancial sector as a whole, which in turn correlates highly with cyclical variables, blurs the contrast between the two major determinants of investment to some extent.

What is clear, however, is that differences in the sample-period averages of the relative q values, $(q_i/q)_{av.}$, are associated with differences in trend rates of growth in the real capital stock between industries much more closely than differences in the trend rates of growth of output or differences in the average real after-tax rates of return on the replacement cost of assets. Compared to the latter variables, q-type variables thus appear to convey information about the business and profit outlook which is not just based on the extrapolation of past trends or levels. The paucity of suitable proxies for anticipations variables has often been lamented in empirical research of investment behavior. This work strongly suggests that q can help fill this gap.

While q plays an important role in determining investment, the tendency for q_i values to be equilibrated between industries over time is very weak and not statistically detectable over the sample period 1956–1976. While certain features of both the corporate and individual income tax systems discriminate between different types of returns on capital and the industries which provide them, quasi-permanent differences in industry q_i's which were found to amount to several hundred percent in extreme cases can hardly be explained by such factors. Generally, research-intensive industries with high rates of return and output growth are also characterized by high rates of growth of the stock of capital, without however diminishing their high relative q's. Conversely industries characterized by low (q_i/q)'s struggle on with lower rates of growth of capital without thereby bringing their q_i/q values to the average. Industries therefore display seemingly chronic differences in their relative q's which are rooted in the dynamics of technological leadership and world-market competition. Since the expectation that q_i's will be equilibrated through shifts in the distribution of investment between industries would itself tend to hold interindustry q differentials within narrow bounds, we find no evidence that such expectations are held by financial investors.[y]

From a dynamic perspective, firms that are located in industries characterized by rapid product innovations (for example, machine building, aircraft), rapid downward shifts in the international supply function on account of cost-saving inventions (textiles, steel), or both (chemicals) apparently cannot hope to improve or even to maintain their average q's by shrinking. Negative net investment is what Tobin's q theory would suggest, however, if their marginal q is less than unity. Since the marginal q is unobservable *ex post* and unknowable *ex ante*, empirically the marginal q has always been identified with the average q. Capital goods used to produce particu-

---

[y] The unweighted regression of the dividend-price ratio on the trend growth rate of capital (both in percentage points) reported below for the eleven two-digit manufacturing industries shows that a positive percentage point difference in the latter between industries is associated with a negative difference in the former which is significantly less than 1. Since the growth rates of the capital stock and of retained earnings may differ within industries, this finding does not necessarily imply that expected capital gains are substituted for dividend pay-out at a rate less than one-to-one. Nevertheless it tends to suggest this perhaps because future dividends are regarded as less uncertain than capital gains.

$$(DIV/MVE)_i = \begin{matrix} 4.930 \\ (11.53) \end{matrix} - \begin{matrix} 0.370 \ g_i; \\ (-3.77) \end{matrix} \ \bar{R}^2 = 0.569 .$$

Though excluded factors, including interindustry differences in fundamental (operating) risk, may well bias the coefficient on g_i, it is conceivable, therefore, that a preference for dividend pay-out is as widespread as Tobin and Brainard [42, 1977] have found even when $q > 1$. By contrast, tax factors alone would lead to the expectation that returns in the form of capital gains are valued more highly than dividend returns.

lar products in a specific way may be quite heterogeneous over time not just in terms of their physical efficiency but also because demand and supply characteristics relating to the profitability of particular processes and products may have changed. If new investments are thus potentially of very different marginal profitability from old investments, the link between the average q and the marginal q may break down.

It is entirely possible that some of the low q industries, though hampered by high costs of capital, can hope to raise their q only by faster, more technology intensive growth and by more rapid replacement of existing capacity. This dynamic implication runs counter to the usual static interpretations of the q theory which are implicitly based on the assumption that the net stock of capital is homogeneous intertemporally once straight-line or some other method of depreciation has been applied.

In fact, the relative q may be chronically low in some unregulated industries because they do not invest enough, just as it may be high in others because they invest so much that progress is too rapid for q to be equilibrated between industries. Surely a program of reduced investment in the computer sectors would help whittle down the very high q's of the machine-building industries of which they form a part, as technological leadership gradually passes to other countries. However, the importance of such paradoxical approaches to equilibrating q_i's should not be exaggerated: by and large industries act as if a low average q_i told them something equally depressing about their marginal q. Hence they grow less rapidly over long periods of time when the industry-characteristic $(q_i/q)_{av.}$ is low; and whenever their own q_i declines, they reduce their gross investment rates even if the q_i's of all other industries fall by the same percentage.

The decline in q_i that started in the mid or late 1960s in almost all industries included in this study has undoubtedly contributed to declining rates of business fixed investment in the aggregate. The advent of a new technological era or a change in the distribution of the capital stock between existing industries can raise the aggregate q. In fact, it is the ongoing redistribution of weights from low to high q_i industries that has made declines in the aggregate q less severe than those registered in most individual industries. Still, given that the tendency of the q_i's to converge to any common value, such as unity, is imperceptible, there is no guarantee that previous declines in q will soon be reversed.

This study has found that any policy that is conducive to raising q will raise investment rates with a high degree of probability in almost all industries, but it has not attempted to identify what such policies may be. While previous research [18, von Furstenberg, 1977, p. 378] has suggested that cuts in corporate tax rates benefit q rather promptly while increasing the rate of the investment tax credit does not, changes in capital gains taxation and in the double taxation of dividends have now also been placed on the national agenda [16, Feldstein and Slemrod, 1978]. They should be evaluated together with other measures to find the most effective way of stimulating the demand for capital (and the supply of private saving) since the evaluations of financial investors matter greatly for productive investment.

Appendix

THE DERIVATION OF INDUSTRY q's

To obtain a representative sample of the firms in two-digit or, in a few cases, three-digit standard industrial classifications (SICs), balance-sheet data were aggregated over all firms included in the total industrial file of Compustat in these SICs. The Compustat tapes cover all industrial companies and utilities listed on the New York and American stock exchanges. However, not all account items are reported for all of the firms for each year since 1956. Thus, firms for which essential information, such as on common stock equity, was missing were eliminated from the annual sample. Even then for a few firms the accounts for inventories and net plant were blank. Since the number of such discrepancies was small in relation to the total number of firms per SIC and since they occurred in only a few industries and years, no attempt was made to shrink the annual sample further to eliminate all instances of missing information in individual accounts.[z]

Compustat annual files cover reports ending from one-half year before to one-half year after the end of each calendar year. On the average, the balance sheet items are thus centered on the end of calendar years while flow magnitudes in the income statement refer to calendar years. The balance sheets derived for two- or three-digit SICs were arranged as follows:

Assets	*Liabilities*
(1) Inventories	(3) Current Liabilities (Total)
	(3) Liabilities (Other)
(2) Plant-Net	(3) Deferred Taxes and Investment Credit
(3) Cash and Short-Term Investments	(3) Minority Interest
(3) Receivables	
(3) Current Assets (Other)	(4) "Marketable" Long-Term Debt
(3) Investments in and Advances to Unconsolidated Subsidiaries	(4) "Nonmarketable" Long-Term Debt
(3) Investments in and Advances to Others	Stockholder's Equity
	(5) —Common
(3) Intangibles	(6) —Preferred
(3) Assets (Other)	

---

[z]However, the problem of missing information on inventories and net plant was too widespread to be ignored for utilities (49) for the years 1956-1960.

For the purpose of estimating q, all items classified as (3) were netted at their book values and identified as "net short-term financial assets." "Marketable" long-term debt consists of the sum of the following Compustat accounts: debt (convertible), debt (subordinated), and debt (debentures), for which market price quotations are generally available. "Nonmarketable" long-term debt consists of debt (notes), debt (other long-term), and debt (capitalized lease obligations), for which market price quotations are generally not available. After revaluing marketable debt as described later, the sum of these two classes yields the long-term debt component in the market value of q as shown below.

Replacement Cost	*Market Value*
(1) Inventories	(4) Long-Term Debt
(2) Plant-Net	(5) Common Equity
(3) Net Short-Term Financial Assets	(6) Preferred Equity

Unlike the book values of assets and liabilities shown in the previous balance-sheet tabulation, the replacement cost of assets and the market value of liabilities need not balance. The derivation of each of the six items shown above follows.

1. Unpublished end-of-quarter estimates of the current-dollar replacement cost of industry inventories have been provided by the Bureau of Economic Analysis for the period starting with the first quarter of 1959. These are divided by the inventory stocks reported for the end of each month by the Bureau of the Census [44]. Although respondents to the Census survey are asked to report inventories of individual establishments at approximate current cost if feasible; otherwise, "at book values," there is little doubt that book values are, in fact, reported by almost all. Hence, the ratios obtained can be used to convert the inventory numbers reported for the industries aggregated from the Compustat files to replacement cost at the end of each year. These inventory conversion factors range up to 1.5 in industries such as primary metals (33) containing many firms which have used the LIFO method of inventory accounting for decades. Because of extraordinary price rises and because many oil com-

---

Thus q values for these years are not reported in Table 6-A-16 nor are they used in regressions for industry (49). However, except for ρ_j and $(R/I)_j$, the averages reported in Table 6-5 for industry 49 include 1956-1960, the same as for all other industries, since the estimates of the market value of liabilities were complete.

panies also use LIFO in accounting for their domestic operations, the inventory conversion factors were even higher in that industry (29) since 1973. The undervaluation of inventories on the balance sheets of some industries is thus considerable. The conversion factors estimated for 1956–1976 are shown in columns 1 of the industry tables that follow. The earliest obtainable inventory conversion factor, calculated for March 1959, is used for the yearends 1956–1958 throughout.

In a few industries additional difficulties arose. Because estimates of the book value of inventories were unavailable for the utilities (industry 49) and estimates of the replacement cost of inventories were missing for basic steel and mill products (industry 331), primary nonferrous metals (333), and aircraft and parts (industry 372), the inventory conversion factor for petroleum and coal products (industry 29) was used for 49, and that of primary metals (industry 33) for both 331 and 332. Since conversion factors could be estimated for transportation equipment as a whole (industry 37) and motor vehicles and parts (industry 371), the conversion factor for 372 was derived as a reconciliation item using book values as weights and assuming 372 accounts for the entire rather than just most of the residual of 37 after 371 is taken out.

2. The balance sheet item, plant-net, is defined in the Compustat tapes to include plant, equipment, land, and other real property used in the production of revenue. Its conversion from book values to replacement cost presents great difficulties since both price differences and differences in depreciation methods are involved. Estimates of the real net stock of capital by 1972 SIC industries were obtained in 1972 dollars for 1967–1975 from Frank Ripley under an NSF-funded project on financial flows and economic activity in the United States, directed by Gary Fromm. These estimates were converted to current dollars using the industry investment deflators also provided by Ripley. This reflation procedure yields estimates of the replacement cost of net capital by industries. It is inexact to the extent the composition of the net stock of industry capital, by type of equipment and between equipment and structures, differs from the composition of annual industry investment.

For 1967, Ripley also provided estimates of the gross book value of depreciable assets adjusted from 1967 to 1972 SICs. Comparing these estimates with those reported by the Bureau of the Census in its *Annual Survey of Manufacturers* [43] revealed small percentage differences due to reclassification in about half the industries which were used to convert Census estimates for the period 1967 through 1971 from the 1967 to the 1972 SIC basis. The next step was to convert these consistent 1967—1975 estimates of gross book values to net values. This was done by applying the percentage of plant-net to plant-gross obtained from the Compustat tapes for each industry and year through 1975. The conversion factors reported in columns 2 of the industry tables that follow are then obtained by dividing the estimates of the replacement cost of net capital by the estimates of the net book value of depreciable assets just explained.

Since our estimation period is 1956—1976, these capital stock conversion factors had to be extended to the missing years for which critical components are as yet unavailable. The extension was guided by the behavior of the ratio of capital consumption allowances, converted to consistent accounting at historical cost, to capital consumption allowances with capital consumption adjustment over the entire period. These depreciation ratios are derived from data reported annually in Table 8.7 of the *Survey of Current Business*. They show what historical-cost depreciation for tax purposes would have been each year compared to replacement-cost depreciation if the same depreciation rules and tax lives had been used. Assuming the depreciation rate is a constant percentage of net capital, the ratio of the book value of net capital to its replacement cost (the inverse of the conversion factor) is the same as the ratio of historical-cost to replacement-cost depreciation. On less restrictive assumptions, these two ratios, though not identical, are at least highly covariant. Hence, years with identical depreciation ratios (that is, identical ratios of the two estimates of depreciation provided by BEA) were judged to be years with equal conversion factors.

On this basis, the conversion factors for 1976 were set equal to those for 1975 in each industry, and the conversion factors for 1968, 1969, and 1970 were used for 1963, 1962, and 1961, respectively. The depreciation ratios rise as the high rates of inflation encountered up to the early 1950s fade into the past and the conversion factors fall until a new surge of inflation commences in the mid-1960s. The U-shaped pattern of the latter thus allowed matching ratios to be estimated from the leg 1967—1975 for the leg 1964—1956. Since the depreciation ratios were lowest in the mid-1960s, 99 percent of the 1967 conversion factors was used for 1965 and 1966 while 100 percent was taken for 1964. For both 1959 and 1960, the sum of 60 percent of the 1973 and 40 percent of the 1974 conversion factors was used. The weights on this sum changed to 40 and 60 percent for 1958, to 15 and 85 percent for 1957, and to 25 and 75 percent for 1956, as the depreciation ratios rise unevenly toward the start of our estimation period.

In 1972, the year in which the data are "hardest" because it is the base of the deflator and the SIC classification here employed, the conversion factors range from 1.7 to 3.7, with the replacement cost of net capital over twice as high as its book value on average.[aa] These data imply that book values are unacceptable as a basis for deriving rates of return on capital or any other analytical financial measure for the manufacturing and utility industries.

The size of the conversion factors for any industry depends positively on the longevity of capital it employs and negatively on the growth rate of the capital stock. Since no data suitable for the derivation of capital stock conversion factors were available for utilities (industry 49), the average of the conversion factors for petroleum and coal products (industry 29) and rubber and plastics products (industry 30) was used to obtain comparable above-average growth and extreme longevity conditions.

3. Although receivables may include uncollectible accounts exceeding the allowance made for doubtful accounts on the balance sheet and although idle land is included in assets (other) at original cost, all items in this category were treated as par items equal to their book value. To the extent intangibles, such as good will, arise from an excess of the purchase price over the book value of second-hand depreciable assets, double-counting would result if these items are then revalued from book to replacement cost in the account, plant-net. Only if second-hand assets were valued at market prices rather than at original cost in interindustry flow matrices of book values would a lower conversion factor be applied to net plant to reflect these transfers.

4. Book value is used for "nonmarketable" long-term debt previously identified. Since this class is composed mainly of notes and other fairly short debt with more than one year to maturity remaining, this procedure is not likely to involve large errors. Even privately placed debt with an initial maturity of, say, fifteen years typically requires substantial repayments before maturity. The detail required to divide total long-term debt into "marketable" and "nonmarketable" components is reported on the Compustat files only since 1969. However, because the percentage of "marketable" debt was fairly constant in each industry over the period 1969–1976, the 1969 percentage was applied to all earlier years in the sample with little risk of error.

[aa] The capital stock conversion factor is highest in aircraft and parts (industry 372). Some of the economic consequences of underdepreciation in that industry have been analyzed by Klaus Heiss [22, 1976].

All "marketable" debt was valued at a premium or discount, with the complement of the discount shown in columns 3 of the industry tables that follow. This "percent of par" was obtained by directly sampling bond prices reported for each industry each year using all the marketable debt of firms included in the S&P 500 stock market index that was reported in the July issues of *Moody's Bond Record.* The percentages of par found for each bond were then weighted by the principal amount of each debt issue outstanding to obtain a price index equal to the average percent of par. This was used to convert the yearend book values of marketable long-term debt to market values for each industry and year.

Except in the utility sector, where extremely long financing is common, and except for crisis years, such as 1970 and 1974, discounts in excess of 20 percent or market values more than 20 percent below par are extremely rare. Even though the face values of bonds outstanding at yearend were converted to market values, current price quotations reported in July of each year were used on the theory that they might yield price quotations which are more representative for the year as a whole than if December prices were used. (Because of a lack of suitable bond price quotations, only the 1956 percent of par value for textile mill products (industry 22) was estimated indirectly from 1957. This was done by applying the unweighted average percentage change in the percent of par observed for all other industries from 1957 to 1956.) The percent of marketable debt in the face value of total long-term debt is shown in columns 4 of the industry tables that follow.

5. A similar price-averaging process was also used to establish the market value of common equity. Here the average of the high and low prices registered during a calendar year was applied to the number of common shares outstanding. As in (4), the product of the yearend quantities and average prices may differ from the yearend market values to the extent the average price differs from the yearend price. However, the use of an average price was judged preferable to the use of a single price at the close of each year. In this respect the result is a kind of average for the year as a whole.

6. Since some firms have many different kinds of preferred stock outstanding, while their common is generally homogeneous, estimating the market value of preferred stock, like that of "marketable" long-term debt, was an extremely time consuming procedure. Here market price quotations were not used to establish premiums or discounts from carrying value but to derive market dividend/price ratios for preferred stock. The preferred dividends reported in the

Compustat files were then divided by these ratios to obtain the market value of preferred stock by industry and year.

Preferred stock newly issued on which no dividends were as yet paid or on which only partial dividends were paid during the initial or final year was ignored in the calculation of the annual dividend/price ratios. However, all other preferred issues of companies in the S&P 500 (and of some additional Compustat corporations in industry 331) were included in the calculations, regardless of whether dividends and arrears were paid or not. The average of the high and the low price of the year for each preferred was multiplied by the number of preferred shares outstanding and the resulting products were summed over the issues selected in each industry. Dividing the sum of the preferred dividends paid on those issues (dividends paid per preferred share times the number of preferred shares outstanding) by these summed products provided the representative dividend/price ratios, which are shown in columns 5 of the industry tables below. (All ratios were estimated directly except for those in aircraft and parts [industry 372] from 1956 and through 1965 where the dividend/price ratio of transportation equipment as a whole [industry 37] was used for lack of more suitable data.) Capitalizing the total dollar amount of preferred dividends paid during a calendar year reported in Compustat by these ratios yielded an estimate of the average value of preferred stock during that year. It is not meaningful to center Compustat flow variables, such as dividends paid, at yearends by averaging figures for adjoining years. Since the number and representativeness of the firms appearing on the Compustat tapes for any industry changes somewhat from year to year, dollar magnitudes cannot be combined or related across years, even though the Compustat corporations always account for such a large percentage of the industry totals that sampling biases are bound to be small in any year.

Evaluation of Estimates

Having explained the procedures used to estimate all components of q, how reliable are the resulting estimates likely to be? On the asset side, the inability to separate land used in the production of revenue from plant-net and idle land from net short-term financial assets and then to estimate the replacement cost of land on its own is likely to lead to some understatement of the replacement cost of assets. On the liability side, some systematic underestimate of the market value of firms at yearend would result if yearend stock and bond prices are generally above the average of the high and low prices for the year as a whole. This, however, while sometimes true for stocks was rarely true for bonds. On balance, therefore, the latter underestimate is likely to be smaller than the former so that the numerator of q is less depressed than the denominator. Some overstatement of the true value of q is therefore possible. However, except for paper and products (industry 26) the share of land value in total asset value is generally small in the industries analyzed in this paper. Hence, the measurement bias is likely to be small also.

The q values shown in columns 6 of the industry tables which follow are generally less than 1 though they differ greatly between industries. Their average level thus accords well with the q values estimated for the nonfinancial corporate sector as a whole by von Furstenberg [18, 1977] and is much lower than the q's of around 2 estimated for individual industrial corporations by Tobin and Brainard [42, 1977]. Although scalar transformations of q, or uniform percentage errors in estimates of q, would not affect the regression results, we would find it difficult to believe that such errors are, in fact, uniform if the estimated level of q were implausibly high. For this reason we regard the reduction in measurement errors in the level of q as important.

The minimization of measurement error is particularly important since cross-sectional relations between industry q's and between components of q, such as the market value of debt and total market value, are of analytical interest also. Furthermore, the attempt to obtain numerically precise estimates of q yields by-products, such as the conversion factors of inventories and net capital stock from book values to replacement cost, which have a variety of uses in financial analysis. Although these conversion factors may be subject to measurement error, they differ so substantially from unity, particularly in the case of fixed capital, as to be greatly at variance with the accounting fictions used in income taxation and in regulatory and antitrust proceedings as well as in government contracting and rate-of-return calculations.

Table 6–A–1. Industry 20: Foods

Year	Conversion Factors Inventories (1)	Net Plant (2)	Long-Term Debt Percent of Par Value (3)	Percent Marketable (4)	Preferred Stock Dividend/Price (percent) (5)	q_i (6)
1956	1.2062[e]	2.0849[e]	99.25	43.0[e]	4.26	0.756
1957	1.2062[e]	2.0943[e]	91.95	43.0[e]	4.77	0.682
1958	1.2062[e]	2.0709[e]	94.09	43.0[e]	3.83	0.791
1959	1.2110	2.0521[e]	90.13	43.0[e]	4.55	0.902
1960	1.2064	2.0521[e]	87.74	43.0[e]	4.76	0.987
1961	1.1922	2.1050[e]	90.60	43.0[e]	4.54	1.219
1962	1.1779	2.0938[e]	94.26	43.0[e]	4.62	1.103
1963	1.1773	2.1324[e]	95.08	43.0[e]	4.45	1.149
1964	1.1729	2.0883[e]	94.58	43.0[e]	4.17	1.219
1965	1.1859	2.0674[e]	93.89	43.0[e]	4.50	1.259
1966	1.1660	2.0674[e]	89.05	43.0[e]	2.96	1.106
1967	1.1718	2.0883	86.85	43.0[e]	3.38	1.156
1968	1.1679	2.1324	84.09	43.0[e]	3.02	1.244
1969	1.1762	2.0938	78.23	43.0	4.00	1.215
1970	1.1647	2.1050	78.75	47.0	4.60	1.032
1971	1.1864	2.1354	89.39	50.0	3.69	1.148
1972	1.2185	2.0676	96.34	49.0	2.73	1.283
1973	1.2256	2.0147	94.57	49.0	4.37	1.132
1974	1.2444	2.1083	87.89	48.0	7.02	0.780
1975	1.1860	2.2275	91.45	51.0	5.13	0.766
1976	1.2096	2.2275[e]	96.74	51.0	5.20	0.805

[e]Estimated by indirect methods explained in the text of this appendix.

Table 6-A-2. Industry 22: Textile Mill Products

	Conversion Factors		Long-Term Debt		Preferred Stock Dividend/Price (percent)	q_i
	Inventories	Net Plant	Percent of Par Value	Percent Marketable		
Year	(1)	(2)	(3)	(4)	(5)	(6)
1956	1.1658[e]	2.4596[e]	86.78[e]	30.0[e]	4.32	0.445
1957	1.1658[e]	2.4866[e]	80.88	30.0[e]	5.16	0.368
1958	1.1658[e]	2.4191[e]	74.63	30.0[e]	4.50	0.392
1959	1.1269	2.3651[e]	85.25	30.0[e]	5.23	0.487
1960	1.1043	2.3651[e]	80.50	30.0[e]	5.26	0.518
1961	1.1153	2.2621[e]	79.75	30.0[e]	4.89	0.529
1962	1.1037	2.1925[e]	67.00	30.0[e]	4.42	0.556
1963	1.1143	2.1852[e]	80.25	30.0[e]	4.27	0.686
1964	1.1009	2.1268[e]	85.50	30.0[e]	4.14	0.773
1965	1.1103	2.1055[e]	94.86	30.0[e]	4.07	0.821
1966	1.0696	2.1055[e]	94.34	30.0[e]	4.55	0.726
1967	1.0901	2.1268	90.18	30.0[e]	5.30	0.712
1968	1.0476	2.1852	93.29	30.0[e]	5.74	0.850
1969	1.0492	2.1925	82.42	30.0	6.33	0.773
1970	1.0437	2.2621	68.61	36.0	7.25	0.620
1971	1.0812	3.3702	92.74	39.0	6.51	0.690
1972	1.0932	2.2438	94.88	38.0	6.70	0.714
1973	1.1459	2.2571	91.18	30.0	6.80	0.554
1974	1.0436	2.5271	78.42	34.0	8.02	0.391
1975	1.1299	2.8819	85.86	35.0	8.07	0.361
1976	1.1321	2.8819[e]	89.82	34.0	7.60	0.413

[e]Estimated by indirect methods explained in the text of this appendix.

Table 6−A−3. Industry 26: Paper and Products

Year	Conversion Factors		Long-Term Debt		Preferred Stock Dividend/Price (percent)	q_i
	Inventories	Net Plant	Percent of Par Value	Percent Marketable		
	(1)	(2)	(3)	(4)	(5)	(6)
1956	1.1467 [e]	2.0179 [e]	97.50	28.0 [e]	3.50	1.032
1957	1.1467 [e]	2.0257 [e]	95.00	28.0 [e]	4.66	0.809
1958	1.1467 [e]	2.0063 [e]	102.93	28.0 [e]	4.50	0.846
1959	1.1344	1.9908 [e]	100.75	28.0 [e]	4.63	0.960
1960	1.1084	1.9908 [e]	96.62	28.0 [e]	4.76	0.862
1961	1.1374	1.8722 [e]	114.91	28.0 [e]	4.46	0.962
1962	1.1045	1.8704 [e]	102.94	28.0 [e]	4.44	0.844
1963	1.1116	1.8449 [e]	105.69	28.0 [e]	4.29	0.857
1964	1.1091	1.7907 [e]	107.13	28.0 [e]	4.25	0.911
1965	1.1086	1.7728 [e]	103.13	28.0 [e]	4.39	0.859
1966	1.0937	1.7728 [e]	93.35	28.0 [e]	3.80	0.791
1967	1.1089	1.7907	90.66	28.0 [e]	4.01	0.753
1968	1.1038	1.8449	86.48	28.0 [e]	5.51	0.779
1969	1.2076	1.8704	81.96	28.0	5.41	0.817
1970	1.1044	1.8722	90.04	35.0	6.92	0.694
1971	1.1128	1.9562	97.14	39.0	6.42	0.686
1972	1.1217	1.9381	102.23	40.0	5.99	0.704
1973	1.1810	1.9598	98.53	43.0	7.02	0.684
1974	1.2037	2.0373	88.17	42.0	8.15	0.540
1975	1.2447	2.2133	90.86	45.0	8.21	0.498
1976	1.2471	2.2133 [e]	95.92	45.0	5.89	0.596

[e]Estimated by indirect methods explained in the text of this appendix.

Table 6-A-4. Industry 28: Chemicals and Products

Year	Conversion Factors		Long-Term Debt		Preferred Stock Dividend/Price (percent)	q_i
	Inventories	Net Plant	Percent of Par Value	Percent Marketable		
	(1)	(2)	(3)	(4)	(5)	(6)
1956	1.0031[e]	2.2750[e]	99.97	38.0[e]	4.34	1.615
1957	1.0031[e]	2.2775[e]	94.22	38.0[e]	4.41	1.387
1958	1.0031[e]	2.2711[e]	94.58	38.0[e]	4.64	1.483
1959	1.0121	2.2660[e]	92.24	38.0[e]	4.61	1.758
1960	1.0129	2.2660[e]	88.59	38.0[e]	4.76	1.639
1961	1.0098	2.2201[e]	99.50	38.0[e]	4.56	1.785
1962	1.0042	2.2271[e]	97.22	38.0[e]	4.12	1.532
1963	1.0051	2.2225[e]	93.72	38.0[e]	4.27	1.630
1964	1.0049	2.1552[e]	95.71	38.0[e]	3.90	1.742
1965	1.0069	2.1336[e]	100.57	38.0[e]	3.51	1.730
1966	1.0198	2.1336[e]	93.80	38.0[e]	3.22	1.468
1967	1.0116	2.1552	92.03	38.0[e]	3.58	1.433
1968	1.0058	2.2225	86.87	38.0[e]	3.61	1.421
1969	1.0283	2.2271	80.14	38.0	3.43	1.352
1970	1.0200	2.2201	74.13	42.0	4.97	1.181
1971	1.0377	2.2952	85.60	45.0	4.36	1.325
1972	1.0318	2.2577	92.26	48.0	4.37	1.537
1973	1.0646	2.2557	90.20	46.0	4.13	1.483
1974	1.1556	2.2814	80.98	44.0	5.07	1.014
1975	1.1413	2.4201	90.81	45.0	4.94	0.919
1976	1.1589	2.4201[e]	94.20	50.0	4.77	0.902

[e]Estimated by indirect methods explained in the text of this appendix.

Table 6–A–5. Industry 29: Petroleum and Coal Products

Year	Conversion Factors		Long-Term Debt		Preferred Stock Dividend/Price (percent)	q_i
	Inventories	Net Plant	Percent of Par Value	Percent Marketable		
	(1)	(2)	(3)	(4)	(5)	(6)
1956	1.2196[e]	2.2608[e]	104.15	47.0[e]	4.26	0.833
1957	1.2196[e]	2.2581[e]	102.44	47.0[e]	4.51	0.794
1958	1.2196[e]	2.2648[e]	100.60	47.0[e]	2.88	0.708
1959	1.1708	2.2701[e]	97.52	47.0[e]	4.53	0.695
1960	1.2172	2.2701[e]	94.70	47.0[e]	3.16	0.600
1961	1.2031	2.2597[e]	100.84	47.0[e]	1.90	0.652
1962	1.1798	2.3168[e]	100.90	47.0[e]	4.01	0.619
1963	1.1714	2.3701[e]	102.92	47.0[e]	2.82	0.697
1964	1.1630	2.4373[e]	102.43	47.0[e]	3.56	0.756
1965	1.1882	2.4129[e]	101.17	47.0[e]	2.34	0.751
1966	1.1949	2.4129[e]	93.64	47.0[e]	3.80	0.669
1967	1.1864	2.4373	93.72	47.0[e]	3.50	0.647
1968	1.1839	2.3701	88.07	47.0[e]	2.02	0.729
1969	1.2050	2.3168	82.23	47.0	3.57	0.692
1970	1.2728	2.2597	73.29	48.0	5.58	0.538
1971	1.2422	2.2797	87.63	50.0	4.93	0.589
1972	1.2595	2.3700	92.23	53.0	5.15	0.580
1973	1.6216	2.2808	90.39	51.0	4.45	0.594
1974	1.6464	2.2541	80.96	47.0	5.51	0.453
1975	1.7051	2.3405	88.81	49.0	4.83	0.427
1976	1.7655	2.3405[e]	92.52	48.0	4.47	0.459

[e]Estimated by indirect methods explained in the text of this appendix.

Table 6–A–6. Industry 30: Rubber and Plastics Products

Year	Conversion Factors		Long-Term Debt		Preferred Stock Dividend/Price (percent)	q_i
	Inventories	Net Plant	Percent of Par Value	Percent Marketable		
	(1)	(2)	(3)	(4)	(5)	(6)
1956	1.0653[e]	2.1026[e]	100.46	31.0[e]	5.09	0.923
1957	1.0653[e]	2.1173[e]	91.18	31.0[e]	5.46	0.875
1958	1.0653[e]	2.0806[e]	93.64	31.0[e]	5.42	0.956
1959	1.0769	2.0513[e]	88.35	31.0[e]	5.37	1.186
1960	1.0199	2.0513[e]	86.87	31.0[e]	5.31	1.041
1961	1.0324	2.0083[e]	94.05	31.0[e]	5.14	1.054
1962	1.0453	2.0154[e]	96.08	31.0[e]	5.06	0.919
1963	1.0271	2.0438[e]	98.26	31.0[e]	4.75	0.888
1964	1.0290	2.0771[e]	96.79	31.0[e]	4.75	0.923
1965	1.0247	2.0563[e]	96.20	31.0[e]	4.55	0.928
1966	1.0138	2.0563[e]	89.29	31.0[e]	5.21	0.894
1967	1.0237	2.0771	86.45	31.0[e]	5.68	0.870
1968	1.0205	2.0438	78.78	31.0[e]	6.15	0.928
1969	1.0237	2.0154	75.14	31.0	6.85	0.854
1970	1.0176	2.0083	77.21	34.0	7.73	0.683
1971	1.0205	2.1035	92.58	43.0	7.51	0.716
1972	1.0287	1.9942	95.76	48.0	6.30	0.735
1973	1.0599	1.9926	92.85	46.0	8.21	0.569
1974	1.1468	2.1393	82.11	38.0	10.06	0.417
1975	1.1903	2.4472	86.78	43.0	10.65	0.387
1976	1.2276	2.4472[e]	90.29	45.0	10.10	0.424

[e]Estimated by indirect methods explained in the text of this appendix.

Table 6–A–7.   Industry 32:   Clay, Glass, and Stone Products

| Year | Conversion Factors | | Long-Term Debt | | Preferred Stock Dividend/Price (percent) | q_i |
| | Inventories | Net Plant | Percent of Par Value | Percent Marketable | | |
	(1)	(2)	(3)	(4)	(5)	(6)
1956	1.0740 [e]	2.1709 [e]	102.00	38.0 [e]	4.35	1.006
1957	1.0740 [e]	2.1806 [e]	90.00	38.0 [e]	4.46	0.874
1958	1.0740 [e]	2.1563 [e]	98.11	38.0 [e]	4.29	1.017
1959	1.0611	2.1368 [e]	94.02	38.0 [e]	4.20	1.141
1960	1.0553	2.1368 [e]	90.44	38.0 [e]	4.01	1.068
1961	1.0557	2.0475 [e]	95.42	38.0 [e]	3.83	1.138
1962	1.0528	2.0110 [e]	98.25	38.0 [e]	4.04	1.004
1963	1.0543	1.9975 [e]	97.94	38.0 [e]	4.17	0.984
1964	1.0511	1.9595 [e]	96.22	38.0 [e]	4.16	1.043
1965	1.0442	1.9399 [e]	94.70	38.0 [e]	4.21	1.021
1966	1.0736	1.9399 [e]	89.24	38.0 [e]	4.76	0.969
1967	1.0484	1.9595	83.53	38.0 [e]	4.61	1.008
1968	1.0876	1.9975	83.02	38.0 [e]	3.53	1.032
1969	1.0491	2.0110	83.05	38.0	4.12	0.956
1970	1.0578	2.0475	78.25	37.0	5.67	0.763
1971	1.0396	2.1794	89.74	45.0	5.14	0.761
1972	1.0422	2.0616	92.68	46.0	5.35	0.770
1973	1.0641	2.0979	89.36	44.0	6.21	0.622
1974	1.0885	2.1952	81.62	46.0	7.39	0.463
1975	1.0920	2.4039	87.36	51.0	7.20	0.424
1976	1.1130	2.4039 [e]	91.50	48.0	6.28	0.487

[e] Estimated by indirect methods explained in the text of this appendix.

Table 6–A–8.   Industry 33: Primary Metals

| | Conversion Factors | | Long-Term Debt | | Preferred Stock Dividend/Price (percent) | q_i |
| | Inventories | Net Plant | Percent of Par Value | Percent Marketable | | |
Year	(1)	(2)	(3)	(4)	(5)	(6)
1956	1.3386[e]	2.3137[e]	104.76	58.0[e]	4.37	0.833
1957	1.3386[e]	2.3228[e]	105.77	58.0[e]	4.78	0.696
1958	1.3386[e]	2.3000[e]	98.78	58.0[e]	4.70	0.691
1959	1.3318	2.2817[e]	93.21	58.0[e]	4.62	0.828
1960	1.2754	2.2817[e]	92.10	58.0[e]	4.68	0.734
1961	1.2731	2.1693[e]	95.23	58.0[e]	4.72	0.723
1962	1.2542	2.1321[e]	97.28	58.0[e]	4.73	0.612
1963	1.2680	2.1858[e]	98.14	58.0[e]	4.52	0.586
1964	1.3039	2.2155[e]	96.64	58.0[e]	4.54	0.622
1965	1.3065	2.1933[e]	95.67	58.0[e]	4.47	0.599
1966	1.2589	2.1933[e]	89.51	58.0[e]	4.64	0.566
1967	1.2992	2.2155	87.40	58.0[e]	4.78	0.559
1968	1.3017	2.1858	83.00	58.0[e]	6.41	0.530
1969	1.3843	2.1321	78.20	58.0	4.98	0.511
1970	1.3379	2.1693	70.71	60.0	8.32	0.422
1971	1.3659	2.2356	82.41	63.0	8.75	0.384
1972	1.3732	2.2153	86.89	62.0	8.31	0.388
1973	1.5225	2.2452	85.69	61.0	8.65	0.375
1974	1.4613	2.3365	78.65	62.0	9.13	0.335
1975	1.4056	2.5725	83.79	55.0	8.29	0.332
1976	1.4683	2.5725[e]	89.24	55.0	6.91	0.371

[e]Estimated by indirect methods explained in the text of this appendix.

Table 6–A–9.   Industry 331: Basic Steel and Mill Products

	Conversion Factors		Long-Term Debt		Preferred Stock Dividend/Price (percent)	q_i
	Inventories	Net Plant	Percent of Par Value	Percent Marketable		
Year	(1)	(2)	(3)	(4)	(5)	(6)
1956	1.3386[e]	2.4535[e]	106.66	63.0[e]	4.50	0.654
1957	1.3386[e]	2.4640[e]	109.70	63.0[e]	4.84	0.584
1958	1.3386[e]	2.4376[e]	98.96	63.0[e]	4.68	0.625
1959	1.3318[e]	2.4164[e]	93.85	63.0[e]	4.82	0.758
1960	1.2754[e]	2.4164[e]	92.08	63.0[e]	4.88	0.663
1961	1.2731[e]	2.2658[e]	95.66	63.0[e]	4.86	0.661
1962	1.2542[e]	2.2144[e]	97.74	63.0[e]	4.81	0.554
1963	1.2680[e]	2.3145[e]	98.73	63.0[e]	4.57	0.507
1964	1.3039[e]	2.3348[e]	97.18	63.0[e]	5.93	0.529
1965	1.3065[e]	2.3115[e]	96.31	63.0[e]	6.11	0.488
1966	1.2589[e]	2.3115[e]	89.55	63.0[e]	6.66	0.433
1967	1.2992[e]	2.3348	85.44	63.0[e]	7.20	0.419
1968	1.3017[e]	2.3145	80.64	63.0[e]	6.23	0.409
1969	1.3843[e]	2.2144	75.40	63.0	4.40	0.408
1970	1.3379[e]	2.2658	67.63	66.0	9.25	0.326
1971	1.3659[e]	2.3226	79.42	67.0	9.84	0.309
1972	1.3732[e]	2.3552	84.02	64.0	8.82	0.321
1973	1.5225[e]	2.3741	82.67	64.0	9.21	0.296
1974	1.4613[e]	2.4799	75.65	71.0	9.45	0.272
1975	1.4056[e]	2.6925	80.61	62.0	8.31	0.282
1976	1.4683[e]	2.6925[e]	87.60	62.0	7.15	0.324

[e]Estimated by indirect methods explained in the text of this appendix.

Table 6–A–10. Industry 333: Primary Nonferrous Metals

	Conversion Factors		Long-Term Debt		Preferred Stock Dividend/Price (percent)	q_i
	Inventories	Net Plant	Percent of Par Value	Percent Marketable		
Year	(1)	(2)	(3)	(4)	(5)	(6)
1956	1.3386[e]	1.8237[e]	99.42	55.0[e]	3.80	1.190
1957	1.3386[e]	1.8370[e]	93.20	55.0[e]	4.53	0.881
1958	1.3386[e]	1.8038[e]	98.56	55.0[e]	4.93	0.930
1959	1.3318[e]	1.7773[e]	91.70	55.0[e]	4.08	1.097
1960	1.2754[e]	1.7773[e]	92.15	55.0[e]	4.26	0.995
1961	1.2731[e]	1.8069[e]	93.43	55.0[e]	4.36	0.923
1962	1.2542[e]	1.7801[e]	95.28	55.0[e]	4.49	0.795
1963	1.2680[e]	1.7566[e]	95.41	55.0[e]	4.40	0.787
1964	1.3039[e]	1.7767[e]	94.09	55.0[e]	4.38	0.882
1965	1.3065[e]	1.7589[e]	92.15	55.0[e]	4.47	0.880
1966	1.2589[e]	1.7589[e]	89.33	55.0[e]	4.64	0.902
1967	1.2992[e]	1.7767	96.20	55.0[e]	4.78	0.884
1968	1.3017[e]	1.7566	89.76	55.0[e]	5.29	0.784
1969	1.3843[e]	1.7801	86.29	55.0	5.88	0.745
1970	1.3379[e]	1.8069	79.65	56.0	6.53	0.647
1971	1.3659[e]	1.8713	89.44	65.0	6.71	0.548
1972	1.3732[e]	1.7301	92.52	65.0	7.16	0.547
1973	1.5225[e]	1.7242	92.34	64.0	7.40	0.591
1974	1.4613[e]	1.8569	84.56	59.0	8.35	0.498
1975	1.4056[e]	1.9813	88.84	51.0	8.24	0.483
1976	1.4683[e]	1.9813[e]	92.85	50.0	6.36	0.522

[e]Estimated by indirect methods explained in the text of this appendix.

Table 6–A–11.   Industry 35: Nonelectrical Machinery

	Conversion Factors		Long-Term Debt		Preferred Stock Dividend/Price (percent)	q_i
Year	Inventories	Net Plant	Percent of Par Value	Percent Marketable		
	(1)	(2)	(3)	(4)	(5)	(6)
1956	0.9729e	2.2527e	99.67	41.0e	4.60	1.308
1957	0.9729e	2.2538e	97.30	41.0e	4.65	1.322
1958	0.9729e	2.2511e	104.61	41.0e	4.62	1.381
1959	0.9668	2.2490e	107.11	41.0e	4.65	1.701
1960	0.9739	2.2490e	101.60	41.0e	4.80	1.699
1961	0.9691	2.1871e	105.54	41.0e	4.62	2.151
1962	0.9719	2.2361e	101.30	41.0e	4.89	1.765
1963	0.9827	2.2641e	103.25	41.0e	4.71	1.726
1964	0.9872	2.1698e	101.32	41.0e	3.76	1.868
1965	0.9917	2.1481e	100.22	41.0e	2.71	1.894
1966	1.0133	2.1481e	96.13	41.0e	2.64	1.753
1967	1.0121	2.1698	95.61	41.0e	1.47	2.112
1968	1.0091	2.2641	89.39	41.0e	4.24	2.237
1969	1.0296	2.2361	81.48	41.0	4.73	2.049
1970	1.0291	2.1871	77.34	46.0	6.39	1.621
1971	1.0355	2.2294	86.00	45.0	5.64	1.620
1972	1.0400	2.2362	90.08	44.0	4.99	1.823
1973	1.0713	2.2447	86.65	41.0	5.31	1.647
1974	1.1291	2.2554	81.44	39.0	6.04	1.064
1975	1.1483	2.4722	88.06	42.0	6.26	0.899
1976	1.1836	2.4722e	96.08	46.0	5.32	1.020

eEstimated by indirect methods explained in the text of this appendix.

Table 6–A–12. Industry 36: Electrical Machinery

	Conversion Factors		Long-Term Debt		Preferred Stock Dividend/Price (percent)	q_i
	Inventories	Net Plant	Percent of Par Value	Percent Marketable		
Year	(1)	(2)	(3)	(4)	(5)	(6)
1956	1.1698[e]	2.2613[e]	93.50	44.0[e]	4.00	1.408
1957	1.1698[e]	2.2698[e]	95.46	44.0[e]	4.88	1.342
1958	1.1698[e]	2.2486[e]	94.83	44.0[e]	4.74	1.461
1959	1.1469	2.2316[e]	87.80	44.0[e]	4.80	1.862
1960	1.1366	2.2316[e]	87.95	44.0[e]	4.84	1.609
1961	1.1640	2.1263[e]	91.49	44.0[e]	4.66	1.672
1962	1.2926	2.1844[e]	92.80	44.0[e]	4.59	1.369
1963	1.0996	2.1700[e]	93.61	44.0[e]	4.15	1.591
1964	1.0943	2.1482[e]	94.41	44.0[e]	4.14	1.691
1965	1.0901	2.1267[e]	92.14	44.0[e]	3.99	1.870
1966	1.0777	2.1267[e]	88.38	44.0[e]	3.12	1.785
1967	1.0892	2.1482	91.16	44.0[e]	2.31	1.746
1968	1.0707	2.1700	85.91	44.0[e]	2.32	1.651
1969	1.1098	2.1844	80.09	44.0	3.33	1.433
1970	1.1009	2.1263	72.15	44.0	3.27	1.173
1971	1.1103	2.2268	88.97	47.0	2.96	1.311
1972	1.1113	2.1988	93.48	50.0	2.38	1.496
1973	1.1497	2.1977	90.75	45.0	4.18	1.240
1974	1.1304	2.2825	84.99	44.0	7.10	0.803
1975	1.1499	2.5506[e]	85.45	46.0	6.94	0.743
1976	1.1670	2.5506[e]	89.10	48.0	6.02	0.863

[e]Estimated by indirect methods explained in the text of this appendix.

Table 6–A–13.   Industry 37: Transportation Equipment

Year	Conversion Factors Inventories (1)	Conversion Factors Net Plant (2)	Long-Term Debt Percent of Par Value (3)	Long-Term Debt Percent Marketable (4)	Preferred Stock Dividend/Price (percent) (5)	q_i (6)
1956	1.0421[e]	3.0343[e]	104.17	39.0[e]	4.29	0.963
1957	1.0421[e]	3.0507[e]	92.82	39.0[e]	4.65	0.756
1958	1.0421[e]	3.0096[e]	92.69	39.0[e]	4.52	0.815
1959	1.0157	2.9768[e]	91.35	39.0[e]	4.75	0.983
1960	1.0298	2.9768[e]	90.34	39.0[e]	4.30	0.892
1961	1.0298	2.6514[e]	94.51	39.0[e]	4.70	0.966
1962	1.0335	2.6467[e]	91.44	39.0[e]	4.55	0.932
1963	1.0423	2.7115[e]	97.10	39.0[e]	4.16	1.080
1964	1.0494	2.6713[e]	99.56	39.0[e]	3.92	1.164
1965	1.0463	2.6446[e]	101.12	39.0[e]	4.12	1.182
1966	1.0276	2.6446[e]	92.51	39.0[e]	4.55	0.967
1967	1.0222	2.6713	96.84	39.0[e]	4.48	0.896
1968	1.0602	2.7115	93.64	39.0[e]	2.86	0.914
1969	1.0570	2.6467	83.34	39.0	5.02	0.780
1970	1.0916	2.6514	77.49	39.0	6.72	0.651
1971	1.1310	2.7522	88.36	39.0	5.69	0.721
1972	1.1159	2.8237	93.65	38.0	5.27	0.722
1973	1.1246	2.9110	89.67	41.0	6.15	0.555
1974	1.1316	3.0754	83.37	41.0	6.51	0.382
1975	1.1518	3.2616	87.76	41.0	7.48	0.377
1976	1.1747	3.2616[e]	92.35	41.0	5.53	0.468

[e]Estimated by indirect methods explained in the text of this appendix.

Table 6-A-14.   Industry 371: Motor Vehicles and Parts

	Conversion Factors		Long-Term Debt		Preferred Stock Dividend/Price (percent)	q_i
	Inventories	Net Plant	Percent of Par Value	Percent Marketable		
Year	(1)	(2)	(3)	(4)	(5)	(6)
1956	1.2209e	3.1339e	102.69	47.0e	4.29	0.913
1957	1.2209e	3.1623e	90.15	47.0e	4.65	0.718
1958	1.2209e	3.0912e	90.29	47.0e	4.52	0.765
1959	1.1748	3.0344e	86.56	47.0e	4.75	0.989
1960	1.1935	3.0344e	89.21	47.0e	4.30	0.896
1961	1.1798	2.6615e	90.97	47.0e	4.70	0.968
1962	1.1738	2.6232e	90.18	47.0e	4.55	0.953
1963	1.1703	2.6428e	98.39	47.0e	4.16	1.158
1964	1.1725	2.5961e	97.75	47.0e	3.92	1.254
1965	1.1466	2.5701e	97.98	47.0e	4.12	1.237
1966	1.0893	2.5701e	92.11	47.0e	4.55	1.001
1967	1.0903	2.5961	89.87	47.0e	4.48	0.901
1968	1.0943	2.6428	90.80	47.0e	3.06	0.942
1969	1.0903	2.6232	83.69	47.0	5.21	0.806
1970	1.0916	2.6615	83.87	48.0	6.43	0.704
1971	1.0902	2.7410	91.75	44.0	5.50	0.785
1972	1.1018	2.7670	96.83	43.0	5.31	0.762
1973	1.0941	2.9207	93.60	46.0	6.15	0.582
1974	1.0963	3.2049	86.47	45.0	5.97	0.376
1975	1.1270	3.3259	89.29	45.0	7.61	0.373
1976	1.1347	3.3259e	93.24	46.0	5.84	0.480

eEstimated by indirect methods explained in the text of this appendix.

Table 6–A–15. Industry 372: Aircraft and Parts

Year	Conversion Factors		Long-Term Debt		Preferred Stock Dividend/Price (percent)	q_i
	Inventories	Net Plant	Percent of Par Value	Percent Marketable		
	(1)	(2)	(3)	(4)	(5)	(6)
1956	0.9726[e]	3.7524[e]	107.75	36.0[e]	4.29[e]	1.067
1957	0.9726[e]	3.7402[e]	116.63	36.0[e]	4.65[e]	0.778
1958	0.9726[e]	3.7706[e]	97.39	36.0[e]	4.52[e]	0.687
1959	0.9408[e]	3.7949[e]	99.34	36.0[e]	4.75[e]	0.692
1960	0.9528[e]	3.7949[e]	92.30	36.0[e]	4.30[e]	0.627
1961	0.9559[e]	2.8623[e]	100.45	36.0[e]	4.70[e]	0.911
1962	0.9580[e]	2.6615[e]	93.42	36.0[e]	4.55[e]	0.904
1963	0.9734[e]	2.6728[e]	94.51	36.0[e]	4.16[e]	0.810
1964	0.9740[e]	2.6228[e]	102.66	36.0[e]	3.92[e]	0.850
1965	0.9822[e]	2.5966[e]	105.59	36.0[e]	4.12[e]	1.258
1966	0.9972[e]	2.5966[e]	93.82	36.0[e]	5.59	1.097
1967	0.9970[e]	2.6228	104.65	36.0[e]	3.16	1.117
1968	1.0476[e]	2.6728	99.75	36.0	1.64	0.974
1969	1.0453[e]	2.6615	82.77	36.0	4.17	0.749
1970	1.0916[e]	2.8623	60.48	31.0	8.31	0.464
1971	1.1485[e]	3.2716	80.18	30.0	6.61	0.477
1972	1.1225[e]	3.6583	85.15	29.0	5.13	0.540
1973	1.1410[e]	3.8435	75.96	30.0	6.12	0.409
1974	1.1506[e]	3.7220	65.87	29.0	7.60	0.345
1975	1.1629[e]	3.9166	73.70	29.0	7.29	0.373
1976	1.1944[e]	3.9166[e]	85.32	29.0	5.18	0.430

[e] Estimated by indirect methods explained in the text of this appendix.

The Distribution of Investment between Industries 457

Table 6–A–16. Industry 49: Utilities

Year	Conversion Factors		Long-Term Debt		Preferred Stock Dividend/Price (percent)	q_i
	Inventories	Net Plant	Percent of Par Value	Percent Marketable		
	(1)	(2)	(3)	(4)	(5)	(6)
1956	1.2196[e]	2.1817[e]	92.16	88.0[e]	4.37	NA
1957	1.2196[e]	2.1877[e]	85.50	88.0[e]	4.68	NA
1958	1.2196[e]	2.1727[e]	86.42	88.0[e]	4.59	NA
1959	1.1708[e]	2.1607[e]	82.80	88.0[e]	4.88	NA
1960	1.2172[e]	2.1607[e]	82.78	88.0[e]	5.15	NA
1961	1.2031[e]	2.1340[e]	86.19	88.0[e]	4.84	0.695
1962	1.1798[e]	2.1661[e]	89.00	88.0[e]	4.51	0.653
1963	1.1714[e]	2.2070[e]	92.98	88.0[e]	4.49	0.683
1964	1.1630[e]	2.2572[e]	92.01	88.0[e]	4.09	0.680
1965	1.1882[e]	2.2346[e]	91.56	88.0[e]	4.56	0.686
1966	1.1949[e]	2.2346[e]	85.43	88.0[e]	5.14	0.593
1967	1.1864[e]	2.2572[e]	81.15	88.0[e]	5.50	0.550
1968	1.1839[e]	2.2070[e]	77.35	88.0[e]	5.45	0.538
1969	1.2050[e]	2.1661[e]	74.16	88.0	6.44	0.501
1970	1.2728[e]	2.1340[e]	67.32	93.0	6.35	0.447
1971	1.2422[e]	2.1916[e]	76.05	90.0	6.54	0.468
1972	1.2595[e]	2.1821[e]	82.73	87.0	6.77	0.472
1973	1.6216[e]	2.1367[e]	82.48	80.0	6.80	0.451
1974	1.6464[e]	2.1967[e]	63.97	70.0	9.05	0.354
1975	1.7051[e]	2.3939[e]	72.35	70.0	9.21	0.340
1976	1.7655[e]	2.3939[e]	78.40	69.0	9.09	0.375

[e]Estimated by indirect methods explained in the text of this appendix.

REFERENCES

1. AUERBACH, ALAN J. "Share Valuation and Corporate Equity Policy." NBER Working Paper No. 255. Cambridge: National Bureau of Economic Research, April 1978.
2. BAUMOL, WILLIAM J., et al. "Earnings Retention, New Capital and the Growth of the Firm," *Review of Economics and Statistics*, Nov. 1970, *52* (4), pp. 345-55.
3. BOARD OF GOVERNORS OF THE FEDERAL RESERVE SYSTEM. *Industrial Production: 1976 Revision.* Washington: Federal Reserve System, Dec. 1977.
4. BODDY, RAFORD, and GORT, MICHAEL. "Obsolescence, Embodiment, and the Explanation of Productivity Change," *Southern Economic Journal*, April 1974, *40*(4), pp. 553-62.
5. BRAINARD, WILLIAM C., and TOBIN, JAMES. "Pitfalls in Financial Model Building," *American Economic Review*, May 1968, *58*(2), pp. 99-122.
6. CICCOLO, JOHN H. "Four Essays on Monetary Policy." Unpublished doctoral dissertation, Yale University, 1975.
7. ____. "Money, Equity Values, and Income: Tests for Exogeneity," *Journal of Money, Credit and Banking*, Feb. 1978, *10*(1), pp. 46-64.
8. ____, and FROMM, GARY. "'q' and the Theory of Investment," *Journal of Finance*, May 1979, *34*(2), pp. 535-47.
9. CLARKSON, KENNETH W. *Intangible Capital and Rates of Return.* Washington: American Enterprise Institute, 1977.
10. DHRYMES, PHOEBUS J., and KURZ, MORDECAI. "Investment, Dividend, and External Finance Behavior of Firms," in *Determinants of Investment Behavior.* Edited by ROBERT FERBER. New York: National Bureau of Economic Research and Columbia Univ. Press, 1967.
11. EISNER, ROBERT. "Investment and the Frustrations of Econometricians," *American Economic Review*, May 1969, *59*(2), pp. 50-64.
12. ELTON, EDWIN J., and GRUBER, MARTIN J. "Valuation and the Cost of Capital for Regulated Industries," *Journal of Finance*, June 1971, *26*(3), pp. 661-70.
13. ERIKSSON, GORAN. *Growth and Finance of the Firm.* New York: Halsted Press—Wiley, 1978.
14. FAMA, EUGENE F. "The Effect of a Firm's Investment and Financing Decisions," *American Economic Review*, June 1978, *68*(3), pp. 272-84.
15. FELDSTEN, MARTIN S. "Tax Incentives, Stabilization Policy, and the Proportional Replacement Hypothesis," *Southern Economic Journal*, April 1974, *40*(4), pp. 544-52.
16. ____, and SLEMROD, JOEL. "Inflation and the Excess Taxation of Capital Gains on Corporate Stock," *National Tax Journal*, June 1978, *31*(2), pp. 107-18.
17. FRIEND, IRWIN. "The Economic Consequences of the Stock Market," *American Economic Review*, May 1972, *62*(2), pp. 212-19.
18. VON FURSTENBERG, GEORGE M. "Corporate Investment: Does Market Valuation Matter in the Aggregate?" *Brookings Papers on Economic Activity*, 1977 (2), pp. 347-97.

19. _____ , "Corporate Taxes and Financing under Continuing Inflation," in *Contemporary Economic Problems.* Edited by WILLIAM FELLNER. Washington, D.C.: American Enterprise Institute, 1976.

20. GRABOWSKI, HENRY G., and MUELLER, DENNIS C. "Life-Cycle Effects on Corporate Returns on Retentions," *Review of Economics and Statistics*, Nov. 1975, 57(4), pp. 400-409.

21. GREENBERG, EDWARD; MASHALL, WILLIAM J.; and YAWITZ, JESS B. "The Technology of Risk and Return," *American Economic Review*, June 1978, 68(3), pp. 241-51.

22. HEISS, KLAUS P. *Aerospace Capital Formation, Impact of Inflation and Depreciation.* Vol. I: Executive Summary. Washington: Aerospace Research Center, Aerospace Industries Association of America, Inc., April 1976.

23. KLEIN, LAWRENCE R., and LONG, VIRGINIA. "Capacity Utilization: Concept, Measurement, and Recent Estimates," *Brookings Papers on Economic Activity*, 1973 (3), pp. 743-56.

24. _____ , and PRESTON, ROSS S. "Some New Results in the Measurement of Capacity Utilization," *American Economic Review*, March 1967, 57(1), pp. 34-58.

25. LITTLE, I.M.D., and RAYNER, A.C. *Higgledy Piggledy Growth Again.* Oxford, England: Basil Blackwell, 1966.

26. LIVINGSTON, MILES. "Industry Movements of Common Stocks," *Journal of Finance*, June 1977, 32(3), pp. 861-74.

27. LOVELL, MICHAEL C. "Comments and Discussion," *Brookings Paper on Economic Activity*, 1977 (2), pp. 398-401.

28. MALKIEL, BURTON G.; VON FURSTENBERG, GEORGE M.; and WATSON, HARRY S. "Expectations, Tobin's *q*, and Industry Investment," *Journal of Finance*, May 1979, 34(2), pp. 549-61.

29. MAYSHAR, JORAM. "Investors' Time Horizon and the Inefficiency of Capital Markets," *Quarterly Journal of Economics*, May 1978, 92(2), pp. 187-208.

30. McFETRIDGE, DONALD G. "The Efficiency Implications of Earnings Retention," *Review of Economics and Statistics*, May 1978, 60(2), pp. 218-24.

31. MODIGLIANI, FRANCO, and MILLER, MERTON H. "The Cost of Capital, Corporation Finance, and the Theory of Investment," *American Economic Review*, June 1958, 48(3), pp. 261-97.

32. NATIONAL SCIENCE FOUNDATION. *Research and Development in Industry, 1972.* NSF 74-312. Washington: NSF, 1974. Subsequent issues: NSF 75-315, NSF 77-324.

33. OULTON, NICHOLAS. "Aggregate Investment and Tobin's *Q*: the Evidence from Britain." Unpublished paper, University of Lancaster and University of Michigan, June 1978.

34. REINHART, WALTER J. "A Relative Valuation Concept." Unpublished paper, Virginia Polytechnic and State University, Jan. 1978.

35. RESEK, ROBERT W. "Investment by Manufacturing Firms: A Quarterly Time Series Analysis of Industry Data," *Review of Economics and Statistics*, Aug. 1966, 48(3), pp. 322-33.

36. STIGLITZ, JOSEPH E. "On the Irrelevance of Corporate Financial Policy," *American Economic Review*, Dec. 1974, 64(6), pp. 851-66.

37. SULLIVAN, TIMOTHY G. "The Cost of Capital and the Market Power of Firms," *Review of Economics and Statistics*, May 1978, *60*(2), pp. 208-17.

38. TAUB, ALLAN J. "Determinants of the Firm's Capital Structure," *Review of Economics and Statistics*, Nov. 1975, *57*(4), pp. 410-16.

39. THOMADAKIS, STAVROS B. "A Value-Based Test of Profitability and Market Structure," *Review of Economics and Statistics*, May 1977, *59*(2), pp. 179-85.

40. TOBIN, JAMES. "A General Equilibrium Approach to Monetary Theory," *Journal of Money, Credit and Banking*, Feb. 1969, *1*(1), pp. 15-29.

41. ____ . "Macroeconomic Models and Policy," in *Frontiers in Quantitative Economics*, Vol. IIIb. Edited by MICHAEL D. INTRILIGATOR. Amsterdam: North-Holland, 1977.

42. ____ , and BRAINARD, WILLIAM C. "Asset Markets and the Cost of Capital," in *Economic Progress, Private Values, and Public Policy; Essays in Honor of William Fellner*. Edited by BELA BELASSA and RICHARD NELSON. Amsterdam: North-Holland, 1977.

43. U.S. BUREAU OF THE CENSUS. *Annual Survey of Manufacturers*, 1949/50-. Washington, D.C.: U.S.G.P.O., 1976 and earlier years.

44. ____ . *Manufacturers' Shipments, Inventories, and Orders: 1958-1976* (Revised). Current Industrial Reports No. M3-1.6. Washington, D.C.: U.S.G.P.O., 1976.

45. U.S. PRESIDENT. *Economic Report of the President: Transmitted to the Congress, January, 1977; together with the annual report of the Council of Economic Advisers*. Washington, D.C.: U.S.G.P.O., 1977.

46. ____ . *Economic Report of the President*. Washington, D.C.: U.S. G.P.O., 1978.

✳ *Chapter 7*

Investment in Producer Durable Equipment 1976–1990

Clopper Almon and
Anthony J. Barbera

Approximately two-thirds of nonresidential fixed investment, or about 40 percent of all capital formation, takes the form of producers' durable equipment (PDE). This investment is largely determined by (1) expansion of industry, (2) the need to replace worn-out or obsolete equipment, and (3) changes in relative prices of capital and labor.

This chapter uses these factors to explain equipment investment by eighty-seven industries covering the entire economy. Equations estimated on historical data extending through 1976 are used to forecast investment through 1990. To do so, they are imbedded into an input-output forecasting model distinguishing 190 products and showing the sales of each product going into other products as materials (for example, steel to automobiles) or as capital goods (for example, machine tools to automobiles) or to exports or consumer or government demand.[a] The investment forecasted by the investment equations is used in the determination of the outputs of the capital goods industries.

If we were interested only in the total magnitude of PDE investment, we might well be content with a simple aggregate equation, for it is possible to explain total PDE expenditures quite well with only gross private product and its lagged values. The advantage of having

[a]The input-output model used for this study was developed by INFORUM, the Interindustry Forecasting Project of the University of Maryland. The model distinguishes, along with the 190 products and eighty-seven investing industries, thirty types of construction purchased, nine government categories, exports, imports, inventory change, and consumption. The model is explained in [2, Almon et al., 1974]. The price submodel is explained in [1, Almon, 1978].

separate equations for different industries lies in the range of questions we can ask and in the confidence we can have that we are indeed estimating structural relationships rather than statistical coincidences. We can ask, for example: What will be each industry's needs for capital funds? How does the investment expenditure match internal fund availability on an industry-by-industry basis? What types of capital goods will be needed? How would investment demands be changed by shifts in energy prices and outputs of various forms of energy? The assurance that we are estimating structures comes from a comparison of the investment behavior for different industries. If we have only one equation, there is always the suspicion that a slight difference in data might change the estimated parameters substantially. If, however, equations for a number of industries show similar structures, our confidence in them may increase.

In this chapter we shall first, in Section I, explain the theory of our equations, then in Section II describe the data we have used. Section III displays the results of estimating the investment equations, and Section IV presents the forecasts.

I. THEORY OF DEMAND FOR CAPITAL

Our investment equations begin from the much-used constant elasticity of substitution (CES) production function, which may be conveniently written in the form

$$Q_t^\beta = A_t^\beta (v L_t^\beta + (1 - v) K_t^\beta), \tag{1}$$

where

> Q is output,
>
> L is labor,
>
> K is the gross stock of capital,
>
> A is a function only of time, and
>
> v and β are constants.

The level of capital desired is readily expressed as a function of output and the marginal productivity of capital. To do so, differentiate (1) with respect to K, holding L constant, and solve for K to get

$$K_t = B_t Q_t (\partial Q / \partial K)_t^{-\sigma}, \tag{2}$$

where σ, the elasticity of factor substitution, is given by $1/(1-\beta)$, and B_t, a product involving β, v, and $A(t)$, is a function of time alone. By assuming optimal investment planning, we can replace the marginal physical product of capital in (2) by a function of prices, interest rates, inflation rates, depreciation rates, and tax rules. Just to illustrate the procedure, let us consider the simplest case in which there are no taxes, the capital stock wears out at an exponential rate d, the nominal interest rate is i, and the inflation rate is f. Then an industry should invest up to the point at which the cost of one additional unit of equipment, P_e, is equal to the present value of the stream of returns resulting from the investment. The return in the year of the investment is $P_v\, \partial Q/\partial K$, where P_v is the "value added price" of the product; that is, it is the price of the product less the cost of materials needed to make a unit of the product. In year t after the purchase of the unit of equipment, only e^{-dt} of that unit is left, so it is reasonable to assume that the return, in prices of the installation year, will be $P_v\, \partial Q/\partial K e^{-dt}$. Finally, if prices are rising at rate f, the return in year t in current prices will be $e^{ft}\, \partial Q/\partial K$ e^{-dt}. If firms now invest up to the point at which the price of equipment is equal to the present value of the stream of return, we will have

$$P_e = \int_0^\infty e^{ft} P_v\, (\partial Q/\partial K)\, e^{-dt}\, e^{-it}\, dt$$

or

$$P_e = P_v\, (\partial Q/\partial K)\,/\,(i-f+d).$$

Therefore

$$\partial Q/\partial K = P_e\, (i-f+d)\,/P_v. \tag{3}$$

The numerator of the right side of (3) may be called the user cost of capital, since it is the price of the capital times the real interest rate $(i-f)$ plus the depreciation rate. Since the whole right side is this cost relative to the value-added price, we may call it the "relative user cost of capital," which we shall denote by r. Thus (2) becomes

$$K_t = B_t\, Q_t\, r_t^{-\sigma}, \tag{4}$$

where

$$r_t = [P_e\, (i-f+d)\,/P_v]_t. \tag{5}$$

As soon as we introduce taxes and different tax treatment for different expenses, the formula for r_t gets more complicated, although the logic of its derivation remains unchanged. We shall apply the formula for the case in which there is a corporate profit tax at rate T and an investment tax credit at rate C. Both depreciation and interest expense are deductible from earnings before taxes. The fraction b of the purchase price will be paid for by borrowing at the financing rate i.[b] Because of the common practice of refinancing debt when it comes due, there is no necessary relation between the life of an asset and the life of the debt used to finance its purchase. We shall assume, however, that at the time of purchase, the firm desires to have net changes in debt a proportion, b, of the net changes in the book value of the asset. The firm will therefore borrow the proportion b of gross investment and retire debt equal to the proportion b of depreciation. Thus, net borrowing will be the proportion b of the net changes in the book value of assets; from this relation we estimate b. Although b may vary historically, we shall assume that, for planning purposes, the firm expects its b to remain constant in the future, so that it expects its repayment to be the proportion b of depreciation. That depreciation should be, given the way we estimate b from book value data, *legal* depreciation; but the legal depreciation formulae are mathematically cumbersome, so we use instead physical depreciation at rate d. Physical depreciation will be exponential at rate d; legal depreciation for tax purposes will follow the path $\delta(t)$. Because of the tax credit C and borrowing, the firm's initial outlay is only $(1 - b)P_e - CP_e = (1 - b - C)P_e$. Capital is purchased up to the point at which this outlay is equal to the discounted cash flow resulting from the investment and the loan, thus

$$(1 - b - C)P_e = \int_0^\infty [P_v e^{ft} (\partial Q/\partial K)e^{-dt} - P_e b(i+d)e^{-dt}$$

$$-T(P_v e^{ft} (\partial Q/\partial K)e^{-dt} - P_e b i e^{-dt} - P_e \delta(t)] e^{-it} dt$$

$$= \frac{(1-T)P_v \partial Q/\partial K}{i - f + d} - P_e b + TP_e bi/(i+d) + TP_e Z,$$

[b]Miller and Modigliani [8, 1966] discussed the issues associated with determining the proper cost of financing and have found that with a tax on business income that allows interest payments to be deducted, the cost of funds may be considered a weighted average of the costs of debt and equity, with the weights being the relative amounts of debt and equity in the firms desired capital structure. They further determined that the cost of debt is the cost of equity times one minus the tax rate. To determine the proper cost of funds, Charles W. Bishoff in [5, Fromm, 1971], for example, has used a weighted sum of Moody's

where

$$Z = \int_0^\infty \delta(t)\, e^{-it}\, dt \ ,$$

which equals the present value of the stream of tax depreciation from a \$1.00 investment. Solving for $\partial Q/\partial K$ gives

$$\partial Q/\partial K = \frac{P_e}{P_v} \frac{(i-f+d)}{(1-T)} \left[1 - C - Tbi/(i+d) - TZ \right]$$

or

$$r = \frac{P_e\,(i-f+d)}{P_v\,(1-T)} \left[1 - C - Tbi/(i+d) - TZ \right] \ . \tag{3a}$$

Equation (3a) makes it clear that increasing the fraction borrowed, b, reduces the relative user cost. Of course, it also increases the risk of default and bankruptcy. A determination of the optimal b would require knowledge of the degree of risk aversion of firms and would therefore reach far beyond the bounds of the present study. We have rather accepted the level of b as determined from historical data and have calculated the implied values of r.

So far, we have assumed that capital can be instantaneously adjusted to the levels dictated by Q_t and r_t. In fact, there may be substantial delays. The lags in responding to output are, first, in recognizing and believing that an increase in sales has occurred and is likely to endure, and then in planning, ordering, building, and installing the new equipment. Although many firms invest now for future sales, their expectations about future sales may rest on present sales, so that, statistically, investment may lag behind sales. The relative user cost of capital also acts with a lag that may be even longer. Perception of the fact that faster depreciation means lower capital costs may take a while. Once it is perceived, it may still require time before the increase in the capital-labor ratio which it implies can be brought about. This lag is connected in part with the "putty-clay"

---

industrial bond yield, Moody's industrial dividend price ratio, the corporate income tax, and a time trend to estimate an aggregate investment equation. For our purposes, however, the merits of such an approach would not justify the effort. It would require a determination of the dividend price ratio for eighty-seven separate industries which would in turn lead to eighty-seven separate costs of financing. Yet, the specification of the cost of financing makes little difference, relative to other possible modifications of an investment equation. See, Robert Coen's discussion in [5, Fromm, 1971]. We have, therefore, taken Moody's Baa bond yield as the cost of financing for all eighty-seven industries.

question. Everyone agrees that capital and labor can be combined in variable proportions *before* the physical form of the capital is selected and the machine bought. Capital is "putty" at that stage. But can it really be used, as our equation assumes, with varying amounts of labor, after it is bought, or does the putty "set" so that the capital bought in any year is fated to be always used with exactly the same amount of labor? Does the putty become clay? The idea that it does become clay sometimes seems to be thought more realistic than the opposite view, which we hold. Numerous examples, however, point to the validity of our view. The introduction of the diesel engine in railroads changed about 6 percent of railroad capital yet made a huge change in the capital-labor ratio for the industry. Direct distance dialing had similar impacts on the telephone industry, while influencing only a small portion of the capital. One tractor requires one farmer to drive it, but that fact by no means prevents the farmer from purchasing a cotton picker and thereby increasing the capital-labor ratio on his farm long before the tractor is worn out. Thus, if we look at an establishment or industry as a whole, we usually see that the capital-labor ratio is technologically quite flexible without changing all of the capital. Nonetheless, there does remain the fact that when the farmer *does* replace the tractor, it will be with a more powerful one if the relative user cost of capital has declined. Consequently, this part of the lag would depend upon replacement and would be, presumably, rather slow. The lag in reaction to r is also likely to be slower than the reaction to Q simply because not having the optimal capital-labor ratio does not create the same kind of crisis in the firm that an unfillable order does.

In view of all these sources of lags, we replace (4) by

$$K_t = B_t \prod_{i=o}^{m} Q_{t-i}^{w_i} \prod_{i=o}^{n} r_{t-i}^{-\sigma_i} \tag{6}$$

as our fundamental equation. Here $\sum_{i=o}^{m} w_i = 1$, $\sum_{i=o}^{n} \sigma_i = \sigma$, and r_t is defined by (5). We shall presume that $B_t = B_o e^{at}$, where a is a small number on the order of 0.01. By taking logarithms of both sides and taking first differences we obtain

$$\underline{\Delta} K_t = a + \sum_{i=o}^{m} w_i \underline{\Delta} Q_t - \sum_{i=o}^{n} \sigma_i \underline{\Delta} r_t, \tag{7}$$

where the symbol Δ means first difference of the logarithms, which we shall approximate by the fraction change; thus

$$\underline{\Delta} Q_t = (Q_t - Q_{t-1})/Q_{t-1} \, .$$

We then multiply (7) by K_{t-1} to obtain the change in the net stock of capital in natural units (Δ):

$$\Delta K_t = a \, K_{t-1} + K_{t-1} \sum_{i=o}^{m} w_i \, \underline{\Delta} Q_t - K_{t-1} \sum_{i=o}^{n} \sigma_i \, \underline{\Delta} \, r_t \, . \tag{8}$$

II. DATA

Confidence in the accuracy of the estimated coefficients and the forecasting properties of any investment equation rests heavily upon the data used to estimate it. In order to estimate (8), data for net investment, ΔK_t, constant-dollar output, Q_t, and the relative user cost of capital, r_t, for each of the eighty-seven investing industries had to be constructed. A description of this undertaking follows.

Net Investment

The first step in constructing eighty-seven separate series of net investment was to ascertain separate series for gross investment in equipment in current dollars. Data for these series were collected from a variety of sources, taking care that the total matched the investment in producers' durable equipment (PDE) shown in the national accounts. For the manufacturing industries, seventy-five of the eighty-seven equations estimated, data were taken directly and exclusively from the *Census of Manufacturers* and *Annual Survey of Manufacturers.* Equipment spending for the remaining industries rested heavily upon the new plant and equipment (NPE) figure for the appropriate industry in the BEA–SEC investment survey. For example, airlines data are exactly the NPE figure; while railroads, communications, electric utilities, and gas and other utility data are taken to be the NPE figure less the construction figure for the appropriate industry found in Table 1 of the U.S. Department of Commerce, Bureau of the Census, *Construction Reports.* An exact, series-by-series description may be found in [2, Almon et al., 1974, pp. 86–89].

The next step is to transform these current dollar series into constant dollars. (All data for this study are in 1976 dollars.) To construct the necessary deflators, we combine the 200-order output prices with weights given by the INFORUM capital flow matrix, which distributes equipment investment by buyers to the various types of equipment. Thus we define

$$p_e^j = \sum_{i=1}^{n} b_{ij}\, p_q^i \;, \tag{9}$$

where

p_q^i = price index of the ith product, equal to $1.00 in 1976,

b_{ij} = the share of the ith product in a dollar's worth of capital bought by sector j, and

p_e^j = the price index of equipment to the jth investing industry.

This equation says that the price of equipment to the jth industry is a weighted average of the prices of the outputs of the 200 industries, where the weights are the shares of the ith product in a dollar's worth of capital bought by industry j in 1972. For example, since about 80 percent of airline equipment purchases are aircraft, the price of equipment to the airline industry will be greatly influenced by the output price of aircraft (with a weight of 0.8), and only slightly influenced by the output prices of other industries from which equipment is purchased. These deflators were used to convert the gross investment series to constant, 1976 dollars.

The final task in determining net investment, the dependent variable in (8), is to calculate the capital stock, and with it, retirement of equipment. The difference between gross investment and replacement investment is net investment.

The capital stock is calculated by a method that approximates the productive capacity rather than the book value of the stock. We distinguish two classes of capital: the first may be thought of as equipment which has not yet been written off while the second has been written off but is still in service. The first class of stock, K_1, grows by gross investment, V_t, and falls by the percentage depreciated or "spilled," s_t:

$$K_{1t} = K_{1\,t-1} + V_t - s_t K_{1\,t-1}\;.$$

The second class of stock, K_2, grows by the depreciation of the first-class stock and falls by the same percentage depreciation:

$$K_{2t} = K_{2\,t-1} + s_t K_{1\,t-1} - s_t K_{2\,t-1}\;.$$

The total stock of capital is then the sum of the two classes:

$$K_t = K_{1t} + K_{2t} \, .$$

In the above equation, s_t is the double-declining-balance rate of depreciation determined by the physical life of capital,

$$s_t = \frac{2}{L_t} \, .$$

For the physical life of capital, we project a gradual shortening of the equipment service lives given by

$$L_t = \begin{cases} [0.8 e^{\, 0.008(1980 - t)^{1.1}}] L_{1960} & t \leq 1980 \\[2em] 0.8 \, L_{1960} & t > 1980 \end{cases} \qquad (10)$$

where

L_{1960} = physical life of capital, initially taken from the *Depreciation Guidelines* but subject to change in the course of fitting the equations.

Finally, net investment, ΔK, the dependent variable of the equation, is the difference between gross investment, V_t, and retirement, R_t, where R_t is the depreciation or spillage out of the second-class stock:

$$\Delta K_t = V_t - s_t K_{2t-1} \, .$$

Relative User Cost of Capital

The relative user cost of capital, calculated by equation (3a), requires no less than nine ingredients:

T, the corporate profits tax rate,

C, the investment tax credit rate,

P_e, the price of equipment,

P_v, the value-added price,

i, the nominal rate of interest,

f, the expected rate of inflation,

d, the depreciation rate,

Z, the present value of the depreciation stream from a dollar of investment, and

b, the ratio of debt financing to total financing.

The first two, T and C, were taken directly from Internal Revenue Service publications. The third, the price of equipment, P_e, was derived as in (9) above, and simply reflects the cost of equipment to each of eighty-seven investing industries.

The fourth component, the "value added price" of each product, P_v, is found by making use of the input-output coefficient matrix in the following manner:

$$p_v^j(t) = p_q^j(t) - \sum_{i=1}^{n} a_{ij}(t) \, p_q^i(t), \tag{11}$$

where

$p_v^j(t)$ = price index of value added of the jth industry at time t,

$p_q^i(t)$ = price index of the ith product at time t,

$a_{ij}(t)$ = input of product i per unit of product j produced at time t, and

n = number of sectors.

Since there are 200 output industries, equation (11) gives 200 valued added prices for each year of the estimation period. What is needed, however, is value added prices for eighty-seven investing industries for each year. This aggregation was accomplished by using as weights the share of the outputs of the eighty-seven-order investing sectors in the 200-order sectors, as follows:

$$p_v^k(t) = \frac{\sum_{i \in I_k} x_i(t) \, p_v^i(t)}{\sum_{i \in I_k} x_i(t)}, \tag{12}$$

where

$p_v^k(t)$ = price of value added of the product of the kth investing industry at time t,

$x_i(t)$ = output of the ith industry at the 200 order industry level at time t,

I_k = set of 200 order sector numbers in investment industry k, and

$p_v^i(t)$ = price of value added for the ith 200 order industry at time t.

As explained in Section I, the value added price represents the price of the product less the cost of materials needed to make a unit of the product. If $\partial Q/\partial K$ is the marginal product of capital, then $P_v \, \partial Q/\partial K$ is the value of the marginal product of an additional unit of capital less material costs, as required by equation (3a). In addition, because P_v gives the *share* of value added in *gross* output, the appropriate weights for aggregating the P_v are gross outputs, not value added.

The fifth and sixth components, i and f, the nominal interest rate and the expected rate of inflation, appear together as i–f, the real rate of interest. In the first instance, we have constructed series for i and f separately, but we have also done some experiments in which we modified only their difference, the real rate. For i we have Moody's Baa bond rate. For f, the expected rate of inflation, we have used a weighted average of past rates of growth of the GNP deflators. To find appropriate weights, we reasoned that, since f was to be compared to i, the weights should show inflation expectations as they are reflected in i. We therefore estimated a simple equation for i, making it depend upon money market conditions as shown by the ratio GNP/M_2 and lagged values of inflation, thus

$$i_t = \sum_{j=o}^{n} \alpha_j \left(\frac{GNP}{M_2}\right)_{t-j} + \sum_{j=o}^{m} \beta_j \, \underline{\Delta} \, p_{t-j}, \tag{13}$$

where

M_2 = currency plus demand deposits plus time deposits at commercial banks,

p_t = the quarterly GNP price deflator,

$\underline{\Delta} p_{t-j}$ = $(p_{t-j} - p_{t-j-1}) / p_{t-j-1}$,

GNP = gross national product ,

   n = length of lag on GNP/M_2 ,

   m = length of lag on p_t ,

   t = time in quarters, and

   i_t = Moody's Baa bond rate entered in percentage points.

Therefore, the estimated expected rate of inflation, as reflected in i, is given by

$$f_t = \sum_{i=o}^{m} \hat{\beta}_i \, \Delta \, p_{t-i} \, ,$$

where

$$\hat{\beta}_i = \text{estimated coefficients determined in (13).}$$

The results of the regression estimated over the period 49:3 to 76:4 are (t statistics shown in parentheses):

α_0 = -8.40 (-2.87)		β_0 = 46.67 (3.48)
α_1 = 3.51 (0.687)		β_1 = 42.40 (2.97)
α_2 = 1.00 (0.195)		β_2 = 42.68 (2.91)
α_3 = -0.695 (-0.137)		β_3 = 35.30 (2.37)
α_4 = -0.776 (-0.148)		β_4 = 30.38 (2.04)
α_5 = -0.852 (-0.165)		β_5 = 24.87 (1.67)
α_6 = -0.773 (0.150)		β_6 = 23.33 (1.60)
α_7 = 1.20 (0.235)		β_7 = 36.04 (2.52)
α_8 = -1.74 (-0.338)		β_8 = 35.40 (2.52)
α_9 = 8.87 (-0.280)		β_9 = 38.34 (2.80)
α_{10} = 8.87 (3.04)		

R^2 = 0.9289 $\bar{R}^2$ = 0.9127 SEE = 0.6567 RHO = 0.85.

The sum of the β's are, as one would expect, positive. Furthermore, the lag distribution of the coefficients (as well as the T statistics) is U shaped, suggesting that the most recent past quarters and the most distance past quarters of price change are most important in forming expectations. The sum of the coefficients, 355.41, would seem to support the contention that past price changes are not fully reflected in the nominal interest rate used for this study.[c]

---

[c]Alternatively, one may argue that the sums of coefficients supports the view that price expectations, as reflected in the nominal interest rate, do not fully reflect past price changes. This result is not directly apparent from the estimated

The implied real rate of interest is, then, computed using the esti-mates of the β's shown above. Figure 7–1 shows a plot of the real rate of interest estimated in this way. It shows considerable variabil-ity and an unmistakable positive time trend. The figure also shows a smoothed-out alternative to the estimated real rate. Investment equa-tions were estimated using both the smooth rate and the estimated rate. More is said about the results below.

The seventh component of the relative user cost of capital, d, the depreciation rate, is a function of the reciprocal of equipment's aver-age tax life. We have adopted Thomas Mayor's [7, 1971] estimate of d for the period of 1947 to 1960. We extended the series beyond 1960 by letting it rise in proportion to the reciprocal of the average life of equipment, L_t, for which we used formula (10) above.

Thus each industry has a distinct rate of depreciation. Further-more, since this rate is related to the life of the capital stock, and since the initial life is subject to change in the course of fitting the equations, the rates of depreciation are likewise subject to change.

The present value of the stream of depreciation, Z, was computed using the sum of years digits depreciation formula. Robert Hall and Dale Jorgenson [6, 1967] found that this method dominated the double declining balance and straight-line formulas in the range of discount rates and life times with which we are concerned. Hence, the rate of depreciation formula used to compute Z in (3a) is

$$\delta(t) = \begin{cases} \dfrac{2(L^* - t)}{L^{*2}} & \text{for } 0 \leq t \leq L^* \\ \\ 0 & \text{otherwise} \end{cases} \tag{14}$$

where

L^* = the length of period over which the depreciation is taken; which is the initial guess from *Depreciation Guidelines.*

The present value of the stream of depreciation expression implied by the rate of depreciation in (14) is then

$$Z = \frac{2}{iL^*} \left[1 - \frac{1}{iL^*} (1 - e^{-iL^*}) \right].$$

equation since quarterly observations of annual nominal rates are regressed on quarterly changes in the GNP price deflator. To obtain results more commensu-rate with other studies, one should annualize our quarterly change in the GNP price deflator, and scale the nominal interest rate, which is in percentage points in our equation, by the factor 0.01. Estimating our equation with these trans-formations gives a sum of coefficients on the price variable which is less than 1.

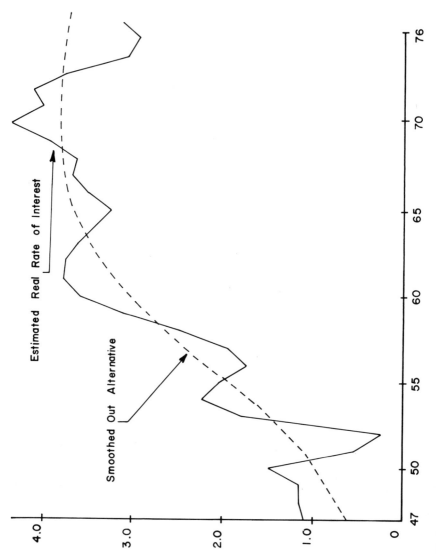

Figure 7–1. Estimated and Smoothed Real Rate of Interest

Note that the appropriate rate of interest for the computation of Z is the *nominal* rate, for the value of the depreciation depends upon its being deducted from profits before taxes, and this deduction is fixed in dollar terms, not real terms.

The final component of the cost of capital, the ratio of debt financing to total financing, b (for borrowing), was approximated by making use of the data on the change in total liabilities and total equities in the balance sheet table of the *Quarterly Financial Report*. The total liabilities include long-term and short-term debt, tax liabilities, and trade accounts and trade notes payable. Total equities include retained earnings, capital stock, and other capital. The fraction of borrowing is then given by

$$b = \frac{\Delta D}{\Delta D + \Delta E}$$

where

$$\Delta E = \text{change in equity, and}$$

$$\Delta D = \text{change in debt.}$$

Since a considerable amount of variability was evidenced by these numbers computed directly, we chose to smooth out the changes over time to show only the secular movement in this ratio (see Figure 7–2). This smoothed time series was then used for the b in (3a).

Output

Unfortunately, no one source can be consulted to provide all the data needed for the outputs of the eighty-seven investing industries. And data that are available are often not comprehensive. Consequently, many of our sources provide indexes by which we move forward the outputs given in the 1967 BEA table.

In the case of nonmanufacturing industries, the 1967 outputs are frequently moved forward by statistics on operating revenue, while for some of the service sectors we used unpublished data on Gross Product Originating (GPO) or Personal Consumption Expenditures (PCE) from the *Survey of Current Business* as mover. For the manufacturing industries, data on product shipments by five-digit SIC are used, and are found in the *Annual Survey of Manufacturers*.

To convert these current dollar series to constant dollars, proper deflators are required. For the manufacturing industries, we used deflators provided by the BEA which they have used in their GPO

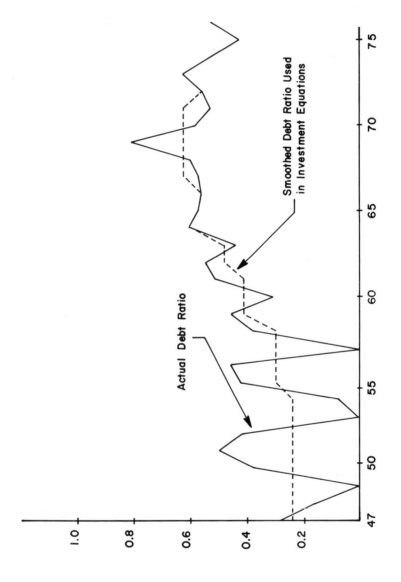

Figure 7–2.   Ratio of Debt Financing to Total Financing

work. For this chapter, we have made use of deflators at the five-digit level of detail, which are in turn based upon detailed WPI. For nonmanufacturing industries, numerous sources were consulted. A complete description of these sources may be found in [2, Almon et al., 1974].

Given these deflators and the outputs described above, we computed constant dollar outputs for 200 output industries. We then compared our constant dollar outputs with FRB Indexes of Industrial Production. In several instances we found puzzling differences in the trends of these two series for recent years. When the FRB indexes were based on some reasonable measure of quantity, and where the FRB and INFORUM series moved together for earlier years, we have modified the deflators so that our real output movement would approximate the movement in the FRB indexes.

Finally, we aggregated up the 200 output series to eighty-seven industries outputs used for the investment equations.

III. THE ESTIMATED EQUATIONS

Equation (8) of Section I has been fitted to the data of Section II. The equation is linear in all of the parameters being estimated except for L_{1960}, the life of the capital bought in 1960. This one parameter was simply varied at half year intervals until the life was found which gave the best fit.

The fit, however, was not simply the fit to the data but also the fit to our a priori expectations of what would be reasonable values of the parameters. These a priori expectations were:

1. The coefficient on the stock of capital should be close to zero;
2. The sum of weights on the present and lagged changes in output should be approximately 1.0, so that an x percent change in output should eventually give rise to an x percent change in investment; and
3. The length of life in 1960, which gives the minimum value of our objective function, should be close to that of the *Depreciation Guidelines.*

The expectations were introduced into the estimating procedure by inserting them into the objective function to be minimized, in addition to the sum of squared errors, in the following manner:

$$\text{minimize } H = (1 - R^2) + G_1\,(a/s_n)^2 + G_2\,(1 - \sum_i w_i) + G_3\,(L/L^* - 1)^2 \,,$$

where the G_1, G_2, and G_3 are weights which we can specify, L^* is the *Guideline* life, and L is the optimal life.

According to this objective function, we are willing, for example, to give up G_1 (Δa^2) in R^2 to obtain a decrease of Δa^2 in a. Hence, the larger the G_i, the greater the weight placed upon minimizing the ith component of the objective function, and the greater the importance, in our view, of the ith expectation.

To aid in understanding our assignment of values to G_1, G_2, and G_3, a helpful approach may be to ask and answer a specific question, such as: If $R^2 = 0.85$ and $a = 0.05$, how much of a drop in R^2 would be tolerated to get down to $a = 0.04$? Suppose we want the answer to be 0.018. What value of G_1 would be implied? The drop in a^2 is $0.05^2 - 0.04^2 = 0.0025 - 0.0016 = 0.0009$. Therefore, $0.0009 G_1 = 0.018$ or $G_1 = 20$. For the equations estimated for this chapter, we used $G_1 = 10$, $G_2 = 5$, and $G_3 = 5$. Thus, $G_1 = 10$ means that we are indifferent between a 0.01 decrease in R^2 and a 0.05 decrease in the ratio of the intercept over the variance in net investment, when the ratio is 0.01. G_2 and G_3 have analogous interpretations and are fully explained in [1, Almon et al., 1974].

Early experimentation with various values of the G's indicated that G_1 and G_2 have little effect; the data naturally lead the sum of weights to be close to 1 and a to be close to 0, when L, the length of life, is held close to the a priori life. Relaxation of G_3, holding the other G's constant, leads to substantial and unreasonable changes in the length of life and the fit. Finally, simultaneous relaxation of all the G's leads to considerable changes in the length of life and sum of weights without, however, substantially improving the fit.

The consideration of the a priori expectations thus produces parameter estimates which imply reasonable behavior and fit the historical data tolerably well. This claim may sound less ambitious than the usual claim to have produced efficient, unbiased estimates of the parameters. However, claims to efficiency and unbiasedness rest on the assumption that the equations have been correctly specified and that the economy really operates just as we have assumed that it does. To our way of thinking, such a claim is simply preposterous. All that we hope for is that the theory will provide us with equations for which parameter estimates can be found which both imply plausible behavior and fit historical experience fairly well. If a priori expectations can help us find these parameter estimates, we should certainly use them.[d]

[d] In addition to the a priori expectations discussed, the first five weights on output and on the cost of capital were required to lie on separate second degree polynomials. We made use of the method of Lagrangean polynomials explained

The investment equation described in Section I was reestimated four times, in each case with a slightly modified cost of capital. For our forecast, we selected that equation for each industry which provided the best fit.

As was mentioned in Section II, we have both an estimated time series of real rates of interest and a smoothed time series. Thus the investment equations were estimated for each real rate of interest. As can be seen in Figure 7–1, the estimated time series exhibited considerable variability. We reasoned that although our method might accurately approximate the long-run trend in the real rate, still a considerable amount of "noise" might be picked up in the short run. Furthermore, this extreme variability may significantly undermine the quality of the estimated equations by forcing the data to conform to large fluctuations in the real rate, when those fluctuations either did not actually occur or were not, in any case, perceived by firms. It was hoped, therefore, that smoothing the time series would improve the quality of the equations.

We further modified the cost of capital by first including and then excluding the (smoothed) debt ratio b in (3a). Again, we felt that the introduction of this parameter might improve the quality of the equations. The tax savings of increased debt clearly belongs in any cost of capital variable, as the derivation of the cost of capital in Section I showed. Its exclusion would, therefore, lead to an incomplete measure for the cost of capital. Yet, there are considerable difficulties with actually trying to measure the ratio of debt financing to total financing. If these difficulties are severe enough, then including b may conceivably worsen our measure of the cost of capital rather than improve it, and hence lead to poorer fitting equations.

Just two difficulties will be mentioned here. First, we were not totally convinced that the actual data being used correctly corresponded to the concept of b implied by the derivation of (3a). One should not expect, for example, the ratio to be below zero or above 1. In fact, however, ratios in this excluded region were computed. In some cases, firms experienced a decrease in debt over a twelve-month period, and an increase in equity greater in absolute value than the debt decrease, leading to a negative b. And in other cases, a decrease in equities over a twelve-month period, along with an increase in debt, lead to a ratio greater than 1.[e] As stated in Section II, we at-

---

in [3, Almon, 1965] to accomplish this. The final weight is left free except for requiring it to be no greater than the preceding one. For a detailed discussion of the method used in this chapter for estimating the equations, see [4, Dantzig. 1963].

[e] Negative values for b for "all manufacturing" occurred in 1949, 1953, and 1957 and were set to zero in Figure 7-2. No values for b at the level of "all

tempted to counteract some of these difficulties by smoothing out the movement in *b* over the estimating period, so that for each year we had a ratio between zero and 1. Second, all data used to compute *b* actually pertained to manufacturing industries exclusively, which are only seventy-four of the eighty-seven industries for which equations are here estimated. Hence, the debt ratio which is computed may be completely inappropriate for, say, the agriculture or transportation industries. As we will see, the introduction of the debt ratio could actually lead to a diminution in the quality of the equations for even the manufacturing industries.

We therefore have four alternative sets of estimates of our investment equations from which to select one set to make our forecast. The four equations are henceforth referred to as

1. NDVR; no debt ratio in the cost of capital and fully variable real rate of interest;
2. DVR; debt ratio in the cost of capital and fully variable real rate of interest;
3. NDSMR; no debt ratio in the cost of capital and smoothed real rate of interest;
4. DSMR; debt ratio in the cost of capital and smoothed real rate of interest.

A summary of the set of equations used for the forecast, selected from the four runs mentioned above, is found in Table 7-1. The first column gives sigma, the elasticity of substitution. The second column, labeled "fit," gives a measure of the closeness of the fit, namely the root mean squared error divided by the average gross investment by the industry over the period 1953-1976. The third column, labeled "stock," is the coefficient on last year's stock of capital. Next follow the six weights on the changes in output, their sum, and the six weights on the changes in the cost of capital. Thus a lag of up to six years was allowed for the response of investment to both changes in output and changes in the cost of capital. Finally, in the last two columns appear the "original" or a priori life of capital equipment and the "adjusted life," the adjustment coming in the course of fitting the equations.

---

manufacturing" were greater than 1; however, at the two-digit SIC level, such magnitudes frequently occurred. There was, in fact, far more variability in the debt ratio at the two-digit SIC level than there was at the aggregate level shown in Figure 7-2. We therefore chose to use the "all manufacturing" ratio for all industries rather than try to match our eighty-seven investing industries with the proper two-digit SIC time series.

Table 7–1.   Summary of Investment Equations Used for the Forecast

Sec. No. and Title	Sigma	Fit	Stock	W1	W2	W3	W4	W5	W6	Sumw
1 Agriculture (NDVR)	.287	13.3	−.013	.338	.298	.229	.129	.000	.000	.994
2 Mining (NDVR)	.000	19.8	−.001	.152	.168	.175	.172	.159	.159	.985
3 Petroleum & gas (NDVR)	.835	14.9	.003	.000	.150	.242	.248	.177	.177	1.004
4 Construction (NDVR)	.072	12.7	.012	.181	.231	.235	.193	.105	.020	.964
5 Ordnance (DSMR)	4.180	44.7	−.097	.313	.235	.157	.078	.000	.000	.784
6 Meat (DVR)	.114	11.5	.009	.026	.185	.266	.268	.191	.033	.969
7 Dairy (NDVR)	.000	30.4	.004	.169	.169	.168	.168	.167	.167	1.008
8 Canned & frozen foods (NDVR)	.031	20.5	.006	.215	.191	.166	.141	.116	.116	.945
9 Grain mill products (NDVR)	.146	9.1	.010	.113	.197	.230	.213	.144	.081	.978
10 Bakery (NDVR)	.107	11.5	.005	.185	.238	.237	.181	.070	.064	.874
11 Sugar (NDVR)	.408	23.0	.027	.296	.241	.185	.130	.075	.075	1.003
12 Candy (DVR)	.098	15.0	.009	.202	.188	.173	.158	.144	.144	1.009
13 Beverages (NDVR)	.320	9.9	.003	.006	.178	.259	.249	.147	.147	.987
14 Misc. food products (NDVR)	.022	18.7	.006	.094	.122	.151	.180	.209	.209	.964
15 Tobacco (NDVR)	.269	19.4	.021	.377	.286	.195	.104	.013	.013	.987
16 Fabrics & yarns (NDVR)	.000	17.7	−.006	.356	.275	.195	.115	.035	.035	1.010
17 Floor coverings (NDVR)	.000	31.3	−.076	.170	.241	.247	.188	.063	.063	.972
18 Misc. textiles (NDVR)	.000	21.2	−.001	.208	.236	.223	.173	.083	.083	1.006
19 Knit fabric & apparel (DSMR)	.369	44.4	−.047	.402	.302	.201	.101	.000	.000	1.005
20 Apparel (NDVR)	.000	17.0	−.006	.281	.231	.181	.131	.081	.081	.986
21 Hsehld. text. & upholstry (NDVR)	.000	32.8	−.020	.168	.168	.168	.131	.168	.168	1.010
22 Logging & lumber (NDVR)	.349	13.0	.027	.023	.216	.294	.257	.105	.105	.999
23 Plywd., millwork, struct. (NDVR)	.000	19.1	.015	.324	.270	.208	.137	.058	.000	.998
24 Wooden containers (NDSMR)	.000	43.9	−.004	.570	.185	.000	.015	.229	.000	.998
25 Hsehld. & ofc. furniture (NDVR)	.000	16.1	−.010	.344	.268	.192	.117	.041	.041	1.004
27 Paper/products ex. cont. (NDVR)	.294	15.7	.008	.063	.237	.306	.269	.127	.000	1.002
28 Paper containers (NDVR)	.000	16.4	−.015	.087	.200	.247	.230	.148	.102	1.014
29 Newspapers (NDVR)	.126	13.1	.013	.389	.303	.210	.109	.000	.000	1.012
30 Printing & publishing (NDVR)	.000	10.5	−.000	.201	.186	.172	.157	.142	.142	1.000

(Table 7–1.   continued overleaf)

Table 7-1. continued

Sec. No. and Title	V1	V2	V3	V4	V5	V6	Orglif	Adjlif
1 Agriculture (NDVR)	.018	.062	.078	.068	.030	.030	9.0	8.5
2 Mining (NDVR)	.000	.000	.000	.000	.000	.000	8.0	7.5
3 Petroleum & gas (NDVR)	.043	.113	.157	.177	.172	.172	8.0	7.5
4 Construction (NDVR)	.000	.021	.029	.021	.000	.000	7.5	7.0
5 Ordnance (DSMR)	.069	.849	1.182	1.068	.506	.506	7.0	3.5
6 Meat (DVR)	.004	.013	.020	.024	.026	.026	14.0	14.5
7 Dairy (NDVR)	.000	.000	.000	.000	.000	.000	14.0	13.5
8 Canned & frozen foods (NDVR)	.012	.009	.006	.003	.000	.000	15.0	15.5
9 Grain mill products (NDVR)	.027	.026	.025	.024	.023	.023	16.0	16.0
10 Bakery (NDVR)	.000	.008	.015	.023	.030	.030	14.0	14.0
11 Sugar (NDVR)	.000	.041	.072	.090	.101	.101	15.0	15.0
12 Candy (DVR)	.000	.007	.014	.021	.028	.028	15.0	15.5
13 Beverages (NDVR)	.000	.074	.104	.088	.027	.027	15.0	15.0
14 Misc. food products (NDVR)	.000	.002	.004	.007	.009	.000	14.0	13.5
15 Tobacco (NDVR)	.006	.081	.104	.077	.000	.000	12.5	12.5
16 Fabrics & yarns (NDVR)	.000	.000	.000	.000	.000	.000	13.0	13.5
17 Floor coverings (NDVR)	.000	.000	.000	.000	.000	.000	9.5	8.0
18 Misc. textiles (NDVR)	.000	.000	.000	.000	.000	.000	13.0	13.5
19 Knit fabric & apparel (DSMR)	.148	.111	.074	.037	.000	.000	9.0	9.0
20 Apparel (NDVR)	.000	.000	.000	.000	.000	.000	9.0	9.0
21 Hsehld. text. & upholstry (NDVR)	.000	.000	.000	.000	.000	.000	9.0	9.5
22 Logging & lumber (NDVR)	.058	.081	.084	.067	.029	.029	8.5	8.5
23 Plywd., millwork, struct. (NDVR)	.000	.000	.000	.000	.000	.000	10.0	10.5
24 Wooden containers (NDSMR)	.000	.000	.000	.000	.000	.000	9.5	9.0
25 Hsehld. & ofc. furniture (NDVR)	.000	.000	.000	.000	.000	.000	10.0	10.0
27 Paper/products ex. cont. (NDVR)	.000	.035	.058	.068	.066	.066	14.0	14.0
28 Paper containers (NDVR)	.000	.000	.000	.000	.000	.000	12.0	12.0
29 Newspapers (NDVR)	.050	.038	.025	.013	.000	.000	11.0	11.5
30 Printing & publishing (NDVR)	.000	.000	.000	.000	.000	.000	11.0	11.0

Table 7–1. continued

Sec. No. and Title	Sigma	Fit	Stock	W1	W2	W3	W4	W5	W6	Sumw
31 Industrial chemicals (DVR)	.736	12.9	-.004	.000	.150	.237	.263	.226	.116	.992
32 Agricultural chemicals (NDSMR)	.372	31.8	.018	.289	.245	.201	.157	.114	.000	1.006
33 Glue, ink, & fatty acids (NDVR)	.441	24.3	.000	.129	.254	.290	.237	.096	.000	1.005
34 Plastics & synthetics (DVR)	.430	24.4	-.002	.137	.260	.292	.233	.083	.000	1.006
35 Drugs (DVR)	.430	17.3	-.026	.195	.277	.279	.201	.043	.000	.995
36 Cleaning & toilet items (DSMR)	.243	19.8	.006	.000	.072	.143	.215	.286	.286	1.002
37 Paints & allied prod. (NDVR)	.000	29.3	-.015	.039	.092	.145	.199	.252	.252	.979
38 Petroleum refining (DVR)	.676	30.9	.031	.000	.300	.401	.301	.000	.000	1.002
39 Tires & tubes (DSMR)	.426	25.5	.001	.372	.302	.216	.116	.000	.000	1.005
40 Rubber prod., ex. tires (DSMR)	.221	13.1	-.004	.101	.132	.163	.194	.225	.167	.984
41 Plastic products (NDVR)	.052	11.4	-.017	.334	.262	.191	.119	.048	.048	1.001
42 Leather tan. & ind. prod. (NDVR)	.011	20.6	-.004	.401	.301	.200	.100	.000	.000	1.002
43 Shoes & other lea. prod. (NDVR)	.000	17.3	.008	.200	.202	.203	.204	.206	.000	1.015
44 Glass & glass products (DSMR)	.000	13.4	-.002	.314	.262	.201	.130	.049	.049	1.005
45 Stone & clay products (NDVR)	.000	13.4	-.002	.314	.262	.201	.130	.049	.049	1.005
46 Iron & steel (NDSMR)	.063	23.1	.014	.091	.196	.242	.228	.155	.098	1.012
47 Nonferrous metals (NDVR)	.000	17.0	.001	.099	.179	.215	.208	.158	.158	1.017
48 Metal containers (NDVR)	.000	16.5	.001	.392	.296	.200	.104	.008	.008	1.008
49 Plumbing & heating (NDVR)	.093	25.5	-.035	.035	.158	.224	.233	.185	.160	.995
50 Structural metal prod. (NDSMR)	.229	15.9	.003	.197	.188	.180	.171	.162	.083	.981
51 Stampings (NDVR)	.000	22.2	-.004	.215	.197	.178	.160	.141	.112	1.004
52 Hdwre., plating, wire prod. (DSMR)	.047	4.8	.002	.220	.200	.180	.161	.141	.099	1.001
53 Engines & trubines (DSMR)	.124	15.2	-.002	.282	.233	.185	.136	.087	.087	1.010
54 Farm machinery (DVR)	.227	16.2	-.022	.162	.199	.205	.179	.123	.123	.992
55 Construct. mining material (DSMR)	.197	11.2	.019	.101	.245	.287	.229	.070	.070	1.001
56 Metalworking mach. & equip. (NDVR)	.360	14.6	-.020	.199	.190	.177	.161	.140	.140	1.007
57 Spec. ind. machinery (NDVR)	.000	15.0	-.012	.235	.205	.175	.145	.115	.115	.990
58 Ger. indus. machinery (NDVR)	.012	10.9	-.001	.184	.196	.191	.168	.126	.126	.991
59 Misc. machinery & shop (NDVR)	.519	27.2	-.008	.219	.192	.166	.139	.112	.112	.940
60 Ofc. & computing mach. (DSMR)	.065	18.4	-.037	.105	.134	.163	.191	.220	.168	.981

(Table 7–1. continued overleaf)

Table 7–1. continued

Sec. No. and Title	V1	V2	V3	V4	V5	V6	Orglif	Adjlif
31 Industrial chemicals (DVR)	.056	.113	.146	.153	.135	.135	11.0	11.0
32 Agricultural chemicals (NDSMR)	.147	.111	.074	.038	.001	.000	11.0	11.0
33 Glue, ink, & fatty acids (NDVR)	.028	.048	.067	.086	.106	.106	10.5	10.5
34 Plastics & synthetics (DVR)	.034	.052	.071	.089	.108	.108	10.5	10.5
35 Drugs (DVR)	.000	.031	.061	.092	.123	.123	11.0	10.5
36 Cleaning & toilet items (DSMR)	.097	.073	.049	.024	.000	.000	11.0	11.0
37 Paints & allied prod. (NDVR)	.000	.000	.000	.000	.000	.000	11.0	11.0
38 Petroleum refining (DVR)	.055	.122	.152	.145	.101	.101	11.0	11.0
39 Tires & tubes (DSMR)	.000	.128	.171	.128	.000	.000	13.5	13.5
40 Rubber prod., ex. tires (DSMR)	.049	.066	.064	.042	.000	.000	14.0	14.0
41 Plastic products (NDVR)	.021	.016	.010	.005	.000	.000	14.0	14.0
42 Leather tan. & ind. prod. (NDVR)	.000	.001	.002	.002	.003	.003	10.5	10.5
43 Shoes & other lea. prod. (NDVR)	.000	.000	.000	.000	.000	.000	10.5	10.5
44 Glass & glass products (DSMR)	.000	.000	.000	.000	.000	.000	14.5	14.0
45 Stone & clay products (NDVR)	.000	.000	.000	.000	.000	.000	14.5	14.0
46 Iron & steel (NDSMR)	.000	.006	.013	.019	.025	.000	16.5	16.0
47 Nonferrous metals (NDVR)	.000	.000	.000	.000	.000	.000	13.5	13.5
48 Metal containers (NDVR)	.000	.000	.000	.000	.000	.000	11.5	11.5
49 Plumbing & heating (NDVR)	.000	.007	.013	.020	.027	.027	9.5	9.0
50 Structural metal prod. (NDSMR)	.000	.069	.092	.069	.000	.000	12.0	12.0
51 Stampings (NDVR)	.000	.000	.000	.000	.000	.000	11.5	11.5
52 Hdwre., plating, wire prod. (DSMR)	.000	.014	.019	.014	.000	.000	11.5	11.5
53 Engines & turbines (DSMR)	.000	.037	.050	.037	.000	.000	12.0	12.5
54 Farm machinery (DVR)	.039	.042	.045	.049	.052	.052	11.5	11.0
55 Construct. mining material (DSMR)	.000	.057	.077	.059	.004	.004	12.0	12.0
56 Metalworking mach. & equip. (NDVR)	.011	.071	.089	.065	.000	.000	12.0	12.0
57 Spec. ind. machinery (NDVR)	.000	.000	.000	.000	.000	.000	11.5	11.0
58 Gen. indus. machinery (NDVR)	.005	.004	.002	.001	.000	.000	12.0	11.5
59 Misc. machinery & shop (NDVR)	.093	.110	.110	.093	.057	.057	9.5	8.5
60 Ofc. & computing mach. (DSMR)	.000	.019	.026	.019	.000	.000	12.0	12.0

Table 7–1. continued

Sec. No. and Title	Sigma	Fit	Stock	W1	W2	W3	W4	W5	W6	Sumw
61 Service ind. machinery (NDVR)	.317	26.5	-.012	.167	.167	.168	.168	.168	.168	1.006
62 Elec. meas. transformers (NDVR)	.000	13.2	-.027	.186	.177	.169	.161	.152	.152	.997
63 Elec. apparatus & motors (NDVR)	.000	8.8	-.012	.183	.186	.180	.164	.139	.139	.991
64 Household appliances	.000	26.3	-.040	.201	.186	.172	.157	.142	.142	1.001
65 Elec. light & wiring (NDVR)	.000	19.0	-.008	.267	.225	.183	.141	.099	.099	1.014
66 Radio, TV sets, & records (DVR)	.271	27.0	-.003	.360	.277	.195	.112	.029	.029	1.003
67 Communication equipment (DSMR)	.020	22.0	-.007	.170	.163	.157	.150	.143	.143	.926
68 Electronic components (DSMR)	.331	19.0	-.018	.291	.236	.182	.128	.073	.073	.983
69 Batteries, X-ray, & elec. equip. (NDSMR)	.624	24.2	.011	.000	.154	.236	.247	.187	.187	1.010
70 Motor vehicles & parts (NDVR)	.000	29.3	-.036	.190	.225	.225	.189	.118	.055	1.002
71 Aircraft & parts (NDVR)	.393	42.2	-.007	.400	.300	.200	.100	.000	.000	1.000
72 Ships & boats (NDSMR)	1.397	21.2	.047	.067	.151	.198	.210	.186	.186	.998
73 Locomotives, RR, & stcars (NDVR)	.098	26.9	-.023	.166	.164	.162	.160	.157	.157	.966
74 Cycles, trailers, & parts (NDVR)	.666	17.0	-.006	.355	.278	.200	.123	.045	.000	1.001
75 Engr. & scient. instr. (NDVR)	.000	23.8	.014	.295	.236	.176	.117	.058	.058	.940
76 Mech. measuring devices (NDVR)	.000	20.3	-.005	.193	.179	.165	.151	.137	.137	.961
77 Surgical & medical inst. (NDVR)	.421	12.3	.005	.151	.203	.223	.210	.164	.047	.998
78 Optical & photo. supply (DSMR)	.103	10.3	-.014	.196	.205	.195	.166	.119	.119	.999
79 Misc. manufactured prod. (NDVR)	.000	14.7	-.009	.086	.129	.172	.215	.257	.131	.989
80 Railroads (NDVR)	.137	22.6	-.010	.404	.303	.202	.101	.000	.000	1.011
81 Trucking (NDVR)	.305	18.9	.010	.404	.303	.202	.101	.000	.000	1.010
82 Other transport (NDVR)	.086	55.0	-.006	.000	-.055	.000	.166	.442	.442	.995
83 Airlines (NDVR)	.000	40.3	-.055	.213	.307	.302	.200	.000	.000	1.022
84 Wholesale & retail trade (NDVR)	.000	13.2	.004	.404	.303	.202	.101	.000	.000	1.010
85 Communication (NDVR)	.000	20.5	-.006	.144	.154	.164	.174	.183	.183	1.003
86 Finance, ins., & services (DSMR)	.620	22.2	.004	.403	.302	.201	.101	.000	.000	1.006
87 Electric utilities (NDVR)	.000	25.2	.005	.403	.303	.202	.101	.000	.000	1.008
88 Nat. gas, water & sewer (NDVR)	.308	30.2	-.001	.000	.069	.139	.208	.278	.278	.971

(Table 7-1. continued overleaf)

Table 7–1. continued

Sec. No. and Title	V1	V2	V3	V4	V5	V6	Orglif	Adjlif
61 Service ind. machinery (NDVR)	.127	.095	.063	.032	.000	.000	12.0	12.0
62 Elec. meas. transformers (NDVR)	.000	.000	.000	.000	.000	.000	11.5	11.0
63 Elec. apparatus & motors (NDVR)	.000	.000	.000	.000	.000	.000	12.0	12.0
64 Household appliances	.000	.000	.000	.000	.000	.000	12.0	12.0
65 Elec. light & wiring (NDVR)	.000	.081	.108	.108	.000	.000	12.0	12.0
66 Radio, TV sets, & records (DVR)	.000	.006	.008	.006	.000	.000	8.0	8.0
67 Communication equipment (DSMR)	.000	.099	.132	.099	.000	.000	8.0	7.5
68 Electronic components (DSMR)	.000	.187	.250	.187	.000	.000	8.0	8.0
69 Batteries, X-ray, & elec. equip. (NDSMR)	.000	.000	.000	.000	.000	.000	12.0	12.0
70 Motor vehicles & parts (NDVR)	.000	.028	.056	.084	.112	.112	12.0	11.5
71 Aircraft & parts (NDVR)	.000	.000	.000	.000	.000	.000	10.0	10.0
72 Ships & boats (NDSMR)	.303	.273	.243	.213	.182	.182	12.0	12.0
73 Locomotives, RR, & strcars (NDVR)	.039	.029	.020	.101	.000	.000	10.0	8.5
74 Cycles, trailers, & parts (DSMR)	.266	.200	.133	.067	.000	.000	12.0	12.0
75 Engr. & scient. instr. (NDVR)	.000	.000	.000	.000	.000	.000	10.5	10.5
76 Mech. measuring devices (NDVR)	.000	.000	.000	.000	.000	.000	9.5	8.0
77 Surgical & medical inst. (NDVR)	.150	.126	.093	.051	.000	.000	12.0	12.0
78 Optical & photo. supply (DSMR)	.000	.031	.041	.031	.000	.000	12.0	12.0
79 Misc. manufactured prod. (NDVR)	.000	.000	.000	.000	.000	.000	8.5	8.0
80 Railroads (NDVR)	.000	.024	.036	.035	.021	.021	10.0	10.0
81 Trucking (NDVR)	.000	.022	.044	.065	.087	.087	8.0	8.5
82 Other transport (NDVR)	.000	.026	.034	.026	.000	.000	16.0	16.0
83 Airlines (NDVR)	.000	.000	.000	.000	.000	.000	6.0	6.0
84 Wholesale & retail trade (NDVR)	.000	.000	.000	.000	.000	.000	8.0	8.5
85 Communication (NDVR)	.000	.000	.000	.000	.000	.000	9.5	10.0
86 Finance, ins., & services (DSMR)	.070	.186	.213	.151	.000	.000	16.5	17.0
87 Electric utilities (NDVR)	.000	.000	.000	.000	.000	.000	10.0	10.0
88 Nat. gas, water & sewer (NDVR)	.012	.029	.046	.062	.079	.079	9.5	9.5

The results of estimating the four sets of equations from which Table 7–1 was constructed left little basis for choice, since no set of assumptions generated clearly superior equation estimations. However, the results do suggest a few comments, first about the elasticity of substitution, and second about the fits. Introducing the debt ratio into the investment equations increased the average elasticity from 0.1536 to 0.1859, and smoothing out the real rate of interest increased the elasticity still further to 0.2188. Hence, including the (smoothed) debt ratio and a smoothed real rate of interest in the cost of capital leads to investment equations which, on the average, appear to be more sensitive to changes in the cost of capital. (This is not true, of course, for all industries. For example, the elasticity in natural gas, water and sewer (88) dropped from 0.269 to 0.249 when debt and the smoothed rate are introduced.)

Table 7–2 summarizes further the results of the four separate sets of *a priori* assumptions on the properties of the estimated equations, in this case the size distribution of the elasticities. Introducing debt and a smoothed rate reduces the number of industry equations with zero elasticities by only four, and increases the number of industries with elasticities greater than 0.5 from seven to nine. In addition, the number of industries with elasticities greater than 0.25 varies from twenty-two (NDVR) to twenty-six (DSMR). Thus, introducing these modifications does not drastically alter the size distribution of the elasticities among the eighty-seven industries. Hence, although the presence of debt and/or the smoothed real rate seemingly increases, on average, the explanatory power of the cost of capital, this improvement maintains intact the relative sensitivity of different industry investments to a change in the cost of capital.

Yet while the explanatory power of the cost of capital increases, presumably because of a more accurate expression for the cost of capital, this change does not lead to an unambiguous improvement in the fits of the equations. As Table 7–3 shows, no debt (NDVR plus NDSMR) did the best in thirty-two of the eighty-seven industries while debt (DVR plus DSMR) did the best in twenty-one industries. There was no change due to these modifications in thirty-four industries. Thus we cannot draw any categorical conclusions about the overall impact of inserting debt and/or a smoothed rate into the cost of capital on the quality of the equations. Instead, it appears to be wiser simply to pick for each industry the equations with the best fit.

Finally, Table 7–4 provides a different view of the investment equations and their sensitivity to modifications in the cost of capital. This table contains two measures of the lagged distributions on output and the cost of capital. The eight columns under the heading

Table 7−2. Elasticity Measures of the Investment Equations

Equation	Average Elasticity[a]	Number of Industries with Elasticities Greater Than			
		0.0	0.25	0.5	1.0
NDVR	0.1536	55	22	7	2
NDSMR	0.1813	55	24	8	2
DVR	0.1859	57	24	7	2
DSMR	0.2188	59	26	9	2

[a]This is a weighted average of the sigmas with the capital stock as weights.

Table 7−3. Comparison of Fits of Investment Equations[a]

Equation	Best Fit	
	Manufacturing (5−79)	Nonmanufacturing (1−4, 80−88)
NDVR	17	7
NDSMR	8	0
DVR	8	0
DSMR	12	1
NO DIFFERENCE	29	5

[a]The fit is given by the root mean squared error divided by the mean of gross investment.

"average lag" show the amount of time, on average, it takes investment to respond to output (the first four columns) and the cost of capital (the next four columns). These numbers are simply the weighted average of the length of the lag, from 0 to 5, with the estimated coefficients as weights. The columns under the heading "cumulative weight" give the amount of response of investment to changes in output (and the cost of capital), as a percentage of the total response, in the present and two lagged years. Thus, the higher this number, the faster the industry responds to changes in output (or the cost of capital).

As the table shows, changing from no debt to debt and variable to smoothed real rate has little or no affect on the lag distribution on output for most industries, whether measured as average lag or by the cumulative weight, as would be expected. Introducing the smoothed real rate and debt leads to introducing modifications in the structure of lags on capital cost which are mixed and modest. In eight sectors, introducing the smoothed real rate gives equations implying an earlier and stronger reaction of investment to changes in the cost of capital, as measured by the average lag, while in eighteen others it had an opposite effect. On the other hand, debt in the cost of capital gives equations suggesting a quicker response of investment to changes in the cost of capital in nine industries, and a reverse implication in twelve industries.

The overall impact of the two modifications mentioned is, therefore, to lengthen the lag on the cost of capital. Hence, the results seem clearly to support the contention that investment responds more quickly to changes in output than to changes in the cost of capital. When looking at only those sectors with nonzero elasticities, in every case the average lag on the cost of capital is longer than the average lag on output in a majority of the industries. In addition, a cursory review of Table 7–4 will show that the number of industries with cumulative weights on output greater than 0.5, that is, the number of industries in which at least half the response of net investment to changes in output occurs within the first three years, ranges from seventy (DVR) to sixty-nine (DSMR); while the number of industries with cumulative weights on the cost of capital greater than 0.5 ranges from a low of thirty-four (NDVR) to a high of thirty-five (DSMR).

On balance, it appears that there are no clear grounds, either on the basis of the sigmas or on the basis of the lag structure, to hold that one cost of capital measure is uniformly better than another. Nor do the implications of the equations seem to depend crucially on the measure chosen. In the following analysis of the forecasts for capital requirements under various assumptions, we have used, for each industry, the equation which gives the best fit for that industry.

Table 7–4. Measures of Lag in Response of Investment to Changes in Output and the Cost of Capital: Average Lag and Selected Cumulative Weights

	Average Lag (Years)							
	Output				Cost of Capital			
Sec. No. and Title	*NDVR*	*DVR*	*NDSMR*	*DSMR*	*NDVR*	*DVR*	*NDSMR*	*DSMR*
1 Agriculture	1.2	1.2	1.3	1.6	2.4	2.4	2.4	2.3
2 Mining	2.5	2.5	2.5	2.5	NR[a]	NR	NR	NR
3 Petroleum & gas	3.0	3.0	3.0	2.9	3.0	3.0	2.5	2.4
4 Construction	1.9	1.8	1.8	1.8	2.0	2.0	2.4	2.2
5 Ordnance	1.1	1.1	1.0	1.0	2.7	2.6	2.7	2.6
6 Meat	2.6	2.5	2.6	2.6	2.9	3.2	2.8	3.1
7 Dairy	2.5	2.5	2.5	2.5	NR	NR	NR	NR
8 Canned & frozen foods	2.1	2.1	2.1	2.0	1.0	1.0	2.3	3.0
9 Grain mill products	2.3	2.3	2.3	2.3	2.4	2.5	2.5	2.6
10 Bakery	1.9	1.9	1.8	1.8	3.6	3.6	3.6	3.6
11 Sugar	1.7	1.5	1.6	1.3	3.4	3.4	3.4	3.4
12 Candy	2.3	2.3	2.3	2.3	3.6	3.6	3.6	3.6
13 Beverages	2.8	2.9	2.8	2.9	2.5	2.5	2.7	2.5
14 Misc. food products	2.9	2.9	2.9	2.9	3.0	3.0	3.0	3.0
15 Tobacco	1.1	1.1	1.1	1.1	1.9	2.0	2.1	2.4
16 Fabrics & yarns	1.3	1.3	1.3	1.3	NR	3.6	3.6	3.6
17 Floor coverings	1.9	1.9	1.9	1.9	NR	NR	NR	NR
18 Misc. textiles	1.9	1.9	1.9	1.9	NR	NR	NR	NR
19 Knit fabric & apparel	1.0	1.0	1.0	1.0	1.0	1.0	1.0	1.0
20 Apparel	1.7	1.7	1.7	1.7	NR	NR	NR	NR
21 Hsehld. text. & upholstry	2.5	2.5	2.5	2.5	NR	NR	NR	NR
22 Logging & lumber	2.5	2.4	2.5	2.4	2.0	2.2	2.2	2.3
23 Plywd., millwork, struct.	1.3	1.3	1.3	1.3	NR	NR	NR	NR
24 Wooden containers	1.2	1.1	1.1	1.1	3.6	3.6	2.0	NR
25 Hsehld. & ofc. furniture	1.4	1.4	1.4	1.4	NR	NR	NR	NR
27 Paper/products, ex. cont.	2.2	2.2	2.2	2.2	3.2	3.2	3.4	3.4

Table 7–4. continued

Sec. No. and Title	Cumulative Weight (3 Years)							
	Output				Cost of Capital			
	NDVR	DVR	NDSMR	DSMR	NDVR	DVR	NDSMR	DSMR
1 Agriculture	.870	.869	.831	.740	.552	.553	.549	.568
2 Mining	.502	.502	.502	.502	.000	.000	.000	.000
3 Petroleum & gas	.400	.402	.406	.415	.375	.384	.459	.471
4 Construction	.671	.677	.677	.683	.700	.700	.591	.636
5 Ordnance	.877	.875	.900	.900	.488	.510	.484	.503
6 Meat	.483	.493	.474	.482	.393	.331	.428	.357
7 Dairy	.502	.502	.502	.502	.000	.000	.000	.000
8 Canned & frozen foods	.605	.607	.617	.633	.900	.899	.607	.376
9 Grain mill products	.552	.556	.569	.575	.530	.493	.511	.468
10 Bakery	.677	.681	.698	.696	.215	.214	.214	.214
11 Sugar	.720	.775	.751	.812	.277	.263	.264	.253
12 Candy	.548	.558	.553	.563	.214	.214	.214	.214
13 Beverages	.449	.430	.442	.430	.555	.560	.490	.533
14 Misc. food products	.381	.383	.381	.382	.300	.300	.300	.300
15 Tobacco	.869	.871	.868	.876	.712	.700	.651	.564
16 Fabrics & yarns	.817	.818	.818	.819	.000	.214	.214	.214
17 Floor coverings	.677	.677	.677	.677	.000	.000	.000	.000
18 Misc. textiles	.663	.663	.663	.663	.000	.000	.000	.000
19 Knit fabric & apparel	.900	.900	.900	.900	.900	.900	.900	.900
20 Apparel	.703	.703	.703	.703	.000	.000	.000	.000
21 Hsehld. text. & upholstry	.500	.500	.500	.500	.000	.000	.000	.000
22 Logging & lumber	.533	.560	.539	.576	.643	.607	.604	.572
23 Plywd., millwork, struct.	.804	.804	.804	.804	.000	.000	.000	.000
24 Wooden containers	.726	.756	.756	.756	.214	.214	.000	.000
25 Hsehld. & ofc. furniture	.801	.801	.801	.801	.000	.000	.000	.000
27 Paper/products, ex. cont.	.604	.604	.588	.588	.317	.331	.263	.268

(Table 7-4. continued overleaf)

Table 7–4. continued

Sec. No. and Title	Average Lag (Years)							
	Output				Cost of Capital			
	NDVR	DVR	NDSMR	DSMR	NDVR	DVR	NDSMR	DSMR
28 Paper containers	2.5	2.5	2.5	2.5	NR	NR	NR	NR
29 Newspapers	1.0	1.1	1.1	1.1	1.0	1.0	1.0	1.0
30 Printing & publishing	2.3	2.3	2.3	2.3	NR	NR	NR	NR
31 Industrial chemicals	2.9	2.9	3.0	2.9	2.9	2.8	2.8	2.7
32 Agricultural chemicals	1.6	1.6	1.6	1.5	1.2	1.0	1.0	1.0
33 Glue, ink, & fatty acids	1.9	1.9	1.8	1.8	3.2	3.1	3.0	2.9
34 Plastics & synthetics	1.7	1.6	1.7	1.7	3.6	3.6	3.6	3.6
35 Drugs	2.3	2.3	2.3	2.3	3.6	3.6	3.6	3.6
36 Cleaning & toilet items	3.6	3.6	3.6	3.6	1.0	1.0	1.0	1.0
37 Paints & allied prod.	3.3	3.3	3.3	3.3	NR	NR	NR	NR
38 Petroleum refining	2.0	2.0	2.1	2.0	2.8	2.6	2.7	2.6
39 Tires & tubes	1.1	1.1	1.1	1.1	2.0	2.0	2.0	2.0
40 Rubber prod., ex. tires	2.8	2.8	2.8	2.8	1.4	1.4	1.5	1.4
41 Plastic products	1.4	1.4	1.4	1.4	1.0	1.0	1.0	1.0
42 Leather tan. & ind. prod.	1.0	1.0	1.0	1.0	3.6	3.6	NR	NR
43 Shoes & other lea. prod.	2.0	2.0	2.0	2.0	NR	NR	NR	NR
44 Glass & glass products	1.5	1.5	1.6	1.6	2.0	2.0	2.0	2.0
45 Stone & clay products	1.5	1.5	1.5	1.5	NR	NR	NR	NR
46 Iron & steel	2.4	2.4	2.4	2.4	3.0	3.0	3.0	3.0
47 Nonferrous metals	2.6	2.6	2.6	2.6	NR	NR	NR	NR
48 Metal containers	1.1	1.1	1.1	1.1	NR	NR	NR	NR
49 Plumbing & heating	2.9	2.9	2.9	2.9	3.6	3.6	3.6	3.6
50 Structural metal prod.	2.2	2.2	2.2	2.1	2.0	2.0	2.0	2.0
51 Stampings	2.2	2.2	2.2	2.2	NR	NR	NR	NR
52 Hdwre., plating, wire prod.	2.1	2.1	2.1	2.1	2.0	2.0	2.0	2.0
53 Engines & turbines	1.7	1.8	1.7	1.8	NR	NR	NR	NR
54 Farm machinery	2.4	2.3	2.3	2.2	1.6	2.1	1.5	2.1

Table 7–4. continued

	Cumulative Weight (3 Years)							
	Output				Cost of Capital			
Sec. No. and Title	NDVR	DVR	NDSMR	DSMR	NDVR	DVR	NDSMR	DSMR
28 Paper containers	.527	.527	.527	.527	.000	.000	.000	.000
29 Newspapers	.892	.889	.887	.884	.900	.900	.900	.900
30 Printing & publishing	.560	.560	.560	.560	.000	.000	.000	.000
31 Industrial chemicals	.389	.390	.371	.377	.408	.427	.424	.448
32 Agricultural chemicals	.719	.727	.730	.743	.834	.900	.894	.900
33 Glue, ink, & fatty acids	.669	.686	.706	.723	.324	.339	.369	.393
34 Plastics & synthetics	.740	.754	.730	.740	.214	.214	.214	.214
35 Drugs	.593	.589	.588	.578	.214	.214	.214	.214
36 Cleaning & toilet items	.214	.214	.214	.214	.900	.900	.900	.900
37 Paints & allied prod.	.283	.283	.283	.283	.000	.000	.000	.000
38 Petroleum refining	.690	.700	.665	.689	.448	.486	.442	.495
39 Tires & tubes	.879	.879	.883	.885	.700	.700	.700	.700
40 Rubber prod., ex. tires	.420	.412	.400	.403	.827	.829	.796	.810
41 Plastic products	.786	.787	.789	.791	.900	.900	.900	.900
42 Leather tan. & ind. prod.	.900	.900	.900	.900	.214	.214	.000	.000
43 Shoes & other lea. prod.	.596	.596	.596	.596	.000	.000	.000	.000
44 Glass & glass products	.766	.756	.749	.741	.700	.700	.700	.700
45 Stone & clay products	.773	.773	.773	.773	.000	.000	.000	.000
46 Iron & steel	.523	.529	.524	.531	.300	.300	.300	.300
47 Nonferrous metals	.484	.484	.484	.484	.000	.000	.000	.000
48 Metal containers	.881	.881	.881	.881	.000	.000	.000	.000
49 Plumbing & heating	.419	.415	.412	.408	.214	.214	.214	.214
50 Structural metal prod.	.563	.579	.576	.596	.700	.712	.700	.700
51 Stampings	.588	.588	.588	.588	.000	.000	.000	.000
52 Hdwre., plating, wire prod.	.603	.604	.597	.599	.700	.700	.700	.700
53 Engines & turbines	.709	.687	.708	.692	.000	.000	.000	.000
54 Farm machinery	.547	.571	.564	.579	.721	.556	.755	.576

(Table 7–4. continued overleaf)

Table 7-4. continued

| | Average Lag (Years) | | | | | | | |
| | Output | | | | Cost of Capital | | | |
Sec. No. and Title	NDVR	DVR	NDSMR	DSMR	NDVR	DVR	NDSMR	DSMR
55 Construct. mining material	2.2	2.2	2.2	2.1	1.9	2.1	2.1	2.0
56 Metalworking mach. & equip.	2.3	2.2	2.2	2.2	1.9	1.8	2.3	2.1
57 Spec. ind. machinery	2.0	2.0	2.0	2.0	NR	NR	NR	NR
58 Gen. indus. machinery	2.2	2.2	2.2	2.2	1.0	NR	NR	NR
59 Misc. machinery & shops	2.1	2.1	2.0	2.0	2.2	1.6	2.5	2.0
60 Ofc. & computing mach.	2.7	2.7	2.7	2.8	NR	NR	NR	2.0
61 Service ind. machinery	2.5	2.5	2.5	2.5	1.0	1.0	1.1	1.2
62 Elec. meas. transformers	2.4	2.4	2.4	2.4	NR	2.0	NR	2.0
63 Elec. apparatus & motors	2.3	2.3	2.3	2.3	NR	NR	NR	NR
64 Household appliances	2.3	2.3	2.3	2.3	NR	NR	NR	NR
65 Elec. light & wiring	1.9	1.9	1.9	1.9	NR	NR	NR	NR
66 Radio, TV sets, & records	1.3	1.3	1.2	1.2	2.0	2.0	2.0	2.0
67 Communication equipment	2.4	2.4	2.4	2.4	2.0	2.0	2.0	2.0
68 Electronic components	1.7	1.7	1.7	1.7	2.0	2.0	2.0	2.0
69 Batteries, X-ray, & elec. equip.	3.2	3.2	3.0	2.9	2.0	2.0	2.0	2.0
70 Motor vehicles & parts	2.0	2.0	2.0	2.0	NR	NR	NR	NR
71 Aircraft & parts	1.0	1.0	1.0	1.0	3.6	3.6	3.6	3.6
72 Ships & boats	3.0	2.8	2.9	2.6	2.0	2.3	2.2	2.4
73 Locomotives, RR, & stcars	2.5	2.4	2.5	2.4	1.0	1.0	1.0	1.0
74 Cycles, trailers, & parts	1.4	1.4	1.3	1.2	1.0	1.0	1.0	1.0
75 Engr. & scient. instr.	1.6	1.6	1.6	1.6	NR	NR	2.0	2.0
76 Mech. measuring devices	2.3	2.3	2.3	2.3	NR	NR	NR	NR
77 Surgical & medical inst.	2.2	2.2	2.2	2.3	1.1	1.2	1.2	1.2
78 Optical & photo supply	2.1	2.1	2.2	2.2	2.0	2.0	2.0	2.0
79 Misc. manufactured prod.	2.8	2.8	2.8	2.8	2.0	NR	NR	NR
80 Railroads	1.0	1.0	1.0	1.0	2.8	2.7	3.6	3.6
81 Trucking	1.0	1.0	1.0	1.0	3.6	3.5	3.6	3.6

Table 7–4. continued

Sec. No. and Title	Cumulative Weight (3 Years)							
	Output				Cost of Capital			
	NDVR	DVR	NDSMR	DSMR	NDVR	DVR	NDSMR	DSMR
55 Construct. mining material	.608	.621	.622	.632	.685	.649	.663	.682
56 Metalworking mach. & equip.	.563	.571	.584	.593	.724	.733	.599	.661
57 Spec. ind. machinery	.621	.621	.621	.621	.000	.000	.000	.000
58 Gen. indus. machinery	.576	.581	.581	.581	.900	.000	.000	.000
59 Misc. machinery & shops	.614	.607	.628	.631	.603	.762	.509	.645
60 Ofc. & computing mach.	.430	.430	.430	.409	.000	.000	.000	.700
61 Service ind. machinery	.498	.502	.490	.495	.900	.900	.881	.869
62 Elec. meas. transformers	.534	.534	.534	.533	.000	.700	.000	.700
63 Elec. apparatus & motors	.554	.554	.554	.554	.000	.000	.000	.000
64 Household appliances	.559	.559	.559	.559	.000	.000	.000	.000
65 Elec. light & wiring	.666	.666	.666	.666	.000	.000	.000	.000
66 Radio, TV sets, & records	.826	.830	.836	.845	.700	.700	.700	.700
67 Communication equipment	.526	.525	.529	.529	.700	.700	.700	.700
68 Electronic components	.726	.724	.717	.721	.700	.700	.700	.700
69 Batteries, X-ray, & elec. equip.	.332	.331	.386	.408	.700	.700	.700	.700
70 Motor vehicles & parts	.639	.639	.639	.639	.000	.000	.000	.000
71 Aircraft & parts	.900	.900	.900	.900	.214	.214	.214	.214
72 Ships & boats	.373	.413	.417	.479	.630	.568	.587	.515
73 Locomotives, RR, & stcars	.509	.527	.505	.527	.900	.900	.900	.900
74 Cycles, trailers, & parts	.790	.793	.817	.833	.900	.900	.900	.900
75 Engr. & scient. instr.	.752	.752	.750	.744	.000	.000	.700	.700
76 Mech. measuring devices	.558	.558	.558	.558	.000	.000	.000	.000
77 Surgical & medical inst.	.578	.561	.567	.553	.878	.864	.864	.857
78 Optical & photo supply	.609	.603	.599	.596	.700	.700	.700	.700
79 Misc. manufactured prod.	.390	.390	.390	.390	.000	.000	.000	.000
80 Railroads	.900	.900	.900	.900	.438	.477	.214	.214
81 Trucking	.900	.900	.900	.900	.214	.251	.214	.214

(Table 7–4. continued overleaf)

Table 7-4. continued

| | Average Lag (Years) | | | | | | | |
| | Output | | | | Cost of Capital | | | |
Sec. No. and Title	NDVR	DVR	NDSMR	DSMR	NDVR	DVR	NDSMR	DSMR
82 Other transport	4.4	4.4	4.4	4.4	2.0	2.0	1.2	1.1
83 Airlines	1.5	1.5	1.5	1.5	NR	NR	NR	NR
84 Wholesale & retail trade	1.0	1.0	1.0	1.0	NR	NR	NR	NR
85 Communications	2.6	2.6	2.6	2.6	NR	NR	NR	NR
86 Finance, ins., & services	1.0	1.0	1.0	1.0	2.0	1.7	2.0	1.7
87 Electric utilities	1.0	1.0	1.0	1.0	NR	NR	NR	NR
88 Nat. gas, water & sewer	3.6	3.6	3.6	3.6	3.3	3.6	3.6	3.6

Table 7-4. continued

| | Cumulative Weight (3 Years) | | | | | | | |
| | Output | | | | Cost of Capital | | | |
Sec. No. and Title	NDVR	DVR	NDSMR	DSMR	NDVR	DVR	NDSMR	DSMR
82 Other transport	.000	.000	.000	.000	.702	.700	.853	.887
83 Airlines	.804	.804	.804	.804	.000	.000	.000	.000
84 Wholesale & retail trade	.900	.900	.900	.900	.000	.000	.000	.000
85 Communications	.461	.461	.461	.461	.000	.000	.000	.000
86 Finance, ins., & services	.900	.900	.900	.900	.700	.753	.700	.756
87 Electric utilities	.900	.900	.900	.900	.000	.000	.000	.000
88 Nat. gas, water & sewer	.214	.214	.214	.214	.283	.214	.214	.214

In case of a tie, NDVR was used. On this basis fifty-eight of the equations in Table 7–1 are NDVR, thirteen are DSMR, eight are DVR, and eight are NDSMR. We now turn to the forecasts.

IV. THE FORECAST

The investment equation derived in Section I posits that net investment in an industry at any time t depends upon present and past percentage changes in output, present and past percentage changes in the cost of capital, and the capital stock in existence in the previous year. Hence, to forecast investment, one needs not only the estimated coefficients on the independent variables, but also future values for the independent variables, that is, the previous year's capital, output, and the cost of capital.

The previous year's capital stock and output for each industry are endogenously determined by the INFORUM model. The capital stock grows, essentially, by last year's net investment while future outputs for each industry are the result of past investment, consumption, and government demand.

In the cost of capital (3a), the price of equipment P_e, and the price of value added, P_v, are both determined endogenously by the model following equations (9), (11), and (12) in Section II. The present value of the stream of depreciation, Z in (3a), moves with future movements in the nominal interest rate; and the rate of depreciation, d in (3a), moves with the life of the capital stock explained in (10). The ratio of debt financing to total financing is given the value of zero for those industries with costs of capital excluding the debt ratio, and is given the value of 0.52 for those industries which include the debt ratio in the cost of capital, 0.52 being approximately the average ratio over the recent past (see Figure 7–2). What remains to be determined are future movements in the real rate of interest, and the tax parameters C and T.

Assuming the tax parameters remain unchanged from their existing values, that is, $C = 0.10$ and $T = 0.46$, a set of three forecasts were run with divergent assumptions about the future movements in the real rate of interest. In the "BASE" forecast, the real rate was held constant at 0.035 throughout. In the "ALT1" forecast, the real rate is assumed to increase linearly from 0.035 in 1976 to 0.045 in 1990. In the "ALT2" forecast, the real rate is assumed to decrease linearly from 0.035 in 1976 to 0.025 in 1990. A comparison of these three forecasts for each of the eighty-seven industries is found in Table 7–5, which shows gross investment in 1976 dollars in selected years for each of the three forecasts.

Table 7—5. Different Real Rates

Sec. No. and Title	Equipment Investment, by Purchaser (millions of 1976 dollars)			
	(BASE) 1976	(BASE) 1980	(ALT1) 1980	(ALT2) 1980
1 Agriculture	9585.	10460.	10402.	10520.
2 Mining	1657.	1961.	1962.	1961.
3 Petroleum & gas	3354.	4802.	4765.	4839.
4 Construction	5773.	7779.	7778.	7780.
5 Ordnance	125.	158.	158.	158.
6 Meat	285.	409.	408.	410.
7 Dairy	256.	299.	299.	299.
8 Canned & frozen foods	374.	494.	493.	494.
9 Grain mill products	352.	444.	442.	447.
10 Bakery	266.	257.	257.	258.
11 Sugar	191.	116.	114.	117.
12 Candy	102.	131.	131.	132.
13 Beverages	735.	778.	767.	788.
14 Misc. food products	323.	431.	431.	431.
15 Tobacco	107.	134.	132.	136.
16 Fabrics & yarns	616.	894.	891.	897.
17 Floor coverings	51.	86.	86.	86.
18 Misc. textiles	91.	176.	175.	176.
19 Knit fabric & apparel	165.	178.	174.	182.
20 Apparel	224.	290.	290.	289.
21 Hsehld. text. & upholstry	81.	149.	149.	149.
22 Logging & lumber	674.	1068.	1062.	1074.
23 Plywd., millwork, struct.	303.	574.	573.	574.
24 Wooden containers	7.	12.	12.	12.
25 Hsehld. & Ofc. furniture	208.	306.	305.	307.
27 Paper/products, ex. cont.	2426.	2968.	2947.	2989.
28 Paper containers	282.	403.	403.	403.
29 Newspapers	295.	485.	483.	487.
30 Printing & publishing	742.	962.	963.	962.
31 Industrial chemicals	3646.	3534.	3457.	3612.
32 Agricultural chemicals	285.	415.	411.	420.
33 Glue, ink, & fatty acids	302.	303.	301.	306.
34 Plastics & synthetics	1261.	2205.	2188.	2222.
35 Drugs	340.	341.	340.	342.
36 Cleaning & toilet items	237.	244.	242.	247.
37 Paints & allied prod.	83.	99.	99.	99.
38 Petroleum refining	1611.	1919.	1875.	1964.
39 Tire & tubes	216.	578.	566.	590.
40 Rubber prod., ex. tires	174.	212.	209.	215.

Table 7–5. continued

Equipment Investment, by Purchaser (millions of 1976 dollars)					
(BASE) 1985	*(ALT1)* 1985	*(ALT2)* 1985	*(BASE)* 1990	*(ALT1)* 1990	*(ALT2)* 1990
11059.	10957.	11164.	11307.	11151.	11471.
2286.	2287.	2285.	2582.	2584.	2581.
3972.	3863.	4087.	4330.	4160.	4514.
9437.	9438.	9437.	10358.	10350.	10367.
166.	166.	166.	174.	174.	174.
414.	411.	418.	486.	481.	492.
330.	331.	330.	350.	351.	350.
591.	590.	592.	655.	654.	656.
506.	501.	512.	570.	562.	578.
288.	287.	290.	288.	285.	290.
234.	228.	240.	273.	263.	283.
159.	158.	161.	173.	171.	175.
899.	880.	918	985.	958.	1015.
518.	518.	519.	572.	571.	572.
156.	154.	159.	180.	176.	184.
882.	881.	883.	894.	893.	896.
72.	71.	72.	68.	68.	68.
164.	164.	164.	172.	172.	172.
209.	205.	214.	171.	166.	176.
295.	296.	295.	293.	293.	292.
185.	185.	185.	221.	221.	221.
1323.	1308.	1339.	1562.	1535.	1591.
746.	746.	746.	913.	913.	913.
12.	12.	12.	12.	12.	12.
351.	347.	355.	347.	341.	354.
3122.	3067.	3180.	3516.	3430.	3610.
419.	418.	419.	426.	425.	426.
549.	546.	553.	614.	609.	619.
1121.	1122.	1121.	1229.	1230.	1229.
2510.	2375.	2656.	3591.	3366.	3843.
493.	485.	502.	611.	596.	626.
304.	298.	310.	319.	311.	328.
1629.	1586.	1674.	1612.	1552.	1678.
326.	323.	329.	324.	320.	329.
358.	354.	362.	427.	421.	433.
114.	114.	114.	111.	111.	111.
2544.	2430.	2667.	3340.	3140.	3569.
574.	558.	590.	644.	621.	668.
240.	242.	251.	250.	244.	255.

(Table 7-5. continued overleaf)

Table 7–5.   continued

Sec. No. and Title	Equipment Investment, by Purchaser (millions of 1976 dollars)			
	(BASE) 1976	(BASE) 1980	(ALT1) 1980	(ALT2) 1980
41 Plastic products	652.	986.	982.	991.
42 Leather tan. & ind. prod.	21.	27.	27.	27.
43 Shoes & other lea. prod.	42.	76.	76.	76.
44 Glass & glass products	358.	608.	603.	614.
45 Stone & clay products	854.	1403.	1403.	1404.
46 Iron & steel	2685.	3833.	3824.	3843.
47 Nonferrous metals	934.	1511.	1511.	1511.
48 Metal containers	127.	316.	316.	316.
49 Plumbing & heating	53.	52.	52.	52.
50 Structural metal prod.	454.	498.	493.	503.
51 Stampings	364.	506.	505.	507.
52 Hdwre., plating, wire prod.	586.	778.	775.	781.
53 Engines & turbines	230.	300.	296.	303.
54 Farm machinery	198.	150.	148.	153.
55 Construct. mining material	568.	762.	759.	765.
56 Metalworking mach. & equip.	293.	425.	420.	431
57 Spec. ind. machinery	169.	273.	271.	274.
58 Gen. Indus. machinery	382.	463.	461.	465.
59 Misc. machinery & shops	238.	293.	290.	297.
60 Ofc. & computing mach.	380.	385.	382.	387.
61 Service ind. machinery	144.	201.	197.	204.
62 Elec. meas. transformers	119.	172.	171.	172.
63 Elec. apparatus & motors	222.	261.	260.	262.
64 Household appliances	149.	138.	138.	138.
65 Elec. light & wiring	135.	246.	246.	246.
66 Radio, TV sets, & records	83.	124.	123.	126.
67 Communication equipment	428.	553.	552.	553.
68 Electronic components	551.	690.	682.	698.
69 Batteries, X-ray, & elec. equip.	176.	190.	185.	196.
70 Motor vehicles & parts	1908.	2823.	2815.	2830.
71 Aircraft & parts	380.	611.	608.	614.
72 Ships & boats	257.	311.	301.	320.
73 Locomotives, RR, & stcars	54.	69.	68.	69.
74 Cycles, trailers & parts	52.	90.	87.	93.
75 Engr. & scient. instr.	32.	46.	45.	46.
76 Mech. measuring devices	73.	88.	87.	88.
77 Surgical & medical inst.	112.	139.	136.	143.
78 Optical & photo. supply	337.	403.	398.	408.
79 Misc. manufactured prod.	408.	376.	376.	377.
80 Railroads	1965.	3078.	3064.	3091.

Table 7–5. continued

Equipment Investment, by Purchaser
(millions of 1976 dollars)

(BASE) 1985	(ALT1) 1985	(ALT2) 1985	(BASE) 1990	(ALT1) 1990	(ALT2) 1990
966.	963.	970.	984.	980.	990.
25.	25.	25.	24.	24.	24.
87.	87.	87.	97.	98.	97.
715.	707.	724.	822.	809.	836.
1521.	1521.	1520.	1577.	1577.	1576.
4223.	4192.	4256.	4613.	4574.	4658.
1698.	1693.	1703.	1833.	1830.	1837.
338.	339.	338.	375.	375.	375.
56.	56.	56.	45.	45.	46.
641.	632.	651.	714.	700.	728.
549.	548.	550.	562.	561.	563.
912.	908.	916.	1013.	1008.	1019.
341.	336.	346.	385.	378.	391.
177.	172.	181.	167.	162.	172.
896.	885.	906.	1112.	1096.	1130.
383.	373.	394.	354.	345.	365.
249.	247.	251.	260.	258.	261.
485.	481.	490.	542.	538.	547.
347.	340.	355.	384.	373.	396.
415.	408.	421.	393.	388.	399.
253.	247.	259.	257.	249.	265.
160.	159.	161.	148.	148.	148.
281.	279.	283.	296.	295.	298.
146.	146.	146.	129.	129.	129.
262.	261.	262.	269.	269.	269.
134.	132.	136.	148.	145.	151.
605.	605.	606.	647.	647.	647
780.	768.	792.	853.	835.	873.
293.	282.	304.	338.	322.	355.
2513.	2507.	2520.	2313.	2305.	2323.
475.	468.	482.	449.	439	459.
396.	367.	427.	525.	476.	582.
63.	62.	64.	58.	57.	59.
124.	118.	130.	128.	120.	138.
46.	46.	46.	55.	55.	55.
99.	98.	99.	105.	105.	105.
186.	177.	195.	215.	204.	228.
511.	504.	519.	550.	541.	560.
437.	437.	437.	462.	462.	463.
2852.	2835.	2871.	2860.	2833.	2888.

(Table 7-5. continued overleaf)

Table 7−5. continued

	Equipment Investment, by Purchaser (millions of 1976 dollars)			
Sec. No. and Title	(BASE) 1976	(BASE) 1980	(ALT1) 1980	(ALT2) 1980
81 Trucking	1405.	1789.	1783.	1795.
82 Other transport	1317.	1693.	1693.	1693.
83 Airlines	1300.	1857.	1857.	1856.
84 Wholesale & retail trade	11917.	16231.	16229.	16233.
85 Communication	9523.	12579.	12586.	12573.
86 Finance, ins. & services	7250.	8875.	8193.	9571.
87 Electric utilities	8460.	10544.	10540.	10549.
88 Nat. gas, water & sewer	1744.	1741.	1732.	1750.

As Table 7−5 shows, the differing assumptions about the real rate of interest have the expected results on investments. In all of those sectors with nontrivial elasticities, gross investment for the "BASE" forecast, in the selected years shown, are greater than the corresponding figures for the "ALT1" forecast and smaller than the corresponding figures for the "ALT2" forecast. In those sectors with zero elasticities, the changes have, of course, no affect.[f] These results hold, likewise, for the remaining years of the forecast, and may be verified by turning to the more detailed tables in the appendix.

To obtain a firmer grasp of the degree to which the different exogenous assumptions about the real rate of interest affect the forecast, one should observe the growth in the capital stocks of the respective industries. As we have shown in Section II, the capital stock is simply the accumulation of past net investment; and, hence, its growth over the forecast would give a proper measure of the affect of the three interest rate assumptions discussed above on the aggregate net investment resulting therefrom.

Table 7−6 displays some of these helpful figures for the eighty-seven sectors plus various aggregates. "STOCK(1976)" is the stock in existence at the start of the forecasts. This number is the same for each of the forecasts. "STOCK(1990)" gives the capital stock in existence at the end of each of the forecasts. As expected, the num-

---

[f]To say that the industries with zero elasticities will be unaffected by the different interest rate assumptions is not exactly true. One possibility is that an industry's output in the forecast may change as a result of a general overall increase (or decrease) in economic growth resulting from the different assumptions. This is especially true if a large portion of the output of an industry is equipment purchases by other industries.

Table 7–5. continued

	Equipment Investment, by Purchaser (millions of 1976 dollars)				
(BASE) 1985	*(ALT1)* 1985	*(ALT2)* 1985	*(BASE)* 1990	*(ALT1)* 1990	*(ALT2)* 1990
2354.	2332.	2377.	2884.	2841.	2930.
1787.	1787.	1787.	1881.	1881.	1881.
1479.	1482.	1477.	1282.	1284.	1280.
19282.	19303.	19262.	22071.	22090.	22055.
14965.	14973.	14957.	17163.	17179.	17149.
12909.	11987.	13914.	12297.	11040.	13735.
13086.	13098.	13076.	15000.	15010.	14992.
1705.	1679.	1734.	1727.	1690.	1768.

bers under "ALT2" are at least as large as the corresponding stocks under "BASE" and "ALT1." The columns labeled "% CHANGE IN STOCK (76–90)" give the increase or decrease in the stock over the forecast as a percentage of the original stock, while "% CHANGE IN GROWTH OF STOCK FROM BASE (76–90)" provides a measure of the growth in the capital stock in the "ALT1" and "ALT2" forecasts relative to the growth in the stock in the "BASE" forecast.

Consider as an example the iron and steel industry (46). According to this table, growth in the capital stock, and hence in net investment, over the forecast will be substantial under all three assumptions about the real rate of interest. Under the "BASE" assumption, the capital stock will grow by 60.1 percent while under the "ALT1" and "ALT2" assumptions, the stock will grow at 59.2 and 61.0 percent, respectively. Alternatively, total net investment under the "ALT1" assumption will be 1.4 percent lower than total net investment under the "BASE" assumption, and it will be 1.5 percent higher under the "ALT2" assumption. Consequently, the differing assumptions about future movements in the real rate will have only a marginal impact on the forecasts of investment for the iron and steel industry. The reason for this may be traced to a rather insubstantial elasticity (0.063) for this industry, suggesting that movements in the cost of capital exert only a modest influence on that industry.

The same cannot be said, however, for the plastics and synthetics industry (34, sigma = 0.372). While the three forecasts all suggest continued growth in the capital stocks, with 38.7, 35.2, and 42.4 percent for the "BASE," "ALT1," and "ALT2" forecasts, respectively, the difference in the forecasts may be considered quite significant. Thus, changing one's assumption from constant to decreas-

Table 7–6. Capital Stock Measures under Different Real Rate Assumptions

Sec. No. and Title	Stock (1976) BASE	Stock (1990)			Percent Change in Stock (76–90)			Percent Change in Growth of Stock from Base (76–90)	
		BASE	ALT1	ALT2	BASE	ALT1	ALT2	ALT1	ALT2
1 Agriculture	65552.	74829.	74073.	75618.	14.2	13.0	15.4	−8.1	8.5
2 Mining	10157.	14223.	14235.	14213.	40.0	40.1	39.9	0.3	−0.2
3 Petroleum & gas	16452.	25548.	24783.	26364.	55.3	50.6	60.2	−8.4	9.0
4 Construction	31852.	54007.	53991.	54027.	69.5	69.5	69.6	−0.1	0.1
5 Ordnance	386.	482.	482.	482.	24.9	24.9	24.9	0.0	0.0
6 Meat	2868.	4586.	4555.	4619.	59.9	58.8	61.1	−1.8	1.9
7 Dairy	2980.	3459.	3463.	3456.	16.1	16.2	16.0	0.8	−0.6
8 Canned & frozen foods	3993.	6553.	6546.	6560.	64.1	63.9	64.3	−0.3	0.3
9 Grain mill products	3521.	5827.	5777.	5880.	65.5	64.1	67.0	−2.2	2.3
10 Bakery	2601.	3041.	3028.	3056.	16.9	16.4	17.5	−3.0	3.4
11 Sugar	1321.	2488.	2434.	2546.	88.3	84.3	92.7	−4.6	5.0
12 Candy	1078.	1742.	1732.	1753.	61.6	60.7	62.6	−1.5	1.7
13 Beverages	6155.	9902.	9728.	10086.	60.9	58.1	63.9	−4.6	4.9
14 Misc. food products	3235.	5215.	5213.	5216.	61.2	61.1	61.2	−0.1	0.1
15 Tobacco	1102.	1533.	1511.	1556.	39.1	37.1	41.2	−5.1	5.3
16 Fabrics & yarns	7069.	9133.	9124.	9144.	29.2	29.1	29.4	−0.4	0.5
17 Floor coverings	492.	444.	442.	446.	−9.8	−10.2	−9.3	−4.2	4.2
18 Misc. textiles	1071.	1676.	1674.	1679.	56.5	56.3	56.8	−0.3	0.5
19 Knit fabric & apparel	1992.	1394.	1363.	1428.	−30.0	−31.6	−28.3	−5.2	5.7
20 Apparel	1757.	2066.	2069.	2063.	17.6	17.8	17.4	1.0	−1.0
21 Hsehld. text. & upholstry	736.	1408.	1409.	1407.	91.3	91.4	91.2	0.1	−0.1
22 Logging & lumber	4430.	9119.	8997.	9248.	105.8	103.1	108.8	−2.6	2.8
23 Plywd., millwork, struct.	2619.	6103.	6104.	6102.	133.0	133.1	133.0	0.0	0.0
24 Wooden containers	87.	87.	87.	87.	0.0	0.0	0.0	0.0	0.0
25 Hsehld. & ofc. furniture	1881.	2654.	2620.	2693.	41.1	39.3	43.2	−4.4	5.0

Table 7–6. continued

Sec. No. and Title	Stock (1976)	Stock (1990)			Percent Change in Stock (76–90)			Percent Change in Growth of Stock from Base (76–90)	
	BASE	BASE	ALT1	ALT2	BASE	ALT1	ALT2	ALT1	ALT2
27 Paper/products, ex. cont.	19381.	32597.	32090.	33135.	68.2	65.6	71.0	-3.8	4.1
28 Paper containers	2902.	3846.	3846.	3846.	32.5	32.5	32.5	0.0	0.0
29 Newspapers	2925.	4844.	4816.	4874.	65.6	64.6	66.6	-1.5	1.6
30 Printing & publishing	6526.	9593.	9601.	9586.	47.0	47.1	46.9	0.3	-0.2
31 Industrial chemicals	20038.	27421.	26171.	28785.	36.8	30.6	43.7	-16.9	18.5
32 Agricultural chemicals	1963.	4339.	4262.	4420.	121.0	117.1	125.2	-3.2	3.4
33 Glue, ink, & fatty acids	1644.	2456.	2410.	2505.	49.4	46.6	52.4	-5.7	6.0
34 Plastics & synthetics	10004.	13873.	13522.	14248.	38.7	35.2	42.4	-9.1	9.7
35 Drugs	2378.	2935.	2910.	2961.	23.4	22.4	24.5	-4.5	4.7
36 Cleaning & toilet items	1739.	3097.	3063.	3132.	78.1	76.1	80.1	-2.5	2.6
37 Paints & allied prod.	745.	909.	909.	909.	22.0	22.0	22.0	0.0	0.0
38 Petroleum refining	8960.	23189.	22172.	24313.	158.8	147.5	171.4	-7.1	7.9
39 Tires & tubes	3285.	5791.	5648.	5944.	76.3	71.9	80.9	-5.7	6.1
40 Rubber prod., ex. tires	1850.	2559.	2522.	2598.	38.3	36.3	40.4	-5.2	5.5
41 Plastic products	5671.	9995.	9963.	10030.	76.2	75.7	76.9	-0.7	0.8
42 Leather tan. & ind. prod.	167.	202.	203.	202.	21.0	21.6	21.0	2.9	0.0
43 Shoes & other lea. prod.	476.	717.	718.	717.	50.6	50.8	50.6	0.4	0.0
44 Glass & glass products	3883.	7445.	7368.	7528.	91.7	89.8	93.9	-2.2	2.3
45 Stone & clay products	10339.	15563.	15570.	15556.	50.5	50.6	50.5	0.1	0.1
46 Iron & steel	30518.	48847.	48590.	49125.	60.1	59.2	61.0	-1.4	1.5
47 Nonferrous metals	10096.	16949.	16931.	16971.	67.9	67.7	68.1	-0.3	0.3
48 Metal containers	1821.	2994.	2997.	2992.	64.4	64.6	64.3	0.3	-0.2
49 Plumbing & heating	458.	366.	365.	367.	-20.1	-20.3	-19.9	-1.1	1.1
50 Structural metal prod.	3190.	5772.	5697.	5853.	80.9	78.6	83.5	-2.9	3.1

(Table 7–6. continued overleaf)

Table 7–6. continued

Sec. No. and Title	Stock (1976)	Stock (1990)			Percent Change in Stock (76–90)			Percent Change in Growth of Stock from Base (76–90)	
	BASE	*BASE*	*ALT1*	*ALT2*	*BASE*	*ALT1*	*ALT2*	*ALT1*	*ALT2*
51 Stampings	3726.	4840.	4835.	4846.	29.9	29.8	30.1	-0.4	0.5
52 Hdwre., plating, wire prod.	4741.	8027.	7998.	8060.	69.3	68.7	70.0	-0.9	1.0
53 Engines & turbines	2323.	3305.	3268.	3345.	42.3	40.7	44.0	-3.8	4.1
54 Farm machinery	1501.	1517.	1485.	1551.	1.1	-1.1	3.3	-100.0	212.5
55 Construct. mining material	3699.	8338.	8253.	8429.	125.4	123.1	127.9	-1.8	2.0
56 Metalworking mach. & equip.	3146.	3573.	3511.	3640.	13.6	11.6	15.7	-14.5	15.7
57 Spec. ind. machinery	1631.	2203.	2195.	2213.	35.1	34.6	35.7	-1.4	1.7
58 Gen. indus. machinery	3021.	4446.	4420.	4475.	47.2	46.3	48.1	-1.8	2.0
59 Misc. machinery & shops	1561.	2389.	2336.	2445.	53.0	49.6	56.6	-6.4	6.8
60 Ofc. & computing mach.	2850.	3833.	3799.	3871.	34.5	33.3	35.8	-3.5	3.9
61 Service ind. machinery	1631.	2253.	2207.	2303.	38.1	35.3	41.2	-7.4	8.0
62 Elec. meas. transformers	1143.	1361.	1360.	1363.	19.1	19.0	19.2	-.5	0.9
63 Elec. apparatus & motors	1873.	2603.	2593.	2614.	39.0	38.4	39.6	-1.4	1.5
64 Household appliances	1566.	1365.	1366.	1364.	-12.8	-12.8	-12.9	-0.5	0.5
65 Elec. light & wiring	1628.	2362.	2362.	2362.	45.1	45.1	45.1	0.0	0.0
66 Radio, TV sets, & records	538.	878.	865.	892.	63.2	60.8	65.8	-3.8	4.1
67 Communication equipment	2684.	3675.	3676.	3676.	36.9	37.0	37.0	0.1	0.1
68 Electronic components	3525.	5088.	5004.	5177.	44.3	42.0	46.9	-5.4	5.7
69 Batteries, X-ray, & elec. equip.	1348.	2598.	2508.	2694.	92.7	86.1	99.9	-7.2	7.7
70 Motor vehicles & parts	24839.	22609.	22554.	22672.	-9.0	-9.2	-8.7	-2.5	2.8
71 Aircraft & parts	3484.	3790.	3734.	3848.	8.8	7.2	10.4	-18.3	19.0
72 Ships & boats	1277.	3653.	3399.	3935.	186.1	166.2	208.1	-10.7	11.9
73 Locomotives, RR, & stcars	386.	419.	415.	423.	8.5	7.5	9.6	-12.1	12.1
74 Cycles, trailers, & parts	503.	1047.	997.	1101.	108.2	98.2	118.9	-9.2	9.9
75 Engr. & scient. instr.	234.	397.	396.	398.	69.7	69.2	70.1	-0.6	0.6

Table 7–6. continued

Sec. No. and Title	Stock (1976)	Stock (1990)			Percent Change in Stock (76–90)			Percent Change in Growth of Stock from Base (76–90)	
	BASE	BASE	ALT1	ALT2	BASE	ALT1	ALT2	ALT1	ALT2
76 Mech. measuring devices	506.	638.	637.	640.	26.1	25.9	26.5	−0.8	1.5
77 Surgical & medical inst.	771.	1647.	1581.	1722.	113.6	105.1	123.3	−7.5	8.6
78 Optical & photo supply	2616.	4616.	4560.	4678.	76.5	74.3	78.8	−2.8	3.1
79 Misc. manufactured prod.	2017.	2803.	2802.	2805.	39.0	38.9	39.1	−0.1	0.3
80 Railroads	20276.	22635.	22493.	22786.	11.6	10.9	12.4	−6.0	6.4
81 Trucking	7793.	16353.	16351.	16728.	112.2	109.8	114.7	−2.1	2.2
82 Other transport	16402.	21026.	21032.	21019.	28.2	28.2	28.1	0.1	−0.2
83 Airlines	13136.	6635.	6645.	6625.	−49.5	−49.4	−49.6	0.2	−0.2
84 Wholesale & retail trade	81494.	133064.	133195.	132944.	63.3	63.4	63.1	0.3	−0.2
85 Communications	78197.	119439.	119561.	119325.	52.7	52.9	52.6	0.3	−0.3
86 Finance, ins., & services	138875.	158788.	149748.	168706.	14.3	7.8	21.5	−45.4	49.8
87 Electric utilities	63292.	103831.	103912.	103759.	64.1	64.2	63.9	0.2	−0.2
88 Nat. gas, water & sewer	10830.	12942.	12746.	13153.	19.5	17.7	21.4	−9.3	10.0
89 Nondurable goods	132625.	208830.	204894.	213100.	57.5	54.5	60.7	−5.2	5.6
90 Durable goods	150476.	222654.	220924.	224546.	48.0	46.8	49.2	−2.4	2.6
91 Total	837414.	1194986.	1178583.	1212913.	42.7	40.7	44.8	−4.6	5.0

ing real rate gives a forecast implying a growth in the stock 9.7 percent higher; and changing to increasing real rate implies a growth in the stock which is 9.1 percent lower. The divergence between the increasing and decreasing interest rate scenarios, which are not displayed in the table, may be easily computed from what is shown and would be even more substantial.

The table further shows that there are industries that are both more and less sensitive to the interest rate assumptions than, for example, the industrial chemical industry. Thus, the forecasts of aggregate net investment by aircraft and parts (71, $\sigma = 0.393$), and natural gas, water and sewers (88, $\sigma = 0.308$), vary by as much as 19.0 percent and 10.0 percent, respectively. On the other hand, airlines (83, $\sigma = 0.000$) and electric utilities (87 $\sigma = 0.000$) have essentially the same forecasts under all three assumptions.

There are twenty-four industry forecasts which change by at least 5 percent in either direction solely as a result of changing the one assumption about the real rate of interest. In addition, there are eight industry forecasts which change by more than 10 percent as a result of the modified assumptions. Conversely, there are thirty-one forecasts which were altered by less than 1 percent under the three assumptions.

Table 7–6 also provides totals for aggregates of the eighty-seven industries, namely nondurables goods (89), durable goods (90), and the total for all eighty-seven industries (91).[g] These figures reveal a number of results. First, investment by nondurable goods industries is expected to grow at a faster rate than investment by the durable goods industries. For example, under the "BASE" assumption, the growth in the capital stock over the forecast will be 57.5 percent for the nondurable goods industries compared to 48.0 percent for the durable goods industries. There exists an even greater discrepancy between the nondurable goods industries and total investment, suggesting that investments by nonmanufacturing will grow at a slower rate than manufacturing over the forecast. Second, purchases of equipment by the nondurable goods industries are about twice as sensitive to the various interest rate assumptions as the durable goods industries, and about equal to the sensitivity of total investment to the different interest rate assumptions. This may be seen in the last two columns of Table 7–6. Purchases of durable equipment by the

---

[g]The forecasts for nondurable goods, durable goods and total are not the result of estimating three additional equations. Rather, they are merely aggregates of the forecasts of the eighty-seven industries. Nondurable goods is an aggregate of Sectors 6–21 and 27–43, while the durable goods sector is an aggregate of Sectors 5, 22–25, 44–79.

Table 7–7. Capital/Output Ratio in Selected Years

	1956	1966	1976	BASE	ALT1	ALT2
				1990		
Capital/output ratio	0.469	0.435	0.492	0.465	0.459	0.471

nondurable goods industry will vary by slightly more than 5 percent in either direction, depending upon the interest rate assumption employed. The forecasts under each assumption displaying ten of the fifteen forecast years including aggregates at the two-digit SIC level are found in appendix Tables 7–A–1, 7–A–3, and 7–A–5.

Therefore, our results demonstrate the varied impacts of changing the interest rate assumption on the forecast of investment by eighty-seven industries; and points up the desirability of assessing such changes within a disaggregated framework. One might certainly aggregate up the eighty-seven industry investments, ascertain the various movements in the total capital stocks, and make some general statements about the sensitivity of these forecasts to changing the assumptions about future movements in the real rate of interest. Yet, as we have seen, the conclusions that may be reached would be of little value for, say, the iron and steel or the industrial chemical industries, since neither of these industries behaves in a manner reflected accurately in the aggregate figures. Indeed, only a minority of the industries behave in a manner consistent with the aggregate figures.

These results may also help to suggest an answer to the question, Which of the three scenarios is the most likely in view of the remaining macroeconomic totals, such as, for example, GNP? Appendix Tables 7–A–2, 7–A–4, and 7–A–6 present totals and subtotals for gross national product, consumption, gross private domestic investment, net exports, and government purchases for select years under the three separate interest rate assumptions.[h] Using the proper GNP deflator, one may compare the total capital stocks in Table 7–6, which are in 1976 dollars, with the GNP totals in the appendix. These manipulations produced Table 7–7, which shows the economy-wide capital-output ratio in selected past years as well as the same ratio in 1990 under the three interest rate assumptions. Strong conclusions may not be reached based upon these figures. All fore-

[h]These tables are displayed in 1972 dollars while all remaining tables in the chapter are displayed in 1976 dollars. This approach has been followed in the past by the INFORUM group in order to maintain consistency with the published National Accounts totals.

casts suggest a slight decline in 1990 from the 1976 capital-output ratio, yet this decline may be overstated since 1976 is a year immediately following a severe recession. One would expect output to decline by more than the capital stock, leading to a higher capital-output ratio in this year. It is interesting to note how close the 1990 ratios are to the 1956 ratio.

Therefore, none of the three interest rate assumptions leads to drastically dissimilar conclusions about the future movement in aggregate investment or in the capital-output ratio. Hence, on the basis of these forecasts, we cannot conclude that any of the real rates of interest is the most likely.[i]

These observations about the response of different industry investments to alternative interest rate assumptions are also relevant to questions about the impact of government tax policy upon investment. We will be concerned, in particular, with the impact of changes in the investment tax credit on net investment, yet most of what is discussed could be relevant to changes in the corporate income tax, or modifications in the depreciation laws.

In assessing the response of industry investments to a change in the tax credit, we will address ourselves to two important questions. First, how effective is changing the tax credit in inducing different industry investments? Second, given that an industry does increase investment in response to an increase in the tax credit, in what way is the time path of gross investment then modified? We have, consequently, run a second set of forecasts which differ only in that the investment tax credit was either lowered to 0.05 in 1979 (ALT1), raised to 0.15 in 1979 (ALT2), or held at its existing rate of 0.10 (BASE). In all three cases, the real rate of interest was held constant at 0.035 throughout the forecast.

Complete tables exhibiting the time path of gross investment may be found in appendix Tables 7–A–1, 7–A–7, and 7–A–9, along with aggregates at the two-digit SIC level. However, the most useful measure of the impact of different tax credits on various industry investments is, again, the growth in the capital stocks. Table 7–8 displays this information in the same manner as Table 7–6 did for the previous set of forecasts. We see in Table 7–8 that in answer to our first question above about the efficacy of modifying the investment tax credit to induce investment, we may arrive at more than one correct

---

[i]An attempt to forecast the real rate of interest fifteen years into the future would require, first, a forecast of future movements in the nominal rate of interest as well as the expected rate of inflation. This would require, at a minimum, that a fully integrated financial sector be introduced into the INFORUM model. An attempt to accomplish this task, now in its infancy, is being undertaken.

answer. In the case of the plastics and synthetics industry, for example, an increase in the tax credit from 10 percent to 15 percent leads to a forecast suggesting that there would be 38.5 percent additional net investment as a result. This implies an average increase in net investment of 3.2 percent over the twelve years the 15 percent credit would be in effect. Hence, one might argue that such a tax change would be an effective inducement to invest, at least for the plastics and synthetics industry. On the other hand, the airline industry would hardly notice such a tax change. Given a 15 percent tax credit, net investment summed over the entire forecast, as shown by the growth in the capital stocks in Table 7–8, is 0.4 percent higher than the forecast given the 10 percent tax credit. One might safely argue, then, that the increased credit is a very poor inducement to invest, at least for the airline industry.[j]

These remarks may be applied to the remaining industries. As can be seen, such alterations in the tax credit may have a considerable impact upon net investment over the forecasts for some industries, and a modest impact for others. There are forty-three industries in which a change in the tax credit by 50 percent in either direction would alter the accumulated net investment over the forecast by 5 percent or more. In addition, there are thirty industries in which the forecasts vary by more than 10 percent, and thirteen industries in which forecasts vary by more than 20 percent in either direction. There are only two industries, however, in which changing the tax credit assumption changes the growth in the capital stock from being positive to negative. These are farm machinery (54) and finance/insurance (86), in which the "ALT1" assumption leads to a decline in the capital stocks in the forecast, while the "BASE" and "ALT2" assumptions suggest an increase.[k] On the other hand, there are twenty-two industries in which the forecast varies by less than 1 percent under the three scenarios, and forty-four industries in which the

---

[j]The purpose of this chapter is not to argue for or against tax credit incentives for investment; nor do we intend to evaluate the cost-effectiveness of such a policy. Our only purpose in making the comparison between the response of Plastics and Synthetics to a tax credit change and the response of Airlines to the same change is to show that one tax policy shift may affect different industries radically differently. This may have some bearing on the appropriate way to implement such a policy.

[k]In the case of Finance/Insurance, the change in the sign of the growth rate in the capital stock is due essentially to that industry's extremely high elasticity, 0.620. The growth in the stocks for Farm Machinery changes from positive to negative partly because this industry has a nonzero elasticity, 0.227; but, more importantly, because little or no growth in investment by this industry is expected regardless of the tax scenario used.

Table 7–8. Capital Stock Measures under Different Tax Credit Assumptions

Sec. No. and Title	Stock (1976) BASE	Stock (1990) BASE	Stock (1990) ALT1	Stock (1990) ALT2	Percent Change in Stock (76–90) BASE	Percent Change in Stock (76–90) ALT1	Percent Change in Stock (76–90) ALT2	Percent Change in Growth of Stock from Base (76–90) ALT1	Percent Change in Growth of Stock from Base (76–90) ALT2
1 Agriculture	65552.	74829.	72779.	76933.	14.2	11.0	17.4	-22.1	22.7
2 Mining	10157.	14223.	14263.	14188.	40.0	40.4	39.7	1.0	-0.9
3 Petroleum & gas	16452.	25548.	23792.	27411.	55.3	44.6	66.6	-19.3	20.5
4 Construction	31857.	54008.	53852.	54172.	69.5	69.0	70.0	-0.7	0.7
5 Ordnance	386.	482.	482.	482.	24.9	24.9	24.9	0.0	0.0
6 Meat	2868.	4536.	4480.	4695.	59.9	56.2	63.7	-6.2	6.3
7 Dairy	2980.	3459.	3468.	3452.	16.1	16.4	15.8	1.9	-1.5
8 Canned & frozen foods	3993.	6553.	6546.	6560.	64.1	63.9	64.3	-0.3	0.3
9 Grain mill products	3521.	5827.	5736.	5919.	65.5	62.9	68.1	-3.9	4.0
10 Bakery	2601.	3041.	3008.	3075.	16.9	15.6	18.2	-7.5	7.7
11 Sugar	1321.	2488.	2397.	2582.	88.3	81.5	95.5	-7.8	8.1
12 Candy	1078.	1742.	1699.	1787.	61.6	57.6	65.8	-6.5	6.8
13 Beverages	6155.	9902.	9550.	10264.	60.9	55.2	66.8	-9.4	9.7
14 Misc. food products	3235.	5215.	5216.	5214.	61.2	61.2	61.2	0.1	-0.1
15 Tobacco	1102.	1533.	1499.	1568.	39.1	36.0	42.3	-7.9	8.1
16 Fabrics & yarns	7069.	9133.	9120.	9153.	29.2	29.0	29.5	-0.6	1.0
17 Floor coverings	492.	444.	441.	447.	-9.8	-10.4	-9.1	-6.3	6.3
18 Misc. textiles	1071.	1676.	1674.	1680.	56.5	56.3	56.9	-0.3	0.7
19 Knit fabric & apparel	1992.	1394.	1221.	1582.	-30.0	-38.7	-20.6	-28.9	31.4
20 Apparel	1757.	2066.	2073.	2060.	17.6	18.0	17.2	2.3	-1.9
21 Hsehld. text. & upholstry	736.	1408.	1411.	1405.	91.3	91.7	90.9	0.4	-0.4
22 Logging & lumber	4430.	9119.	8840.	9409.	105.8	99.5	112.4	-6.0	6.2
23 Plywd., millwork, struct.	2619.	6103.	6110.	6098.	133.0	133.3	132.8	0.2	-0.1
24 Wooden containers	87.	87.	88.	87.	0.0	1.1	0.0	0.0	0.0
25 Hsehld. & ofc. furniture	1881.	2654.	2588.	2722.	41.1	37.6	44.7	-8.5	8.8

Table 7–8. continued

Sec. No. and Title	Stock (1976) BASE	Stock (1990)			Percent Change in Stock (76–90)			Percent Change in Growth of Stock from Base (76–90)	
	BASE	BASE	ALT1	ALT2	BASE	ALT1	ALT2	ALT1	ALT2
27 Paper/products, ex. cont.	19381.	32597.	31660.	33564.	68.2	63.4	73.2	-7.1	7.3
28 Paper containers	2902.	3846.	3848.	3845.	32.5	32.6	32.5	0.2	-0.1
29 Newspapers	2925.	4844.	4791.	4899.	65.6	63.8	67.5	-2.8	2.9
30 Printing & publishing	6526.	9593.	9615.	9573.	47.0	47.3	46.7	0.7	-0.7
31 Industrial chemicals	20038.	27421.	23017.	32522.	36.8	14.9	62.3	-59.7	69.1
32 Agricultural chemicals	1963.	4339.	4184.	4496.	121.0	113.1	129.0	-6.5	6.6
33 Glue, ink, & fatty acids	1644.	2456.	2343.	2575.	49.4	42.5	56.6	-13.9	14.7
34 Plastics & synthetics	10004.	13873.	12512.	15361.	38.7	25.1	53.5	-35.2	38.5
35 Drugs	2378.	2935.	2790.	3088.	23.4	17.3	29.9	-26.0	27.5
36 Cleaning & toilet items	1739.	3097.	2921.	3281.	78.1	68.0	88.7	-13.0	13.5
37 Paints & allied prod.	745.	909.	909.	909.	22.0	22.0	22.0	0.0	0.0
38 Petroleum refining	8960.	23189.	21660.	24834.	158.8	141.7	177.2	-10.7	11.6
39 Tires & tubes	3285.	5791.	5251.	6379.	76.3	59.8	94.2	-21.5	23.5
40 Rubber prod. ex. tires	1850.	2559.	2428.	2697.	38.3	31.2	45.8	-18.5	19.5
41 Plastic products	5671.	9995.	9937.	10058.	76.2	75.2	77.4	-1.3	1.5
42 Leather tan. & ind. prod.	167.	202.	203.	202.	21.0	21.6	21.0	2.9	0.0
43 Shoes & other lea. prod.	476.	717.	720.	715.	50.6	51.3	50.2	1.2	-0.8
44 Glass & glass products	3883.	7445.	7247.	7651.	91.7	86.6	97.0	-5.6	5.8
45 Stone & clay products	10339.	15563.	15588.	15541.	50.5	50.8	50.3	0.5	-0.4
46 Iron & steel	30518.	48847.	48467.	49263.	60.1	58.8	61.4	-2.1	2.3
47 Nonferrous metals	10096.	16949.	16936.	16974.	67.9	67.7	68.1	-0.2	0.4
48 Metal containers	1821.	2994.	3002.	2987.	64.4	64.9	64.0	0.7	-0.6
49 Plumbing & heating	458.	366.	363.	369.	-20.1	-20.7	-19.4	-3.3	3.3
50 Structural metal prod.	3190.	5772.	5615.	5938.	80.9	76.0	86.1	-6.1	6.4

(Table 7–8. continued overleaf)

Table 7–8. continued

Sec. No. and Title	Stock (1976) BASE	Stock (1990) BASE	Stock (1990) ALT1	Stock (1990) ALT2	Percent Change in Stock (76–90) BASE	ALT1	ALT2	Percent Change in Growth of Stock from Base (76–90) ALT1	ALT2
51 Stampings	3726.	4840.	4834.	4851.	29.9	29.7	30.2	−0.5	1.0
52 Hdwre., plating, wire prod.	4741.	8027.	7973.	8090.	69.3	68.2	70.6	−1.6	1.9
53 Engines & turbines	2323.	3305.	3205.	3411.	42.3	38.0	46.8	−10.2	10.8
54 Farm machinery	1501.	1517.	1431.	1611.	1.1	−4.7	7.3	−537.5	587.5
55 Construct. mining material	3699.	8338.	8184.	8502.	125.4	121.2	129.8	−3.3	3.5
56 Metalworking mach. & equip.	3146.	3573.	3470.	3712.	13.6	10.3	18.0	−24.1	32.6
57 Spec. ind. machinery	1631.	2203.	2191.	2217.	35.1	34.3	35.9	−2.1	2.4
58 Gen. indus. machinery	3021.	4446.	4405.	4499.	47.2	45.8	48.9	−2.9	3.7
59 Misc. machinery & shops	1561.	2389.	2275.	2508.	53.0	45.7	60.7	−13.8	14.4
60 Ofc. & computing mach.	2850.	3833.	3748.	3935.	34.5	31.5	38.1	−8.6	10.4
61 Service ind. machinery	1631.	2253.	2156.	2357.	38.1	32.2	44.5	−15.6	16.7
62 Elec. meas. transformers	1143.	1361.	1359.	1365.	19.1	18.9	19.4	−0.9	1.8
63 Elec. apparatus & motors	1873.	2603.	2589.	2621.	39.0	38.2	39.9	−1.9	2.5
64 Household appliances	1566.	1365.	1363.	1364.	−12.8	−12.7	−12.9	−1.0	0.5
65 Elec. light & wiring	1628.	2362.	2363.	2362.	45.1	45.1	45.1	0.1	0.0
66 Radio, TV sets, & records	538.	878.	836.	922.	63.2	55.4	71.4	−12.4	12.9
67 Communication equipment	2684.	3675.	3672.	3681.	36.9	36.8	37.1	−0.3	0.6
68 Electronic components	3525.	5088.	4706.	5494.	44.3	33.5	55.9	−24.4	26.0
69 Batteries, X-ray, & elec. equip.	1348.	2598.	2408.	2802.	92.7	78.6	107.9	−15.2	16.3
70 Motor vehicles & parts	24839.	22609.	22502.	22735.	−9.0	−9.4	−8.5	−4.8	5.7
71 Aircraft & parts	3484.	3790.	3633.	3952.	8.8	4.3	13.4	−51.3	52.9
72 Ships & boats	1277.	3653.	3158.	4209.	186.1	147.3	229.6	−20.8	23.4
73 Locomotives, RR, & stcars	386.	419.	413.	431.	8.5	7.0	11.7	−18.2	36.4
74 Cycles, trailers, & parts	503.	1047.	899.	1209.	108.2	78.7	140.4	−27.2	29.8
75 Engr. & scient. instr.	234.	397.	395.	398.	69.7	68.8	70.1	−1.2	0.6

Table 7–8. continued

Sec. No. and Title	Stock (1976)	Stock (1990)			Percent Change in Stock (76–90)			Percent Change in Growth of Stock from Base (76–90)	
	BASE	BASE	ALT1	ALT2	BASE	ALT1	ALT2	ALT1	ALT2
76 Mech. measuring devices	506.	638.	636.	641.	26.1	25.7	26.7	-1.5	2.3
77 Surgical & medical inst.	771.	1647.	1526.	1784.	113.6	97.9	131.4	-13.8	15.6
78 Optical & photo supply	2616.	4616.	4469.	4780.	76.5	70.8	82.7	-7.4	8.2
79 Misc. manufactured prod.	2017.	2803.	2802.	2806.	39.0	38.9	39.1	-0.1	0.4
80 Railroads	20276.	22635.	22351.	22931.	11.6	10.2	13.1	-12.0	12.5
81 Trucking	7793.	16535.	16086.	17000.	112.2	106.4	118.1	-5.1	5.3
82 Other transport	16402.	21026.	21043.	21009.	28.2	28.3	28.1	0.4	-0.4
83 Airlines	13136.	6635.	6663.	6610.	-49.5	-49.3	-49.7	0.4	-0.4
84 Wholesale & retail trade	81494.	133064.	133436.	132735.	63.3	63.7	62.9	0.7	-0.6
85 Communications	78197.	119439.	119781.	119134.	52.7	53.2	52.4	0.8	-0.7
86 Finance, ins., & services	138875.	158788.	131228.	189323.	14.3	-5.5	36.3	-138.4	153.3
87 Electric utilities	63292.	103831.	104070.	103622.	64.1	64.4	63.7	0.6	-0.5
88 Nat. gas, water & sewer	10830.	12942.	12628.	13283.	19.5	16.6	22.7	-14.9	16.1
89 Nondurable goods	132625.	208830.	198328.	220441.	57.5	49.5	66.2	-13.8	15.2
90 Durable goods	150476.	222654.	218931.	226770.	48.0	45.5	50.7	-5.2	5.7
91 Total	837414.	1194986.	1149231.	1245562.	42.7	37.2	48.7	-12.8	14.1

forecast varies by less than 5 percent. Thus the question of the effectiveness of the credit to induce investment admits no simple answer.[1]

Table 7—8 also presents summary results for nondurable goods (89), durable goods (90), and the total of all industries (91). We see again the greater sensitivity of investment by the nondurable goods industries compared to investment by the durable goods industries, as well as the fact that investment by the nondurable goods industries is expected to grow at a faster rate than by the durable goods industries regardless of the tax credit policy followed. The effect of these assumptions on other macro variables resulting from the forecasts are displayed in appendix Tables 7—A—8 and 7—A—10.

To address our second question about the time path of gross investment in response to different tax credits, we must initially remark that a tax credit change will affect investment through essentially two channels.[m]

The first, more immediate yet less enduring channel is the direct impact of a onetime increase in the tax credit. Such an increase leads to a considerable onetime decrease in the cost of capital. This decrease, which is expressed in percent of the cost of capital in our investment equation (8), then directly induces investment for as long as the lag on the cost of capital exists. Lagged percentage changes in the cost of capital resulting from the increase in the credit have little remaining effect after, say, five or six years.

An alternative way of looking at this direct effect of the tax credit is by recalling the origins of our investment equation. Equation (4), Section I, related the *desired* capital stock to the level of output and the "relative user cost of capital." As we know, this equation will

---

[1]Column 9 of Table 7-8 also shows that an increase in the investment tax credit from 10 percent to 15 percent actually results in a decline in aggregate net investment over the forecast period for a number of industries. This paradoxical result, which may be easily explained, is primarily due to an exogenous assumption made early in the forecast. When making a forecast, the INFORUM model makes use of as much current and past information as possible. In the case of investment, the forecasts for gross investment were constrained by a predetermined aggregate level which allowed for only modest growth in investment over 1978 and 1979. Consequently, the unconstrained forecasts of industry investments in 1978 and 1979, which summed to a total greater than desired, were scaled down to be consistent with this constraint. With the tax credit increasing from 10 percent to 15 percent, aggregate investment in 1979 will exceed the constraint by a greater amount, thus requiring a larger scaling factor. In the case of those industries which are not at all sensitive to the cost of capital, gross investment in 1979 will be reduced even further by the larger scaling factor. Hence, an increase in the tax credit will appear to lead to a reduction in investment by certain industries.

[m]The discussion through the remainder of this section will deal with an increase in the tax credit. What is said will be relevant to a decrease in the credit as well.

hold only in equilibrium. But, because of the noninstantaneous adjustment of the capital stock to changes in output and the cost of capital for the reasons cited in Section I, equation (4) was altered by the introduction of lags, to give equation (5). Thus a one-time decrease in the cost of capital generates a new desired level of the capital stock. Yet this new desired level will not be attained (or felt) instantaneously or even in the first year, but perhaps over a five- or six-year period. The attainment of this new desired level resulting from a onetime decrease in the cost of capital is the direct, immediate impact discussed above.

The second, more enduring impact of the tax credit change on investment is through its effect on the capital stocks. As the increased credit leads to increases in net investment, as described above, this increased net investment in turn leads to increased capital stocks. Once the impact of the direct effect of the larger tax credit has dissipated, the resulting capital stocks will have become permanently larger. Since these larger stocks enter into the determination of net investment out into the future, this assures that the initial tax credit change may have an enduring influence upon net investment through its impact on the capital stocks.[n]

Figure 7–3 shows the time path of gross investment for four industries under each tax credit scenario. The corresponding lag distributions on output and the cost of capital may be found in Table 7–1. These plots are fairly representative of the kind of response we observe under different tax credit scenarios, considering those sectors with only nonzero eleasticities. As can be seen from the industrial chemicals plot, for example, once the credit is put into effect, early and large deviations in the forecasts are apparent. This divergence remains substantial until about 1985, at which point all four forecasts move at essentially the same rate but on different paths.

Thus we see that an increase in the tax credit induces a large early response by those industries which are sensitive to the cost of capital, and then the new larger capital stocks sustain a fairly constant divergence among the forecasts. The time path of gross investment appears to be permanently above the original path when the tax credit is increased.

[n] Larger capital stocks will also generate increased gross investment through its effect on replacement investment, which is given by the depreciation of the second class of stock.

Figure 7–3. Annual Gross Investment Relative to 1977 Levels in Forecasts for Three Tax Credit Scenarios:

... c = 0.05   - - - c = 0.10   — c = 0.15

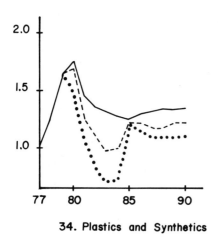

34. Plastics and Synthetics

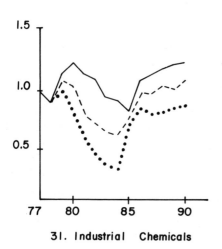

31. Industrial Chemicals

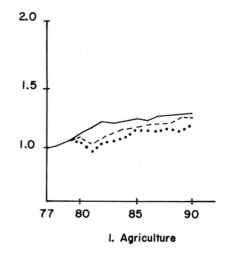

27. Paper and Products

I. Agriculture

V. CONCLUSION

In this chapter we have derived and estimated investment equations for eighty-seven industries using historical data through 1976. In addition, we have described the sources of the historical data, and, in particular, the determination of the parameters which enter the cost of capital.

These equations were then used to forecast, within the context of an input-output forecasting model, purchases of equipment by these eighty-seven industries out to 1990, under various interest rate and government tax policy assumptions. The major conclusions of the chapter are

1. The estimated elasticities among industries display extreme variability with the average elasticity over all industries not exceeding 0.2188.
2. The lag distribution on the cost of capital tends to be longer than the lag distribution on output, suggesting that firms react more quickly to changes in output than they do to changes in the cost of capital.
3. Efforts to introduce either a ratio of debt financing to total financing, or a smoothed version of our estimated real rate of interest, did not uniformly improve the fit of our investment equations to the historical data, nor did it alter conclusions (1) and (2).
4. The sensitivity of forecasts of industry investment to various interest rate assumptions or tax credit modifications varies considerably from industry to industry. However, a onetime increase (decrease) in the investment tax credit ultimately places those industries with nonzero elasticities in a permanently higher (lower) time path of gross investment.
5. Comparison of investments by the nondurable goods and durable goods industries reveals that the former is more sensitive to modifications in the cost of capital, whether it be different interest rate assumptions or alternative tax credit policies. Furthermore, investment by the former is expected to grow at a more rapid rate than the latter.
6. In the light of the forecasts generated by the different interest rate scenarios no clear support is given to any one scenario as being the most likely.

Appendix

TABLES OF FORECAST

Table 7–A–1. Constant Real Rate

Equipment Investment, by Purchaser
(millions of 1976 dollars)

Sec. No. and Title	1976	1980	1981	1982	1983	1984	1985	1986	1988	1990
1 Agriculture	9585.	10460.	10346.	10689.	10750.	10829.	11059.	11109.	11178.	11307.
2 Mining	1657.	1961.	2061.	2101.	2142.	2186.	2286.	2351.	2458.	2582.
3 Petroleum & gas	3354.	4802.	4328.	4399.	4635.	4140.	3972.	4188.	4281.	4330.
4 Construction	5773.	7779.	8232.	8577.	8916.	9235.	9437.	9561.	9886.	10358.
5 Ordnance	125.	158.	160.	161.	163.	165.	166.	168.	171.	174.
6 Meat	285.	409.	366.	350.	369.	385.	414.	452.	468.	486.
7 Dairy	256.	299.	303.	307.	320.	320.	330.	340.	345.	350.
8 Canned & frozen foods	374.	494.	532.	549.	565.	571.	591.	595.	623.	655.
9 Grain mill products	352.	444.	454.	466.	470.	468.	506.	520.	545.	570.
10 Bakery	266.	257.	258.	263.	265.	268.	288.	291.	287.	288.
11 Sugar	191.	116.	139.	229.	230.	224.	234.	243.	254.	273.
12 Candy	102.	131.	136.	143.	146.	141.	159.	165.	167.	173.
13 Beverages	735.	778.	774.	857.	883.	889.	899.	929.	965.	985.
14 Misc. food products	323.	431.	479.	496.	541.	510.	518.	522.	549.	572.
15 Tobacco	107.	134.	143.	152.	151.	153.	156.	160.	170.	180.
16 Fabrics & yarns	616.	894.	823.	838.	841.	854.	882.	853.	861.	894.
17 Floor coverings	51.	86.	77.	78.	74.	69.	72.	68.	66.	68.
18 Misc. textiles	91.	176.	168.	173.	160.	158.	164.	161.	165.	172.
19 Knit fabric & apparel	165.	178.	173.	202.	228.	214.	209.	192.	179.	171.
20 Apparel	224.	290.	282.	291.	285.	286.	295.	285.	290.	293.
21 Hsehld. text. & upholstry	81.	149.	163.	177.	165.	169.	185.	186.	205.	221.
22 Logging & lumber	674.	1068.	1140.	1197.	1241.	1245.	1323.	1339.	1433.	1562.
23 Plywd., millwork, struct.	303.	574.	612.	644.	682.	718.	746.	757.	823.	913.
24 Wooden containers	7.	12.	13.	12.	12.	12.	12.	12.	12.	12.
25 Hsehld. & ofc. furniture	208.	306.	296.	322.	349.	348.	351.	347.	334.	347.

(Table 7–A–1. continued overleaf)

Table 7–A–1.   continued

Equipment Investment, by Purchaser
(millions of 1976 dollars)

Sec. No. and Title	1976	1980	1981	1982	1983	1984	1985	1986	1988	1990
27 Paper/products, ex. cont.	2426.	2968.	2960.	2937.	2895.	2958.	3122.	3197.	3343.	3516.
28 Paper containers	282.	403.	427.	435.	424.	413.	419.	416.	420.	426.
29 Newspapers	295.	485.	492.	500.	517.	531.	549.	559.	579.	614.
30 Printing & publishing	742.	962.	1035.	1053.	1072.	1082.	1121.	1143.	1182.	1229.
31 Industrial chemicals	3646.	3534.	2862.	2535.	2225.	2145.	2510.	3447.	3494.	3591.
32 Agricultural chemicals	285.	415.	445.	450.	460.	474.	493.	522.	564.	611.
33 Glue, ink, & fatty acids	302.	303.	251.	236.	235.	287.	304.	306.	309.	319.
34 Plastics & synthetics	1261.	2205.	1684.	1470.	1356.	1371.	1629.	1622.	1591.	1612.
35 Drugs	340.	341.	333.	324.	314.	314.	326.	327.	331.	324.
36 Cleaning & toilet items	237.	244.	288.	323.	357.	338.	358.	381.	404.	427.
37 Paints & allied prod.	83.	99.	108.	113.	108.	107.	114.	112.	112.	111.
38 Petroleum refining	1611.	1919.	2103.	2434.	2372.	3083.	2544.	2707.	3026.	3340.
39 Tires & tubes	216.	578.	481.	489.	532.	546.	574.	577.	599.	644.
40 Rubber prod., ex. tires	174.	212.	239.	256.	244.	241.	246.	240.	245.	250.
41 Plastic products	652.	986.	989.	973.	967.	947.	966.	953.	958.	984.
42 Leather tan. & ind. prod.	21.	27.	25.	25.	25.	24.	25.	24.	24.	24.
43 Shoes & other lea. prod.	42.	76.	82.	80.	81.	85.	87.	89.	93.	97.
44 Glass & glass products	358.	603.	622.	650.	681.	693.	715.	722.	761.	822.
45 Stone & clay products	854.	1403.	1490.	1530.	1547.	1480.	1521.	1474.	1496.	1577.
46 Iron & steel	2685.	3833.	4297.	4465.	4498.	4288.	4223.	4225.	4358.	4613.
47 Nonferrous metals	934.	1511.	1640.	1761.	1717.	1649.	1698.	1695.	1744.	1833.
48 Metal containers	127.	316.	314.	314.	319.	328.	338.	345.	356.	375.
49 Plumbing & heating	53.	52.	54.	56.	58.	55.	56.	52.	47.	45.
50 Structural metal prod.	454.	498.	544.	593.	622.	629.	641.	644.	676.	714.

Table 7–A–1. continued

Equipment Investment, by Purchaser
(millions of 1976 dollars)

Sec. No. and Title	1976	1980	1981	1982	1983	1984	1985	1986	1988	1990
51 Stampings	364.	506.	533.	545.	545.	538.	549.	537.	548.	562.
52 Hdwre., plating, wire prod.	586.	778.	832.	877.	894.	886.	912.	913.	958.	1013.
53 Engines & turbines	230.	300.	310.	322.	337.	338.	341.	346.	360.	385.
54 Farm machinery	198.	150.	166.	171.	178.	178.	177.	173.	168.	167.
55 Construct. mining material	568.	762.	875.	865.	883.	865.	896.	917.	1009.	1112.
56 Metalworking mach. & equip.	293.	425.	468.	460.	439.	389.	383.	351.	343.	354.
57 Spec. ind. machinery	169.	273.	281.	278.	275.	250.	249.	246.	250.	260.
58 Gen. indus. machinery	382.	463.	492.	498.	511.	485.	485.	488.	513.	542.
59 Misc. machinery & shops	238.	293.	308.	331.	338.	344.	347.	351.	366.	384.
60 Ofc. & computing mach.	380.	385.	442.	432.	405.	406.	415.	406.	393.	393.
61 Service ind. machinery	144.	201.	234.	262.	259.	244.	253.	239.	248.	257.
62 Elec. meas. transformers	119.	172.	181.	192.	167.	164.	160.	151.	147.	148.
63 Elec. apparatus & motors	222.	261.	281.	291.	299.	281.	281.	272.	282.	296.
64 Household appliances	149.	138.	148.	154.	148.	140.	146.	140.	135.	129.
65 Elec. light & wiring	135.	246.	253.	264.	257.	252.	262.	252.	260.	269.
66 Radio, TV sets, & records	83.	124.	123.	128.	126.	130.	134.	137.	142.	148.
67 Communication equipment	428.	553.	572.	600.	587.	587.	605.	601.	626.	647.
68 Electronic components	551.	690.	694.	723.	769.	773.	780.	792.	818.	853.
69 Batteries, X-ray, & elec. equip.	176.	190.	213.	230.	279.	272.	293.	298.	320.	338.
70 Motor vehicles & parts	1908.	2823.	2745.	2530.	2481.	2502.	2513.	2400.	2311.	2313.
71 Aircraft & parts	380.	611.	475.	446.	450.	464.	475.	477.	462.	449.
72 Ships & boats	257.	311.	318.	356.	378.	385.	396.	392.	460.	525.
73 Locomotives, RR, & stcars	54.	69.	76.	77.	72.	64.	63.	59.	58.	58.
74 Cycles, trailers, & parts	52.	90.	101.	107.	114.	119.	124.	123.	122.	128.
75 Engr. & scient. instr.	32.	46.	45.	44.	44.	46.	46.	49.	52.	55.

(Table 7–A–1. continued overleaf)

Table 7−A−1. continued

Equipment Investment, by Purchaser
(millions of 1976 dollars)

Sec. No. and Title	1976	1980	1981	1982	1983	1984	1985	1986	1988	1990
76 Mech. measuring devices	73.	88.	93.	95.	99.	100.	99.	99.	102.	105.
77 Surgical & medical inst.	112.	139.	142.	145.	152.	168.	186.	200.	202.	215.
78 Optical & photo. supply	337.	403.	447.	471.	509.	501.	511.	525.	531.	550.
79 Misc. manufactured prod.	408.	376.	401.	422.	423.	426.	437.	440.	453.	462.
80 Railroads	1965.	3078.	2960.	2905.	2876.	2847.	2852.	2825.	2813.	2860.
81 Trucking	1405.	1789.	1921.	2000.	2116.	2243.	2354.	2426.	2627.	2884.
82 Other transport	1317.	1693.	1712.	1731.	1750.	1769.	1787.	1806.	1844.	1881.
83 Airlines	1300.	1857.	1755.	1563.	1565.	1515.	1479.	1437.	1348.	1282.
84 Wholesale & retail trade	11917.	16231.	16684.	17227.	17989.	18555.	19282.	19627.	20673.	22071.
85 Communication	9523.	12579.	13073.	13441.	13675.	14241.	14965.	15520.	16286.	17163.
86 Finance, ins., & services	7250.	8875.	9434.	10720.	12759.	12699.	12909.	12837.	12392.	12297.
87 Electric utilities	8460.	10544.	11240.	11904.	12293.	12678.	13086.	13468.	14101.	15000.
88 Nat. gas, water & sewer	1744.	1741.	1693.	1727.	1751.	1730.	1705.	1700.	1706.	1727.

Table 7–A–1. continued

Equipment Investment, by Purchaser, Summary by Major Sectors
(millions of 1976 dollars)

Title	1976	1980	1981	1982	1983	1984	1985	1986	1988	1990
Agriculture	9585.	10460.	10346.	10689.	10750.	10829.	11059.	11109.	11178.	11307.
Mining	5011.	6763.	6389.	6500.	6777.	6326.	6258.	6539.	6739.	6912.
Construction	5773.	7779.	8232.	8577.	8916.	9235.	9437.	9561.	9886.	10358.
Ordnance	125.	158.	160.	161.	163.	165.	166.	168.	171.	174.
Food	2884.	3359.	3440.	3660.	3791.	3777.	3941.	4055.	4203.	4352.
Tobacco	107.	134.	143.	152.	151.	153.	156.	160.	170.	180.
Textiles	758.	1156.	1068.	1088.	1075.	1082.	1118.	1083.	1092.	1134.
Apparel	470.	617.	619.	670.	678.	670.	690.	664.	674.	684.
Lumber	984.	1655.	1765.	1853.	1935.	1976.	2081.	2109.	2268.	2487.
Furniture	208.	306.	296.	322.	349.	348.	351.	347.	334.	347.
Paper	2708.	3371.	3387.	3371.	3319.	3371.	3541.	3613.	3763.	3942.
Print & publ.	1037.	1447.	1527.	1553.	1589.	1614.	1671.	1702.	1760.	1843.
Chemicals	6154.	7141.	5971.	5450.	5055.	5037.	5734.	6716.	6804.	6995.
Petroleum	1611.	1919.	2103.	2434.	2372.	3083.	2544.	2707.	3026.	3340.
Rubber & plastics	1042.	1776.	1709.	1718.	1743.	1734.	1786.	1770.	1803.	1878.
Leather	63.	103.	107.	105.	105.	110.	111.	113.	117.	122.
Stone	1212.	2012.	2112.	2180.	2228.	2173.	2236.	2196.	2257.	2399.
Metals	3619.	5344.	5937.	6226.	6216.	5937.	5921.	5919.	6102.	6447.
Metal prd.	1584.	2149.	2277.	2385.	2439.	2436.	2496.	2491.	2586.	2709.
Nonelec. mach.	2602.	3251.	3575.	3619.	3623.	3498.	3545.	3517.	3648.	3854.
Electrical	1863.	2374.	2465.	2580.	2632.	2598.	2660.	2643.	2729.	2828.
Transp. equip.	2651.	3903.	3714.	3516.	3495.	3533.	3571.	3451.	3412.	3473.
Instruments	554.	675.	727.	755.	804.	815.	842.	872.	887.	925.
Misc. mfg.	408.	376.	401.	422.	423.	426.	437.	440.	453.	462.
Transportation	5987.	8417.	8347.	8199.	8306.	8373.	8473.	8494.	8631.	8907.
Communications	9523.	12579.	13073.	13441.	13675.	14241.	14965.	15520.	16286.	17163.
Utilities	10204.	12285.	12933.	13632.	14044.	14408.	14792.	15169.	15807.	16728.
Trade	11917.	16231.	16684.	17227.	17989.	18555.	19282.	19627.	20673.	22071.
Fin, ins, re., services	7250.	8875.	9434.	10720.	12759.	12699.	12909.	12837.	12392.	12297.

Table 7–A–2. GNP Summary: Constant Real Rate *(billions of 1972 dollars)*

	1976	1980	1981	1982	1983
Gross national product	1270.60	1479.51	1527.30	1576.28	1623.49
Personal consumption expenditures	819.30	952.79	983.63	1015.28	1047.38
Gross private domestic investment	172.40	217.36	225.05	233.05	239.68
Structures	85.00	106.49	112.21	117.13	120.08
Residential	46.70	58.42	61.87	65.49	67.20
Producers durable equipment	80.70	103.97	106.09	109.70	113.29
Agriculture	6.60	7.20	7.12	7.36	7.40
Mining	3.40	4.59	4.33	4.41	4.60
Construction	3.90	5.26	5.56	5.79	6.02
Nondurable goods	11.60	14.49	13.83	13.92	13.70
Durable goods	11.10	15.59	16.45	16.86	17.07
Transportation	4.20	5.90	5.86	5.75	5.83
Communication	7.40	9.77	10.16	10.44	10.63
Utilities	7.10	8.55	9.00	9.48	9.77
Trade	9.00	12.26	12.60	13.01	13.59
Finance and services	7.40	9.06	9.63	10.94	13.02
Inventory change	6.70	6.89	6.75	6.21	6.31
Net exports	16.00	18.30	18.58	19.01	18.62
Government purchases	262.90	291.06	300.03	308.95	317.81

Table 7–A–2. continued

	1984	1985	1986	1988	1990
Gross national product	1669.66	1717.58	1754.33	1832.81	1917.39
Personal consumption expenditures	1079.89	1112.87	1136.32	1187.06	1240.82
Gross private domestic investment	244.09	249.84	252.34	259.47	269.40
Structures	122.74	125.35	125.80	129.01	132.96
Residential	68.80	70.34	69.88	71.65	73.78
Producers durable equipment	115.06	118.21	120.54	124.57	130.33
Agriculture	7.46	7.61	7.65	7.70	7.79
Mining	4.29	4.25	4.44	4.57	4.69
Construction	6.24	6.38	6.46	6.68	7.00
Nondurable goods	14.22	14.67	15.56	16.13	16.86
Durable goods	16.78	17.06	16.96	17.44	18.33
Transportation	5.87	5.94	5.96	6.05	6.25
Communication	11.07	11.63	12.06	12.66	13.34
Utilities	10.03	10.29	10.55	11.00	11.64
Trade	14.01	14.56	14.82	15.61	16.67
Finance and services	12.96	13.18	13.10	12.65	12.55
Inventory change	6.29	6.28	6.00	5.88	6.11
Net exports	19.11	19.44	21.26	24.57	28.06
Government purchases	326.57	335.43	344.41	361.72	379.10

Table 7-A-3. Decreasing Real Rate

Equipment Investment, by Purchaser
(millions of 1976 dollars)

Sec. No. and Title	1976	1980	1981	1982	1983	1984	1985	1986	1988	1990
1 Agriculture	9585.	10520.	10411.	10765.	10834.	10923.	11164.	11226.	11318.	11471.
2 Mining	1657.	1961.	2060.	2099.	2141.	2185.	2285.	2349.	2456.	2581.
3 Petroleum & gas	3354.	4839.	4384.	4479.	4727.	4242.	4087.	4316.	4437.	4514.
4 Construction	5773.	7780.	8230.	8575.	8914.	9234.	9437.	9563.	9892.	10367.
5 Ordnance	125.	158.	160.	161.	163.	165.	166.	168.	171.	174.
6 Meat	285.	410.	368.	353.	372.	388.	418.	456.	472.	492.
7 Dairy	256.	299.	302.	307.	320.	320.	330.	339.	345.	350.
8 Canned & frozen foods	374.	494.	532.	550.	566.	572.	592.	596.	625.	656.
9 Grain mill products	352.	447.	457.	470.	475.	473.	512.	526.	552.	578.
10 Bakery	266.	258.	259.	264.	266.	269.	290.	293.	289.	290.
11 Sugar	191.	117.	142.	233.	235.	230.	240.	249.	262.	283.
12 Candy	102.	132.	137.	144.	147.	142.	161.	166.	169.	175.
13 Beverages	735.	788.	786.	872.	899.	907.	918.	950.	991.	1015.
14 Misc. food products	323.	431.	479.	496.	541.	510.	519.	522.	549.	572.
15 Tobacco	107.	136.	145.	153.	153.	155.	159.	163.	174.	184.
16 Fabrics & yarns	616.	897.	826.	839.	842.	855.	883.	855.	863.	896.
17 Floor coverings	51.	86.	77.	78.	74.	70.	72.	68.	66.	68.
18 Misc. textiles	91.	176.	168.	174.	160.	159.	164.	162.	165.	172.
19 Knit fabric & apparel	165.	182.	177.	206.	232.	219.	214.	197.	184.	176.
20 Apparel	224.	289.	282.	291.	285.	286.	295.	285.	290.	292.
21 Hsehld. text. & upholstry	81.	149.	163.	177.	165.	169.	185.	186.	205.	221.
22 Logging & lumber	674.	1074.	1148.	1207.	1253.	1259.	1339.	1358.	1456.	1591.
23 Plywd., millwork, struct.	303.	574.	612.	644.	682.	718.	746.	757.	823.	913.
24 Wooden containers	7.	12.	13.	12.	12.	12.	12.	12.	12.	12.
25 Hsehld. & ofc. furniture	208.	307.	303.	327.	354.	353.	355.	353.	340.	354.

Table 7–A–3. continued

Equipment Investment, by Purchaser
(millions of 1976 dollars)

Sec. No. and Title	1976	1980	1981	1982	1983	1984	1985	1986	1988	1990
27 Paper/products, ex. cont.	2426.	2989.	2994.	2983.	2944.	3010.	3180.	3262.	3422.	3610.
28 Paper containers	282.	403.	427.	435.	424.	413.	419.	416.	420.	426.
29 Newspapers	295.	487.	495.	502.	520.	534.	553.	562.	583.	619.
30 Printing & publishing	742.	962.	1035.	1053.	1072.	1082.	1121.	1143.	1181.	1229.
31 Industrial chemicals	3646.	3612.	2969.	2669.	2359.	2278.	2656.	3621.	3707.	3843.
32 Agricultural chemicals	285.	420.	450.	456.	467.	482.	502.	532.	577.	626.
33 Glue, ink, & fatty acids	302.	306.	255.	241.	240.	292.	310.	312.	317.	328.
34 Plastics & synthetics	1261.	2222.	1715.	1512.	1397.	1410.	1674.	1672.	1649.	1678.
35 Drugs	340.	342.	335.	327.	316.	317.	329.	331.	334.	329.
36 Cleaning & toilet items	237.	247.	291.	326.	360.	342.	362.	385.	409.	433.
37 Paints & allied prod.	83.	99.	108.	113.	108.	108.	114.	112.	112.	111.
38 Petroleum refining	1611.	1964.	2162.	2514.	2465.	3194.	2667.	2848.	3208.	3569.
39 Tires & tubes	216.	590.	494.	502.	546.	561.	590.	595.	620.	668.
40 Rubber prod., ex. tires	174.	215.	243.	260.	248.	246.	251.	244.	250.	255.
41 Plastic products	652.	991.	993.	976.	970.	950.	970.	957.	963.	990.
42 Leather tan. & ind. prod.	21.	27.	25.	25.	25.	24.	25.	24.	24.	24.
43 Shoes & other lea. prod.	42.	76.	81.	80.	81.	85.	87.	89.	93.	97.
44 Glass & glass products	358.	614.	628.	657.	688.	701.	724.	732.	773.	836.
45 Stone & clay products	854.	1404.	1491.	1530.	1547.	1479.	1520.	1473.	1496.	1576.
46 Iron & steel	2685.	3843.	4321.	4496.	4532.	4322.	4256.	4253.	4395.	4658.
47 Nonferrous metals	934.	1511.	1643.	1765.	1722.	1653.	1703.	1696.	1747.	1837.
48 Metal containers	127.	316.	314.	314.	319.	327.	338.	344.	356.	375.
49 Plumbing & heating	53.	52.	54.	56.	58.	55.	56.	53.	48.	46.
50 Structural metal prod.	454.	503.	550.	600.	630.	638.	651.	654.	688.	728.

(Table 7–A–3. continued overleaf)

Table 7–A–3. continued

Sec. No. and Title	Equipment Investment, by Purchaser (millions of 1976 dollars)									
	1976	1980	1981	1982	1983	1984	1985	1986	1988	1990
51 Stampings	364.	507.	534.	546.	545.	539.	550.	537.	549.	563.
52 Hdwre, plating, wire prod.	586.	781.	836.	881.	898.	890.	916.	916.	963.	1019.
53 Engines & turbines	230.	303.	313.	326.	341.	343.	346.	351.	366.	391.
54 Farm machinery	198.	153.	170.	175.	181.	182.	181.	177.	173.	172.
55 Construct. mining material	568.	765.	880.	874.	893.	874.	906.	928.	1022.	1130.
56 Metalworking mach. & equip.	293.	431.	476.	468.	448.	398.	394.	358.	351.	365.
57 Spec. ind. machinery	169.	274.	283.	280.	276.	252.	251.	246.	251.	261.
58 Gen. indus. machinery	382.	465.	495.	502.	515.	488.	490.	491.	516.	547.
59 Misc. machinery & shops	238.	297.	312.	336.	344.	350.	355.	360.	376.	396.
60 Ofc. & computing mach.	380.	387.	446.	436.	410.	413.	421.	409.	398.	399.
61 Service ind. machinery	144.	204.	238.	266.	264.	249.	259.	245.	255.	265.
62 Elec. meas. transformers	119.	172.	181.	192.	167.	165.	161.	151.	147.	148.
63 Elec. apparatus & motors	222.	262.	282.	292.	300.	282.	283.	273.	283.	298.
64 Household appliances	149.	138.	148.	154.	148.	140.	146.	140.	135.	129.
65 Elec. light & wiring	135.	246.	253.	264.	257.	252.	262.	252.	260.	269.
66 Radio, TV sets, & records	83.	126.	124.	129.	128.	131.	136.	139.	145.	151.
67 Communication equipment	428.	553.	572.	599.	586.	588.	606.	601.	626.	647.
68 Electronic components	551.	698.	701.	731.	779.	784.	792.	805.	835.	873.
69 Batteries, X-ray, & elec. equip.	176.	196.	220.	237.	288.	282.	304.	309.	335.	355.
70 Motor vehicles & parts	1908.	2830.	2759.	2544.	2494.	2512.	2520.	2406.	2319.	2323.
71 Aircraft & parts	380.	614.	480.	453.	457.	470.	482.	485.	471.	459.
72 Ships & boats	257.	320.	331.	375.	401.	411.	427.	426.	504.	582.
73 Locomotives, RR, & stcars	54.	69.	77.	77.	72.	65.	64.	59.	58.	59.
74 Cycles, trailers, & parts	52.	93.	104.	111.	119.	124.	130.	130.	130.	138.
75 Engr. & scient. instr.	32.	46.	45.	44.	45.	46.	46.	49.	52.	55.

Table 7–A–3.   continued

Sec. No. and Title	Equipment Investment, by Purchaser (millions of 1976 dollars)									
	1976	1980	1981	1982	1983	1984	1985	1986	1988	1990
76 Mech. measuring devices	73.	88.	93.	96.	100.	101.	99.	99.	102.	105.
77 Surgical & medical inst.	112.	143.	148.	151.	159.	176.	195.	209.	213.	228.
78 Optical & photo. supply	337.	408.	453.	477.	515.	508.	519.	532.	540.	560.
79 Misc. manufactured prod.	408.	377.	401.	423.	424.	426.	437.	440.	453.	463.
80 Railroads	1965.	3091.	2975.	2921.	2892.	2864.	2871.	2846.	2837.	2888.
81 Trucking	1405.	1795.	1931.	2015.	2132.	2262.	2377.	2453.	2662.	2930.
82 Other transport	1317.	1693.	1712.	1731.	1750.	1769.	1787.	1806.	1844.	1881.
83 Airlines	1300.	1856.	1753.	1561.	1562.	1512.	1477.	1435.	1346.	1280.
84 Wholesale & retail trade	11917.	16233.	16679.	17214.	17972.	18535.	19262.	19608.	20655.	22055.
85 Communication	9523.	12573.	13063.	13429.	13663.	14231.	14957.	15502.	16271.	17149.
86 Finance, ins., & services	7250.	9571.	10130.	11453.	13597.	13613.	13914.	13927.	13648.	13735.
87 Electric utilities	8460.	10549.	11241.	11899.	12285.	12667.	13076.	13459.	14092.	14992.
88 Nat. gas, water & sewer	1744.	1750.	1708.	1748.	1774.	1755.	1734.	1730.	1741.	1768.

(Table 7-A-3. continued overleaf)

Table 7–A–3. continued

Equipment Investment, by Purchaser, Summary by Major Sectors
(millions of 1976 dollars)

Title	1976	1980	1981	1982	1983	1984	1985	1986	1988	1990
Agriculture	9585.	10520.	10411.	10765.	10834.	10923.	11164.	11226.	11318.	11471.
Mining	5011.	6800.	6444.	6578.	6868.	6427.	6372.	6666.	6893.	7095.
Construction	5773.	7780.	8230.	8575.	8914.	9234.	9437.	9563.	9892.	10367.
Ordnance	125.	158.	160.	161.	163.	165.	166.	168.	171.	174.
Food	2884.	3377.	3463.	3689.	3823.	3812.	3979.	4098.	4254.	4412.
Tobacco	107.	136.	145.	153.	153.	155.	159.	163.	174.	184.
Textiles	758.	1160.	1072.	1091.	1077.	1083.	1120.	1084.	1094.	1137.
Apparel	470.	621.	622.	673.	681.	674.	694.	668.	679.	689.
Lumber	984.	1661.	1773.	1864.	1948.	1990.	2097.	2127.	2292.	2516.
Furniture	208.	307.	303.	327.	354.	353.	355.	353.	340.	354.
Paper	2708.	3393.	3421.	3418.	3369.	3424.	3598.	3678.	3842.	4035.
Print & publ.	1037.	1450.	1530.	1555.	1591.	1616.	1674.	1705.	1764.	1848.
Chemicals	6154.	7247.	6124.	5644.	5247.	5229.	5948.	6965.	7105.	7349.
Petroleum	1611.	1964.	2162.	2514.	2465.	3194.	2667.	2848.	3208.	3569.
Rubber & plastics	1042.	1796.	1729.	1738.	1765.	1757.	1812.	1796.	1834.	1914.
Leather	63.	103.	107.	105.	105.	110.	111.	113.	117.	122.
Stone	1212.	2018.	2119.	2187.	2235.	2180.	2244.	2205.	2269.	2412.
Metals	3619.	5355.	5964.	6261.	6254.	5975.	5959.	5950.	6141.	6495.
Metal prd.	1584.	2153.	2287.	2397.	2451.	2449.	2511.	2504.	2604.	2731.
Nonelec. mach.	2602.	3279.	3614.	3663.	3672.	3549.	3602.	3564.	3708.	3926.
Electrical	1863.	2390.	2482.	2598.	2653.	2623.	2689.	2670.	2765.	2871.
Transp. equip.	2651.	3927.	3752.	3560.	3542.	3582.	3623.	3505.	3483.	3561.
Instruments	554.	684.	738.	768.	818.	830.	859.	889.	907.	949.
Misc. mfg.	408.	377.	401.	423.	424.	426.	437.	440.	453.	463.
Transportation	5987.	8436.	8371.	8228.	8337.	8405.	8512.	8540.	8689.	8979.
Communications	9523.	12573.	13063.	13429.	13663.	14231.	14957.	15502.	16271.	17149.
Utilities	10204.	12299.	12949.	13648.	14059.	14422.	14810.	15189.	15833.	16761.
Trade	11917.	16233.	16679.	17214.	17972.	18535.	19262.	19608.	20655.	22055.
Fin., ins., re., services	7250.	9571.	10130.	11453.	13597.	13613.	13914.	13927.	13648.	13735.

Table 7–A–4. GNP Summary: Decreasing Real Rate *(billions of 1972 dollars)*

	1976	1980	1981	1982	1983
Gross national product	1270.60	1480.36	1528.24	1577.30	1624.59
Gross private domestic investment	172.40	218.35	226.17	234.24	240.98
Structures	85.00	106.53	112.26	117.17	120.11
Residential	46.70	58.42	61.87	65.49	67.20
Producers durable equipment	80.70	104.86	107.09	110.83	114.54
Agriculture	6.60	7.24	7.17	7.41	7.46
Mining	3.40	4.61	4.37	4.46	4.66
Construction	3.90	5.26	5.56	5.79	6.02
Nondurable goods	11.60	14.64	14.04	14.18	13.97
Durable goods	11.10	15.67	16.56	17.00	17.21
Transportation	4.20	5.92	5.87	5.77	5.85
Communication	7.40	9.77	10.15	10.44	10.62
Utilities	7.10	8.56	9.01	9.50	9.78
Trade	9.00	12.26	12.60	13.00	13.57
Finance and services	7.40	9.77	10.34	11.69	13.88
Inventory change	6.70	6.96	6.82	6.25	6.34
Net exports	16.00	18.16	18.41	18.82	18.41
Government purchases	262.90	291.06	300.03	308.95	317.81

(Table 7–A–4. continued overleaf)

Table 7-A-4. continued

	1984	1985	1986	1988	1990
Gross national product	1670.83	1718.87	1755.72	1834.46	1919.29
Gross private domestic investment	245.49	251.40	254.03	261.49	271.77
Structures	122.77	125.38	125.83	129.05	133.00
Residential	68.80	70.34	69.88	71.65	73.78
Producers durable equipment	116.40	119.71	122.16	126.51	132.62
Agriculture	7.52	7.69	7.73	7.79	7.90
Mining	4.36	4.32	4.52	4.68	4.81
Construction	6.24	6.38	6.46	6.68	7.00
Nondurable goods	14.51	14.99	15.93	16.59	17.41
Durable goods	16.93	17.23	17.11	17.64	18.57
Transportation	5.90	5.97	5.99	6.10	6.30
Communication	11.06	11.62	12.05	12.64	13.33
Utilities	10.03	10.30	10.57	11.02	11.66
Trade	14.00	14.55	14.81	15.60	16.66
Finance and services	13.89	14.20	14.22	13.93	14.02
Inventory change	6.32	6.31	6.03	5.92	6.15
Net exports	18.88	19.18	20.95	24.20	27.59
Government purchases	326.57	335.43	344.41	361.72	379.10

Table 7–A–5. Increasing Real Rate

Equipment Investment, by Purchaser
(millions of 1976 dollars)

Sec. No. and Title	1976	1980	1981	1982	1983	1984	1985	1986	1988	1990
1 Agriculture	9585.	10402.	10282.	10614.	10669.	10739.	10957.	10996.	11044.	11151.
2 Mining	1657.	1962.	2062.	2102.	2144.	2187.	2287.	2354.	2460.	2584.
3 Petroleum & gas	3354.	4765.	4273.	4321.	4547.	4041.	3863.	4067.	4135.	4160.
4 Construction	5773.	7778.	8234.	8580.	8918.	9237.	9438.	9560.	9882.	10350.
5 Ordnance	125.	158.	160.	161.	163.	165.	166.	168.	171.	174.
6 Meat	285.	408.	364.	347.	366.	383.	411.	448.	463.	481.
7 Dairy	256.	299.	303.	307.	321.	321.	331.	340.	346.	351.
8 Canned & frozen foods	374.	493.	531.	548.	565.	570.	590.	594.	622.	654.
9 Grain mill products	352.	442.	451.	461.	466.	464.	501.	514.	538.	562.
10 Bakery	266.	257.	257.	262.	263.	266.	287.	289.	285.	285.
11 Sugar	191.	114.	136.	224.	226.	219.	228.	236.	246.	263.
12 Candy	102.	131.	136.	143.	145.	140.	158.	164.	166.	171.
13 Beverages	735.	767.	762.	843.	867.	872.	880.	908.	941.	958.
14 Misc. food products	323.	431.	479.	496.	541.	510.	518.	521.	548.	571.
15 Tobacco	107.	132.	142.	150.	149.	151.	154.	158.	167.	176.
16 Fabrics & yarns	616.	891.	820.	836.	840.	853.	881.	852.	860.	893.
17 Floor coverings	51.	86.	76.	77.	74.	69.	71.	68.	66.	68.
18 Misc. textiles	91.	175.	167.	173.	160.	158.	164.	161.	164.	172.
19 Knit fabric & apparel	165.	174.	170.	198.	223.	210.	205.	188.	174.	166.
20 Apparel	224.	290.	282.	291.	286.	287.	296.	286.	290.	293.
21 Hsehld., text. & upholstry	81.	149.	163.	177.	165.	170.	185.	186.	205.	221.
22 Logging & lumber	674.	1062.	1132.	1187.	1229.	1232.	1308.	1322.	1411.	1535.
23 Plywd., millwork, struct.	303.	573.	611.	644.	682.	719.	746.	757.	823.	913.
24 Wooden containers	7.	12.	13.	12.	12.	12.	12.	12.	12.	12.
25 Hsehld. & ofc. furniture	208.	305.	289.	317.	345.	344.	347.	342.	329.	341.

(Table 7–A–5. continued overleaf)

Table 7–A–5. continued

Sec. No. and Title	Equipment Investment, by Purchaser (millions of 1976 dollars)									
	1976	1980	1981	1982	1983	1984	1985	1986	1988	1990
27 Paper/products, ex. cont.	2426.	2947.	2927.	2891.	2847.	2907.	3067.	3136.	3271.	3430.
28 Paper containers	282.	403.	426.	434.	424.	413.	418.	416.	419.	425.
29 Newspapers	295.	483.	490.	497.	514.	529.	546.	555.	574.	609.
30 Printing & publishing	742.	963.	1035.	1054.	1073.	1083.	1122.	1144.	1183.	1230.
31 Industrial chemicals	3646.	3457.	2756.	2405.	2099.	2021.	2375.	3286.	3301.	3366.
32 Agricultural chemicals	285.	411.	440.	444.	453.	467.	485.	513.	552.	596.
33 Glue, ink, & fatty acids	302.	301.	247.	232.	230.	282.	298.	300.	302.	311.
34 Plastics & synthetics	1261.	2188.	1653.	1429.	1317.	1333.	1586.	1575.	1538.	1552.
35 Drugs	340.	340.	331.	321.	311.	311.	323.	324.	327.	320.
36 Cleaning & toilet items	237.	242.	286.	320.	354.	335.	354.	376.	399.	421.
37 Paints & allied prod.	83.	99.	108.	112.	107.	107.	114.	112.	112.	111.
38 Petroleum refining	1611.	1875.	2045.	2357.	2285.	2979.	2430.	2578.	2864.	3140.
39 Tires & tubes	216.	566.	469.	477.	518.	532.	558.	560.	580.	621.
40 Rubber prod., ex. tires	174.	209.	236.	253.	240.	237.	242.	235.	241.	244.
41 Plastic products	652.	982.	984.	969.	963.	944.	963.	949.	954.	980.
42 Leather tan. & ind. prod.	21.	27.	25.	25.	25.	24.	25.	24.	24.	24.
43 Shoes & other lea. prod.	42.	76.	82.	80.	81.	85.	87.	89.	93.	98.
44 Glass & glass products	358.	603.	616.	644.	674.	685.	707.	713.	751.	809.
45 Stone & clay products	854.	1403.	1489.	1530.	1548.	1481.	1521.	1475.	1497.	1577.
46 Iron & steel	2685.	3824.	4273.	4435.	4465.	4256.	4192.	4198.	4325.	4574.
47 Nonferrous metals	934.	1511.	1637.	1757.	1713.	1645.	1693.	1693.	1742.	1830.
48 Metal containers	127.	316.	314.	314.	320.	328.	339.	345.	356.	375.
49 Plumbing & heating	53.	52.	54.	56.	58.	55.	56.	52.	47.	45.
50 Structural metal prod.	454.	493.	538.	586.	615.	621.	632.	635.	665.	700.

Table 7–A–5. continued

Equipment Investment, by Purchaser
(millions of 1976 dollars)

Sec. No. and Title	1976	1980	1981	1982	1983	1984	1985	1986	1988	1990
51 Stampines	364.	505.	532.	544.	544.	637.	548.	536.	547.	561.
52 Hdwre., plating, wire prod.	586.	775.	829.	874.	891.	882.	908.	909.	954.	1008.
53 Engines & turbines	230.	296.	306.	318.	333.	335.	336.	342.	355.	378.
54 Farm machinery	198.	148.	163.	167.	174.	174.	172.	169.	163.	162.
55 Construct. mining material	568.	759.	869.	857.	873.	856.	885.	908.	996.	1096.
56 Metalworking mach. & equip.	293.	420.	460.	452.	431.	380.	373.	344.	335.	345.
57 Spec. ind. machinery	169.	271.	280.	277.	273.	249.	247.	245.	249.	258.
58 Gen. indus. machinery	382.	461.	489.	494.	507.	481.	481.	485.	509.	538.
59 Misc. machinery & shops	238.	290.	303.	326.	333.	337.	340.	344.	356.	373.
60 Ofc. & computing mach.	380.	382.	439.	428.	400.	399.	408.	403.	389.	388.
61 Service ind. machinery	144.	197.	229.	257.	254.	238.	247.	234.	241.	249.
62 Elec. meas. transformers	119.	171.	180.	191.	166.	164.	159.	151.	146.	148.
63 Elec. apparatus & motors	222.	260.	279.	289.	297.	279.	279.	272.	281.	295.
64 Household appliances	149.	138.	148.	154.	148.	140.	146.	140.	135.	129.
65 Elec. light. & wiring	135.	246.	253.	264.	257.	252.	261.	252.	260.	269.
66 Radio, TV sets, & records	83.	123.	122.	127.	125.	128.	132.	135.	140.	145.
67 Communication equipment	428.	552.	573.	600.	587.	587.	605.	602.	626.	647.
68 Electronic components	551.	682.	686.	715.	760.	763.	768.	779.	803.	835.
69 Batteries, X-ray, & elec. equip.	176.	185.	207.	222.	271.	263.	282.	287.	306.	322.
70 Motor vehicles & parts	1908.	2815.	2731.	2518.	2470.	2494.	2507.	2395.	2303.	2305.
71 Aircraft & parts	380.	608.	469.	439.	443.	457.	468.	469.	453.	439.
72 Ships & boats	257.	301.	305.	338.	357.	360.	367.	362.	421.	476.
73 Locomotives, RR, & stcars	54.	68.	76.	76.	71.	63.	62.	58.	57.	57.
74 Cycles, trailers, & parts	52.	87.	97.	103.	110.	114.	118.	117.	115.	120.
75 Engr. & scient. instr.	32.	45.	45.	44.	44.	46.	46.	49.	51.	55.

(Table 7-A-5. continued overleaf)

Table 7–A–5. continued

Equipment Investment, by Purchaser
(millions of 1976 dollars)

Sec. No. and Title	1976	1980	1981	1982	1983	1984	1985	1986	1988	1990
76 Mech. measuring devices	73.	87.	93.	95.	99.	100.	98.	99.	101.	105.
77 Surgical & medical inst.	112.	136.	137.	139.	145.	160.	177.	191.	193.	204.
78 Optical & photo. supply	337.	398.	442.	465.	503.	495.	504.	518.	523.	541.
79 Misc. manufactured prod.	408.	376.	400.	422.	423.	425.	437.	440.	452.	462.
80 Railroads	1965.	3064.	2944.	2889.	2860.	2831.	2835.	2806.	2790.	2833.
81 Trucking	1405.	1783.	1911.	1986.	2100.	2225.	2332.	2400.	2593.	2841.
82 Other transport	1317.	1693.	1712.	1731.	1750.	1769.	1787.	1806.	1844.	1881.
83 Airlines	1300.	1857.	1757.	1565.	1567.	1517.	1482.	1439.	1350.	1284.
84 Wholesale & retail trade	11917.	16229.	16690.	17240.	18007.	18577.	19303.	19647.	20692.	22090.
85 Communication	9523.	12586.	13083.	13454.	13687.	14252.	14973.	15538.	16303.	17179.
86 Finance, ins., & services	7250.	8193.	8763.	10023.	11973.	11851.	11987.	11846.	11275.	11040.
87 Electric utilities	8460.	10540.	11239.	11910.	12302.	12690.	13098.	13479.	14111.	15010.
88 Nat. gas, water & sewer	1744.	1732.	1679.	1707.	1730.	1706.	1679.	1673.	1673.	1690.

Table 7-A-5. continued

Equipment Investment, by Purchaser, Summary by Major Sectors
(millions of 1976 dollars)

Title	1976	1980	1981	1982	1983	1984	1985	1986	1988	1990
Agriculture	9585.	10402.	10282.	10614.	10669.	10739.	10957.	10996.	11044.	11151.
Mining	5011.	6727.	6335.	6424.	6690.	6229.	6150.	6420.	6595.	6744.
Construction	5773.	7778.	8234.	8580.	8918.	9237.	9438.	9560.	9882.	10350.
Ordnance	125.	158.	160.	161.	163.	165.	166.	168.	171.	174.
Food	2884.	3341.	3417.	3632.	3760.	3743.	3904.	4015.	4156.	4296.
Tobacco	107.	132.	142.	150.	149.	151.	154.	158.	167.	176.
Textiles	758.	1152.	1064.	1086.	1073.	1081.	1116.	1081.	1090.	1132.
Apparel	470.	613.	616.	667.	674.	666.	686.	660.	669.	680.
Lumber	984.	1648.	1756.	1843.	1924.	1963.	2066.	2092.	2246.	2460.
Furniture	208.	305.	289.	317.	345.	344.	347.	342.	329.	341.
Paper	2708.	3350.	3353.	3325.	3270.	3320.	3486.	3553.	3690.	3856.
Print. & publ.	1037.	1445.	1525.	1551.	1587.	1611.	1668.	1699.	1757.	1839.
Chemicals	6154.	7037.	5822.	5262.	4871.	4856.	5535.	6485.	6530.	6677.
Petroleum	1611.	1875.	2045.	2357.	2285.	2979.	2430.	2578.	2864.	3140.
Rubber & plastics	1042.	1757.	1689.	1698.	1722.	1713.	1763.	1745.	1774.	1845.
Leather	63.	103.	107.	105.	105.	110.	112.	113.	117.	122.
Stone	1212.	2006.	2105.	2174.	2222.	2166.	2228.	2188.	2247.	2386.
Metals	3619.	5334.	5911.	6192.	6178.	5901.	5885.	5891.	6067.	6404.
Metal prd.	1584.	2140.	2266.	2374.	2427.	2423.	2483.	2478.	2570.	2690.
Nonelec. mach.	2602.	3223.	3538.	3576.	3577.	3449.	3490.	3473.	3594.	3788.
Electrical	1863.	2359.	2447.	2562.	2611.	2575.	2632.	2618.	2697.	2789.
Transp. equip.	2651.	3879.	3678.	3475.	3451.	3488.	3522.	3401.	3348.	3396.
Instruments	554.	667.	716.	744.	791.	801.	826.	857.	869.	904.
Misc. mfg.	408.	376.	400.	422.	423.	425.	437.	440.	452.	462.
Transportation	5987.	8398.	8324.	8171.	8277.	8342.	8436.	8451.	8576.	8839.
Communications	9523.	12586.	13083.	13454.	13687.	14252.	14973.	15538.	16303.	17179.
Utilities	10204.	12272.	12918.	13616.	14032.	14396.	14776.	15152.	15784.	16700.
Trade	11917.	16229.	16690.	17240.	18007.	18577.	19303.	19647.	20692.	22090.
Fin., ins., re., services	7250.	8193.	8763.	10023.	11973.	11851.	11987.	11846.	11275.	11040.

Table 7–A–6.   GNP Summary: Increasing Real Rate *(billions of 1972 dollars)*

	1976	1980	1981	1982	1983
Gross national product	1270.60	1478.67	1526.38	1575.32	1622.45
Personal consumption expenditures	819.30	952.79	983.63	1015.28	1047.38
Gross private domestic investment					
Structures	172.40	216.38	223.97	231.91	238.45
Residential	85.00	106.46	112.17	117.10	120.05
Producers durable equipment	46.70	58.42	61.87	65.49	67.20
	80.70	103.10	105.12	108.63	112.11
Agriculture	6.60	7.16	7.08	7.13	7.35
Mining	3.40	4.56	4.30	4.36	4.54
Construction	3.90	5.25	5.56	5.80	6.02
Nondurable goods	11.60	14.34	13.63	13.67	13.43
Durable goods	11.10	15.51	16.33	16.74	16.93
Transportation	4.20	5.89	5.84	5.73	5.81
Communication	7.40	9.78	10.17	10.45	10.64
Utilities	7.10	8.54	8.99	9.47	9.76
Trade	9.00	12.26	12.60	13.02	13.60
Finance and services	7.40	8.36	8.94	10.23	12.22
Inventory change	6.70	6.82	6.67	6.18	6.28
Net exports	16.00	18.45	18.74	19.19	18.81
Government purchases	262.90	291.06	300.03	308.95	317.81

Table 7–A–6. continued

	1984	1985	1986	1988	1990
Gross national product	1668.57	1716.38	1753.07	1831.34	1915.70
Personal consumption expenditures	1079.89	1112.87	1136.32	1187.06	1240.82
Gross private domestic investment	242.78	248.40	250.80	257.65	267.30
Structures	122.71	125.32	125.77	128.98	132.93
Residential	68.80	70.34	69.88	71.65	73.78
Producers durable equipment	113.80	116.83	119.06	122.81	128.29
Agriculture	7.39	7.54	7.57	7.60	7.68
Mining	4.23	4.17	4.36	4.47	4.58
Construction	6.24	6.38	6.46	6.68	6.99
Nondurable goods	13.94	14.37	15.22	15.72	16.37
Durable goods	16.64	16.91	16.81	17.26	18.11
Transportation	5.85	5.92	5.93	6.02	6.20
Communication	11.07	11.64	12.07	12.67	13.35
Utilities	10.02	10.28	10.54	10.98	11.62
Trade	14.03	14.58	14.84	15.63	16.68
Finance and services	12.10	12.24	12.09	11.51	11.27
Inventory change	6.26	6.26	5.98	5.85	6.08
Net exports	19.33	19.68	21.53	24.91	28.47
Government purchases	326.57	335.43	344.41	361.71	379.10

Table 7–A–7.   Tax Credit Equals 0.05

Equipment Investment, by Purchaser
(millions of 1976 dollars)

Sec. No. and Title	1976	1980	1981	1982	1983	1984	1985	1986	1988	1990
1 Agriculture	9585.	9988.	9746.	10139.	10427.	10440.	10831.	10834.	10873.	10996.
2 Mining	1657.	1955.	2054.	2096.	2141.	2187.	2287.	2362.	2469.	2589.
3 Petroleum & gas	3354.	4589.	3999.	3984.	4164.	3623.	3790.	3930.	3989.	4031.
4 Construction	5773.	7701.	8114.	8476.	8899.	9221.	9426.	9550.	9855.	10324.
5 Ordnance	125.	158.	160.	161.	163.	165.	166.	168.	171.	174.
6 Meat	285.	399.	350.	330.	346.	359.	408.	444.	458.	475.
7 Dairy	256.	299.	303.	308.	321.	321.	331.	341.	346.	351.
8 Canned & frozen foods	374.	489.	528.	547.	565.	571.	591.	595.	623.	654.
9 Grain mill products	352.	431.	440.	451.	455.	451.	501.	513.	537.	561.
10 Bakery	266.	254.	253.	255.	254.	257.	287.	289.	285.	285.
11 Sugar	191.	109.	128.	213.	211.	203.	228.	236.	245.	263.
12 Candy	102.	129.	131.	136.	135.	129.	157.	162.	164.	169.
13 Beverages	735.	716.	682.	771.	843.	844.	875.	902.	934.	951.
14 Misc. food products	323.	431.	478.	493.	538.	510.	518.	522.	549.	572.
15 Tobacco	107.	125.	132.	142.	149.	151.	153.	157.	167.	176.
16 Fabrics & yarns	616.	862.	785.	821.	856.	875.	893.	857.	857.	891.
17 Floor coverings	51.	83.	71.	73.	73.	71.	73.	69.	66.	68.
18 Misc. textiles	91.	172.	162.	169.	160.	160.	166.	163.	165.	171.
19 Knit fabric & apparel	165.	116.	134.	174.	208.	192.	185.	169.	157.	149.
20 Apparel	224.	289.	283.	292.	286.	287.	296.	286.	291.	293.
21 Hsehld., text., & upholstry	81.	149.	163.	177.	165.	170.	185.	187.	206.	221.
22 Logging & lumber	674.	1025.	1077.	1124.	1184.	1199.	1297.	1312.	1391.	1511.
23 Plywd., millwork, struct.	303.	567.	602.	638.	685.	725.	753.	761.	822.	913.
24 Wooden containers	7.	12.	13.	12.	12.	12.	12.	12.	12.	12.
25 Hsehld., & ofc. furniture	208.	306.	279.	269.	349.	356.	351.	343.	325.	335.

Table 7–A–7. continued

Equipment Investment, by Purchaser
(millions of 1976 dollars)

Sec. No. and Title	1976	1980	1981	1982	1983	1984	1985	1986	1988	1990
27 Paper/products, ex. cont.	2426.	2880.	2787.	2716.	2676.	2750.	3093.	3147.	3251.	3413.
28 Paper containers	282.	401.	422.	429.	421.	414.	421.	421.	420.	425.
29 Newspapers	295.	467.	477.	490.	515.	529.	546.	553.	572.	607.
30 Printing & publishing	742.	960.	1032.	1052.	1073.	1084.	1123.	1148.	1186.	1232.
31 Industrial chemicals	3646.	2887.	1974.	1593.	1404.	1343.	2292.	3013.	2962.	3013.
32 Agricultural chemicals	285.	382.	417.	428.	447.	460.	477.	505.	544.	589.
33 Glue, ink, & fatty acids	302.	290.	231.	211.	207.	258.	298.	297.	295.	304.
34 Plastics & synthetics	1261.	2092.	1445.	1136.	960.	1001.	1573.	1517.	1441.	1454.
35 Drugs	340.	331.	314.	294.	272.	270.	318.	315.	315.	309.
36 Cleaning & toilet items	237.	210.	260.	300.	341.	321.	339.	360.	382.	402.
37 Paints & allied prod.	83.	98.	108.	111.	106.	106.	113.	113.	113.	111.
38 Petroleum refining	1611.	1756.	1865.	2159.	2132.	2790.	2424.	2555.	2829.	3115.
39 Tires & tubes	216.	450.	302.	350.	508.	514.	533.	530.	544.	583.
40 Rubber prod., ex. tires	174.	179.	204.	227.	234.	229.	234.	232.	235.	236.
41 Plastic products	652.	948.	950.	954.	974.	956.	970.	953.	952.	977.
42 Leather tan. & ind. prod.	21.	27.	25.	25.	25.	24.	25.	24.	24.	24.
43 Shoes & other lea. prod.	42.	76.	82.	80.	81.	86.	87.	89.	93.	98.
44 Glass & glass products	358.	562.	555.	596.	672.	683.	702.	708.	742.	799.
45 Stone & clay products	854.	1394.	1472.	1520.	1551.	1494.	1531.	1483.	1497.	1577.
46 Iron & steel	2685.	3788.	4154.	4260.	4286.	4234.	4222.	4287.	4362.	4563.
47 Nonferrous metals	934.	1501.	1608.	1720.	1684.	1637.	1691.	1719.	1760.	1826.
48 Metal containers	127.	314.	312.	314.	321.	330.	340.	346.	357.	376.
49 Plumbing & heating	53.	51.	53.	55.	57.	54.	56.	52.	47.	45.
50 Structural metal prod.	454.	463.	491.	545.	603.	608.	628.	634.	662.	693.

(Table 7–A–7. continued overleaf)

Table 7–A–7. continued

Equipment Investment, by Purchaser
(millions of 1976 dollars)

Sec. No. and Title	1976	1980	1981	1982	1983	1984	1985	1986	1988	1990
51 Stampings	364.	496.	519.	536.	543.	537.	548.	542.	549.	560.
52 Hdwre., plating, wire prod.	586.	752.	797.	850.	886.	879.	909.	919.	956.	1004.
53 Engines & turbines	230.	270.	268.	290.	329.	332.	335.	341.	351.	373.
54 Farm machinery	198.	131.	141.	144.	153.	170.	168.	168.	161.	158.
55 Construct. mining material	568.	740.	825.	806.	845.	850.	882.	916.	997.	1090.
56 Metalworking mach. & equip.	293.	385.	401.	406.	421.	380.	367.	360.	342.	342.
57 Spec. ind. machinery	169.	264.	267.	266.	268.	248.	250.	250.	251.	258.
58 Gen. indus. machinery	382.	446.	463.	470.	491.	473.	481.	496.	515.	537.
59 Misc. machinery & shops	238.	270.	281.	306.	319.	321.	333.	338.	349.	365.
60 Ofc. & computing mach.	380.	359.	396.	391.	384.	382.	397.	420.	392.	383.
61 Service ind. machinery	144.	173.	208.	242.	247.	231.	239.	236.	240.	245.
62 Elec. meas. transformers	119.	169.	175.	188.	165.	164.	156.	154.	148.	147.
63 Elec. apparatus & motors	222.	254.	268.	280.	292.	276.	278.	278.	284.	295.
64 Household appliances	149.	137.	147.	153.	148.	140.	146.	141.	135.	129.
65 Elec. light. & wiring	135.	242.	248.	262.	258.	253.	262.	254.	260.	269.
66 Radio, TV sets, & records	83.	113.	108.	115.	123.	125.	128.	131.	135.	141.
67 Communication equipment	428.	547.	565.	595.	586.	587.	599.	604.	626.	647.
68 Electronic components	551.	585.	553.	610.	737.	727.	725.	737.	757.	788.
69 Batteries, X-ray, & elec. equip.	176.	156.	158.	175.	252.	252.	275.	289.	302.	311.
70 Motor vehicles & parts	1908.	2746.	2608.	2423.	2445.	2513.	2548.	2447.	2298.	2290.
71 Aircraft & parts	380.	591.	438.	403.	403.	418.	471.	464.	442.	430.
72 Ships & boats	257.	257.	259.	289.	304.	300.	343.	343.	402.	458.
73 Locomotives, RR, & stcars	54.	66.	72.	74.	69.	62.	60.	60.	57.	58.
74 Cycles, trailers, & parts	52.	60.	76.	88.	102.	105.	108.	106.	105.	110.
75 Engr. & scient. instr.	32.	44.	44.	43.	44.	46.	47.	49.	51.	55.

Table 7–A–7. continued

Sec. No. and Title	Equipment Investment, by Purchaser (millions of 1976 dollars)									
	1976	1980	1981	1982	1983	1984	1985	1986	1988	1990
76 Mech. measuring devices	73.	86.	90.	93.	98.	99.	98.	100.	102.	105.
77 Surgical & medical inst.	112.	127.	126.	118.	134.	150.	169.	187.	190.	197.
78 Optical & photo. supply	337.	359.	385.	419.	492.	488.	500.	522.	521.	529.
79 Misc. manufactured prod.	408.	372.	395.	416.	416.	420.	438.	447.	452.	462.
80 Railroads	1965.	2983.	2830.	2804.	2837.	2810.	2849.	2803.	2775.	2822.
81 Trucking	1405.	1753.	1857.	1918.	2013.	2126.	2321.	2373.	2555.	2804.
82 Other transport	1317.	1693.	1712.	1731.	1750.	1769.	1787.	1806.	1844.	1881.
83 Airlines	1300.	1851.	1749.	1559.	1568.	1526.	1490.	1445.	1353.	1287.
84 Wholesale & retail trade	11917.	16129.	16581.	17204.	18072.	18670.	19392.	19704.	20720.	22127.
85 Communication	9523.	12565.	13051.	13433.	13686.	14255.	14962.	15596.	16360.	17208.
86 Finance, ins., & services	7250.	2798.	2605.	5621.	11358.	11018.	10946.	10666.	9972.	9673.
87 Electric utilities	8460.	10467.	11153.	11880.	12350.	12760.	13161.	13517.	14124.	15030.
88 Nat. gas, water & sewer	1744.	1712.	1645.	1657.	1655.	1624.	1676.	1671.	1669.	1685.

(Table 7–A–7. continued overleaf)

Table 7-A-7. continued

*Equipment Investment, by Purchaser, Summary by Major Sectors
(millions of 1976 dollars)*

Title	1976	1980	1981	1982	1983	1984	1985	1986	1988	1990
Agriculture	9585.	9983.	9746.	10139.	10427.	10440.	10831.	10834.	10873.	10996.
Mining	5011.	6544.	6053.	6080.	6305.	5810.	6076.	6293.	6458.	6620.
Construction	5773.	7701.	8114.	8476.	8899.	9221.	9426.	9550.	9855.	10324.
Ordnance	125.	158.	160.	161.	163.	165.	166.	168.	171.	174.
Food	2884.	3258.	3292.	3503.	3667.	3645.	3897.	4003.	4140.	4281.
Tobacco	107.	125.	132.	142.	149.	151.	153.	157.	167.	176.
Textiles	758.	1116.	1018.	1062.	1088.	1106.	1131.	1089.	1088.	1129.
Apparel	470.	554.	579.	642.	660.	649.	667.	643.	654.	664.
Lumber	984.	1604.	1692.	1775.	1881.	1936.	2062.	2085.	2225.	2436.
Furniture	208.	306.	279.	269.	349.	356.	351.	343.	325.	335.
Paper	2708.	3282.	3208.	3144.	3097.	3164.	3514.	3568.	3672.	3838.
Print. & publ.	1037.	1427.	1508.	1541.	1588.	1613.	1669.	1701.	1758.	1838.
Chemicals	6154.	6292.	4749.	4074.	3737.	3758.	5410.	6120.	6051.	6181.
Petroleum	1611.	1756.	1865.	2159.	2132.	2790.	2424.	2555.	2829.	3115.
Rubber & plastics	1042.	1578.	1456.	1531.	1715.	1699.	1737.	1715.	1731.	1797.
Leather	63.	103.	107.	105.	106.	110.	112.	113.	117.	122.
Stone	1212.	1956.	2027.	2116.	2223.	2177.	2233.	2191.	2240.	2376.
Metals	3619.	5289.	5762.	5980.	5971.	5871.	5913.	6006.	6122.	6389.
Metal prd.	1584.	2076.	2172.	2300.	2410.	2408.	2481.	2493.	2570.	2677.
Nonelec. mach.	2602.	3039.	3252.	3322.	3458.	3389.	3452.	3524.	3598.	3753.
Electrical	1863.	2203.	2222.	2378.	2561.	2523.	2568.	2587.	2647.	2727.
Transp. equip.	2651.	3721.	3452.	3277.	3322.	3397.	3530.	3420.	3304.	3345.
Instruments	554.	616.	645.	673.	768.	784.	814.	857.	865.	886.
Misc. mfg.	408.	372.	395.	416.	468.	420.	438.	447.	452.	462.
Transportation	5987.	8280.	8148.	8012.	8167.	8230.	8447.	8427.	8527.	8795.
Communications	9523.	12565.	13051.	13433.	13686.	14255.	14962.	15596.	16360.	17208.
Utilities	10204.	12179.	12798.	13537.	14004.	14384.	14836.	15188.	15793.	16715.
Trade	11917.	16129.	16581.	17204.	18072.	18670.	19392.	19704.	20720.	22127.
Fin., ins., re., services	7250.	2798.	2605.	5621.	11358.	11018.	10946.	10666.	9972.	9673.

Table 7–A–8.   GNP Summary: Credit Equals 0.05 *(billions of 1972 dollars)*

	1976	1980	1981	1982	1983
Gross national product	1270.60	1472.45	1518.66	1569.39	1620.60
Personal consumption expenditures	819.30	952.80	983.63	1015.28	1047.38
Gross private domestic investment	172.40	209.12	214.86	224.87	236.12
Structures	85.00	106.19	111.81	116.91	120.09
Residential	46.70	58.42	61.87	65.49	67.20
Producers durable equipment	80.70	96.59	97.01	101.99	109.50
Agriculture	6.60	6.88	6.71	6.98	7.18
Mining	3.40	4.44	4.11	4.13	4.28
Construction	3.90	5.20	5.48	5.73	6.01
Nondurable goods	11.60	13.43	12.34	12.34	12.36
Durable goods	11.10	14.98	15.49	15.91	16.51
Transportation	4.20	5.81	5.72	5.62	5.73
Communication	7.40	9.76	10.14	10.44	10.63
Utilities	7.10	8.47	8.90	9.42	9.74
Trade	9.00	12.18	12.52	12.99	13.65
Finance and services	7.40	2.86	2.66	5.74	11.59
Inventory change	6.70	6.33	6.05	5.98	6.53
Net exports	16.00	19.49	20.14	20.30	19.29
Government purchases	262.90	291.06	300.02	308.95	317.81

(Table 7–A–8. continued overleaf)

Table 7–A–8. continued

	1984	1985	1986	1988	1990
Gross national product	1666.84	1716.01	1752.41	1830.11	1914.36
Personal consumption expenditures	1079.89	1112.87	1136.32	1187.06	1240.82
Gross private domestic investment	240.58	247.70	249.75	255.89	265.37
Structures	122.79	125.40	125.83	128.98	132.92
Residential	68.80	70.34	69.88	71.65	73.78
Producers durable equipment	111.20	115.84	117.83	121.08	126.39
Agriculture	7.19	7.46	7.46	7.49	7.57
Mining	3.94	4.12	4.27	4.38	4.49
Construction	6.23	6.37	6.45	6.66	6.97
Nondurable goods	12.88	14.27	14.93	15.30	15.95
Durable goods	16.45	16.86	16.94	17.22	17.94
Transportation	5.77	5.93	5.91	5.98	6.17
Communication	11.08	11.63	12.12	12.71	13.37
Utilities	10.01	10.32	10.57	10.99	11.63
Trade	14.10	14.65	14.88	15.65	16.71
Finance and services	11.25	11.17	10.89	10.18	9.87
Inventory change	6.58	6.47	6.09	5.83	6.07
Net exports	19.80	20.02	21.93	25.44	29.07
Government purchases	326.57	335.43	344.41	361.71	379.10

Table 7–A–9.   Tax Credit Equals 0.15

Sec. No. and Title	Equipment Investment, by Purchaser (millions of 1976 dollars)									
	1976	1980	1981	1982	1983	1984	1985	1986	1988	1990
1 Agriculture	9585.	10932.	10955.	11258.	11085.	11232.	11290.	11389.	11491.	11626.
2 Mining	1657.	1967.	2069.	2108.	2145.	2186.	2286.	2341.	2447.	2577.
3 Petroleum & gas	3354.	5015.	4663.	4833.	5138.	4704.	4163.	4460.	4591.	4647.
4 Construction	5773.	7857.	8351.	8682.	8938.	9251.	9449.	9572.	9920.	10394.
5 Ordnance	125.	158.	160.	161.	163.	165.	166.	168.	171.	174.
6 Meat	285.	419.	382.	371.	393.	411.	420.	460.	478.	498.
7 Dairy	256.	299.	302.	307.	320.	320.	330.	339.	345.	349.
8 Canned & frozen foods	374.	498.	535.	551.	566.	571.	592.	596.	624.	656.
9 Grain mill products	352.	458.	468.	481.	487.	486.	512.	516.	552.	579.
10 Bakery	266.	260.	263.	271.	275.	279.	290.	293.	290.	291.
11 Sugar	191.	122.	151.	245.	250.	247.	239.	250.	262.	283.
12 Candy	102.	134.	141.	151.	158.	154.	162.	168.	171.	177.
13 Beverages	735.	839.	867.	946.	925.	937.	923.	957.	997.	1021.
14 Misc. food products	323.	432.	480.	498.	545.	510.	518.	521.	548.	572.
15 Tobacco	107.	143.	155.	162.	152.	155.	159.	164.	174.	184.
16 Fabrics & yarns	616.	928.	866.	861.	827.	831.	870.	849.	865.	899.
17 Floor coverings	51.	89.	83.	83.	76.	68.	70.	67.	66.	69.
18 Misc. textiles	91.	180.	174.	179.	161.	156.	162.	159.	165.	173.
19 Knit fabric & apparel	165.	248.	221.	234.	247.	238.	235.	217.	203.	194.
20 Apparel	224.	290.	282.	290.	284.	286.	294.	284.	289.	292.
21 Hsehld. text. & upholstry	81.	150.	164.	178.	165.	169.	185.	185.	204.	221.
22 Logging & lumber	674.	1111.	1204.	1274.	1305.	1296.	1349.	1366.	1476.	1616.
23 Plywd., millwork, struct.	303.	581.	623.	651.	680.	712.	739.	753.	824.	913.
24 Wooden containers	7.	13.	14.	12.	12.	12.	12.	12.	12.	12.
25 Hsehld. & ofc. furniture	208.	350.	374.	369.	337.	316.	339.	347.	346.	361.

(Table 7–A–9. continued overleaf)

Table 7-A-9. continued

Sec. No. and Title	Equipment Investment, by Purchaser (millions of 1976 dollars)									
	1976	1980	1981	1982	1983	1984	1985	1986	1988	1990
27 Paper/products, ex. cont.	2426.	3055.	3135.	3165.	3126.	3177.	3149.	3244.	3439.	3624.
28 Paper containers	282.	405.	432.	441.	428.	413.	416.	412.	419.	426.
29 Newspapers	295.	503.	509.	511.	519.	533.	552.	563.	586.	621.
30 Printing & publishing	742.	965.	1039.	1055.	1071.	1080.	1120.	1139.	1178.	1227.
31 Industrial chemicals	3646.	4191.	3810.	3614.	3237.	3184.	2749.	3934.	4107.	4266.
32 Agricultural chemicals	285.	449.	474.	473.	473.	489.	509.	540.	584.	633.
33 Glue, ink, & fatty acids	302.	316.	272.	263.	265.	317.	309.	315.	324.	335.
34 Plastics & synthetics	1261.	2318.	1929.	1826.	1795.	1799.	1680.	1729.	1757.	1787.
35 Drugs	340.	350.	353.	355.	357.	361.	335.	340.	347.	342.
36 Cleaning & toilet items	237.	280.	318.	347.	374.	356.	379.	403.	428.	453.
37 Paints & allied prod.	83.	99.	109.	114.	109.	109.	115.	111.	111.	112.
38 Petroleum refining	1611.	2083.	2347.	2727.	2635.	3403.	2669.	2868.	3240.	3585.
39 Tires & tubes	216.	705.	671.	649.	558.	581.	617.	629.	660.	711.
40 Rubber prod., ex. tires	174.	245.	277.	288.	256.	255.	259.	247.	256.	264.
41 Plastic products	652.	1025.	1031.	997.	959.	936.	962.	952.	965.	993.
42 Leather tan. & ind. prod.	21.	27.	26.	25.	24.	24.	25.	24.	24.	24.
43 Shoes & other lea. prod.	42.	76.	81.	80.	81.	85.	86.	88.	93.	97.
44 Glass & glass products	358.	655.	690.	708.	690.	703.	728.	737.	781.	846.
45 Stone & clay products	854.	1413.	1509.	1542.	1544.	1466.	1509.	1465.	1495.	1577.
46 Iron & steel	2685.	3880.	4445.	4684.	4730.	4355.	4229.	4158.	4351.	4670.
47 Nonferrous metals	934.	1521.	1674.	1807.	1756.	1665.	1706.	1670.	1725.	1842.
48 Metal containers	127.	318.	316.	315.	318.	326.	337.	344.	355.	374.
49 Plumbing & heating	53.	52.	55.	57.	59.	56.	56.	52.	48.	46.
50 Structural metal prod.	454.	533.	598.	644.	645.	653.	655.	655.	691.	736.

Table 7–A–9. continued

Equipment Investment, by Purchaser
(millions of 1976 dollars)

Sec. No. and Title	1976	1980	1981	1982	1983	1984	1985	1986	1988	1990
51 Stampings	364.	516.	548.	556.	547.	540.	550.	531.	547.	565.
52 Hdwre., plating, wire prod.	586.	804.	870.	909.	905.	895.	916.	907.	961.	1024.
53 Engines & turbines	230.	329.	352.	357.	346.	346.	347.	351.	370.	397.
54 Farm machinery	198.	171.	193.	200.	205.	187.	187.	178.	175.	177.
55 Construct. mining material	568.	784.	925.	928.	925.	881.	910.	918.	1020.	1136.
56 Metalworking mach. & equip.	293.	466.	539.	522.	468.	417.	414.	352.	341.	362.
57 Spec. ind. machinery	169.	281.	297.	292.	282.	252.	247.	241.	249.	261.
58 Gen. indus. machinery	382.	480.	523.	530.	535.	500.	490.	479.	510.	548.
59 Misc. machinery & shops	238.	316.	335.	358.	359.	367.	362.	366.	383.	404.
60 Ofc. & computing mach.	380.	413.	491.	478.	430.	435.	437.	392.	394.	406.
61 Service ind. machinery	144.	229.	261.	284.	271.	257.	268.	242.	255.	269.
62 Elec. meas. transformers	119.	175.	187.	196.	169.	165.	163.	148.	145.	149.
63 Elec. apparatus & motors	222.	269.	294.	304.	307.	286.	285.	267.	280.	298.
64 Household appliances	149.	139.	149.	154.	148.	139.	146.	140.	134.	129.
65 Elec. light. & wiring	135.	250.	258.	267.	257.	250.	261.	250.	259.	270.
66 Radio, TV sets, & records	83.	136.	139.	142.	129.	134.	140.	144.	149.	156.
67 Communication equipment	428.	559.	580.	605.	587.	589.	612.	599.	626.	648.
68 Electronic components	551.	795.	842.	849.	803.	821.	838.	849.	883.	923.
69 Batteries, X-ray, & elec. equip.	176.	224.	271.	290.	312.	296.	313.	306.	337.	367.
70 Motor vehicles & parts	1908.	2902.	2891.	2655.	2525.	2491.	2475.	2350.	2325.	2341.
71 Aircraft & parts	380.	631.	513.	492.	499.	512.	478.	489.	482.	468.
72 Ships & boats	257.	366.	382.	432.	465.	486.	457.	448.	524.	601.
73 Locomotives, RR, & stcars	54.	71.	81.	80.	74.	67.	68.	59.	59.	59.
74 Cycles, trailers, & parts	52.	123.	131.	131.	127.	134.	141.	141.	141.	149.
75 Engr. & scient. instr.	32.	47.	47.	45.	45.	46.	45.	48.	52.	55.

(Table 7–A–9. continued overleaf)

552 Investment by Industries

Table 7–A–9. continued

Equipment Investment, by Purchaser
(millions of 1976 dollars)

Sec. No. and Title	1976	1980	1981	1982	1983	1984	1985	1986	1988	1990
76 Mech. measuring devices	73.	90.	96.	98.	101.	102.	100.	99.	102.	105.
77 Surgical & medical inst.	112.	169.	188.	193.	182.	186.	187.	192.	217.	238.
78 Optical & photo. supply	337.	447.	513.	530.	529.	516.	524.	528.	541.	573.
79 Misc. manufactured prod.	408.	380.	407.	430.	431.	433.	438.	433.	453.	464.
80 Railroads	1965.	3173.	3095.	3016.	2916.	2884.	2853.	2847.	2853.	2899.
81 Trucking	1405.	1826.	1987.	2087.	2223.	2364.	2387.	2480.	2701.	2966.
82 Other transport	1317.	1693.	1712.	1731.	1750.	1769.	1787.	1806.	1844.	1881.
83 Airlines	1300.	1863.	1762.	1569.	1563.	1504.	1469.	1429.	1343.	1277.
84 Wholesale & retail trade	11917.	16335.	16804.	17273.	17911.	18442.	19169.	19550.	20633.	22024.
85 Communication	9523.	12595.	13101.	13459.	13671.	14235.	14974.	15449.	16212.	17123.
86 Finance, ins., & services	7250.	15118.	17065.	16923.	14291.	14536.	15064.	15237.	15092.	15229.
87 Electric utilities	8460.	10624.	11338.	11945.	12239.	12594.	13009.	13420.	14083.	14976.
88 Nat. gas, water & sewer	1744.	1770.	1742.	1799.	1851.	1842.	1740.	1735.	1749.	1770.

Table 7–A–9. continued

Equipment Investment, by Purchaser, Summary by Major Sectors
(millions of 1976 dollars)

Title	1976	1980	1981	1982	1983	1984	1985	1986	1988	1990
Agriculture	9585.	10932.	10955.	11258.	11085.	11232.	11290.	11389.	11491.	11626.
Mining	5011.	6982.	6732.	6940.	7283.	6890.	6449.	6802.	7037.	7224.
Construction	5773.	7857.	8351.	8682.	8938.	9251.	9449.	9572.	9920.	10394.
Ordnance	125.	158.	160.	161.	163.	165.	166.	168.	171.	174.
Food	2884.	3461.	3590.	3822.	3919.	3915.	3985.	4108.	4268.	4425.
Tobacco	107.	143.	155.	162.	152.	155.	159.	164.	174.	184.
Textiles	758.	1196.	1123.	1123.	1063.	1055.	1102.	1075.	1096.	1141.
Apparel	470.	687.	667.	702.	697.	693.	715.	687.	696.	706.
Lumber	984.	1705.	1840.	1938.	1996.	2020.	2101.	2131.	2312.	2541.
Furniture	208.	350.	374.	369.	337.	316.	339.	347.	346.	361.
Paper	2708.	3461.	3567.	3607.	3554.	3590.	3565.	3656.	3858.	4050.
Print. & publ.	1037.	1468.	1548.	1566.	1591.	1614.	1672.	1703.	1763.	1848.
Chemicals	6154.	8003.	7265.	6992.	6611.	6616.	6076.	7371.	7657.	7927.
Petroleum	1611.	2083.	2347.	2727.	2635.	3403.	2669.	2868.	3240.	3585.
Rubber & plastics	1042.	1976.	1978.	1933.	1773.	1772.	1839.	1828.	1881.	1968.
Leather	63.	103.	107.	105.	105.	109.	111.	112.	117.	121.
Stone	1212.	2068.	2200.	2251.	2235.	2168.	2237.	2201.	2276.	2423.
Metals	3619.	5401.	6119.	6491.	6486.	6019.	5935.	5827.	6076.	6512.
Metal prod.	1584.	2223.	2386.	2480.	2473.	2469.	2513.	2489.	2602.	2745.
Nonelec. mach.	2602.	3470.	3916.	3948.	3821.	3644.	3661.	3521.	3698.	3959.
Electrical	1863.	2546.	2720.	2808.	2712.	2681.	2758.	2702.	2815.	2939.
Transp. equip.	2651.	4093.	3997.	3790.	3690.	3691.	3618.	3486.	3531.	3617.
Instruments	554.	752.	844.	867.	857.	850.	857.	867.	911.	971.
Misc. mfg.	408.	380.	407.	430.	431.	433.	438.	433.	453.	464.
Transportation	5987.	8554.	8556.	8402.	8452.	8521.	8496.	8563.	8741.	9024.
Communications	9523.	12595.	12101.	13459.	13671.	14235.	14974.	15449.	16212.	17123.
Utilities	10204.	12394.	13079.	13744.	14090.	14436.	14749.	15155.	15833.	16746.
Trade	11917.	16335.	16804.	17273.	17911.	18442.	19169.	19550.	20633.	22024.
Fin., ins., re. services	7250.	15118.	17065.	16923.	14291.	14536.	15064.	15237.	15092.	15229.

Table 7–A–10.   GNP Summary: Credit Equals 0.15 *(billions of 1972 dollars)*

	1976	1980	1981	1982	1983
Gross national product	1270.60	1486.76	1536.77	1584.34	1626.75
Personal consumption expenditures	819.30	952.79	983.63	1015.27	1047.38
Gross private domestic investment	172.40	225.82	236.22	242.60	243.70
Structures	85.00	106.80	112.66	117.42	120.07
Residential	46.70	58.42	61.87	65.49	67.20
Producers durable equipment	80.70	111.56	116.05	118.66	117.53
Agriculture	6.60	7.53	7.54	7.75	7.63
Mining	3.40	4.74	4.57	4.71	4.94
Construction	3.90	5.31	5.64	5.87	6.04
Nondurable goods	11.60	15.56	15.40	15.67	15.23
Durable goods	11.10	16.25	17.53	17.93	17.69
Transportation	4.20	6.00	6.00	5.89	5.93
Communication	7.40	9.79	10.18	10.46	10.62
Utilities	7.10	8.62	9.10	9.56	9.80
Trade	9.00	12.34	12.69	13.04	13.53
Finance and services	7.40	15.43	17.42	17.27	14.59
Inventory change	6.70	7.46	7.51	6.53	6.09
Net exports	16.00	17.08	16.88	17.51	17.86
Government purchases	262.90	291.07	300.04	308.96	317.81

Table 7–A–10. continued

	1984	1985	1986	1988	1990
Gross national product	1672.84	1719.24	1756.42	1835.81	1920.75
Personal consumption expenditures	1079.89	1112.87	1136.32	1187.06	1240.82
Gross private domestic investment	248.04	252.14	255.16	263.42	273.88
Structures	122.68	125.28	125.76	129.05	133.01
Residential	68.80	70.34	69.88	71.65	73.78
Producers durable equipment	119.41	120.78	123.50	128.42	134.71
Agriculture	7.73	7.77	7.84	7.91	8.01
Mining	4.67	4.38	4.62	4.77	4.90
Construction	6.25	6.38	6.47	6.70	7.02
Nondurable goods	15.80	15.09	16.24	17.06	17.89
Durable goods	17.17	17.29	16.97	17.69	18.75
Transportation	5.98	5.96	6.01	6.13	6.33
Communication	11.06	11.64	12.01	12.60	13.31
Utilities	10.04	10.26	10.54	11.02	11.65
Trade	13.93	14.48	14.76	15.58	16.63
Finance and services	14.84	15.38	15.55	15.40	15.54
Inventory change	5.94	6.07	5.90	5.95	6.16
Net exports	18.34	18.81	20.52	23.61	26.94
Government purchases	326.57	335.43	344.41	361.72	379.10

REFERENCES

1. ALMON, CLOPPER. "Prices in Input-Output," a paper presented at the Second U.S.–USSR Exchange Symposium on Econometric Modeling, Skyland, Virginia, May 16, 1978.

3. _____ ; BUCKLER, MARGARET B.; HORWITZ, LAWRENCE M.; and REIMBOLD, THOMAS C. *1985: Interindustry Forecasts of the American Economy.* Lexington, Mass.: D.C. Heath, 1974.

3. ALMON, SHIRLEY. "The Distributed Lag Between Capital Appropriations and Expenditures," *Econometrica*, January 1965, *33*(1), pp. 173-96.

4. DANTZIG, GEORGE B. *Linear Programming and Extensions.* Princeton: Princeton Univ. Press, 1963.

5. FROMM, GARY, ed. *Tax Incentives and Capital Spending.* Washington, D.C.: Brookings, 1971.

6. HALL, ROBERT E., and JORGENSON, DALE W. "Tax Policy and Investment Behavior," *American Economic Review*, June 1967, *57*(3), pp. 363-75.

7. MAYOR, THOMAS H. "Equipment Expenditures by Input-Output Industries," *Review of Economics and Statistics*, Feb. 1971, *53*(1), pp. 26-36.

8. MILLER, MERTON H., and MODIGLIANI, FRANCO. "Some Estimates of the Cost of Capital to the Electric Utility Industry, 1954-57, *American Economic Review*, June 1966, *56*(3), pp. 333-91.

Index

About the Editor

George M. von Furstenberg is a Professor of Economics at Indiana University, Bloomington, from where this study was directed. He is currently serving as Chief of Financial Studies in the Research Department of the International Monetary Fund. During previous tours of duty in Washington he served as Senior Staff Economist at the President's Council of Economic Advisers and was associated with both the Brookings Institution and the American Enterprise Institute at various times.

While his chief interest is macroeconomics and public finance, he has contributed to the professional literature also in the fields of income redistribution, mortgage financing, and capital formation. In recent years he has been concerned mainly with the study of saving and investment.